A History of the Oklahoma State University School of Journalism and Broadcasting

CENTENNIAL HISTORIES SERIES

Centennial Histories Series

Committee

W. David Baird
LeRoy H. Fischer
B. Curtis Hamm
Harry Heath
Beulah Hirschlein
Vernon Parcher

Murl Rogers
J. L. Sanderson
Warren Shull
Milton Usry
Odell Walker
Eric I. Williams

Robert B. Kamm, Director
Carolyn Hanneman, Editor
Carol Hiner, Associate Editor

CENTENNIAL
1890 • 1990

A History of the Oklahoma State University School of Journalism and Broadcasting

by Harry E. Heath Jr.

OKLAHOMA STATE UNIVERSITY / Stillwater

Published by Oklahoma State University
Centennial Histories Series, Stillwater, Oklahoma 74078

Library of Congress Cataloging-in-Publication Data

Heath, Harry E. (Harry Eugene)
    A history of the Oklahoma State University School of Journalism and Broad-
casting / by Harry E. Heath, Jr.

      p. cm.—(Centennial histories series)
    Includes bibliographical references and index.
    ISBN 0-914956-52-3 :
    1. Oklahoma State University. School of Journalism and Broadcasting—
    History.
I. Title.   II. Series.
PN4791.044H4 1992
071'.6634'0711—dc20   92-18645
                                            CIP

Contents

Foreword

Although some would not expect to find a nationally recognized School of Journalism and Broadcasting at a university in the "A. and M." tradition, the fact is that several, including Oklahoma State University, defy that expectation. One only needs to look at the students (both past and present) to recognize the strength of OSU's programs. Many prominent names immediately come to mind, including Paul Miller, former Associated Press president and head of Gannett newspapers; Walker Stone, former editor-in-chief of Scripps-Howard publications; and Earl Richert who succeeded Stone as head of Scripps-Howard. There are hundreds of others who have excelled and brought honor to their alma mater.

Interestingly, it was those in agricultural journalism who provided the impetus to the university's early journalistic efforts. With the advent of programs in broadcasting, it was personnel in agriculture who again helped to establish the foundations for the strong programs to follow.

The Centennial Histories Committee was most fortunate in securing the services of Harry E. Heath Jr., longtime director of OSU's School of Journalism and Broadcasting, in writing *A History of the Oklahoma State University School of Journalism and Broadcasting*. With his experience in both on-campus and off-campus journalism and broadcasting, with his commitment to high quality research and writing, and with his deep appreciation for the contributions of others who have helped to make OSU's School of Journalism and Broadcasting what it is today, he is able to present for readers an accurate and exciting account of the growth and development of OSU's present-day programs in journalism and broadcasting.

In this, the twenty-fifth and final volume of the Centennial Histories Project, special thanks and appreciation are expressed to the editors of the volumes. Carolyn Hanneman, current editor, has been involved in all of the twenty-five volumes and has had a great impact on the total project. Carol Hiner, current associate editor, has been involved in twenty-two volumes and has also contributed much to the series. Judy Buchholz who served half-time in the early stages of the project was involved with only one of the manuscripts but played an important role in getting the project under way. Ann Matoy succeeded her and contributed much in establishing a solid foundation for the series. She was involved in thirteen of the twenty-five volumes.

Special appreciation at this time of conclusion of the Centennial Histories Project is expressed to those of the Oklahoma State University administration who have supported for ten and one-half years the production of the twenty-five volumes. Vice President Richard Poole originally conceived the idea of a series of books to commemorate OSU's Centennial in 1990, rather than the single volume usually produced on such occasions. He had been appointed earlier by President L. L. Boger to serve as the overall coordinator for all upcoming Centennial planning and events, including the writing of one or more historical volumes. On February 2, 1982, Dr. Poole asked me to direct the project. He has been of tremendous encouragement and help throughout the effort, and deep appreciation is expressed to him.

In September 1987, Mr. Dale Ross succeeded Dr. Poole as executive director of the Centennial Coordinating Office and served through March 1991. He, too, was a strong supporter and friend of the project, and great appreciation is expressed to him.

On April 1, 1991, administrative responsibility for the final stages of the Centennial Histories Project was transferred to Vice President Harry Birdwell. In some ways, the concluding months and years of any long-term project such as the Centennial Histories Project are the most difficult for the staff as time runs short and funds run low. Dr. Birdwell and his associate, Dr. Ralph Hamilton, former director of Public Information Services at OSU, have been most understanding and helpful, and deep appreciation is expressed to them. The OSU Foundation and its president, Charles Platt, assisted with timely supplementary funding, and again special thanks are extended.

President L. L. Boger, during whose presidency much of the project was accomplished, gave his support at all times. His successor, President John R. Campbell, although coming into the project late, helped considerably in completing the project. Warm appreciation is expressed to both men.

Gordon White, of University Printing Services, Heather Lloyd, librarian in Special Collections and Archives, and Carla Chlouber, of Agricultural Publications, together with their respective staffs, have assisted greatly. Also, John Holbird's dust jacket art adds much to the present volume. Assisting greatly, too, have been Kathryn Merrill, secretary; her predecessor, Jeri Fortney; and Gayle Hiner, graphic designer.

Finally, appreciation is expressed to Dr. Marlan D. Nelson, director of the School of Journalism and Broadcasting at OSU, for his interest in and support of the production of this volume.

Robert B. Kamm, Director
Centennial Histories Project
President Emeritus
Oklahoma State University

July 1992

Preface

As a teacher I had told my students that journalism is history in a hurry. I used that remark to underscore the importance of accuracy, for I had observed that so much of the material historians work with in assessing people and events is taken from newspapers and periodicals. Journalists face the possibility that what they write today could lead to an incorrect assessment by historians decades later. That in itself—aside from integrity, honesty, ethical journalistic behavior, and a host of other considerations—underscores the need for accuracy. Tomorrow's journalists need to know this.

In writing this book, I became a historian—a new role for me—and I took to heart that lesson I had used in the classroom. Journalism may be history in a hurry, but history decidedly is not expanded journalism written in a hurry. It is a long, hard, sometimes disappointing search for truth.

I had amassed a large collection of facts and opinions about the people and events in this book. In total, there were six file drawers and nine large boxes crammed with documents, newspaper clippings, magazine articles, letters, interview notes, and many items of memorabilia. I almost became hostage to my material. At times, it overwhelmed me, making the task of finishing the project seem hopeless. In the final stages, the deadline hung over me with more weight than any of the thousands of newspaper and broadcasting deadlines I had faced through the years.

How to turn away from the seemingly endless but interesting material I wished to incorporate into the manuscript became a problem. The manuscript was running much too long. Already, the editors and I had agreed to discard chapters covering such interesting and worthwhile enterprises as public information, telecommunications, graduate studies in mass communication, student publications, and professional and honorary societies in journalism and broadcasting. Insofar as was possible, some of this history was incorporated into the final manuscript. This was a hard compromise for me to make, for I had spent hundreds of hours in researching and writing these discarded chapters. In some cases, the chapters were virtually complete. In others, only a good start had been made.

I finally rationalized the necessity for dropping this material by resolving to deposit the manuscripts in the Special Collections and University Archives Department of the Edmon Low Library, along with miscellaneous notes and other research materials, including tape recordings of several interviews. I would have preferred to spend another six to twelve months on the project, integrating the essence of the discarded chapters, but time was running out. The ambitious and unparalleled Centennial Histories Project was closing down.

It is my earnest hope that you will find the end product, despite the necessary compromises, both useful and interesting. I have tried to make this volume more than a recital of names and dates. These were real people, people who in the main gave their hearts and minds to instruction of students whose words on paper would, in some cases, span the globe. Often they were people of skills and intellects far surpassing the fleeting and misty images conjured as we reflect upon the past. I have sought to relate their disappointments and defeats as well as their triumphs. I have not turned away from the tragedies that came to some of the principal characters, whose stage was an ambitious land-grant institution that fate had placed in what once was the home of the Indian.

There were so many kind people who helped me over the difficult times of authorship that naming all of them would be impossible. I hope that any serious oversights will be forgiven. My deep appreciation extends from those who checked a single name or fact to those who sacrificed large blocks of time to assist with the research.

I am especially indebted to the director of the Centennial Histories Project, President Emeritus Robert B. Kamm, and to two superb editors, Carolyn Hanneman and Carol Hiner, whose skill and patience brought this final volume in the series to fruition. Working closely with them was Kathy Merrill, secretary to the administrators emeritus. She took copy that was often covered with the author's red ink and, uncomplainingly, worked her way through it efficiently and accurately. No writer could have asked for a better team. They were supported in the production by Gayle Hiner, a graphic artist whose skills merit the highest accolades, and my longtime friend, Gordon M. White, coordinator of University Printing Services.

Heather Lloyd, head of Special Collections and University Archives, and members of her staff were both willing and courteous in locating needed reference materials. The task could not have been accomplished without the joint efforts of Kathleen Bledsoe, David Peters, Greg Hines, Wray Larman, Kelly Secrest, Susan Walker, Brenda Nixon, Kayla Barrett, Louisa Payne, Bob Brown, and their numerous student assistants. In addition to the professionals of the Edmon Low Library, Richard Sutton of the Stillwater Public Library, Max Nichols of the Oklahoma Historical Society, and scores of librarians in various parts of the country proved to be prompt and reliable.

To my colleagues and friends in the School of Journalism and Broadcasting, I owe a major debt. First, I want to extend thanks to Dr. Marlan D. Nelson, director, for his support from the inception of the project. For various reasons, the work stretched out far longer than expected, but his helpful assistance never wavered. Amber Hoover was the original compositor, followed by Jone Hawkins and Lea Godsey, whose enthusiasm for the content warded off discouragement on many occasions. Donna Jelley, Joy Stewart, and Dorothy Nixon were invaluable in locating documents to answer my many questions. Various faculty members spurred me on with their inquiries as to progress.

I am deeply indebted, too, to the many alumni and former students who responded to my requests for their reflections upon the people and events of their college days. Their letters and questionnaire responses may be found in the School of Journalism and Broadcasting Centennial History Collection. In addition, both color and perspective were added by the numerous individuals I interviewed, some on three or four occasions. To them, most of whom are listed in the Bibliography, I give thanks once more. Similarly, my appreciation goes to Carmen Dorris, whose help in studying musty class rolls for needed information was of great value.

The foresight of my good friend John W. Hamilton, who loved this institution with a deep and unwavering passion, made possible the use of a number of rare photographs, some of which had been passed on to him by Clement E. Trout. In an age inclined toward the purging of files, it was fortunate that Hamilton not only saved so much, but passed so much on to me. The OSU library will have an opportunity to catalog these materials. Other help in illustrating the book came from D. Earl Newsom, John Catsis, and Todd Johnson.

Ralph Hamilton, director of special projects in the Office of the Vice President for University Relations and Public Affairs, is another whose support was indispensable. Not only did he contribute useful background for one of the chapters, but his careful and insightful reading of proofs was both a gift of time and professional competence.

My one great disappointment is that so many of those in my personal hall of fame—James C. Stratton, Wauhillau LaHay, Sam Byerley, Earl Richert, "Scoop" Thompson, and many others—did not receive the attention they deserved in this volume. Some old-timers reading the book will know this. More recent members of the passing parade will not. But the author knows, as he sits at his typewriter mentally calling the roll of the many who gave so much, both on the campus and in the wider world out there.

If I could, I would set the type large for these closing words: "To the students, faculty and staff, past and present, of the School of Journalism and Broadcasting, and to Jody, who cheerfully sacrificed so much because she understood."

Harry E. Heath Jr.
Regents Service Professor Emeritus
School of Journalism and Broadcasting

July 1992

A History of the Oklahoma State University School of Journalism and Broadcasting

1 The Seed Is Planted

The history of journalism and broadcasting at Oklahoma State University—including the wide range of information activities to be found on any major campus—is a fascinating story. It is a tapestry woven from the hopes and dreams of energetic planners, disagreements over both ideology and methods, brilliance as well as humdrum monotony in the classroom, and a myriad of social and political conflicts which have left their mark for good or ill, to be dealt with in varying degrees of success by each new generation of visionaries. It is a story of men and women who believed their teaching would strengthen democracy in the Jeffersonian tradition.

Exactly when the story begins is a matter of viewpoint. While the story's beginning may be open to question, there is no doubt about the cast of characters. Nor is there any doubt about their abilities, for the pioneers whose work will be examined in the early chapters were exceptionally capable men with creative minds, a sense of adventure, and an abundance of energy. Their names were Freeman E. Miller, Angelo C. Scott, Frank D. Northup, Edwin R. Barrett, Noble W. Rockey, John A. Craig, and Harry R. O'Brien. Each added color to the tapestry. Each believed in the importance of words on paper, placed there with substance, grace, and clarity. But before we turn to their stories and the origins of today's School of Journalism and Broadcasting, a look at earlier efforts elsewhere is in order.

A rudimentary effort in journalism education began soon after the Civil War. In 1867, General Robert E. Lee, president of Washington College (known today as Washington and Lee University), recommended to his board of trustees that fifty scholarships be made available to young men planning to make printing or journalism their profession. The plan was approved. A year earlier, Lee had tested the idea by arranging for six students to receive printing instruction, no doubt believing that the encouragement of publishing would be crucial in the Reconstruction era. These students, all enrolled in the college's classical course, were admitted to the program and allowed to work out their tuition. The lectures were given on campus, with the students gaining hands-on experience at Lafferty & Company, a print shop in downtown Lexington, Virginia. Credit was allowed for the classroom work, but the success of the course depended heavily upon the practical application of skills developed in what today might be called a practicum or laboratory. Lafferty & Company made no charge for the "laboratory" instruction, perhaps feeling that some of the young men would learn enough to work later as part-time employees while financing their college studies. The cooperation between the Lafferty firm and the college lasted ten years. Word of the idea spread westward, and Kansas Agricultural College started a similar printing course in 1873.[1]

Lee died in 1870. Although his program apparently disappeared from the Washington College catalog after 1878, what was to become a widespread movement had been given its start. The University of

COURTESY VIRGINIA HISTORICAL SOCIETY, RICHMOND

Robert E. Lee, the great military hero of the Confederacy, saw the printer-editor as a major force in rebuilding the South following the Civil War. Accordingly, in 1867, he established a course in printing at Washington College, Lexington, Virginia, and obtained scholarship money to support it. The idea spread, giving birth to journalism education.

Missouri had picked up where General Lee's pioneering efforts had left off, but with a different emphasis. The first Missouri course was in the hands of a thirty-year-old man of rare talents. Although his given name was David Russell McAnally, he had adopted the name David R. McAnally Jr. in honor of his father, David Rice McAnally, educator, Methodist minister, and journalist. Young McAnally had worked on the *St. Louis Christian Advocate*, which his father edited, and then had joined the *St. Louis Globe-Democrat* in 1875 as a feature and editorial writer. He established a reputation for his well-researched articles on history, music, and science as well as literature and religion. He was not new to education when he joined the Missouri faculty in 1877 as professor of English, history, and elocution. He had been principal of Arcadia College in Missouri before joining the *Globe-Democrat* and already had achieved acclaim as an organist and composer.

As chairman of the English department, he had decided to add a course in journalism to the curriculum. It was listed in the university catalog for 1878-79 and was described in these terms: "Fifth year, Special Studies: History of Journalism—Lectures with practical explanations of daily newspaper life. *The Spectator*, *The London Times*, the *New York Herald*." McAnally's department also was responsible for bookkeeping, United States history and constitution, elocution, political economy, and vocal music. He organized a choir that was in demand for university functions and wrote three anthems for it. He was an excellent speaker and gave public lectures at the university and five other state institutions. He established a trust fund for the McAnally Medal, which was awarded on the same basis as the Oklahoma A. and M. College Magruder Medal, begun at about the same time. McAnally also founded the *Missouri University Review* and served as its managing editor. In 1883, he was named dean of the Normal School in addition to his duties as chairman of English at the same salary he had received since 1877. It was not the first time a productive faculty member had been expected to achieve more and more out of a sense of loyalty alone. This fact probably led to McAnally's casting about for his next move.

A lifetime bachelor, McAnally lived alone during his years in Columbia, avoiding social gatherings. He believed in moderation in all things except work. Although he was never known to have a feminine attachment, he wrote such books as *How Men Make Love and Get Married*; *Modern Techniques of Love Making*; *Women and Their Ways*; *Love, Courtship and Marriage*; and *Unaccountable Humors of Womankind*. His most widely read books were *Philosophy of English Poetry*; *Irish Wonders*; *Popular Tales as Told by the People;* and *A Compendium of Useful Knowledge*.

In 1885, he submitted his resignation, intending to return to the *Globe-Democrat*. More pay and the chance to be near his aging father no

The first course listed as "journalism" was introduced by David R. McAnally Jr. at the University of Missouri in 1878. McAnally, an accomplished organist and sometimes composer, was a man of many talents: teacher, author, columnist, feature writer, and editor.

doubt played a part in his decision. In the summer of 1886, he traveled abroad, writing a series of articles on his experiences for the *Christian Advocate*. Upon his return, he lived in the family home with his father and a housekeeper and joined the *Globe-Democrat*, where he wrote Sunday features and, according to one source, editorials again. He had moved his organ from Columbia to St. Louis and built it into the parlor of his father's home. Neighbors enjoyed the "concerts" wafting through the parlor windows. His greenhouse and his hobby of growing flowers were among his diversions. After his father's death in 1895 he withdrew further from society.

On February 20, 1930, twenty-one years after his own death, McAnally was honored at the fourth annual University of Missouri Journalism Banquet for his contributions to the journalism profession. Casper S. Yost, a famous editor of the day, said, "In good sooth he was, as old Chaucer said of another, 'A very gentle, parfit knight.'"

There are two reasons for devoting this much detail to McAnally in this brief survey of journalism education's early days. While there were earlier attempts to prepare future journalists in other colleges and universities, he was the first to start a course that specifically was titled *journalism*. In addition, his broad-ranging talents were typical of several other early journalism educators, including those at Oklahoma A. and M. College.[2]

The University of Missouri had set the stage for what was to follow. One or more journalism courses also were taught prior to 1900 at Cornell, Pennsylvania, Indiana, Iowa, Kansas, Nebraska, and Ohio State. Joseph F. Johnson, who established the nation's first comprehensive journalism curriculum in the University of Pennsylvania's Wharton School of Commerce, had written in a *Spokane Spokesman* editorial on May 14, 1890: "It is a popular notion in newspaper offices that a college or chair of Journalism is humbug; that the only effective School of Journalism is the newspaper itself. . . . Journalism is a profession as much as law or medicine. . . . There could undoubtedly be a successful College of Journalism. . . . It will be established some day."[3]

Johnson's prophecy was to become reality, but whether he was looking ahead to an academic career when he wrote the editorial is not known. Regardless of how he saw his role in bringing the prophecy to pass, history notes that he left the Pacific Northwest in 1893 to accept a position at the University of Pennsylvania. Together with Eugene Camp, an editor of the *Philadelphia Times*, he is credited by Albert Sutton (*Education for Journalism in the United States*) with setting up a five-course curriculum.[4] The courses included Art and History of Newspapermaking; Law of Libel and Business Management; Newspaper Practice (exercises in reporting, editing, etc.); Current Topics (lectures on important national and international issues); and Public Lectures (guest speakers from the newspaper field).

When Johnson left the University of Pennsylvania in 1901 to become dean of the School of Commerce at New York University, journalism was discontinued. But the idea of an integrated curriculum had been noted even in the higher echelons of commercial journalism. One leading publisher of the day, Joseph Pulitzer, was among those examining journalism's position in higher education. Degree work in journalism received a tremendous boost in 1903 when he agreed to endow a school of journalism at Columbia University with $2,000,000. Pulitzer first had

The first curriculum in journalism is credited to Joseph F. Johnson, who left the Pacific Northwest to join the faculty of the Wharton School of Commerce at the University of Pennsylvania in 1893. It consisted of five courses and included guest lectures by visiting editors.

sought the advice of Charles W. Eliot, president of Harvard University, and had received a proposal from him for a curriculum embracing news and editorial writing, methods of the business and advertising offices, and close work with the mechanical department. Pulitzer rejected Eliot's plan because it failed to distinguish between the newspaper as a business and editorial work as a profession.[5]

Pulitzer was one of the earliest and strongest champions of the professional view. He wanted his endowment to be used "to begin a movement that will raise journalism to the rank of a learned profession, growing in the respect of the community as other professions far less important to the public interests have grown."[6] His school, finally established at Columbia University in 1912, became a model for many similar programs. Undergraduate journalism was dropped at Columbia twenty-three years later, and a Graduate School of Journalism was formed.[7]

Meanwhile, the popularity of Professor McAnally's work at the University of Missouri in the 1880s had not been forgotten. The Missouri Press Association, as well as individual editors, began pressing for a formal program on the Missouri campus. The idea was promoted for several years, and in 1908 the first School of Journalism was established at Missouri with Walter Williams of the *Columbia Herald* as dean.[8]

The growing interest in journalism education was reflected on the opening day of the 1910 Oklahoma Press Association (OPA) convention. On that occasion, the highly respected Missouri dean delivered in a "masterly style" the principal address. Notes on the meeting stated that Williams had "won a high place in the estimation of all American journalists." Ironically, at the next year's meeting, the OPA voted down as impracticable the idea of establishing a school of journalism at the University of Oklahoma. Intense opposition was aroused immediately by the suggestion. Most editors believed that an aspiring journalist should learn the trade by working at all the jobs on a newspaper. The OPA's endorsement of a school of journalism was postponed for several years.[9]

Despite frequent skepticism of this kind, by the fall of 1912 journalism instruction had made important gains on many highly regarded campuses. Departments had been established at the Universities of Wisconsin, Kansas, Notre Dame, Washington, and Oregon, and at Iowa State and Kansas State College. In addition, professional schools had been created at Columbia University, Marquette University, and the University of Missouri. In a report to the American Association of Teachers of Journalism that year, Williams identified thirty-one colleges and universities offering instruction.[10] Oklahoma A. and M. College qualified to be listed among these.

Some of the early journalism courses were taught in departments of English and/or rhetoric, often by reluctant teachers who had had little or no experience in the journalism field. This no doubt contributed to the widespread skepticism of newspapermen who saw academic training in the field little better—or perhaps worse—than no training at all. To the skeptics, only the apprenticeship system made sense. Certainly this was the attitude in pre-statehood Oklahoma and for several years to come.[11]

At first, the primary aim of some educators in approving journalism instruction was to promote interest and competence in English composition. But some college presidents—among them men who had had editorial experience—began to see other benefits. For one thing, the quality of campus publications could be improved through some instruction in journalism, even if on a small scale. For another, the quality of news reports being sent to major newspapers and the wire services by student correspondents could be upgraded. Moreover, the early and rudimentary public information offices on various campuses relied heavily upon student help. Journalism instruction would be a plus in those offices.[12]

In many cases, students were pressing for more work in journalism. Their interest, combined with the practicality of a faculty member to pull together the various journalistic functions on campus, had a certain appeal among college presidents willing to test the uncharted waters of

Walter Williams left his editorship of the *Columbia Herald* to become founding dean of the world's first School of Journalism at the University of Missouri in 1908. A leader in state and national press organizations, he served as president of the university from 1931 to 1934. He was a lecturer, world traveler, and author of numerous journalism books.

journalism education. Most campuses had someone responsible for editing and publishing academic catalogs, bulletins, and promotional materials of one type or another. Some, as soon would be true at Oklahoma A. and M., were setting up printing facilities on campus. Administrators were looking for qualified journalists to wear all of these hats—run the public information program, coordinate the publishing and printing operation, monitor student publications, and be the guiding hand in the fledgling academic program as well. This was to be the pattern at the Oklahoma A. and M. College for a least three decades.

Journalism's appearance in the academic world was part of a great surge in education for the professions and what have been called the "emerging professions."[13] This national trend was reflected in the growing regional interest in journalism education. It could not be totally ignored. Iowa State, probably the most frequent land-grant model for Oklahoma A. and M., had begun a course in agricultural journalism in 1905. With programs at Missouri, Kansas, and Kansas State gaining momentum, it seemed certain that Oklahoma A. and M. College eventually would follow suit. Innovation on the struggling Stillwater campus, however, was hampered by territorial status and limited funds. A few halting steps had been taken at the students' own initiative before the first of the pioneers, Freeman Miller, joined the faculty in 1894. It would be nearly four years after Miller's arrival before limited classroom instruction in journalism would begin under Angelo Scott and Frank Northup, and sixteen years before a full-term course in the subject would be offered by John Craig.

Journalism education had not yet arrived at Oklahoma A. and M., but it was coming.

Endnotes

1. George S. Turnbull, *Journalists in the Making* (Eugene: The School of Journalism, University of Oregon, 1965), p. 1; *Universal Standard Encyclopedia* (New York, NY: Unicorn Publishers, Incorporated, 1955), vol. 14, p. 4967; William R. Lindley, *Journalism and Higher Education: The Search for Academic Purpose* (Stillwater, OK: Journalistic Services, 1975), pp. 1, 2; Leon William Lindsay, "A Biography of David R. McAnally Jr." (Master of Arts thesis, University of Missouri, 1956), pp. 2,3; Frank Luther Mott, *American Journalism*, third edition (New York, NY: The Macmillan Company, 1962), p. 406; *Southern Newspaper Publishers Association Special Bulletin*, Chattanooga, Tennessee, 8-10 November 1948, p. 3. Turnbull lists 1868 as the beginning of Lee's pioneering effort in printing instruction. Some sources refer to 1869.

2. Turnbull, pp. 1, 2; Edwin Emery and Henry Ladd Smith, *The Press and America* (New York, NY: Prentice Hall Incorporated, 1954), p. 736; *Annual Catalog, the Missouri University, Columbia, Missouri, 1878-79*, pp. 49, 50; Lindsay, pp. 2, 4, 5, 11, 16, 19, 32, 49, 57, 62, 63, 68, 71, 79, 82, 84, 86-88, 90-93, 95-97, 99, 104-110, 111, 112, 117, 119, 120, 124, 126, 127, 132, 134, 136, 140, 141, 144, 147, 148, 150, 153. These sources place the date of the first Missouri journalism course variously as 1877, 1878, and 1879. Based upon the Missouri catalog, 1878 is the correct date.

3. Turnbull, p. 2; Lindsay, pp. 3, 25, 26, 46.

4. Turnbull, p. 2; Lindsay p. 3; Gail M. Pietrzyk to Harry E, Heath Jr., 7 May 1991, School of Journalism and Broadcasting Centennial History Collection, Special Collections, Edmon Low Library, Oklahoma State University, Stillwater, Oklahoma.

5. DeForest O'Dell, *The History of Journalism Education in the United States* (New York, NY: Teachers College, Columbia University, 1935), pp. 14-19; 84 ff.

6. Joseph Pulitzer, "The College of Journalism," *North American Review*, vol. 178, no. 570 (May 1904), p. 657; Lindsay, p. 4.

7. *Universal Standard Encyclopedia*, vol. 14, p. 4967.

8. Turnbull, pp. 2, 3; Lindley, p. 2; Lindsay, pp. 3, 4; *Universal Standard Encyclopedia*, vol. 14, p. 4967. Lindley reports that soon after McAnally's resignation, a move for a journalism curriculum was begun, resulting in the first classes in the Department of Journalism on September 14, 1908.

9.   Margaret M. Larason, "The Life and Work of Undril Stanley Russell" (16 July 1960), p. 76, School of Journalism history and biography papers, University of Oklahoma, Norman, Oklahoma; J. B. Thoburn and John Winthrop Sharp, *History of the Oklahoma Press and the Oklahoma Press Association* (Oklahoma City, OK: Industrial Printing Company, 1930), pp. unnumbered. This reference may be found in the cited work below the reports of the 1910 and 1911 meetings of the association. In addition, see L. Edward Carter, *The Story of Oklahoma Newspapers* (Muskogee, OK: Western Heritage Books, Incorporated, 1984), p. 193.

10. Edwin Emery and Joseph P. McKerns, *ACEJMC: 75 Years in the Making* (Columbia, SC: Accrediting Council for Education in Journalism and Mass Communication, 1987), pp. 2-4.

11. Carter, p. 193.

12. Turnbull, pp. 4, 5.

13. Lindley, p. 3.

2 A Faltering Start

The enabling act providing for an agricultural and mechanical college in Payne County, Oklahoma Territory, was signed into law by Governor George W. Steele on Christmas Eve 1890. Twenty months and two days had passed since the dramatic April 22, 1889, opening of the Unassigned Lands by the newly elected Benjamin Harrison. The area consisted of 2,000,000 acres ceded to the Creeks and Seminoles but sold back to the government on demand after those tribes had supported the South during the Civil War. This large tract had not been reassigned to smaller Indian tribes, as planned, nor was it available for non-Indian settlement prior to the "run." Ten years of clamor by leaders of the Boomer Movement plus a lobbying effort had preceded the congressional action on March 3, 1889, that enabled President Harrison to open the Unassigned Lands to settlement. For nearly a year after the opening, when 50,000 claim seekers in one day had swarmed across the land, settlers were without federal, state, or territorial legal jurisdiction. The "Law of the West" ruled. Finally, on May 2, 1890, Oklahoma Territory was formed out of the Unassigned Lands, and a territorial government under federal jurisdiction was established. Six counties were designated, with Stillwater—twenty miles from the nearest railroad—as the seat of Payne County.[1]

The months following the opening of the Unassigned Lands were memorable. The exciting but hard days of settling in and proving up claims plus the political ferment as a territorial structure evolved added an air of suspense to daily life, especially in Payne County. Hopeful pioneers in their newly established communities competed for the big prize that political maneuvering in Guthrie had assured the county. The balance of power in the territorial assembly was in the hands of the People's Party Alliance, and three of the four alliance delegates were from Stillwater. Competition for the college had settled down to a dogfight between Perkins and Stillwater. Governor Steele had appointed three site-location commissioners who, after studying the possibilities of both communities, had chosen Stillwater on June 26, 1891.[2] Steele then named a board of regents for the college. Robert J. Barker, who held a homestead in Crescent, was chosen as president and secretary; and Amos A. Ewing, Kingfisher, treasurer. Other members were John A. Wimberly, Kingfisher, and J. P. Layne, Norman. Steele, an ex officio member, left one position vacant.[3]

Meanwhile, James C. Neal had been playing a crucial role in the governor's planning. He had known Steele since their Indiana boyhood days, and throughout 1890 had advised him by mail on the mission of land-grant colleges. At that time, Neal was on the staff of the experiment station at the Florida State Agricultural College. His letters had convinced Steele that he was needed in Stillwater. He became the director of the Oklahoma experiment station on August 14, 1891.[4]

After the enabling act had been passed and signed into law by Governor Steele, Oklahoma A. and M. College came to life in a series of seven steps described in the 1891-1892 catalog. On November 25, 1891, the regents met to plan the college's opening. Because he was president and secretary of the regents, Barker was elected to serve as president of the college as well. His academic title would be professor of moral and mental science. Faculty members elected were Steele's friend, Neal, professor of natural science; Edward F. Clark, professor of English literature and mathematics; Alexander C. Magruder, professor of agriculture and horticulture; and Captain Lewis J. Darnell, tactician and commandant. The regents adopted the courses of study for the preparatory and college departments, decided to postpone the requirement that military uniforms be required, and set Monday, December 16, as the first day of the first session. The quarter system would be followed, military discipline applied, and the theory-with-practice concept confirmed. Barker and Neal were ordered to "prepare a history of the organization of the College, with a list of students, course of studies, daily programs, prospectus and other information necessary, and to send copies, duly attested by the Board of Regents, to the proper authorities." The seventh step, of course, was to convene and register the college's first student body.[5] On Saturday, December 14, 1891, twenty-two males and twenty-three females were registered on schedule by President Barker and Dr. Neal.[6]

The years 1891 to 1894 may be viewed as a trial-and-error period, a period in which the faith, patience, and stamina of Neal enabled the infant college to overcome a wide array of obstacles. An early faculty member, Frank A. Waugh, wrote: "Here was a college with no buildings, no equipment, no course of study, no history, no traditions—nothing but a charter and a picked-up faculty. But that faculty was not dismayed. . . . They began without handicaps to make a college as it ought to be. . . . They had a merry time and for the most part enjoyed it. They founded a great institution, to be sure, but without much thought for the gravity of their actions and certainly without any feeling for the hardships and discouragements usually imputed to the pioneers."

It was a time when many things were being tested for workable perimeters, among them student-faculty relationships, the extent to which military discipline would be enforced, the use of temporary quarters for teaching, town-and-gown cooperation, and the difficult task of grooming green preparatory enrollees for college-level work. There were more than enough challenges to go around. In the beginning, most of the students were from Stillwater. They merely followed Clark from his temporary public school classroom in the First Methodist Church at Eighth and Duncan to his temporary Oklahoma A. and M. preparatory facilities in the Congregational Church just north of the courthouse. Clark, despite his title, had now been given responsibility for history and all sub-freshman subjects in addition to English and mathematics.[7] There were no buildings north of the Congregational Church. What was to become the campus was unbroken prairie.[8] During this period of borrowed space, classes also were held in the Presbyterian Church and both the Methodist Episcopal Church and the Methodist Episcopal Church, South. Occasionally, secular locations were used, but the town's churches seemed to sense a special responsibility in helping launch this new educational enterprise.[9]

Before the little college was to have a permanent home in the summer of 1894, it had grown from forty-five preparatory students and a faculty of five to an enrollment of fifty-four collegiate students and ninety preparatory students served by a faculty of twelve. Clark now taught at both preparatory and collegiate levels in English and mathematics. In the college department, only a senior class remained to be formed.[10] Hard pressed for teaching space as they awaited the completion of the College Building (now known as Old Central), the faculty adopted a report by a new faculty member, Willis W. Hutto, in which he announced that he had secured the *Oklahoma Hawk* office for college work.[11] Whether this referred to space only or to journalistic work by his students is not known, although in the context of the meeting it seems likely he was referring to space. At this juncture, Hutto, who had relieved Clark of his English duties, also taught history and constitutional law and, for a short time, military tactics as well. He required original declamations to be delivered from the chapel rostrum during the junior and senior years.[12]

That same faculty meeting revealed a growing sensitivity to the college's public relations. Professor Magruder was appointed to inform the city council of the faculty's action in a case involving two young men apprehended while stealing poultry for a chicken roast. Some faculty members wanted to keep the matter quiet. However, a motion to "see city editors about restraining publications of [the] late trouble" lost. How the vote split was not included in the minutes, but it seems obvious that the early faculty took a dim view of telling editors what they should or should not print.[13]

Another feature of the Barker administration was the work duty assigned to students. Agricultural students were required to perform two hours of farm labor each weekday on a variable pay scale. Maximum pay in the beginning was ten cents an hour. This later was increased to fifteen cents. Mechanical arts students worked four hours a week in the college shops. This work was considered to be "instructive" and, therefore, was without pay.[14]

It was time to increase the flow of basic information about the college and its programs. The college catalog for 1893-1894 was prepared with a surer grasp of what the college could deliver. Harry E. Thompson, principal of the Preparatory Department, and President Barker collaborated on the catalog, spending most of the summer working out details

SPECIAL COLLECTIONS, OSU LIBRARY

Important faculty figures in the early days of the Oklahoma A. and M. literary societies (*from the left*) were George L. Holter, Alexander C. Magruder, Willis W. Hutto, and Frank A. Waugh. Holter chaired the Literary Societies Committee; Magruder established the Magruder Medal for literary excellence; Hutto served as informal advisor and critic; and Waugh, though a Webster member, gave strong support to the petition of the Sigma Literary Society.

and preparing copy for the printer. That fall, the number of collegiate students finally had caught up with the dominant preparatory enrollment of the first two years. The freshman class had forty-one students and the sophomore class, twenty-five. Sixty-six preparatory students were also enrolled. A new governor, William C. Renfrow, had named a new board of regents; the territorial assembly had enacted legislation giving the regents authority to fix salaries, prescribe duties, and fill all vacancies at the college. No longer was the president of the board, simply by virtue of that position, to be president of the college.[15]

From its first classes on December 14, 1891, until the spring term of 1895, the Oklahoma A. and M. College offered students nothing that could be identified as journalistically focused. This did not mean that a student could not set his sights on a journalism career, unlikely as such a choice was in the student body of that day. However, opportunities for journalistic expression, if any, would have to be developed outside the courses then available.

A first step toward such extracurricular opportunities developed with the birth of the first literary society. The little agricultural college in Stillwater was quick to follow the example of older and more prestigious institutions of higher learning, where such societies flourished. It is not surprising, then, that in January 1892, less than a month following the beginning of classes in the Congregational Church, the faculty granted a charter to the Star-Crescent Literary Society, made up of nearly every member of the sub-freshman preparatory class. Apparently, the Crescents had established a good reputation, for the faculty four months later requested them to "have charge of all exercises" during one day of commencement activities. At that time, Stillwater was a town of 500 to 600 inhabitants, and the first freshman class had not yet been created out of the raw material of the first preparatory class. Despite this, commencement exercises were held for the next four years as the college awaited its first graduating class.[16]

The Star-Crescent Society was short-lived. It reorganized the following year but disbanded in the spring of 1893. In referring to its death, James H. Adams, a member of the first graduating class, reported on a surprise box supper sponsored by the Crescents but gave no reason for the society's demise. A new society, the EFC Debating Club, was organized soon after, but it, too, had a short existence. The void was filled on October 16, 1893, when a small group of male students met at the Methodist Episcopal Church, South, which by then was the principal seat of the college, to organize a new society.[17] Members chose the name Webster Debating Society. Weekly meetings were held, usually on Saturday evening, and membership excluded females. Until the College Building was occupied in the summer of 1894, the Websters met in a variety of places. In addition to the church where the first meeting was held, the group met at the experiment station laboratory, the county courthouse and the North Schoolhouse.[18]

Later that October, two students, Maggie Hutto and Elsie Parker, petitioned President Barker for permission to organize a similar organization that would admit both male and female students. Permission was somewhat grudgingly granted by Barker. Speaking in his slow voice that emphasized the last syllable of important words, he said his approval was contingent upon a constitution and bylaws acceptable to the faculty. The Sigma Literary Society was over its first big hurdle. Professor Frank A. Waugh, whose horticultural articles frequently appeared in national publications, had been elected as the first president of the Webster Debating Society. He could hardly sit by without guiding the discussion in a favorable direction as the faculty considered the Sigma petition.[19] It was becoming apparent to faculty members that a supervisory mechanism would be needed, for there likely would be other societies formed. Professor George L. Holter was appointed chairman of the newly created Committee on Literary Societies, which would consider the Sigmas' rules of procedure and then report to the full faculty.[20]

The Sigmas held their first formal meeting on October 20, 1893, and began the job of drafting a constitution similar to that of the Websters. The document was received and referred to the Committee on Literary Societies at the faculty's October 23 meeting. It was approved with minor changes at the faculty's November 13 meeting. At that meeting, the Websters' constitution and bylaws were presented by Professor Holter.

Elsie Parker, with strong support from Maggie Hutto, appeared before the faculty asking that their petition to establish the Sigma Literary Society be approved. Frank Waugh helped lead the request to a happy ending.

They, too, were referred to the Committee on Literary Societies for study. Approval was granted at the faculty's meeting on December 11, when the society was formally recognized.[21] The Friday evening Sigma programs were more varied than those of the Websters. They included opening music, roll call, a declamation, a dramatic reading, more music, a debate, practice in extemporaneous speaking, drill in parliamentary procedure, the minutes, the report of the critic appointed to evaluate the evening's program, general criticism from the audience and, finally, assignments of future responsibilities.[22]

The variety of the Sigma programs plus the fact that the society was co-educational made for stiff competition. Soon the Websters broadened their vistas and changed their name to reflect a literary rather than simply a debating focus.[23] Programs began to include declamations, readings, essays, music, mock trials, and an occasional guest lecture by a faculty member.[24]

One of the faculty that students looked to for guidance in the literary societies' programs was Willis W. Hutto, whose brother Frank was a territorial leader in the Republican Party and later would become a faculty member. Hutto's courses were useful to the goals of the two groups. Others sympathetic with the literary societies were Professors Magruder, Holter, Waugh and, later, Freeman E. Miller. Magruder gave

The first Magruder Medal, established by Alexander C. Magruder to promote literary excellence, was presented to Kate Neal by Freeman E. Miller. Miss Neal was the daughter of James C. Neal, the first director of the experiment station and a powerful force in the college's early history.

the societies both recognition and motivation by awarding a gold medallion for literary merit. The first of these was won by Kate Neal in 1893. The award was continued for two years before Magruder, dismissed by the board of regents in the summer of 1895, left for Tulane University to study medicine.

In their first year, the Sigmas grew from nine charter members to thirty-three, including faculty members Hutto, Thompson, and James M. Halbrook. Halbrook, an assistant in the preparatory department, served as one of the society's early presidents, once again suggesting that faculty membership was sometimes classed as more than "honorary." Despite faculty participation, apparently there was less than smooth sailing at times. Within two months after the Sigmas organized, the faculty went into a committee of the whole to discuss the literary societies. Some wanted all debate topics to be submitted for faculty approval. The motion lost. The next suggestion that problems existed came fifteen months after the Sigmas' first meeting. A faculty motion that the Sigmas live up to the letter of their constitution and bylaws carried. How the group had voted was not reported.[25]

While it would be nice to think that journalistic stirrings played a part in the establishment of these organizations, it is closer to the truth to say that the regents' policy against secret Greek letter societies, strongly supported by the students themselves, played a more important role.[26] On the work-oriented Oklahoma A. and M. campus, as was true of earlier land-grant colleges, students were searching for relief through entertainment and social contacts. They knew that literary societies, with their professed humanistic aims, were likely to be looked upon favorably by the regents because of their informal extension of educational goals.

In one sense, the literary societies were a showcase for the college while at the same time bringing entertainment to hundreds of towns-people, still swelling with pride over the good fortune of having landed Oklahoma A. and M. in the tug-and-pull of territorial politics. Stillwater residents turned out in goodly numbers for the programs of the Websters and the Sigmas.[27]

The increasing attention paid to the societies would soon lead to conflict. As competition for promising new members became more spirited, tensions began to develop. When an 1893 debate between the two societies ended in a Sigma victory, the Websters reported that they had not understood the ground rules. They had prepared for long arguments, but were limited to ten minutes each. They were not prepared to concentrate their remarks. Members voted to have their secretary inform the Sigmas that they did not desire another joint meeting. Tempers cooled after a time, and the earlier friendly rivalry was resumed.[28]

Soon the societies were looking for ways to build more interest in

Competition between the Sigmas and the Websters was intense, especially when joint meetings were held. Considerable planning preceded the meetings, and resentment and anger sometimes followed. Discussing details of future competition are Sigma member Clarence R. Donart (*left*) and Arthur B. McReynolds, a Webster member.

their programs. It appeared to some that the missing ingredient was a journalistic component. To meet this need, student writers submitted briefs to the *Stillwater Eagle-Gazette*. These personal columns were printed under the heading "College Notes" and were signed with pseudonyms such as "No Man," "Mirza," "Vanquished," "The Populist," and "Pagoda." The items published sometimes boomeranged, for readers complained when the opinionated squibs were too barbed or too far-fetched to be acceptable. When editor Charles M. Becker decided that all future submissions must be signed with the name of a student currently enrolled, the correspondence ended.[29]

However, students with a journalistic bent were not easily deterred. "Manuscript newspapers" prepared by the literary societies became the medium for a continuation of this highly personal journalism. There was little news in the modern sense in these papers. They most closely resembled country correspondence in rural community newspapers, plus a bit of gossip covering the romantic interests of certain students and an occasional good-natured, humorous jab at a faculty member. Though crude by modern standards, this development made an important contribution to early journalism at Oklahoma A. and M. These unpublished, handwritten newspapers were read aloud at meetings by one of the members who had assembled the news. Apparently, this responsibility was rotated. The name of the news sheet often changed at the whim of the person assigned to collect the items. The manuscript newspapers were not considered by their creators to be a passing fad. The one remaining issue of the "Riverside Review," published by the Sigmas and edited by Willa Adams and an unnamed colleague, is numbered Volume 10, Number 5, and is inscribed on ruled tablet paper. Apparently, the staff did not follow traditional practice, for the society was not old enough to have reached a tenth volume.[30] Some evidence suggests that the Websters, too, produced manuscript newspapers. The reading of these papers added to the joviality of the meetings and probably helped keep attendance up.

The editor of one weekly manuscript newspaper described it years later as "the highlight of the whole program." To be mentioned in one of the papers was the secret desire of most students. Knowing this, the editors sought to use as many names as possible in each issue.[31] The old axiom that "names make news" was clearly evident.

This was a time when large paintings of George Washington and Abraham Lincoln graced the walls of many a classroom across the land and a sense of nationalism was keenly felt by students and faculty alike. It seemed perfectly natural in this context that one of the joint efforts of the literary societies would be an anniversary program commemorating Washington's Birthday. The first such program was presented in the College Hall on the evening of February 22, 1895, before a large crowd of Stillwater citizens, students, and faculty, but not before a faculty disagreement over supervisory responsibility had been settled. On January 28, the faculty considered a resolution to make the event an annual affair under the supervision of the Committee on Literary Societies. The program, under this plan, would be dominated by literary society members. On February 4, the resolution was reconsidered. Professors Freeman E. Miller, Edward F. Clark, and Harry E. Thompson opposed the plan. Miller's growing strength on the faculty was apparent in the outcome. The resolution was revised so that the celebration would be "by the student body of the college under the supervision and control of the Chair of English," which Miller occupied. Miller's egalitarianism and his ability to advance a point of view strongly seemed clear from the outcome of this small faculty tiff. The plan finally adopted was to have a program "rendered by two declaimers, two essayists, two orators and two debaters, together with one reader, the last of whom shall read all or a portion of Washington's Farewell Address."[32]

Later that year, perhaps with encouragement from the versatile Professor Miller, the two groups made plans to upgrade their manuscript newspapers. Their efforts led to the establishment of the *Oklahoma A. and M. College Mirror,* the first student publication given general distribution.

Oklahoma A. and M. students, under strict military discipline and a

SPECIAL COLLECTIONS, OSU LIBRARY

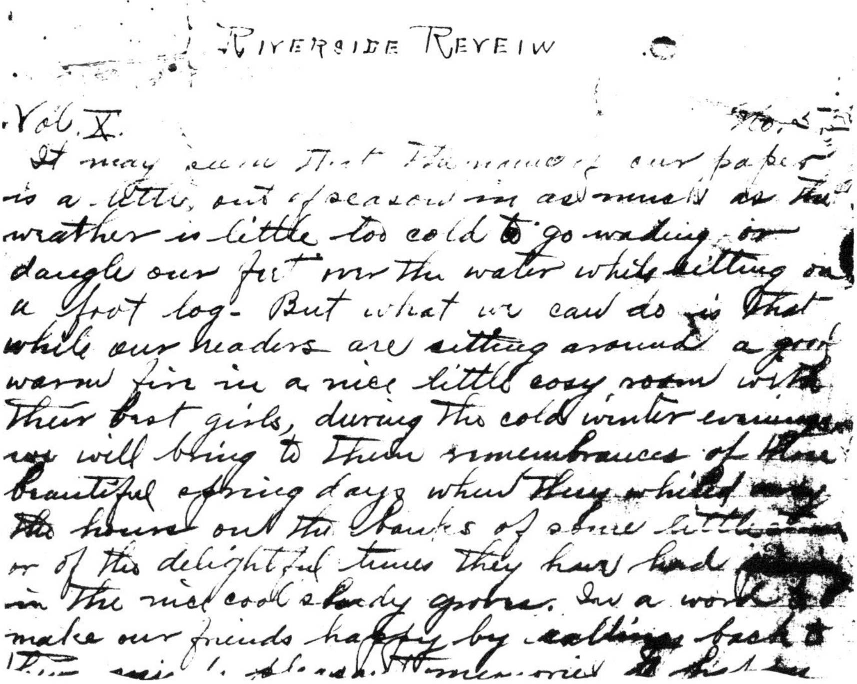
Riverside Review

Vol. X. No. 2

It may seem that the name of our paper is a little out of season inasmuch as the weather is little too cold to go wading or dangle our feet over the water while sitting on a foot log. But what we can do is that while our readers are sitting around a good warm fire in a nice little cosy room with their best girls, during the cold winter evenings we will bring to their remembrances of those beautiful spring days when they whiled away the hours on the banks of some little [illegible] or of the delightful times they have had in the nice cool shady groves. In a word [illegible] make our friends happy by calling back to them [illegible] pleasant memories [illegible]

A forerunner of the first campus newspaper was the "Riverside Review," a so-called manuscript newspaper. These manuscript papers, with varying names and editors from month to month, were a feature of literary society meetings that boosted attendance. The issue shown here probably was edited by Willa Adams, who later wrote the booklet *The Sigma Literary Society.*

Several pranks growing out of the intense rivalry between the Websters and Sigmas are described in considerable detail in *The Sigma Literary Society 1893-1897.*[33] Obviously, the members were not immune to these cyclic outbreaks. After a period of relative calm during which they had contributed immeasurably to the publishing of the newly established campus newspaper, tensions once more increased, causing faculty concern. Finally, in 1896, the Websters asked for trouble. They had purchased and were publicly wearing badges. Five Websters, in fact, later wore the shining insignias during commencement exercises. Their action, technically at least, was not in violation of campus rules, but it did not conform to the spirit of expected student behavior. This was followed by a disturbance at a Sigma meeting. Someone had wired the electric bell system to set the gongs going, temporarily disrupting proceedings. The Sigmas, blaming the Websters, retaliated by stealing some Webster refreshments. Then came a "reconciliation" gift of a bushel of apples in which the Websters had spiked the fruit with quinine and cayenne pepper. Near violence was the result at a meeting in the College Building on December 4, 1896.[34]

Professors Holter and Miller were appointed to conduct an investigation. When members refused to inform on one another, the faculty suspended nine male students for one month and, in an order issued January 25, 1897, ordered both societies to disband.[35]

This action meant a change in responsibilities on the *Mirror*. The literary societies along with the College Press Bureau, one of Miller's several responsibilities, had been early sponsors of the paper. Indeed, in its early history, most of the editorial work had been done by the literary groups. The masthead no longer reflected this when the 1897-98 academic year began. It now read: "Published by the faculty and students under the supervision of the department of English." Below this statement, in boldfaced type, Miller for the first time was listed as editor. No student staff was shown, nor was there any mention of the College Press Bureau. Little change was apparent in succeeding issues. Miller's steady hand gave the paper continuity. He was a dogmatic perfectionist, but the students of that period were accustomed to discipline. Oklahoma A. and M. was, as its catalog stressed, run along military lines.[36]

As concern over the Webster-Sigma tensions finally eased and feelings had healed somewhat, a move to form another literary society led to the first real challenge of military-style faculty authority over students. A group vaguely identified in faculty minutes as "the literary society" had met in a room over the Payne County Bank. Their meeting came one day after the faculty had adopted and posted a resolution which placed students "under control of the faculty" from their enrollment until severed by withdrawal, suspension, expulsion, or graduation. In addition, the resolution prohibited such student meetings in college buildings "or elsewhere" without prior faculty approval. The faculty assumed the resolution would be followed to the letter. Instead, it had been violated by the off-campus meeting on November 6, 1897.

At a special meeting three days later, the faculty ruled that its order of November 5 had been violated. The following day, E. E. Bogue, Henry E. Glazier, and Lowery L. Lewis were appointed to conduct an investigation. On November 11, the three committee members met in the mathematics room of the College Building with eighteen students who had violated the rule, then on November 12 the three faculty members had prepared a report that reflected a desire to resolve the impasse. The report, rather than being sharply critical, revealed sensitivity to student aspirations. The students had told the investigators that—in the words of the report—the faculty appeared to be "hostile toward the formation of a literary society and that the restrictions would practically prevent such an organization because they would prevent general interest among the students, the growth of the society, and the training they expected to get by appearing before audiences."

Then came an argument that was even more thought-provoking. The students told Bogue, Glazier, and Lewis that they had exercised their right to meet as citizens and that "no violation of any order of the faculty" had been intended. The students being interrogated expressed a desire to hold literary meetings in the Assembly Hall (formerly the College Building and ultimately Old Central) and to work for the "best good of the institution." Showing further willingness to compromise, they said they would limit attendance of non-members to persons "especially invited by members of the society." They also told the committee they were willing to await the further action of the faculty.

In an appendage to the report, Bogue, Glazier, and Lewis recommended "that the faculty grant to the students the use of the Assembly Hall one evening per week for a literary meeting to continue not later than 10 o'clock and that visitors be allowed to attend only on invitation of a society member." The report as read was accepted, but an amendment was offered. Admission by visitors would be restricted to those holding tickets issued by members. These tickets would be collected at the door by the sergeant-at-arms, and the order granting this permission would become effective "on and after the ratification of a constitution." The recommendation passed as amended. Although the students had not yet heard the term *in loco parentis*—popularized during the campus unrest of the 1960s—they had placed a chink in its armor at Oklahoma A. and M. College.

History would show that the off-campus meeting November 6, 1897, was the beginning of the Omega Literary Society. The Omegas, the second group to choose a Greek name, held their first faculty-approved meeting in the College Building on November 27. Ten months had passed since the death of the rival societies. Tempers finally had cooled, and most of the officers in the new literary society had been Websters and Sigmas who had taken part in the scrap a year earlier.[37]

In 1899, faculty concerns surfaced again, this time in connection with another society, at first unidentified in faculty minutes. Holter, Thompson, and Glazier had received a revised constitution from the group. A week later, faculty minutes revealed that the "Oratorical Association" had been investigated in connection with charges of disorder involving the "Literary Society." The faculty committee that looked into the unspecified disorder recommended no further action be taken and that the matter be dropped. Its report was accepted.[38]

In later years, the Philomatheans and Alphas formed, as did others with similar objectives. The Omega Literary Society, which survived for nearly thirty years, had the greatest longevity.[39] But as the college grew, the literary societies were less central to the needs of students. The

Sigmas and Websters had dominated student life for a brief period. With their death, student interest never would reach such intensity again. The heyday was over. A variety of interest groups now provided social and cultural outlets. Students formed clubs based upon their courses of study, later to be known as departmental clubs. And as the prejudice against fraternities and sororities subsided, local chapters were formed preparatory to seeking national Greek letter affiliation.[40]

Although new organizations with different interests and goals began to capture student support, the literary society movement continued to play an important role in Oklahoma A. and M. student life for more than three decades. The last of the societies, Omega, apparently closed its books sometime between 1929 and 1930. It did not appear in the club section of the 1930 *Redskin*, although the Debate and Oratory Club continued active for several years, finally giving up between 1935 and 1936, based upon yearbook data.[41]

With the passing of time, the literary societies outlived their usefulness. But for years to come many an old grad would pay glowing tribute to training received in the programs.[42]

Despite the breakup of the Websters and Sigmas, student journalism was now launched. Except for one brief interruption, it would develop beyond the imaginations of those few students and faculty members who had given it wings.

Endnotes

1. Philip Reed Rulon, *Oklahoma State University—Since 1890* (Stillwater: Oklahoma State University Press, 1975), pp. 3-16; Oklahoma A. and M. College *Daily O'Collegian,* 14 December 1941, pp. 1, 6; *Centennial Clarion,* Oklahoma City Economic Development, Incorporated, November 1988, pp. 10, 11; *Ponca City News,* 11 January 1989, p. 2-C; *Stillwater NewsPress,* undated clipping in Scrapbook, Willa Adams Dusch Collection, Special Collections, Edmon Low Library, Oklahoma State University, Stillwater, Oklahoma; *Universal Standard Encyclopedia* (New York, NY: Unicorn Publishers, Incorporated, 1955), vol. 17, p. 6287; Grant Foreman, *A History of Oklahoma* (Norman: University of Oklahoma Press, 1942), p. 243; Stephen Jones, "Captain Frank Frantz, The Rough Rider Governor of Oklahoma Territory," *Chronicles of Oklahoma,* vol. 43, no. 4 (Winter 1965-1966), p. 382.

2. LeRoy H. Fischer, Oklahoma State University *Historic Old Central* (Stillwater: Oklahoma State University, 1988), pp. 10-13, 22-26; *Daily O'Collegian,* 14 December 1941, p. 1; *1923 Redskin,* pp. 21, 22, Oklahoma A. and M. College Yearbook.

3. *Annual Catalog, Oklahoma A. and M. College, 1891-1892,* unnumbered page describing the college; *Daily O'Collegian,* 14 December 1941, p. 1.

4. Rulon, p. 4; Francis Richard Gilmore, "A Historical Study of the Oklahoma Agricultural Experiment Station" (Doctor of Education dissertation, Oklahoma State University, 1967), p. 21; *Oklahoma A. and M. College Mirror,* 15 May 1895, p. 1.

5. *Annual Catalog, Oklahoma A. and M. College, 1891-1892,* unnumbered page following History section, and unnumbered page describing the college; *Stillwater NewsPress,* 13 May 1951; *Daily O'Collegian,* 14 December 1941, pp. 1, 2, 18 April 1942, p. 2.

6. *Stillwater NewsPress*, 27 April 1988, p. 5B; *Daily O'Collegian*, 13-14 November 1941, p. 1, 14 December 1941, p. 1, 21 February 1942, pp. 1, 2; James K. Hastings, "Oklahoma A. and M. College and Old Central," *Chronicles of Oklahoma*, vol. 28, no. 1 (Spring 1950), p. 82; *Stillwater NewsPress (NewsPlus)*, 11 December 1991, p. 1B. The *O'Collegian* articles cited offer valuable insights into the crucial 1891-1894 period.

7. Oklahoma A. and M. College *Orange and Black,* September 1908, p. 4; *Daily O'Collegian*, 18 April 1942, pp. 2, 3, 21 February 1942, pp. 1, 2; *Stillwater NewsPress (NewsPlus)*, 11 December 1991, p. 1B.

8. *Orange and Black,* September 1908, p. 4.

9. *Annual Catalog, Oklahoma A. and M. College, 1891-1892,* six unnumbered pages of historical narrative. See also J. Homer Adams, "In Retrospect and Prospect," *Oklahoma A. and M. College Magazine*, vol. 13, no. 4 (January 1942), p. 8; *Stillwater NewsPress (NewsPlus)*, 11 December 1991, p. 1B.

10. *Annual Catalog, Oklahoma A. and M. College, 1894-1895,* pp. 2, 3, 116-121.

11. Oklahoma Agricultural and Mechanical College Faculty, "Minutes of the First Faculty," 9 January 1893, Special Collections, Edmon Low Library.

12. *Annual Catalog, Oklahoma A. and M. College, 1893-1894,* p. 41; Rulon, p. 89.

13. Oklahoma Agricultural and Mechanical College Faculty, "Minutes of the First Faculty," 9 January 1893.

14. *Annual Catalog, Oklahoma A. and M. College, 1892-1893,* pp. 12, 13; *Annual Catalog, Oklahoma A. and M. College, 1893-1894*, pp. 31, 32; *Daily O'Collegian,* 12 November 1941, p. 1.

15. *Annual Catalog, Oklahoma A. and M. College, 1893-1894,* pp. 5, 6 and two unnumbered pages following frontispiece listing regents and faculty; *Daily O'Collegian,* 9 December 1941, p. 1. Thompson incorrectly asserted that this was the first catalog. It was the third.

16. *Daily O'Collegian*, 13 November 1941, p. 1; Rulon, p. 100, citing the *Stillwater Gazette,* 22 January 1892 and 15 April 1892; *Orange and Black,* September 1908, pp. 3-5; George L. Holter, "When the School Was Young," *Oklahoma A. and M. College Magazine*, vol. 1, no. 3 (November 1929), pp. 12, 31; Oklahoma Agricultural and Mechanical College Faculty, "Minutes of the First Faculty," 12 May 1892. See also Willa Adams Dusch, *The Sigma Literary Society 1893-1897* 1987, edited by Berlin B. Chapman (Stillwater: The Research Foundation, Oklahoma A. and M. College, 1951), p. 3.

17. *Daily O'Collegian*, 13 November 1941, p. 1; *Oklahoma A. and M. College Mirror*, 15 May 1895, p. 10; *Stillwater NewsPress* , 11 December 1949, p. 4; Berlin B. Chapman, "Literary Records Preserved in Library," *Oklahoma A. and M. College Magazine*, vol. 17, no. 7 (April 1945), p. 4; Patrick M. Murphy, *A History of Oklahoma State University Student Life and Services* (Stillwater: Oklahoma State University, 1988), p. 46. Faculty minutes for 16 October 1893 show that Professor George L. Holter had received a request for a male literary society. A faculty motion that the president appoint a Committee on Literary Societies carried. Based upon subsequent minutes, it appears certain that Holter was appointed to chair the committee. The 1894-95 college catalog (pp. 114, 115) was the first to mention the role of literary societies at Oklahoma A. and M.

18. Chapman, p. 4; *Oklahoma A. and M. College Mirror,* 15 May 1895, p. 7; Rulon, pp. 100, 101; J. Homer Adams, "When the College Was Young," *Oklahoma A. and M. College Magazine*, vol. 1, no. 4 (December 1929), pp. 9, 21.

19. Rulon, p. 103; Dusch, pp. 3-6; Frank D. Northup, talk presented at Historical Packet Ceremonies, 15 December 1941, p. 1, Special Collections, Edmon Low Library.

20. Dusch, pp. 3-6.

21. Oklahoma Agricultural and Mechanical College Faculty, "Minutes of the First Faculty," 23 October, 13 November and 11 December 1893. See also Berlin B. Chapman, "A 1951 Reunion Day Attraction," *Oklahoma A. and M. College Magazine*, vol. 22, no. 9 (May 1951), p. 23; *Oklahoma A. and M. College Mirror,* 15 May 1895, p. 10.

22. Dusch, p. 14; Chapman, "A 1951 Reunion Day Attraction,"

23. Dusch, pp. 11, 20, 21.

24. Chapman, "Literary Records Preserved in Library," p. 13.

25. Dusch, pp. 7, 36; Rulon, pp. 28, 29; *Stillwater NewsPress,* 14 January 1987, p. 1B; Oklahoma Agricultural and Mechanical College Faculty, "Minutes of the First Faculty," 18 December 1893, 29 January 1894.

26. Rulon, p. 100.

27. Dusch, p. 15; Chapman, "A 1951 Reunion Day Attraction," p. 22.

28. Rulon, pp. 103, 104; *Daily O'Collegian,* 14 November 1941, p. 1.

29. Rulon, p. 105; *Stillwater Eagle-Gazette,* 14 February 1895, p. 5.

30. Richard D. Wilson, "Early Oklahoma A. and M. College Newspapers—A Perspective," unpublished manuscript submitted to fulfill requirements in MC 4360 in 1980, pp. 3-5, Special Collections, Edmon Low Library; Chapman, "A 1951 Reunion Day Attraction," p. 23; Rulon, p. 105.

31. Chapman, "A 1951 Reunion Day Attraction," p. 23.

32. Oklahoma Agricultural and Mechanical College Faculty, "Minutes of the First Faculty," 28 January 1895, 4 February 1895; Dusch, p. 15; Scrapbook, Willa Adams Dusch Collection. This clipping is unidentified as to source and date.

33. Dusch, pp. 20-30; *Oklahoma A. and M. College Mirror,* 15 June 1896, p. 13; "Early Military Training," *Oklahoma A. and M. College Magazine,* vol. 1, no. 7 (March 1930), p. 4.

34. Rulon, pp. 31, 104; *Stillwater NewsPress (News Plus),* 14 February 1987, p. 1B; Dusch, pp. 21, 22, 25; *1916 Redskin,* p. 215; *Oklahoma A. and M. College Mirror,* 15 January 1896, p. 5, 15 June 1896, pp. 12, 13.

35. Dusch, pp. 25, 26; Rulon, p. 104; *Stillwater Eagle-Gazette,* 17 January 1895, p. 5; Oklahoma Agricultural and Mechanical College Faculty, "Minutes of the First Faculty," 25 January 1897; Frances Campbell interview with Willa Adams Dusch, undated clipping, Willa Adams Dusch Collection.

36. Oklahoma Agricultural and Mechanical College Faculty, "Minutes of the First Faculty," 25 January 1897; Chapman, "A 1951 Reunion Day to Remember," pp. 22, 23; *Oklahoma A. and M. College Mirror,* 15 September 1897, p. 8, January 1898, pp. 3, 6.

37. Dusch, p. 30; Rulon, pp. 103-105; Oklahoma Agricultural and Mechanical College Faculty, "Minutes of the First Faculty," 5, 9, 10, 11, 23 November 1897; Chapman, "A 1951 Reunion Day Attraction," p. 23.

38. Oklahoma Agricultural and Mechanical College Faculty, "Minutes of the First Faculty," 19 May 1899, 27 May 1899, 2 June 1899; *1916 Redskin,* p. 216.

39. Dusch, p. 31.

40. Rulon, p. 105.

41. *1928 Redskin,* p. 339; *1929 Redskin,* p. 206; *1930 Redskin,* p. 176; *1935 Redskin,* p. 227.

42. Chapman, "Literary Records Preserved in Library," p. 13.

3 A Press Bureau and a Mirror

It would be difficult to find more singularly interesting characters for this story than three of those who were drawn by the lure of the frontier to Oklahoma Territory and subsequently to the fledging land-grant college in Stillwater. In the order of their appearance on stage, they were Freeman E. Miller, Angelo C. Scott, and Frank D. Northup. Each was important in the early development of journalism and related studies at Oklahoma A. and M. College.

Miller was enigmatic as well as charismatic. He was one of the restless young who left such well-established states as Indiana and Ohio to seek their fortunes in the push westward. He could have remained at home and achieved prominence—regional if not national—in law, politics, journalism, or the more delicate art of poetry. He had established himself as a "comer" and was seen by his elders as one of Indiana's most promising young men. However, the frontier drew him, for whatever reasons, and his life was to be lived out in the robust give-and-take of this developing landscape.[1]

He was born on May 19, 1864, on a farm in Fountain County near Newtown, Indiana, one year before the Confederacy would stack arms at Appomattox and five years after Horace Greeley's much-quoted admonition, "Go west, young man, go west!" He was destined to be the first journalist at the new agricultural college in Oklahoma Territory's red dirt country. Greeley's admonition and John Clark Ridpath's influence would lead him to what Miller later was to call the Southwest Country.[2]

By the age of five, he was reading from the family Bible and composing rhymes to show to his mother. When he was ten, his father gave him a copy of Ridpath's *History of the United States*. He literally learned it by heart. By the time he was twelve, the precocious lad had read everything he could beg or borrow, from dime novels to Gibbon's *Decline and Fall of the Roman Empire*. He wanted to own a volume of Shakespeare but he did not have the necessary $1.25, so he chopped and peddled stove wood until he had earned enough to buy it. It seems obvious that his reading menu, considering his age, was unusually large and sophisticated. His expanding talents continued to be challenged. That year, he read an original composition, much of it in verse, at a meeting of his country school's literary society.[3]

In 1880, when he was sixteen, Miller was graduated from his township high school and immediately began teaching an eighteen-month term there for $42 a month, a princely sum for those times. The following summer he taught a term in an adjoining school district. His salary was $20.[4]

But the would-be poet had a fire in his belly: he wanted to go to college. Teaching in a country school was not enough to quench the fire. College was out of reach without money. How was he to earn it? The answer came when he signed on with a railroad crew, hacking ties, saving piling, and performing other menial tasks. The strong stand he took against the railroads in his law career years later may have had its beginning here. The raw language and sometimes crude behavior of the crew constituted a new kind of education for the sensitive youth, one that no doubt brought with it considerable discomfort. However, the attitude of the owners toward labor—and toward the farmers over whose fields the tracks pushed their way—may have had even more impact.[5]

In any event, in the fall of 1881 Miller entered DePauw University in Greencastle, Indiana, where twenty-eight years later journalism's most prestigious professional society, Sigma Delta Chi, would have its beginning. He was a preparatory student for two terms in 1881-82 before starting college-level work in the 1883-84 academic year. DePauw brought him into contact with his idol, John Clark Ridpath. James E. Watson, later to gain fame as majority leader of the United States Senate, was a classmate, and Albert J. Beveridge, who later served with distinction for twelve years in the United States Senate while becoming a noted public speaker and author, held membership in the same literary society as Miller. His parents had fostered a respect for knowledge and now Miller's well-tuned intellect was being stimulated in Greencastle's heady atmosphere.[6]

DePauw was a whole new world for this country boy starving for knowledge and culture. The ferment was all around. As a state, Indiana was awakening to her literary heritage. Lew Wallace, James Whitcomb Riley, and a dozen others were writing furiously, and Riley had recognized in Miller the makings of a future poet.[7]

Being gifted intellectually was not without its down side. A life-long problem for Miller was how to deal with the multitude of talents birth had dealt him. This became apparent during the DePauw years. It carried over later into his career at Oklahoma A. and M., where he sometimes was short-tempered with the less gifted around him.[8]

The youth was a workaholic long before there was a word for that trait. He was achievement-oriented and restless. Despite this, he apparently found time for fraternity life. The DePauw yearbook for 1884 listed him as an active member of Phi Delta Theta. He was a sophomore in the class of 1886. While working toward the A.B. degree, he had once again taught at a country school near his home "on the banks of the Turkey Run" and in 1884-85 had been principal of schools in Hillsboro. He also had begun a study of law outside the classroom and was admitted to the Indiana bar in 1886. By graduation time in 1887, he had practiced about a year at Veedersburg, where he also leased and actively operated a country weekly, the *Veedersburg Courier*. Profits from the *Courier* and income from his other work made it possible for him to meet his college expenses but left no time for him to work on the student magazine, the *DePauw Monthly*, or the yearbook, the *Mirror*. It is interesting to note that the first student publication at Oklahoma A. and M. was under Miller's supervision and was given the name *Mirror*.[9] His industry also made it possible for him to court and win Estelle Shroyer, a twenty-two-year-old Hopkins, Missouri, school teacher. They were married on March 22, 1886. Whether it was his work as Hillsboro principal, his intensive, independent law studies the following year, his newspaper work, or the obligations of married life—probably it was a combination of these— Miller's graduation was delayed. Rather than 1886, when he would have finished had he not had so many diversions, he was graduated as valedictorian in 1887.[10]

Perhaps influenced by Ridpath's grasp of the nation's unfolding and of the romance and excitement of adventure, young Miller decided to strike out for Canadian, Texas. He was never to return to his roots, except for brief visits, although he maintained a strong loyalty to his parents throughout their lives.[11]

The decision to leave Indiana meant more than a geographical change in his life. His young wife did not share his enthusiasm for adventure. She wanted no part of Texas. The phlegmatic writer-lawyer refused to be deterred by Estelle's veto. She filed for divorce, and he left for the Southwest. She would later regret having forced the issue.[12]

Miller arrived in Texas in October 1887. Once more, he mixed law and journalism. He shared a law office with Temple Houston, son of the famed hero of the Texas Republic, and in addition to his legal practice he founded a newspaper, the *Canadian Crescent*, writing most of the copy himself. In a matter of months, he had become so well established that he was serving as Hemphill county attorney.

Miller had planned to leave for the newly opened Oklahoma country, but he was diverted from becoming an "89er" at the urging of James S. Hogg, the Texas attorney general who soon would be governor. He was asked to serve as attorney for the thirty-first judicial district, and he accepted the appointment. He held this office in 1889 and most of 1890. His district encompassed nine far-flung west Texas counties.[13]

His role as district attorney was not the only diversion. His personal life was in turmoil. His first wife, after what must have involved a complete reversal of attitude, had sought to win Miller back by impassioned letters, then had traveled to Texas to bid for his love face to face. This posed problems, for Miller had met seventeen-year-old Allee Carey in Canadian, and they had married on September 30, 1888. Miller's young bride apparently was unaware that he had been married before. She may have discovered this later by reading one of Estelle's letters. In any case, the marriage, judging from court records, was a stormy one. Miller resented Allee's deeply held fundamentalist religious beliefs, while Allee resented the sudden intrusion of Estelle Shroyer into a

SPECIAL COLLECTIONS, OSU LIBRARY

Freeman E. Miller's most significant contribution to campus journalism was his dual role as director of the College Press Bureau and supervisor of the *Oklahoma A. and M. College Mirror*. He was frequently published and was widely known as Oklahoma Territory's poet laureate.

marriage that already was complicated by incompatibility and pregnancy. In a series of lawsuits, serious charges and counter charges were made by each against the character of the other. On April 21, 1890, Miller sued for divorce in Bent County, Colorado, with summons to be served by publication in the *Las Animas Leader* for four successive weeks. The divorce decree became final on July 16. About four days earlier, Allee had left Miller to live with relatives in Canadian. Miller's immediate reaction was to convey to Estelle—"fraudulently," Allee charged—what Allee believed to be her own as community property.

On November 21, Allee went to court to preserve her right to the property against the claims of Miller and Estelle. The court record shows that a jury trial was waived. The courtroom once more was filled with charges and counter charges of impropriety. If there was a winner in the messy proceedings, it was Allee. She won her share of the community property, including real estate, and custody of her infant son, Floyd E. Miller, while all court costs were to be assumed by Miller.[14] Details of his personal problems in Texas would be used against him later by political opponents.

The year 1890 was crucial for both Miller and Stillwater's newly approved land-grant college. His youthful instincts for yet a new adventure had been delayed for a year by Hogg's urging and by his own tangled and chaotic personal affairs. By December, when he and Estelle struck out for Oklahoma Territory, they were more than ready to brush the Canadian dust from their garments. He already had tentative plans for the future. He was interested in a struggling Stillwater newspaper, the *Oklahoma Hawk*, which he had intended to buy from Patrick H. and E. Bee Guthrey. The sale apparently never materialized, although three years later he was co-editor of the *Hawk's* successor, the *Oklahoma State Sentinel*. In 1890, too, DePauw conferred the A.M. degree upon Miller. Whatever the degree requirements, they must have been satisfied in absentia. It seems unlikely that he returned to the Greencastle campus for further classes during the busy three years following the A.B. degree.[15] It also seems unlikely that he could have known that the remainder of his life would be spent in Stillwater, punctuated by summer months in his Colorado Springs home at the foot of Pike's Peak.

When Miller started his second youthful adventure late in 1890, Stillwater was a town of 480 souls, most of them from Kansas. Local boosters liked to describe it as the center of a fertile valley fed by the Stillwater, Brush, and Boomer creeks. To put a good face on the matter, they spoke of the area's soil as a "rich chocolate brown."[16] On his arrival, he noted a crude frame structure at the corner of what is now Sixth and Duncan. It was the Congregational Church and would play a historic role in a college that was yet to be. Six streets had been named, and a legal battle was raging over Garnett Burks's claim of legal rights to the townsite. Frame buildings—already there were more than fifty—were going up as fast as carpenters and their helpers could construct them. Horse-drawn wagons and buggies as well as men on horseback were common Main Street sights. Ninth Street was the town's north-south dividing line. Carpenters were the most numerous tradesmen. There were six teamsters, five grocery stores, four physicians, four sawmills, three churches, two blacksmith shops, two stage and mail lines, two hotels, two newspapers, two attorneys, two bakeries, two freighters, and one combination hardware and grocery store. Also on the scene were one deputy U.S. marshal, one bank, one barber shop, one dry goods store, one photographer, one real estate agent, one water well driller, one druggist, one restaurant, one billiard parlor, one furniture store, and one jewelry store. Telephone service was still eight years in the future. The city directory, a single sheet, contained the complete roster of Stillwater's families.[17]

At twenty-six years of age, Miller soon was a man to be reckoned with in his new hometown. Almost immediately, he was involved in politics as a Democrat with Populist sympathies. He hung out his law shingle, became a leader in the temperance movement, was active in church and civic activities, and was developing an eye for real estate.[18]

One authority on early Oklahoma publications lists twenty-five papers, mostly weeklies, published in Stillwater prior to statehood. Another historian lists the number as "more than 50." Miller was identified with four of these, either as editor or editor and publisher, but in one case he was out after only four weeks in a shared editorship. Neither historian mentioned him in connection with the *Hawk* and the *Democrat.*[19]

By mid-year in 1893, Stillwater was seeing its lawyer-journalist in a new light. Charles M. Becker, editor and publisher of the *Gazette*, wrote: "It may not be generally known, but is a fact nevertheless, that Stillwater harbors a poet of no mean talents." Becker then referred readers to a new Miller poem, "If We Don't or If We Do," elsewhere on the editorial page. The poem, carefully structured with precise meter, might have appeared to confidants to reflect the earlier turmoil in his personal life.[20]

Even before he joined the faculty, Miller had been a staunch supporter of the college. In 1893, he was one of fifty individuals who "went down into our pockets" in order to float the $10,000 in bonds required of the town of Stillwater, assuring the college's location. At his own expense that year, he went to Guthrie while the legislature was in session to assist Payne County members in getting an appropriation to construct the Central Building, now known as Old Central. The last night of the session, the council was deadlocked under a "call of the house"; Miller's suggestions as to procedure broke the deadlock, however, and the bill passed.[21]

President Robert J. Barker was elated by the news that the legislature had passed the appropriations bill, assuring Oklahoma A. and M. $15,000 for the College Building. He immediately called a meeting of the regents for March 21. At that time, he cited figures to show the federal government's generosity in land grants to Idaho, Wyoming, North Dakota, South Dakota, Montana, and Washington, while expressing the hope that it would be as generous with Oklahoma Territory.[22]

When a site for the campus and buildings was to be selected, Miller appeared before the board of regents to represent a group of Stillwater citizens who favored what was to become the present campus location, an area then covered by tall prairie grass and leather-root, referred to by Fred Stallard as "mangelwurzel." Attorney Frank Hutto spoke for a site half a mile farther northwest. By the casting vote of the president, the present site was chosen. In the early years, this action would save every student at least a mile of unnecessary travel daily.[23]

Two years following his arrival, the town Miller had claimed for his future still consisted of cottonwood shacks and tents. The only brick building in town was located on Main Street and was built by Louis J. Jardot. The Farmers and Merchants Bank was under construction with a 25-foot frontage.[24] Despite its isolation from the railroad, the college already was being advertised as the "largest and best attended" in Oklahoma Territory, which consisted of only six counties but included both Edmond and Norman. Mail came to the campus along with passengers in a three-seated hack drawn from Orlando by a pair of native mules at a hard gallop. Sessions were being held in the Congregational Church, the classes divided by moveable screens. Before the 1892-93 academic year had begun, increasing enrollment made it necessary to move some classes to the Presbyterian Church and to the Methodist Episcopal Church, South, on a leased-space arrangement. By the fall of 1893, the district courtroom in the courthouse also was used for classes, and some even met in the front room of the professor's home.[25] On the campus, the federal government had erected a building for the experiment station. It served both as the station office and home for Director James C. Neal and his family. Within a year, the basement walls of the College Building were going up, and many local citizens were complaining that the college was to be located "so far out in the country." There were only two houses between the courthouse and the campus, although a shack or two had been built on Hester Street. People going to the campus did not follow the treeless streets but cut across open land to shorten the "long journey." Most dwellings were in the south and east parts of town, for it was generally believed that no good water could be found "up on the hill," where years later many of the most substantial residences would be built.[26]

The contract for the College Building had been let June 20, 1893, and students—among them Thomas J. Hartman—served as hod carriers for the bricklayers at ten cents an hour. Curious students watched workers mold and fire bricks at the Jardot kiln. The college would have Stillwater's second brick building.[27] From the first year, when classes were held in the Congregational Church, enrollment had grown from 76 to 112. Thirty-five of these were college students, and the remainder preparatory school students or preps, as they were called. The "Year of the Turnip" and its harsh realities was still fresh in their memories.[28]

The creative energies of the man from Indiana were at a peak at this time in his life. His sense of social responsibility was taut, and hard-hitting articles in which he was essayist more than newswriter often became the focus of conversation around town. The fact that he was deputy Payne County attorney from 1892 to 1894 did not keep him from contributing to the public forum through letters and speeches. He was active in the Union Christian Temperance League of Stillwater and a guest lecturer at Oklahoma A. and M. At the college's commencement week program in June 1893—a commencement without a graduate—Miller presented the first "elegant gold" Magruder Medal to Kate Neal for her winning declamation in competition with five others from the freshman class. His carefully prepared remarks of approximately 480 words, dominated by his poetic touch, impressed the overflow audience at the new 250-seat Methodist Episcopal Church, South. In slightly less than four minutes, he had convinced the townspeople that he was the community's most talented writer of rhythmic, measured prose. He was co-editor of the *Oklahoma State Sentinel*, successor to the *Oklahoma Hawk*, and only months away from a faculty appointment at the time. Similarly, his 1894 treatise, "An Argument For Single Statehood," boosted his standing in state politics and helped to squelch the dual state arguments of citizens in the twin territories.[29] Neither had his abilities gone unnoticed by the college's board of regents, whose political complexion had changed with President Grover Cleveland's appointment of Governor William Renfrow to replace Abraham J. Seay. By April 1894, the Democratic Party was firmly in control of the board and ready to make major changes at Oklahoma A. and M. President Robert J. Barker, slated for the axe, was a lame duck spending most of his remaining time at his homestead in Crescent. In May, the popular Willis W. Hutto was released, ostensibly because of his brother Frank's position in the Republican hierarchy. Hutto's wife was seven months pregnant at the time.

Meanwhile, politics had held up the completion of the College Building. The bond issue had been delayed in a dispute over which board of regents—Seay's or Renfrow's—was in control. There was no money to pay the contractor. Needless to say, the conflict finally was resolved. At long last, the College Building was dedicated on June 15, 1894, giving a sense of permanence to the sometimes-challenged dream of local civic leaders who had worked so hard to assure that Stillwater would have the agricultural college. Two weeks later, July 1, 1894, Miller replaced Hutto in the college's English chair. While the Huttos were adjusting to this discouraging news, their first child, a boy, was born on July 15.[30] Miller was elected at the same time as Henry E. Alvord, who was chosen to succeed the institution's first chief executive. Barker had served from the time the first classes were formed until the day the College Building was dedicated.[31]

Although Hutto had taught some useful journalistic skills in his classes in the Presbyterian Church and the Payne County Courthouse— among them exposition, argument, and literary criticism—there is no evidence that he gave instruction in journalism as such. His hands had been full. He had been responsible for a heavy teaching load plus his duties as commandant.

Hutto, a Kansas Agricultural College graduate, had a large number of friends who protested his removal. His participation in community programs had been appreciated. Typically, those affiliated with the college contributed mightily to community betterment. At a Sunday evening Congregational Church service in November 1893, for example, Professors Hutto and Frank A. Waugh, their wives, and students Myrtle and Maggie Hutto sang—some solo, some in quartets. The innovative worship service featured brief biblical passages interspersed with a variety of musical selections. In addition to their singing, Mrs. Hutto played the organ and Waugh the flute. The musically versatile Waugh also played the piccolo on various occasions. Such interaction between town and gown was frequent in early Stillwater.[32]

Hutto no doubt was well aware of the man who would replace him. Miller had achieved prominence both in law and newspaper work during Hutto's two years on the faculty. But neither man may have expected the changes to come. The Republican-oriented *Gazette* protested the board's action, calling it politically motivated, while citing Hutto's popularity with students and patrons alike. The Democratically inclined *Sentinel* welcomed the appointment with high praise for the transplanted Hoosier. There was a tragic epilogue to the Hutto story. On June 11, 1929, he was found close to death from self-inflicted bullet wounds on a highway near Lawton. He died within minutes. The former Fletcher superintendent of schools, who was a prominent citizen, had been despondent and in ill health. He was sixty-two. The *Stillwater Gazette* failed to mention his pioneering role at Oklahoma A. and M.[33]

One year after Miller had been elected by the regents, only Neal and Holter of the first faculty were left. Neal had been demoted when President George E. Morrow took over his title as experiment station director. Neal's neutral political stance and the technical nature of Holter's work probably accounted for their having survived the earlier

George E. Morrow was the first of three journalists to serve as president of Oklahoma A. and M. College. He had been co-publisher of the *Western Farmer* before joining the faculty at the Iowa State Agricultural College. His tenure overlapped those of Freeman E. Miller and Angelo C. Scott, the lawyer-journalist who gave Oklahoma City the first newspaper published from a territorial press. Morrow, a strong influence upon early campus journalism, would later be succeeded by Scott as president.

faculty dismissals. Perhaps exhausted from the 1894-95 chaos during which he provided faculty continuity, Neal died after a brief illness in December 1895. Miller wrote the eulogy that was made a part of the faculty record, conveyed to the family, and published in local newspapers.[34]

Miller's appointment is significant in the history of journalism at Oklahoma A. and M. for two reasons: first, he became the first public information officer for the college, and second, he supervised the first real campus newspaper, one set in type rather than handwritten. While his selection no doubt was linked to his political persuasion, it also reflected his competence in the fields Hutto had taught. It is unlikely that Alvord and Miller knew one another, although Miller, familiar with the news figures of the day, may have had some knowledge of the newly chosen president's background.

Although Miller's responsibility for the College Press Bureau came about through faculty action, it seems likely that the regents had seen the need for an organized effort in the dissemination of news.[35] The assignment came during President Edmund D. Murdaugh's six months in office following Alvord's short tenure. On March 4, 1895, the faculty appointed Murdaugh, Waugh, and Miller to a committee that would "consider the matter of general news correspondence from the College." One week later, the committee recommended "the organization of a Press Bureau under the charge of the Department of English." Its report was adopted. Two months later, the faculty requested that President Murdaugh assist Miller in supervising the flow of information from the College Press Bureau to weekly papers. Little is known of the bureau's effectiveness. One of the rare assessments merely stated: "The college correspondence in the town papers is growing in interest since the press bureau was organized."[36]

One advantage the college had in Miller's services as head of the bureau was the fact that, in spite of his law career, he had been active in newspaper work throughout his early life. He was active in the Oklahoma Territorial Press Association and knew many of the state's editors personally.

Miller enjoyed writing long poems for special occasions. When the press association met in Hennessey on November 15, 1897, he amazed the territorial editors by presenting "Calling the Roll at Hennessey." This poem of approximately 2,650 words included the names of virtually all the editors who were present and some who were not. It is likely that Miller read the poem to the group, as he often did on such occasions. It was printed in booklet form by "Gazette Print, Stillwater," and distributed at the meeting. It was the kind of thing that brought attention not only to him but to the college. The poem decidedly was a plus in furthering the college's ties with the territorial newspaper fraternity. That evening, Miller was said to have responded to one of several toasts "with ability, eloquence and humor."[37]

As for the *Oklahoma A. and M. College Mirror*, Alvord may indirectly have had a hand in its founding, although he had resigned four months before the paper's birth. As a student, he had served as editor of both the *Reveille* and *University Quarterly* at Norwich University. He knew the value of campus publications.[38] It is likely that in more than one conversation with Miller he had mentioned the possibility of a newspaper for Oklahoma A. and M. Miller no doubt saw the potential of a close relationship between publicity functions off campus and on. A campus newspaper would help him carry out his public information duties. Alvord had spent July and the first part of August in Washington, D. C., cleaning up his remaining responsibilities as deputy assistant to U.S. Secretary of Agriculture J. S. Morton. He reached the campus shortly after the opening of the fall term.[39]

Things had been running smoothly for Miller. However, there were problems on the horizon for the young college. It was a pattern that soon would seem endemic, one of many stressful periods throughout the first thirty years of Oklahoma's land-grant institution. Some would be at the local level while others would reach all the way to the legislature and the governor's office. One in the latter category was in the making soon after

Miller joined the faculty. It has been called the "Crisis of 1894."[40]

More than anything, this crisis was a battle of wills: President Alvord vs. the board of regents. Alvord and Miller, elected by the board on the same hot summer day, were highly intelligent and goal-oriented. These traits were less threatening to Miller at that time than to the new president. Alvord brought to Oklahoma A. and M. a rich and varied background. The twin territories were not totally foreign to him. His first experience in the Southwest was as a captain, 10th Cavalry, at Forts Arbuckle, Cobb, and Gibson. Later, in 1869, he returned to Indian Territory as a special Indian agent, assigned by President Ulysses S. Grant to meet with Satanta, the incarcerated Kiowa chieftain, and to bring representatives of nine selected Indian tribes to Washington for a conference. Upon his successful completion of that mission, he returned to the Northeast to study agriculture. Following his studies, he accepted a faculty position at the Massachusetts Agricultural College.[41] While there, he began to publish widely in the dairy field. His article, "The American Cattle Trade," brought a medal from the Royal Agricultural Society of Great Britain.[42] Fifteen years after his mission to Satanta, he would see the raw prairie college through the eyes of an Army officer. He retained his title of rank and preferred to be called Major Alvord. He seemed to believe that West Point discipline was what the farm boys and girls needed if he was to create a serious academic atmosphere—and a more glamorous image—in Stillwater. Nevertheless, that is an oversimplification, for Alvord also was well schooled in the agriculture of his day. He knew the land-grant system and its procedures forward and backward. He had served at a high level in the U.S. Department of Agriculture and maintained his contacts there after coming to Oklahoma A. and M. He was, in fact, highly regarded by the secretary of agriculture himself.[43]

Of the eight faculty members on hand in the fall of 1894, two of the most influential—James C. Neal and Alexander C. Magruder—were well aware of Alvord's abilities. They had attended meetings of the Association of American Agricultural Colleges and Experiment Stations (AAACES), an organization in which Alvord had a leadership role.[44] President Barker had had no experience of this kind. He was feeling his way through the regulatory twists and turns of the federal government in its dealings with a territorial college. Matters that may have mystified Barker in considering the school's obligations as a recipient of federal funds were well understood by Alvord. On the other hand, Barker's successor may have been unprepared for the machinations of territorial politicos, some of whom wanted a patronage plum more than they wanted a school. It seems safe to surmise that the small Oklahoma A. and M. faculty was pleased with Alvord's election and that their new colleague, Miller, joined them with an optimistic view toward the new academic year.

Approximately 120 students had begun their work on September 12 before President Alvord had completed all of the details of his move from the nation's capital. Upon his arrival in Stillwater, Alvord found that the college's required annual report had not been prepared by Barker, although the former president had left in his desk much of the data needed by his successor. Alvord would have found it expedient merely to have read the annual report in orienting himself to his new responsibilities, but he faced the job of writing the report himself. While the task deterred him from some of the amenities that might have smoothed his path later, it did alert him to major changes that needed to be made at Oklahoma A. and M. As a result, numerous recommendations for corrective action were included in the report.[45]

Alvord moved ahead with gusto. He reorganized the faculty and courses, caused rules governing student conduct and the literary societies to be revised, and took action to free the faculty from various administrative duties to make time for research. The faculty committee system was continued, and Miller was appointed to the Room and Board Committee along with Edward F. Clark and Frank Waugh. The president also asked Miller to develop a plan for strengthening the library, which until then had been Clark's responsibility.[46]

Exactly how much muscle Washington had used, if any, in the Alvord appointment is not clear. No doubt the regents were aware of Alvord's standing in the United States Department of Agriculture (USDA), and may have received subtle cues that his appointment would be desirable. Even that subtle nudging may have created an unlikely climate for success. Beyond such speculation was the fact that Alvord and the regents soon clashed over policy. President Alvord and Professor Neal, in charge of the experiment station, were directed by the board to swear to the accuracy of all vouchers passing over their desks for payment. To comply, Alvord and Neal would have to see that each voucher was notarized. Both men resented the directive as an affront to their integrity. They knew that other land-grant college administrators had no such requirement. Alvord stated that he could not comply, then in an act inconsistent with his military background he went out of channels to appeal the ruling.[47]

Officials in the Office of the Secretary of Agriculture studied Alvord's request for a policy clarification. On November 9, a letter supporting Alvord was posted by the USDA. Alvord promptly forwarded the letter to the board of regents in Guthrie. He did not know it at this point, but he had won the battle and lost the war. During the time a compromise might have been worked out had positions not become too rigid, Alvord went to Washington as a member of the AAACES steering committee to help plan the group's upcoming convention, during which he served as chairman of the executive committee. He asked the delegates to accept his resignation from the chairmanship because of the press of duties in Stillwater. They did, but in a show of recognition for past service elected him as the association's next president.[48]

While things festered in Guthrie, Alvord's behavior in Washington suggests that he did not sense the growing dissatisfaction of the regents. He attended to several items of college business, including acquisitions for the college library, coordinating a major purchase with Freeman Miller by letter.[49] He probably visited with his friends at the USDA, including the secretary of agriculture. If so, the conflict with the territorial board of regents no doubt came in for discussion. When Alvord returned to Stillwater, any real chance for compromise seems to have slipped away. He soon prepared a long written report outlining questionable college practices that should be discontinued. He had coupled this with a demand that the board turn the daily operation of the college over to him.[50] Soon after this, a face-to-face showdown took place in Guthrie. Board members, resenting any attempt to curtail their powers, refused to adopt Alvord's recommendations. In an atmosphere that bristled with tension, President Alvord verbally tendered his resignation, apparently without premeditation, following it on December 21, 1894, with a formal resignation letter of three paragraphs. The *Oklahoma State Sentinel* and *Oklahoma City Times-Journal* cautioned that Alvord's resignation should not be accepted without an investigation. Their efforts to postpone action on Alvord's status failed. One week earlier, the *Stillwater Messenger* had called for an immediate investigation by the territorial legislature, a move that had strong support from many Stillwater citizens.[51]

At the board's meeting in Stillwater on January 18, Major Alvord's resignation was made a matter of record, and the regents quickly elected Edmund D. Murdaugh as his successor. The new president, from a well-known Baltimore family, was polished both in dress and manner.[52] Murdaugh's election did not end the year of crisis. Alvord's official letter of resignation was published by the *Stillwater Eagle-Gazette*, making public serious charges about the college's handling of public funds. Copies of the letter, along with Alvord's last report as president, were mailed to the secretary of the interior and the secretary of agriculture in Washington. Alvord followed this up with a public letter of appreciation from Spring Hill Farm, Lewinsville, Fairfax County, Virginia. It was dated January 11, 1895, and was published in three Stillwater newspapers and probably others as well. He asked the "good people of Oklahoma" to insist through their legislators that the college "not be used for selfish, personal, or political ends, but. . . solely for the public good." A number of immediate reforms were suggested, some dealing bluntly with personalities. The *Eagle-Gazette* showed its support for Alvord in an editorial and predicted that an investigation would follow.[53]

As one historian has written, the "Crisis of 1894" and the investigation of 1895 proved to be pivotal points in the history of Oklahoma A. and M. College. Though his aggressiveness was not appreciated nor the full reach of his earlier accomplishments understood by his superiors, Major Alvord had completed in six months a reorganization that might have taken a weaker president years to accomplish. Now the institution more closely approximated a real center of higher education.[54]

Representative Angelo C. Scott, a member of the assembly, introduced a motion calling for Alvord to withdraw his resignation. The resolution passed but to no avail. The legislators had not yet learned that the board had elected Murdaugh to replace Alvord.[55] It was not too late, however, to carry out an investigation. An ad hoc group made up of members of the house and council agricultural committees was set in motion by a joint resolution of the two bodies. On February 5, 1895, the investigating committee called the public hearing to order in Guthrie. Three weeks later, after hearing extended testimony by both state and college officials, the investigating committee issued its report. The report condensed the testimony of the fifteen witnesses and offered the committee's observations on several issues. The views expressed by the ad hoc committee found a number of targets on both sides of the controversy, but the concluding section laid most of the blame on the board of regents. While the investigators reported that no laws had been broken, there was a strong implication of moral laxity.[56]

In spite of the benefits Alvord's short presidency had brought to the campus, the legislative report had sharpened the conflict between Republicans and Democrats, resulting in an effort by Democrats to move the institution to El Reno, a more populous area that was said to have better soil. In this cauldron of emotion, another move threatening Stillwater developed. Representative William A. Knipe introduced a plan in the legislature to expand Payne County and to move the county seat to Perkins, his home town. Stillwater leaders mustered the political punch to quash both moves, largely through the good offices of Robert Lowry, a Stillwater pioneer serving in the house of representatives.[57]

Murdaugh's short five-and-a-half months in office had ended on June 30; on August 8, 1895, the *Gazette* reported on the arrangements "whereby the newly elected president would accept his position." George E. Morrow would be "President, [Experiment Station] Director and Agriculturist at a salary of $2,400 and Henry E. Glazier, Vice-director and Horticulturist." At the same session, the regents confirmed all faculty except Magruder and Waugh and approved a conditional contract for an artesian well 2,000 feet deep.[58] The loss of Magruder and Waugh was unfortunate. Magruder's dismissal was the trade-off the board required if Morrow was to unify the station and the college. Glazier, probably unknown to Morrow and far less competent than Waugh, was strictly a political appointment. To the board, he was "one of the boys."

President Morrow was convinced that he must reestablish equilibrium following the months of crisis. To him, this meant a consolidation of power. He was concerned about the power the Farmers' Institutes held over board members. He sought to be cautious in public statements about the institutes in Oklahoma Territory, endorsing their value "when properly conducted." But he said that members of the college faculty and experiment station staff would speak on Institute programs only "so far as their duties. . .will permit."[59] This statement represented a shift in Oklahoma A. and M. policy.

The unrest over the college's location had disturbed Stillwater's leading citizens. The *Gazette* reprinted a lengthy article from the *Orlando Herald*, apparently as a warning to local leaders that they could not afford to rest on their laurels. The article alleged that thousands of dollars had been wasted by the experiment station. The Territorial Horticulture Society had visited the station and, the article implied, had found numerous lapses of judgment. At that time, Captain S. H. Kelsey, a new regent, was pushing for a faculty shakeup, citing the need for greater economy. The *Herald* article showed an anti-scientific bias: "The days of. . .theoretical farming are past and the agriculturist or horticulturist who is not practical must step down and 'out.' The people demand it, the Board of Regents emphasize it by action, and the *Herald* says Amen." The paper criticized those who protested Waugh's and Magruder's removal and praised Glazier for the courage of his convictions.[60] The *Herald's* attitude certainly did not agree with Morrow's. The new president strongly favored scientific agriculture, but this was not so for Glazier. Whatever Miller's feelings were about the tensions of the brief Alvord administration and the investigation that followed, Morrow's appointment had returned a semblance of calm to the campus. Now he could set his mind to carrying out his duties in a less emotionally charged atmosphere. That he accomplished as much journalistically as he did is surprising. It was a time when faculty members often wore several hats, and Miller was among the most versatile. If he had thought he was being hired merely to teach English, he long since had learned such was not the case. The catalog, in four different sections, listed him as the responsible faculty member.

Only five academic programs at the time—none under Miller—had departmental status. There were only 144 students in the college served by nine faculty, not counting the president. Ninety of the 144 were sub-college preparatory students.

Miller's library duties must have come almost immediately. In the first faculty meeting he attended in August 1894, he was asked to obtain all territorial publications for the library. His press association contacts were helpful here. At a faculty meeting the following month, he reported that 114 publications had been processed for the college file.[61]

English Language and Literature.

FREEMAN E. MILLER, A. M., Professor.

History and Political Science

FREEMAN E. MILLER, A. M., Professor.

Logic

FREEMAN E. MILLER, A. M., Professor.

The College Library

FREEMAN E. MILLER, A. M., Acting Librarian.
MISS JESSIE THATCHER, Assistant.

The versatility expected of some early faculty members is evident from this list of college catalog headings. In essence, Freeman E. Miller was a one-man head of three academic departments plus librarian and director of the College Press Bureau. Academically speaking, he is best remembered for his work in English and literature.

Thirty-five years later, reflecting on his early career at Oklahoma A. and M., Miller wrote that his office was "somewhat of a dumping ground for about every thing that did not fall strictly within the other departments. . .and no stretch of imagination was needed to show that the library did not belong with. . .them. Therefore, it must accrue to the Department of English and Literature; and it was so ordered." In addition, Miller was responsible for public speaking, political economy, some Latin (disguised as etymology), mythology, and "many lesser courses."[62] His duties were more than enough to fill a normal workday.

In spite of his busy schedule, Miller continued to find time for outside activities. He was working on a comprehensive history of Oklahoma, and he continued to give public speeches. He was a featured speaker at the Payne County Teachers' Association meeting in October 1895, one of many such programs in which he participated. Ten months later, he was elected vice president of the association. In addition, he took an active part in faculty meetings, sometimes initiating action and at other times accepting various assignments. In August 1896, he was elected secretary of the faculty, but this in no way restricted his action in such matters as faculty deliberations, committee duties, and special assignments. For example, his faculty colleagues asked him to deliver the Oklahoma Day address on April 22 following chapel. During the year, he planned the first program honoring Washington's birthday, served on committees to study elective courses and absences, and with Holter investigated the disorderly conduct at the public Sigma Literary Society program the evening before Thanksgiving.[63]

Miller was even more active the following year. First, the faculty requested that instead of a debate on Washington's birthday, Miller deliver an address. Then he served with President Morrow and Holter on a committee to review the college's course of study. The report was accepted with the amendment that all seniors be required to submit a thesis before qualifying for a degree. Miller was authorized to use four hours each week in a freshman composition practicum, and again he was involved in Oklahoma Day, this time on the planning committee. He served on committees studying commencement exercises, textbooks, and the demerits system. On September 4, 1897, Miller prepared his last minutes, passing his secretarial duties on to Lowery L. Lewis. His participation in faculty meetings continued unabated. His programs for senior speakers and junior exercises were approved. In his final committee assignment, Miller and two other faculty members planned the winter term recitations schedule.[64]

Miller's performance left no doubt that he was a vital member of the faculty, providing rigorous and exacting standards in the classroom and leadership among his faculty peers. He was a popular public speaker, in Stillwater and beyond, and held offices in the Oklahoma Press Association as well as the Territorial Teachers' Association. His obvious popularity with students in a variety of activities during the early part of his tenure suggests that he probably was well accepted in the classroom, where he sometimes used a touch of subtle humor. Nevertheless, his greatest contribution may have been the widespread attention he brought to the college through his creative writing and public speaking.[65]

In journalistic terms, the creation of the first campus newspaper, the *Oklahoma A. and M. College Mirror*, was most significant. Miller established the *Mirror* in May 1895, a month and a half before Murdaugh's departure and two years before the University of Oklahoma started a similar monthly literary publication, the *Umpire*. He saw the paper as an opportunity to involve the literary societies and, at the same time, to lighten the load he carried. To Miller, it was more than a campus newspaper. It was a publicity medium for the college throughout the region.[66] Jessie Thatcher, a student active in the Sigma Literary Society, took the lead in the organizational stage of the *Mirror*, seeing that during the month of April ample news was gathered for the first edition. Charles M. Becker, editor of the *Stillwater Gazette*, probably at Miller's request, instructed the students in the relatively simple layout techniques of the day. He predicted that Volume 1, Number 1, would come out about May 13.[67] This suggests that arrangements had been made to have the paper printed at the *Gazette.*

Becker, later to become a printer in the yet-to-be-established college printing plant, was on target. The first issue, using a two-column format in literary magazine style, was dated May 15, 1895. The masthead on the editorial page placed responsibility for the publication. It read: "Published by the Literary Societies under the supervision of the College Press Bureau." Simply put, that meant Miller was in charge, for the bureau was his responsibility. Norris T. Gilbert, one of the college's most promising students, and Samuel R. Querry were listed as editors, with E. G. Lewis and Emma Swope as local news editors. Business matters were handled by Arthur W. Adams and Charles E. Regnier. Regnier and Lewis were Websters, and the others were members of the Sigma Literary Society. The *Mirror* was to be published monthly during the college year at five cents a copy or fifty cents for the year.

Gilbert and Querry, in their first editorial, entitled "Salutatory," saw "importance for us and for the institution which we love" in launching the paper. They stated their goals were self-improvement as well as the growth, extension, and influence of the Oklahoma A. and M. College. They believed that both goals could be sought "by the same labor at the same time." They invited the "hearty support" of students and friends of the institution "in the most substantial way."[68] The *Mirror* was distributed to editors throughout the territories and to selected publications in border states. In a sense, the paper was somewhat self-serving, for

SPECIAL COLLECTIONS, OSU LIBRARY

First editors of the *Oklahoma A. and M. College Mirror* were Samuel R. Querry and Norris T. Gilbert (*pictured*). They were strong boosters of the young college's aims and objectives. Their goals, they said, were to seek self-improvement as well as the growth, extension, and influence of the college. The *Mirror* was typical of the nation's college literary magazines of the day. In Oklahoma Territory, the courteous but vigorous competition among the institutions at Norman, Edmond, and Stillwater was reflected in the *Mirror.*

Miller's poetry often appeared in it, sometimes for the first time, sometimes reprinted from other publications. Whatever his motives, his poems added to the cultural tone of the campus environment.

Not only did Miller use the *Mirror* as an outlet for his poetry, but for narratives relating to his college days as well. These stories sometimes took the form of parables in which Miller hoped to have a positive influence on Oklahoma A. and M. students. In one such narrative, Miller told of a DePauw University professor of Greek whose influence kept him in school when, as a disheartened sophomore, he was ready to quit for lack of funds. Miller had told the professor that he intended to "study up on the subjects embraced in the Junior and Senior years. . .and [that he] would know as much about them as anyone who. . .went out into the world with a degree."

The old professor, intently gazing with kind, regretful eyes into Miller's young face, said: "Nothing is impossible when you desire knowledge if you have the energy to continue to the end. I have been over the road, my boy. Nothing can defeat your purpose except yourself. Get the stamp! You can if you will; and into the world you will carry not your own influence alone, but the faith and influence of this great institution will stand by your side and speak for you and fight for you all your after life."

SPECIAL COLLECTIONS, OSU LIBRARY

Jessie Thatcher, a student who believed Oklahoma A. and M. should have a real student publication, took the lead in organizing support for the *Oklahoma A. and M. College Mirror* in 1895. The second women's dormitory, occupied in 1926, was named after her, honoring her status as the first female graduate of the college.

Professor Miller concluded the story with its unmistakable lesson for the disheartened Oklahoma A. and M. sophomores of 1895: "I have never forgotten his words nor his illustration. I completed my college course, and on my study wall hangs a diploma which is the stamp challenging the world to test my value. That was more than ten years ago, and it has repaid me already more than all it cost."[69]

The *Mirror* was typical of most, if not all, college "newspapers" of the day. A cross between a literary magazine and a folksy country weekly, it was made up largely of editorials; essays (some by Miller himself); poems; and chit-chat, under the heading "In and About the College." Objective newswriting in the inverted pyramid fashion was not to be found. Stories that today might dominate page one with lengthy detail often were handled in a single paragraph or even a single sentence. By today's standards, writing that approximated acceptable journalistic reportage on the Oklahoma A. and M. campus newspaper was still years away.[70]

The 1894 crisis and the subsequent legislative investigation of financial affairs at Oklahoma A. and M. received considerable off-campus newspaper coverage. The *Mirror* gave the investigation one paragraph of four sentences on the editorial page. No names were mentioned.[71] Such a situation probably would become a major page-one story on most campus newspapers today.

From the beginning, the *Mirror* carried advertising. Most of it was of the business card variety, although display advertising also appeared. Among the ads was one for Miller's new book, *Oklahoma and Other Poems*, including comments from seven critics. The *Kansas City Journal* called it "a creditable beginning for the future of the literature of the embryo commonwealth," while the *Guthrie Sunlight* offered the view that Miller "is more than a rhymester," adding that "some of the writings compare favorably with America's most gifted bards." His early hero John Clark Ridpath had written to praise his work, calling some of the poems "quite superior."[72]

The *Mirror* was circulated to schools as well as to commercial publications. Now it was time to await the response of other editors. The June edition, the second of the two-issue volume, devoted a page to the laudatory comments of a dozen Oklahoma Territory newspapers. Typical was this paragraph from the *Edmond Sun-Democrat*: The "*Oklahoma A. and M. College Mirror* is to hand. It is a credit to the students and college; it is in pamphlet form and contains 16 pages, neatly printed and well gotten up."[73]

In September, the *Mirror* opened volume 2 with a ringing editorial endorsement of Alvord's and Murdaugh's successor. The aging President Morrow, described by one well-known Stillwater pioneer as "straight-laced and ministerial," had gained an international reputation

THE OKLAHOMA

A. AND M. COLLEGE MIRROR.

VOL. 1.　　　　STILLWATER, OKLAHOMA, MAY 15, 1895.　　　　NO. 1.

BY THE OVERLAND TRAIL.

This was the path of empire. Fifty years
Have hung their halos where heroic rolled
The white-topped wagons of the pioneers,
Who walked the desert ways for dreams of
　gold.
How gaunt and ghastly gleamed the far fron-
　tiers
With care and carnage for the pale-face bold,
When savage warriors with embattled spears
Brought death and danger to the days of old!

Here crossed the prairies toward the Golden
　Gates
The fathers, founders of the Greater West;
They conquered kingdoms in their mighty
　quest,
And sowed the seeds of cities, towns, and
　states.
Lo, by their prowess is the present blest,
And on their glory all the future waits!
　—Freeman E. Miller in Overland Monthly.

A & M COLLEGE BUILDING.

HISTORICAL AND ADVISORY.

Most great discoveries are accidental,
and often slight causes lead to tremendous changes in the plans of both mice
and men.

The members of the stormy first session of the territorial legislature, especially those from Payne county,
builded much wiser than they knew
when they asked for the Agricultural
college, and "through thick and thin"
worked, schemed, intrigued, and nobody knows what else they did to get
it.

Still, few knew what a bonanza it
was, and in my correspondence with
the first governor, in 1890, his ideas
were so very hazy as to its value and
importance that I gave him line upon
line, letter after letter, even to the extent of an outline of a law, embracing
the results of some years of experience of one of the oldest, and best conducted, and stable colleges in the
United States. These suggestions were
not utilized to any great extent, and
the law passed is a queer medley of bad
English, uncertain phrase and indirect-
ness that makes it one of the curiosi-
ties of legislation.

Some day this may be remedied. The
present law placed the college within
the grasp of Stillwater, and this plucky
little town, with a grit and go ahead
that is unsurpassed in the records of
the territory, assumed the task of providing place and habitation for an institution that now, and in all the future, will give opportunity for a

The first student publication was, typical of its day, in literary magazine format and filled with essays, articles boosting the progress of the college, poems, and short personal items. It would continue in this format under two other names before becoming a broadsheet newspaper known as the *Orange and Black*. The *Oklahoma A. and M. College Mirror* preceded a similar publication at the University of Oklahoma, the *Umpire*, by about two years.

in agriculture during his eighteen years at the University of Illinois. He had had journalistic experience earlier as a writer on the *Western Rural* staff and as co-publisher of the *Western Farmer*. [74] He was ready to build upon Alvord's well-thought-out restructuring of Oklahoma A. and M. College. Morrow had better luck with the regents than Alvord. For one thing, he was less combative. For another, he knew what he needed and because of his wide experience in national and international affairs had great influence. He was widely published and a frequent lecturer at important national agricultural meetings. He had traveled widely in Europe and was the invited guest of Sir John Laws of England as he inspected demonstration and experimental farming. Under Morrow, the Morrill and Hatch funds were used as originally intended, easing the college's relationships with the federal government. [75]

Morrow had spoken to a joint social meeting of the Sigma and Webster societies. This put him in close touch with the *Mirror* staff. The paper reported that "President Morrow's address was brimming over with fun and he made a friend of every student by his kind and social manner." [76]

Although duties had shifted, only one new name appeared in the

Mirror masthead: George W. Bowers had replaced Adams. The *Mirror* had moved from the library to the English office. Earlier, English had shared the southeast room on the first floor of the new Central Building with the library. Expansion of the library called for a readjustment of space, and by moving the college secretary to the library, across the hall from his office, Morrow had been able to give English a room of its own.[77]

Editorially, the paper called for the formation of an Oklahoma Oratorical Association encompassing all territorial colleges with local branches on the various campuses and in some of the high schools. It also issued a call for students outside the literary societies to work for the *Mirror*, and a plea was made for a more animated school spirit. That theme would be repeated over and over for years to come. The masthead encouraged contributions of a literary or scientific nature from students, teachers, and others "that have the educational interests of Oklahoma at heart."[78]

Finally, in the college year 1895-1896, Oklahoma A. and M. had four college classes. The June commencement would launch an embryo alumni association of six young men who had known four presidents— Barker, Alvord, Murdaugh, and Morrow—the last three in two years.

Although the College Press Bureau as an entity apparently had died late in Morrow's administration, the college's responsibility for informing the public in agricultural matters continued to have a high priority. This was clear from a policy statement published in the summer of 1899: "Frequent press bulletins will be issued by the Experiment Station and sent to the newspapers of the territory. This arrangement will, it is believed, enable the college to. . .bring its work into closer connection with the people through the medium of the papers of the territory, which have so uniformly found space for press bulletins in the past. Without the assistance of the county papers, much of the work of the Experiment Station cannot be made available to the farmers, and in turn, subscribers of these papers do not derive the benefits from this institution which they should."[79] There was no such thing as a Cooperative Extension Service at this time, and the roles of extension and research obviously were integrated. Thirty-three years later, evolving a workable public information program for both extension and research would cause problems for Clement E. Trout.

To appreciate how much Miller contributed to campus life from the 1894-1895 school year through December 1897 when he resigned, all one needs to do is read his poems and essays and the news reports of his literary and forensic successes in the *Mirror*. Miller's range of skills was summarized by a Stillwater historian in this fashion: "As head of the English department he was a man of letters who could appreciate quality of expression. As a newspaper man he knew the value of factual precision, and as a lawyer he was attentive to detail. He was a poet of repute also, which endowed him with a feeling for what he saw." Other glimpses of the Miller style come readily to life in the minutes of faculty meetings and in occasional mentions in Stillwater newspapers.

Nor was Estelle Miller reluctant to enter into community and campus life. She taught a girls Sunday School class and willingly gave her time to campus projects. Typical was her participation when faculty wives were asked to design and sew military-style uniforms for female students.[80] The Millers played a part in helping students develop the social amenities while gaining self confidence. They would combine entertainment with learning by inviting his classes to their home at 206 North Duck. These the *Mirror* called "literary entertainment." One of several such events took place on January 21, 1896. That evening, the entertainment was Longfellow's *Tales of the Wayside Inn*. Miller would read, then pass the reading on from student to student. From time to time he would interject explanations and interpretations he considered useful, and the reading would continue, followed by refreshments and animated conversation.[81] However, the thing most students talked about the following day was Andrew Caudell's dousing. Caudell, although a good student, was a prankster who often had fun at the expense of others. Someone decided to turn the tables that night. It was raining hard, and Caudell wore his rubber boots, depositing them at the door. During the festivities, according to Thomas J. Hartman, "some ornery cuss went out and put a little water into each boot." When the party was over, Caudell raised a boot toward the sky to see if it was right or left, and the water poured into his face. He was so mad he left the party without his girl. But he returned for her later and in a fit of laughter called it the best prank he had ever known. But pranks were not restricted to students. Sometimes they were directed at faculty—even the president. Morrow found a pig in his parlor, while Miller walked until his buggy wheels were retrieved from the telephone lines. Despite such nonsense, warm feelings and loyalty existed between faculty and students. The upper classes were small, ranging in number from six to ten. Each professor knew the peculiar traits of character and habit of each student in his classes. As C. R. Donart wrote: "They overlooked our faults or helped us to correct them and recognized and commended our virtues. . . ."[82]

With the sudden resignation of Miller shortly after the first term of the 1897-1898 academic year, Oklahoma A. and M. lost its foremost figure in the world of letters. He was hard working and demanding of others—sometimes to the point of being abrasive—but his tender side came out in his poetry, which earned acclaim for him as the finest poet in Oklahoma Territory, if not in the entire Southwest. No other early faculty member had attracted so much national attention as a writer. The *Mirror* praised his work as teacher, friend, and newspaper supervisor, then commented: "In an unusual degree Professor Miller combines the qualities of a careful, discriminating student of literature and a writer of both prose and poetry of much merit. Recently he has given evidence of marked ability as a reader of his own poems before public audiences. His volume of verse—*Oklahoma and Other Poems*—has attracted very favorable comment from competent critics. Putnam's, the well known New York publishers, are bringing out a second volume of his poetry."

The *Mirror* masthead was changed once more as Angelo C. Scott replaced Miller. Mention of the College Press Bureau had been dropped earlier. Authority had shifted later to the English department. Now that reference, too, was missing. The January 1898 masthead read: "Published by the Faculty and Students."[83]

Praise for Miller's literary talent continued. The first issue of *Oklahoma Literature*, a territorial magazine published by the English Club at Kingfisher College four months after his resignation, gave its opening page to Miller's poem, "The Dreamer," and an assessment of his work. He was thirty-four years old at the time. The unsigned article, presumably the work of H. C. House, editor-in-chief, referred to *Songs From the South West Country*, published by the Knickerbocker Press, as his latest and best volume. House had special praise for "The Opening of Oklahoma," "Ballad of the Alamo," and "The Battle of the Washita" as having caught the spirit of the time. As for his dialectic poem, "The Banks of Turkey Run," the editor saw it as "Rileyesque."[84] This came as no surprise to friends of Miller. They were aware of his friendship with James Whitcomb Riley as well as his admiration for Riley's talent.

Apparently the editor had interviewed Miller personally, for the Stillwater poet had declined to name his favorite work in his newest book, referring to "several favorites" instead. "If a real partiality was shown at all," the critic commented, "it was for "The Old Range Road."" That poem, Miller told his interviewer, had been written in two hours as he visited at his childhood home in Indiana the previous summer. House called Miller a "pleasing maker of rhymes. . .full of brave faith in himself. . ., not merely [with] the delicate instincts and yearnings of the artist, but his power as well." Referring to "The Dreamer," the critic said, "We print it entire. . ., believing it by odds the 'farcry' beyond anything else in the volume."[85]

Miller, in announcing his resignation, had said it was for personal reasons. There had been no elaboration of what such reasons might be. A clue was provided in *Oklahoma Literature*. He had told his interviewer that he retired from academic life to write full time. Prophetically, House wrote: "When a man does this he makes himself either a brave figure or a pathetic one. Whatever the outcome, such a one deserves the sympathy of all who care for the highest in art."[86]

Miller's departure on January 1, 1898, after playing a prominent faculty role for three years and six months, may well have been linked to the twists and turns in territorial politics, as many departures from state campuses were. Higher education in that period was inextricably linked to politics—was, in fact, often a pawn in the hands of politicians—and Miller had strong enemies as well as friends in the rowdy, rough-and-tumble political arena of the day. He was a man with deep political convictions and had no skill in or stomach for compromise.

His short tenure had, perhaps without his fully grasping the fact, been a step on the road toward the college's recognition of professional education for journalism. There was a vigorous, untamed vitality about the new institutions at Norman, Edmond, and Stillwater that matched the mood of Oklahoma Territory. In spite of campus conditions that students today would consider primitive and disorderly, if not chaotic, there was a sense of pride both on and off campus. The *Mirror* reflected and reinforced this vitality. In this sense, it was typical of frontier journalism.

The stage was set for Angelo C. Scott, whose arrival signaled an era of humanism that was an invigorating counterpoise to the important scientific and technological emphasis of the proud prairie college. Scott's arrival also would signal the first glimmering of formal instruction in newspaper work.[87]

Endnotes

1. Susan L. Moore to Harry E. Heath Jr., 12 June 1987, School of Journalism and Broadcasting Centennial History Collection, Special Collections, Edmon Low Library, Oklahoma State University, Stillwater, Oklahoma; Scrapbook, F. Edwin Miller, 1884-1887, Archives, DePauw University, Greencastle, Indiana, Document Case no. 50, "Three Young Poets." This undated clipping from an unidentified Indiana newspaper praises the poetry of Miller, then a junior at DePauw. According to Kenneth C. Kaufman, some of his verse was known to have been published in the *Indianapolis Journal* and the *Indianapolis Herald*. College records occasionally listed Freeman E. Miller's name as Freeland.

2. DePauw University, *1920 Alumnal Record*, p. 106; Joseph B. Thoburn, *A Standard History of Oklahoma* (Chicago and New York: The American Historical Society, 1916), vol. 5, pp. 2079-2081.

3. Oklahoma City *Daily Oklahoman*, 23 May 1937, p. D-7.

4. *Daily Oklahoman*, 23 May 1937, p. D-7; Thoburn, vol. 5, p. 2081.

5. *Daily Oklahoman*, 23 May 1937, p. D-7; Philip Reed Rulon, *Oklahoma State University— Since 1890* (Stillwater: Oklahoma State University, 1975), pp. 135, 136; Stillwater *The People's Progress*, 20 June 1906, p. 1.

6. Eleanor Ypma to Harry E. Heath Jr., 5 June 1987, School of Journalism and Broadcasting Centennial History Collection; *Daily Oklahoman*, 23 May 1937, p. D-7.

7. *Daily Oklahoman*, 23 May 1937, p. D-7.

8. Author interview with Raymond Bivert, 25 March 1987, Stillwater, Oklahoma; Author interview with Sid Miller, 19 October 1988, Stillwater, Oklahoma; Author interview with Leon York, 24 July 1984, Stillwater, Oklahoma; Author interview with James M. Springer Jr., 2 August 1984, Stillwater, Oklahoma.

9.   *Daily Oklahoman*, 23 May 1937, p. D-7; Thoburn, vol. 5, p. 2081; *1920 Alumnal Record*, p. 106; *Depauw Monthly*, October 1885, p. 21; Wesley W. Wilson to Harry E. Heath Jr., 17 January 1991, School of Journalism and Broadcasting Centennial History Collection; DePauw University *Mirror*, 1894, pp. 25, 49; Oklahoma A. and M. College *Daily O'Collegian*, 14 December 1937, p. 6.

10. *Daily Oklahoman*, 23 May 1937, p. D-7; Thoburn, vol. 5, p. 2081; *Alumnal Record*, p. 106. The *Alumnal Record* incorrectly listed the marriage date as 22 March 1896 rather than 1886, as reported in the *Daily Oklahoman*. 1886 is correct for his first marriage to Estelle Shroyer. He remarried her after divorcing his second wife, Allee Carey, in Canadian, Texas. His second wife was not mentioned in the *Alumnal Record*.

11. *Daily Oklahoman*, 23 May 1937, p. D-7; Thoburn, vol. 5, pp. 2080, 2081. Loyalty to his parents also is supported by various personal documents in the possession of a granddaughter, Glee Miller Garnett, as well as in newspaper "personals" in the *Stillwater Gazette*.

12. Author interview with Lorraine Miller Newkirk, 12 May 1987; Author interview with Glee Miller Garnett, 30 May 1987; Coyle *Cimarron Valley Clipper*, 9 October 1902, p. 1.

13. *Daily Oklahoman*, 23 May 1937, p. D-7; *1920 Alumnal Record*, p. 106; *Daily O'Collegian*, 14 December 1937, p. 6; *Cimarron Valley Clipper*, 9 October 1902, p. 1.

14. *Daily Oklahoman*, 23 May 1937, p. D-7; *1920 Alumnal Record*, p. 106; Garnett interview; Newkirk interview; *Cimarron Valley Clipper*, 9 October 1902, p. 1. A report in the *Clipper* indicated that Miller also served as a Texas judge, although this was unconfirmed in other sources.

15. *1920 Alumnal Record*, p. 106; Carolyn Thomas Foreman, *Oklahoma Imprints* (Norman: University of Oklahoma Press, 1936), p. 410; *Daily O'Collegian*, 14 December 1937, p. 6. This *O'Collegian* article by George Ewing stated that Miller purchased the *Hawk* and changed its name to the *Oklahoma State Sentinel*, later changing its name to the *Stillwater Democrat* and merging it with the *Stillwater Advance*. Wesley W. Wilson to Harry E. Heath Jr., 17 January 1991, School of Journalism and Broadcasting Centennial History Collection. Wilson reported that A.M. degrees "were routinely awarded to all alumni a few years after graduation in those days."

16. *Annual Catalog, Oklahoma A. and M. College, 1891-1892*, p. [1]; LeRoy H. Fischer, *Oklahoma State University Historic Old Central* (Stillwater: Oklahoma State University, 1988), p. 6.

17. Berlin B. Chapman, *The Founding of Stillwater* (Oklahoma City, OK: Times Journal Publishing Company, 1948), pp. 70, 71; *Stillwater NewsPress*, 17 April 1988, p. 5; D. Earl Newsom, *A Pictorial History of Stillwater, One Hundred Years of Memories* (Norfolk, VA.: The Donning Company, 1989), p. 65; Robert E. Cunningham, *Stillwater: Where Oklahoma Began* (Stillwater, OK: Arts and Humanities Council of Stillwater, Oklahoma, 1969), p. 65.

18. Foreman, p. 408; *Daily Oklahoman*, 23 May 1937, p. D-7.

19. Foreman, pp. 408, 410, 411; Cunningham, p. 44.

20. *Stillwater Gazette*, 3 June 1893, p. 4.

21. Fischer, pp. 30, 32; Freeman E. Miller, *The Founding of Oklahoma A. and M. College* (Stillwater, OK: Hinkel and Sons, 1928), pp. 17-22; Rulon, pp. 12-16; Stillwater *Oklahoma Hawk*, 16 March 1893, p. 1; *Daily O'Collegian*, 18 April 1942, p. 2; *Oklahoma A. and M. College Mirror*, 15 May 1895, pp. 1, 2; *Stillwater Gazette*, 28 February 1913, p. 1.

22. *Oklahoma Hawk*, 16 March, 1893, p. 1.

23. *Stillwater Gazette*, 31 March 1893, p. 4; 21 January 1916, p. 1; Fischer, p. 36.

24. Newsom, pp. 58, 80, 83; Fischer, pp. 7, 8; Chapman, *The Founding of Stillwater*, p. 10.

25. Rulon, p. 37; J. Homer Adams, "In Retrospect and Prospect," *Oklahoma A. and M. College Magazine*, vol. 13, no. 4 (January 1942), p. 8; *Daily O'Collegian*, 12 November 1941, pp. 1, 2, 11 December 1941, p. 1; *Stillwater Gazette*, 18 August 1893, p. 4. See "Fiftieth Anniversary" in the *Daily O'Collegian* 11 December 1941 for an excellent review of makeshift classrooms as recalled by J. Homer Adams, a member of the college's first graduating class.

26. Miller, pp. 12, 13, 16, 22, 23.

27. Fischer, p. 38; *Stillwater NewsPress (NewsPlus)*, 4 February 1987, p. 1B; *Daily O'Collegian*, 14 December 1937, p. 5, 6 December 1941, p. 4, 14 December 1941, p. 3.

28. *Stillwater Gazette*, 23 June 1893, pp. 1, 4, 6; Miller, p. 17; *Daily O'Collegian*, 6 December 1941, p. 1; Cunningham, p. 37.

29. Thoburn, vol. 2, pp. iii-viii; *1920 Alumnal Record*, p. 106; *Stillwater Gazette*, 31 March 1893, p. 4, 8 December 1893, p. 4, 29 December 1893, pp. 1, 4, 8; *People's Progress*, 20 June 1906, p. 2; Max J. Nichols to Harry E. Heath Jr., 3 December 1991, School of Journalism and Broadcasting Centennial History Collection.

30. Rulon, pp. 48, 49; *Stillwater Gazette*, 29 December 1893, p. 5; *Stillwater Eagle-Gazette*, 12 July 1894, p. 3, 19 July 1894, p. 5; *Payne County Journal*, 28 August 1894, p. 5.

31. Fischer, pp. 43-50; *Stillwater Gazette*, 9 February 1894, p. 4; Rulon, pp. 46, 48-50; *Stillwater NewsPress*, 13 May 1951, p. 15; *Stillwater NewsPress (NewsPlus)*, 11 December 1991, p. 1B; *Stillwater Eagle-Gazette*, 20 December 1929, p. 4. This article contains an address by Freeman E. Miller at the Founder's Day banquet on 14 December 1929 describing the dedication of Old Central.

32. *Annual Catalog, Oklahoma A. and M. College, 1893-1894*, p. 3; *Stillwater Gazette*, 10 November 1893, p. 1.

33. *Stillwater Gazette*, 14 June 1929, p. 4.

34. Rulon, pp. 48, 49; Fischer, p. 56; *Daily O'Collegian*, 11 December 1941, p. 3; Oklahoma Agricultural and Mechanical College Faculty, "Minutes of the First Faculty," 2 January 1895, pp. 229-231, Special Collections, Edmon Low Library; Berlin B. Chapman, "The Neal Family and the Founding of Oklahoma A. and M. College, *Chronicles of Oklahoma*, vol. 68, no. 4 (Winter 1990-91), pp. 353, 354. One of the best records of Neal's death and the community's reaction may be found in an eleven-page letter written by Miller's wife, Stella. The letter is part of the Neal Collection in Oklahoma State University's Edmon Low Library.

35. *Stillwater Eagle-Gazette*, 19 July 1894, p. 5; *Daily O'Collegian,* 21 February 1942, p. 2.

36. *Stillwater Eagle-Gazette*, 19 July 1894, p. 5; Fischer, p. 72; Oklahoma Agricultural and Mechanical College Faculty, "Minutes of the First Faculty," 4 March 1895, 11 March 1895, 14 May 1895; *Oklahoma A. and M. College Mirror*, 15 May 1895, p. 1.

37. J. B. Thoburn and John Winthrop Sharp, *History of the Oklahoma Press and the Oklahoma Press Association* (Oklahoma City, OK: Industrial Printing Co., 1930), pp. unnumbered. This reference may be found in the cited work under the heading "A Semi-Annual Meeting, 1897."

38. Rulon, p. 51.

39. Rulon, p. 49; Fischer, p. 57; *Stillwater Eagle-Gazette*, 9 August 1894, p. 5.

40. Rulon, pp. 48-65; Fischer, pp. 61-64.

41. Rulon, pp. 50, 51; *Daily O'Collegian*, 9 December 1941, p. 1, 11 December 1941, p. 3; W. B. Hazen, "Some Corrections of 'Life on the Plains,'" *Chronicles of Oklahoma*, vol. 3, no. 4 (December 1925), pp. 295-318. This article contains considerable information on Alvord's military career, including high praise for his competence from Brevet Major General W. B. Hazen.

42. Rulon, p. 52.

43. Rulon, pp. 52, 56.

44. Rulon, pp. 52, 53; Fischer, pp. 51, 52.

45. Rulon, pp. 52, 53; Fischer, p. 57; *Stillwater NewsPress (NewsPlus)*, 11 December 1991, p. 1B.

46. Oklahoma Agricultural and Mechanical College Faculty, "Minutes of the First Faculty," August 1894; Freeman E. Miller, "Founding the College Library," *Oklahoma A. and M. College Magazine*, vol. 1, no. 3 (November 1929), pp. 18, 19, 27; *Stillwater NewsPress*, 13 December 1967, p. 3; *Daily O'Collegian*, 13 December 1941, p. 1; Oklahoma A. and M. College Library: A Short History, Vertical Files, Special Collections, Edmon Low Library.

47. Rulon, p. 55; *Daily O'Collegian*, 9 December 1941, p. 1.

48. Rulon, pp. 55, 56.

49. Rulon, p. 56; Miller, "Founding the College Library," p. 19.

50. Rulon, p. 56; *Stillwater Eagle-Gazette*, 17 January 1895, p. 1.

51. *Stillwater Messenger*, 11 January 1895, p. 2; Rulon, p. 56; *Oklahoma State Sentinel*, 17 January 1895, p. 1; *Stillwater Eagle-Gazette*, 17 January 1895, pp. 1, 4.

52. Fischer, p. 71; Rulon, pp. 56, 57; *Daily O'Collegian*, 12 November 1941, p. 2, 18 April 1942, p. 2; *Stillwater Messenger*, 18 January 1895, p. 2. The *Stillwater Eagle-Gazette*, 24 January 1895, p. 4, reprinting a story from the *State Capital* of Guthrie for 21 January 1895, shows January 17 as the date of the meeting at which Murdaugh was named president. The *State Capital* charged that the hasty action was taken to thwart Scott's motion in the Assembly calling for Alvord to withdraw his resignation.

53. Rulon, pp. 57, 58; *Stillwater Eagle-Gazette*, 17 January 1895, pp. 1, 4.

54. Rulon, p. 64; *Daily O'Collegian*, 11 December 1941, p. 3.

55. Rulon, p. 58.

56. Fischer, pp. 61, 62; Rulon, pp. 62, 63; *Daily O'Collegian,* 14 December 1937, p. 1.

57. Fischer, pp. 62-64; Rulon, pp. 63, 64; *Stillwater Messenger*, 15 February 1895, p. 2; *Stillwater NewsPress*, 18 March 1963, p. 3.

58. *Stillwater Gazette*, 8 August 1895, p. 1.

59. *Stillwater Gazette*, 24 October 1895, p. 2; Oklahoma Agricultural and Mechanical College Faculty, "Minutes of the First Faculty," 26 October 1897.

60. *Stillwater Gazette*, 5 September 1895, p. 2; Rulon, p. 69.

61. *Annual Catalog, Oklahoma A. and M. College, 1894-1895*, pp. [4], 78, 89, 106, 116-121; Oklahoma Agricultural and Mechanical College Faculty, "Minutes of the First Faculty," August 1894 and 10 September 1894; *Stillwater Messenger*, 11 January 1895, p. 3; *Stillwater NewsPress*, 13 December 1967, p. 3; *Oklahoma A. and M. College Mirror*, 16 March 1896, p. 6, 15 September 1897, p. 3.

62. Miller, "Founding the College Library," pp. 18, 19, 27; *Stillwater NewsPress*, 13 December 1967, p. 3.

63. Oklahoma Agricultural and Mechanical College, "Minutes of the First Faculty," 10 February 1896, 13 April 1896, 18 May 1896, 25 May 1896, 31 August 1896, 4 September 1896, 7 December 1896, 16 December 1896; *Oklahoma A. and M. College Mirror*, 15 October 1895, p. 11, 15 November 1895, pp. 1, 12, 13, 15 January 1896, pp. 5, 6.

64. Oklahoma Agricultural and Mechanical College Faculty, "Minutes of the First Faculty," 11 January 1897, 15 February 1897, 22 February 1897, 8 March 1897, 15 March 1897, 29 March 1897, 12 April 1897, 4 September 1897, 8 September 1897, 14 September 1897, 7 December 1897, 9 December 1897, 21 December 1897.

65. *Oklahoma A. and M. College Mirror*, 16 March 1896, p. 6.

66. Nancy Jane Wagner, "A History of the University of Oklahoma School of Journalism: The First Fifty Years, 1913-1963" (Master of Arts thesis, University of Oklahoma, 1964), p. 2; *Oklahoma A. and M. College Mirror*, 15 June 1895, 15 October 1895, p. 13.

67. Rulon, pp. 105, 106.

68. *Oklahoma A. and M. College Mirror*, 15 May 1895, p. 8.

69. *Oklahoma A. and M. College Mirror*, 15 December 1895, pp. 5, 6, 15 January 1896, pp. 2, 3; *Daily O'Collegian,* 14 December 1937, p. 6. Numerous examples of Miller's poetry may be readily found by a cursory examination of the *Oklahoma A. and M. College Mirror.*

70. *Oklahoma A. and M. College Mirror*, 15 June 1895, 16 September 1895, pp. 8, 14. In September, this column title was shortened to read "About the College."

71. *Oklahoma A. and M. College Mirror*, 15 May 1895, p. 8.

72. *Oklahoma A. and M. College Mirror*, 15 May 1895, p. 13.

73. *Oklahoma A. and M. College Mirror*, 15 June 1895, p. 7.

74.   *Oklahoma A. and M. College Mirror*, 16 September 1895, p. 8; Rulon, p. 72; Fischer, p. 73; *Daily O'Collegian*, 9 December 1941, pp. 1, 2, 18 April 1942, p. 3.

75.   *Daily O'Collegian*, 9 December 1941, pp. 1, 2; *Oklahoma A. and M. College Mirror*, 15 October 1895, p. 8.

76.   *Oklahoma A. and M. College Mirror*, 16 September 1895, p. 14; *Daily O'Collegian*, 9 December 1941, pp. 1, 2.

77.   *Oklahoma A. and M. College Mirror*, 16 September 1895, pp. 8, 14.

78.   *Oklahoma A. and M. College Mirror*, 16 September 1895, p. 8.

79.   Oklahoma A. and M. College *College Paper*, 15 May 1899, pp. 1, 2; *Daily O'Collegian*, 12 November 1941, p. 2, 11 December 1941, p.3.

80.   *Stillwater Gazette*, 27 September 1912, p. 4; Rulon, p. 40; Oklahoma Agricultural and Mechanical College Faculty, "Minutes of the First Faculty," 15 October 1894; Clarence Bassler Scrapbooks, vol. 1, 11 September 1969, p. 83, Public Library, Stillwater, Oklahoma. See also Chapter 3 citations of faculty meetings, especially Endnotes no. 63 and no. 64.

81.   *Oklahoma A. and M. College Mirror*, 15 February 1896, pp. 6, 7; *Stillwater Gazette*, 18 May 1951, p. 7.

82.   *Stillwater NewsPress (NewsPlus)*, 4 February 1987, p. 1B; Rulon, p. 40; *1916 Redskin*, pp. 215, 216, Oklahoma A. and M. College Yearbook; *Oklahoma A. and M. College Mirror*, 15 February 1896, p. 7.

83.   *Oklahoma A. and M. College Mirror*, 15 September 1897, January 1898, pp. 3, 6.

84.   *Oklahoma Literature*, vol. 1, no. 1 (April 1898), pp. 4-6; Mary Hays Marable and Elaine Boylan, *A Handbook of Oklahoma Writers* (Norman: University of Oklahoma Press, 1939), p. 276; Donald L. DeWitt to Harry E. Heath Jr., 20 June 1990, School of Journalism and Broadcasting Centennial History Collection; *1920 Alumnal Record*, p. 106. In the *Record*, Miller listed "Oklahoma and Other Poems," 1895; "Songs from the Southwest Country," 1898; and "Oklahoma Sunshine," 1906.

85.   *Oklahoma Literature*, p. 6.

86.   *Oklahoma Literature*, p. 6: *Oklahoma A. and M. College Mirror*, January 1898, p. 3.

87.   *Daily O'Collegian*, 18 April 1942, p. 3.

4 A Foot in the Classroom Door

When Angelo C. Scott succeeded Freeman E. Miller in the English chair at Oklahoma A. and M. College in January 1898, there was reason to believe that the regents saw heavier responsibilities ahead for him. They knew that the aging George E. Morrow would complete his tenure only a few months down the road, and that Scott, marked as excellent presidential timber, would have time to size up the strengths and weaknesses of the institution as he carried out his professorial duties. Whether such a view was sheer speculation or based upon an element of truth, Scott's elevation to the top job did come about, ushering in what some have called the college's "Golden Age."[1]

All of this notwithstanding, the versatile Scott's main concern as his snow-covered buggy neared Stillwater from the Orlando depot some twenty miles away was less upon what may have been implied by the regents in asking him to take Miller's place than upon the immediate concerns of housing, setting up his office, and planning for a successful tenure as professor of English. He could justifiably feel a surge of pride in his appointment. Applications had come from New York to Texas and from California to North Carolina. He had not applied. The position came to him unsought.[2] No other faculty appointment in those early years was based upon such a range of successful experience as that of the transplanted Kansan. As one historian has said, he was a man of unique and extraordinary ability.[3] Miller, the staunch Democrat with Populist leanings, had been replaced by a vigorous and loyal Republican. As an orator, Scott was regarded as one of the territory's best, and he enjoyed the many opportunities he had for public appearances. In addition to church, civic, business, and educational groups, he had spoken extensively in every local and congressional campaign prior to his faculty appointment. He had been a member of the Territorial Council, the upper chamber of the legislature, as well as president of the territorial Republican Club. It was typical of Scott that his high sense of ethical behavior led him to resign that position. He later wrote, "From that time on [I] completely ignored politics, in the College and out of it."[4]

In spite of his outstanding record as a founder and leading citizen of Oklahoma City, Scott received close scrutiny. Before being hired, he was invited to lecture at the college. In that way, faculty members could assess the talents of this man regarded by some as the territory's cultural leader. The lecture was well received and probably had some bearing upon his appointment. A plus, of course, was the fact that Scott had the same party affiliation as Governor Cassius M. Barnes and President William McKinley, who had a firm grip on political appointments in the territory.[5] For his part, President Morrow had asked Chancellor Francis Huntington Snow of the University of Kansas for a personal appraisal of Scott. Snow, in an effusive response, stated that Scott was both highly respected and talented, with "remarkable abilities and attainments of a literary character." Snow added that Oklahoma A. and M. would be "exceedingly fortunate to secure [Scott's] services."[6]

Scott was given a profuse official welcome to the faculty. The faculty minutes predicted "pleasant and profitable official and personal associations" and pledged the faculty's hearty cooperation in his efforts to still further develop the program in English.[7]

Angelo Scott was the son of John W. Scott, the first town president of Iola, Kansas. Scott had become a surgeon during the Civil War. He practiced medicine in Iola as well as operated a drug store, acted as a veterinarian, and served in the state legislature. He helped write the first laws of Kansas, just as his son would help write the constitution of Oklahoma. In those days there were talented generalists who seemed to be able to fill any vacant post in public service. John Scott was one of them. He was considered a leader throughout the state as well as a prime mover in Iola and Allen County.

Angelo held the A.B. and M.A. degrees from the University of Kansas and the LL.B. and LL.M. degrees from the Columbian School of Law in the nation's capital. He was a rare combination of scholar and public figure, and he knew politics from close up, not only on the plains but from his law school years in Washington, D.C.

Following his studies at Columbian, today a part of George Washington University, and work in a congressional office, the young attorney returned to his home town. He taught high school classes for a time, although the chronology is not clear. He and his brother, Charles F. Scott, bought the weekly *Iola Register* in 1882 and operated it jointly for about two years. When Charles bought Angelo's share, Angelo then devoted himself to law.[8] Young Scott practiced until the family was challenged by the opening of the Unassigned Lands. They settled in Oklahoma City, where Angelo was chosen to preside at the first town meeting and to serve on the townsite board. He established a law office, then built and operated the Angelo Hotel. He was one of the founding fathers of the Oklahoma City Chamber of Commerce and the Young Men's Christian Association and was seriously considered by President Benjamin Harrison for appointment as territorial governor in 1892. In 1893, he organized the Oklahoma exhibit at the World's Columbian Exposition in Chicago. Later, he would found the Oklahoma City Men's Supper Club, a select group dedicated to the study of public affairs. The club continues to play a vital role in the 1990s.[9]

Scott's role as the first *classroom* teacher of journalism at the Oklahoma Agricultural and Mechanical College may be more clearly understood in the context of Oklahoma newspaper history. The Kansan's role here, as in many aspects of territorial and state life during the next six decades, was significant.

The race to establish Oklahoma Territory's first newspaper, frequently conceded to be the *Daily State Capital* of Guthrie, was more complicated than is generally believed. Instant replay cannot resolve the claims and counter claims. Where the early newspapers were "put to bed" is at the heart of the confusion.[10]

Frank Hilton Greer's *State Capital* was printed in Winfield, Kansas,

Angelo C. Scott, perhaps the most revered of the '89ers, advanced the cause of journalism education in Oklahoma through his rhetoric courses. He introduced units on newspaper writing and manuscript preparation, which he continued to teach throughout his presidency.

a week before the opening of the Unassigned Lands and was predated April 22, 1889, before being sent by rail into Oklahoma Territory. Four months earlier, on December 29, 1888, Hamlin W. Sawyer had started the *Oklahoma City Times* as a weekly before the town was organized. It was written and edited locally but printed in Wichita and shipped down from Kansas. Sawyer was an enterprising publisher who anticipated the shifting political winds in Washington. The paper was moved to Purcell in Indian Territory in February 1889 when the Boomers, those adventurous illegal settlers, were evicted by U.S. troops. The paper returned to Oklahoma City as a daily on June 30, 1889, about two months after the run.[11]

Meanwhile, Winfield W. Scott and his brother Angelo had preceded their own arrival on April 22 by shipping a well-assorted printing plant by rail to the future Oklahoma City, then a stop on the line known as Oklahoma Station. They set up part of their operation in a 9- by 12-foot tent not unlike that of Frank Greer's first shop in Guthrie. The remainder of the equipment was placed in an unenclosed building intended, when completed, to become the paper's home. They called their paper the *Oklahoma Times*.[12]

The Scotts were proud of their pioneer printing establishment. The business interests were left to Winfield Scott while Angelo was the gifted writer. These words from Volume 1, Number 1, probably were Angelo's: "In a business way, the *Times* is most thoroughly equipped. We venture to say that we have the finest and most complete plant that will be found in the territory for a long time. Our Campbell press, run by steam, is a magnificent machine, with a capacity of twenty-thousand copies daily. We are prepared to begin daily publication at the earliest moment our city will justify it. We are equipped for doing all kinds of commercial work, and for publishing any sized paper that may be demanded. All we ask is the hearty cooperation of the business men and citizens of Oklahoma City."[13]

In that first issue on Thursday, May 9, 1889, "set up and printed in Oklahoma City," Angelo Scott admitted that an earlier number of the *Times* had been published outside of Oklahoma, "but owing to its arrival here late and in a mutilated condition it was not distributed." That issue of the *Oklahoma Times*, a name sure to lead to confusion, probably was printed on the *Register's* press. It is not known what date the "trashed" edition carried, but an educated hunch is that it was April 22, 1889.[14]

To make their claim even stronger, the Scotts published this ear at the left end of the paper's nameplate: "KEEP THIS PAPER. It is the first paper ever PUBLISHED IN OKLAHOMA CITY. Send copies to your friends." In column one, under the headline "Our Name," the Scotts had more to say: "We want it thoroughly understood that this paper is not the *Oklahoma City Times*. That paper is published at Wichita, Kansas. The conflict in names is unfortunate, but without wearying our readers with details, it is sufficient to say that there are equities on both sides. In view of this, we offered to arbitrate the matter with the publisher of that paper either here or at Guthrie, and also proposed that both papers change names. He did not see fit to accept any of these offers, and so we have had our name copyrighted and will stand upon our legal rights."[15]

As a practicing attorney with an excellent reputation, Angelo Scott knew his legal rights. Be that as it may, the second issue on May 16 carried a new nameplate: The *Oklahoma Journal*. Apparently the Scotts had decided their future would be brighter without the unnecessary confusion.[16]

The confusion '89ers faced in the wake of the opening of the Unassigned Lands is suggested in other notes from Angelo Scott's pen. On Page 1 of the first issue he pointed out that Oklahoma City, contrary to Guthrie and Kingfisher, had no regularly appointed Associated Press agent. The one telegraph wire had been "swamped with railroad business, and news messages could not be accomodated."[17] The Scotts had been on the ground from the first day, but the heavy freight traffic had delayed their plans. Their building materials had arrived late and their presses and supplies were partly in a railroad car and partly in three different places in the city. Now their building was being erected and Scott predicted that "next week we will be in ship shape, and ready for all demands."[18]

The *Journal* became a daily on June 3, 1889, and on September 15 of that year the Scott brothers leased the paper and plant to J. J. Burke and E. E. Brown. Shortly after Burke and Brown acquired the *Journal*, they bought the *Oklahoma City Times* from Sawyer and established the *Times-Journal*. The only complete copy of Volume 1, Number 1 of the *Oklahoma Times* is in the Kansas State Museum.[19]

Scott's eight years and nine months since the big land run had been busy and satisfying. He knew his move to the territory had been right for him. Now, as his buggy approached Stillwater through the falling snow, Scott was in sight of a light shining from the student janitor's alcove in the Central Building. A new career was ready to unfold.

With his exciting background in territorial journalism, it is understandable that Scott would take an interest in student journalism at Oklahoma A. and M. Some of the material in the *Oklahoma A. and M. College Mirror* following Freeman Miller's resignation appears to have been written by Scott. The literary societies along with the College Press Bureau had been the early sponsors of the paper. In fact, in its early history, most of the editorial work had been done by the literary groups. But the faculty had banned the Websters and Sigmas when their competition with one another had taken a disruptive turn. Their names no longer appeared in the masthead after March 16, 1896; the paper had become a joint effort of "Faculty and students under the supervision of the department of English," with Miller as editor. The College Press Bureau was not mentioned. A faculty committee under E. E. Bogue had been set up to assist with the paper's financial problems. When the December 1897 *Mirror* went to press, Miller was still in charge. The January 1898 issue, however, reported his resignation, and Scott's appointment. The masthead eliminated any mention of departmental involvement, reading simply, "Published by the faculty and students."[20]

As the new curricular head of English and literature, Scott had agreed to supervise editing and layout work on the *Mirror*. The final *Mirror* appeared in June 1898. Apparently no campus newspaper existed from that issue until May 15, 1899, a month and a half before Scott was elevated to the presidency.[21] For the last six months of the *Mirror's* existence, Scott had contributed his skills, as needed, to get the paper out. Student participation had faltered with the dismantling of the literary societies, and the paper was in such financial distress that faculty members were asked to contribute money to keep it alive. Now Scott was president, and though he strongly favored a campus newspaper—he and two classmates had printed the first student newspaper at the University of Kansas—he was too busy with his new responsibilities to give the matter his immediate attention. When the paper resumed, after an eleven-month absence, the college had its own press and the paper a new name, the *College Paper*. But it recognized that it was a continuation of the *Mirror*. It identified its first issue as Volume 4, Number 1. While the

The College Paper.

Vol. IV. The Oklahoma Agricultural and Mechanical College. 10 Cents
No. 1. STILLWATER, OKLAHOMA, MAY 15, 1899. a Year.

STUDENT EDITORS.

CORA MILTIMORE, '99. A. W. ANDERSON, '00. GEO. B. GELDER, '00.
F. L. RECTOR, '02. BEN SHIVELY, '02.

FRANK D. NORTHUP, SUPERINTENDENT OF PRINTING.
[COLLEGE PRESS.]

Entered at the Postoffice at Stillwater, Okla., as second-class matter.

STATEMENT.

This is the initial number of THE COLLEGE PAPER, successor to the good will and back subscriptions of the College Mirror. It is published by the students of the Oklahoma Agricultural and Mechanical College. The composition and press work is done by students as a part of their course of instruction in the department of printing. The responsibility for the paper and its contents rests with a committee of the faculty, and its publication is under direction of the superintendent of printing.

The department of printing in the college was established for the purpose of giving instruction in the minor matters of printing and job work. It is not the intention to make the work other than purely instructive, and work in this department does not count as a part of the regular course leading to the degree of Bachelor of Science, but is taken either as extra work in the regular courses or by special students, along with stenography and typewriting and English. Frequent press bulletins will be issued by the Experiment Station and sent to the newspapers of the territory. This arrangement will, it is believed, enable the college to offer better and broader facilities for in-

The campus had been without a student publication for months when Angelo C. Scott was instrumental in establishing the successor to the *Mirror*. It was called the *College Paper* at the suggestion of John Fields. It continued in literary magazine format with little change in content and objectives.

Centennial Histories Series

content had changed but little, the new publication had reverted to a one-column book page style, dropping its two-column format.[22]

Keeping the *College Paper* afloat was a taxing matter, but the new staff refrained from pleading with students to pay their annual ten cent subscription fee or risk being dropped from the circulation list, contrary to the approach the *Mirror* ahead of it had taken.

Throughout the life of the paper, it continued to display the same qualities the *Mirror* had extolled. It gave the college administration and faculty strong support, encouraged school spirit, fostered student activities and provided essays and editorial comment that encouraged ethical and moral behavior. Along with all this was a large dose of boosterism, in which the paper consistently sought to show Oklahoma A. and M. in a favorable light vis-à-vis the University of Oklahoma at Norman and the Central Normal School at Edmond. The focus of the latter effort was in the outcome of debates, oratory, athletic contests and, of course, enrollment. The paper made it clear that loyal Oklahoma A. and M. students were expected to recruit students from their home counties by praising the virtues of the Stillwater college.[23]

Scott's brilliant mind and teaching skills had quickly made him popular among students. His two rhetoric courses were his favorites. He decided to introduce journalistic writing as a part of both the beginning and advanced rhetoric classes.[24] This move probably grew out of several keenly felt attitudes. For one thing, he was from a Kansas newspaper family and had known the thrill of publication from his early years. For another, one of his reasons for making the run into Oklahoma Territory on April 22, 1889, had been to establish a newspaper, the first printed at the townsite of what would become Oklahoma City. Then, too, there had been his awareness of the early efforts to establish journalism courses at other institutions of higher learning. Finally, although additional reasons may have been in his mind, he considered newspaper writing to be a practical way to teach English to his students.

Scott soon had legitimized journalism instruction at Oklahoma A. and M. Until Scott's arrival, any journalism instruction offered by Miller would have been informal. There is no evidence that the gifted predecessor to Scott had introduced journalistic writing in the classroom on a regular basis, although as a former newspaperman he may have on occasion made a tangential reference to journalistic practices. Miller's rhetoric class did, however, include original work in descriptive and narrative composition, and on one occasion he assigned freshmen in a joint meeting with seniors in political economy to write a story covering the seniors' recitations. Some became so absorbed in what the seniors were saying that they forgot to take notes for the story.[25] While Miller must be credited with the birth of the first campus newspaper, Scott is without question the father of classroom instruction in journalism at Oklahoma

A. and M., for he not only formally taught the first journalistic writing but may have provided the impetus for instruction in typography and printing production.[26]

During the summer of 1899, Morrow retired as president. The student body, with substantial faculty assistance, had clamored for Scott as his successor. The clamor was satisfying but unnecessary; Scott was named the fifth and last territorial president of the college on July 1, 1899. The regents' vote was unanimous.[27] When he replaced Morrow, the campus contained 200 acres, possessed one medium-sized building and several smaller ones, and had a faculty of 14 or 15 to teach the 200 students enrolled.

The new president's background, unlike that of many of his counterparts nationally, was not in agriculture, although in his boyhood he had lived on a Kansas farm in the rural community of Carlyle, six miles north of Iola. He believed that state universities, which many of the older land-grant institutions such as Ohio State University had become, should play an important role in preparing citizens for participation in the nation's political system and in building an environment that would serve the public weal. He was among the land-grant educators of the late 1800s whose writing and public speaking led to progressive reforms. Scott—with strong support from John Fields, the brilliant young experiment station director—used extension courses, short-term winter institutes, and experiment station bulletins to bring change to the territory.[28]

In addition to the talents, training, and experience Scott brought to the presidency, he had the support of his father, also a Republican, who held a seat in the territorial House of Representatives. He could be counted upon to work for the interests of the Stillwater college. His brother Charles served Kansas as a Republican in the United States House of Representatives from 1901 to 1911, giving Oklahoma A. and M. a friendly contact in Washington outside its ties with the U. S. Department of Agriculture. In addition, an all-Republican board of agriculture chaired by Stillwater's Frank J. Wikoff, who had attended a land-grant university, provided conscientious support during Scott's presidential years. Without this confluence of power, the institution might well have kept to a plodding pace for years.[29]

Scott wanted to expand and strengthen the faculty with young scholars. The regents agreed. The faculty soon was unexcelled by any land-grant college in the surrounding territories and states.[30] Academic standards and student performance showed marked improvement. As important as all of these achievements were, another long-awaited improvement was to play a major role in the next stage of the college's wider acceptance. Soon after Scott moved into the president's office in the Central Building, a railroad came to Stillwater. Since its founding in 1889, Stillwater had been isolated, the nearest railroad stops being at

Mulhall, Orlando, and Perry, each about twenty miles or more distant. With the completion of the 40.4 mile length of track in 1900—a bend in a new line from Ripley to the Pawnee area—Oklahoma A. and M. and its role changed dramatically. Athletic teams took to the road, but more importantly, the Agricultural Experiment Station began to send demonstration specialists, equipment, and crops and animal exhibits throughout the territory. The college now was able to bury the canard that it was strictly a local institution, important to Stillwater but wasteful in terms of its territory-wide value.[31]

Scott's immediate problems in picking up the college reins were far too pressing for him to give much thought to an academic program in journalism, whatever was happening at the University of Missouri, Cornell University, or the University of Pennsylvania. In addition to the units on newspaper writing in his rhetoric classes, which he continued to teach, he gave enthusiastic support to the new campus printshop, an auxiliary service that was to play its part in building student interest in both journalism and publishing.[32]

Whether the decision to establish the campus printshop was made solely by Morrow, or at Scott's urging and with Morrow's approval, is not clear. Morrow would have had good reason to favor the move, based upon his earlier publishing experience. However, this late in Morrow's tenure the two men may have reached the decision together. Scott was convinced the move would be, in today's jargon, cost effective. His judgment, no doubt in agreement with Morrow's, was correct.[33]

The confusion surrounding the printing plant is based upon earlier accounts. In 1898, for example, one review of Oklahoma A. and M. history suggests "Angelo Scott found a solution to many of the problems which surrounded the publication of a student newspaper. He felt that high printing costs could be reduced if Oklahoma A. and M. had its own printing press. Such machinery, too, could be used to publish experiment station bulletins, for costs had risen sharply due to the unreasonably high prices charged for work done under the contract for printing made by the Territorial Legislature in 1897. This move not only proved financially expedient, but it also provided the campus with hardware for a new vocational program. The existence of the press greatly aided the effort to improve the quality of [the college's] newspapers and it created an interest in professional journalism as well."[34]

The writer here seems to have given Scott undue credit, for Scott was not yet president. However, Scott was held in high regard by Morrow, and no doubt he offered the president counsel on such matters. The college catalog for 1898-99, published in Morrow's last year as president, resolves this confusion. It refers to a Department of Printing, established "within the [academic] year." "The primary purpose," stated the catalog, "is to give instruction in printing, with its incidental benefits." Particular attention should be given the word *instruction*. Later in the same catalog, printing was listed under "Departments of Instruction," with Frank D. Northup as superintendent of the printing department and instructor in printing.[35] Whether Northup was Morrow's choice to head the new facility or was selected upon Scott's recommendation is clouded by conflicting dates in various accounts.[36]

Scott was a strong proponent of progress. At a May meeting in 1898, the faculty ruled that each senior must submit a typewritten copy of the required thesis by June 1. It first would have to be approved "by the department under which the subject comes" before the student would receive a diploma.[37] Scott no doubt strongly supported this move. Scott was a builder. He was a teaching president as well. Not only did he teach the first lessons on newspaper writing and play a major role in establishing the printing department, but he must be given credit as founding father of speech instruction.

Scott's strong interest in effective speech was reflected in a joint report signed by him and President Morrow on September 17, 1898. The report recommended that freshmen as well as the three upper classes participate in required orations, and that at least one oration be prepared and rehearsed each term under the supervision of Scott "or such other instructors appointed by him." Three days later, the faculty approved the report.[38] Both the 1898-99 and 1899-1900 catalogs referred to hopes that course work in speech would begin soon. The following year, President Scott himself gave the first instruction in public speaking, required of juniors and seniors in the science and literature major. He continued as the lone instructor for four years. In the 1904-05 academic year, he turned some of the work over to James F. Lawrence, a mathematics instructor. Scott and Lawrence shared the speech work for three years. Lawrence, in the perceptive eyes of Scott, was a versatile man, for in 1906 he added the title of director of music to Lawrence's mathematics and speech duties. Both Scott and Lawrence finally got relief when Howard G. Seldomridge joined the faculty as an assistant in English and instructor in public speaking. The 1907-08 catalog presented a more extensive statement on the work in speech. Scott had found his man. During the next year, Seldomridge developed five courses in public speaking. Those appeared in the 1908-09 catalog, the first year speech received recognition as a separate department. Seldomridge, who held a certificate from the Curry School of Expression, also taught English. He continued as a part of that faculty even after the Department of Public Speaking appeared as a separate department.[39]

Scott, a people person, was readily accessible to both students and faculty who needed his counsel. To make himself even more accessible, he was one of the town's first citizens to add a telephone, both at home and in his office. His office number was 23. His line was from the

Angelo C. Scott derived great pleasure from encouraging young writers. His greatest discovery during his years in Stillwater was Vingie Roe, whose poetry was obviously the work of a creative genius. Roe went on to an outstanding career as an author of fiction, whose books sometimes were adapted for Hollywood motion pictures. One book was dedicated to Scott.

Arkansas Telephone Company at 814 1/2 South Main Street to the Central Building, a mile of wire to this lone campus connection. His home number was 14. Mrs. Scott could be reached at 72.[40]

In addition, he took pleasure in discovering promising young talent. A primary example was Vingie Roe, a gifted young woman who lived in Perkins. He "discovered" Miss Roe while scanning the *Perkins Journal*. She had submitted a poem, "The Fight of the Wolves," and editor John P. Hinkel had elected to publish it. It was clearly the work of an extremely gifted writer. Scott sent the poem to Victor Murdock, editor of the *Wichita Eagle*, where it was published for a much wider readership. Scott also contacted Roe and invited her to prepare for a writing career by studying at Oklahoma A. and M. She enjoyed her writing conferences with Scott, but bridled at the formality of classroom work. After a few months she left, but Scott had given her more than most classrooms could have given. She left with a new-found confidence in her creative destiny. Between the years 1912 and her death in 1958, she wrote thirty-one novels and numerous screen plays. One of the books, *The Great Trace*, published in 1948, was dedicated to Scott. The famous author later wrote that Scott had believed in her creative gift, "the one great flame of my life."[41]

Angelo Scott was a stickler for correct and graceful expression. He not only used chapel appearances to stress the importance of effective written and spoken communication, but he used his rhetoric classes to bring the lesson home even more forcefully. He was convinced—as was

Harry O'Brien, his successor as the principal journalism teacher a few years later—that applied English was more productive of student success than theory and personal essays. The catalog description of his Beginning Rhetoric classes contained these words: "careful and painstaking instruction is given in punctuation, in letter writing, and in the preparation of manuscript for the press." Advanced Rhetoric was described, in part, as a class in which students produced practical themes, narratives, newspaper writing, argumentative writing and abstract themes.[42]

As Scott's presidential burdens increased, he began to cut back on his ancillary activities. He was looking for someone to take over some of his responsibilities. Relief came in the first year from Kellis Campbell, who was in charge of Latin and German and an assistant in English and literature. Campbell was replaced the next year by Robert H. Tucker, who held the M. A. degree from William and Mary College. He quickly established a reputation for steady and reliable teaching in English as well as Latin and German, and Scott saw broader responsibilities for him.[43] Within a year he was listed as associate professor of languages, and the following year as professor of German and Latin and associate in English. By 1905, Scott had elevated him to dean of the science and literature course, and one year later had given him vice presidential duties. In spite of his new responsibilities, Tucker continued as professor of German and English while Scott was titular head of the latter program.[44] From the college's earliest days, faculty members were expected to go the extra mile. Overloads were common for six decades, finally beginning to slack off in the 1960s.

As president, Scott could easily have elected not to teach. But that was not in his nature. He valued the classroom contact with students. It gave him a feel for the academic progress of the institution and was a barometer of student morale as well. Throughout his years as president, he continued to hold the reins as head of the English and literature program.

As the first automobile came to Stillwater, Scott was only a year away from a period he later would consider to be the most important of his administration. He had set the stage for 1905-06 by extending an invitation to the Legislative Assembly to visit the campus. Nine members of the council and 11 house members plus about 100 employees and 300 Guthrie citizens took advantage of the free junket on the Santa Fe special. Following a luncheon, Scott reviewed the needs of the college. Nine legislators responded to his remarks, then the delegation made a tour of buildings and grounds. The outcome of the visit would be known, the Stillwater *Daily Democrat* reported, "when the appropriation bills are made up." The legislative visit not only had proven to be a public relations coup but had prepared the way for Scott's next and most crucial move. He had asked and had been authorized by the regents to make a prolonged lobbying trip to the nation's capital. In Scott's own words, this is what transpired:

"[They] had authorized me to go for the purpose of securing, through Congress, four things. They were kind enough to say that if I secured any one of the four, it would more than justify my going. . . . These four matters were as follows: first, the securing of the section of school-land adjoining the college farm; second, the repealing, so far as the A. and M. College was concerned, of a certain federal statute which declared there should be no more public buildings erected by Oklahoma until after statehood. The repealing of this statute enabled us to go before the legislature and secure the appropriation for Morrill Hall; third, the readjustment of the income from the old college lands in a manner more equitable and fair to the A. and M. College; and fourth, the securing of a new land endowment for the college in connection with the pending statehood bill. This last enactment gave the college 250,000 acres of land, in addition to its share in the 'old college' lands. I have heard it has been intimated by those not quite friendly to me that I had little to do with this legislation, which added over a hundred thousand dollars to the building and local land equipment of the college and perhaps a million dollars to its landed endowment—that this was brought about chiefly by others. I never expected to take the trouble to deny this. But. . .I have a feeling that history should be written justly and accurately."

Scott went on to say that his brother had given him valuable introductions to certain representatives and senators, but it had not seemed best that he "actively interest himself in these matters beyond these introductions." Angelo Scott personally succeeded in getting the bills introduced. He presented his goals to the several committees of the House and Senate, interviewed scores of congressmen in behalf of the measures, and secured the men to present and take charge of them on the floor of both houses. He had worked for the four objectives night and day for five weeks. Summing up, Scott said: "Of course I was indebted to many men in both houses of Congress for assistance—but it was the very gist of my job to enlist this aid. . .I may add that the building and teaching equipment increased from about $25,000 to a quarter of a million. . . ."[45]

Scott's tenure as president coincided almost exactly with the life of the *College Paper*, successor to the *Mirror*, although the date of the last issue cannot be absolutely determined from available records. Scott's tenure was marked by considerable progress on a number of fronts, with the student body increasing to 571 collegiate students (1,008 including the longer short course students and the sub-freshman class) before he left in 1908. Under Scott, Oklahoma A. and M. became known by the sobriquet "Princeton of the Prairies." In a paper he wrote at the request of President Henry G. Bennett years after leaving Stillwater, Scott made no mention of being directly involved in journalism at the college.[46]

Among his recollections: "It was indeed a day of small beginnings. The College farm comprised 20 acres, of less than average fertility. The only buildings were Old Central; a tiny building just east of Old Central used as a biological laboratory; a flimsy two-story residence where the director of the experiment station lived; and a small, ramshackle barn. In the year preceding the beginning of my service on the faculty there were between 125 and 150 students, most of them in the preparatory department. The catalog of that year was a mere folder of four pages, not even containing names of the students."[47]

President Scott had found it difficult to persuade students to enroll in agricultural courses. Farming was hard, unglamourous, and in many cases unprofitable. Parents often preferred their offspring to pursue what they considered to be loftier goals.[48] While he was trying to build a multi-purpose institution to serve the territory's needs better, he faced an image problem. This is reflected in a 1907 interview published in *School Journal.* He was aware that his administration would end when Oklahoma Territory became a state, so he spoke frankly to the *Journal* writer. He said that many people thought of Oklahoma A. and M. as a place where students farmed some and did high school-level work. This image, he said, made it difficult for him to implement the late nineteenth century concept of what a Morrill college should be. He said he would like to see the name of the institution changed to Oklahoma State College, broadening its appeal and its public acceptance through a curriculum which would emphasize both the liberal arts and sciences. He hoped that someday the college would become a multi-purpose state university.

Although a journalism curriculum was still seven years away, some students of the Scott era did achieve as writers and editors. One of these was Frank J. Clark, class of 1908, who spent six years on the *Oklahoma Farm Journal* before a career with Webb Publishing Company, St. Paul, as associate editor of *The Farmer.*[49]

Angelo Scott had ridden the uncertain tides of territorial politics as president longer than any of his predecessors. Now the tides had changed. The "Golden Age" his admirers said Scott had brought to Oklahoma A. and M. was at an end.

Oklahoma became the forty-sixth state on November 16, 1907, and the elections later that month gave the Democratic Party full control of state offices. Scott immediately received word that he would be replaced. The shift in power, as was to be expected, saw the Republicans on the board of agriculture supplanted by a full slate of Democrats. Scott resigned at once, effective July 1, 1908. His widespread popularity was undeniable, and this no doubt led the new board to accept his terms, permitting him to continue to the end of the fiscal year. A lesser figure might have been summarily dumped. A glowing review of Scott's leadership in the second issue of *Orange and Black,* the new student

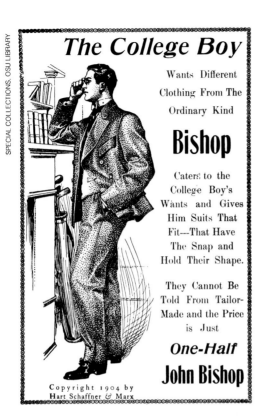

The College Boy

Wants Different Clothing From The Ordinary Kind

Bishop

Caters to the College Boy's Wants and Gives Him Suits That Fit---That Have The Snap and Hold Their Shape.

They Cannot Be Told From Tailor-Made and the Price is Just

One-Half

John Bishop

Copyright 1904 by Hart Schaffner & Marx

Although the *Mirror* had carried advertising, the first full-page display ad appeared in the *College Paper* on the inside front cover of its October 1904 issue. This advertisement caused many local merchants to reevaluate their use of sales strategy aimed at Oklahoma A. and M. students.

newspaper, reflected the great admiration students had for him.[50]

The regents had selected an agricultural journalist, John H. Connell, editor of *Farm and Ranch Magazine*, to replace Scott. For the remainder of Scott's tenure the two men worked as a team, Connell dealing with the legislature and other public officials and Scott with students and faculty.[51]

Scott graciously invited Connell to deliver the 1908 commencement address. After Connell had spoken, Scott took the lectern. He told the assembly that his choicest memory would be of the friendship and loyalty of the students he had served. "I shall never see your brave orange and black," he said with obvious emotion, "without claiming it also as mine, or hear your multitudinous yell without feeling moved to join in it."

The Scott years had been years of simplicity and economy, of doing things without waste or extravagance. They were, as one observed of the period recalled, years of plain living and high thinking. But during those years, materials of strength and virtue went into the foundation on which the superstructure of today has been built.[52]

Now Scott was ready for his next adventure. Perhaps a bit hastily, he had accepted a position on the English faculty at the University of Oklahoma. One can only offer conjecture about his feelings, but he must have had second thoughts about the position at Norman. Would that institution, too, be a toy in the hands of politicians who often were overzealous and at times capricious? Whatever the reasoning he pursued, he did not report to the university. Instead, he returned to Oklahoma City, where young Epworth University was preparing to open its fifth academic year under sponsorship of the two branches of Methodism. Church politics may have seemed to promise a less turbulent future than the rowdy politics of a new state. Be that as it may, when September arrived Scott was facing classes at Epworth as the modern languages professor in the College of Arts and Sciences.[53]

But even church-sponsored universities are not totally free from strife. In 1911, the two branches of Methodism fell into conflict over the university, and the Southern branch withdrew. The Methodist Episcopal Church relocated Epworth in Guthrie and renamed it the Methodist University of Oklahoma. School records in 1913 show Scott as a professor of political science and economics.[54] However, he must have reconsidered the move to Guthrie following this conflict, for he assumed duties instead at the University of Oklahoma in the Extension Division, where he served as director from 1912 to 1923. Before and after his duties at Norman, he handled teaching and administrative assignments at what became Oklahoma City University, lending his prestige to the growth of that Methodist-sponsored institution.[55]

Angelo Scott, described by friends as "one of the wonders of the frontier," died in Oklahoma City on February 6, 1949, at the age of 91. A scholar in the classical mode—he knew both Greek and Latin—Scott had played a continuing role in shaping the cultural development of Oklahoma. In his long and productive life, he had been journalist, lawyer, law maker, orator, educator, poet, essayist, author, musician, composer, and civic leader—all packed into a slim, frail body sparked by an indomitable spirit. He was, in short, Oklahoma's most authentic Renaissance Man.[56]

Endnotes

1. Philip Reed Rulon, *Oklahoma State University—Since 1890* (Stillwater: Oklahoma State University Press, 1975), pp. 76, 111, 112; A. C. Scott, *The Story of an Administration of the Oklahoma A. and M. College* (Oklahoma City, OK: no publisher, March 1942), pp. 3, 6; Oklahoma A. and M. College *Daily O'Collegian*, 9 December 1941, p. 2, 18 April 1942, pp. 2, 3. Scott's story of his administration was given wider distribution in a series of *Daily O'Collegian* articles based upon his booklet, not yet in print. They appeared 20 and 21 November 1941 and 14 and 15 December 1941. All are available in the "Record Book," Special Collections, Edmon Low Library, Oklahoma State University, Stillwater, Oklahoma.
2. LeRoy H. Fischer, *Oklahoma State University Historic Old Central* (Stillwater: Oklahoma State University, 1988), pp. 83-85, 188; *Oklahoma A. and M. College Mirror*, January 1898, p. 6.

3. Fischer, p. 83.

4. Scott, pp. 6, 7; Rulon, p. 58; Fischer, p. 83; Heather Lloyd, "Angelo C. Scott: Oklahoma City's Most Useful Citizen, 1937," a paper prepared for History 5110, Fall 1973, pp. 7, 8, Special Collections, Edmon Low Library.

5. Rulon, p. 111; Fischer, pp. 83-85; Lloyd, p. 8.

6. Rulon, pp. 111, 112.

7. Oklahoma Agricultural and Mechanical College Faculty, "Minutes of the First Faculty," 1 February 1898, Special Collections, Edmon Low Library.

8. Lloyd, pp. 1, 2; Emerson Lynn Jr. to Harry E. Heath Jr., 18 March 1987, D. G. Mounger to Harry E. Heath Jr., 1990, and Della Boyer to Harry E. Heath Jr., 8 August 1990, in School of Journalism and Broadcasting Centennial History Collection, Special Collections, Edmon Low Library; Charles F. Scott and L. Wallace Duncan, *History of Allen and Woodson Counties* (Iola, KS: Allen County Historical Society, 1901), pp. 52, 491-495, 577, 578; *Oklahoma A. and M. College Mirror*, January 1898, p. 6.

9. Fischer, pp. 83, 84; Rulon, pp. 117, 118; Oklahoma City *Daily Oklahoman*, 7 February 1949, p. 1.

10. Harry E. Heath Jr., "Debate Unresolved Over First Paper in Oklahoma," *Publishers' Auxiliary*, 2 October 1989, p. 19.

11. Heath, p. 19.

12. Carolyn Thomas Foreman, *Oklahoma Imprints* (Norman: University of Oklahoma Press, 1936), p. 379; Heath, p. 19; Lloyd, p. 4.

13. Oklahoma City *Oklahoma Times*, 9 May 1889, p. 1; *Daily Oklahoman*, 7 February 1949, p. 1.

14. *Oklahoma Times*, 9 May 1889, p. 1; Heath, p. 19.

15. *Oklahoma Times*, 9 May 1889, p. 1; Heath, p. 19; Lloyd, p. 4.

16. Foreman, pp. 377, 379; Heath, p. 19; Lloyd, p. 4.

17. *Oklahoma Times*, 9 May 1889, p. 1.

18. *Oklahoma Times*, 9 May 1889, p. 1.

19. Foreman, pp. 366, 381; Lloyd, pp. 4, 5.

20. *Oklahoma A. and M. College Mirror*, 16 March 1896, p. 4, 15 September 1897, p. 8, January 1898, pp. 3, 6; Rulon, pp. 106, 107; Scott, p. 4.

21. Rulon, pp. 106, 107; *Oklahoma A. and M. College Mirror*, June 1898, p. 1.

22. *Stillwater Gazette*, 18 May 1899, p. 2; Richard D. Wilson, "Early Oklahoma A. and M. Newspapers—A Perspective," unpublished manuscript submitted to fulfill requirements in MC 4360 in 1980, pp. 11-17, Special Collections, Edmon Low Library; Oklahoma A. and M. *College Paper*, 15 May 1899, pp. 1-16; Rulon, p. 319 (endnote no. 50). The *Gazette* referred to the paper as a new publication of sixteen pages "nicely gotten up."

23. Oklahoma A. and M. *College Paper*, February 1907, p. 43; Rulon, p. 110; Wilson, p. 12.

24. *Annual Catalog, Oklahoma A. and M. College, 1898-1899*, pp. 20, 21.

25. *Annual Catalog, Oklahoma A. and M. College, 1897-1898*, pp. 9, 10; Heath, p. 19; Scott, p. 5; *Oklahoma A. and M. College Mirror*, 16 March 1896, p. 6.

26. Rulon, p. 107.

27. Rulon, p. 112; *College Paper*, January 1898, p. 6; *Stillwater Gazette*, 18 May 1899, p. 2.

28. Rulon, pp. 112-114, 119; Angelo C. Scott, *A Boyhood in Old Carlyle* (Iola, KS: Iola Register Press, 1940), p. 5; Lloyd, p. 1.

29. Fischer, pp. 85, 86, 103; Rulon, pp. 117-119.

30. Rulon, p. 119; Fischer, p. 86.

31. Fischer, pp. 86-88.

32. Rulon, p. 107.

33. *College Paper*, 15 May 1899, pp. 1, 2; Rulon, p. 107; Fischer, p. 271; Foreman, p. 243.

34. Rulon, p. 107.

35. *Annual Catalog, Oklahoma A. and M. College, 1898-1899*, pp. 6, 10, 31.

36. *Daily O'Collegian*, 23 November 1941, p. 1.

37. Oklahoma Agricultural and Mechanical College Faculty, "Minutes of the First Faculty," 10 May 1898.

38. Oklahoma Agricultural and Mechanical College Faculty, "Minutes of the First Faculty," 20 September 1898.

39. *Annual Catalog, Oklahoma A. and M. College, 1898-1899*, pp. 29, 30; *Annual Catalog, Oklahoma A. and M. College, 1899-1900*, p. 40; *Annual Catalog, Oklahoma A. and M. College, 1900-1901*, p. 48; *Annual Catalog, Oklahoma A. and M. College, 1901-1902*, p. 43; *Annual Catalog, Oklahoma A. and M. College, 1902-1903*, p. 43; *Annual Catalog, Oklahoma A. and M. College, 1903-1904*, pp. 42, 43; *Annual Catalog, Oklahoma A. and M. College, 1904-1905*, p. 47; *Annual Catalog, Oklahoma A. and M. College, 1905-1906*, p. 47; *Annual Catalog, Oklahoma A. and M. College, 1906-1907*, pp. 69, 70; *Annual Catalog, Oklahoma A. and M. College, 1907-1908*, pp. 88, 89; *Annual Catalog, Oklahoma A. and M. College, 1908-1909*, pp. 107, 108.

40. Robert E. Cunningham, *Stillwater, Where Oklahoma Began* (Stillwater, OK: Arts and Humanities Council of Stillwater, Oklahoma, 1969), pp. 103-105.

41. Vingie E. Roe, "Former Aggie Is Famous Writer," *Oklahoma A. and M. College Magazine*, vol. 1, no. 3 (November 1929), pp. 8, 9; *Daily O'Collegian*, 5 November 1941, pp. 1, 2; Berlin B. Chapman, "Author Discovered by A. C. Scott," *Oklahoma A. and M. College Magazine*, vol. 17, no. 6 (March 1945), pp. 3, 4, 13, 14; *Stillwater NewsPress*, 5 November 1986, p. 8B; Kay Nettleton, "Vingie Roe," *Oklahoma State University Outreach*, vol. 52, no. 2 (December 1980), p. 17; Rulon, pp. 116, 117.

42. *Annual Catalog, Oklahoma A. and M. College, 1898-1899*, p. 20; Rulon, p. 95.

43. *Annual Catalog, Oklahoma A. and M. College, 1898-1899*, pp. 6, 20; *Annual Catalog, Oklahoma A. and M. College, 1899-1900*, pp. 6, 26.

44. Rulon, p. 117; *Annual Catalog, Oklahoma A. and M. College, 1898-1899*, pp. 6, 20; *Annual Catalog, Oklahoma A. and M. College, 1899-1900*, pp. 6, 26; *Annual Catalog, Oklahoma A. and M. College, 1900-1901*, pp. 5, 29, 42, 48; *Annual Catalog, Oklahoma A. and M. College, 1901-1902*, pp. 5, 25, 38, 43; *Annual Catalog, Oklahoma A. and M. College, 1905-1906*, p. 5; *Annual Catalog, Oklahoma A. and M. College, 1906-1907*, pp. 5, 34, 56; *Daily O'Collegian*, 3 December 1941, pp. 1, 3; Lloyd, pp. 9, 10.

45. Stillwater *Daily Democrat*, 17 February 1905, p. 1; *1916 Redskin*, pp. 221, 222, Oklahoma A. and M. College Yearbook; *Daily O'Collegian*, 18 April 1942, p. 2; Cunningham, pp. 83, 223. The *Redskin* account, "Reminiscences of a Former President," was extracted from an address by A. C. Scott at the Quarter-Centennial Anniversary, 7 January 1916.

46. Scott, pp. 3-19; Rulon, pp. 112, 114, 117, 125; Fischer, pp. 101-103; Wilson, p. 14.

47. Scott, pp. 7-9; *Annual Catalog, Oklahoma A. and M. College, 1900-1901*, pp. 6, 49, 50; *Annual Catalog, Oklahoma A. and M. College, 1901-1902*, pp. 6, 44, 45; *Annual Catalog, Oklahoma A. and M. College, 1902-1903*, pp. 6, 44; *College Paper*, November 1906, p. 25. Scott, whose memory usually could be relied upon, was wrong about the catalog. Although the experiment station report was the largest section in the 1897-98 catalog, the academic section included 13 numbered pages. From 1891-92 through 1897-98 not counting the missing 1895-96 issue, the catalog averaged 53 pages, ranging from a low of 13 numbered pages to a high of 123 pages.

48. Fischer, p. 84.

49. Blanche Little, "The Oklahoma A. and M. College," *The School Journal*, vol. 74, no. 2 (1907), p. 664; Rulon, p. 113.

50. Fischer, pp. 102, 103; Rulon, pp. 123, 124; Oklahoma A. and M. College *Orange and Black*, May 1908, pp. 1-3.

51. Rulon, p. 124; Fischer, p. 103; *Orange and Black*, April 1908, pp. 5, 6, May 1908, pp. 19, 20; *Daily O'Collegian*, 20 November 1941, pp. 1, 2, 21 November 1941, pp. 1, 2; Lloyd, p. 11.

52. Rulon, pp. 124, 125; *Daily O'Collegian*, 18 April 1942, p. 3.

53. H. E. Brill, *The Story of Oklahoma City University and Its Predecessors* (Oklahoma City: Oklahoma City University Press, 1938), p. 40; Lloyd, p. 11.

54. Brill, p. 101; Lloyd, pp. 11, 12.

55. Tressie Mayo-Walker to Harry E. Heath Jr., 16 June 1988, School of Journalism and Broadcasting Centennial History Collection; Brill, pp. 40, 42, 101, 165, 232; Lloyd, p. 13.

56. Heath, p. 19; *Daily Oklahoman*, 7 February 1949, p. 1; *Oklahoma A. and M. College Boomer*, January-February 1922, p. 16.

5 Printing Comes to the Campus

The third pioneer in Oklahoma A. and M. College journalism was Frank D. Northup. Unlike Freeman E. Miller and Angelo C. Scott, Northup was rarely in the spotlight. Although widely respected in the community, he had not yet gained significant recognition beyond county lines. He never claimed to be teaching journalism in his printing classes. In fact, he made it a point to disclaim any such objective.[1] A careful study of early college catalogs, however, clearly shows that what he taught was typical of the typography courses in journalism programs of that period and for decades beyond.

The early history of what is now the School of Journalism and Broadcasting is not unlike that of journalism at Washington College in the time of Robert E. Lee's presidency following the Civil War. Certainly there is a close parallel. In this context, Northup's brief career at Oklahoma A. and M. is crucial.

He was born to Lyman D. and Marie Adeline Baird Northup in the hill town of Cheshire, near Pittsfield, Massachusetts, on July 14, 1870. The westward movement took his parents from their mountain-type farm to Cuba, Kansas. Northup was a mere child, probably no older than three or four, when the family moved to Kansas. His only memory of the Massachusetts days was of a country dance during which he strayed onto the floor to be caught up by his mother and her dancing partner. He wrote many years later that they each took a hand and "sort of galloped me around the room." He thought the whole affair fun and judged his mother to be the nicest person there.[2]

The years in Kansas were hard ones. Northup saw them as soul-trying.

"What they must have done to the women was incomparably more so," he wrote. But his mother lived through them, rearing eight of the nine children she bore, "a human endurance marvel" that Northup could not understand. Without much help, she came through those trying times without losing her zest for life and a healthy sense of humor. "The fight was terrific, the courage undaunted."[3]

The Kansas years gave him valuable lifelong skills. At age fourteen, he became a printer's devil, learning the trade from the ground up. A near child prodigy, he was setting type when he could barely see into the top case. He could compose a story, word by word, as he set the type letter by letter. During the day he attended Cuba's public schools. Evenings and weekends, he advanced his printing know-how. He was always a voracious reader. He never attended college but never stopped being a student.[4]

On April 19, 1892, shortly before his twenty-second birthday, he made the run into Cheyenne and Arapaho country. A great crowd swarmed over the land and finally centered in D County at Taloga, where the 320-acre townsite had been laid out by government surveyors. If Northup made his claim and filed for it with his friend, Probate Judge Jerome S. Workman, he later relinquished it. Nevertheless, he went right to work, probably in a tent. Overnight he had become the pioneer editor and publisher of the *Taloga Occident*, the first newspaper published in that part of the territory. He joined the Oklahoma Territorial Press Association that year. Territorial Governor Abraham J. Seay estimated that 7,600 settlers lived in Oklahoma Territory's six counties. Some 2,815,873 acres were still unclaimed. Many claims were bypassed because they were too far from the railroad. Around Taloga, a county seat, 90 percent of the settlers lived in dugouts. Sod houses also were common.[5]

Northup later described what might well have been his Taloga experience—with some Stillwater reflections thrown in—when he was asked to reminisce about early territorial journalism. The pioneer editor began his work, he said, with no traditions to block him. There were no ruts to follow. His trail was not easy, but it was a trail of his own blazing. The editor brought a few fonts of news type, several fonts of display type, and either a Washington or an Army handpress, not an imposing array of materials with which to work. If he was fortunate, he was also able to bring with him lumber with which to erect his office-home. Less fortunate, he camped in a tent. Even the three "essentials" mentioned were not always essentials. Bee Guthrey, who founded the *Payne County News*, arrived in Oklahoma Territory without the handpress. His ingenuity, which contrived wheels and cylinders out of logs, was responsible for a hand-fashioned press which rolled out the first editorials and social notes in Payne County.[6]

A newspaperman at the opening of the territory was printer, press-man, and advertising salesman. His only aid in getting out his paper was the readyprint which filled the inside of a four-sheet paper. There were times when even more rugged individualism was demanded—when the readyprint did not arrive. Then the news was printed on common wrapping paper.

In the newspaper shack on muddy Main street, the editor was the congenial pivot around which community opinions gravitated and were caught up and molded into form. The editor's office was the community hall—the recreational center for business men, farmers, professional men, and hangers-on who wanted to exchange gossip and solve their neighbor's problems. Is it any wonder that political organizations were formed there, political candidates chosen there, school buildings planned there, and that the first-born churches received their baptism within its tobacco-stained walls?

The editor saw a future for his community and realized that future would depend upon new industries and new institutions to give it additional vitality. It was because of the support of ambitious editors, Northup said, that the Oklahoma A. and M. College at Stillwater, the teachers college at Edmond, and the first territorial capital in Guthrie were placed as they were.[7]

After thirteen months in Taloga, Northup chose Stillwater as a more promising site for newspapering. Another enticement was the prospect of homesteading in the Cherokee Outlet, which soon was to be opened to settlement. On the last day of May 1893, Northup rode his horse "Damon" through the Oklahoma A. and M. campus on the road to a dusty little wooden town of about 1,000. The college had been organized almost two years. As he glanced about the campus on his way to town he saw a barn, a small 20- by 30-foot flat, one-story frame building housing the weather bureau and the beginnings of the chemistry department, and a house for the experiment station director. That was all.

Northup lost little time in making his presence felt. He joined the staff of the *Stillwater Gazette*, a weekly started four years earlier by Daniel W. Murphy. When Northup walked in the door at 703 South Main Street, J. E. Sater, a civil engineer, was in the editor's chair. He was impressed by the young man's credentials and signed him on as a printer-reporter.[8] Northup put on his printer's apron and went to the backshop when needed, for every hand counted when the struggling little papers of the day were close to press time.

Young Northup did not have to wait long to see that he had made the right move in leaving Taloga. On September 1, 1893, shortly after joining the *Gazette*, he covered his first big story and began to establish a name for himself as a newspaper reporter. It was the greatest gun battle between outlaws and peace officers in the history of Oklahoma Territory. Six men were killed, three of them deputy marshals, but the two most notorious outlaws, Bill Doolin and Bill Dalton, escaped. The story has been relived in considerable detail by both historians and feature writers. Northup talked about it in a speech thirty-one years later. "I had a hunch," he said, "that there was going to be some shooting when the posse of marshals from Stillwater went over to Ingalls to 'get' the Dalton gang, and I followed them over. I saw a part of the fight, and I wrote the first accounts of it, not only for the *Gazette* but I also sent it out to other papers."[9]

When the Cherokee Strip was opened on September 16, 1893, Stillwater was four years old. The town was overrun by more than 6,000 transients who camped in or near Stillwater, some of them having arrived several days before the opening. Stillwater was just three miles south of the southern boundary of the strip.

At high noon, more than 100,000 land hungry settlers poured into the Cherokee Strip in one of history's greatest land runs. The "run" was started by gunshots fired by soldiers stationed along the line. The day was hot and dusty. All along the boundary line men were stationed about fifty feet apart, while at certain points of anticipated advantage the "runners" were jammed ten deep awaiting the signal to start the race for claims. Nearly every Stillwater man of legal age, and many women, too, were eager for claims. Many of them were successful.

The thousands who flocked to Stillwater from the south, arriving in ever-increasing numbers as the days until the opening grew fewer, caused Stillwater's first water shortage. Wells formed the only source of supply. Every well in Stillwater, except one in the 900 block on Main Street, was pumped dry. Folks stood in long lines awaiting a turn at the one flowing well.

About one person in every five who started got a claim. Many of the fortunate ones sold their filing privileges to others and did not "prove up" their claims. No person who had acquired land in former openings was allowed to take part.

Northup had made the run and secured a claim that he proved up. It was eleven miles north of Stillwater in Eden Township. Life looked rosy. He had a young wife, he had the land he wanted, and his newspaper career was progressing. On January 1, 1894, the *Gazette* merged with another weekly, the *Oklahoma Eagle*, established in 1892. The new paper became the *Eagle-Gazette*. On February 9, 1894, Northup's name appeared in the masthead of the combined papers as editor and manager. The former publisher, Charles M. Becker, was now associate editor. Newspaper ownership and management changed frequently in frontier journalism, however, and Northup gave up the editorship on June 14, 1894, to Joe E. Litsinger and C. F. Neerman. He had been associated with Litsinger in Taloga, where Litsinger had started the *Occident*. Despite this, Northup continued his association with the paper for five years, serving as printer, reporter, and co-owner while maintaining his homestead and holding office in the Columbian Lodge, Knights of Pythias. There is a possibility that he also served in a part-time publicity capacity for the college.[10] He was considered one of Stillwater's leading men in the Fourth Estate during these years.

Northup often covered news of the young Oklahoma A. and M. College, sometimes taking sides in the college's internal bickering. The local churches that provided space for early-day classes were far from ideal, and Northup decried the lack of comfort. At one location, he noted, only a woodburning stove was available in the winter, and in the summer "the winds sifted fine dust over students, seats, and books with indiscriminate regularity." He also interjected himself into a conflict over the power of the farm superintendent versus the experiment station director.[11] Soon he was extending his influence beyond Stillwater's limited boundaries. He later would have a role in naming John H. Connell to the Oklahoma A. and M. presidency.

He had married twenty-one-year-old Myrtle May Hutto on December 25, 1895, but their happy days on the homestead soon were to end. With her death during childbirth on June 24, 1897, he was at loose ends. As soon as he could dispose of his property, some of which he gave away,

Frank D. Northup and Myrtle May Hutto struck a pose for this wedding picture in 1895. Northup had homesteaded north of town at the opening of the Cherokee Strip in 1893 while he was making a name for himself in Stillwater journalism. The marriage ended tragically with Myrtle May's death in childbirth two years later. Northup lost both his wife and baby son, disposed of his belongings, and joined the Army. In 1898, he became the college's first superintendent of printing.

he enlisted for service in the Spanish-American War. Home on furlough fourteen months later, he had earned his stripes as a sergeant in Company C, Oklahoma Volunteers.[12] He was mustered out a few months later but never returned to the homestead.

While Northup was in uniform, the *Mirror* had listed fifteen needs of the college, including "a printing plant, fixtures, and suitable rooms." When that need was met a few months later, Northup would be in charge.

Northup's official connection with the college began in 1898, when he became superintendent of the printing department and instructor in printing. This was the first highly visible recognition of classroom or laboratory teaching in a journalistic area.[13] George E. Morrow, who had succeeded Edmund D. Murdaugh as president on July 1, 1895, came to Oklahoma A. and M. at a time when Northup's work on the *Gazette* was being increasingly felt on campus. As the college's first president with a solid background in professional journalism, Morrow may have been more sensitive to the college's image throughout the region than had been his three predecessors. His experience as a pioneer agricultural journalist, editor, and publisher before turning to an academic career had given him a practical, firsthand appreciation of public opinion and its ability to determine the fortunes of institutions, particularly institutions dependent upon public funds.

The young college already had had its share of adverse publicity in its first four years. Henry E. Alvord's clash with the board of regents, Murdaugh's indolence, and recent legislative investigations had been particularly trying. Morrow was the third president who had served in the two-year period following Robert J. Barker's resignation. He had taken a chaotic situation and brought the institution new respectability and a measure of stability. Now, after four years in office, Morrow had decided to return to his native Illinois. Northup's appointment with a $1,000 budget for printing equipment came before Morrow had retired in June 1899. The aging president had been able to support the regents in appointing Northup.[14]

Northup was a good choice to serve as the first superintendent of printing at Oklahoma A. and M. While his academic background was far different than that of Miller and Scott—both university certified intellectuals—his reading program was wide. He was a self-made intellectual with the common touch. He was a territorial pioneer from Kansas, as was Scott, and he had established a newspaper in Oklahoma Territory, an experience that paralleled Scott's adventure in Oklahoma City newspapering. Northup had worked both front and back shops, as Scott, too, had done on occasion on the *Iola Register* and the *Oklahoma Times*. His reporting often covered Oklahoma A. and M. problems in a realistic way. In short, he had become a figure to be reckoned with in the formation of public attitudes on campus and off. As he matured in his professional life, he was widely respected for the breadth of his knowledge and for his common sense as well.[15] Once again, the college had been fortunate in adding to its faculty an unusually talented man.

Northup had worked on two Stillwater newspapers, holding editorships on both, by the time Scott left his beloved Oklahoma City in 1898 to take up his duties as professor of English at Oklahoma A. and M., replacing Freeman Miller.[16] Northup's stories about the fledgling college attracted local attention, often providing a major topic for the evening's conversation around town. Scott respected Northup's reportage. They became good friends.

Northup saw his move to the campus as a transitional period in his life. He certainly had no intention of making a career of the position. He was willing to get things moving in the new printery, which he established in the Mechanics Building, often referred to as "the shops." He knew, too, that once he had settled in, the simple job work would expand into more complex efforts. One of these was sure to be a student publication. The *College Mirror* had died a few months after Miller's departure. It had become increasingly difficult to staff the paper and meet its monthly printing bill. Scott knew the value of a campus newspaper. Along with two of his 1876 classmates at the University of Kansas, he had printed the first student newspaper on Mount Oread.[17] Now he was settling into his new faculty routine and was in no position to pick up immediately where Miller had left off.

His goal of reestablishing the student newspaper had been delayed, but it was not forgotten. After eighteen months on campus, Scott had replaced Morrow as president. He saw the college's new print shop as the focal point for a series of practical printing courses. Students with this vocational goal could earn money to meet some of their college expenses while working in the shop.[18] He considered such an on-campus setting to be ideal for the re-birth of the student newspaper. Soon the new paper was born.

The instructional role of the new Department of Printing was clearly apparent in the first issue of the *College Paper*. An editorial statement read, in part: "This [is] successor to the good will and back subscriptions of the *College Mirror*. It is published by the students. . . . The composition and press work is done by students as part of their course of instruction in the department of printing. The responsibility for the paper and its contents rests with a committee of the faculty, and its publication is under the direction of the superintendent of printing.

"The department of printing. . .was established [to give] printing instruction and do job work. It is not the intention to make the work other than purely instructive, and work in this department does not count as part of the regular course leading to the degree of Bachelor of Science, but is taken either as extra work in the regular courses or by special students

Students hand-set type for the *College Paper* in the Oklahoma A. and M. College printshop under the supervision of Frank D. Northup. A talented printer-editor in territorial days, Northup said his work could not be dignified by the term "journalism." Despite this, his classes were typical of typography courses that became standard fare in schools and departments of journalism for many years to come.

along with stenography and typewriting and English." This may have been seen by some special students as a rudimentary journalism curriculum, although no evidence has been found to support such a tentative conclusion. The first journalism curriculum was still fifteen years in the future.

Describing Northup's domain, the catalog stated: "A printing plant has been installed during the past year, and occupies pleasant quarters in the mechanics building. Such students as desire are given instruction in the art of printing and matters relating thereto free of charge. The college and station jobbing work, including catalogues and announcements, is done here, and a monthly publication, the *College Paper*, is issued from the press. Students assist in all this work, and *The College Paper* is a student publication, though speaking officially for the college."[19] The college catalog for the following year, 1899-1900, leads one to believe that the program had been expanded somewhat, or that the catalog the previous year did not include complete information. It added this new information: "Two courses are pursued. In one the student is taught the use of the implements or tools used in typography, composition and imposition, correcting proof, and presses and their workings. The other course embraces instruction in spelling, capitalization, syllabication, punctuation, and proof reading."[20]

Throughout his nine years as president at Oklahoma A. and M., Scott wore two hats: one as professor in charge of English and literature and the other as chief executive. In either role, using his influence to bring a newspaper back to the campus was not surprising. The *Mirror's* last issue (if surviving files may be used as a reference) was June 1898. The first issue of its successor was dated May 15, 1899. It was issued in the literary magazine or bulletin format of the *Mirror* because of the shop's limited press equipment. Until the students had learned to set type, Northup did all of the mechanical work and edited much of the student-generated copy. At the suggestion of John Fields, popular and influential director of the Agricultural Experiment Station and business agent for the college, the new publication was called the *College Paper*. Fields offered the opinion that the paper would be referred to informally that way, so why not call it that. President Scott agreed to the name and wrote some of the articles in early issues of the paper to help the staff get it under way. The new paper continued the linage of the old, numbering its first issue Volume 4, Number 1.[21]

For the next two years, Scott and Northup were the key figures in journalism at Oklahoma A. and M. Scott stressed classroom theory, based upon his practical knowledge of newspapering and his thorough grounding in the rules of composition. Northup, in his new position, stressed the practical side of printing production, based upon the backshop tools of the day. The two men complemented one another perfectly, for each valued precision in his own area of academic responsibility.

While Northup's work closely paralleled the early effort at Washington College, hands-on printing experience was available to students on their own campus rather than in an off-campus commercial printery.[22] Morrow's and Scott's foresight and interest made the difference. Years later, Northup wrote: "The equipment was set up in the original stone building erected for the machine shop. It was on the second floor and consisted of a Gordon (it may have been a Chandler-Price) 10 x 15 job press powered by the feeder's foot, and several fonts of type. Here was printed the *College Paper*. . . . Whatever instruction I gave the students in writing stories and in the mechanics of the newspaper business was not dignified by the term 'journalism.' It was merely teaching the youngsters to write campus news, the value of the various types of stories and how to put things down on paper so, after set in type, they would be interesting as well as accurate." Equipment obviously was minimal. At this time Northup had never seen the new mechanical marvel, Mergenthaler's Linotype machine.[23]

Northup's busy life had helped him shed the intense sorrow that came with the loss of both Myrtle May and his infant son. He had "found himself" following military service. His work as college printer had kept him in touch with the optimism of youth. He began to set new goals. Romance once more had entered his life and on June 27, 1900, he married Elsie M. Parker, a Stillwater teacher. She had been a prime mover in founding the Sigma Literary Society. They moved into a cottage in west Stillwater. Less than a month later, his closest friend, John Fields, had married Carol Emmerson at her parents' home in Winfield, Kansas.[24] The *College Paper* had reported both weddings with obviously enthusiastic comment. Soon Northup would make another important decision that would shape his life and that of the state as well.

The Scott-Northup team was about to break up. Northup was growing restless again. He saw larger vistas ahead, with broader opportunities for service. A year earlier, John Fields and Northup had talked briefly of starting a farm paper. Then the idea was put on hold. Now it was time to act. After talking the idea over again with Fields and, perhaps, with Frank Waugh, Northup decided to leave the college and launch a new publication in the fast-growing farm magazine field. In January 1901, he founded the *Southwest Farmer-Stockman* in Stillwater and listed himself as editor and publisher. He was editor in name only, for Fields, sub-rosa, actually handled most of the editorial content. They had a written agreement that Fields, though outstanding in his experiment station duties, would join Northup, taking a half interest when—and if—the publication could support two families.[25]

At the college, Northup was succeeded by one of his earlier printing students, George B. Gelder, who quickly assumed the role of mentor for the small group of students who sought to know more about publishing. His title was the same Northup had carried, superintendent of the printing department and instructor in printing. Wording with reference to the department in the 1902-03 catalog changed slightly under Gelder but continued to include some emphasis upon editorial skills. However, mastery of mechanical skills was given top priority. Essentially the same wording is found in the catalogs issued from 1903-04 through 1907-08.[26]

That students made themselves at home in the college print shop during Gelder's tenure is suggested by an editorial comment in the 1906 student newspaper: "We feel called upon again to impress upon the minds of the students that it is a big breach of printing etiquette to come into the composing room and read copy over the compositors' shoulders or to handle any of the printed sheets laid out to dry. This thoughtlessness on the part of others is often the cause of the printer's using language that is neither elegant nor elevating nor conducive of friendship. As a matter of fact, we are not going to have any more of it in the college printing office."[27]

Meanwhile, Northup, representing the *Farmer-Stockman* of Stillwater, was one of three vice presidents elected by the Oklahoma Territorial Press Association in 1902. That year, in association with Fields, who would continue his ties with the college for five more years, Northup bought the *Oklahoma Farm Journal*, owned by A. J. Henthorne and edited by J. B. Thoburn. He moved the *Farmer-Stockman* to Oklahoma

George B. Gelder, a student of Frank D. Northup's, succeeded Northup as superintendent of printing when he resigned to establish a state farm publication, which would flourish with the aid of John Fields.

City and merged the two publications as the *Oklahoma Farm Journal and Southwest Stockman*. The *Journal* already had built an impressive record. It was founded in 1893 in Oklahoma City and issued semi-monthly. By 1898, it had reported a circulation of 2,000. Under Northup, the paper was issued the first and fifteenth of each month from its office at First and Harvey Streets. In 1905, the circulation was advertised as 14,700 and the next year it was 24,027. The success of the publication was spectacular, winning recognition on the prestigious *Printers' Ink* "Roll of Honor" for its growth.[28] The message was clear. John Fields, with his broad knowledge of the technical aspects of agriculture and with his hard-earned but widespread respect, was needed in Oklahoma City. Already co-owner of the fast-growing journal, he left Oklahoma A. and M. in 1906 to become editor in name as well as fact. He would hold that position for nine years, gaining a wide following with "Uncle John's Letter," as well as with his interpretative reporting and editorials.[29]

In 1915, Fields and Northup sold the *Oklahoma Farm Journal* to Arthur Capper, well-known Kansas publisher and political figure, who merged it with his *Oklahoma Farmer*, founded by Frank Greer in Guthrie in 1905. On December 25, 1915, the masthead read: "The Oklahoma Farmer with which is combined the Oklahoma Farm Journal." It listed Fields as editor. He held that position until June 10, 1924, when the

Oklahoma Publishing Company bought the publication from Capper and combined it with the *Oklahoma Farmer-Stockman*, a name borrowed from Northup's first farm journal.[30]

Northup and Fields were true pioneers in the regional farm journal field, among the most powerful of their day. But their impact was broader than agriculture. The two examples which follow, both of which reached fruition in 1913, will suggest their growing influence.

It seems unmistakably true that without the efforts of Northup and Fields, consolidated schools and their vastly improved educational facilities for rural children may have been years longer in coming. In the June 1, 1906, *Oklahoma Farm Journal* the two agricultural journalists began their campaign. They ran the first of literally hundreds of editorial appeals for "country schools that will provide the same advantages for country children that the cities and towns have." To many, this was an assault on the sacred image of the "little red school house." The next five and a half years were filled with unanticipated sacrifices in time and money before success was achieved.[31]

On January 1, 1906, while the state Constitutional Convention was in session, the *Journal* published an article headlined "A State School System." The first paragraph urged consolidated country schools. Fields, in demand as a public speaker, pushed the program. Before the end of the year there were consolidations in five counties where his talks had built favorable sentiment. By 1908, Fields was making at least 150 speeches annually, most of them before rural groups. He missed no chance to promote the *Journal's* school plan. However, the proposal had failed to penetrate political minds. Finally, Northup and Fields decided that the only way to achieve an awareness among political leaders was for Fields to declare himself a candidate for governor and make it his leading issue. Fields did not win, in fact had not expected to win, but his showing was strong enough that the consolidated school proposal became a part of the platforms of each major party.[32]

In 1911, with Fields writing the bill and with Northup joining him in lobbying for its passage, the measure reached the governor's desk. Errors in transcription, however, which the *Journal's* leaders thought may have been intentional, rendered the legislation invalid. More than three years of hard work had been lost.

Northup and Fields continued the fight. Finally, the 1912-13 legislature responded to the movement's growing support from the general population as well as from teachers. Once more Fields drafted the legislation. When the bill was ready to come to a vote in the closing hours of the session, a timely front-page editorial in the *Journal* urged readers to contact their legislators. On a single day, more than 10,000 letters were delivered to both the house and senate. The final vote on House Bill 149 spelled victory, the senate voting 30 to 11 and the house 65 to 16 for the measure. Governor Lee Cruce signed the bill in March 1913.[33]

The Northup-Fields team had the ear of political leaders on many occasions. For example, Dick Thompson Morgan, who had been reelected to his third term from the old First District, came into the *Oklahoma Farm Journal* office one day. He told Northup and Fields, "Boys, I need me an issue in Congress." Fields said, "All right, Dick, we've got one for you. Just come in here." They went into Fields's office. He pulled out his old "Smith and Wesson" double-decked typewriter and typed out a bill proposing an addition to the postal system. It would give farmers equal service to that enjoyed by their city cousins. With help from other farm state congressmen, Morgan got the bill passed and the U.S. Parcel Post System became a reality in 1913.[34]

Northup was a mover and doer with workaholic tendencies. He was a charter member of the Oklahoma Historical Society, which he served as director and secretary from 1903 to 1914. During this period he also was a director of the press association. In 1905, he was chosen as one of seventeen delegates to the annual meeting of the National Editorial Association scheduled for Guthrie the first week in June. He and Fields were among the charter members of the Oklahoma City Advertising Club, founded in 1907, and in 1957 Northup was the only remaining charter member. Upon the sale of the *Oklahoma Farm Journal*, he turned to interests outside the publishing field for a time. From 1916 to 1919 he was a dealer in oil and gas leases, president of the Choctaw Oil Producing Company of Tulsa, and vice president of the Midwest Oil and Gas Company. This was a period of unhappy memories for him. He followed with an automobile manufacturing and sales venture in Tulsa that was destined to fail. Next he served in the U.S. Internal Revenue Bureau from 1923 to 1927 before returning to journalism. He was editor and co-owner of the *Enid Events* from 1928 to 1935, then moved to California where in 1936 he became associate editor and business manager of the *Daily Times-Star* at Alameda. In 1939 Northup returned to the Bush Hills section of Oklahoma City to live out his years. His last contribution to Oklahoma A. and M. was as a member of Berlin B. Chapman's Record Book Committee in 1941 and 1942. He was honored at the State Fair Press Day September 30, 1955, for "exemplification of constructive journalism at its best during his service of more than half a century." A certificate of appreciation was presented by Ray J. Dyer, Oklahoma Press Association (OPA) president. Mrs. Northup, the Elsie Parker who had petitioned President Barker for approval of the Sigma Literary Society in 1893, was at his side for the presentation.[35]

The friendship they had forged on the Stillwater campus had led to wider acclaim for both Frank Northup and John Fields, but it failed by a margin of 4,000 votes to give Oklahoma its first Republican governor in 1914. Northup's role as campaign manager for Fields was one of his few direct involvements in politics. Northup died on August 3, 1965, in an Oklahoma City nursing home. He was ninety-six years of age and was writing a history of Oklahoma at the time of his death.[36]

It would be inappropriate to close this chapter without a few additional words about Fields and Waugh, two Oklahoma A. and M. men who became important journalists despite their professional training in scientific fields. Fields was born in Iowa on July 29, 1871, and reared in Pennsylvania. He attended Pennsylvania State College where, in his student days, he was co-discoverer with Leonard Pierson of tuberculosis in cattle. He was graduated from Pennsylvania State in 1891, then taught and served as assistant chemist in the experiment station there until 1894. After a year with a New York advertising agency, he was elected assistant chemist at Oklahoma A. and M. College in 1896. At twenty-eight, he was promoted to chemist, then was elected Agricultural Experiment Station director and college agent, serving in one or both capacities from 1899 to 1906. During this time, he wrote numerous bulletins published by the experiment station. Then he left to enter the commercial world. He was editor and co-owner of the *Oklahoma Farm Journal and Southwest Farmer-Stockman* from 1906 to 1915, and editor of the *Oklahoma Farmer* until 1924. Twice, in 1914 and 1922, he was the enthusiastic choice of the Republican Party for governor. During World War I, he worked for the National Food Control Administration, where he was in charge of publicity in addition to supervising grain production. He was vice president and a director of the Farmers' National Bank of Oklahoma City from 1924 to 1926, and was appointed vice president and director of the Federal Land Bank and the Federal Intermediate Credit Bank at Wichita, Kansas, in 1926. He was in demand as a lecturer on agricultural topics by farmers' and bankers' organizations, and was author of the volume *Sure Food Crops*. He died in 1935.[37]

Northup's admiration for Fields ran deep. Were it not for Angelo Scott's similar assessment of Fields's exceptional intellect, judgment, and humanitarian motives, one might write off Northup's evaluation as growing out of a long-term business partnership that was exceptionally congenial. However, Northup was a good judge of talent and was not wearing rose-colored glasses in 1941 when he wrote: "John Fields was the most unselfish man and the greatest I was ever to know. When I. . . [say that], you may think I knew few men. On the contrary, in the intervening years it had been my privilege to meet several presidents, many senators, congressmen, governors and men of successful businesses almost without number. None seemed to grasp present trends and penetrate the future as could this man.

"The misinformation of one man in a position of great power kept him from becoming Secretary of Agriculture, after a president had approved [the appointment]." The naysayer afterward apologized and

Widely read and possessing a keen analytical mind, Frank D. Northup became a powerful molder of opinion from territorial days until well after statehood.

later, as president, invited Fields to take one of the country's most important financial positions. He declined.[38]

Northup said that Fields cared little for public recognition of his accomplishments. "The point," Fields often told Northup, "is to get the job done." In addition to the school consolidation and parcel post legislation, Fields co-authored the Federal Land Bank Law and later administered it in Oklahoma, Kansas, Colorado, and New Mexico. In Northup's view, Fields laid the foundation for Oklahoma's agriculture in its broadest sense while director of the experiment station.[39]

The second scientist-journalist, Frank A. Waugh, joined the Oklahoma A. and M. faculty in February 1893. At twenty-three, he had just completed the requirements for his master of science degree at Kansas State College. Waugh was popular in the classroom, but even more so outside the classroom. He was in demand as a chaperon and often was sought out for personal counseling. A measure of his popularity was the fact that, although a faculty member, he was elected president of the student Webster Debating Society in 1893. A leader in horticultural research, Waugh believed that science classes should be taught both as technical and liberal arts courses instead of being limited to a vocational classification.[40]

Along with Freeman Miller, Waugh was the most widely published of early faculty members. He did not restrict himself to scientific journals but often wrote articles for popular farm publications. He was editor of the first Oklahoma Territory farm paper, *Home, Field and Forum*, established in the spring of 1893 by J. S. Soule. Unsuccessful financially, the paper was sold, and the new owner installed a new staff.[41]

A faculty rift developed during the Murdaugh administration, and in the summer of 1895 Waugh was among those fired outright along with Murdaugh. After leaving Stillwater, he studied in France and Germany and went on to write more than thirty books and a hundred scientific articles. He served the Massachusetts Agricultural College as head of the Division of Horticulture from 1902 until his death from pneumonia on April 3, 1943. He also was horticultural editor for the *Country Gentleman*. Waugh was a prolific writer of newspaper and magazine articles and a widely known lecturer.[42]

The growth and acceptance of Oklahoma A. and M. was, in a significant way, tied to the energy, enthusiasm and competence of individuals such as Northup, Fields, and Waugh. A more stable political climate would have held some of them for longer periods. Despite this, each added something special to the mystique of the people's college. Northup's contribution was through his skills as a printer-editor. What he had begun as a vocational effort in printing was later to move in an academic direction, and there was to be no hedging on the use of the term "journalism." Oklahoma A. and M. College would soon join the growing list of colleges and universities in which journalism was seen as a legitimate academic pursuit—with or without the blessings of skeptical newspapermen.

There is no reason to deny Northup the honor of being the founding father of journalism education at Oklahoma State University if the Lee model is followed. If, on the other hand, a theoretical model is to be used—that is, one in which formal studies place emphasis upon writing and editing—the honor must go to Scott.

It is difficult in the flush of success which modern journalism education has achieved to look upon these early efforts as anything but crude. To the students of that day, however, the work of Miller, Scott, Northup, and Gelder—and still later the English professors who taught the first full-term journalism courses—must have seemed very much up to date and more than adequate. It was a time in which young people were less blase about their opportunities and more accepting of the competence of their teachers. These early opportunities generated excitement among those with an interest in publications work, coming as they did after a period in which students had had no opportunity to write a story, pick up a type stick, set the story from the California job case, pull a proof, and ultimately see the effort distributed across the campus and often to the farthest reaches of the territory.

Endnotes

1. Ruth Howard, "The Development of the Oklahoma Agricultural and Mechanical College," unpublished manuscript (April 1942), p. 62, Special Collections, Edmon Low Library, Oklahoma State University, Stillwater, Oklahoma.

2. Northup Family Record in genealogical files of L. D. Melton, Oklahoma City, Oklahoma; Author interview with L. D. Melton, 29 July 1987, Oklahoma City, Oklahoma; Frank D. Northup to "Dear Family," 31 July 1945, p. 1, School of Journalism and Broadcasting Centennial History Collection, Special Collections, Edmon Low Library.

3. Frank D. Northup to "Dear Family," p. 1.

4. Oklahoma City *Daily Oklahoman*, 5 August 1965, p. 9.

5. Frank D. Northup, "An Incident in the Early History of Dewey County," *Chronicles of Oklahoma*, vol. 3, no. 4 (December 1925), pp. 289, 290; John Melton to Harry E. Heath Jr., 26 October 1990, School of Journalism and Broadcasting Centennial History Collection; Carolyn Thomas Foreman, *Oklahoma Imprints* (Norman: University of Oklahoma Press, 1936), p. 413; *Oklahoma Journal*, 5 August 1965, p. 4; *Oklahoma City Times*, 4 August 1965, p. 17. The *Times* reported that Northup was eighteen at the time of his move to Taloga, "bringing the first printing press in the area with him." This is supported in John Melton's letter; J. B. Thoburn and John Windsor Sharp, *History of the Oklahoma Press and the Oklahoma Press Association* (Oklahoma City: Industrial Printing Company, 1930), biographical section, unpaged; Michael H. Reggio, "Troubled Times: Homesteading in Short Grass Country, 1892-1900," *Chronicles of Oklahoma*, vol. 57, no. 2 (Summer 1979), pp. 197-200.

6. Bill H. Borglund radio interview with Frank D. Northup, publisher, *Enid Events*, broadcast 7 November 1935 over WNAD, School of Journalism and Broadcasting Centennial History Collection.

7. Borglund interview with Northup; Oklahoma A. and M. College *Daily O'Collegian*, 22 November 1941, p. 1.

8. Foreman, p. 411.

9. *Stillwater Gazette*, 8 September 1893, p. 2, 5 September 1924, p. 3, 29 August 1924, pp. 1, 4.

10. Foreman, pp. 409, 411; *Stillwater Eagle-Gazette*, 5 January 1894, p. 4, 9 February 1894, p. 4, 27 April 1894, p. 4, 5, 14 June 1894, p. 4, 6 December 1894, p. 1, 1 August 1895, p. 3; L. D. Melton to Harry E. Heath Jr., 1 November 1990, School of Journalism and Broadcasting Centennial History Collection. Melton placed the claim "on Long Branch Creek 8 miles north of town."

11. Philip Reed Rulon, *Oklahoma State University—Since 1890* (Stillwater: Oklahoma State University Press, 1975), pp. 26, 27, 37; *Daily O'Collegian*, 23 November 1941, p. 1.

12. *Stillwater Gazette*, 26 December 1895, p. 1, 1 July 1897, p. 2; Melton interview; *Stillwater Democrat*, 2 September 1898, p. 1; Irvin Hurst to Harry E. Heath Jr., 21 August 1984, School of Journalism and Broadcasting Centennial History Collection.

13. *Annual Catalog, Oklahoma A. and M. College, 1898-1899*, pp. 6, 31; *Oklahoma A. and M. College Mirror*, 15 September 1897, p. 5.

14. LeRoy H. Fischer, *Oklahoma State University Historic Old Central* (Stillwater: Oklahoma State University, 1988), p. 73; Rulon, pp. 72, 73, 80; *Daily O'Collegian*, 7 January 1942, p. 2.

15. Melton interview; Author interview with John Hamilton, 20 January 1988, Stillwater, Oklahoma.

16. Foreman, pp. 409, 411.

17. Rulon, p. 319, endnote no. 50; *Daily O'Collegian*, 7 January 1942, p. 2; Melton interview.

18. Rulon, p. 107.

19. Oklahoma A. and M. College *College Paper*, 15 May 1899, p. 1; *Annual Catalog, Oklahoma A. and M. College, 1898-1899*, p. 31.

20. *Annual Catalog, Oklahoma A. and M. College, 1899-1900*, p. 41.

21. *Daily O'Collegian*, 7 January 1942, p. 2; *College Paper*, 15 May 1899, p. 1.

22. George S. Turnbull, *Journalists in the Making* (Eugene: The School of Journalism, University of Oregon, 1965), p. 1.

23. Howard, pp. 61, 62; *Daily O'Collegian*, 23 November 1941, pp. 1, 3; *Annual Catalog, Oklahoma A. and M. College, 1899-1900*, pp. 6, 41.

24. *College Paper*, 25 July 1900, pp. 55, 56.

25. Frank D. Northup to Lucille Downing [7 July 1949], School of Journalism and Broadcasting Centennial History Collection; *Daily O'Collegian*, 7 January 1942, p. 2.

26. *Annual Catalog, Oklahoma A. and M. College, 1900-1901*, pp. 6, 49, 50; *Annual Catalog, Oklahoma A. and M. College, 1901-1902*, pp. 6, 44, 45; *Annual Catalog, Oklahoma A. and M. College, 1902-1903*, pp. 6, 44.

27. *College Paper*, November 1906, p. 25. Similar comments appear in issues of December-January 1905-06, p. 45, February 1906, p. 59, February 1907, p. 43.

28. J. B. Thoburn and John Winthrop Sharp, under "Thirteenth Annual Meeting, 1902," pages unnumbered; Frank D. Northup to Lucille Downing [7 July 1949], School of Journalism and Broadcasting Centennial History Collection; Foreman, p. 376.

29. Frank D. Northup, untitled manuscript transmitted by letter on 6 March 1950 to Lucille Downing, and "Early Farm Papers," summary revised "to include Mr. Northup's addition," with notation, "this summary approved by Mr. E. K. Gaylord," in School of Journalism and Broadcasting Centennial History Collection.

30. Frank D. Northup to Lucille Downing [7 July 1949], and addendum to manuscript, "History of Early Farm Papers in Oklahoma," transmitted to the author by Ferdie J. Deering with cover letter, 16 February 1977, in School of Journalism and Broadcasting Centennial History Collection.

31. Frank D. Northup, "First Consolidated School Law in the United States," *Chronicles of Oklahoma*, vol. 27, no. 2 (Summer 1949), p. 163.

32. Northup, "First Consolidated School Law in the United States," pp. 164-166; *Stillwater Gazette*, 1 April 1910, p. 6, 8 April, p. 1, 22 April, p. 7.

33. Northup, "First Consolidated School Law in the United States," p. 167.

34. *Daily Oklahoman*, 30 December 1962, p. A7.

35. Melton interview; *Daily Oklahoman*, 17 February 1957, p. 19, magazine section; Northup, "First Consolidated School Law in the United States," p. 162 (see editor's note); *Stillwater Gazette*, 20 January 1922, p. 8; *Stillwater NewsPress*, 13 January 1988, p. 4B; "Official Minutes, Annual Meeting, Oklahoma Historical Society, April 26, 1956," *Chronicles of Oklahoma*, vol. 34, no. 2 (Summer 1956), p. 250.

36. LeRoy H. Fischer, editor, *Oklahoma's Governors, 1907-1929: Turbulent Politics* (Oklahoma City, OK: Oklahoma Historical Society, 1981), pp. 62, 71, 119; *Stillwater Gazette*, 5 May 1922, p. 1; *Oklahoma City Times*, 4 August 1965, p. 17. The *Times* obituary identified Northup as a former manager of the Western Newspaper Union and an early member of the Oklahoma City Men's Dinner Club, founded by Angelo Scott. Following retirement, he was a member of Sigma Delta Chi, professional journalism society, and the First Methodist Church. He was a frequent contributor to the letters-to-the-editor columns of the *Oklahoman* and *Times*.

37. Northup, "First Consolidated School Law in the United States," p. 162 (see editor's note); *Daily O'Collegian*, 23 November 1941 pp. 1, 3; Rulon, pp. 144, 145, 172.

38. *Daily O'Collegian*, 22 November 1941, p. 2; *Stillwater Gazette*, 11 February 1921, p. 2.

39. *Daily O'Collegian*, 22 November 1941, p. 2.

40. *Daily O'Collegian*, 13 March 1942, p. 2; Rulon, pp. 29, 30, 101.

41. "Early Farm Papers," p. 1.

42. Rulon, p. 30; *Daily O'Collegian*, 13 March 1941, p. 2; "Deaths," *Oklahoma A. and M. College Magazine*, vol. 14, no. 7 (April 1943), p. 16.

6 Journalism Loses Ground

The territorial political power that derived from a succession of Republican administrations in the White House was over. Statehood had brought with it the power of the vote to replace the power of Washington-centered appointments and it was soon to be a clean sweep for the Democratic Party. It was at this juncture that two important figures in Oklahoma A. and M. history played a behind-the-scenes role in John H. Connell's selection as successor to the popular Angelo C. Scott. John Fields and Frank D. Northup, while no longer affiliated with the college, were working closely with the experiment station and certain unnamed faculty leaders. Their support of the station and their statewide leadership through the *Oklahoma Farm Journal* was crucial to agricultural interests on the campus. They had almost a paternal interest in the college's agricultural program and its future. It was not surprising, then, that Fields and Northup would protect what they believed to be in the college's best interests.

When it appeared that S. M. Barrett, a well-respected school teacher, would be the successor to Scott, the two publishing partners went into action. Barrett had been a leading contender for nomination on the Democratic ticket to become state superintendent of schools but withdrew in a political deal that was to pave the way for his appointment as Oklahoma A. and M. president. Northup and Fields were alarmed because Barrett had no background in agriculture. They set out to find someone who would overshadow him. There were plenty of good prospects in the north, but their politics were not right and the state's new power brokers did not think kindly of looking northward. Fields and

Northup, at the latter's suggestion, settled on Connell after a careful survey of likely prospects. For one thing, Connell had served the Texas Agricultural College as professor of agriculture and director of the Texas Experiment Station from 1893 to 1902. For another, he now was editor-in-chief of *Texas Farm and Ranch* and had a solid reputation as a writer and speaker on agricultural topics. Finally, he was favorably known to William H. Murray, then president of the Constitutional Convention. They had taught common school together in Texas, and during the transition to statehood Murray had called upon Connell for advice.[1]

Connell could not, however, be the candidate of Fields and Northup, both dedicated Republicans. Politics had to be considered. Fields wrote the Texas editor to sound him out, asking that he say nothing about the feeler. Fields then contacted Ewers White, president of the board of agriculture, a friend of both himself and Northup. White also was disturbed about the possibility of Barrett's election. White was instructed to see Murray and "just incidentally break the matter to him." Murray not only was agreeable, White said, but happy about the suggestion. Connell was elected by the board, thanks to Murray's recommendation.[2]

Angelo Scott, after a lame duck status of seven months, was gone, and Connell finally was in full control on the Stillwater campus. One of the first indications of the jubilant mood statehood had ushered in was reflected in the motto, "The New State is Our Parish," boldly proclaimed

SPECIAL COLLECTIONS, OSU LIBRARY

John Fields, along with Frank D. Northup, played a behind-the-scenes role in the selection of John H. Connell as Angelo C. Scott's successor. Fields later would come close to becoming Oklahoma's first Republican governor.

in the 1908-09 Oklahoma A. and M. catalog. The coming of the railroad to Stillwater eight years earlier now was making this motto a reality.[3]

The new president had seen several improvements he would make as soon as his shared leadership with Scott was at an end. For one thing, he wanted a more dramatic catalog. He got it. The new catalog was printed on slick paper and carried twenty pages of pictures that could not have been reproduced well on the cheaper paper used during Scott's tenure, although Scott sometimes printed halftones on special stock and had the pages tipped in. In a sense, Connell's first catalog was a forerunner of the first college yearbook, which would come two years later. But the catalog changes were more than cosmetic. Connell had seen that the college's organizational structure needed to be overhauled. In earlier years with smaller enrollments, the major academic units of the college were the courses of study, roughly analogous to curricular majors. A full-blown departmental structure awaited Connell's shaping. He created six divisions (later to be called schools and still later colleges) and grouped the courses of study, or departments, under appropriate divisions.[4]

The initial catalog of Connell's presidency recognized journalism for the first time as an academic discipline worthy of a full-term course. While Scott had introduced journalism merely as a unit in his rhetoric classes, it now would merit a full quarter of instruction. Its academic home would be the Division of Agriculture rather than the Department of English. Entitled Agricultural Journalism, it was listed among "Subjects Common to all Departments" in the division. Whether Connell, with his background in agricultural journalism, had asked that the course be added is uncertain. John A. Craig, the new dean of the Division of Agriculture and director of the experiment station, may have originated the course. Or, perhaps, it was mutually agreed upon in a dialogue between the two. At any rate, Craig, who was well qualified in the field, taught the course. It was restricted to seniors and was offered during the winter term.

The catalog description of Agricultural Journalism stated that the three weekly lectures would bring students "into closer relation with the agricultural press." Its goal was to give "such instruction as will enable [students] to prepare acceptable copy on farm topics." In writing the catalog statement, Craig stressed the college's up-to-date printing plant. The large number of publications—including technical bulletins and press bulletins—would provide "abundant material to familiarize the student with the work involved," Craig wrote.[5]

Craig, who had replaced W. L. English, the first Oklahoma A. and M. dean of agriculture, was born on December 25, 1868, at Russell, Ontario, Canada. He was reared on a ranch and held the bachelor of science degree in agriculture from the Ontario Agricultural College. In 1889, nineteen years before his arrival in Stillwater, he had joined the staff of the *Canadian Livestock Journal.* After a year, he left for the University of Wisconsin to establish the nation's first academic department in animal husbandry. This was followed by work at Iowa State College, where he organized the first interstate intercollegiate livestock judging contest at the Trans-Mississippi Exposition at Omaha, and a year as editor of the *Iowa Homestead.* After two years in stock farming, he became dean of the School of Agriculture and director of the Texas Agricultural Experiment Station in 1903. Connell had left Texas A. and M. shortly before Craig's arrival, but they had frequent contacts during Connell's editorship in Dallas and probably had known one another earlier. After three years at College Station, Texas, Craig returned to stock farming for two years, then accepted his appointment at Oklahoma A. and M.[6]

The Agricultural Journalism course Craig had started was listed in the catalog for only two years. Craig's name was identified with the course only the first year, but it probably was offered the second year as well, for three students in December 1910 petitioned to substitute other agriculture courses for it. After the 1909-10 catalog, the course no longer appeared. It disappeared with Craig's departure in the 1909-10 purge in

1910 REDSKIN

The first course at Oklahoma A. and M. College with "journalism" in its title was taught by John A. Craig in 1909. His Agricultural Journalism course "died" in 1910 with his controversial firing.

which eighteen faculty members were fired or resigned under the pressure of John P. Connors, who as president dominated the board of agriculture and exerted strong pressure upon Connell.[7]

In Connell's reorganization of the academic structure, the Department of English and Literature was placed, as was to be expected, under the Division of Science and Literature. President Scott had used instruction in journalism as a practical teaching tool in his rhetoric classes, and some students had discovered a talent for newspaper work there. Now no reference to newspaper writing was to be found in the twelve quarters of composition and literature listed in the catalog, although two years later journalism would return to the English program. In addition, the *College Paper* had taken a hiatus.[8]

The date of the last issue of the *College Paper* remains something of a mystery, as a complete file of issues is unavailable. The last issue in the Special Collections section of the OSU Library is Volume 11, Number 3, for February 1907. No mention was made in the 1907-08 or 1908-09 college catalogs of either the *College Paper*, which ceased publication sometime in the latter part of the 1907-08 academic year, or its successor, the *Orange and Black*, the first issue of which is dated April 1908. Both the *Mirror*, the first campus newspaper, and the *College Paper* were monthlies, and both had served in a dual capacity as student *and* official college publications. Both used a literary magazine format, though the size of the latter varied from time to time.[9]

The Philomathean Literary Society, resurgent under a new constitution and with new leadership, took on the responsibility of pushing for a new college paper. The Philos, as members were called, selected the name *Orange and Black* for the monthly successor to the *College Paper*. President Connell suggested that the idea for a new student publication be placed before the student body for consideration. A unanimous vote followed, and the paper—first as a monthly and later as a weekly—contributed mightily to campus life for sixteen years. The vigor of the Philos was such that late in 1910 the society removed its constitutional barrier that had limited membership to fifty. In a short time, membership had grown to seventy-two.[10]

Succeeding President Scott as head of the Department of English and Literature was William W. Johnston, who had prestigious academic credentials plus a brother, Henry, who was gaining political power. Under Johnston, the interest in journalism was fast dissipated. The English program had taken a more classical turn, reflecting his work both at Baker University and Harvard University. In fact, Scott's rhetoric courses had disappeared from the catalog. George B. Gelder's work with students in printing also was at an end. The printing department, listed in Connell's first catalog with the optimistic statement that a full vocational program would be developed under the new superintendent of printing, Edward J. Westbrook, was soon to be changed radically. In the next year's catalog, no visibility as an *instructional* unit was given to the Department of Printing, sometimes referred to as "The College Press." Whatever lofty hopes had been held for a vocational program now had seemingly evaporated as the increasing demands for college printing strained Westbrook's resources.[11]

William Johnston, like Scott and Northup, was a Kansan. He was born on a farm near Erie in Neosho County on January 5, 1876, the son of Matthew and Jennie May Lodge Johnston. He was the youngest of three children. When he was eight, his family moved to town. As a youth, he worked on the farm and later clerked in his father's grocery store in Erie. After training in the common school, young Johnston entered Baker University in 1899. By his junior year in 1901, he had developed a reputation as a debater. That year, he was one of 170,000 people who registered in Oklahoma Territory's land lottery. He was surprised to learn that he held a winning number, giving him the right to a 160-acre claim, one of 13,000 tracts given away. His summer vacation had just begun when he journeyed southward to establish ownership of his windfall. Thirty thousand people were waiting in Lawton for final allotments. When his assignment finally was made, several choices at the top of his list had gone to other winners. His land was about twenty miles southeast of Lawton and twenty miles from Duncan, the nearest railroad town. He had only one neighbor within twenty miles. He moved to the claim, residing there long enough to comply with the law. He also acquired a lease on a school quarter-section, then returned to Kansas by freight. While making his claim, Johnston had traveled the prairies in a buck-board. Later, he was to say that two wagon tracks meant a main highway and one track meant a road. That summer, he had practiced a speech he would give at Baker. His audience was "a goodly number" of stray cattle, and he spoke from the roof of a four-by-fourteen shack he had built to protect his land rights. He occupied his claim again during the Christmas holidays.[12]

While his older brother, who was to become Oklahoma's seventh governor, had decided upon a career in politics, William still was undecided about his life's work. One year out of his classical course at Baker University, he returned to his homestead, but not to develop it. He sold it for $1,100 and drove to Lawton with a team of horses and a wagon, where he remained for a few days contemplating his next move. For a recent college graduate—he had taken the A.B. degree at Baker in 1902— he was in a favorable position. He had been offered a banking job in Kansas City or he could return to circulation management with the *Kansas City Journal*, where he had worked the previous year. He rejected both. He had decided to be an English teacher and would use the money from his sale to enroll at Harvard University in 1902 as a special student.

After a year of study in English literature, he returned to Baker University for his first teaching experience. The next year he was back in Cambridge once more, this time as a graduate student specializing in poetry and creative writing. He completed the master's degree in 1905 and left for the Pacific Northwest by way of Kansas, where he married Ethelyn Genevieve Thorne of Waterville, Kansas. She had attended Boston University and, in 1905, had finished her degree at Baker. They had met at a joint meeting of Biblical and Clionion literary societies. The young couple set off for the Pacific Northwest, where he had planned to teach in Tacoma, Washington. A better position at Washington State College in Pullman had opened, and he accepted an appointment in the English department there. At Washington State, he taught English composition and literature and coached the debate team. In three years he had advanced from an instructorship to professorial rank.

William and Ethelyn spent a ten-day honeymoon on the slopes of Mount Rainier. Mountain travel was to become a passion with Johnston, not only in the western United States but in Switzerland and Greece, where he visited places of literary note along the way. In Greece he would sleep at the medieval Monastery of Saint Luke on the slopes of Mount Parnassus facing Mount Helicon, mythical home of the muses.[13]

Meanwhile, his brother Henry was collecting more political power. He had presided over the Democratic caucus as the state constitution was written. Among the sections he penned was one establishing Langston University. He was to become presiding officer in the first Oklahoma Senate.[14]

By now William was well established on the Washington State faculty, but his brother's letters spoke of the opportunities for a young educator in the new state, and he was tempted. As he and Ethelyn talked about the distance between Washington and their Kansas friends, they decided to trade apple country for the wheatlands and cattle ranges as soon as they could. At age thirty-two, the opportunity came to Johnston with the changing of the guard at Stillwater. He joined Connell's new administration as head of the English faculty. The Johnstons moved into a home at 412 West Street, an easy walk to his office in the Central Building.[15]

Johnston had been on the job only about a month when the *Orange and Black* editor, W. L. Lahman, suggested the possibility of converting the publication from a literary-magazine format to a weekly newspaper by year's end. He envisioned a monthly edition in the current mode as well. But he knew that subscriptions at twenty-five cents a term or fifty cents a year barely covered production costs. "Our paper," he wrote, "depends almost entirely upon advertising for its finances." He urged students to show their appreciation to the publication's advertisers.

As 1909 arrived, the *Orange and Black* was editorializing in favor of

ORANGE & BLACK

✛✛✛✛✛✛✛✛✛✛✛✛✛✛

APRIL ✎ 1908
VOLUME I   NUMBER I

With the urging of the revitalized
Philomathean Literary Society, the
campus was to have a new student
publication. In April 1908, the
Orange and Black made its debut.
Later, it would become a broadsheet
newspaper, the first in the line that
eventually evolved into the *Daily
O'Collegian*.

Stillwater Oklahoma

a college annual. Lahman urged students to sharpen their skills on the
paper in preparation for work on the yearbook staff. He was calling, too,
for a stronger *Orange and Black* with "more cartoons, more poems, and
more literary articles." He told his readers that a special publication was
being planned for May, "one that each student will want to keep." This
statement may have referred to the *Brown and Blue*, a forerunner of what
would become the *Red Skin* in 1910. By spring of his first year, Johnston
had clearly been accepted as faculty leader of the student paper. At the
Orange and Black dinner for the editorial board on April 7, 1909,
Professor and Mrs. Johnston were guests of honor.

Johnston may have been somewhat surprised, if not disappointed, by
the department he had inherited. The year before his arrival, it had listed
four faculty members, including President Scott. Now, in addition to
Scott, Professor Robert H. Tucker, Scott's strong right-hand man, and
Ethel V. Walker were gone. The only holdover in the fall of 1908 was
Howard G. Seldomridge, whose principal interest was public speaking.
Scott had placed considerable emphasis upon public speaking and had
listed that work in the 1907-08 catalog in a separate section, although
"Seldy," as students liked to call him, remained on the English faculty.
The work in printing continued to hold its place in the catalog but with
less stress upon its instructional function.[16]

The next year, 1909-10, L. Frank Stewart, who probably had arrived too late to be listed in the 1908-09 catalog, had been added to the faculty as an assistant, and Ada Belle House served both in English and mathematics. The small faculty had stabilized. Johnston, too, would teach, and students often commented upon his classroom style. He occasionally would use a parody on a major news event, and when suddenly struck by an idea that moved him, he was inclined to say, "By Jolly," then proceed to his narrative. When visiting with students in his office, he frequently would lean back and clasp his hands over his head. To some, he projected an air of quiet dignity, to others, he seemed reticent.

No changes were listed in the 1910-11 catalog. However, there were significant changes in titles. Johnston had been assigned additional duties by President Connell as the first dean of the Division of Science and Literature. In addition, the Department of English Language and Literature now was to be known as the Department of English and Public Speaking, a change that Seldomridge may have found disappointing after his brief experience with a free-standing academic unit.[17]

The department's growing role of college-wide service was reflected in increasing enrollments. Apparently Johnston, as dean, now could make a stronger case for more help to meet the changing demands upon the English and speech faculty. In his last year at Oklahoma A. and M. College, he had added Carl Ostrum, Noble W. Rockey and B. F. Brown, all assistants, and had lost only Stewart. P. J. Davis divided his time between physical education and English. Of the new hires, only Rockey would have an extended tenure and play a major role in the post-Scott development of journalism. Ostrum was soon to become a popular teacher and well-known debate coach at Kansas State College. While he had no formal ties with English or student publications, J. E. McCutchen was added in 1911 as editor of college publications. His successors often contributed valuable services to student publications as well as to writing classes, but there is no evidence that McCutchen set such a precedent.

By the time Rockey joined the English staff, he had had seven years on other faculties plus two years of administrative experience in secondary education. Oklahoma A. and M. was different. He had never experienced such fresh, enthusiastic, and loyal college spirit as was evident in both faculty and student body. Although the English department was small, the connection between public speaking and the department was not clear. Seldomridge, rightly or wrongly, considered himself to be independent of the department. There was no intercollegiate literary activity, but the athletic department had organized what it called the Northeast Oklahoma Interscholastic, which included athletic competition and contests in oratory and dramatic readings. Professor Johnston sent Rockey to the Library Building auditorium as a one-man judge of the latter contests. The interscholastic at this time was not very large. There were perhaps only fifteen contestants in oratory and declamations. Both students and their teachers showed strong interest in this opportunity offered by the college to show what they could do. The result, Rockey believed, was excellent. More important to the college, however, was the good spirit created toward it among the high school contestants.[18]

Although within two years Johnston had become the first dean of what was briefly called the Division of Science and Literature, he accepted these heavier administrative responsibilities which had been added to his departmental headship as a matter of duty rather than choice. He preferred coaching students in debate, drama, and public speaking. He was well liked by both students and faculty, and the feeling was mutual.[19] As had been Freeman E. Miller and Scott ahead of him, he was a poet, with about 150 poems to his credit. Many a student developed skills writing poetry with his encouragement.

With his brother deeply involved in state politics, Professor Johnston no doubt was somewhat better informed concerning the political quicksand than the average faculty member. In spite of this advantage, he may have had no advance warning of two of the biggest campus upheavals of his four years in Stillwater. The first came in his first year, when the *Stillwater Gazette* reported in a major front-page story on April 23, 1909, that eleven faculty members had been "canned." As one of those who lost his job told the *Gazette*: "One could hear the can rattling behind him as he came down the street." The most serious loss in what the headline called a "wholesale dismissal" was George L. Holter, head of the chemistry department and unofficial dean of the faculty. Holter had been bluntly outspoken in his dissatisfaction over Connell's appointment and leadership. The *Gazette* report included this vignette:

"The day before he received his notice, Prof. Holter had been summoned by President Connell to make out his schedule or budget for the next year. When he received notice that his resignation would be accepted, Prof. Holter went to President Connell and asked him the reason. The president said there were charges against him. Charges against his efficiency? No. Charges against his character? No. The only conclusion Prof. Holter or his friends could come to was that the reason he is persona non grata is that of all the members of the faculty he is, and has been for years, the best loved by the students. He has been their friend and mentor, and has always had the courage to stand by them." The dismissals led to informal complaints from both town and gown, but the protests gradually faded away.[20]

Soon after this unsettling news, the faculty adopted a document entitled "Rules of the Board of Regents and Faculty for the Government of the Oklahoma Agricultural and Mechanical College." Secret societies, including "Greek Letter Societies," were prohibited, as was smoking on campus by students and employees. The lengthy document charged the Committee on Literary Societies and Student Publications, under Johnston's chairmanship, with supervisory power over all student publications. The rule read: "It shall be the duty of this committee to supervise and to give all assistance and encouragement possible to student societies and to supervise and assist the publication of all papers, annuals, etc. . .gotten out by the students of the College." In addition, the Committee on Catalogs and College Bulletins was to aid in compiling and arranging the content of publications "authorized by the College."[21]

One year after Holter's departure, the firing of three additional faculty members led to a mass meeting on April 26, 1910. Students calling for the ouster of President Connell gathered at Sixth and Duncan. Soon the students with their petitions moved to the court house, where the court room overflowed. In the wake of this action, two delegations— one of businessmen and one of faculty, including those scheduled for dismissal—were invited to meet with the board of agriculture in Guthrie. The businessmen planned a low-key approach, privately laying out the student position before Board of Agriculture President John P. Connors, Ewers White, and other board members "so they might see and understand the feeling of the student body."

The train from Stillwater was four hours late. Nerves were on edge. A board member told each of the delegations to select a spokesman to present their views to the board when called. After waiting about an hour, the delegations received a message that the board had given President Connell a vote of confidence and would not meet with the spokesmen who had been chosen.[22]

Reaction by the student petitioners was one of anger. Another mass meeting was held April 30, disclaiming a report by the board of agriculture to the press that the students had apologized and that members of the board's college committee had visited Stillwater and found everything in order. The students struck back. They vigorously defended all of the dismissed professors. Thirty agriculture students signed a resolution expressing contempt for the board's accusations of disloyalty against Professors John A. Craig, L. A. Moorhouse, and H. P. Miller.[23]

In the same issue (May 6), the *Gazette* also ran the college faculty's resolutions, approved unanimously at a faculty meeting May 4, expressing disapproval of the student agitation, calling for all students to discourage such demonstrations and expressing their loyalty to, and confidence in, President Connell. At the May 4, 1910, faculty meeting, an advisory committee was selected to assist in settling the student agitation. At the May 17 meeting, a progress report by the committee was read. Couched in vague terms, the minutes of that meeting stated: "This report set forth clearly the causes of agitation, and the work of the Committee." The report was received, accepted, and filed for record. A reassuring

John H. Connell, who had been editor of *Texas Farm and Ranch*, became the third journalist to serve as president of Oklahoma A. and M. College. He gave a solid boost to the college's public information program but exerted little influence upon journalism as an academic subject until late in his presidency.

letter setting forth the college's version of the conflict and a review of accomplishments under Connell was sent to all parents of students on May 25.[24]

The students were not alone in their criticism of the board. The influential *Oklahoma Farm Journal*, in a hard-hitting editorial reprinted in the *Gazette*, chastised board members for their in-breeding and for their unjustified action in the firing of loyal and effective faculty members. The *Tulsa World* was equally critical, calling the condition of the board chaotic "as a result of partisanship and politics."[25]

The conflict made for lively conversation among the town's 2,500 inhabitants both on campus and off. It also nurtured hope for reform in the system. On April 4, 1910, John Fields, one-time experiment station director and more recently editor of the *Oklahoma Farm Journal*, had announced that he was a candidate for governor. In a long letter published in the *Tulsa World*, former president Angelo C. Scott had spoken out strongly in support of Fields's candidacy, stressing both his competence and his unflinching devotion to scrupulously honest public service.[26] He would be in a position to make Oklahoma A. and M. governance a campaign issue, or at least to suggest the need for less political meddling in higher education. He was not pleased with the board he had helped to create as the territory achieved statehood.

Journalistically, the big news in 1910 was that the *Orange and Black* planned to convert to weekly publication, abandoning its literary magazine format for a broadsheet newspaper dress. (This change was delayed until September 11, 1912.) Another major journalistic topic was the advent of the *Red Skin*, later to be a one-word title. The senior class entered into this pioneer publishing venture after discarding the name "The Retrospect" in favor of a name that would more closely capture the state's Indian heritage. That venture had survived eighty years as the curtain came down on the Centennial Decade.[27]

The 1910 yearbook called attention to the *New Education*, a widely circulated bi-monthly paper "printed in the interest of A. and M. in general and its work." President Connell served as editor-in-chief, with C. J. Bushnell as editor. In the genteel language of the day, the *Red Skin* said "the paper is made interesting and instructive in every respect, and is a great benefit to the institution and the people at large."[28]

That year, Connell once more considered the possibility of a course in printing. He appointed a three-man committee—B. C. Pittick, Edward J. Westbrook, and Bushnell—to "take under consideration" such a course "to begin next September." They were to report to the Committee on Courses. The outcome apparently was never reported, officially at least. No further mention of the matter appeared in subsequent minutes. While this was a setback for those interested in journalism, there was good news to help offset the bad. Recognition of the academic value of certain student endeavors came in 1910. Students could earn one credit for active participation in any of fifteen approved activities, among them the Philomathean and Omega literary societies, the *Orange and Black*, and the *Red Skin*. [29]

After his first year as dean, Johnston toured Europe for the first time,

1910 REDSKIN

The first *Red Skin* staff was diligently at work in the fall of 1909 when this photograph was made. It depicts the typical flavor of student publications work areas.

taking leave from his Sunday School teaching duties at the Stillwater Methodist Episcopal Church for the summer. He was a lay preacher as well, and frequently went by horse and carriage or by train to preach in neighboring towns and villages.[30]

Ethelyn and William Johnston had become an important part of Stillwater's religious and social life. Two children—a boy and a girl—were born in Stillwater and, given a more stable college system in the state, they may have stayed. But in 1912, when cheeky students on the *Redskin* staff jokingly referred to Johnston as "Weary Willie," Professor Carl Gundersen suggested that Johnston look into an opening at Michigan State College, where a headship in the Department of English, Modern Languages and Public Speaking existed. Johnston applied and got the job. The *Orange and Black*, reporting on his departure, praised his "good work." The story cited his membership on "most of the important Faculty Committees" and his support of "all worthy student enterprises."[31] Ironically, at Michigan State he placed heavy emphasis upon journalism, contrary to his seeming lack of interest in it at Oklahoma A. and M.

Johnston was at the peak of his career when the unexpected happened. En route to Florida, he and his wife were seriously injured in an automobile accident near Fort Wayne, Indiana, on March 24, 1935. From Edward W. Sparrow Hospital in Lansing, Ethelyn Johnston expressed the couple's appreciation for the "tokens of friendship" that had been sent. As flowers continued to come, she requested that friends bring only one flower. The Johnstons' gratitude and appreciation had been conveyed through the *Lansing State Journal*. It clearly reflected a shift from traditional Methodism into a metaphysical approach to life.[32]

While at Michigan State, Johnston spent the summers teaching in various universities—he preferred West Virginia University because of the scenery—or continuing his foreign travel. He devoted the summer of 1927 to Europe and England. During his absences, whether for health reasons or travel, Johnston's replacement often was another former Oklahoma A. and M. man, Albert H. Nelson, whose career at Michigan State was unbroken from 1919 until his death in 1935.

In a sense, Johnston was a world traveler. He particularly liked to visit the haunts of literary figures. He took a leave of absence from June 21, 1938, to September 1, 1939, for travel and study in Europe. He and his wife were visiting Paris when war broke out. The French government ordered all foreign tourists to leave. William and Ethelyn decided to return to Holland. Frontiers were closely guarded, and "red tape" increasingly made it difficult to cross international boundaries. The trip was complicated by their arrest in the French-Belgian town of Dunquerque, later to become an early landmark in World War II history. A spy scare was sweeping Europe. The Johnstons had driven to a wharf for information when they were stopped by a gendarme and taken to headquarters.

They were detained for twenty-four hours while their passports were being checked. The Johnstons accepted their arrest as a reasonable precaution on the part of the French. They had been in Germany the previous year during the Munich Crisis where the atmosphere, Ethelyn observed, "did not make one feel comfortable." Despite this, she had been impressed with the warm hospitality of most Europeans.[33]

The inconvenience at Dunquerque had not been without its pleasures. Johnston had seen the Isle of Wight as Alfred Noyes had seen it poetically, "glimmering like a ghost," and had written a poem dedicated to Noyes. The poem later was broadcast over WKAR. Will and Ethelyn visited Corves, scene of the great British yachting regattas, finally arriving in Holland, where they remained until their return to the United States. During their stay, they drove along the longest dike, visited Boleomendal in the colorful flower-growing area, and Huizen, where they visited with dislocated people from Italy, England, Poland and India.[34]

Johnston had grown weary of administrative duties in 1937. He gave up the headship of the Department of English in July 1939, retiring in 1940, one year early, because of ill health that had followed the auto accident. Ethelyn and William moved to Ojai, California, to spend their remaining years. They visited Stillwater in 1950, and ten years later

1910 REDSKIN

William W. Johnston, the first dean of science and literature, did little to encourage journalism in the classroom. He was, however, supportive of student publications.

Ethelyn, traveling alone, toured a dozen states, placing books of the Theosophical Gift Book Institute in libraries along the way. Apparently William Johnston's health would not permit him to make this trip. He died on September 8, 1966.[35]

The faculty of the Connell era handled a wide variety of concerns, as had earlier faculties. Some of the matters taken up at general faculty meetings would have been restricted to departmental action today. There was still a strong military flavor in the approach to student discipline. For example, a student could sever his connection with the college in only one of six ways: by graduation, honorable discharge, suspension, expulsion, desertion, or death. To be absent, a student was required to obtain a furlough. Without an honorable discharge, the student was automatically classed as a deserter and his parents were notified. A first offense for smoking was twenty-five demerits; a second offense was fifty demerits. The commandant of cadets could inspect rooms in the men's dormitory at any time without warning.[36]

One case that returned to faculty attention on several occasions was that of Roy F. Miller, son of Freeman E. Miller, a prominent faculty member from 1894 to 1898. Miller's petition for the reinstatement of his son was denied at the September 9, 1909, faculty meeting. The faculty ruled "there was no evidence that the young man had complied with the action of the Faculty placing him under discipline last year." On September 10, 1910, Freeman Miller once more appeared before the faculty seeking readmission for his son, who was at the time manager of the Miller Mercantile Agency in partnership with his father. He presented a letter from a Miss Foster of Butler, Missouri, in connection with the appeal. Action was deferred "until Roy Miller appear before the Faculty in person." Miller tried again and apparently succeeded, according to the faculty minutes for September 19, 1910. However, the faculty at its next meeting nullified this action without explanation. On October 8, Roy presented his case personally. His petition for readmission was not granted. On September 6, 1911, he was denied again.[37] Similar problems would plague Freeman Miller during his reprise as head of English four years later.

The hard feelings that had developed over the firing of several key faculty and staff members in 1909 and 1910 had not died. As Connell strengthened his grip on campus affairs, an undercurrent of hostility toward him among some Stillwater business leaders had grown in intensity. One of this group was C. A. Melton. Writing on a Chamber of Commerce letterhead, Melton sought the support of W. T. Leahy, a prominent Pawhuska businessman and member of the board of agriculture, in the campaign against Connell. Leahy responded with a letter strongly supporting the president. Leahy wrote: "If Dr. Connell is the man that you and your followers claim him to be, I request you to make affidavit charging him with the different things that he has done, including the mis-appropriation of school funds,. . .present the charges to the Board at the July meeting and they will get due consideration, but so far as my taking into consideration the letters that I have received signed by people who have fallen out with Dr. Connell or who are not satisfied with his management of the school, I am frank to say that I for one will not pay any further attention to them. If Dr. Connell is wrong as you people say and will prove it he will lose his job. If he is right as the Board thinks he is he will stay there. Now it is up to you people as to whether an investigation is held or not."

Apparently Leahy sent copies of the Melton correspondence to Connell, for three days later the president wrote to Leahy thanking him for his support and returning the Melton correspondence. Connell stated: "I have made no statement in the public press concerning this matter. The question is being discussed quite hotly on our streets and some indignation has been expressed against Melton and [C. A.] Strickland for having gone far beyond the purposes and intentions of the Commercial Club in. . .assuming undue responsibilities concerning the administration of affairs in the A. and M. College."[38]

Connell survived the Melton attack, but his tenure was nearing its end. In one year the board would be seeking a new president.

As for Johnston, he had given journalism and related studies scant encouragement. This seemed paradoxical in view of President Connell's actions. Connell not only had stepped up the college's public information program but had created the *New Education*, a news-packed paper with statewide circulation, unmistakably a major journalistic effort. Why, some wondered, had there been no comparable academic effort in journalism other than the ill-fated effort in the Division of Agriculture? The paradox became more perplexing as news of Johnston's work in East Lansing filtered back to Stillwater. But the facts were clear, despite his earlier newspaper experience. He had been a printer's devil at the *Erie Republican-Record*, Neosho County, Kansas, as a boy. In his college days he took pride in his position as correspondent for the *Kansas City Star*, and following graduation from Baker University he had worked a year for the *Kansas City Journal*, responsible for circulation in the south half of Kansas City, Kansas. He had considered a career in journalism, but his work at Harvard had convinced him that his future was in teaching. Poetry, not news, had become his forte. This was reflected in his work at Oklahoma A. and M., where he poured his energies into developing literary and oratorical skills—not journalism—among students in the Department of English and Public Speaking. Thinking back on his days in Erie, he recalled setting type, "turning the big press to run off the papers" once a week and hearing the voice of a veteran printer singing "Kathleen Mavoureen." He remembered, too, wrapping the "single list," and said: "I seem to smell still the paste used on wrappers."[39] But from 1908 until 1912—four academic years—the only evidence of journalism instruction at Oklahoma A. and M. was Craig's short-lived effort, in which Johnston had no part. Some students working on the monthly *Orange and Black* may have entertained hopes of journalistic careers, but they were to receive minimal instruction to help them on their way. All of that would change with the arrival of Edwin R. Barrett. Journalism was to have a rebirth that would give it both shape and texture as well as promise of future academic status and success.

Endnotes

1. Record Book Committee, compiler, "Selections From the Record Book of the Oklahoma Agricultural and Mechanical College, 1891-1941. Compiled on the Occasion of the Fiftieth Anniversary of the College," vol. 1, pp. 2, 3, Special Collections, Edmon Low Library, Oklahoma State University, Stillwater, Oklahoma; Charles R. Schultz to Harry E. Heath Jr., 26 November 1990, School of Journalism and Broadcasting Centennial History Collection, Special Collections, Edmon Low Library; Philip Reed Rulon, *Oklahoma State University—Since 1890* (Stillwater: Oklahoma State University Press, 1975), pp. 127, 128. Rulon mentions Connell's regional reputation at Texas A. and M. College in "institute work" and dairy experiments.

2. Record Book Committee, compiler, pp. 3, 4; Rulon, p. 127.

3. *Annual Catalog, Oklahoma A. and M. College, 1908-1909*, unnumbered page following list of faculty, instructors and other officers; LeRoy H. Fischer, *Oklahoma State University Historic Old Central* (Stillwater: Oklahoma State University Press, 1988), p. 87.

4. *Annual Catalog, Oklahoma A. and M. College, 1908-1909*, pp. 91, 96.

5. *Annual Catalog, Oklahoma A. and M. College, 1908-1909*, pp. 71, 72.

6. Donald E. Green, *A History of the Oklahoma State University Division of Agriculture* (Stillwater: Oklahoma State University, 1990), pp. 47, 48; *Annual Catalog, Oklahoma A. and M. College, 1908-1909*, faculty list, unpaged; *Annual Catalog, Oklahoma A. and M. College, 1909-1910*, p. viii with notation "resigned May 1."

7. Minutes, Oklahoma A. and M. College Faculty, 19 December 1910, p. 129, Special Collections, Edmon Low Library; *Annual Catalog, Oklahoma A. and M. College, 1908-1909*, pp. 71, 72; Green, pp. 106, 107.

8. *Annual Catalog, Oklahoma A. and M. College, 1908-1909*, pp. 96-98.

9. Richard D. Wilson, "Early Oklahoma A. and M. College Newspapers—A Perspective," p. 16, unpublished manuscript submitted to fulfill requirements in MC 4360 in 1980, Special Collections, Edmon Low Library.

10. *1911 Red Skin*, p. 150, Oklahoma A. and M. College Yearbook.

11. *Annual Catalog, Oklahoma A. and M. College, 1908-1909*, p. 28; *Annual Catalog, Oklahoma A. and M. College, 1909-1910*, pp. x, 10.

12. *Stillwater NewsPress*, 9 February 1964, p. 9; *Michigan State News*, 7 December 1933, pp. 1, 6; William J. Beal, *History of the Michigan Agricultural College* (East Lansing: Michigan Agricultural College, 1915), pp. 465, 467.

13. *Stillwater NewsPress*, p. 9; *Michigan State News*, 7 December 1933, pp. 1, 6; Copy of transcript, Baker University, and W. W. Johnston to Homer Hoch, 11 May 1938, in Henry S. Johnston Collection, Special Collections, Edmon Low Library.

14. *Stillwater NewsPress*, 9 February 1964, p. 9.

15. *Stillwater NewsPress*, 9 February 1964, p. 9; *Hoffhine's Stillwater and Payne County Oklahoma Directory for 1910* (Oklahoma City: Hoffhine Directory Company, 1910), p. 44.

16. *Annual Catalog, Oklahoma A. and M. College, 1907-1908*, pp. 49, 88, 89, 91, 92; *Annual Catalog, Oklahoma A. and M. College, 1908-09*, pp. 107, 108; Oklahoma A. and M. College *Orange and Black*, October 1908, pp. 20, 22, January 1909, pp. 26, 27, 34; Oklahoma A. and M. College *Brown and Blue*, 1 June 1908, throughout.

17. *Annual Catalog, Oklahoma A. and M. College, 1909-1910*, pp. 108-111, 117, 118; *Annual Catalog, Oklahoma A. and M. College, 1910-1911*, pp. v, 93, 105-108; *Stillwater NewsPress*, p. 9; *Michigan State News*, 7 December 1933, pp. 1, 6.

18. *Annual Catalog, Oklahoma A. and M. College, 1911-1912*, p. x; *Orange and Black*, 11 September 1912, p. 1; Noble Warren Rockey, untitled and undated handwritten historical review, 1911-1921, family papers of Esther Jones Rockey, School of Journalism and Broadcasting Centennial History Collection.

19. *Stillwater NewsPress*, 9 February 1964, p. 9.

20. *Stillwater Gazette*, 23 April 1909, pp. 1, 5; Rulon, p. 130.

21. Minutes, Oklahoma A. and M. College Faculty, June 1909, p. 77; *Annual Catalog, Oklahoma A. and M. College, 1910-1911*, p. x.

22. *Stillwater Gazette*, 29 April 1910, pp. 1, 8.

23. *Stillwater Gazette*, 6 May 1910, p. 5.

24. *Stillwater Gazette*, 22 April 1910, p. 7, 6 May 1910, p. 5; Minutes, Oklahoma A. and M. College Faculty, 4 May, 17 May 1910.

25. *Stillwater Gazette*, 22 April 1910, p. 7, 6 May 1910, p. 7.

26. *Stillwater Gazette*, 7 April 1910, pp. 1, 7, 8 April 1910, p. 1, 9 April 1910, p. 7; Robert E. Cunningham, *Stillwater Through the Years* (Stillwater, OK: Arts and Humanities Council of Stillwater, Oklahoma, Incorporated, 1974), p. 232.

27. *1916 Redskin*, p. 213.

28. *1910 Red Skin*, p. 17; Minutes, Oklahoma A. and M. College Faculty, 20 November 1909.

29. Minutes, Oklahoma A. and M. College Faculty, 13 January 1910. A search of all minutes through 25 October 1910 failed to shed any light on the work of the committee. Westbrook, pressed with his other duties, may have suggested privately to Connell that the matter be dropped.

30. *Stillwater NewsPress*, 9 February 1964, p. 9.

31. *Orange and Black*, 11 September 1912, p. 1; *1912 Redskin*, p. 11.

32. *Lansing State Journal*, 5 April 1935.

33. *Lansing State Journal* [1940], and W. W. Johnston to Nelson P. Horn, 17 June 1938, in Henry S. Johnston Collection.

34. *Lansing State Journal*, 27 February 1940, p. 15.

35. Juliette Teorey, "75 Years of MSU Journalism," *J-School Update*, Michigan State University, p. 1; *Michigan State University Alumni Magazine*, November 1935, p. 8; *Stillwater NewsPress*, 9 February 1964, p. 9; Dorothy T. Frye to Harry E. Heath Jr., 25 February 1992, School of Journalism and Broadcasting Centennial History Collection; W. W. Johnston to Homer Hoch, 11 May 1938, Henry S. Johnston Collection.

36. Minutes, Oklahoma A. and M. College Faculty, 2 March 1910, 13 April 1910. The latter includes "Rules of the Board of Regents and the Faculty for the Government of the Oklahoma A. and M. College" (adopted June 1909).

37. Minutes, Oklahoma A. and M. College Faculty, 9 September 1909, 10 September 1910, 19 September 1910, 23 September 1910, 8 October 1910, 6 September 1911; *Hoffhine's Stillwater and Payne County Oklahoma Directory for 1910*, advertisement on outside back cover.

38. C. A. Melton to W. T. Leahy, undated, W. T. Leahy to C. A. Melton, 7 June 1913, W. T. Leahy to *Stillwater Daily Press*, 7 June 1913, and John H. Connell to W. T. Leahy, 10 June 1913, in School of Journalism and Broadcasting Centennial History Collection; Rulon, p. 30.

39. Erie, Kansas *Erie Record*, 28 December 1945, p. 7.

7 The Builders: Barrett, Rockey, and O'Brien

The stage was set. Freeman E. Miller, Angelo C. Scott, Frank D. Northup, and John A. Craig had taken the lead in establishing journalism's presence on the young Oklahoma A. and M. campus, but there had been no real curriculum available to students with journalistic aspirations. Work on the student newspaper helped an occasional early grad such as Arthur B. McReynolds of the class of 1899 to enter the field, but these students entered journalism on a wave of enthusiasm and desire— sometimes by chance—and not upon a solid educational foundation for publications work.[1]

A journalism program that went beyond printing alone began to take on a more permanent shape at Oklahoma A. and M. shortly before the outbreak of World War I. The idea had originated at Iowa State College in 1905 with a gift from John Clay, head of a large livestock-commission firm. The result was a course in agricultural journalism, believed to be the first such course at any land-grant institution. It was taught by Will H. Ogilvey, a perceptive Scottish agriculturalist who was serving as experiment station editor in Ames. Iowa State quickly became a leader in training journalists with an agricultural specialty.[2]

It took five years for Oklahoma A. and M. College to adopt the Iowa State idea, and then it had quickly died. This is surprising when one considers the prestige and leadership Iowa State enjoyed among fledgling land-grant schools. But the time for a more permanent effort finally came, heralded by curriculum changes reflected in the 1912-13 general catalog. These changes coincided with the arrival of Edwin R. Barrett as head of the Department of English and Public Speaking.[3]

His appointment was announced in the *Stillwater Gazette* on September 6, 1912. William W. Johnston, the man he was to replace, was en route to East Lansing, Michigan, where he would take a leading role in building a journalism program at the Michigan State Agricultural College. The *Orange and Black* reported the departure of Carl Ostrum for Kansas State and three significant arrivals: Raymond A. Swink, Harry R. O'Brien, and Ralph E. Tieje.[4]

Barrett was to find his new home somewhat more primitive than Kirksville, Missouri, where for six years he had taught English. But the town fathers were making progress in improving conditions. Stillwater had just completed its third annual Chautauqua. Work on a new water supply, called "the big well," was progressing and eventually would furnish 300,000 gallons a day. A new movie house, the Camera, was being built at 719 Main, and construction on paving from Main to the college was getting under way. Within two months after Barrett's arrival, Woodrow Wilson, a Democrat, would win the presidency while Payne County would show a strong Republican preference. Local citizens had had enough of pool halls in their college town and would vote them out of existence.[5]

Major strides also were being made on campus during the academic year that Barrett arrived. The Auditorium and the new Engineering Building were occupied that year, completing what would be known as the quadrangle, the heart of the campus. Barrett's department, which

This is the Stillwater that greeted Edwin R. Barrett and his family upon their arrival in 1912. It must have seemed somewhat primitive to the three young Ohioans—Harry R. O'Brien, Ralph E. Tieje, and Raymond A. Swink—who joined Barrett to advance the cause of campus journalism.

formerly had occupied part of Morrill Hall, had been given space on the second floor of Engineering. Journalism classes were to be held in Room 216.[6]

While he and his wife would become involved in church and civic affairs later, there was no time for such things now. His new work would demand all of his energies for a while.[7]

Barrett's early life had not been easy. He was born in Indianapolis in 1871, and his father had died before he was four years old. He lived with his mother and sisters and sold papers on the city streets. The youngster got printers ink on his fingers, and it never washed off. He attended school in Indianapolis until he was fourteen, when the family moved to Parkville, Missouri, where he entered the academy at Park College, later starting the college's first newspaper. His mother was a dormitory house mother for five or six years, and the dormitory later was called "Barrett Home" in her honor.[8]

In 1895 he received his B.A. degree at Park. Although he majored in mathematics and planned to take up engineering, his first loves were literature and reading, reinforced by his mother, who read to him daily during his boyhood. (Park College would call him back in May 1939 to bestow upon him the honorary doctor of letters degree.)[9] He left Parkville, baccalaureate degree in hand, and got a high school job teaching mathematics, then realized he lacked the patience required of a math teacher. While he did not have the patience for quadratics, he did have the patience to drill students on the parts of speech and conjugations. "After the first mastering," he once said, "the binomial theorem holds no promising future, but literature never grows old."[10] Next he taught printing in a reform school briefly before accepting a teaching assignment at Lawson College. In 1898 he took a newspaper job on the *Pilot* in Manitowoc, Wisconsin, probably also serving as a string correspondent for the *Milwaukee Journal*, before returning to Park College to head the literature division of the English department in 1901. His love for newspapers and printing was exceeded only by his love for good literature and the grace and beauty of the English language. This love was reflected in one of his poems, "My Books," part of which read: "They open the gate to the fountain of youth; They dazzle my eyes with gold; They roll me far from today's black mar, And things more real unfold. Shall I miserly hover these riches alone? Or be guide to the golden way? Come hither, youth, and learn the truth. Oh, hear what these may say." He believed in the beauty and lasting qualities of good books.[11]

Following a year on the Park College faculty, he studied at the University of Chicago in the summer of 1902, then returned to Park for two more years. He had found his career, but he knew he must have an advanced degree to ensure his future success. The opportunity came when an English fellowship at the University of Kansas was offered to

With the appointment of Edwin R. Barrett, journalism fortunes took an upturn. He considered journalism to be a practical way to enhance the teaching of English composition.

him. He took his master of arts degree in 1905 before joining the English faculty at Teachers College, Kirksville, Missouri, later that year. On leave in 1908, he studied for three months in European schools under sponsorship of the American Civic Federation.[12]

Barrett quickly became a respected member of the English faculty at Kirksville. He had a natural gift for teaching that was quickly recognized by his colleagues. Later in his career it would make him a legendary figure in Emporia, Kansas, second only to his friend, William A. White. During the years in Kirksville he was active in the Presbyterian Church, serving as an elder for four years and on the pulpit committee. He also was a leader in the Law and Order League, a group organized to fight the sale of intoxicants within Kirksville's city limits. The league prevailed on June 6, 1912, in a city-wide election, 736 to 669. Soon after, he was preparing for the move to Oklahoma.[13] Such was the background of the man who was to bring to fruition the first journalism curriculum at the Oklahoma A. and M. College.

That Barrett saw promise in his new assignment is apparent from a letter written to a Kirksville friend in early September. "The prospects for a pleasant year here are very bright," he wrote. "This is a big, bustling new school in a new country. Life, energy and enthusiasm are abundant. I feel as though I have a number of good, warm friends already." Then in an effort to pay tribute to the good days in Kirksville, he concluded: "I should like very much to be there tomorrow, enrollment day. . .but the 'fates and the sisters three' have decreed otherwise."[14]

As in other evolving programs at Oklahoma A. and M., a combination of events made the difference, but Barrett most likely was the catalyst. Johnston had served not only as professor in charge of English and speech but as dean of the science and literature division as well. With Johnston's departure, the popular Lowery L. Lewis, who served as dean of veterinary medicine, added a second deanship. Lewis had won the hearts of the student body and equally strong faculty support. He was progressive and open-minded. Barrett found the mild-mannered "Doctor Lew" to be a good listener as he unfolded his plans for curricular changes.

Barrett's plans for journalism may have been favored, too, by the fact that President John H. Connell had served as editor of *Farm and Ranch Magazine* in Dallas.[15] Having a chief executive with journalistic experience was sure to be of some help, whether or not he took an active part in the decision. At the least, he was not likely to block the move.

But there were other key figures as well. One was Harry R. O'Brien, who had studied English and journalism at Ohio State University. Another was Noble W. Rockey, an Ohio State man also aware of journalism's success at his alma mater. Both were favorably disposed to testing the curricular waters. Rockey, who earlier had professed hopes for a writing career, had been an assistant in the department since 1911.[16] He was solid and well respected by students and faculty alike. But the most important element in the curricular ferment was Barrett himself.

While there is no documentation for exactly what was happening at the time, one can easily imagine Barrett, O'Brien, and Rockey in animated discussion over the need for journalism instruction at Oklahoma A. and M. on more than a hit or miss basis. Certainly O'Brien, fresh from his master's program at Ohio State, was enthused about the journalism course he had taken there and about his future plans to use as a free lance writer and teacher the skills he had developed. Barrett, as an ex-newspaperman, may have taken the lead in the discussions. If not, he could at least listen to such proposals with positive feelings. However it came about, Barrett—with the help of O'Brien and Rockey—gave Oklahoma A. and M. a full-term journalism course, its first since John A. Craig's brief pioneering effort in 1908. Soon, the college's first rudimentary journalism curriculum would follow.

Concurrent with these faculty deliberations was an emerging interest in the Division of Agriculture. A new student publication was about to be born. Volume 1, Number 1 of the *Progressive Agriculturist* appeared in September 1912 with a staff of thirteen students. It would be a motivating factor in O'Brien's early journalism instruction and in the growing interest in journalism as a career among Oklahoma A. and M. students. One of the early successes out of this ferment was Clarence

Noble W. Rockey joined the faculty in
1911 as a member of William W.
Johnston's English faculty.

Roberts, who served on the *Agriculturist* staff before becoming editor of
the *Orange and Black* in 1914. He had added journalism to his dairy
specialty and was said to be "the first of the Oklahoma A. and M.
journalists to put his special training to work" when on January 1, 1916,
he was named as assistant to Carl Williams of the *Oklahoma
Farmer-Stockman.* [17]

For the immediate future, journalism education at Oklahoma A. and
M. was to experience growing pains. Certainly the growth was not
spectacular. It was a matter of gaining a foothold in the academic
community under the aegis of the Department of English and Public
Speaking and holding on. Journalism courses were being set up in a
number of English departments elsewhere, and this natural evolution of
a new academic interest was to be the pattern at Stillwater. The growing
interest in journalism programs on other campuses, including the University of Oklahoma, had been noted.[18] President Connell may have felt
the time was right for journalism to receive some attention at Oklahoma
A. and M., and that English was the obvious home for such a program in
its early stages.

The catalog for 1912-13 suggests that Barrett's predecessor was trying
to keep pace with the "increasing attention" that was being paid to
English in other institutions. "The teaching force in the Department has
been increased," the catalog reported.[19] Johnston, or perhaps Rockey,
depending upon the deadline college editor Walter Stemmons had set,
was responsible for the catalog copy, which expanded upon Scott's
earlier work in journalism. In essence, it was a return to Craig's course in

Agricultural Journalism. It had a new name and had changed homes, but it would occupy a full term.[20]

Barrett was fortunate in the young talent converging upon Oklahoma A. and M. In addition to the versatile and energetic O'Brien, both Swink and Tieje proved to be extremely popular. This was apparent on several public occasions. At the annual February party for freshmen, held in the women's gymnasium, Swink and O'Brien tied for first place in the riddle contest. To the delight of the crowd, they had to give a musical performance to break the tie. O'Brien played the piano, and Swink, undaunted, sang "Wished I Had a Nickle." Again they tied, so a penny was produced and "with Mr. O'Brien's 'Tails I win, heads you lose,' the penny was flipped." Tails won and amidst loud laughter he was presented with a 1916 pennant. Swink then was called upon to present class emblems. After offering several examples of humorous double entendre, he gave the triangular emblems in the freshman class colors to women of the class basketball team, the men of the class football team, and finally to the men who had been pulled through the water in the traditional freshman-sophomore tug-of-war.[21]

A similar show of light-hearted fun involving the English faculty occurred during Senior Chapel Day the same week. The faculty occupied the senior corner. Roll was taken and, to the delight of the students, demerits were issued to those who had cut chapel. When announcements were called for, Professor Howard G. Seldomridge announced that the

ANNUAL CATALOG, OKLAHOMA A. AND M. COLLEGE, 1914-1915

203 News Writing. Class 2 hours. Credit 2.
Prerequisite: 101, 102.
A study of the elements of news writing and style form the basis of the work. Proper attention is given to writing leads, structure of news stories, reporting and gathering of news, interviewing, reporting speeches, and other forms of elementary journalism.
Text: "Essentials in Journalism", Harrington and Frankenberg, supplemented by "Typical News Stories", Harrington.

204 Magazine Writing. Class 2 hours. Credit 2.
Prerequisite: 101, 102, 203.
This course takes up the problem of turning scientific and technical information into practical articles for publication in magazines. Preparation of manuscripts and submitting them for acceptance forms part of the work. Special attention is given to agriculture and allied subjects.
Farm Writing, Neal.

205, 206 Current Literature. Class 1 hour. Credit 1.
Prerequisite: 101, 102.
A course offered as an aid to more intelligent magazine reading and to stimulate an interest in the best current literature.
Text: Current magazines.

301 Editorial and Publicity Work. Class 2 hours. Credit 2.
Prerequisite: 203, 204.
Copy prepared by students in course 203 is edited for publication in student papers. Practical work is given in editing, proofreading, makeup, along with special assignments in writing. Publicity work for the College is undertaken in connection with the course.

302 Feature and Publicity Writing. Class 2 hours. Credit 2.
Prerequisite: English 203, 204, 301.
Writing feature articles for newspapers and magazines forms the basis of the work. Upon arrangement a separate section is formed for those interested in the short-story and offering English 201, 202 as prerequisite. This takes up a study of the history, the structure and forms of the short story, the reading of short stories, and the writing of stories on assignment by the instructor. Editing for student publications and College publicity work is continued by those in that phase of the course.

The first journalism curriculum appeared in the 1914-1915 catalog. The junior-level courses were used to give support to student publications as well as the college's off-campus publicity efforts. Harry R. O'Brien of the English faculty worked closely with Walter Stemmons, college editor, to make the plan work.

play to be given February 28 had been written by Professors "Swiege and Tink." Another roar of laughter went up.[22] Such instances as these provide a clue to the state of student-faculty relationships in the Oklahoma A. and M. of that decade. Journalism obviously stood to benefit from the popular young professors on Barrett's faculty team. Swink, a loyal supporter of student activities, was a graduate of Ohio Wesleyan University. His student record was unspectacular until his junior year when, the Wesleyan yearbook reported, "he suddenly broke into the hall of fame as a silver tongued orator and an accomplished debater." He completed his academic requirements at the University of Chicago during the summer of 1912, transferring his credits to Wesleyan, then taking a position with the Lyon School for Boys in Spokane, Washington. His B.A. degree was awarded by Wesleyan in 1913 at the end of his first year on the Oklahoma A. and M. faculty. The Wapakoneta, Ohio, youth had been on the varsity debate team and had been named Varsity Orator. He was selected to give the Washington Birthday Oration. In addition he was active in two Greek-letter organizations. It was easy to see why, fresh from his successes in student activities at Wesleyan, he interacted readily with Oklahoma A. and M. students. In an informal poll reported in the 1913 *Redskin* he was named the most popular professor on campus, edging out the revered Lowery Lewis, who finished a close second.[23] While he was primarily a debate coach and teacher of public speaking, he also taught journalism.

Swink was the kind of teacher Oklahoma A. and M. could build upon. But he was overshadowed in the speech area by Seldomridge, a man protective of his academic territory. Swink's teaching assignments were not, to his own way of thinking, ideal. Barrett's plans to leave in the near future, which Swink may have been privy to, plus an attractive offer from W. W. Johnston, led him to move north. Michigan would bring him closer to his Ohio roots. He resigned in January 1914 to accept a position teaching agricultural journalism under Johnston, who had served since leaving Oklahoma A. and M. as head of the English faculty at Michigan State Agricultural College.[24]

Swink's stay in Michigan was brief. On October 3, 1914, the *Orange and Black* reported that he had left Michigan State to accept a position as professor of public speaking and oratory at Heidelberg University, Tiffin, Ohio.[25] He served at Heidelberg, where he was praised for his leadership in debate and drama, until the end of the 1915-16 academic year. The *Aurora*, Heidelberg yearbook, reported that he was a severe critic in his public speaking classes, but respected by his students. One of his former professors said: "He is a young man of splendid character, great industry and especially fine intellect. I have never known a student who was his superior." Despite the praise and popularity that surrounded him at Tiffin, he left his position as head of the Department of

Oratory that summer to join the speech faculty at Ohio Wesleyan University. After two years as an assistant professor of public speaking and associate director of development, Swink entered the business world. Three years later he took the M.A. at Ohio State University to assist him in his business career. He would never return to the classroom except as a part-time teacher in evening programs at the University of Cincinnati and at the Cincinnati YMCA School of Commerce.[26]

Of the newcomers, Ralph E. Tieje was perhaps the most promising. When he came to Stillwater he held A. B. and A. M. degrees from the University of Illinois. He had taken the baccalaureate degree in English in June 1910 with special honors, final honors and a Phi Beta Kappa key, and had completed the master's two years later while serving for $800 a year as an assistant in English 1 and 2 and Rhetoric. During the last five months of his undergraduate work, he was on the department's theme-reading staff and had written his senior thesis on "The Common Grammatical and Rhetorical Errors in Freshman Themes at the University of Illinois." He knew both French and German, and spoke the latter fluently.[27]

He may have come to Oklahoma A. and M. on Rockey's recommendation, for both were from Dayton, Ohio, where Tieje was born on January 24, 1887. He had attended Steele High School in Dayton and later Urbana High School. At Illinois, he was a member of the Scribblers Club and Der Deutsche Verein, and had served on the *Illinois Magazine* board.[28]

But for Tieje, who served on the Oratorical Board with Barrett, Oklahoma A. and M. was only a way station, as it was for so many promising young intellectuals of the day. Following the 1912-13 academic year he spent one year as an instructor of English at Washington State College and then returned to the University of Illinois where he was an English instructor for two years and a fellow in English during 1916-17 while he completed his Ph.D. degree. Most of his sections were open only to engineering students. In the fall of 1917, he became head of the English department at the Washington State Normal School, Cheney, and married Helen Virginia Nourse, whom he had met while at Washington State.[29]

The loss of Swink and Tieje was unfortunate, for both showed rare promise and both had assisted in journalism, although it was not their primary interest. But for journalism's immediate future the key faculty addition was O'Brien, who had come to Oklahoma A. and M. at the same time as Swink and Tieje. What sort of man was O'Brien? What experiences had shaped his approach to campus life in the Southwest? As a student at Ohio State University, he had set a fast pace. The 1910 *Makio*, student yearbook, pictures him in a serious pose and records that he was a member of Athenean, English Club, French Club, Debate and Oratory Council (1908-09), Political Science Club, and Delta Kappa, a local social

Three of the most popular teachers of journalism and public speaking were (*left to right*) Harry R. O'Brien, Raymond A. Swink, and Ralph E. Tieje. They built a groundswell of popular sentiment for their courses but stayed only a short time.

fraternity founded in 1908. He was president of the Atheneans in the fall of 1909 and sergeant-at-arms during the winter term. In addition, he was Ivy Orator, a senior class honor of high prestige. As Ivy Orator, he delivered a Class Day address at the 7:30 A.M. ivy-planting ceremony at the Student Building on Monday, June 20, 1910. Then he settled in for two years of graduate work.[30]

In the context of today's emphasis upon professional experience for acceptance on a journalism faculty, O'Brien was a somewhat unlikely candidate to become the cornerstone of journalism's revival at Oklahoma A. and M. He was born in Union, Ohio, December 12, 1889, and while his professional credentials were considerable in later years, he had virtually no experience to back up his journalism teaching when at twenty-three he arrived at the little prairie college in Stillwater. He had taken the A.B. degree at Ohio State and then had accepted a library reference fellowship there so he could work toward the M.A. O'Brien had entered Ohio State with the intention of becoming an English teacher, but along the way he had taken journalism. He was hooked. He completed the master's in 1912 and joined the English faculty at Oklahoma A. and M. to tackle a new Advanced Composition course that would provide instruction in journalism. The course already was listed in the catalog when he reported for duty.[31]

The Stillwater that greeted O'Brien provided a marked contrast to Columbus, Ohio. Oklahoma had been a state for only five years and its rough-and-tumble politics were difficult for an outsider to fathom. O'Brien's home state had entered the Union in 1803, more than a hundred years before Oklahoma and Indian Territories were linked to form the forty-sixth state. Columbus, the state capital, was a city of nearly 200,000.

Ohio State University, chartered in 1870, boasted 3,969 students. It was a university in the true sense of the word and had dropped the descriptive "agricultural and mechanical college" from its name in 1878. Earlier corruption in Ohio politics had been brought under control and both political and economic stability were now taken for granted by most citizens. The Ohio of 1912 had well-established cities and towns, abundant industry, the natural beauty of numerous forests, major rivers, rolling hills and undulating plains. It capped its pride with the many advantages that Lake Erie offered. Stately homes in long-established communities were commonplace to O'Brien's youthful experience.[32]

By comparison, Oklahoma was not long removed from sod huts, dugouts, and shanties, and was in political turmoil—a turmoil that made for frequent upheaval on the Oklahoma A. and M. campus. O'Brien had little more than organized the bookshelves in his office than a referendum was on to move the county seat from Stillwater to Ripley and the courts were ruling on which of three groups claiming to be the board of agriculture was *legally* entitled to carry out the responsibilities vested in the board, including the power to control Oklahoma A. and M. College. Stillwater itself was a proud but somewhat raw frontier town with a population of about 6,000, a campus enrollment of 1,253, a mixture of buggies, horseless carriages, livery stables, and a telephone system of approximately 350 subscribers.[33]

As O'Brien started his teaching career, the agricultural journalism movement was gaining momentum nationally. The American Association of Teachers of Journalism, twenty-four strong, met in the Historical Library at the University of Wisconsin November 28 and 29, 1913, and two of the papers presented dealt with agricultural journalism. This was not surprising, for by then many of the early journalism units, following the Iowa State model, were on land-grant campuses. One of the leaders in the field was the University of Wisconsin. Topics discussed in addition to agricultural journalism included the value of owning a printing plant, the college newspaper as a training device, and journalism's relationship to English departments.[34]

Before his three years in the young state of Oklahoma had ended, O'Brien had played a part in drawing up a bona fide journalism curriculum in the Department of English similar to the Ohio State program. Most of the courses were taught, or scheduled to be taught at some time, by O'Brien. He would have some assistance from Rockey as well as Swink and Tieje, but it is likely he was expected to carry most of the load. The early exits of Barrett, Swink, and Tieje would shift most of the courses to O'Brien and Rockey.

The young teacher was from an area known as Slabhollow, twelve miles north of Dayton, Ohio, on the Stillwater River. His plain-folks roots were readily apparent in his open, friendly approach. He believed in breaking down the barriers between the lectern and the seats in front of him. He once told a reporter that he was a failure if, after the first two weeks, students were not calling him by his first name and borrowing his smoking tobacco. He smoked a pipe in his Oklahoma A. and M. days, but in later years was addicted to cigars. He wore a green eyeshade when reading or pecking out a magazine story or column at his typewriter. On another occasion, a *Columbus Dispatch* reporter credited O'Brien with "originating" the work in journalism at Oklahoma A. and M. That point, however, depends upon one's interpretation. Mable Caldwell told the Stillwater Writers Club, which she helped organize, that she was a student in the first journalism course taught at Oklahoma A. and M., and that Noble W. Rockey was the teacher. The class she apparently referred to was English 203, News Writing, listed on her transcript in the summer of 1915. But Craig's 1908 effort had come first followed five years later by an English course that would stress journalistic writing. The best evidence is that O'Brien was the teacher.[35]

O'Brien signed on early enough to be listed in the 1912-13 catalog as an assistant in the Department of English and Public Speaking. Whether he was hired to provide the new emphasis in journalism or had asked Barrett to give him that assignment after his arrival may never be known. What is known is that the catalog stated that a new course in Advanced Composition would be offered in the next academic year. The new course, English 8a-b-c, was designed primarily for junior-level students, although it was open to seniors as well. The enrollment was fairly well balanced between male and female students. The course description read: "The aim is to make this course intensely practical. The themes that

NEW EDUCATION

Student journalists helped the Chamber of Commerce and the college administration give a royal welcome to state newspaper editors in the early summer of 1915. The visiting editors were met at the train depot and then driven to the campus for a "Grown in Oklahoma" dinner, music, talks, and guided tours of the college.

are written by the class are used in the College publications whenever it is possible to do so. This course is co-elective with English 9a-b-c, and any term of one may be taken instead of the corresponding term of the other. Seniors may elect any term. Fall: The elementary principles of journalism are taken up. Papers of the nature of special articles for popular magazines, agricultural journals and Government bulletins are written. Winter: The winter term is devoted largely to argumentation. The principles of this form of discourse are studied. The composition work will consist of short arguments, editorials, and one or two debates. Spring: A study of the short story and general narrative composition." The catalog also included the year's schedule of classes. It shows that English 8 was offered during that academic year, two sections each of 8a in the fall, 8b in the winter and 8c in the spring. A search in the registrar's office turned up no transcripts listing English 8a that fall. Many records prior to 1914 are missing because of the fire that gutted Morrill Hall on August 7, 1914. There *are* transcripts, however, to verify that 8a was taught in the fall of 1913. The teacher that semester, if only one section was offered, probably was O'Brien.[36]

O'Brien faced the English 8 class in what the catalog called a large, beautiful recitation room on the second floor of the new Engineering Building.[37] It seems likely that Barrett, Seldomridge, Rockey, Tieje, and Swink gave most of their attention to the other six English and four public speaking courses in the department, and that O'Brien was selected to develop the work in journalism. The course in printing, which had offered some help to aspiring journalists in past years, had been abandoned in 1908 as production demands pressed the printing staff for time and facilities.

O'Brien taught five hours of theory per week to juniors in English 8, Advanced Composition, for at least two and perhaps all of the three quarters. The course was required in domestic science and arts, and was elective in animal husbandry, agronomy, dairy, horticulture, science and literature, and the normal school. Freshman and sophomore English were prerequisites.[38]

Based upon available class schedules, 8a-b-c was offered regularly from 1912 until the introduction of the first journalism curriculum with its new numbering system in 1914. Just how the new curriculum fared is difficult to trace from 1915 through spring of 1919, for class schedules and class rolls are unavailable for those years. With few exceptions, schedules are available since the 1919-20 academic year. They provide evidence of uninterrupted course work in journalism, limited at times, expanded at other times, depending upon changing conditions.

"Streaking," a campus social phenomenon somewhat comparable to an earlier penchant for goldfish swallowing, was still six decades away when the *Orange and Black* reported what may have been the first case at Oklahoma A. and M. Early in 1913, a page-one story headlined "Not Even Fig Leaves" told of two unnamed male students, "prominent in social and athletic circles," and their unconventional dash across campus. They had visited the women's dormitory kitchen, where "Daddy" Swope had a fire under the boiler to keep the water pipes from freezing. They resolved to stay up with him all night. At about 5:30 A.M., one dared the other to "make it to the boys' dorm stark naked." Both stripped and, clothes draped over their arms, started across campus. According to the *Orange and Black* report, they emitted a few war whoops that "would have done justice to a tribe of Comanche Indians." These were made more realistic when their feet slipped from under them and they suddenly were wallowing in the snow. When Room 311 was visited at about 7 A.M., one of the young men was found in bed with all his clothes on. He said his feet were cold. It was not often that such campus high jinks made the front page.[39]

Although he stressed news and feature coverage in technical fields, O'Brien knew how to appreciate off-beat stories and could enjoy a good belly laugh. While Barrett may have cringed, O'Brien probably congratulated the *Orange and Black* for its handling of a bit of tomfoolery. The fun-loving young professor had a hand, too, in a spoof publication known as the *Earthquake*. It was published in connection with one of the big campus events of the pre-World War I years, the Harvest Carnival, a fund-raising benefit for the *Redskin*, started in the fall of 1914 and continued yearly until shortly after 1921. It evolved into the annual homecoming celebration. The 1915 carnival was typical. Both afternoon and evening were given over to "fun and frolic." Festivities opened with

EARTHQUAKE

| NINTH ERUPTION | MAY, 1920 | | PRICELESS |

LET'S BOOST A. & M.

Cut Down the Swivel Chair Salary. Hire Coaches for Chess Players.

DORM INVADED

Girls in Pink Stolen From Beds.

SOCIETY

COURT ITEMS

BOLSHEVISTIC MOVE

Hits Football Squad. Football May be Eliminated At A. & M.

BLOODY AFFAIR

Lewis and Moorehouse Out on Bond of $550.

Students studying journalism under Harry O'Brien enjoyed the "spoof" editions they published as part of the fall and spring carnivals on campus. They produced the *Earthquake*, which poked fun at both student leaders and faculty members.

a parade at 11 a.m. with floats representing the different academic departments. A balloon ascension was the first attraction of the evening. Edward C. Gallagher and John Dean, both instructors in the athletic department, were the stars of a one-ring circus with 100 clowns. There were sack and potato races and 50-yard dashes. Prizes were given to the winner of each race. Only high school participants were eligible. Everyone was expected to climb the greased pole and to catch the greased pig.

Each college class was known by its dress or action. The seniors carried canes, the juniors wore black bow ties, the sophomores wore masks, the freshmen donned suits of green, and preps wore overalls.

As a leader, Edwin Barrett kept a low profile. A colleague who knew him well said that he made no great show of his work. He performed "quietly, steadily, effectively, and influentially—without fanfare, but always with solid and measurable results." He was easy to work for, but hard to satisfy; his standards were reasonable, but his insistence that they be lived up to by his staff was inexorable. Although he was not a productive scholar as the publish-or-perish school of academicians would measure results, the Barrett-Ryan tests, circulated in the millions, probably did more to improve English composition than a library full of scholarly articles. He was not a brilliant teacher, but no student earned a grade without a sound and thoroughgoing knowledge of the course's content. Gentleness characterized his approach.[40]

In 1914, the Barretts and their two sons left for Kansas and a job that would last for thirty years. The work of the English department had been successful, but he saw signs of political interference with the progress of the college. He accepted a position at the Emporia State Teachers College and so avoided the trying conditions Oklahoma A. and M. would face in the 1914-15 academic year. In his administration of the English department at Emporia there was a kind of Lincolnian simplicity and strength. His staff was made to know at once that there was a difficult and demanding job to be done, and that it must be done by strong and fundamental means—by conscientious teaching and by old-fashioned, hard-working learning on the part of the students. No other "methods" or "approaches" were ever mentioned. Ingenuity, experimentation and communicativeness were essential, he told his faculty, if they expected to get the job done.[41]

Barrett was convinced that organizing teachers of English was essential to progress in the field. While at Kirksville, he had helped organize the Missouri Society of Teachers of English. He repeated with a state organization for English teachers while at Oklahoma A. and M. Later, he was one of the founders and leaders of the Kansas Association of Teachers of English, which he served as president on two occasions. He also was a founder of the National Council of Teachers of English and served on various committees in the council for more than three decades.

He exerted a wide and stimulating influence upon English teaching at both the high school and college levels.[42]

In addition, the college administration relied on him when it had a printing job calling for taste and quality craftsmanship. When vacations from class work came, he often could be found at work in the printing plant. He felt deep satisfaction in turning out distinctive printing. He was a man of many skills. During his long tenure at Emporia, he was at various times director of publicity; sponsor of the campus newspaper, the *Bulletin*; freshman advisor; chairman of the Catalog Committee; and a member of both the Curriculum Committee and the Committee of Seven, with whose guidance President Butcher managed the institution.[43]

Meanwhile, the work in journalism at Oklahoma A. and M. continued as the 1913-14 academic year moved along. The English and public speaking courses remained essentially the same, the only change being the addition of Shakespeare to replace a course on English poets. Seldomridge, Tieje, and Swink had left the faculty. They were replaced by Isadore Samuels and J. Emerson Nye. O'Brien continued to handle the embryonic journalism work.[44] Oklahoma A. and M. was shifting from the old farm-oriented quarter system to the semester system. The change reflected the Stillwater college's growing sophistication. The 8 a-b-c type of listing had been replaced in the 1914-15 catalog by a more informative numbering system. Numerous courses had been added college-wide to reflect the demands of increasing enrollments. Rockey was listed as associate professor and acting head, and his top assistant was O'Brien, now holding the rank of instructor. While public speaking was still the department's responsibility, it no longer was part of the English unit's title. With the shift to the semester system, O'Brien's course had been reduced from five to three hours of theory per week. Commerce and Marketing students now were required to take the course along with the young women in domestic science and arts.[45]

New faces on the faculty were Albert H. Nelson, Lawrence A. Wachs, Mary Bell Barlow, and Nellie Rockey, Noble W. Rockey's sister. The catalog for the year showed the first solid growth in journalism offerings, with a rudimentary curriculum beginning to take shape. Fourteen English, four public speaking and four journalism courses were listed. All of the courses were grouped together and listed sequentially. The journalism courses were English 203, News Writing; English 204, Magazine Writing; English 301, Editorial and Publicity Work; and English 302, Feature and Publicity Writing. Another course, English 205-206, placed a strong emphasis on current events.[46]

Among the newcomers, Nelson would play a journalistic role. A native of Wolcott, Indiana, he was twenty-three years old and straight out of the master's program at Wabash College in Indiana. His thesis was titled "The Historical Point of View in English Literary Criticism from

1800-1832." As an undergraduate at Wabash, he was elected to Phi Beta Kappa and held the Ophelia Fowler-Duhme Fellowship in English literature in his senior year. He not only compiled an outstanding academic record, but was one of the college's most active students in extracurricular affairs. He was in the Cross Country Club, treasurer of the Dramatics Club, represented the junior class in track, served as president of both the Caliopean Literary Society and the Prohibition Association, had a part in the Greek play all four years, and served on the *Wabash Magazine* board. Nelson was on the committee in charge of the "Media" of Euripides, the Greek play during his senior year, in which he won the role of Aegeus, King of Athens. Wabash had drawn widespread attention for this annual event. "Electra," in which Nelson played in his junior year, had gained attention in *The Theater*, a national magazine.[47]

It seems likely that Nelson was recommended by Rockey and elected by the Oklahoma A. and M. board because of his interest and apparent competence in literature. He had no professional journalistic experience to offer. In his three years on campus, he strongly supported student activities, and was popular with students in the classroom. They had nicknamed him "Bat" for no apparent reason. Nelson was especially interested in campus YMCA activities throughout his years at Oklahoma A. and M. Following O'Brien's departure a few months later, he would fill that important gap in the journalism program.[48]

O'Brien was popular with his students, most of whom had no plans for a full-time journalism career. They merely wanted to learn writing skills that would aid them in reaching farmers, homemakers, and other special-interest groups as they pursued work as county agents or in

COURTESY ESTHER ROCKEY JONES

Picnics were popular with the faculty families in the Department of English and Public Speaking, whether in town or out. The Noble W. Rockeys sometimes invited the faculty to their home. Picnics also were held in a scenic spot near the Cimarron River in the Ripley countryside.

scientific or technical fields. To some, a required journalism course was distasteful—a demand that was resented. But O'Brien had a knack for involving students, and his approach was vigorous and fresh. Soon, even those who saw little value in such courses were won over. The word around campus was that O'Brien was a good teacher. The young Ohioan would open his lecture with the same words each day, even before he reached the lectern. He would stride in facing the class and all but shout out the single-word questions "Who? What? When? Where?" as he moved through the classroom door.[49]

O'Brien, along with most of the faculty of his day, believed in practical experience for his students. When a class exercise in news or feature writing was well done, he would pass it on to the *Orange and Black* or encourage the writer to do so himself, hoping this might inspire him to join the student newspaper staff. In some cases, stories were sent to the college publicity office for evaluation and possible distribution to one or more state newspapers. Occasionally they were mailed directly to off-campus publications. Assignments were, whenever possible, geared to the student's own major field. O'Brien knew that writers work best at the things they know best.[50]

He quickly involved himself in campus activities. There were no fraternities or sororities, but two campus literary societies flourished, and he took a special interest in both. One society would "pump" him to get a tip on what the other would do in an upcoming debate, but he played no favorites. When consulted by students, as he often was, he would emphasize the importance of substance as well as delivery. He knew the value of research as the basis for persuasion. Nevertheless, declamatory techniques were considered important and O'Brien would sharpen the delivery of prospective debaters by having them memorize and deliver, with gestures, Marc Antony's oration at the death of Caesar.

He taught students to avoid filling their speeches with "and uhs" and to move their hands naturally rather than with exaggerated gestures. Elizabeth Oursler Taylor would recall that he made it a practice to "point out our weak points, our selection of words, the formation of our sentences, and to [evaluate] the points we were trying to make." He emphasized that it was unwise to cover too many different points in a speech. Rather, he advised his young friends, "be sure of the main points you want to make, and then put them down—carefully." The young Ohioan, scarcely older than some of his charges, generally was gentle and kind in his criticism, both inside the classroom and out. He enjoyed helping students who sought him out. But when the occasion called for toughness, he could be tough in a quiet way.

Further evidence of his interest in helping students was the fact that O'Brien coached a small circle of writers who had formed a club. It started with about fifteen students, later leveling off at about half that number.

The group met in various Stillwater homes. His generally tactful and unabrasive criticism at these meetings could be biting, though restrained, especially when a matter of ethics was involved. It was customary for the members to read their works for the appraisal of all the students present, to be followed by the professor's remarks. One coed read a particularly professional article that drew high praise. O'Brien listened to the group's flattering remarks, then finally commented: "Yes, that's a good story. I read it in the *Century* magazine."[51]

He urged students to write at every opportunity. One said, "He always encouraged us to write our thoughts—particularly the *new* thoughts we would have." He often suggested keeping a diary or daily journal. He felt that this, if thoughtfully done, was valuable writing practice.[52]

Despite his youthfulness (or, perhaps, because of it) he was sought out as a chaperon. Yost Lake, seven miles northeast of Stillwater, was a popular site for student recreation, but a picnic or party there required a chaperon. Some mothers thought such a young faculty member was not equal to the task, but Professor O'Brien served in that capacity more than once. The young men and women on these occasions found him to be both strict and alert, despite the concerns of questioning Stillwater matrons.[53]

Some professors of that era used sarcasm in the classroom to establish their superiority. This was not O'Brien's style. He was easy going, "a quiet sort of fellow with sparkling eyes." Having a crush on a young professor then, as now, was fairly common among coeds, and many a girl in his classes was infatuated with him. He was both intelligent and well educated, but he never went out of his way to impress his classes with his learning. Said one admirer, reflecting upon the teachers she had had at both the undergraduate and graduate levels: "My land, how he stands out as *the* teacher."[54] Jesse J. Canfield, one of O'Brien's students during the Oklahoma A. and M. days, remembered him as a rather small, wiry individual and a good teacher. Another contrasted him with Freeman E. Miller, O'Brien being someone students could approach easily while Miller was said to be "rigid and standoffish."[55]

O'Brien was not a lecturing professor. Rather, he encouraged class discussion. To provoke discussion, he sometimes used unusual methods. For example, he thought it would be a novel idea if his sophomore class nominated a candidate for the presidency of the agricultural student body. Joseph L. Robinson was one of those in O'Brien's classroom when the idea was broached. He was nominated as a byproduct of this class discussion and was elected. O'Brien also encouraged Robinson to try out for the debating team. After some gentle prodding, Robinson did. He became an outstanding member of the Tri-State team during his sophomore, junior, and senior years. Robinson not only took a journalism course under O'Brien at Oklahoma A. and M. but later enrolled as a graduate student in a journalism class taught by O'Brien at Iowa State College. He recalled that O'Brien used the same teaching methods on both campuses. He also challenged his students by giving them something extra occasionally, such as a stimulating guest speaker. One of these at Iowa State was Henry A. Wallace, an agricultural journalist and economist who later served in two cabinet posts and as vice-president of the United States under Franklin D. Roosevelt.[56]

Throughout his teaching career, early and late, O'Brien waged war against the word *very*. He detested its use, recommending that his students use the word *damn* instead. If they did that, he said, the editor would always delete damn and their writing would be improved. There is good evidence that students at Oklahoma A. and M., Iowa State and Ohio State all had this lesson drilled into them. One Oklahoma A. and M. student, more than seventy years after she had sat in his class, confessed that "I never write the word *very* that I don't remember him."[57]

O'Brien's role in this narrative is necessarily limited for the most part to his years at Oklahoma A. and M. College. However, his later work adds clarity to his brief stay in Stillwater. That brief stay had had an impact upon many Oklahoma A. and M. students and upon the future of journalism in the vigorous new state. His students were sad to see him leave, for he was a caring individual who participated fully in campus life. Balanced against this emotional tug were several things: Iowa State's more extensive program in agricultural journalism, its prestige in this growing field, and the greater freelance opportunities the richly endowed and older agricultural state afforded. These were attractions too

In the twilight of his long career as journalist and teacher, Harry R. O'Brien served as garden editor for the *Columbus Dispatch*, in Columbus, Ohio. He also was a part-time journalism teacher at Ohio State University.

strong to resist. Nevertheless, his tenure there was destined to last only one year longer than at Stillwater. After only four years, the last as acting department head while Frederick W. Beckman was overseas in YMCA work, he moved into what would be his lifetime niche as a writer and speaker.[58]

At Iowa State, O'Brien and Beckman co-authored the first book on agricultural journalism. In later editions, Blair Converse joined in the book's revision, and it became a national standard on land-grant campuses as *Technical Journalism*.[59] The Iowa State years were challenging ones for O'Brien. A humanitarian by nature, he was both encouraging and helpful. Students there felt at ease with him just as had those at Oklahoma A. and M. One of his 1916 students recalled that he was "beloved by all journalism students," especially by the coeds. He encouraged young women to prepare for journalism in spite of the fact that it was largely a male-dominated profession. Beckman also encouraged women's aspirations in the field. While acting head at Iowa State, O'Brien took the lead in bringing to the campus a chapter of Theta Sigma Phi, now known as Women In Communications, Incorporated.[60]

An illustration of how helpful he could be occurred during a humor magazine controversy. The Theta Sigs sought to join talents with Sigma Delta Chi, then a professional journalism society restricted to men, in producing the campus humor magazine, *The Green Gander*. Their offer was "scornfully turned down." The coeds, their egos crushed, turned to Professor O'Brien for help. He set about establishing the Theta Sigs in a great venture: creating a competing magazine. "He inspired us to hours of hard work and we produced, successfully, *The Emerald Goose*. After a few issues, the members of Sigma Delta Chi relented and begged us to join them on the *Gander*," one of his students recalled years later.

Another example illustrates the concern he showed for students and was typical of his Oklahoma days as well as those in Ames. For two years, he planned and arranged for a booth at the Iowa State Fair where students presided in an effort to gain subscriptions for the *Iowa Agriculturist*, the *Iowa Engineer*, and the *Iowa Homemaker*, all magazines written and edited by students combining journalism with technical specialties. Four students—two women and two men—made up the sales force. The student booth was in a corner of the big tent housing the display of Iowa State's Extension Service. Dormitory quarters for the four were in a corner of the Extension Service's living-tent. All had been arranged by O'Brien, who supervised the week's activity. His arrangements had included a trip up to Manchester in northeast Iowa to assure a coed's parents that she would be "properly chaperoned and cared for while at the State Fair."[61]

But O'Brien's impact upon the field was only beginning. He was to become even more widely recognized as his career unfolded. More than four decades of productive journalism stretched out before him as he left Iowa State College in 1919. Ahead lay forty years as a staff writer for *Country Gentleman*, thirty-one years as writer of the popular "Diary of a Plain Dirt Gardener" in *Better Homes and Gardens*, development of a business known as the Four O'Clock Garden Nursery in Worthington, Ohio, twenty-two years as garden columnist for the *Columbus Dispatch*, and an extensive speaking career that took him to all parts of the country at the request of women's groups, garden clubs and horticultural organizations. In one seven-year period he spoke to 120 clubs in seventeen states before more than 25,000 people, traveling 50,000 miles. He was active in five educational and scientific societies and averaged 15,000 to 20,000 miles a year most of his adult life gathering material for magazine articles and delivering his gospel of the joys of gardening to various organizations along the way.[62]

In one year, in addition to his work for *Country Gentleman* and *Better Homes and Gardens*, twenty-two articles appeared under his pen names in other magazines of national distribution. Despite this flurry of activity, he could not get teaching out of his blood. From 1925 until 1958, with the exception of two years, he taught at nearby Ohio State University. He returned for another year in 1960 to close out what he had started when he taught one of Oklahoma A. and M.'s earlier full-term journalism courses nearly half a century earlier. He retired once more in 1961—eight years before his death—after having sent many of his students into prestigious executive positions in journalism.[63]

By the time he had returned to his alma mater, O'Brien's professional depth was apparent in his teaching. Ralph Hamilton, former director of public information at Oklahoma State University, took his first journalism under O'Brien at Ohio State and credited him with whetting his appetite for a career in communications. O'Brien was listed as a lecturer in the School of Journalism. His course in technical journalism may have been the only one he taught at that time, for his other pursuits placed heavy demands upon him. It was a rather casual class, Hamilton recalled. The lectures were informal but O'Brien communicated clearly, just as he had at Oklahoma A. and M. from 1912 to 1915. The points he made about journalistic writing and reporting were simple and few in number and they were easily understood and easy to remember.[64]

He had a peculiarity in his grading system. Poorly-done or unacceptable assignments were given a "37," but he never explained the reason for his having selected that figure. Along with this peculiarity was a droll sense of humor, which he often injected into his lectures. His immense experience in seeking out stories, in interviewing, in writing, and in working with publications made his lectures informative and useful. He would constantly draw upon his experience to give accounts of how he had found a story or how he interviewed a subject. No doubt based upon one of his interviews, he suggested that students avoid wearing lapel pins or other insignia to show affiliation with an organization. The interviewee might not like that organization, he advised, thus putting the interviewer at a disadvantage in establishing a good reporter-subject relationship.[65]

Those glimpses at O'Brien's post-Stillwater years give numerous insights into the personality that played such an important part in early campus journalism at Oklahoma A. and M. Encouraged by Professor Barrett, who had President Connell's approval, O'Brien soon saw a curriculum begin to take shape. He joined in this effort with Barrett and Rockey, who was to rise from the rank of departmental assistant—the same rank initially held by O'Brien—to professor and head of the Department of English. By the time O'Brien left to join the faculty at Iowa State he held the rank of assistant professor, and journalism courses no longer passed as composition courses. They were given titles that clearly delineated them as journalistic.[66]

Rockey himself, years later, provided a brief history for this exciting period, which began one year after his arrival in 1911. Several "new, young and very active instructors" had been added in 1912, he would recall. With Seldomridge's departure, the work in public speaking had been divided among the new men, who increased the work in debate, leading later to the college's participation in intercollegiate competition. The rationale for Professor Barrett's introduction of news writing, Rockey said, was to provide a practical objective for what had been traditional theme writing.

In 1913-14 a new man—J. Emerson Nye—was added for public speaking, but he was interested only in dramatic readings. The remaining speech courses were divided among others. Nye lasted only a year. News writing was increased, but also was divided among instructors. Rockey, now an associate professor, had his share in it. As acting head of the department following Barrett's resignation, Rockey had decided that it was time to put public speaking and journalism upon a more solid footing. He had excellent men for both subjects. He transferred all public speaking to Isadore Samuels and most of the journalism to O'Brien. The result was excellent, he recalled. Interest in both subjects grew rapidly. These promising developments soon were slowed as politics again affected the college, ending Rockey's year as department head but not his views about the respective roles of speech and journalism.[67]

Journalism finally had arrived. Barrett's leadership in giving Oklahoma A. and M. its first journalism curriculum seems plausible, for his catalog copy likely would have been submitted before he left for Emporia, where he was destined to become the "grand old man of the campus."[68] The program that Barrett, Rockey, and O'Brien had worked so hard for was in place. The future for journalism at Oklahoma A. and M. looked promising.

Endnotes

1. *Annual Catalog, Oklahoma A. and M. College, 1901-1902*, p. 6; *Annual Catalog, Oklahoma A. and M. College, 1902-1903*, p. 61; *Annual Catalog, Oklahoma A. and M. College, 1903-1904*, p. 62; *Annual Catalog, Oklahoma A. and M. College, 1904-1905*, p. 68; *Annual Catalog, Oklahoma A. and M. College, 1905-1906*, p. 7; *Annual Catalog, Oklahoma A. and M. College, 1906-1907*, p. 104; *Annual Catalog, Oklahoma A. and M. College, 1907-1908*, p. 124; *Annual Catalog, Oklahoma A. and M. College, 1908-1909*, p. 138; *Annual Catalog, Oklahoma A. and M. College, 1909-1910*, p. 161; *Annual Catalog, Oklahoma A. and M. College, 1910-1911*; *Annual Catalog, Oklahoma A. and M. College, 1911-1912*, p. 166; *Annual Catalog, Oklahoma A. and M. College, 1912-1913*, p. 163; *Annual Catalog, Oklahoma A. and M. College, 1913-1914*, p. 180; *Annual Catalog, Oklahoma A. and M. College, 1914-1915*, p. 174; Undated clipping in Minutes, Webster Literary Society, 16 October 1894, Special Collections, Edmon Low Library, Oklahoma State University, Stillwater, Oklahoma; Author telephone interview with John Perry, 22 November 1991. McReynolds came to Stillwater with his parents, the Reverend and Mrs. S. J. McReynolds, in 1894. He was a leader in pioneer music circles and composed several numbers, including a song dedicated to Captain Carter C. Hanner. He served as chemist at the experiment station from 1899 until 1902, then moved to California. He married Ida Calgari, Guadalupe, California, in 1905, soon after becoming owner of the *Guadalupe Gazette* in 1904. He also published papers in Lomoc (circa 1904), King City (circa 1907-1914), and Santa Maria, California (date unknown), returning to Guadalupe in 1914.

2. *Newsletter '80* (Ames: Department of Journalism and Mass Communication, Iowa State University), p. 11; *Technical Journalism at Iowa State College 1905-1955* (Ames: Department of Technical Journalism, Iowa State College, 1955), pp. 1, 2; Loretta Goodwin, "The Origin and Development of Journalism Education at Iowa State University" (Master of Science thesis, Iowa State University, 1984), pp. 9-12; "Departmental History" (File: 1991-92 Accreditation Disk, June 25, 1991, 21:21), p. 3, and "Publications History" (File: 1991-92 Accreditation Disk, June 26, 1991, 17:02), p. 4, materials located at Iowa State University, Ames, Iowa, and sent to author; Tom Emmerson to Harry E. Heath Jr., 21 March 1992, School of Journalism and Broadcasting Centennial History Collection, Special Collections, Edmon Low Library.

3. *Annual Catalog, Oklahoma A. and M. College, 1912-1913*, pp. 96, 98.

4. *Stillwater Gazette*, 6 September 1912, p. 1; Oklahoma A. and M. College *Orange and Black*, 11 September 1912, pp. 1, 4, 25 September 1912, p. 4, 2 October 1912, p. 1.

5. *Stillwater Gazette*, 28 June 1912, p. 1, 12 July 1912, p. 1, 26 July 1912, p. 1, 4 October 1912, p. 1, 1 November 1912, p. 1, 8 November 1912, p. 1, 9 November 1912, p. 2; Robert E. Cunningham, *Stillwater Through the Years* (Stillwater, OK: Arts and Humanities Council of Stillwater, Oklahoma, Incorporated, 1974), p. 33.

6. *Orange and Black*, 18 September 1912, pp. 2, 4; *1913 Redskin*, pp. 9, 10, Oklahoma A. and M. College Yearbook; *Annual Catalog, Oklahoma A. and M. College, 1912-1913*, p. 96.

7. *Orange and Black*, 9 October 1912, p. 1; *Stillwater Gazette*, 18 April 1913, p. 1.

8. *Emporia Gazette*, 26 July 1944, p. 6.

9. *Emporia Gazette*, 26 July 1944, p. 6, 29 May 1939; *Bulletin*, Kansas State Teachers College, Emporia, 11 May 1934, p. 1.

10. *Bulletin*, Kansas State Teachers College, 11 May 1934, p. 1.

11. *Bulletin*, Kansas State Teachers College, 11 May 1934, p. 1.

12. *Bulletin of the First District Normal School*, Kirksville, Missouri, vol. 9, no. 1 (June 1909), pp. 61, 177.

13. P. O. Selby, *Kirksville Presbyterians* (Kirksville, MO: First Presbyterian Church, 1971), pp. 27, 33, 75; *Kirksville Normal School Index* (Kirksville, MO: 7 June 1912) p. 1.

14. *Kirksville Normal School Index*, 13 September 1912, p. 3.

15. Philip Reed Rulon, *Oklahoma State University—Since 1890*, (Stillwater: Oklahoma State University Press, 1975) pp. 123, 124; LeRoy H. Fischer, *Oklahoma State University Historic Old Central* (Stillwater: Oklahoma State University Press, 1988) p. 103.

16. *Annual Catalog, Oklahoma A. and M. College, 1911-1912*, pp. ix, 103; *Annual Catalog, Oklahoma A. and M. College, 1912-1913*, pp. viii, 96.

17. *Orange and Black*, 18 September 1912, p. 2, 15 November 1915, p. 2.

18. Edwin Emery and Joseph P. McKerns, *AEJMC: 75 Years in the Making* (Columbia, SC: Accrediting Council for Education in Journalism and Mass Communication, 1987), p. 3; Nancy Jane Wagner, "A History of the University of Oklahoma School of Journalism: The First Fifty Years 1913-1963" (Master of Arts thesis, University of Oklahoma, 1964), pp. 1-3.

19. *Annual Catalog, Oklahoma A. and M. College, 1912-1913*, p. 96.

20. See course descriptions for Rhetoric and Advanced Rhetoric in Annual Catalogs, Oklahoma A. and M. College, for years 1898-1899 through 1907-1908.

21. *Orange and Black*, 16 October 1912, p. 1.

22. *Orange and Black*, 19 February 1913, pp. 1, 4.

23. *Orange and Black*, 11 September 1912, p. 4; *1913 Redskin*, p. 109; *1913 Le Byeu*, Ohio Wesleyan University, p. 179; Sarah E. Niebuhr to Harry E. Heath Jr., 3 October 1990, School of Journalism and Broadcasting Centennial History Collection.

24. Noble Warren Rockey, untitled and undated handwritten historical review, 1911-1921, family papers of Esther Rockey Jones, pp. 1, 2, School of Journalism and Broadcasting Centennial History Collection; *Orange and Black*, 7 January 1914, p. 1.

25. *Orange and Black*, 3 October 1914, p. 4.

26. *1916 Aurora*, Heidelberg University, Tiffin, Ohio, p. 114; *1917 Aurora*, p. 28; *Kilikilik*, Heidelberg University, 28 September 1914, pp. 2, 3, 2 October 1916, p. 2; "Acts and Proceedings of the Board of Regents, Heidelberg University, 1903-1922," unpublished manuscript, pp. 238, 239, School of Journalism and Broadcasting Centennial History Collection; Alumni Card File, Ohio Wesleyan University; *Cincinnati Times-Star*, 21 March 1929, copy unpaged; *Cincinnati Post*, 6 December 1933, p. 4, 19 September 1935, copy unpaged; *The Torch*, Cincinnati, Ohio, December 1926, p. 7; Ohio Wesleyan University Alumni Records, 1951; *Ohio Wesleyan Magazine* (Autumn 1964), p. 80. After thirty years as a specialist in medical economics, Swink died in Good Samaritan Hospital, Cincinnati, on June 12, 1964.

27. Robert T. Chapel to Harry E. Heath Jr., 5 October 1988; biographical information sheet, University of Illinois (3 pages), 9 March 1911; *Announcement of Courses, University of Illinois*, September 1914, pp. 180-182, September 1915, pp. 183-185.

28. *1918 Alumni Directory*, University of Illinois, p. 401.

29. *1913 Redskin*, p. 185; *1918 Alumni Directory*, University of Illinois, p. 401.

30. *1910 Makio*, pp. 43, 71, 188-189, 214-215, 249, Ohio State University Yearbook; *Ohio State University Bulletin*, vol. 14, no. 26 (9 June 1910), page unnumbered; "Class Day," *Ohio State University [Alumni] Monthly* (July 1915), p. 12.

31. Biographical information sheet, Ohio State University News Bureau, 11 June 1938, School of Journalism and Broadcasting Centennial History Collection; *Columbus [Ohio] Dispatch*, 3 December 1967, p. 25A-2; *Orange and Black*, 11 September 1912, p. 2; *Annual Catalog, Oklahoma A. and M. College, 1912-1913*, p. 98.

32. *The Universal Standard Encyclopedia*, vol. 17 (New York, NY: Unicorn Publications, Incorporated, 1955), pp. 6275, 6279, 6280; George Bridges to Harry E. Heath Jr., 1 October 1990, School of Journalism and Broadcasting Centennial History Collection.

33. Rulon, pp. 141, 142.

34. Emery and McKerns, p. 11.

35. *Columbus Dispatch*, 15 April 1938, p. B-7, 3 December 1967, p. 25A-2; Transcript for Mable Caldwell, Office of the Registrar, Oklahoma State University; Author interview with Charles Dutreau, 27 October 1990, Stillwater, Oklahoma; *Annual Catalog, Oklahoma A. and M. College, 1912-1913*, p. 98; *Columbus Dispatch*, 3 December 1967, p. 25A-2.

36. *Annual Catalog, Oklahoma A. and M. College, 1912-1913*, pp. viii, 96, 98; Shirilyn Dehls to Glen Jones to Harry E. Heath Jr. [8 October 1990], and Robin Lacy to Harry E. Heath Jr., 4 October 1990, in School of Journalism and Broadcasting Centennial History Collection; Rulon, p. 147; Fischer, p. 160; Minutes, Oklahoma State Board of Agriculture, 23 September 1912, Special Collections, Edmon Low Library.

37. *Annual Catalog, Oklahoma A. and M. College, 1913-1914*, p. 96.

38. *Annual Catalog, Oklahoma A. and M. College, 1913-1914*, p. 98.

39. *Orange and Black*, 5 February 1913, p. 1.

40. *Orange and Black,* 20 April 1915, p. 1; Doris Dellinger, *A History of the Oklahoma State University Intercollegiate Athletics* (Stillwater: Oklahoma State University, 1987), p. 71; Roy Dunham, editor, *Qualities of Greatness* (Emporia: Kansas State Teachers College, 1963), p. 60; *Bulletin,* Kansas State Teachers College, 11 May 1934, p. 1.

41. Dunham, pp. 60, 61; Rockey, p. 3.

42. Dunham, pp. 60, 61; *Emporia Gazette,* 26 July 1944, p. 6; *Bulletin,* Kansas State Teachers College, 11 May 1934, p. 1.

43. *Emporia Gazette,* 26 July 1944, p. 6; Dunham, p. 61.

44. Rockey, pp. 2-6; *Annual Catalog, Oklahoma A. and M. College, 1913-1914,* pp. v, vii, viii, 101, 103.

45. *Annual Catalog, Oklahoma A. and M. College, 1914-1915,* pp. 83-86.

46. *Annual Catalog, Oklahoma A. and M. College, 1914-1915,* pp. 83-85.

47. Johanna Herring to Harry E. Heath Jr., 6 October 1988, School of Journalism and Broadcasting Centennial History Collection; *Wabash Magazine* (June 1913), pp. 456, 457, 496, 497 and unnumbered page with senior picture. The *Wabash* was a quarterly publication and served as a yearbook in June.

48. "Data on Faculty of Michigan State College 1934," mimeographed form completed by Nelson for MSC news service, School of Journalism and Broadcasting Centennial History Collection; *Orange and Black,* 23 March 1918, p. 3, 12 April 1919, p. 3, 20 June 1916.

49. Author interview with Haskell Pruett, 21 October 1987, Stillwater, Oklahoma.

50. Pruett interview.

51. Author interview with Elizabeth Oursler Taylor, 23 October 1987, Stillwater, Oklahoma.

52. Pruett interview.

53. Taylor interview.

54. Taylor interview.

55. Jesse J. Canfield to Harry E. Heath Jr., 31 May 1987, School of Journalism and Broadcasting Centennial History Collection; Taylor interview.

56. Joseph L. Robinson to Harry E. Heath Jr., undated 1988, School of Journalism and Broadcasting Centennial History Collection; *Orange and Black,* 12 February 1916, p. 2.

57. Ralph Hamilton to Harry E. Heath Jr., undated 1987, School of Journalism and Broadcasting Centennial History Collection; Taylor interview.

58. Rodney Fox to Harry E. Heath Jr., undated 1988; *Iowa State College General Catalogue, 1916-1917,* pp. 19, 101; *Iowa State College General Catalogue, 1917-1918,* pp. 20, 107; *Iowa State College General Catalogue, 1918-1919,* pp. 21, 93; *Stillwater Gazette,* 20 August 1915, p. 8; Orange and Black, 17 May 1919, p. 1.

59. Frederick W. Beckman, Harry R. O'Brien, and Blair Converse, *Technical Journalism* (Ames: Iowa State College Press, 1942), throughout.

60. Ruth P. Seaward to Harry E. Heath Jr., 4 March 1988, School of Journalism and Broadcasting Centennial History Collection.

61. Ruth P. Seaward to Harry E. Heath Jr., 4 March 1988, School of Journalism and Broadcasting Centennial History Collection.

62. *Columbus Dispatch,* Columbus, Ohio, 15 April 1938, p. B-7; *Columbus Citizen-Journal,* 17 March 1969, p. 2.

63. Ralph Hamilton to Harry E. Heath Jr., undated 1987, School of Journalism and Broadcasting Centennial History Collection; *Columbus Citizen-Journal,* 17 March 1969, p. 2.

64. Ralph Hamilton to Harry E. Heath Jr., undated 1987. School of Journalism and Broadcasting Centennial History Collection.

65. Ralph Hamilton to Harry E. Heath Jr., undated 1987. School of Journalism and Broadcasting Centennial History Collection.

66. *Annual Catalog, Oklahoma A. and M. College, 1914-1915,* pp. 83-85; *Stillwater Gazette,* 20 August 1915, p. 8; *Orange and Black,* 17 May 1919, p. 1.

67. Rockey, pp. 2, 3.

68. *Bulletin,* Kansas State Teachers College, 11 May 1934, p. 1.

8 A Friendly Fight Over Territory

A lost figure in campus journalistic lore is Harold W. Moorhouse, who came to Oklahoma A. and M. College in 1913 as a professor of political economy and social science. Less than a year later he became the first dean of an upgraded academic program, the School of Commerce and Marketing. In addition, he carried the title of professor of political economy and marketing. In his six years on the campus he became a favorite of students—the *1916 Redskin* was dedicated to him—and a leader among faculty members. He played a major role in developing the curriculum for what today has evolved into a highly respected College of Business Administration, but he also found time to serve as chairman of the athletic board and to become a founding father and twice president of the Redlands Club, an organization made up of faculty members and business leaders. Club members opened their new home at Fourth and Knoblock with a "Ladies Night" in early June 1916, featuring music, dancing, cards, pool, and billiards. Ice cream, wafers, and punch were the evening's refreshments.[1]

Moorhouse is significant to journalism at Oklahoma A. and M. College in that he added advertising and related courses to the School of Commerce and Marketing and openly advertised in the campus newspaper for students to prepare for a journalism career in his school. No doubt he was aware of journalism's early ties to commerce programs on a number of campuses. Journalism faculty members and those in the Oklahoma A. and M. business program worked closely together during the Clement E. Trout years, jointly budgeting for courses where the two disciplines overlapped. But at the time that Moorhouse made his first

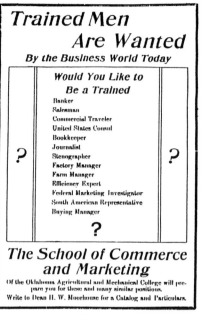
As competition among academic departments grew, the School of Commerce and Marketing turned to the *Orange and Black* to recruit students for careers in various fields, including journalism. This was an outgrowth of studies in marketing and advertising that Harold W. Moorhouse had introduced. Science and literature responded with a competing ad.

move to promote journalism, some faculty members in the School of Science and Literature must have been wary, for journalism courses were under the wing of the Department of English, which was in the province of the science and literature dean. Both schools ran advertisements listing journalism as a career option. It was not until the arrival of Charles L. Allen, a man with a national reputation in advertising and management, that business no longer provided funding for split appointments with journalism. By then, marketing techniques had advanced in sophistication, and the College of Business believed it could concentrate upon marketing and give advertising to the Department of Journalism.[2]

Moorhouse, a studious and personable young man, had been a popular student at Beloit College, a Wisconsin school well regarded for its excellent liberal arts program. He had been third baseman on the 1903 baseball team, and his teammates had nicknamed him "Tommy." For the following three years he had played center field, his last year serving as team captain. His .292 batting average in his first year had slipped to .111 in his last. He had come to Beloit from his home in Breckenridge, Missouri, after studies at Kidder Institute. He was a member of Sigma Chi fraternity and had served as local editor of the *Round Table* during his junior year. He gained additional journalistic experience in his senior year on *The Codex*, the Beloit yearbook, with a byline on his review of the 1906 baseball season. In addition, the senior section of the yearbook indicated that he had participated in a traditional Greek play and was treasurer of three organizations: Archaean Union, Delian, and the class of 1906, in which he received the B.A. degree. He specialized in economics under Professor Robert C. Chafin.[3]

Following his graduation from Beloit, Moorhouse spent a summer session doing graduate work at the University of Wisconsin. Then he began work for the Farmers and Merchants Bank of Imperial, California, Pioneer Farm, where he remained until coming to Oklahoma A. and M. at the age of twenty-nine. While in the Imperial Valley he helped start an agricultural college at Heber, California. He loved the outdoors and both Wisconsin's lakes and California's beaches tugged at his loyalties.[4]

California was a young man's field of dreams. Moorhouse quickly took advantage of his opportunities for leadership. He engaged in general stock farming in the Imperial Valley while taking on other major responsibilities. He was a director of the Imperial Farmers and Merchants Bank, the Imperial Farmers' Marketing Corporation and the Imperial Creamery Association. He appeared to be filling a deep-felt need for leadership in the area, adding to his other responsibilities the presidency of the Imperial Valley Farmers' Association. As if these roles were not enough, he was elected to the state legislature in 1909, where he served for two years.

His political career ended because a new opportunity beckoned. John H. Connell was president of the National Marketing Association, in which Moorhouse was active. Connell was impressed by the transplanted Missourian whose know-how stimulated the association. He suggested that Moorhouse join the Oklahoma A. and M. College faculty. Connell was overhauling the college's academic structure, and Moorhouse's training and experience in economics and marketing held promise for a new program that would be highly beneficial to agriculture. Connell no doubt dangled this exciting possibility as the "carrot" that would bring Moorhouse to Oklahoma. The president, nearing the end of his tenure, was successful. Moorhouse declined to seek reelection. He cut his ties to the Imperial Valley and left for Stillwater.

Connell's confidence in Moorhouse was confirmed. In the academic years 1914-15 and 1915-16, enrollment in the School of Commerce and Marketing had shown a higher percentage of growth than any school at Oklahoma A. and M. Despite this record, the program was so new that many, including Judge Joseph Green Ralls, an ex officio member of the State Board of Education, wondered if it could justify its existence. Moorhouse was quick to respond with copious statements as to the program's value, citing a wide variety of jobs students could prepare for,

Harold W. Moorhouse became the first
dean of the School of Commerce and
Marketing, where he established the
college's first work in advertising in 1914.

including that of industrial journalist, an idea that Clement Trout later
would devote years to promoting, both on and off campus. Moorhouse,
a perceptive educator, stressed the nation's economic problems with
particular attention to foreign as well as domestic markets.[5]

Moorhouse was clean-cut and slender. He looked as though he could
put on his Beloit baseball uniform once more and trot jauntily onto the
field. He was careful about his appearance on campus and off, preferring
both jacket and vest, white shirt, and a black bow tie. He was clean-shaven
and well groomed, with regular features, sharp but not too sharp. That he
was popular with both students and faculty was apparent. The senior
class, which had responsibility for the yearbook, paid him this tribute:
"To our great friend, H. W. Moorhouse, universally conceded to be the
head of his profession, admired by his followers, and esteemed by his
pupils, we dedicate the Redskin of 1916."[6]

Moorhouse, like Freeman E. Miller, enjoyed having student groups
visit his home. He entertained seniors on a pleasant May day in 1916 with
a lawn party at which the young women hid their food boxes and baskets
among bushes and vines to be sought by the black-robed senior men
following a ceremony in which they knelt with bowed heads as the food
was hidden. Coffee and ice cream were served as the chaperons—
including President and Mrs. James W. Cantwell and Dr. and Mrs. L. L.
Lewis—joined in the festivities.[7]

It is not difficult to see why the popular professor-dean was widely known and admired on campus. Beginning in 1914 he regularly served on the athletic council. He also was on the standing committees on grades and reports, student plays and social entertainments (chairman), catalog and college publications, and rules and regulations. Later he was added to the courses of study, library and advanced standing committees. In 1917 he was named chairman of the athletic council. As he assumed this responsibility he dropped some of his earlier committee work.[8]

Lacking better evidence, advertising instruction at Oklahoma A. and M. appears to have been the brainchild of Moorhouse. Early in the second half of the academic year 1912-13, he had joined the Department of Pedagogy, History, Political Economy and Social Science under John H. Bowers, who wore a second hat as dean of the Teachers' Normal Division. Before the catalog for the next year had been assembled by Walter Stemmons, editor of college publications, a School of Commerce and Marketing had been created with Moorhouse as dean. The new school included a Department of Political Economy and Marketing under Moorhouse, who, like Bowers, wore two hats. In the school's first year, the man from California had established a course entitled Markets and Marketing.[9]

The 1914-15 catalog, in which the first real curriculum in journalism appeared under Edwin R. Barrett's leadership, saw a considerably expanded School of Commerce and Marketing and a new numbering system. The Department of Political Economy and Marketing now was known as the Department of Economics and Marketing, still headed by Dean Moorhouse. It included 202 Elements of Marketing, 405 Salesmanship, and 410 Market Investigations. The Salesmanship course is significant, for it included instruction in advertising copy writing. An interesting note is that Moorhouse had introduced advertising as a unit in Salesmanship, just as Angelo C. Scott had introduced newspaper writing as a unit in his rhetoric courses.[10] It seems likely that the first instruction in advertising was given by Moorhouse himself.

In succeeding years, the Salesmanship course carried the numbers 416 and 312. Elements of Marketing became Principles of Marketing and then Principles of Commerce. In the 1919-20 catalog, the lineup was 202 Principles of Commerce, 311 Market Organization, and 312 Principles of Selling, the new name given to Salesmanship, which continued to include instruction in advertising copy writing. The advertising work at this time probably was handled by Lloyd M. Graves, who served from 1918 to 1921. Graves was appointed an assistant in commerce and marketing on August 25, 1918, upon the recommendation of President Cantwell. He was a 1914 arts and sciences graduate of the University of Oklahoma from Orlando, Oklahoma. He had been reporter for the Senate, a men's junior-senior literary society, and had served as president of both

A graduate of the University of Oklahoma, Lloyd M. Graves joined the faculty in 1918. Among his assignments was course work in advertising.

the Social Science Club and the Progressive Club. His senior picture in the *Sooner* depicted a serious-looking, neatly dressed young man with regular features and a full head of hair combed straight back. His three years were served under Moorhouse. Following Moorhouse's resignation, Graves departed as twenty-eight year old Henry F. Holtzclaw assumed the deanship in 1921. Along with Noble W. Rockey, Graves was one of eight faculty who fell under the "guillotine" in June of 1921.[11]

Moorhouse had begun to attract attention and was being wooed by offers from afar. Before he ended his connection with Oklahoma A. and M., however, he had planned a more important role for advertising in his school. Principles of Commerce had been dropped, but a new series of courses was to establish advertising more solidly in the curriculum. In addition to 311 Market Organization, Moorhouse had received approval for 312 Principles of Selling (3 credits), 313 Advertising (2 credits), and 425 The Psychology of Advertising and Selling (2 credits). Advertising was paralleling the growth of journalism, although on a slightly more modest scale.[12]

Moorhouse apparently felt that he must have stronger academic credentials, for he used the summers of 1918, 1919, and 1920 for studies at the University of Chicago. When he left Oklahoma A. and M. at the end of the 1919-1920 academic year, advertising was firmly in place. The program he had shaped appeared in the new catalog along with the name of his successor, Fred D. Merritt, acting dean and professor of economics.[13] Advertising was to remain in the business school for forty years, surviving through a series of organizational changes that finally would lead to what, in the centennial year, was known as the College of Business Administration.

One of the key faculty appointments in the fall of 1921 was thirty-five year old Avery L. Carlson, who was hired to teach advertising in addition to four other courses. He received his liberal arts baccalaureate in 1911 and his M.A. in economics in 1915, both from the University of Iowa. He followed these with postgraduate work in law at the University of Chicago, where he was granted the doctor of jurisprudence degree in 1918. Professor Carlson taught in Drake University's School of Commerce, Finance, and Journalism before coming to Oklahoma A. and M. The Drake catalog listed him on one page as an associate professor holding A.B. and J.D. degrees, but listed the A.M. and J.D. on another. The Drake yearbook faculty list for commerce and finance listed all three of his degrees. Students enjoyed Carlson, a heavy-set man who could handle a joke or a prank. On one occasion, a marketing student put a tack on his chair. He sat down to lecture, and remained seated as though nothing had happened. He knew how to play the game of one-up-manship. Before Carlson's three years at Oklahoma A. and M. had ended, he may have played a part in one of the world's first singing commercials. A member of the Men's Glee Club Quartet had written the Anglo American Drug Company with the suggestion that the quartet sing "Mrs. Winslow's Soothing Syrup" on the glee club's state tour and at the home concert. The number, written by a student identified only as Hamilton, had an "exquisite" melody and a "soothing" theme, the *Orange and Black* reported. The drug company sent the quartet a check for twenty-five dollars, creating a minor sensation on campus. Carlson later returned to his studies at the University of Iowa, where he was awarded the Ph.D. in economics on August 22, 1929.[14]

Oscar J. Merrell, who joined the faculty as a full professor in 1925, was to become the mainstay of advertising instruction for 26 years. He had received the B.S. degree from John Tarleton College, followed by B.A. and M.A. degrees from the University of Texas. His credentials included standing as a certified public accountant.

The University of Texas listed Merrell as a resident of University Hall from Stephenville, Texas, in 1910 and 1911. His senior yearbook picture carried the notation: "Your name should be silent Oscar." In 1912, in his first year of graduate work, he was living in Marlin and was "absent on leave." He had returned to Austin in 1913, was back in school part time, and lived at 203 East Fourteenth Street while teaching at Austin High School. The following year he had moved to 2207 Speedway in Austin, where he remained for the rest of his graduate studies. He received the M.A. in education, economics, and institutional history. His thesis was titled: "Commercial Education in Secondary Schools, with Special

Reference to Conditions in Texas."

University of Texas records show that Merrell was elected to Phi Delta Kappa, honorary education society, and that he had been a member of the Salton Club. Following his graduate studies, he taught full time in the commercial department at Austin High, where he also had administrative duties. The 1918 Austin city directory showed that he had taken a wife, Maggie, at some point between completion of his graduate work and 1918. They made their home at 2207 Lampasas. Later, and the date is unclear, the Merrells moved to Newark, Delaware, where O. J. taught at the University of Delaware. He was on the faculty there immediately before accepting his appointment at Oklahoma A. and M. College.[15]

Merrell is remembered and admired by many of his former students, some after seventy years. One recalled his tolerance and patience, another that he was "down to earth." If something funny came up in class, he would join in the laughter. Another alumnus saw him, in retrospect, as "a very lonesome man."

Some of his instructional methods were forward-looking and practical. He would send small groups of students to local stores as would-be buyers. They were instructed to listen carefully to the clerk's sales pitch, noting the "explanation of items of interest set forth that might be helpful to a prospective customer." Later the students would report on their findings, with an evaluation of the sales effectiveness of the clerk's presentation. This method gave the class clues as to points to stress in advertising copy.[16]

1922 REDSKIN

Avery L. Carlson, a widely educated man with a good sense of humor, replaced Lloyd M. Graves in 1921. His tenure lasted until 1924 when he left for doctoral work at the University of Iowa.

Merrell's classes were small enough for free exchange of ideas between teacher and students, and he commanded student attention with thoughtful discussion. Following class, a cluster of students usually would continue the discussion with him as they strolled from the room. While he followed his course outline, he often would include some of his personal experiences to illustrate points in the lesson. Students sometimes would challenge his accuracy, if not his truthfulness, when the account appeared to be beyond belief. His response would be, "I was just telling you that for purposes of illustration." To some, Merrell was brilliant, but the best of him did not always come out in his teaching.[17]

A measure of his relationship with students was the fact that they felt they could pull a prank on him without risking retribution. Once in a class in the northwest corner room on the second floor of Morrill Hall, the students decided to get him to cancel class. It was a blustery, cold winter day. Someone had the idea that if one north and one west window were raised, it would make the room too cold for class. One student acted as sentry, watching for Professor Merrell's arrival at the east end of the floor. When he appeared, the windows were lowered and each student was in his proper place as Merrell entered the room. As usual, he sat down at his desk. Then he buttoned his wool sweater and his suit coat over the sweater and proceeded to conduct his hour of class. "I thought then and still think that Professor Merrell surmised what had taken place, so he kept us in the room for a full, cold hour as punishment. I'm sure that he chuckled for the rest of the day."[18]

While some students saw him as the typical college professor, others thought he did not look or act the part. His hair was always hanging down over one eye, he spoke with a drawl and, to some, did not seem to fit. Behind his back, he was "Freight Train" to some of the students in his Transportation class. But, as one recalled, he was sharper than he appeared. He built and financed a home out of thin air at a time it was hard to do. He engaged in business ventures outside the classroom. He audited books for small firms and served as consultant to several clients. He also purchased real estate and built duplex homes near the college campus. He not only was teaching business courses but was brave enough to put into practice the subject matter he taught. In that sense, he was more involved in the community than most professors.[19]

Life for Merrell was, to use a cliche, no bed of roses. He had an invalid daughter who could neither walk nor talk. He would spend time with her each evening after his college day had ended, trying to bring laughter and happiness to her. Students who knew him best wondered how he could cope with the demands upon him at home. One older married student said his four-year-old daughter played with "Dolly May" by the hour. That pleased the Merrell family.

Another insight into Merrell's personality may be drawn from this vignette. One student who liked him called him Oscar rather than Professor Merrell. "It pleased him very much. He said he was tired of being called professor and never hearing his name."[20]

He was a congenial teacher who liked to linger after class to visit with the gaggle of students who inevitably wanted to follow up on some idea. They remembered him long after they had left to face life in the "real world."

During his long tenure, Merrell saw the competitiveness between deans controlling journalism and business diminish, finally blending into cooperative efforts. A prime example was the program in business journalism, through which many graduates—Max E. Stansbury, Joe Synar, D. Earl Newsom, Joe Taylor, Bruce Heydenburk, Gene Allen, Dorothy Harvey, Joe Woolard, and Warren Shull, to name a few—became leaders in journalism, broadcasting, advertising, promotion, and public relations. In 1942, the Department of Technical Journalism began to share the responsibility for advertising courses by a split-appointment arrangement. The first person on the split appointment was Donald D. Burchard, who taught in both commerce and journalism from 1942 through 1945. He was followed by Lemuel D. Groom from 1946 through 1959. Both were well accepted by students and faculty whether the degree was under Dean Schiller Scroggs or Dean Raymond D. Thomas and, during the last two years in commerce, Eugene Swearingen.

1926 REDSKIN

After O. J. Merrell arrived in 1925, the classes in advertising achieved stability. An energetic and popular classroom teacher, he used practical exercises to teach his students salesmanship, advertising, and marketing.

Harold Moorhouse no doubt would have taken a keen interest in the contributions of Carlson and Merrell to the development of advertising and marketing in the school he had founded. But his tenure did not overlap with either of them.

In the year following his departure from Oklahoma A. and M., Moorhouse studied at Northwestern University, where he was awarded the master of business administration degree in 1921, following up in the fall term with a seminar in economics. The School of Commerce at Northwestern, located in suburban Evanston, Illinois, no doubt led him to his next career stop. In 1921 he began a four-year period in Chicago. The American Farm Bureau Federation was setting up a research department and Moorhouse was chosen to head the new unit at $6,000 a year. He also carried the title of assistant federation director. In addition, he was a lecturer in Northwestern's commerce curriculum.[21] Harry R. O'Brien, who had left Oklahoma A. and M. College five years earlier, wrote in *Country Gentleman* magazine that one of the most important improvements in the Farm Bureau program had been the addition of a department of research and statistics under Moorhouse. The *Orange and Black* published the report from O'Brien, who at that time was a staff writer for the magazine. The student reporter had this to say: "Mr. Moorhouse was the man who started and placed on its feet the present School of Commerce and Marketing. . . . He was dean from the time it was started here until the summer of 1920."[22]

With the Brookmire Economic Service, Incorporated, in New York City from 1924 to 1931, Moorhouse was promoted from vice president to president, a position that more than doubled his salary at $16,000. Then he returned to California where, for the next ten years, he was with the Eberle Economic Service in a partnership arrangement. Apparently things did not go well there, for he accepted a position with the U.S. Civil Service Commission in Washington, D.C., in 1942 for $5,228 a year, serving as a senior review and negotiations officer. In 1943, he moved to the Food Distribution Administration as an agricultural economist. There he advanced from $6,440 to $7,341.60 a year. In 1945 he moved from the FDA to the Commodity Credit Corporation and later that year to the Office of Requirements and Allocations. He left government service on March 31, 1947, in one of the early postwar reduction-in-force moves by the U. S. Department of Agriculture. His job description in the Production and Marketing Administration judged his duties to be "of a highly important and significant nature." His responsibilities had been wide ranging. He had supplied information for news releases, bulletins, memoranda, summaries of commodity positions, and other written material for publication.[23]

In baseball terms, life had taken a bad bounce for the man who had started such a promising academic career at Oklahoma A. and M. thirty-four years earlier. He may have reflected upon the creative challenges the prairie college had offered him as he molded the School of Commerce and Marketing out of a course or two in the Teachers' Normal Division. At sixty-three years of age, he was ready to play out the string, and the playing field that most suited him was a college campus.

While the government was cutting back, colleges and universities everywhere were scrambling to handle the vast influx of veterans eager to use the G. I. Bill for the secure future they had fought for. Moorhouse joined the College of Business Administration at the University of Georgia on January 1, 1947, where he was named professor of economics. He taught two junior level courses—Banking and Principles of Marketing—in the Commerce-Journalism Building on the North Campus. He probably taught some sections of freshman and sophomore economics courses as well. A Georgia historian noted that he was "not totally at home in the teaching stream." During the years 1948-52, he also served as assistant director of the university's Bureau of Business Research.[24]

He retired to the Orlando, Florida, area in 1952, where he died in July of 1961.[25] Of the host of successful OSU graduates in the advertising field today, it is doubtful that a single one knows that Harold Moorhouse started it all.

Endnotes

1. *Annual Catalog, Oklahoma Agricultural and Mechanical College, 1912-1913*, pp. 112-114; *Annual Catalog, Oklahoma A. and M. College, 1913-1914*, pp. vi, 122, 123, 125-128; Minutes, Oklahoma A. and M. College Faculty, 7 June 1913, p. 299, Special Collections, Edmon Low Library, Oklahoma State University, Stillwater, Oklahoma; *1916 Redskin*, pp. 4, 5, Oklahoma A. and M. College Yearbook; *Stillwater Gazette*, 2 June 1916, p. 1; Oklahoma A. and M. College *Orange and Black*, 10 September 1913, p. 1, 13 December 1915, p. 1, 1 March 1919, p. 4. The *Orange and Black* reported: "We can justly be proud of our Athletic Association when we stop and think that it is the only athletic association in four States that is out of debt. All other[s]. . .are in debt to amounts ranging from $100.00 to $10,000.00."

2. *1920 Redskin*, p. 24; *Orange and Black*, 26 June 1915, p. 2, 24 July 1915, p. 2, 23 October 1916, p. 1; *JB News* (1983-86), pp. 21-26; *Annual Catalog, Oklahoma State University, 1961-1963*, pp. 69, 70.

3. *1906 Codex*, pp. 48, 170-172, Beloit College Yearbook; *Orange and Black*, 13 December 1915, p. 1; Joe Kobylka to Harry E. Heath Jr., 22 December 1988, School of Journalism and Broadcasting Centennial History Collection, Special Collections, Edmon Low Library.

4. U.S. Department of Agriculture, Production and Marketing Administration, Summary of Qualifications, 25 June 1946, and Joe Kobylka to Harry E. Heath Jr., in School of Journalism and Broadcasting Centennial History Collection; *Stillwater Gazette*, 18 August 1916, p. 8.

5. *1916 Redskin*, pp. 4, 5; *Orange and Black*, 13 December 1915, p. 1; "Necrology Section," *Chronicles of Oklahoma*, vol. 11, no. 4 (December 1933), pp. 1129-1131.

6. *1916 Redskin,* dedication and photograph following Foreword.

7. *Orange and Black*, 20 May 1916, p. 2.

8. *Annual Catalog, Oklahoma A. and M. College, 1913-1914*, p. xii; *Annual Catalog, Oklahoma A. and M. College, 1914-1915*, p. xiv; *Annual Catalog, Oklahoma A. and M. College, 1915-1916*, p. xxii; *Annual Catalog, Oklahoma A. and M. College, 1916-1917*, p. xxiv; *Annual Catalog, Oklahoma A. and M. College, 1917-1918*, p. xviii; *Annual Catalog, Oklahoma A. and M. College, 1918-1919*, p. xx; *Annual Catalog, Oklahoma A. and M. College, 1919-1920*, p. xxii.

9. *Annual Catalog, Oklahoma A. and M. College, 1912-1913*, pp. 112-114; *Annual Catalog, Oklahoma A. and M. College, 1913-1914*, pp. vi, 106, 107, 109-112.

10. *Annual Catalog, Oklahoma A. and M. College, 1914-1915*, pp. 109, 111, 112.

11. *Annual Catalog, Oklahoma A. and M. College, 1919-1920*, pp. vii, ix, 142, 144, 145, 146; Virginia M. Boyd to Harry E. Heath Jr., 22 January 1992, School of Journalism and Broadcasting Centennial History Collection; *1914 Sooner*, pp. 67, 216, 217, University of Oklahoma Yearbook; Minutes, Oklahoma State Board of Agriculture, 25 August 1918, Special Collections, Edmon Low Library.

12. *Annual Catalog, Oklahoma A. and M. College, 1920-1921*, pp. 154, 156.

13. Maxine H. Sullivan to Harry E. Heath Jr., 17 January 1989, School of Journalism and Broadcasting Centennial History Collection; *Annual Catalog, Oklahoma A. and M. College, 1920-1921*, p. 150. An erratum sheet tipped in following p. iv, "Changes in Staff for 1921-1922," lists Henry Fuller Holtzclaw as dean.

14. *1921 Redskin*, p. 27; *Orange and Black*, 22 September 1921, p. 1; *Annual Catalog, Oklahoma A. and M. College, 1921-1922*, p. 9; Author telephone interview with Bernard T. Dodder, 4 March 1989; Earl M. Rogers to Harry E. Heath Jr., 21 January 1992, Holly Davis to Harry E. Heath Jr., 7 February 1992, Inga Hoifeldt to Harry E. Heath Jr., 28 January 1992, and Jerald W. Dallam to Harry E. Heath Jr., 21 February 1991, in School of Journalism and Broadcasting Centennial History Collection; *Annual Catalog, Drake University, 1920-1921*, pp. 13, 65; *1922 Quax*, p. 260, Drake University Yearbook.

15. Ralph L. Elder to Harry E. Heath Jr., 20 February 1992, 16 March 1992, School of Journalism and Broadcasting Centennial History Collection; *Bulletin of the University of Texas*, 15 October 1910, p. 37, 22 October 1911, p. 37, 1 December 1912, p. 46, 22 November 1913, p. 51, 10 December 1914, p. 54, 1 November 1915, p. 58, 1 November 1916, p. 62; Program, Twenty-Eighth Annual Commencement, University of Texas, 13 June 1911; Program Thirty-Second Annual Commencement, University of Texas, 8 June 1915; Morrison and Fourmy Directory Company, Incorporated, *General Directory of the City of Austin 1914*, p. 578; General Register of the Students and Former Students of the University of Texas, 1917, p. 130; *Morrison and Fourmy Austin City Directory 1918*, p. 324; *University of Texas Ex-Student Directory 1883-1925*, p. 237; *1911 Cactus*, p. 23, University of Texas Yearbook; *1915 Cactus*, p. 116.

16. Aubrey L. McAlister to Harry E. Heath Jr., 23 March 1989, Thomas L. Bessire to Harry E. Heath Jr., 15 March 1989, J. W. Nesbitt to Harry E. Heath Jr., 31 July 1989, and James R. Enix to Harry E. Heath Jr., [1 August 1989], in School of Journalism and Broadcasting Centennial History Collection.

17. James R. Enix to Harry E. Heath Jr. [1 August 1989], and Erman Tucker to Harry E. Heath Jr., 28 July 1989, in School of Journalism and Broadcasting Centennial History Collection.

18. Erman Tucker to Harry E. Heath Jr., 28 July 1989, School of Journalism and Broadcasting Centennial History Collection.

19. J. W. Nesbitt to Harry E. Heath Jr., 31 July 1989; and Erman Tucker to Harry E. Heath Jr., 28 July 1989, in School of Journalism and Broadcasting Centennial History Collection.

20. Erman Tucker to Harry E. Heath Jr., 28 July 1989, Thomas L. Bessire to Harry E. Heath Jr., 15 March 1989, and J. W. Nesbitt to Harry E. Heath Jr., 31 July 1989, in School of Journalism and Broadcasting Centennial History Collection.

21. Patrick M. Quinn to Harry E. Heath Jr., 4 December 1988, and USDA Summary of Qualifications, in School of Journalism and Broadcasting Centennial History Collection; *Orange and Black*, 12 January 1922, p. 4.

22. *Orange and Black*, 8 December 1921, p. 1.

23. Patrick M. Quinn to Harry E. Heath Jr., 4 December 1988, USDA Personnel Notification, 18 March 1947; and USDA Summary of Qualifications, Job Description, Bu. No. 1012, in School of Journalism and Broadcasting Centennial History Collection.

24. Gilbert Head to Harry E. Heath Jr., 1 February 1989, and Larry B. Dendy to Harry E. Heath Jr., 8 February 1989, in School of Journalism and Broadcasting Centennial History Collection; *General Catalogue, University of Georgia, 1947-1948*, pp. 18, 120.

25. Gilbert Head to Harry E. Heath Jr., 1 February 1989, Larry B. Dendy to Harry E. Heath Jr., 8 February 1989, and Patrick M. Quinn to Harry E. Heath Jr., 4 December 1988, in School of Journalism and Broadcasting Centennial History Collection.

9 A Brief Reprise

After Edwin R. Barrett's departure for Emporia, Dean Lowery L. Lewis had chosen Noble W. Rockey as professor in charge of the English faculty. He had seniority as well as ability. He took charge immediately and the faculty had responded to his leadership. It probably came as a surprise to his colleagues when he lost the well-deserved promotion after only a year. But the college's administration at the top had changed and that meant a review of middle-echelon and departmental leadership.

Freeman E. Miller, who had resigned and had been replaced by Angelo C. Scott seventeen years earlier, now returned to the campus. His job was the same as before: professor and head of English. Rockey's title had been *acting* head, but Miller's prestige demanded a full professorship and an unequivocal headship. Rockey stayed on at the rank of associate professor.[1]

Miller was elected by the Oklhaoma State Board of Agriculture on May 17, 1915, just two days after it had been reorganized by Governor Robert L. Williams. Miller was no stranger to Williams, for he had observed his ability as an attorney in a case that reached the State Supreme Court while he was chief justice. The appointment was received with enthusiasm by the *Stillwater Gazette*, the same *Gazette* which had harshly criticized his appointment in 1894. In an editorial full of lavish praise, the *Gazette* called the board's decision one of wisdom, a cause for celebration by both students and patrons of the college. Citing scripture, the paper implied that he had been a prophet without honor in Stillwater. "Mr. Miller. . .has been a resident of Stillwater since the early days of the town; he has been lawyer, real estate dealer, farmer, justice of the peace, teacher, and editor and publisher. . . . Outside of Stillwater, and outside the borders of Oklahoma, he is known as one of the few poets Oklahoma has produced—not a mere versifier or clever rhymster, but a poet. . .whose philosophy and wisdom are expressed in pleasing meter. . . . It is outside that [he is] best known and appreciated. . . . [It] is rarely that the 'home town' has the honor of furnishing a member of the faculty of a college. It is the belief of this newspaper that this appointment will greatly add to the appreciation of Freeman E. Miller at home."[2]

In the news report of his appointment, effective June 1, the *Gazette* stated that the action "came as a complete surprise" to him. "He was not an applicant for the position and the first he knew that his name was being considered was when a telephone message came from Oklahoma City asking if he would accept the position."[3]

Miller had filled his years since 1898 with his practice of law, investments, an active role in politics and a continuing interest in poetry, which he contributed to state and national literary journals. His greatest creative skills may have been dulled somewhat by his business and legal involvements but he continued his avocative role as poet and philosopher and as a voracious reader of his favorite writers. Miller's original intention—to become a full-time poet following his departure from Oklahoma A. and M.—turned out to be only a writer's dream. The dream was short lived. In 1901, as a member of the Territorial Council, he pushed through a $54,000 appropriation for the college despite opposition in the governor's office. Seeking reelection the following year, he had been attacked by the *Cimarron Valley Clipper* through extensive publication of court records involving his turbulent Texas divorce from Allee Carey. The *Stillwater Gazette* had used the *Clipper's* ugly attack as the basis for numerous anti-Miller paragraphs and the smear campaign had led to his loss to John P. Hickham of Perkins. In 1903, he returned to newspaper work as co-editor of the *Stillwater Daily Democrat*, followed in 1906 by his editorship of the *People's Progress*. That year, he started what was expected to be a periodical of political and governmental essays and miscellany, the *Third House*. Only one issue appeared. During this period he played an increasingly active role in the Oklahoma Territorial Press Association.

In 1907, state newspapers speculated that Miller would be appointed by Governor Charles N. Haskell as assistant attorney general responsible for enforcing the new state's prohibition laws. The appointment failed to materialize. His disappointments piled up. The greatest of this period came in 1912 with the death of Stella, who as his wife had contributed so much to his early tenure on the Oklahoma A. and M. faculty. But typical of the stoic Miller, he plunged into his work with scarcely a pause. He waived his fees to represent Ruth Gray, the daughter of his good friend and political ally, Dr. J. T. Gray. The suit tested the validity of incidental fees levied upon prospective Oklahoma A. and M. students prior to entrance. The fees were knocked out as illegal. The next year he represented the Ewers White board of agriculture in a dispute over which of three boards claiming authority was the legal board. Then, in 1914, he married again. His bride was Mrs. Ada M. Kelly, a prominent local matron. He obviously had remained in the public eye during his years away from the campus.[4] Miller's reprise, filled with great promise, would in reality become a year of triumphs and defeats. The defeats would shape his future in an unmistakable way.

His greatest triumph came when he was asked by the Honorable Jesse J. Dunn, provisional commissioner, to prepare and deliver an appropriate poem on Oklahoma Day July 19, 1915, at the Panama-Pacific International Exposition in San Francisco. One week before the exposition, Miller finished his work on "Oklahoma: An Ode." It was read by Mrs. Blanche Lucas, a Ponca City civic leader, at the Oklahoma Building on the impressive exposition grounds. He had accepted the assignment with the understanding that he would be unable to attend.[5] The following month, he read the poem at the first meeting of the Oklahoma State Folk Lore Club on the University of Oklahoma campus. The *Norman Transcript* reported that Miller was the principal speaker at the evening session and that his poetry "kept his audience interested during the entire evening, applause being given many times."

Miller was an advocate of the good life—his way—and seemed to care little for what people may have thought of his affairs, whether involving business, profession, or his personal life, all of which provided ample opportunity for tongues to wag. For him, part of the good life was to spend summers at 2818 West Pike's Peak Avenue in Colorado Springs, Colorado. His commodious two-story summer home was on the edge of town at the foot of the mountain named for Zebulon Pike, who mapped the mountainous terrain in 1806. Year after year the *Stillwater Gazette* would record these annual retreats in its "Jottings About Town" column. A typical item reads: "Mr. and Mrs. Freeman E. Miller left Stillwater Wednesday afternoon for Colorado Springs, Colo., where they will stay at the foot of Pike's Peak, until September." Usually the Millers would leave in early July and return in September. On at least one occasion, Mrs. Miller made the trip with a granddaughter. Miller joined them later. On another occasion, Miller and his father, Lewis, left for Colorado Springs in early June.[6]

The new president, James W. Cantwell, arrived in Stillwater in June of 1915 to succeed Lewis. The popular "Doctor Lew" had served as president temporarily while the board of agriculture searched for a successor to John H. Connell. Cantwell, a former public school superintendent from Fort Worth, saw immediately that his most pressing need was to strengthen the faculty. He was successful in attracting those he sought. Several full professors with solid credentials from institutions of high standing joined the Oklahoma A. and M. ranks.[7]

In his return to the campus, Miller had a strong faculty lineup. His departmental letterhead as the 1915-16 academic year began listed, in addition to himself, Rockey, Harry R. O'Brien, Isadore Samuels, Albert H. Nelson, and Laurence A. Wachs, apparently in the order of their length of service. (O'Brien had resigned after the letterheads had been printed. He was replaced by Alva P. Taylor, a graduate of Colorado College with an M.A. from Westminster College and additional graduate work at the University of Chicago).[8] In spite of his good fortune faculty-wise, Miller faced a major morale problem: pay for Oklahoma A. and M. faculty and staff was four months overdue. The state treasurer insisted on keeping the Morrill fund rather than releasing it to the treasurer of the board of agriculture. To get by, teachers in this distressing situation were paying interest on borrowed money, which amounted to a cut in pay. Miller wrote President Cantwell:

"Personally I sympathize with the Board of Agriculture and believe they are right and the State Treasurer is wrong in the controversy; but I believe that the Board ought to devise some plan whereby these men who have waited four months for their salaries can be paid up to date. If then it is necessary to litigate the matter through the slow reaches of the courts, doubtless a result can there be reached before another four months shall expire.

"Would it not be possible to pay these temporarily from some other

1917 REDSKIN

President James W. Cantwell washed his hands of the Frank Gault attack upon Freeman E. Miller. He instructed Miller not to meet his classes until Gault and the board of agriculture had settled the matter, then told the board it was an issue they must decide.

fund? Or from the Morrill fund, under protest, in the manner insisted upon by the State Treasurer until a court decision can be had? In my opinion the latter course would not prejudice their legal rights in the matter at all.

"I trust that you will bring this matter to the earnest attention of the Board and I ask that you insist upon these salaries being paid at once in some way. As matters now stand, both individuals and the College itself, both innocent, are the only sufferers from the controversy."[9]

Students looking forward to journalism studies under the effusive Harry O'Brien were disappointed to learn that he had left to accept an assistant professorship at Iowa State College. The *Orange and Black* was calling for student help. It had placed boxes in strategic places for students to use as drop points for news items. Help was especially needed, the editor pointed out, because journalism classes in the O'Brien tradition had not yet been organized to assist the staff. Miller was faced with yet another problem. The popular Isadore Samuels, instructor in public speaking, had resigned and left for Columbia, Missouri, where he was scheduled to teach while working toward a law degree. His outstanding service as debate coach and director of the Men's Glee Club would be sorely missed. The problem evaporated when his plans at Missouri did not work out. After a brief absence, he rejoined the Oklahoma A. and M. faculty. Fearn Hamilton, daughter of the legendary Hays Hamilton and an able writer who had been outstanding on student publications at Oklahoma A. and M., was added as an assistant and would help fill O'Brien's shoes. But the faculty would be hard pressed to handle the growing demand for courses in English, speech, and journalism. No significant changes were made in the journalism course descriptions. A new course in technical writing for engineering students was added, but this likely was assigned to a composition teacher.[10] Stories in the student newspaper make it clear that Miller taught at least one journalism class during his ill-fated return to campus life. Unfortunately, no class schedules or class rolls were available during the centennial year to document the extent of the journalism offerings. It seems probable that most of the courses created the year before were offered, with Rockey, Hamilton, and Nelson the likely teachers.

Office space was limited, as Morrill Hall, heavily damaged by fire in August of 1914, had not yet been rebuilt, although parts of it were in use. Miller moved into a small office on the first floor of the new Engineering Building, later to be known as Gundersen Hall. As head of the English department, he was responsible for the success or failure of journalism courses. No such courses had existed during his earlier tenure. English 301, Editorial and Publicity Work, had 5 students enrolled; 203, News Writing, had 67, and 205, Current Literature (a study of magazines), 11.[11]

The importance of journalism instruction to student publications is suggested by a report in the *Orange and Black,* successor to the *College Paper.* In the paper's first staff meeting of the year, plans were discussed for "handling news until journalism classes are working." Journalism classes the previous year, largely due to the energetic work of Professors O'Brien and Rockey, had played an important part in news gathering for the *Orange and Black.*[12]

The Old Engineering Building, constructed in 1902, was now to be the home of student publications. No sooner had the *Orange and Black, Redskin,* and the *Oklahoma Agriculturist* moved to the downstairs southeast corner of the building than the newspaper issued a call for help. "It will be appreciated especially now when the journalism classes are not organized into a working unit," editor Glen Briggs wrote from his office in Room 11.[13]

Although Room 15 in the new Engineering Building was known as the Journalism Room for instructional use, campus space was so much in demand that the *Orange and Black* Room in the Old Engineering Building also had to be used for classes. This was not entirely satisfactory. In an editorial, Briggs complained that classes sharing space with the *Orange and Black* were taking pencils, pens, and paper that belonged to the newspaper staff. "These are our work tools," Briggs wrote, "and we would appreciate it very much if you would leave them there for us to use." He noted, too, that mail and papers belonging to the newspaper were being moved or discarded from the *Orange and Black* desk. The papers presumably included notes and stories belonging to staff members.[14]

As for the academic year as a whole, it was a full one. The new president's theme was "theory with practice." The Student Handbook was replaced by a Student Directory, published by the YMCA. Coach Edward C. Gallagher, one of the great athletic heroes of his student days, if not the greatest, returned to his alma mater. And the college shifted from the quarter to the semester system.

It was a year in which the legendary Boh Makovsky, who had led the Oklahoma State Fair Band for several years, came to Oklahoma A. and M. to create an aura that still is felt in the music department; when senior males would carry their rank of authority with matching canes, while freshmen wore their green caps from the first football game until the OU game on Thanksgiving Day; when the terms Tigers and Tigerland were slowly yielding to Aggies and Aggieland; when a whistle system signalled the outcome of football games. Three very short blasts equalled zero and seven short ones meant seven, etc., with the opponent's score first followed by a thirty-second wait and then the Oklahoma A. and M. score.

Professor W. L. Blizzard, who once was on the advertising staff of Capper's Publications, brought his cattle-judging fame from Iowa State

College to Oklahoma A. and M.; enrollment was up from 910 to 1,065; Randle Perdue, secretary to the president and a former Tiger baseball star, was elected manager of the baseball team by the Athletic Association; the traditional stag banquet of the School of Agriculture became a co-educational affair because Bertha Rogers and Katherine Carlyle were ag majors.

Male agriculture seniors decided that canes were not enough to set them apart and added overalls and a red bandanna to their symbols of stature. They even wore them to chapel where they entered with a robust cheer: "Farmer! Hayseed! Pumpkin! Squash! Senior Aggies, yes, by gosh!"

It was a heady period. The first local Greek-letter clubs were forming and the literary societies no longer were the sole outlet for acceptable social contacts. Reflecting the changing attitudes on campus, where as "democracy's college" the early students supported the regents' view that secret societies were undemocratic, the Philomathean Literary Society now felt free to debate the topic, "Resolved, that Nationalized Fraternities should be allowed in Oklahoma A. and M." Line parties, in which women's social clubs would walk in line to a local theater, were an outlet for comradery and youthful exuberance.

It was a year in which the fame of Oklahoma A. and M. College continued to spread. Students came to Stillwater from nineteen states and from every Oklahoma county except Cherokee, Cimarron, Hughes, Latimer, and Marshall. By mid-November, 1,085 students were attending classes. The traditional Harvest Carnival was successful, showing a profit of $82.36, which would be passed along to help the 1916 and 1917 *Redskin* staffs. Gas wells were being dug seven miles east of Stillwater, promising a new source of heat and revenue for the community.

Perhaps the biggest event, in terms of wider public awareness of— and enthusiasm for—the Stillwater school occurred in Oklahoma City on Thanksgiving Day. The fact that OU's football team defeated Oklahoma A. and M. 26-7 was painful. But the college's Cadet Corps salvaged the day with a performance that captured the admiration of all, whatever their school loyalties.

Approximately 1,000 Oklahoma A. and M. rooters, including the Corps and band, travelled to Oklahoma City in a special train made up of twelve coaches and an express car. The proud Corps, Army rifles shouldered, paraded through the streets of the capital behind Mokovsky's spirited forty-piece military band. The regiment passed in review before Governor Robert L. Williams and his staff, President Cantwell, President Frank M. Gault of the state board of agriculture, and Mayor Ed Overholser of Oklahoma City. The Sooners would win the day's game, but the Cadet Corps had won the day.

As for instruction in journalism, Miller had not overlooked the building program of Barrett and Rockey as he had presided over the Department of English in his return to academic life. The *Orange and Black* was looking forward to continued cooperation with English. The editors acknowledged that journalism classes had "played an important part in the newsgathering last year." They were looking forward to the same arrangement under Miller for the mutual advantage of both the newspaper and the journalism classes. Newspaper jargon was creeping into the news columns as Briggs referred to the assignment of *beats*. Both staff members and those in Miller's journalism classes would be held responsible for any news occurring on their *runs*, he said.[15]

But after one semester, there were signs that Miller had been a problem for the *Orange and Black*. Briggs said the arrangement had been less than satisfactory. Nevertheless, he hoped to build a closer relationship during the spring term.[16]

In this up-and-down academic year, Miller scored an Oklahoma A. and M. "first." He planned and carried out the college's first journalism short course January 3-8. He called it "Newspaper Week," and incorporated it into the upcoming Farmers' Short Course. It included five lectures daily. The student newspaper used this announcement to boast of the growth of journalism at Oklahoma A. and M. It was typical of the paper to boost journalism instruction at every opportunity. Obviously there were students who wanted a full-fledged journalism department and they sought to influence the administration through their boosterism. Typical was this paragraph from the story announcing "Journalism Week": "Although instruction in journalism is a small part of the work undertaken by the Department of English, yet interest taken in it is so great that the number of students enrolled for it exceeds that of many institutions having fully organized schools of journalism and conferring the degree of master of journalism on those finishing the course. The School of Journalism of the Texas State University has only fifty-three students in the course, while more than seventy are taking phases of the work here as part of the course in English. The School of Journalism of the Kansas State Agricultural College, organized for many years, has only 126 students in its courses this year."[17]

In addition to planning a major speech for the college's twenty-fifth anniversary, scheduled for January 7, 1916, Miller was busy making improvements in the routine of the Department of English. He had ordered a card index of all students taking work in the department. That Miller himself was teaching journalism is verified by an *Orange and Black* story telling of his class's visit to the College Printing Plant, where Arthur McEwen and Charles Becker explained Mergenthaler's Linotype machine to the students. The student reporter covering the field trip, probably a member of Miller's class, said the machine "is to the printer what the cotton gin is to the Southern agriculturist, and has revolutionized the methods of the printing industry. The reporter had observed carefully, giving readers an accurate description of how the technology of that day worked. Sixty years later, students would try their hand at computerized typesetting on the latest equipment in a traveling "new technology" van provided by the Gannett Company, whose chief executive officer was Paul Miller, an Oklahoma A. and M. graduate.[18]

While he was building contacts with newspapermen through his "Newspaper Week" plan, Miller did not overlook his responsibilities in making his presence felt among English teachers. When Miller, Nelson, Samuels, and Miss Hamilton attended the Oklahoma Education Association convention in Oklahoma City, they took an active part in the association's English section. Miller, always a commanding presence among state educators, was chosen secretary-treasurer by the 150 English teachers attending their sectional session.[19] On the other hand, "Newspaper Week," a program that sought to meet the needs of country newspapers, had met with only limited success. Only about twelve newspapermen from over the state attended, but seventy-two persons—including "students taking the current work in journalism"—had registered. Miller integrated some of his classroom lectures into the program. Editor J. S. Chilton of the *South Pottawatomie Progress*, a weekly published at Asher, was impressed by the program. The *Orange and Black* quoted Chilton: "If the newspaper people of the State knew what was being offered them by the College they would have come here in great numbers to obtain the benefits so freely extended. . .I hope that the governing

Frank M. Gault, president of the board of agriculture, ordered President James W. Cantwell to suspend Freeman E. Miller, pending investigation of charges concerning his son, Roy. Some considered it Gault's way of getting rid of a strong faculty member for political or personal reasons.

board of the College will place sufficient funds at the disposal of the department having this work in charge that the course may be strengthened and outside help obtained from newspaper men of national reputation."[20] Chilton also expressed his belief in "school training in journalism," saying that while theory could not replace practical newspaper experience, "it is useful to know theory as well as the practice." He praised Miller's short-course lectures.[21]

The state's press cooperated with Oklahoma A. and M. by providing complimentary subscriptions to the library. Students in journalism classes had access to 103 newspapers, all but a few from Oklahoma communities. Miller's many friendships developed through his earlier participation in the Oklahoma Press Association may have helped establish this cooperation. Nor can one discount the early work of Frank D. Northup as a key association member. The library's newspaper collection was useful in journalism studies, but it also made it possible for other students to keep up with what was happening back home.[22]

Miller's interest in the library could be traced back to his days as acting librarian in 1895, when he had emphasized the importance of the college's periodical collection. He no longer had such responsibilities, but his interest continued high, as it did in other aspects of campus life. During his short reprise on campus, Miller presented a chapel program in which he illustrated the mission of poetry. The *Orange and Black* reported: "He said that poetry was not to teach a lesson, but to give voice to beauty. The man who paints in words of rhyme the beautiful things he sees or feels is a true artist." Miller read a variety of poems—from those of Woodsworth to his own—at least a dozen in all, the paper reported. His selections were upbeat, and the student reporter remarked that they illustrated "the spirit underlying the name of 'Sunshine Miller,'" a nickname associated with his "Oklahoma Sunshine" column in the *Oklahoman.* [23]

Miller, in his earlier years at Oklahoma A. and M., had served as head of the College Press Bureau as well as filling the chair in English. He was still a college publicity agent at heart. He approached the college's county clubs with a suggestion. Each club president would write an article featuring the work of his club, and Miller would edit the articles and send them to county papers across the state. The *Orange and Black* reported: "It is the desire of Professor Miller to advertise The County Club contests and to announce the fact that Board of Agriculture President Gault would offer Hereford calf prizes again next year to those who had recruited the largest number of Oklahoma A. and M. freshmen."[24]

Late in Miller's ill-fated return to the classroom, Oklahoma publishers began a movement urging a vocational program in printing at Oklahoma A. and M. similar to the one that had been abandoned earlier. It had been eight years since such course work had been offered under

George Gelder and, earlier, Frank Northup.

As the academic year was winding down, some campus journalists were looking forward to the fun-filled spoof publication known as the *Earthquake*, published in connection with the May Day Carnival in the spring and the Harvest Carnival in the fall. The *Orange and Black* reported that "These yellow journalists have been sneaking around with eyes and ears alert for anything they can find that touches on the sensational or dark side of life. . . . No skeleton in the closet is too sacred for exposition; no name too mighty to escape publicity. The highest and the mightiest may as well expect to get theirs." Profits from the five-cents-per-copy "Truth" edition would go to support the *Redskin*.[25]

On a more serious note, representatives of the *Orange and Black, Oklahoma Agriculturist*, and the *Redskin* had formed a Journalism Club that at some future time hoped to become a chapter of the national journalistic fraternity Sigma Delta Chi, which had established a chapter at the University of Oklahoma in 1913. Three decades would pass before that goal would be reached.[26]

In his last issue of the year, Editor Briggs spoke his mind about what in September had seemed to hold promise of cooperation with Miller and the journalism classes. He referred to the 1914-15 year under Noble W. Rockey as one in which the journalism class "furnished enough material to more than fill the paper every week." Pulling no punches, he accused the class under Miller of loafing on the job, asserting that no more than 700 words a week had been turned in during the spring semester.

The possibility of tensions between Miller and the staff—tensions that may have led to the faltering cooperation—was suggested by an

Freeman E. Miller could get scarcely a line in the news columns of the *Stillwater Gazette* in his 1916 political campaign. He bought space and used a series of advertisements to gain recognition.

indirect remark in Briggs's editorial, "Our Swan Song." Briggs commented: "We soon learned that to even try to run a paper there cannot be too many bosses." The inference was that there had been a disagreement as to the authority of the editor. Whether the disagreement involved Miller was not spelled out, but in view of Briggs's criticism of the journalism class, one may assume that Miller, who years earlier had run the *Mirror* with an authoritarian style, did not encourage the class's cooperation with Briggs and his *Orange and Black* staff because of some unstated disagreement.[27]

What had started as a promising year for Miller began to shatter in the spring. On April 27, President Gault of the board of agriculture sent this telegram to President Cantwell: "Suspend Freeman E. Miller, chair of English, Stillwater Oklahoma A. and M. College, also his son if he is a student at the College. Will not tolerate insubordination on part of students or members of faculty. The College interests must be held superior to that [*sic*] of any individual."

The wheels were in motion and the rest of the story unfolded quickly. At its May 1 meeting in Oklahoma City, President Gault read the telegram he had sent to Cantwell ordering Miller's suspension. The board approved the action by roll-call vote. At the same meeting, President Cantwell's monthly report to the board, dated April 29, was presented. The final paragraph read: "The one unfortunate incident marring the smooth course of the College during the present month grew out of alleged misconduct of a man related to a professor. The final disposition of this matter must be undertaken by the Board."

Acting upon Gault's telegram, Cantwell presumably had suspended Miller. The board voted that Miller stand suspended until an investigation could be conducted. C. B. Campbell thereupon was appointed by Gault to chair an investigating committee, including J. J. Savage and R. H. McLish. Gault turned over to Campbell "a copy of the evidence, affidavits, complaint, and all papers pertaining to the complaint" with the request that the committee report its recommendation to the board "as soon as possible."[28]

Facts were hard to come. The campus newspaper carried no information at all, while the *Stillwater Gazette*, rather than aggressively reporting the board of agriculture's attack upon one of the city's leading citizens, chose to reprint a story from the *Daily Oklahoman*. Gault refused to comment beyond the fact that, at its meeting the following Monday, the board would consider whether to make the suspension permanent. Meanwhile, Miller told the *Oklahoman* that he would not conduct his Friday classes, but that he would be in his office "attending to other duties connected with my position" as head of the English department.

If the *Oklahoman* report was accurate, President Cantwell did not serve the notice of suspension. Miller reportedly told the *Oklahoman* that Cantwell merely had suggested he not conduct classes until the board had met.

Miller's responses to the *Oklahoman's* telephone interview provided Stillwater citizens, both on and off campus, with the most factual information they had had amidst fast-traveling rumors, some of them outrageous. Miller told the *Oklahoman* that the suspension order grew out of the fact that he had represented his son, Roy F. Miller, following his arrest the previous Saturday night. Roy Miller had been arrested when several young women students charged that he had made improper remarks within earshot as he had crossed the campus. Young Miller was taken before the local insanity board and Professor Miller appeared as his attorney.

Professor Miller told the *Oklahoman* reporter: "I represented my son because I am his father and am an attorney, but I would not have represented him if I had been able to secure the presence of my own attorney who was out of town at the time. [My son] was declared to be of sound mind and was discharged. The question of whether he made the remarks is a question of fact to be proved, in court. There are now no charges pending against him. He has not attended school for several years. He is 25 years old and has a wife and child. At the time he was

1917 REDSKIN

Near the end of the turbulent 1915-16 academic year, a new campus organization appeared. The Journalism Club was organized May 10 to create "a bond between the various publications and to forward interests in journalism." It would later evolve into the Press Club, which in the Clement E. Trout administration became a chapter of Sigma Delta Chi, known today as the Society of Professional Journalists. Members were (*front row, left to right*) Randle Perdue, Fred L. Jones, J. E. Martin, and Mortimer Woodson; (*top row*) O. D. McNeely, M. G. Harnden, and Workman Rapp.

crossing the campus he was looking for a stray horse."[29]

In the meantime, in an apparent effort to reduce the pressures directed against his father, Roy Miller decided to leave Stillwater. On May 12, the *Gazette* reported in its "Jottings About Town" column: "Mr. and Mrs. Roy F. Miller and baby left Sunday [May 7] for Ada, where they will make their home. Roy is a Stillwater boy, born and reared here, and his friends wish him all prosperity in his new location."[30]

Freeman Miller, as the maelstrom gathered around him, carried on in his unruffled, pragmatic way. The embattled professor could see the probable outcome. He had watched, and participated in, Oklahoma politics from territorial days through the first decade of statehood. The coming and going of presidents and faculty members at Oklahoma A. and M. had a way of matching the ebb and flow of Republican and Democratic fortunes and their attendant spoils system. On May 17 he traveled to Kaw City to deliver an address to the high school graduating class there.

One week later, Freeman Miller would be on the road again, this time returning from Ada with his son's body. On May 23 Roy, his wife, and his four-month-old child had gone on a family outing to a lake near Ada. At about 5:30 P.M., Roy decided to go for a swim. The *Gazette* of May 26 reported that "presumably he was taken with cramps, for he called for aid and his wife and an old man who was there tried to succor him, but could not save him." His body was recovered five hours later.

Funeral services conducted by the Reverend John E. Thackrey were held at the family home at 230 Duck Street. Roy Miller would have been twenty-five years old in October, the *Gazette* reported.[31]

At its June 1 meeting in Oklahoma City, the board of agriculture reelected Cantwell as president of the Oklahoma Agricultural and Mechanical College. Cantwell presented a list of "teachers and employees for re-election for the ensuing year." The board acted favorably upon Cantwell's list. Freeman Miller's name was not on it. On the third day of the meeting, the board made final its decision in the Miller suspension, ending the academic career of one of the most talented—and controversial—figures in Oklahoma A. and M. history. The report of the Special Committee read, in part: "Your committee has examined the statements, affidavits and letters, and has read the testimony and proceedings in such insanity hearing, and having considered all such matters, the same being the information upon which the President of the State Board of Agriculture ordered President Cantwell to suspend Professor Miller, your committee concludes that the facts contained in such statements, letters and testimony and proceedings in such insanity hearing authorized and warranted the President of the State Board of Agriculture in directing the suspension of Professor Miller, and that President Cantwell complied with the rules of the Board of Agriculture in suspending Professor Miller on the order and direction of the President of the Board, and your committee recommends that the action of the President of the State Board of Agriculture in directing President Cantwell to suspend Professor Miller, and the action of President Cantwell under the direction of the Chairman of the State Board of Agriculture be approved.

"Your committee attaches hereto and makes a part of this report the motion adopted by the State Board of Agriculture on May 1, 1916, the written statement of A. W. Turner, a copy of the affidavit of D. H. Self, a statement of I. D. Andrew, a letter from John P. Hickham, a letter of W. R. Jones, County Judge of Payne County, and a certified copy of the testimony and proceedings in the County Court of Payne County, Oklahoma in the insanity matter of Roy Miller, Number 223 taken and had on the 26th day of April, 1916."[32]

McLish moved and Savage seconded that the report be approved. The roll-call vote was unanimous. The board agreed to pay Miller his salary to July 1 and then adjourned.[33] No mention was made of Roy Miller's death nor of Miller's statements to the *Oklahoman,* which constituted the closest thing to a defense on his behalf. Not only did the *Orange and Black* avoid the drama that had unfolded over a three-month period, but no mention of the threat to Freeman Miller's faculty status appeared in the minutes of Oklahoma A. and M. faculty meetings. The poet from Indiana had become, in a sense, a non-person while his professional career was being sullied, presumably for the behavior of his second son. As many things did in the rowdy Oklahoma days of 1916, Gault's action, supported by members of the board of agriculture, smacked of politics.

With Miller out as head of the English department, President Cantwell presented a familiar name to the regents as his replacement: Noble W. Rockey, who had earlier served as acting head of English on two occasions. Rockey had been on the Oklahoma A. and M. faculty since 1911 and wanted to strengthen the journalism program which Barrett had conceived with his help and that of Harry O'Brien. The board elected Rockey as head on July 1 at a salary of $2,000 for twelve months. At the same meeting, Cantwell recommended W. D. Little of Ada to "take the place of Mr. Rockey's present position" at a salary of $1,400 for twelve months. The board approved Little's appointment. Apparently Little did not readily accept, for on August 2 the board approved Cantwell's recommendation that the Ada newspaperman "be advanced from $1,400 to $1,500 for 12 months." Despite this move, Little apparently did not accept the appointment.[34]

Miller's response to his humiliation by the board was to take his case to the people of Payne County. On June 5 he filed for a place on the Democratic ticket in the upcoming race for the legislature. The county, formerly with only one representative in the house, was now entitled to two. In the words of Roy T. Hoke, he wanted to "get back at certain

1917 REDSKIN

Freeman E. Miller and his political crony, Dr. J. T. Gray, were buried in effigy in downtown Stillwater in 1916. The *Redskin* ran this picture in its humor section. Miller had sought election to the state legislature following his dismissal by the board of agriculture and had lost.

individuals."[35] He survived the Democratic primary, running second to A. J. Hartenbower, 594 to 420, in a field of four candidates. The general election would be more difficult for him.[36]

Following the primary race, Miller may have spent about a month planning his campaign and working quietly to organize a network of support. Or, perhaps, the strongly Republican *Gazette* simply chose not to give his activities any real visibility during this crucial period. In an editorial, "Purely Advertising," the *Gazette* had openly stated that it would accept paid advertising from Democratic candidates but that they could expect no endorsements. It appears that they could expect only muted news coverage as well. In contrast, the newspaper carried the entire Republican slate on its editorial page each week without charge, and openly supported Republicans in its news columns while pushing the campaign for a new courthouse as well. Whatever the reasons, Miller's campaign efforts, viewed from available evidence today, appeared to be concentrated late in the race. First came two major display advertisements, seemingly unrelated to politics, in which he offered more than 400 lots for sale at $50 to $150 each. The lots adjoined the Oklahoma A. and M. campus or were within easy walking distance, Miller pointed out, stressing the fact that the lots "comprise the only considerable body of vacant property left in the immediate vicinity of the college."

Playing the role of prophet, Miller wrote: "As the college develops to its possibilities, and thousands of students instead of hundreds throng its halls from state and nation, these lots will increase in value many times." In display type at the bottom, the ad read: "Buy Some of These Lots and Get the Benefit of the Bigger and Better Oklahoma A. and M. College that Is Coming Within the Next Two Years. Let Its Prosperity Be Your Fortune, and Take Advantage of the Opportunity at Hand."[37] It may be conjectured that Miller was unloading some of his vacant property to raise money for his campaign.

Less than a month later, Miller ran a similar ad in which he said, "I have held this property for more than seven years, waiting through fat and lean seasons for the college and city to grow. It has been a long wait, but now that the good time is at hand, I am willing to give everyone who wants to share the prosperity a chance to get his portion of the added values that will come with city and college development." He reported that an armory and gymnasium with swimming pool, a new science hall, and other buildings would be provided by the next legislature at an expense of a quarter of a million dollars. "The proposed new court house costing $100,000 will also add to the values," the ad predicted.[38]

As his campaign peaked, Miller purchased another large display advertisement in the *Gazette*. On this occasion, an error in the headline may have negated what otherwise might have been more productive of votes. The ad was a letter of approximately 750 words in which Miller traced his support of the college from 1893 to 1916. Unfortunately for him, the headline read: "HOW FREEMAN E. MILLER HAS 'FOUGHT THE COLLEGE.'" Obviously the word FOR had been omitted. A modern journalism class studying ethical matters could spend half an hour discussing the *Gazette's* responsibility for such a crucial error. Or was it an error? The staunchly Republican *Gazette* had little desire to see Miller return to a place of power in state politics. The facts in the case may never be known. Apparently no correction or apology was forthcoming in the next issue of the *Gazette*.[39]

In another ad in the October 20 issue, Miller used the words of Angelo Scott to validate his fitness for the legislature. Miller quoted from Scott's remarks of February 1, 1901, at a meeting attended by both students and members of the legislature in the Assembly Hall at Oklahoma A. and M. On that occasion, the president had referred to Miller as "One who from his long association with the institution understands its constitution, its operation, and its needs. . . . Senator Miller. . .fully understands and can explain to his fellow legislators just how this institution is maintained—just how the government contributes to its support, and just how the territory must come to its assistance—just how the government funds can and cannot be used, and just how the territorial funds must be applied.

"Heretofore we have generally suffered before the legislature by reason of not having a man on the floor of either house who understood all these distinctions and could make others see them. It is my purpose tonight to make statements so clear that not only Senator Miller. . .will fully understand them, but that all other members of the legislative assembly present here will thoroughly understand the situation, and incidentally I think it perfectly right and proper that all of our students and friends here should understand all about it."

Following that review of past events, the ad concluded with these words, probably written by the candidate himself: "Three new buildings and a heating plant were secured for the college that session. . . . [Miller] knows as much about the college and its needs as President Cantwell or Frank Gault. . . . If the college was fortunate to have him represent its interests in the legislature of 1901, how much more fortunate will it be to have him represent it in the next legislature, fresh from its class rooms and with his added experience?" Two other display ads followed. They were headlined "Vote for Freeman E. Miller" and listed his qualifications point by point in identical copy.[40] Meanwhile, M. J. Otey, with whom

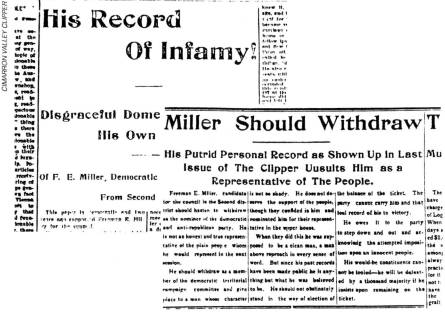

Stories such as these in the 1902 *Cimarron Valley Clipper* led to the defeat of Freeman E. Miller as he sought reelection to the Territorial Council. Scurrilous charges based upon these stories were used in an anti-Miller campaign by Oklahoma A. and M. students in 1916.

Miller had served along with Lowery L. Lewis on the committee that had planned the college's twenty-fifth anniversary celebration, had decided to fight Miller's candidacy. Otey had been popular as a student and now was serving his alma mater as financial secretary and purchasing agent. He organized a county-wide anti-Miller campaign. The *Gazette* reported that the campaign had its beginning in the Student Senate and had been endorsed by the Student Association. The *Gazette* made vague reference to the bill as "pertaining to the morals of the institution."[41]

Because the Student Association had "heartily endorsed" the Student Senate's legislation, volunteers began speaking almost immediately against Miller's candidacy. The *Gazette* reported that the substance of the speeches was based upon extracts from court records which were printed in the *Cimarron Valley Clipper,* a Coyle newspaper, in 1902. These records, had cost Miller an earlier election. From the many students who volunteered, Eric L. Castile, an agriculture student from Stillwater, selected the speakers. He chose for the first wave Harry E. Johnson, Jeff Campbell, Roy T. Hoke, V. J. Booth, Joe Blackburn, and L. V. Surtees. Castile also spoke.[42]

One week later, the *Gazette* reported that three to five school-house meetings had been held each night during the week plus "large and enthusiastic mass meetings on the streets of Yale, Cushing and Stillwater." The story indicated that the remaining half of the county would be covered in the next seven days.

In a somewhat subdued attempt to balance the story, the *Gazette* reported that Mrs. Miller and Dr. J. T. Gray had "taken up the fight" for the embattled Democratic candidate. Floyd Miller, Freeman Miller's first son, born to Allee Carey Miller during a tempestuous Texas marriage, also joined the counter-attack. Floyd, now a junior at the University of Oklahoma, agreed to appear with his father at a public meeting in the Opera House on November 1. The *Gazette* reported that they would discuss "matters of a personal nature that have been brought into the campaign." Public meetings also were scheduled by the Millers in Glencoe, Marena, Ingalls, and Perkins.[43] The Stillwater meeting "broke all records for attendance and enthusiasm," the *Gazette* reported, "exceeding all political gatherings held so far at Stillwater during the campaign. The house was crowded to capacity, and the friends of Mr. Miller listened with interest to the matters discussed."[44]

On November 10, in a page-one story, the *Gazette* reported Freeman Miller's defeat. He had finished fourth in a close race. A. J. Hartenbower, in first place, had only 212 more votes than Miller. Hartenbower, a fellow Democrat, and C. C. Platt, a Republican, would occupy seats in the state senate.[45] There were reports that Miller would contest the election "on the ground that illegal votes had been cast." Nothing came of the report. Over 100 anti-Miller speeches had been made by 28 different students

1917 REDSKIN

M. J. Otey, an Oklahoma A. and M. alumnus who served as financial secretary, organized a campaign against Freeman E. Miller in 1916. Students visited towns and villages throughout Payne County giving anti-Miller speeches.

sent out by the Student Association. "Speeches were made in nearly every school house in Payne County, as well as upon the streets of the various towns and villages," the paper reported. In addition to the speakers listed earlier, the *Gazette* named G. C. Smith, Oscar Carlton, Sherman Krisher, W. E. West, E. M. West, Phil Hayes, Oscar Mittendorf, H. H. Finnell, Ray Bryant, Floyd Keller, Gus Gloeckner, Ray Skinner, Paul Hoggard, A. L. Smith, William Beck, O. J. Meyer, T. H. Mittendorf, J. E. Martin, A. P. Brodell, Arthur Ellis, B. F. Harrison, and G. O. Ranes.[46]

Years later, as Miller recalled the losing campaign while visiting with Hoke in front of the Roy T. Hoke Lumber Company at 218 West Ninth Avenue, tears ran down his cheeks.[47] Beneath his stern exterior, he was more sensitive than the public image he projected throughout his life.

Miller did not fight what he and his friends considered to be an injustice. He used a paragraph in the *Gazette* to publicly thank the 1,613 people who had voted for him, calling their loyalty "worth more than all possible honors." Then he signaled defeat, or at least acquiescence, with this notice in the *Stillwater Gazette* for December 1: "I have reopened my office at Number 623 1/2 Main Street (over Searcy's grocery store) for the general practice of the law, where I shall be pleased to serve old and new clients. Respectfully, Freeman E. Miller."[48] Miller's academic career had reached its end. Whether his 1915-16 reprise had signaled his desire to spend the remainder of his professional life close to the ivy-covered walls of Old Central and the original Library Building, turreted like a castle on the Rhine, is murky. Perhaps he considered it a transitional period in his life. He was fifty-one at the time, and he might have seen the year as a chance to prepare for a return to politics. His efforts to woo the Oklahoma Press Association during the year could be interpreted that way. On the other hand, he had had connections with the OPA as early as 1897, if not before.[49] In either event, the year's outcome was far different than he had hoped for.

He would never return to the faculty, but his public life continued unabated. He had helped organize and had spoken at the twenty-fifth anniversary celebration on campus, and would speak again at the fiftieth in 1941. He would gain a statewide following with his "Oklahoma Sunshine" column in the *Daily Oklahoman*, and would do legal work involving the college on several occasions.

Politically, he had the satisfaction of being named district judge for Payne and Logan counties by Governor William H. "Alfalfa Bill" Murray in 1932. His friendship with Stillwater attorney James Springer, a close friend of Murray's, had played an important role in the appointment. He had the satisfaction, too, of seeing a major article on his career in the *Daily*

Freeman Miller's two sons became the focus of interest during his disappointing return to the campus in 1915-16. Roy Miller (*below right*) was accused of improper remarks to coeds and was subjected to a sanity hearing that, in part, became the excuse for his father's dismissal by the board of agriculture. He died tragically soon after. Floyd Miller (*above right*) campaigned for his father in the legislative election later that year.

Oklahoman, an article which identified him as "Dean of Oklahoma Poets."[50]

Those who knew Miller best, men like J. T. Gray and James Springer, could see his life as one in which the elements of a Shakespearean tragedy were readily apparent. But he shrugged off his disappointments and frustrations and continued to have a strong local and regional impact for years. While he dabbled at poetry until senility set in late in life, there is no evidence that he offered his work to a major book-publishing house again.

In its October 1952 issue, the *DePauw Alumnus* noted the passing of Judge Freeman E. Miller. In a vast understatement, the news note read: "He. . .was also author of several poems."[51]

Endnotes

1. *Annual Catalog, Oklahoma A. and M. College, 1914-1915,* p. vi; *Annual Catalog, Oklahoma A. and M. College, 1915-1916,* p. vi.

2. *Annual Catalog, Oklahoma A. and M. College, 1915-1916,* p. vi; *Stillwater Gazette,* 21 May 1915, pp. 2, 5; Oklahoma A. and M. College *Orange and Black,* 26 June 1915, p. 1; Philip Reed Rulon, *Oklahoma State University—Since 1890* (Stillwater: Oklahoma State University Press, 1975), p. 151. Page 95 of the 1915-16 catalog lists N. W. Rockey as "Associate Professor in Charge," his role of the previous year. This suggests that the Miller appointment as head of the Department of English came after the main body of the catalog had been printed.

3. *Stillwater Gazette,* 21 May 1915, p. 5.

4. Rulon, pp. 119, 120, 140, 141, 142, 151; LeRoy H. Fischer, *Oklahoma State University Historic Old Central* (Stillwater: Oklahoma State University, 1988), p. 88; Joseph B. Thoburn, *A Standard History of Oklahoma,* vol. 2 (Chicago and New York: American Historical Society, 1916), pp. iii-viii, 920; Oklahoma City *Daily Oklahoman,* 23 May 1937, p. D-7; *1920 Alumnal Record,* De Pauw University, p. 106; *Stillwater Gazette,* 9 October 1902, pp. 2, 8, 9, 16 October 1902, pp. 1, 9, 30 October 1902, pp. 1, 4, 7, 6 November 1902, pp. 1, 4, 13 November 1902, p. 1, 20 November 1902, p. 5, 27 November 1902, p. 4, 4 December 1902, p. 1, 22 November 1907, p. 1, 6 September 1912, p. 1, 13 September 1912, p. 1, 27 September 1912, p. 4, 4 October 1912, p. 1, 11 October 1912, p. 1, 7 February 1913, p. 1, 14 February 1913, pp. 1, 8, 21 February 1913, pp. 1, 5, 28 February 1913, p. 1, 4 April 1913, p. 1, 4 July 1913, p. 8, 18 July 1913, p. 1, 7 August 1914, p. 1, 21 May 1915, pp. 2, 5; Carolyn Thomas Foreman, *Oklahoma Imprints* (Norman: University of Oklahoma Press, 1936), pp. 408, 411; Oklahoma A. and M. College *Daily O'Collegian,* 14 December 1937, p. 6; Stillwater *Daily Democrat,* 29 September 1903, p. 1; Stillwater *People's Progress,* 6 June 1906, pp. 1, 5, 13 June 1906, p. 5, 20 June 1906, pp. 1, 2, 4. For the *Record,* Miller had listed 1905-06 and 1906-07 for his years on the two newspapers. George Ewing in the *O'Collegian* reported that Miller started his last newspaper, the *Progress,* before settling down to his law practice. According to Ewing, it lasted until November 1907. See "The Consolidation of the Two Territorial Press Associations" [1906] and "Annual Meeting of 1907" in J. B. Thoburn and John Winthrop Sharp, *History of the Oklahoma Press and Oklahoma Press Association* (Oklahoma City, OK: Industrial Printing Company, 1930). As a long-time prohibitionist, Miller may have played a role in the choice of Mrs. Nation as a speaker. See also Freeman Edwin Miller, *The Third House* (Stillwater, OK: no publisher [1906]), 20 pp., listed in *National Union Catalog Accumulated Author List,* vol. 384, Pre-1956 Imprints [1906] p. 233. The *Record* lists 24 September 1912 as the date of Estelle's death. Miller and his son Roy had attended the burial in Hopkins, Missouri. Five months later, Miller returned to Hopkins for the funeral of Estelle's mother; Minutes, Oklahoma A. and M. College Faculty, 9 September, 19 November 1912, 3 February 1913, Special Collections, Edmon Low Library, Oklahoma State University, Stillwater, Oklahoma; Contested fees in Rulon differ from those in the faculty minutes; Oklahoma A. and M. College *Orange and Black,* 22 May 1915, p. 4. The *Record* lists his return to the faculty as 1906. This obviously was intended to read 1916, covering the academic year 1915-1916.

5. Thoburn, pp. ii-viii; *Stillwater Gazette*, 9 July 1915.

6. *Stillwater Gazette*, 13 August 1915, p. 1; Author interview with Lorraine Miller Newkirk, 12 May 1987; *Universal Standard Encyclopedia* (New York, NY: Unicorn Publishers, Incorporated, 1955), vol. 18, p. 6650.

7. Minutes, Oklahoma State Board of Agriculture, vol. 2, p. 156, Oklahoma Department of Libraries, Oklahoma City, Oklahoma; *Orange and Black*, 12 June 1915, p. 1; *Stillwater Gazette*, 11 June 1915, p. 7; Rulon, pp. 150, 151; Minutes, Oklahoma State Board of Agriculture, vol. 3, pp. 221, 253; *Stillwater Gazette*, 11 June 1915, p. 7, 7 December 1917, p. 1; Rulon, pp. 150-151.

8. *Orange and Black*, 20 September 1915, p. 1.

9. Freeman E. Miller to James W. Cantwell, 29 October 1915, President's Papers, Special Collections, Edmon Low Library.

10. *Orange and Black*, 20 September 1915, p. 2; *Stillwater Gazette*, 20 August 1915, p. 8; *Orange and Black*, 13 September 1915, p. 2; *Annual Catalog, Oklahoma A. and M. College, 1915-16*, p. 96.

11. Annual Catalog, Oklahoma A. and M. College, 1915-16, pp. 96, 97; *Orange and Black*, 4 October 1915, pp. 3, 4.

12. *Orange and Black*, 20 September 1915, p. 2.

13. *Orange and Black*, 13 September 1915, p. 2.

14. *Orange and Black*, 11 October 1915, p. 2, 18 October 1915, p. 3.

15. *Orange and Black*, 20 September 1915, p. 1.

16. *Orange and Black*, 29 January 1916, p. 1.

17. *Orange and Black*, 1 November 1915, p. 1, 19 November 1915, p. 2, 6 December 1915, p. 4, 10 January 1916, p. 4, 19 February 1916, p. 4; *Stillwater Gazette*, 24 December 1915, p. 1, 27 December 1915, 31 December 1915, p. 1.

18. *Orange and Black*, 22 November 1915, p. 4, 13 December 1915, 14 January 1916, p. 1; Rulon, p. 153; *1916 Redskin*, p. 214. Freeman Miller, L. L. Lewis, and M. J. Otey were members of the committee planning the anniversary celebration.

19. *Orange and Black*, 6 December 1915, p. 3.

20. *Orange and Black*, 6 December 1915, p. 4, 10 January 1916, p. 4; *Stillwater Gazette*, 31 December 1915, p. 1.

21. *Orange and Black*, 19 February 1916, p. 4.

22. *Orange and Black*, 8 May 1915, p. 3.

23. *Orange and Black*, 4 March 1916, p. 1.

24. *Orange and Black*, 25 March 1916, p. 2.

25. *Orange and Black*, 29 April 1916, p. 2.

26. *Orange and Black*, 13 May 1916, p. 1.

27. *Orange and Black*, 20 May 1916, p. 2.

28. Minutes, Board of Agriculture, 1 May 1916, pp. 9, 12, 22, 29.

29. *Stillwater Gazette*, 6 May 1916, p. 5.

30. *Stillwater Gazette*, 12 May 1916, p. 8.

31. *Stillwater Gazette*, 26 May 1916, pp. 1, 8.

32. Minutes, Oklahoma State Board of Agriculture, 3 June 1916, pp. 30-31; *Stillwater Gazette*, 9 June 1916, p. 1; James M. Springer Jr. to Harry E. Heath Jr., 3 March 1992, School of Journalism and Broadcasting Centennial History Collection, Special Collections, Edmon Low Library.

33. Minutes, Oklahoma State Board of Agriculture, 3 June 1916, pp. 30, 31.

34. Minutes, Oklahoma State Board of Agriculture, 3 June 1916, pp. 30, 31; *Stillwater Gazette*, 5 May 1916, p. 5; Minutes, Oklahoma State Board of Agriculture, 1 July 1916; *Orange and Black*, 18 July 1918, p. 1.

35. Author interview with Roy T. Hoke, 15 March 1988; *Stillwater Gazette*, 9 June 1916, p. 8.

36. *Stillwater Gazette*, 11 August 1916, p. 1.
37. *Stillwater Gazette*, 15 September 1916, p. 8, 20 October 1916, p. 2.
38. *Stillwater Gazette*, 6 October 1916, p. 4.
39. *Stillwater Gazette*, 20 October 1916, p. 5.
40. *Stillwater Gazette*, 20 October 1916, p. 4, 27 October 1916, p. 7, 3 November 1916, p. 7.
41. *Stillwater Gazette*, 31 December 1915, p. 1, 27 October 1916, p. 8; *Orange and Black*, 30 October 1916, p. 1; Rulon, p. 153.
42. *Orange and Black*, 23 October 1916, p. 1, 30 October 1916, p. 1, 13 November 1916, p. 1.
43. *Stillwater Gazette*, 27 October 1916, p. 8; *Orange and Black*, 30 October 1916, p. 1.
44. *Stillwater Gazette*, 3 November 1916, p. 4.
45. *Stillwater Gazette*, 10 November 1916, p. 1.
46. *Stillwater Gazette*, 10 November 1916, p. 1; *Orange and Black*, 13 November 1916, p. 1.
47. Hoke interview, 15 March 1988.
48. *Stillwater Gazette*, 17 November 1916, p. 8, 1 December 1916, p. 8.
49. Thoburn and Sharp, *History of the Oklahoma Press and Oklahoma Press Association*, pp. unnumbered. This reference may be found in the cited work under the heading "A Semi-Annual Meeting" [1897].
50. *Stillwater Gazette*, 27 February 1913, p. 1; *Daily Oklahoman*, 23 May 1937, p. D-7.
51. *De Pauw Alumnus*, October 1952, unpaged copy.

10 A Steady Hand Takes Over

On May 13, 1961, an eighty-one year-old professor emeritus of English at Kansas State University died after being hospitalized for about two weeks.[1] The story held little if any interest for news editors in Stillwater, where only a few oldsters with long memories might have recalled the name, even if the story had been used in print or on the air.

In spite of all that, the name was fraught with historical significance for journalism, although few living alumni had ever heard it. For Noble W. Rockey, who had just died in Riley County Hospital, Manhattan, Kansas, had played a major role in developing the first journalism curriculum at Oklahoma A. and M. College. In a sense, he was a forgotten hero.

Ironically, just eleven days after Rockey's death, the school's most prominent journalism alumni along with Oklahoma newspaper leaders and students would congregate on the campus to celebrate "Ed Hadley Day." Edmund E. Hadley was to be honored as the man who had started the journalism program at Oklahoma A. and M. There was ample reason to honor him, for the two most famous journalists in Aggie history, both internationally known, were strongly influenced by him. There was little doubt that student interest in journalism instruction had been revived under Hadley and that the celebration would draw favorable statewide attention. The truth is, however, that a rather fully developed journalism program was in place years before Hadley arrived on the scene.[2] It was a program that could be favorably compared with the journalism curricula at other leading land-grant colleges of that day. The road that Rockey took from his native Ohio to early-day Oklahoma and then to his final

Noble W. Rockey, who had joined the faculty in 1911, was named head of the Department of English in the summer of 1916. He had been acting head on two earlier occasions. He guided the journalism program during and after the difficult World War I period.

professional duties in Manhattan was a meandering one. Circuitous though it may have been, it traced a career with commendable highlights. It was a career, too, that saw unfulfilled dreams.

Following Freeman E. Miller's dismissal by the board, Noble W. Rockey's time finally had come. On July 1, 1916, the board of agriculture approved President James W. Cantwell's recommendation that Rockey replace Miller at a salary of $2000 for twelve months. After three brief periods in charge of the English department, Rockey would have his chance to shape the faculty and its programs.[3] Now he could return to the reorganization he had started during the 1914-15 academic year. He had never felt that public speaking belonged in an English department. Moreover, as the number of hours a student was allowed to take in one department was limited and public speaking hours were being charged against the English department, considerable freedom of choice was lost to the students. Various departments were fighting for student credit hours. Rockey felt the department would gain more time for its legitimate work and the students would gain greater flexibility if the departments were divorced. English would lose the publicity value of intercollegiate debating, but Rockey considered that the gain to both students and department was the real thing to be considered. The increase in interest and enrollment during that year convinced him that the time for separation had come. He told Isadore Samuels that if he would plan a curriculum for a one-man public speaking department and could get President Cantwell to approve it, he could start such a department with himself as head. The plan was approved, but for family reasons Samuels did not return to the college as expected.

Fortunately, John R. Pelsma, the man chosen to take his place, was just right for the job ahead. Rockey and Pelsma worked closely together during the transition; Rockey, reticent to take credit for what he had brought about, praised Pelsma not only for placing the new department upon a firm foundation but also for creating an enthusiastic and successful season of intercollegiate debating, now made financially possible by the allotment of a small percentage of the funds of a student general activity ticket demanded by the student body to replace the old limited athletic ticket. In addition, Pelsma succeeded in bringing Pi Kappa Delta, the national honorary forensic fraternity, to the campus. Later he organized the first national honorary dramatics fraternity, Theta Alpha Phi, at Oklahoma A. and M. in 1920.

As a member of Pi Kappa Delta, Rockey was included in the group of honorary fraternity members which succeeded in bringing Phi Kappa Phi, national honorary scholarship society, to the campus. Dean Alfred Boyd of the engineering division headed the group.[4]

As Rockey succeeded Freeman Miller, the *Orange and Black* reviewed his role at Oklahoma A. and M. since 1911. The paper praised him for improvements "not only in the English Department, but in other lines as well." Among the successes enumerated were the cooperation between journalism classes and the *Orange and Black*, the higher standards and subsequent growth of public speaking classes, the success of the high school literary contests in recent years, the spirited competition between the literary societies in 1914-15, and his efforts in bringing the Ben Greet Players to Stillwater.

Asked what one thing at Oklahoma A. and M. had given him the most pleasure, Rockey replied: "The formation of the constitution of the present Student Association. I had the honor of presiding as chairman over the committee that formed the association constitution." Professor Rockey also expressed satisfaction in the way the English department had moved forward and in the cooperation of other departments.[5]

There were serious distractions on every campus in the fall of 1916. The war in Europe with its tanks, long-range artillery, machine-gun-equipped aircraft, chemical weapons, and reports of atrocities against women and children had held the attention of people everywhere for two years. Trench warfare was punctuated by newspaper accounts of hand-to-hand combat in the contest for enemy territory. Dwarfed by this

World War I scenario, U.S. colleges and universities looked nervously on, hoping not to be drawn into the conflict. It was a significant period in world history. It was an important period in journalism history at Oklahoma A. and M. College as well.

In the midst of this turmoil on the world stage, Rockey would prove to be an able department head, guiding his faculty and students through a period of military preparedness and finally through twenty-two months during which 1,438 Oklahoma A. and M. students would serve in the nation's armed forces. One of this number, Lee Gilstrap, would receive the Distinguished Service Cross for bravery above and beyond the call of duty. Many would join Gilstrap in combat, and twenty-nine would die in uniform.[6] Through all of this, Rockey was paving the way for journalism's acceptance on campus.

Rockey, the fifth of seven children, was born on January 23, 1880, to Henry Sylvanus Rockey and Julia Maria Patridge Rockey. He was a descendant of Henrich Nickel Raque, one of three brothers who fled from Alsace-Lorraine during the persecution of the Huguenots. His great-great-grandfather Raque and family had arrived in Philadelphia on September 20, 1764, aboard the ship *Sarah* out of Rotterdam and had settled in the southwestern corner of York County close by the Maryland border. John and Elizabeth Snyder Rockey, Noble Warren Rockey's paternal grandparents, migrated into Fairfield County, Ohio, about 1810. Rockey's father was born to this union in Lithopolis, Ohio, on December 7, 1839. Following his marriage to Julia Maria Patridge in 1866, he moved to Dayton, Ohio, on March 22, 1870, where the family lived at 21 Howard Street while the children were growing up. The year Noble Warren Rockey was born, his parents joined the Rapel Methodist Church, a religious preference that would loom large in the Rockey family's genealogy for many years to come on the sub-continent of India and later in West Pakistan. One of Rockey's five sisters, Nellie, the last of the children, was born November 27, 1888. Years later, she was destined to join her brother on the English faculty at Oklahoma A. and M.[7]

Before Rockey had joined the Oklahoma A. and M. faculty in 1911 at the age of thirty-one, he already had compiled a varied and interesting record in education. His first teaching experience was on a government assignment in Puerto Rico, where he began as a grade-school teacher and later was advanced to district supervisor. He had taken the assignment to earn money to complete his college studies. Returning to the United States in 1902, he reentered Ohio State University, where he was awarded the A. B. degree in 1905. He then joined the English faculty at the Pennsylvania State Normal School at Bloomsburg. There he built a foreign department that, partly because of his reputation among Puerto Rican students, became a mecca for Spanish-Americans who came to the United States to study. This program grew until it required fifteen instructors to do the work. It was a forerunner of today's proliferating programs in English as a second language. Later he taught English at the prestigious Ohio Wesleyan University from 1908 to 1911.

Four men had led the English faculty in five years, but now it could look forward to five years of continuity in its leadership despite the faculty instability that would become increasingly acute as World War I progressed. Noble Rockey had sufficiently broad interests to advance the specialized programs in his department. He earlier had sought and achieved independent status for the public speaking curriculum. Now he was interested in seeking greater stature for journalism. Rockey had more than a routine understanding of journalism's needs, for he had taught some journalism classes in addition to his English assignments and had served as chairman of the *Orange and Black* board.[8]

He had risen from associate, the lowest academic rank, to a headship, and during that time had watched with considerable satisfaction the development of the journalism program he had helped to bring into existence under the gentle but deft leadership of Professor Edwin R. Barrett. He and his wife, Edna, were well settled. They had bought a lot and planned to build a home on it, and had started a family. Their home at 216 Duncan was the scene of English department socials from time to

ORANGE AND BLACK

1919 REDSKIN

Albert H. Nelson (*left*) developed an interest in journalism after joining the English faculty. He succeeded Harry R. O'Brien and achieved popularity with students while setting high standards. He took a leading role in campus YMCA activities as well. Mary Mustain was the first female journalism teacher with extensive credentials as a writer. During her brief stay, she was outstanding in a wide range of responsibilities.

time, and departmental picnics on Squaw Creek and in the Ripley countryside added a touch of collegiality.[9] Those who taught journalism usually taught one or two English courses as well, so no sense of divisive rivalry was apparent.

Rockey missed his fellow Ohio State alumnus, Harry O'Brien, but Albert H. Nelson had O'Brien's congenial qualities and in his third year on campus had achieved solid support among the students. Other members of the faculty at the beginning of the Rockey era in 1916 were Merle A. Sweney, replacing Lawrence A. Wachs, and an erstwhile *Orange and Black* editor, Fearn Bernard Hamilton, starting her second year.[10]

Rockey felt at home as department head. He had held the title of acting head for a brief period after the resignation of Professor W. W. Johnston in 1912, again for the year 1914-15 following Barrett's resignation, and finally in the months before his promotion to the headship after Miller's dismissal by the board of agriculture.

While planning for the fall term, Rockey had acted quickly to take up the slack in the journalism side of his program. The summer *Orange and Black* was without a staff, for there were no experienced student journalists available. The paper reported that "Professor N. W. Rockey, being chairman of the *Orange and Black* Board, and also in charge of the English Department, made short work of the matter. He organized a journalism class in chapel and placed its members under Professor Nelson. Since then, things have been lively." Albert Nelson apparently gave the recruited newspaper staff, in the reporter's words, "a spirit and enthusiasm that bids fair to recall the times when Harry R. O'Brien and his journalists kept the College and town guessing." Wrote the reporter, "Yes, it is a live class. The College is being turned upside down for news."

Nelson was alert, efficient, and factual. His journalism students invariably thought of him as businesslike and austere at the beginning of a course. They usually discovered his warmth and personal concern before they finished. There was something of the stoic about him. He would simply say: "Here are the facts. See what you can do." His reserve would completely vanish if a neophyte writer or editor displayed a flash of ingenuity, a clever lead, an eye-catching headline. The stoicism, the cold exterior impression, the aloof attitude melted away once a student displayed the interest and energy to apply himself.

Slender, ramrod straight, blond, cold blue eyes, thin lipped, Albert Nelson was a rather awesome character to freshmen just off the farm. That may have been good. Students knew that he meant business when he strode into the classroom, right to the minute. A gray three-piece suit was his standard uniform. The gold watch he flicked from a vest pocket and laid on the desk told students that the class period was under way and would be concluded in exactly fifty minutes.

He came to class well prepared. He would open a file folder with comparative samples of leads and sequence structures of how various papers had handled the same story. If the class was editing, he had headline samples from any one of several newspapers. Always he conducted a campaign against unnecessary adjectives.[11]

Nelson's zest for campus life infused the faculty as well. He was a popular member of the Redlands Club and participated fully in its activities. One example documented in the *Stillwater Gazette* tells of a program that attracted 100 members "and their lady guests" to the clubhouse at Fourth and Knoblock. Highlight of the evening was a pantomime presentation of the John Smith-Pocahantas legend. The play was so successful that President Cantwell asked that it be presented at the college auditorium for the benefit of Stillwater school children. The idea had originated with Harry B. Bullen, titular head of Stillwater's H. B. Bullen Lumber and Coal Company, but the script had been written by Nelson. Professor John R. Pelsma directed the cast of thirteen.[12]

During the summer of 1916 Rockey had completed the M.A. degree at Ohio State. In the fall, in keeping with his seniority and his appointment as department head, Rockey was advanced to full professor. The sophomore level journalism courses remained essentially intact, but Magazine Writing was now known as Magazine and Editorial Writing and included work in editing and proofreading. The junior level courses were renamed Feature and Publicity Writing and offered as a two-term sequence, English 301 and 302. All continued to carry two academic credits.[13]

The war in Europe, near to everyone on campus though an ocean away, invaded virtually every conversation. When Stillwater was visited by its first airplane in 1917, it created intense excitement. Word spread fast, and a large crowd of students and townspeople gathered.

As the military situation became more serious, keeping a faculty together was increasingly difficult. Curriculum development would be put on hold. On April 26, 1917, the Oklahoma A. and M. faculty voted to notify the Oklahoma congressional delegation that it favored President Woodrow Wilson's selective draft measure. Also that month, Captain Arthur J. Davis, a West Point graduate sent to Oklahoma A. and M. to organize the ROTC program, called an assembly for all males. He asked them to join the Army, Navy, or the National Guard within the next week or to enroll in the new ROTC program. About 100 men enlisted, including four faculty members. Nelson was one of the four. He resigned to enter military service at Camp Logan as assistant director of the YMCA. Walter Stemmons notified U.S. Senator Thomas Gore of Oklahoma, in response to a query, that 400 Oklahoma A. and M. males were eligible for military training. Before going overseas, Nelson apparently had requested combat

Glen Briggs, editor of the *Orange and Black*, found it difficult to work with Freeman E. Miller's journalism class during the 1915-16 academic year. The year before, Harry R. O'Brien's students had contributed greatly to the student newspaper. Miller's class seemed indifferent.

duty and had been assigned to the 33rd Infantry Division. He asked Lillian Bass, class of 1915, a Stillwater school teacher from Enid, to marry him. They were wed in Houston on March 23, 1918. While on active duty, Nelson rose from private to sergeant. Following the Armistice, Stillwater friends learned that he was in a program sponsored by the Army Education Commission. Like Lester Getzloe, who would join Rockey's faculty in 1920, Nelson was studying at the Sorbonne in Paris.[14]

While Nelson did not return to Stillwater after the war, his Oklahoma A. and M. connections still played a role in his future. In 1919, he joined the Department of English and Modern Languages at Michigan State College as an instructor under W. W. Johnston, who was by then well established as head of the division. Within two years, Nelson had been promoted to assistant professor. By 1926 he was an associate professor.[15]

He had arrived in East Lansing in time to see the burgeoning interest in journalism, which Johnston had nurtured since 1912. From a single agricultural journalism course in 1910 the program had grown to three courses by 1916 and 10 by 1929. Because of its rapid growth in enrollment, journalism was removed from the Department of English and Modern Languages and a Department of Journalism and Publications was established on July 1, 1929.[16]

While Nelson's education had been in English literature, his interest in journalism had grown at Oklahoma A. and M., and he saw at Michigan State better opportunities in that line. He began to prepare by moving more and more into writing courses and by working as a reporter on the

Worcester Daily Telegram during the summer of 1926. Despite his limited professional experience, he joined the new journalism unit in 1929 and was the sole instructor of most of the ten journalism courses offered from 1929 to 1934, including advertising. Occasionally someone else would help out if Nelson was teaching several large sections of a course.[17]

On January 1, 1933, Nelson became acting head of journalism and publications after having served as assistant extension editor. In addition to his duties as department head, he was extension editor, editor of the college experiment station, publicist for the college, director of the summer session, and supervisor of radio station WKAR, a pioneer educational broadcasting facility. In addition, he was expected to teach half time and supervise the photo and mimeograph services.[18] In 1934 the board of agriculture made his headship official, but his career was nearing its end. After a long bout with cancer, Nelson died at his East Lansing home, 711 Sunset Road, on October 18, 1935. By then, journalism enrollment—with a total of 338 students for all courses—had more than doubled in ten years. At the same time, annual reports stated that the department's publicity production was increasing, too. One such report, for example, said that weekly papers had devoted "16,470 more column inches of space" to college news than in any previous year.[19] Nelson had died young. He was only forty-three. But he had achieved on a grand scale.

1919 REDSKIN

During the United States participation in World War I, faculty members such as Albert H. Nelson, as well as servicemen who had been active in student publications, kept in touch with the *Orange and Black* through frequent letters. These letters were among the paper's best-read content. At times, they would arrive heavily censored.

Nelson's zest for work at Michigan State was, in retrospect, an indication of the promise he held for the future of journalism at Oklahoma A. and M., had World War I not intervened. Rockey saw him as a talented and well-rounded teacher. His decision to volunteer for military service had put a sizeable dent in Rockey's plans. Rockey had hoped he would become a fixture at Oklahoma A. and M. College. In the 1917-18 academic year, the English faculty reached its lowest point in five years. Only three persons were listed in the catalog. Rockey and Hamilton had returned, to be joined by a new colleague, Homer G. Hall, an instructor. The description of the three journalism courses, each for two credits, remained unchanged.[20]

Rockey looked for new ways to add interest to journalism classes. One method in 1917 was to assign students to write a critical review of the freshman play, "The Order of the Yellow Robe." The best review would win a prize offered by the *Orange and Black* staff.[21]

These were difficult times for all department heads. The United States had entered the war on April 6, 1917, and patriotic fervor ran high. Both students and faculty were caught up in the high emotions that followed. Stabilizing a faculty was impossible. Hall's appointment illustrates the difficulties department heads had in staffing their programs during the war years. The thirty-one year-old teacher was hired in January 1918 to replace Nelson. Hall had attended Northern Illinois State Normal School, then entered the University of Illinois on September 20, 1910. He was awarded the B.A. degree in English on June 12, 1912, followed by the M.A. on June 11, 1913. At Illinois he was an Ionian, a member of the Scribblers' Club and on the staff of the *Illinois* magazine. He had taught at Kansas State Agricultural College before coming to Stillwater. His stay in Stillwater was short, only about six months. Then he had left for Camp Grant at Rockford, Illinois, seven miles from his home town of Belvidere.[22] The frequent faculty changes in English must have seemed like a game of "musical chairs" to Oklahoma A. and M. students, but they understood the demands of war upon faculty members as well as students. Despite these patch-work changes, the course offerings in journalism were still in place. Nothing had been added or taken away. Even the course descriptions continued without revision. Only course titles had been overhauled.

A parade of young faculty stars passed through Stillwater during the college's first twenty-five years. This parade was accentuated during the Great War. Merle Sweney was one of them. He was born October 8, 1890, at Tamora, Nebraska, to Albert Barclay Sweney and Anna Austine Sweney. His early schooling was at Hastings, Nebraska. The family had moved to Smithfield, Illinois, and he enrolled in the academy at Hedding College, Abingdon, Illinois, in September 1906. He completed his academy work in 1910 and entered the college freshman class in the fall. In addition to the regular academic subjects, he took courses in oratory throughout his years at Hedding, where he received the B.A. degree in June 1913. During his years at Hedding, Sweney won Premier Honor for Scholarship both in June 1909 and June 1912. He placed third in the Grand Army Prize in 1913 and won the Emma Saunders Brown Contest in oratory. He was a member of the YMCA and had served on one of its gospel teams. He was a member of "Der Deutsche Verein" and the Lincolnian Literary Society and had served on its inter-society debate team. He proved himself to be a promising poet in the *Hedding Graphic* and had a part in the senior play, "As You Like It."[23]

From Hedding, Sweney moved to the University of Illinois, where he married Edith Irene Sendenburgh on Christmas day 1916, five months after being awarded the M.A. degree on June 14. Then came a year and a half on the Oklahoma A. and M. faculty, where Sweney, twenty-six years old when he signed on, taught both English and journalism. He was poised, articulate and handsome, and quickly became a popular and valuable faculty member. The war touched him, as it had Nelson and Hall, but in a different way. He wanted to serve but had moral reservations about combat duty. When the Sweneys left Stillwater in February 1918 with their six-weeks-old daughter, Professor Sweney had resigned to do alternative war service on a farm in Champaign County, Illinois.[24]

SPECIAL COLLECTIONS, OSU LIBRARY

1919 REDSKIN

Merle A. Sweney (*left*) was a brilliant young teacher who helped with journalism classes in the procession of faculty who came and went during the World War I years. He was a conscientious objector and volunteered for alternate service. His promising career ended in tragedy. John R. Pelsma brought a chapter of Pi Kappa Delta to the campus and was founder of Theta Alpha Phi, a dramatics fraternity which soon spread across the nation.

With the end of the war, he returned to the University of Illinois in 1919 to pursue the Ph.D. degree. As part of his doctoral work he took his family to Europe for a year in 1920-21 for independent study. He spent three months in Switzerland learning German, three months in Rome learning Italian, three months in Paris learning French, and three months in Madrid learning Spanish. These language skills he added to his knowledge of Latin and Greek. His purpose was to prepare for a study of novels in the romance languages. While working toward the doctorate in comparative literature from 1919 to 1926, Sweney taught English at the University of Illinois.[25]

In the summer of 1926, he abandoned the university, perhaps to get relief from the pressure of his doctoral research. He bought the Saint J. Moffit farm three miles south of Fithian, Illinois, near Muncie, where he raised oats and ran several hundred head of sheep. His three months on the farm had been disastrous. The excessive rainfall ruined the oat crop and when it could not be threshed, Sweney turned the sheep into the area to feed. Several of the animals died either of pulpy kidney disease or acidosis, a development that added to the doldrums he had been in for at least five months.[26]

If Sweney had hoped the farm would erase the mental depression he was in, the move had not been successful. On the day of his death he had planned to take his wife, daughter, and two sons to Champaign for Thanksgiving dinner. Forty-five minutes after he and a tenant on the farm had fed the sheep, he died in his basement. His daughter said the death was accidental, but the *Danville Morning Press* attributed it to a self-inflicted shotgun wound.[27]

Another star performer during the Rockey years, one of the most colorful journalism teachers to serve at Oklahoma A. and M., was never listed as a member of Rockey's department. She was Mary Eleanor Mustain, who came to Stillwater in December of 1917, eleven months before the Armistice. She was recovering from pneumonia and her physician in Chicago had ordered her south. Mrs. Mustain was a friend of Professor George Washington Dunlavy and his family, which may have played a part in her decision. She was the first female faculty member with significant journalistic experience.[28]

The *Orange and Black*, headlining her as a "prominent writer and author," reported that she had been added to the English faculty as an instructor. The paper, citing her credentials, listed her as a graduate of both Wellesley College and Pratt Institute, Brooklyn, New York. She had taught in Illinois schools for twelve years and later held the chair of English at the Manor School in Connecticut, probably a private school. Its existence can no longer be verified. During those years, she developed her journalistic skills. She covered news, wrote book reviews, served as a drama critic and gained some attention as an author, using the pen name

Mary Eleanor Kramer. The *Orange and Black*, listing five books by name plus "a great many more," stated that "her facile pen has truly enriched the literature of today."

She was a staff writer on the *Chicago Evening Post*, the *Mediator* and the *Associated Educational Press*. In addition, she had served as editor of the women's department of the *Lakeview Times and News* and the *Leader*, both Chicago publications, and as literary editor of *Educational Foundations*. Among other publications, she was a regular contributor to the *Woman's Home Companion, Woman's World, Holland's Magazine, Youth's Companion,* and *Good Housekeeping*.

Mrs. Mustain had a keen interest in promoting women's rights in all aspects of American life. She often gave financial support to feminist movements and was a member of the Women's Political Equality League of Illinois. She also belonged to the Illinois Women's Press Association, Midland Authors' Club, and the Brownlee Club.[29]

It was no wonder, then, that she quickly swung into action after arriving on campus. Within a month she was writing an erudite column, "Literary Notes," in the *Orange and Black*. It was obvious to any reader that she was a skillful writer. In 1918, she took charge of the third war loan drive at Oklahoma A. and M. She had become one of the best-known figures on campus.[30]

Professor Rockey gave her the job of organizing two classes in magazine and editorial writing. The student newspaper reported that meritorious articles would be published in a monthly issue. Each class elected an editor-in-chief and departmental heads for their work and entered into friendly competition. The *Orange and Black* reported: "Mrs. Mustain plans to send all worthy material written by members of the classes to magazines for publication. The members of the class will receive whatever remuneration the work brings. . . ." As the class progressed, the *Orange and Black* printed some of the best articles, most of which had been submitted to national magazines.[31]

In another class, Advanced Publicity, Mrs. Mustain's students took on the responsibility for publicizing the traditional Oklahoma A. and M. May Carnival, a practical hands-on assignment, under the supervision of Professor Rockey. In still another effort to give her students practical experience, Mrs. Mustain conducted a poster competition advertising the annual Interscholastic Contests held in connection with the carnival. The artistic posters were widely displayed in Morrill Hall.[32]

In none of its frequent coverage of Mrs. Mustain's activities did the *Orange and Black* refer to her as Professor Mustain. She was always Mrs. Mustain. She was a strong personality, and students instinctively showed deference to her. She may have been a female counterpart of Henry Iba, another highly respected personality of a later day. Iba, one of the greatest basketball coaches in the nation's history, was always Mr. Iba to his players and the student body in general. Mrs. Mustain was a featured speaker on Philomathean and Omega Literary Society programs, sponsored the Vocational Literary Society, was a campus leader in a drive for Armenian relief, led a discussion group of twenty-one female business students on postwar social conditions, and gave a "stunt" social for her vocational English short course students, many of them returning soldiers. In addition to humorous stunts, the party featured baskets of apples decorated with orange and black. The student newspaper reported, "After a jolly get-acquainted time, every one went out on the campus and played games in the moonlight."[33] When a story about Oklahoma A. and M. appeared in the overseas edition of the *Chicago Tribune*, students said, "Mrs. Mustain probably got it in there."[34]

She occasionally used her literary column in the *Orange and Black* to teach lessons in journalism. Under the heading, "The Idling Life of a Reporter," she wrote this: "Some members of the Columbia school of journalism went on a strike recently because they considered an essay on 'Journalism in Philadelphia' too arduous an assignment. They would probably seek a new profession after reading in a New York daily an account of a quarter-hour's work of a reporter on that paper: 'This reporter, who earlier in the night had recorded a dozen individual New York stories without threatening to strike, discovered a fire, turned in an

The Science Hall with its stately columns neared completion in 1919 and was dedicated in 1920. In 1958, it would become the first home of the newly created School of Communications. By the time the Paul Miller Journalism and Broadcasting addition was dedicated in 1976, the Georgian columns had disappeared from sight, encompassed in the mechanical room with its air conditioning and other necessary utility controls.

Centennial Histories Series

alarm, blew a police whistle, ran to the burning residence, alarmed the sleeping family, carried a fainting servant from the fourth floor to the street, assisted the police in rescuing five other persons, and then telephoned a detailed account of all happenings to *The Herald* office— all in fifteen minutes.'

"This incident is cited, not to indicate this *Herald* reporter is more dexterous than other men in the profession, but to give to the school of journalism students an idea of the work a real reporter can perform when he has nothing else to do."[35]

Soon after the campus newspaper had reported her birthday party at Mrs. Stansbury's boarding table on January 29, she had chided the staff for erroneously listing her age as fifty. The *Orange and Black* published an abject apology under the heading "We're Sorry, Mrs. Mustain." In a style typical of the editorial comment students mixed with news in those days, the apology ended with these words: "But honestly, Mrs. Mustain, was that an underestimate or a mite too much?"[36]

The stocky Chicago journalist was, in short, a human whirlwind, but she was spreading herself thin during a period when she had been advised to rebuild her health. The *Orange and Black* for March 22, 1919, published news of a farewell party planned for Mrs. Mustain by her vocational students. It was to be held in Rooms 201 and 203 of the Library Building and all college students were invited. A week later, the paper reported that the party had been cancelled because of her "continued ill health." It had been necessary to forfeit her last chance of meeting with students and faculty before returning to Chicago, where she had taken a position with the International Harvester Company.[37]

In her short time in Tigerland, Mrs. Mustain had become one of the best known journalism teachers since the days of the popular Harry O'Brien. While journalism students studied under other female English professors before her, she was the first woman with impressive journalistic credentials to stand before a journalism class at Oklahoma A. and M. Others have since been given credit for that honor. But earlier writers on the subject were lacking the historical background that this volume has presented.

In the 1918-19 catalog, the only changes were in course titles. English 301 and 302 became Publicity and Bulletin Writing, and English 204, Magazine and Editorial Writing, was renamed Magazine and Feature Writing. There were three new faces on the faculty as well, with only Rockey returning. New instructors were Benjamin H. Van Dyke, a 1911 Colorado College graduate; Stella Priest and Grace Mountcastle, both Oklahoma A. and M. graduates. Van Dyke joined the English faculty to help plug the gaps created by the war. He was born in Nebraska, but his father, a farmer, had moved the family to Grand Junction, Colorado. Before coming to Oklahoma A. and M. College he had taught at La Verne

College in southern California for four years. He held the A.B. degree in English and had done graduate work at the University of California in Berkeley during the summer of 1914. Later, at Pomona College, he was a charter member of the Ciceronian Literary Club and won both a master's degree and a wife, Edna Schrock, in 1918. He was listed in the Oklahoma A. and M. catalog for two years. The Van Dykes shared chaperon duties with the DeWitt Hunts at the "crowning social of the season," a masked party in the armory given by the class of 1921 in the spring of 1919. Van Dyke was active in church work, faculty activities, and the American Association of University Professors (AAUP). No class rolls are available to document his teaching assignment. In spite of frequent wartime faculty changes in English, the journalism program had survived. It had taken patience and ingenuity to preserve the curriculum, plus the use of Mary Mustain and others, some of whose primary interests were not journalistic.

When the 1919-20 catalog was issued, more than one student and faculty member must have been surprised. Not a single change had been made in either full-time faculty or journalism courses. The Armistice of November 11, 1918, had made planning less difficult.[38]

The following year gave journalism its greatest catalog visibility up to that time. Grace Mountcastle, elevated from assistant to assistant professor, and Stella Priest, promoted from instructor to assistant professor, were listed along with Rockey under the Department of English, as was a new faculty member, Verda V. Wilbourn, instructor. Wilbourn had received her diploma in home economics from Ouachita College, Arkadelphia, Arkansas. She had entered Ouachita in 1913 after completing high school in Magnolia and was a member of the Jam Girl's Club and the Alpha Kappa Literary Society. Following her studies at Ouachita, she had enrolled at Oklahoma A. and M., taking the B.S. degree in 1915. Van Dyke had departed. After leaving Oklahoma A. and M., he taught in the Department of English Language and Literature at the University of Southern California and studied at the University of Washington in 1925. For the first time, a sub-department heading appeared: JOURNALISM. Under that category was the name Lester C. Getzloe.[39]

This was no spur-of-the-moment decision. For some time, Rockey had thought of journalism and its relationship to the English department. He had been one of the first to teach a full-term course in journalism at Oklahoma A. and M. He had played a role along with Barrett and O'Brien in shaping a curriculum. Now, after four uninterrupted years as professor in charge of English courses, including journalism, he was ready to make an innovative change. He knew he must add a journalism specialist to the faculty as the first step in starting a Department of Journalism. He took that first step just before the 1920-21 academic year.[40]

As was true of most knowledgeable faculty members interested in curricular trends of the day, Rockey was familiar with the journalism program created by Willard G. Bleyer at the University of Wisconsin in Madison. Bleyer had pioneered in the journalism textbook field while building a curriculum held in high esteem by the academic community. Nine years before Rockey had decided to liberate journalism, H. H. Herbert at the University of Oklahoma had been scorned by editors when he proposed support for a full-fledged school of journalism. Some newspaper editors still were of the opinion that the only place to learn journalism was on the job.[41] Whether Rockey contacted Bleyer for help, or, as a job-seeking young man Getzloe had learned of the opening at Oklahoma A. and M. in some other way, the outcome was the same. Rockey chose Getzloe as the man who would head the journalism section of his department. He chose wisely.

A page-one story in the *Stillwater Gazette* just before the opening of the fall term reported that Getzloe had been hired as an assistant professor of English. More significantly, the *Gazette* reporter stated: "He will be in charge of the journalism work. Mr. Getzloe has had practical experience in newspaper work and has also been a teacher of journalism."[42] There is no solid evidence for the last part of that statement unless Getzloe had been a student laboratory assistant at Wisconsin.

Because he was chosen by Rockey to be the first full-time leader in

Fearn Bernard Hamilton (*left*), who had been an outstanding student journalist and short story writer, was added to the English faculty to assist with journalism courses, among other duties. Later, Verda Wilbourn joined the faculty and worked with student journalists. Contrary to earlier customs, Noble W. Rockey relied heavily upon female faculty members during the World War I emergency.

Oklahoma State University

journalism at Oklahoma A. and M., it seems appropriate to take a closer look at Getzloe. He was born on September 27, 1894, to W. J. and Bertha Matthews Getzloe in Kiel, Wisconsin, where he spent his early youth. Following graduation from Kiel High School, he attended Ripon College for two years, enrolling as one of forty-nine students pictured in the 1911 freshman class, the same year Rockey had left Ohio for his ten-year association with Oklahoma A. and M. College. Getzloe was one of ten active members of the Woodside Club, a campus men's social group. It is likely that he worked on the student newspaper at Ripon, for he decided to transfer to the University of Wisconsin School of Journalism following his sophomore year at the well-respected liberal arts college.[43]

At Wisconsin, Getzloe served as correspondent for the *Milwaukee Sentinel* from 1914 to 1916. His studies included English, French, German, journalism, mathematics, political economy, political science, philosophy, comparative literature and history. Most of his grades ranged from the middle 80s to the high 90s. He took the B.A. degree in journalism. His senior thesis, "Lord Northcliffe and the Daily Mail," was thoroughly researched and impeccably written. It was approved by Willard G. Bleyer on May 28, 1917, its quality far surpassing many of the master's theses of the 1980s. That month he joined the Wisconsin National Guard's medical detachment, training for seven months in the United States and serving the next nineteen months in France as a private first class in an Army hospital. One report suggests that service in the hospital corps in 1916-17 may have delayed his graduation, but official biographical data in Ohio State files fail to support this. While on active duty in the combat zone, he was caught in a German gas attack upon Allied troops and became a new kind of casualty. Once the Armistice was signed, he enrolled in special course work for soldiers at The Sorbonne and the Alliance Francaise in Paris. He studied from February through July of 1919, winning diplomas from both. While in Paris, he began research on the French press during the revolution. He would visit fourteen different countries, most of them during this six-month period. Returning home, he took a job as editor of the *Wisconsin Rapids Daily Tribune*, then accepted the appointment at Oklahoma A. and M.[44]

Getzloe had a well-built five foot, six inch frame and a nicely chiseled face dominated by a strong chin. He was a popular classroom teacher despite his low-key approach. He had a mystique that may have been related to his experiences as a corpsman during the war. He had seen suffering at the maximum and had carried away a sardonic if not sometimes sarcastic view of life that occasionally spilled over into the journalism he criticized in the classroom. His purpose was to get students to think. While a few students may have resented this, most revered him for his obvious competence. There was an undercurrent of soft-spoken style that led them to use their own intelligence to see through the weaknesses he highlighted in some major story of the day. One particular Ohio State student, Margaret Stribling, found his approach enchanting. She would marry him on December 20, 1930.[45]

In a brilliantly written article years after Getzloe had left Stillwater, Frank J. Tate profiled "the professor with the nose of a prizefighter and the soul of an artist who delighted in sticking needles into sacred cows." The catalog referred to him as Lester C. Getzloe. But to any student who ever had a course with him he was simply Getz. The formal teaching of journalism was only a tolerated sideline. His main goal was a philosophy of news reporting: creating the ability to discern phoniness of any sort.[46]

He had an unquenchable zest for life, good writing, the punch lead, and the reporter who could balance objectivity with a humane regard for all, whether high or low. It is doubtful that he gave ten formal lectures during the years he met with his "kids." Sometime during the hour he was sure to pull from his pocket a torn, crumpled clipping that had lain long among others in one of the stuffed pigeonholes of his rolltop desk. He would digress from his lecture to read the clipping and then, in a passionate voice, look about the room and ask, "My God, could this be?" Then he would get to the heart of the real issue and the sham became apparent. When his chuckling "kids" left the classroom, they may not have received all the lecture called for, but they had learned an insight that somehow escapes most textbooks.

Lester C. Getzloe was the first faculty member assigned exclusively to journalism. A graduate of the University of Wisconsin, he brought a touch of professionalism to the *Orange and Black*.

He demanded the utmost honesty in reporting, completely accurate quotations, and a sense of fairness that transcended the immediate account. One of the many clippings that illustrate the Getzloe approach to journalism was the short lead that an Associated Press writer sent from San Quentin prison: "John Doe, age 25, went to his death in the gas chamber tonight screaming, 'I'm too young to die,' to pay for the rape slaying of Dancer Sally Smith, 19, who was also young." That dramatic lead, Getzloe thought, revealed the writer's sense of fairness and perspective.

Getzloe's sense of humor was unbounded. One of his greatest delights was to see the typographical errors or silly sentence structures he had clipped from newspapers and forwarded to *The New Yorker*, where they were inevitably published.

During World War II, he gave in and completed work for a master's degree at Ohio State but did not attend the commencement. Those who read his thesis said it would have fulfilled requirements for a doctoral dissertation.[47]

As Getzloe moved to Stillwater in 1920, the town's population was recorded as 7,000, up from 2,500 ten years earlier. During his one year at Oklahoma A. and M., he apparently was given an opportunity to make further changes in the journalism program, for the title Magazine and Feature Writing no longer appeared. It had been recast as the second term of a two-quarter sequence in News Writing, now listed as English 203 and 204. English 301 was no longer listed, and 302, Publicity and Bulletin Writing, had been given the title Magazine and Bulletin Writing.[48]

Getzloe's passion for clear writing, whether by professionals or students, was exactly what his department head had hoped for. Rockey wanted plenty of student writing, even in courses that might have skirted around it. One example was the Modern Drama class taught by Stella Priest. Although made up of only seven students, the class put together a book, "Stage Stars," on the lives of great actors. The book, in manuscript form, was added to the College Library. It was the fourth book composed by her classes, the earlier books focusing upon writers, motion picture artists, and playwrights.[49]

Journalism students then as now were sometimes naive and provided an occasional laugh among both students and faculty. One coed who gave the campus a sympathetic chuckle interviewed Dean Lowery L. Lewis.

"In her best journalistic tone of voice," the *Orange and Black* reported, she asked Lewis what changes or improvements in the School of Science and Literature he hoped to bring about in the 1921-22 academic year. Lewis volunteered that he especially hoped for funds to add a taxidermist so that birds and animals could be stuffed and mounted as a first step toward building a museum.

1921 REDSKIN

Chester Gould contributed to both the *Orange and Black* and the *Redskin* before leaving to complete his work at Northwestern University and to work for the *Chicago Tribune*. Gould is shown as an Oklahoma A. and M. student in 1921 and as the famous creator of "Dick Tracy" in his Woodstock, Illinois, studio in 1981.

"Desiring to bluff a little intelligence," the paper reported, "the young lady leaned forward. . .and asked, 'And how much does one cost?'"

"We could get one for about the same amount. . .we pay. . .instructors," the dean replied.

"Oh, I see, you just rent it by the year." "Well, hardly. That is. . . ."

Dean Lewis kindly explained that a taxidermist was a person, not a machine.

The *Orange and Black* report concluded: "And with the best grace possible, the would-be reporter thanked the dean and fled from the office."[50]

Under Barrett's and Rockey's leadership, journalism courses had been well accepted. That the close cooperation of students enrolled in journalism had contributed to the success of the *Orange and Black* was readily apparent. For example, when Walter Weaver, an outstanding athlete affectionately known to fellow students as "Fat," was elected editor in a run-off with Madelaine Bradley and Beulah Snider, the campus newspaper noted that "he has completed all of the courses offered at Oklahoma A. and M. in journalism."[51]

One can gain some idea of student journalistic concepts at the end of the Rockey era from the farewell message of editor George H. C. Green and his staff in the *Orange and Black's* final edition of the 1920-21 academic year. It might well have been shaped from notes made during a Getzloe lecture. It was presented in a series of cryptic paragraphs:

"Our purpose has been to give you the truth briefly so that you would read it.

"To give you the truth clearly so that you would understand it.

"To give you the truth forcibly so that you would appreciate it.

"To give you the truth picturesquely so that you would remember it.

"And to give you the truth accurately so that you could be wisely guided by its light.

"We have done all this. . . . We have enjoyed working for you and with you. . . ."[52] Despite this service-oriented philosophy, the *Orange and Black* did not share in the money derived from Student Enterprise Tickets, a forerunner of today's student activity fees. At a meeting May 10, 1921, the governing board of the Student Enterprise Association approved this breakdown for the fall ticket sale: athletics 65 percent, lyceum 15 percent, band 7 percent, dramatics 4 percent, glee clubs 3 percent each, oratorical association 2 percent, and orchestra 1 percent.[53]

It is difficult to record in detail Rockey's final year as head of the English department. Only Numbers 32 and 33 of the *Orange and Black's* Volume 14—the best source for this period—are extant in the library holdings. It seems safe to say, however, that Rockey's diligence in seeking to keep Oklahoma A. and M. journalism in step with the developing field nationally maintained a steady pace. His choice of Professor Getzloe to bring greater expertise to the faculty was one indication, and the catalog visibility he gave to journalism was another.

There were political storm warnings as Rockey neared the end of his ten years at Oklahoma A. and M. Cantwell, frustrated by Gault's domination of the board of agriculture, had resigned. The capitol was in turmoil. The state senate was controlled by Democrats, the house of representatives by Republicans. Numerous bills had been sidetracked by the senate as the legislative session ended. A special session seemed likely to resolve a disagreement over the $1,913,832 appropriation for education. A week later, the *Gazette* reported James B. Eskridge's appointment as Cantwell's replacement. Thinking this turn of events over, the *Gazette* concluded that Eskridge's appointment smacked of politics.[54]

As recently as May 7, 1921, Cantwell had written Rockey to congratulate him on his "splendid success in conducting the interscholastic meet recently held at the College." He commented upon the event's value in building favor with the state's high schools. "With aggressive action and reasonable financial support," he wrote, "you should be able to make progress each year." One month later, almost to the day, Rockey and seven other faculty members were without jobs, victims of what the *Stillwater Gazette* called the "annual slaughter." Eskridge would fill the vacancies. Friends thought it strange that the Rockeys were not as disturbed by the news as the other victims, but on June 9 a son, Ned, was born and nothing else seemed to matter. Rockey was offered a position as dean of men at the University of Tulsa, among positions elsewhere, but chose to accept an offer from Kansas State College in the Department of English.[55]

If Rockey and Cantwell had remained for at least two more years, there is little doubt that journalism soon would have become independent of the English department just as had public speaking. It seems clear that Getzloe's successful year had set the stage for Rockey's next step in reorganizing his department. In a brief, informal history of his years at Oklahoma A. and M., Rockey clearly outlined how his thinking about journalism's role on the campus had evolved. He wrote: "Professor Barrett introduced news writing into the work of the department for the purpose of giving more objectivity and interest to theme writing. This. . .was divided among instructors. My own experience in teaching domestic science students to organize their knowledge into readable magazine articles led me to more ambitious extension of the work. During these years, the students felt that the *Daily Oklahoman* was biased toward the university—especially in athletics. Personally I thought that if only we could get some A&M men on the staff we might get better publicity. I believed also that colleges graduating lawyers and educators and newsmen have the best opportunity to reach the public. I decided to develop within the department news and other creative writing until some possible future time conditions might be favorable to the establishment of a department of journalism. Certainly journalism and creative writing belonged in A&M as a college of applied science and arts. Fortunately there was a good man [Harry O'Brien] in the department for the purpose and again, as in public speaking, for greater efficiency and as a start for a possible greater future I placed all such writing in the hands of [O'Brien]. Enthusiastic student response was immediate but the next year a local man [Freeman Miller] was made head of the department. [O'Brien] refused to work under him and left. . . . The department marked time for the brief period under the new head. After he was dismissed, I chose an experienced graduate [Lester Getzloe] of the School of Journalism of Wisconsin University to carry on the work. Thus far the development of our courses into a department of journalism was encouraging but as yet too uncertain for definite promises to be made. It still depended upon time, future conditions and [Getzloe's] own work. Unfortunately, a meddling instructor, ignorant or opposed to my plans, selfishly discouraged him from returning. . .the next year. Later he wrote to me explaining the cause of his withdrawal and expressed his desire to return—but it was too late for I myself had left the college. The work [was] in excellent condition but as yet incomplete. However, the later work for the good of Oklahoma of some of the students of those early courses more than justified the effort." (Here Rockey named Clarence Roberts as an example.)[56]

There was a note of sadness on the campus as the *Orange and Black* heralded the end of another academic year. At the top of page one in the final issue, President Cantwell's photograph was run alongside that of President-elect Eskridge's. Cantwell had been both a progressive and popular leader, and his upcoming departure was not accepted by his followers with the grace Cantwell himself had shown. In what the campus paper referred to as his "informal abdication" before a chapel audience "in sympathetic silence," the departing president spoke of his six years at Oklahoma A. and M. as the best period of his life. He recited the progress made in the past and what the college should do in the future "in a straight-forward manner, which precluded any trace of egotism." He said that the faculty had "worked up an efficient organization" and he urged students to stand behind the new administration, doing nothing to hinder it. He called for loyalty and faithfulness on the part of all who would return in the fall. On Saturday, May 28, Cantwell performed his last duties as president, announcing student honors and conferring degrees upon fifty-four men and thirty-five women. Three students received master's degrees.[57]

Some of the leading members of the alumni association would not take the change in leadership without a fight. The *A. & M. Boomer*, the Alumni Corporation's new publication edited by secretary Randle Perdue, clearly showed its hostility to Eskridge's appointment. Special alumni committees were sent to both Chickasha and Weatherford, where the new president had most recently held leadership positions. They returned with an abundance of negative feedback which was reported in the *Boomer*. In addition, the alumni magazine reprinted an anti-Eskridge editorial from the *Daily Oklahoman* of April 26. In the same issue was a glowing account of the accomplishments of Cantwell during the six years of his presidency. Perdue had served as Cantwell's secretary, handling press relationships as well as other duties during the popular president's administration. In the following issue of the *Boomer*, the anti-Eskridge campaign continued with extensive quotations from a June 3 article in *Harlow's Weekly*.[58]

Because of the sensitivity of its activities in opposition to Eskridge, the Alumni Corporation moved its headquarters off campus to 614 Main Street. The corporation wished to be free from the influence of the new administration. At a June 29 meeting, Perdue was reelected by the corporation's board of directors, a clear statement that the alumni leadership did not intend to give up its protest of the Eskridge appointment. The new address was the headquarters of the *Stillwater Advance-Democrat*, where the *Boomer* was being printed. In the May-June issue, the *Boomer* also campaigned for a board of regents free from ties to the board of agriculture.[59]

While the alumni leaders worked for a separate board of regents, they also pushed a name change for the college. The choice was Oklahoma State College, and when Jess Hoke bought the *Advance-Democrat* and assumed the editorship on February 16, 1922, he began using that name in stories relating to the institution.[60]

The aggressive anti-Eskridge stand finally began to taper off. Several alumni at large had suggested that it was their responsibility to support the college's chief executive.[61] But the widespread dissatisfaction had made an impression upon many opinion leaders. The new president, the first to have a formal inauguration, was to be a short-termer.

As Professor Rockey prepared for advanced study at Harvard University during the summer, he could look back upon ten exciting years. He

1919 REDSKIN

The Oratorical and Debating Board brought together two outstanding faculty members and three student leaders in 1915. During his tenure as head of the Department of English and Public Speaking, Noble W. Rockey (*front row, left*) successfully encouraged Isadore Samuels (*seated right*) to form an independent Department of Public Speaking. The students (*from left*) were W. J. Green, L. W. Hilgenberg, and Clarence Roberts, all active in campus journalism as well as debate.

would face the new challenge of classes on a different campus when September rolled around. The changing of the guard at the top of the Oklahoma A. and M. structure called for a personal assessment. The turbulence was still fresh in Rockey's mind as he shared his perspective with a former Oklahoma A. and M. colleague.[62]

From Rockey's point of view, the alumni had played into the hands of the board. They had been interested in replacing Cantwell with a "big name" and had been assured by the board that alumni officers would be consulted in the selection of Cantwell's replacement. When Eskridge was announced as the new president without alumni consultation, the alumni association spoke out vigorously in opposition. They were successful only in arousing the community, the student body, and to some extent the general public. Rockey felt that Eskridge's selection had been engineered "long ago," and that nothing had been allowed to stand in the way. To set the stage, the board had been making it difficult for some time for Cantwell to carry out his objectives. Rockey felt that Whitehurst's ambitions to be governor had been thwarted and that, having replaced Gault, he was "determined to strengthen his machine at any cost." Cantwell had suddenly resigned in frustration, leaving the Oklahoma A. and M. faculty at the mercy of the board. In the aftermath, all deans except two were dismissed and the faculties of the Schools of Engineering, Home Economics, and of Commerce and Marketing had been practically wiped out.[63]

Getzloe was discouraged by recent campus events. While he was sorting things out, a faculty member painting a "worst possible" scenario had urged him to seek new opportunities elsewhere. Getzloe, too hastily, perhaps, decided it was time to move on. His departure was voluntary. He had not been dropped by the board, but he may have had doubts about journalism's prospects under Eskridge. Had it not been for the vagaries of Oklahoma politics intruding upon higher education, he might have had a longer career at Oklahoma A. and M. As a teacher, he was excellent, though unconventional. At Ohio State, where he became a legendary teacher of many of the nation's top journalists, he was an assistant professor from 1921 until 1945, when he was promoted to associate professor—a long time for anyone to remain in rank. The promotion came in 1944 after he somewhat reluctantly had completed the master of arts degree in history while doubling as teacher and part-time student. Upon his retirement twelve years later, despite both his seniority and popularity, he was still an associate professor. Again, outstanding teaching in the Mark Hopkins tradition had not been rewarded for its intrinsic value.[64]

As for Rockey, the greatest indication of what his plans for the future had been may be found in a letter written to a Stillwater friend after his arrival in Manhattan. After mentioning former Oklahoma A. and M. students and faculty members who were then at Kansas Agricultural

College, Rockey went on to a crucial fact in his unrealized hopes during the Stillwater years: "We have fourteen teachers in the English department alone. This is exclusive of journalism teachers, for this subject, which I was trying to establish at A. and M., has a department of its own."[65]

One of the positive developments in Rockey's last year was the success of the *Redskin*, which he served as advisor. For four years the annual had been in debt. Because of World War I and other obstacles, the 1918 and 1919 *Redskins* had started the deficits and there had not been full recovery. A committee composed of Ward Chase, Dick Hurst, Marcus Hinson and, later, A. Frank Martin, editor of the 1920 edition, had by hard work and good management reduced the deficit considerably. But it was left to the 1921 staff to finally bring the *Redskin* out of the hole. They did it by selling season tickets to a series of movies sponsored by the yearbook under the management of editor Leo B. Wertz. Both students and townspeople responded generously, many attending every show in the series. Most of the debt was paid by profits from the motion pictures.[66]

Although Getzloe's name was dropped in the 1921-22 catalog, along with the sub-department heading for journalism, course work had expanded.[67] Whether the growth in journalism offerings should be credited to Getzloe during his year on campus, or to Rockey or his successor, is not clear. It is likely that the strengthened journalism offerings were a joint effort by Rockey and Getzloe. Catalog copy probably had been written before William P. Powell's arrival as the new head. Certainly Rockey's role is strongly supported by the evidence.

Staffing the rudimentary curriculum that Barrett, Rockey, and O'Brien had created was a problem following O'Brien's departure in 1915. It is difficult to know who taught the courses, for no class schedules and class rolls are available for inspection. The best evidence is to be found in occasional stories in the *Orange and Black*. During his reprise in 1915-16, Freeman Miller handled some of the work in journalism. Where the classes were taught is unclear. But late in Rockey's administration, most journalism classes were taught in Morrill 206, 301, 304, and 306 and Engineering 301 and 316.

The fact that the journalism program had been kept alive from 1915 to 1919, with some minor revisions in course titles, is suggested both by stories appearing in the student newspaper and the 1919-20 schedule of classes, which provided evidence of this continuity. News Writing, Magazine and Feature Writing, and Current Literature (a critical review of magazine and periodical articles), all part of the journalism program conceived in 1914, were offered in that first postwar year with their original course numbers. During this period, Rockey, Nelson, Hall, Sweney, Hamilton, Mustain, and Wilbourn taught various journalism classes. Rockey provided the continuity from 1916 to 1920. The others had only brief stays in Stillwater.

There is little doubt about the teaching in 1920-21, for Getzloe was the sole teacher of journalism. He taught two sections of English 203, News Writing, and 205, Current Literature, in the first semester. His second semester schedule included two sections of English 204, News Writing, 206, Current Literature, and 302, Magazine and Bulletin Writing. In addition, he assisted Paul Gilmore Malone with publicity, using his classes as a team to provide hometown stories to state newspapers about student achievements.[68]

During his five years of uninterrupted service as department head, Rockey had a total of eight faculty members serving under him. His most difficult years were 1916-1917 and 1917-1918 when World War I disrupted staffing. But from 1918-1919 through his final year, 1920-1921, he had achieved stability. His faculty lineup the first two of those years was Van Dyke, Priest, and Mountcastle. In his last year, Van Dyke had been replaced by Getzloe, and Wilbourn was added.

The Stillwater days were recalled in 1988 by Esther Rockey Jones, first of three children born during the family's ten-year stay. She described those years as ones in which the people were hospitable and friendships were made quickly but firmly. "Friendships with the Barretts lasted only two years in Stillwater," she wrote, "but a lifetime between Emporia and Manhattan." This was typical of many other friendships that took root at Oklahoma A. and M. For example, when the Rockeys moved to Manhattan, they were greeted by the Loyal Paynes and other transplanted Oklahoma A. and M. exes ready to extend the happy times started in Stillwater. The Rockey home at 216 Duncan was close enough to the campus for Esther to roam at will. Favorite places included her father's office, the library and the classrooms "with their nice big blackboards." She could still see in her mind's eye the boys busily tossing belongings out the windows or over the balcony of the burning Women's Building, later to be known as Gardiner Hall. She remembered, too, a long torch-light parade from the campus to the business district, "perhaps a celebration of the armistice." Easily near the top of her pleasant memories were excursions to Yost Lake on hot, dry summer days and to pecan groves to gather nuts in the fall. For her father, membership in the Order of the Red, Red Rose had brought spirited relaxation. "He had such fun over it that we were quite intrigued."

The only disturbing note in the family's Stillwater sojourn came during World War I. They recoiled from the unfair treatment—the blatant discrimination—directed at Gustav F. Broemel, professor of foreign languages. Broemel's credentials were from the University of Leipzig, the Staats exam at the University of Kiel, and Wittenberg College, where he was awarded the A.M. degree. The Broemels lived near the Rockeys, and Esther was a great admirer of Professor Broemel's beautiful college-age daughter, Agnes. It is difficult today to imagine the emotional stress those of German extraction suffered as patriotic fervor combined with anger toward the Kaiser was transferred into hostility directed at such men as Broemel and Frederick W. Redlich, professor of architecture and campus planner. Public pressure led to the elimination of German courses from the catalog. Broemel, in failing health, resigned in July 1918 and died on December 31 that year. Redlich was fired by Eskridge in 1921, returned as head of industrial art and architecture in 1923, and left for good in 1925.[69]

A brief but tumultuous period was about to begin. Oklahoma's high-stakes politics, with higher education as one of the pawns, was in a state of upheaval again. But just past the lurching months to come was a period of relative calm and stability, with Bradford Knapp and Clarence H. McElroy playing leading roles in setting the Oklahoma A. and M. house in order. As relative calm returned, journalism was to build upon the work of Barrett, O'Brien, Rockey, and the earlier pioneers to establish an academic program that would become internationally known.

Endnotes

1. The *Trumpet*, Kansas State University Endowment Association (August 1961), p. 4; Anthony R. Crawford to Harry E. Heath Jr., 29 January 1988, 3 February 1992, School of Journalism and Broadcasting Centennial History Collection, Special Collections, Edmon Low Library, Oklahoma State University, Stillwater, Oklahoma.

2. Oklahoma State University *Daily O'Collegian*, 24 May 1961, p. 1; *Stillwater NewsPress*, 16 May 1961, p. 16, 21 May 1961, p. 11, 24 May 1961, p. 1; *Annual Catalog, Oklahoma A. and M. College, 1914-1915*, pp. 84, 85.

3. Minutes, Oklahoma State Board of Agriculture, 1 July 1916, Special Collections, Edmon Low Library.

4. Noble W. Rockey, untitled and undated handwritten historical review, 1911-1921, family papers of Esther Rockey Jones, p. 6, School of Journalism and Broadcasting Centennial History Collection.

5. Oklahoma A. and M. College *Orange and Black*, 18 July 1916, p. 1.

6. *Annual Catalog, Oklahoma A. and M. College, 1918-1919*, pp. iv and facing unnumbered page.

7. Aubrey O. Bradley, editor and compiler, "The Rockey Family," typewritten manuscript, July 1964, pp. 14, 15, 22, and Helen C. Rockey, "Pakistan: A Progress Report," undated and unpaged photocopy from an unidentified Methodist magazine, School of Journalism and Broadcasting Centennial History Collection.

8. Office of the Commissioner, Department of Education of Puerto Rico, San Juan, to Noble W. Rockey, 10 September 1901, Tim Lindemuth to Harry E. Heath Jr., 7 January 1988, News Bureau, Kansas State University, biographical data form, April 1957, Carl Rochat, news release (obituary), News Bureau, Kansas State University 13 May 1961, "Puerto Rico," script for radio talk by Noble W. Rockey, KSAC, Manhattan, Kansas, 16 December 1941, undated and untitled handwritten recollections of Noble W. Rockey concerning his years on the Oklahoma A. and M. College faculty 1911-1921, and Department of Speech Communication Program Review, Oklahoma State University, Fall 1989, p. 1, in School of Journalism and Broadcasting Centennial History Collection; *Annual Catalog, Oklahoma A. and M. College, 1918-1919*, pp. 136-138; *Orange and Black*, 18 July 1916, p. 1, 8 September 1916, p. 1.

9. Inscriptions on photographs, Nellie Rockey Evans album, made available to the Harry E. Heath Jr., by Carol McWilliams, her daughter.

10. *Annual Catalog, Oklahoma A. and M. College, 1916-1917*, pp. ix, xi, 95; 1913 *Redskin*, p. 37, Oklahoma A. and M. College Yearbook; *Alumni and Former Student Directory Issue 1891-1935* (Stillwater: Oklahoma A. and M. College, 1935), p. 37

11. *Orange and Black*, 20 June 1916, p. 1; Jerry Marton to Harry E. Heath Jr., 30 January 1992, School of Journalism and Broadcasting, Centennial History Collection.

12. *Stillwater Gazette*, 3 November 1916, p. 4.

13. Kenneth M. Grossi to Harry E. Heath Jr., 9 June 1988, School of Journalism and Broadcasting Centennial History Collection; Minutes, Ohio State University Board of Trustees, Record of Proceedings, 1 July 1916 to 30 June 1917, p. 40; *Annual Catalog, Oklahoma A. and M. College, 1916-1917*, pp. vii, 101-103.

14. Based upon photographs in Special Collections, Edmon Low Library; Robert E. Cunningham, *Stillwater: Where Oklahoma Began* (Stillwater: Arts and Humanities Council of Stillwater, Oklahoma, Incorporated, 1969), p. 160; Philip Reed Rulon, *Oklahoma State University—Since 1890* (Stillwater: Oklahoma State University Press, 1975), p. 156; *Orange and Black*, 23 March 1918, p. 3, 12 April 1919, p. 3.

15. Dorothy T. Frye to Harry E. Heath Jr., 17 October 1988, School of Journalism and Broadcasting Centennial History Collection.

16. *J-School Update*, Michigan State University School of Journalism (Winter 1966), p. 1.

17. Julie Sutton Teorey, "History of the School of Journalism at Michigan State University: A Plan B Master's Paper," September 1985, p. 8, and "Data on Faculty of Michigan State College 1934," mimeographed form completed by Nelson for MSC News Service, in School of Journalism and Broadcasting Centennial History Collection.

18. Teorey, pp. 7, 8; J. E. Yantis interview with A. A. Applegate, 1959, pp. 1, 2. Madison Kuhn Papers; W. Cameron Myers, "Professional Education for Journalism and the Program at Michigan State University" [1972], p. 6, and Department of Journalism Records, "Data on Faculty of Michigan State College 1934," in Michigan State University Archives and Historical Collections, East Lansing, Michigan.

19. Dorothy T. Frye to Harry E. Heath Jr., 17 October 1988, School of Journalism and Broadcasting Centennial History Collection; *State Journal*, Lansing, Michigan, 18 October 1935, pp. 1, 2.

20. *Annual Catalog, Oklahoma A. and M. College, 1917-1918*, p. 105.

21. *Orange and Black*, 17 February 1917, p. 4.

22. *Orange and Black*, 19 January 1918, p. 1, 13 July 1918, p. 1; Robin Haggard to Harry E. Heath Jr., 20 January 1989, School of Journalism and Broadcasting Centennial History Collection.

23. Julie Anderson to Harry E. Heath Jr., 28 December 1988, and Eleanor S. Hutchens to Harry E. Heath Jr., 26 June 1989, in School of Journalism and Broadcasting Centennial History Collection; Arch O. Heck, *The Hedding Roll* (privately published, 1973), pp. 266, 267; *Hedding Graphic*, June 1913, pp. 14-17; *Fifty-Eighth Annual Catalogue of Hedding College, 1913*, pp. 52, 53.

24. Heck, p. 267; *Annual Catalog, Oklahoma A. and M. College, 1916-1917*, pp. x, 101; Robin Haggard to Harry E. Heath Jr., 20 January 1989, School of Journalism and Broadcasting Centennial History Collection.

25. Robin Haggard to Harry E. Heath Jr., 20 January 1989, and Eleanor S. Hutchens to Harry E. Heath Jr., 26 June 1989, in School of Journalism and Broadcasting Centennial History Collection; Heck, p. 267; unidentified alumni catalog, University of Illinois, p. 936.

26. Roberta Allen to Harry E. Heath Jr., 29 December 1988, and Susan Fletcher to Harry E. Heath Jr., 3 January 1989, in School of Journalism and Broadcasting Centennial History Collection; *Danville Morning Press*, 28 November 1926, copy unpaged.

27. *Danville Morning Press*, 27 November 1926, p. 1; Author interview with G. O. Fitch, 3 February 1992.

28. *Orange and Black*, 26 January 1918, p. 4.

29. *Orange and Black*, 26 January 1918, p. 4; Diana T. Mackiewicz to Harry E. Heath Jr., 16 August 1989, School of Journalism and Broadcasting Centennial History Collection.

30. Pauline W. Kopecky, *A History of Equal Opportunity at Oklahoma State University* (Stillwater: Oklahoma State University, 1990), p. 78.

31. *Orange and Black*, 2 February 1918, p. 1, 9 June 1919, pp. 2, 3.

32. *Orange and Black*, 29 March 1919, p. 1.

33. *Orange and Black*, 2 March 1918, p. 4, 9 March 1918, p. 1, 22 February 1919, pp. 1, 2.

34. *Orange and Black*, 17 May 1919, p. 2.

35. *Orange and Black*, 16 March 1918, p. 3.

36. Orange and Black, 3 February 1919, p. 3, 8 February 1919, p. 4.

37. *Orange and Black*, 22 March 1919, p. 2, 29 March 1919, p. 3, 5 April 1919, p. 1.

38. *Annual Catalog, Oklahoma A. and M. College, 1918-19*, p. ix; *Annual Catalog, Oklahoma A. and M. College, 1919-20*, pp. 117-119; Chris Q. Langois to Harry E. Heath Jr., 10 March 1992, and Al Johnson to Harry E. Heath Jr., 12 April 1988, in School of Journalism and Broadcasting Centennial History Collection; *Pamona Alumni Directory, 1894-1930*, p. 319; Pamona College Commencement Program, 17 June 1918; *Orange and Black*, 14 September 1918, p. 2, 5 April 1919, p. 3.

39. *Annual Catalog, Oklahoma A. and M. College, 1920-1921*, p. 124; Chris Q. Langois to Harry E. Heath Jr., 10 March 1992, and Jean Beckner to Harry E. Heath Jr., 3 May 1988, in School of Journalism and Broadcasting Centennial History Collection.

40. *Stillwater Gazette*, 14 October 1921, p. 1; Noble Warren Rockey, undated and untitled handwritten historical review, 1911-1921, family papers of Esther Rockey Jones, pp. 7, 8, School of Journalism and Broadcasting Centennial History Collection.

41. Edwin Emery and Joseph P. McKerns, *ACEJMC: 75 Years in the Making* (Columbia, SC: Accrediting Council for Education in Journalism and Mass Communication, 1987), p. 5; L. Edward Carter, *The Story of Oklahoma Newspapers* (Muskogee, OK: Western Heritage Books, Incorporated, 1984), p. 193.

42. *Stillwater Gazette*, 10 September 1920, p. 1; Paul Peterson to Harry E. Heath Jr., 20 January 1988, in School of Journalism and Broadcasting Centennial History Collection; Biographical data sheet of Lester C. Getzloe, Ohio State University News Bureau, 12 February 1952; James Pollard, obituary of Lester C. Getzloe, in unidentified publication of the Board of Trustees, Ohio State University, 13 May 1957.

43. Ohio State University News Bureau, biographical data form of Lester C. Getzloe, 12 February 1952; *1914 Crimson*, Ripon College, pp. 66, 67 and Freshman Class photo unpaged; James L. Hoyt to Harry E. Heath Jr., 11 February 1988, Paul Peterson to Harry E. Heath Jr., 20 January 1988, and Kary E. Kantorowicz to Harry E. Heath Jr., 3 March 1988, in School of Journalism and Broadcasting Centennial History Collection.

44. Official transcript, University of Wisconsin, Madison, authenticated by D. J. Wenmeno, 15 February 1988; *1918 Badger*, University of Wisconsin, p. 121; Lester Clyde Getzloe, "Lord Northcliff and the Daily Mail," Senior thesis, University of Wisconsin, 28 May 1917; James L. Hoyt to Harry E. Heath Jr., 11 February 1988, School of Journalism and Broadcasting Centennial History Collection; Ohio State University News Bureau, biographical data form, 12 February 1952; *Columbus Dispatch*, 18 April 1957, pp. 1, 2.

45. Norval Neil Luxon to Harry E. Heath Jr., 2 February 1988, in School of Journalism and Broadcasting Centennial History Collection; Ohio State University Archives, Biographical File on Lester C. Getzloe, 17 April 1957.

46. *Ohio State University Monthly*, 15 May 1957, p. 16; Kenneth M. Grossi to Harry E. Heath Jr., 25 January 1988, in School of Journalism and Broadcasting Centennial History Collection.

47. *Ohio State University Monthly*, 15 May 1957, p. 16.

48. *Annual Catalog, Oklahoma A. and M. College, 1920-1921*, pp. 124, 125; Robert E. Cunningham, *Stillwater Through the Years* (Stillwater: Arts and Humanities Council of Stillwater, Oklahoma, Incorporated, 1974), p. 232.

49. *Orange and Black*, 19 May 1921, p. 2.

50. *Orange and Black*, 19 May 1921, p. 3.

51. *Orange and Black*, 12 May 1921, p. 1.

52. *Orange and Black*, 19 May 1921, p. 2.

53. *Orange and Black*, 12 May 1921, p. 1.

54. *Stillwater Gazette*, 8 April 1921, p. 1, 15 April 1921, p. 1, 22 April 1921, p. 1, 29 April 1921, p. 1.

55. *Stillwater Gazette*, 10 June 1921, pp. 1, 8; Esther Rockey Jones to Harry E. Heath Jr., Summer 1988, School of Journalism and Broadcasting Centennial History Collection.

56. Noble Warren Rockey, untitled and undated handwritten historical review, 1911-1921, family papers of Esther Rockey Jones, in School of Journalism and Broadcasting Centennial History Collection.

57. *Orange and Black*, 19 May 1921, p. 4; *Stillwater Gazette*, June 1921.

58. *A. and M. College Boomer*, April 1921, pp. 2-9, 11, 12, 18; *A. and M. College Boomer*, May-June 1921, pp. 2, 6, 8, 12, 15-17.

59. *A. and M. College Boomer*, May-June 1921, pp. 8, 18, 19.

60. *A. and M. College Boomer*, October 1921, pp. 2, 6, 16-18; *A. and M. College Boomer*, November 1921, pp. 5, 8, 9; *A. and M. College Boomer*, December 1921, pp. 10-13.

61. *A. and M. College Boomer*, October 1921, pp. 2, 16-18.

62. *Stillwater Gazette*, 8 June 1921, p. 1.

63. N. W. Rockey to W. W. Johnston, 1921, Henry S. Johnston Collection, Special Collections, Edmon Low Library.

64. *Ohio State University Monthly*, 15 May 1957, p. 16; "Basic Who's Who," Ohio State University Evaluation Program of Lester C. Getzloe, 5 June 1955, Noble Warren Rockey, untitled and undated handwritten historical review, 1911-1921, family papers of Esther Rockey Jones, p. 8, and John A. Green to Harry E. Heath Jr., 23 May 1988, in School of Journalism and Broadcasting Centennial History Collection.

65. *Stillwater Gazette*, 14 October 1921, p. 1.

66. *Orange and Black*, 19 May 1921, p. 4.

67. *Annual Catalog, Oklahoma A. and M. College, 1921-1922*, pp. 201-203.

68. *Annual Catalog, Oklahoma A. and M. College, 1919-20*, pp. 118, 119; *Annual Catalog, Oklahoma A. and M. College, 1920-21*, pp. vii, 124.

69. Esther Rockey Jones to Harry E. Heath Jr., 24 October 1988, School of Journalism and Broadcasting Centennial History Collection; *Orange and Black*, 11 January 1919, p. 1; Adelia N. Hanson and Joseph A. Stout Jr., "A History of the Oklahoma State University College of Arts and Sciences," pp. 40, 92, unpublished manuscript, files of Adelia Hanson, Stillwater, Oklahoma; Minutes, Oklahoma State Board of Agriculture, 3 July 1923, 6 August 1923.

11 Two Difficult Years

With Noble W. Rockey's departure, journalism instruction once more fell upon a brief period of administrative indifference and hard times. Lester C. Getzloe had left for Ohio State University, where he was to become a popular fixture on that journalism faculty for the next thirty-five years. Rockey was to have a distinguished career as an English teacher at what later was to become Kansas State University, serving from 1921 until 1947, when he retired to emeritus status. Had it not been for the return of Professor Mable Caldwell from her extension information work at Kansas State, Oklahoma A. and M. College would have been without a teacher with an active interest in journalism. Unfortunately, Caldwell was not listed on the college English faculty. She had been assigned to the secondary school program as an English instructor.[1] Later she would become an important part of the journalism teaching team.

Rockey's replacement was William P. Powell, a thirty-nine-year-old southern gentleman who had been graduated in 1903 from Richmond College, the founding college of what today is the University of Richmond. Little is known of his academic career at Richmond College except that he took the classical course of study. He was mentioned in the *1899 Spider*, the college yearbook, but no yearbook was published in his remaining years there. The *Spider* listed him as one of sixty-three members of the Philologian Literary Society for 1898-99, the largest membership in the society's history. It had been organized in 1848 and, except for the Civil War years, had been active continuously since that time. That it played an important campus role is suggested by these words from the *Spider*: "The reception following the annual public debate given by this Society each year to the student body and their lady friends is regarded by many as one of the most pleasant and brilliant events of the session."[2]

Richmond College catalogs show Powell to have been enrolled in Latin, physics, history, literature, Greek, English, chemistry, philosophy, Bible studies, and mathematics during his undergraduate days. He was editor of the college magazine, won the Orators Medal, and served as president of the Philologians. On June 16, 1903, he received the bachelor of arts degree, one of three graduates that year in the English language and literature major. Following graduation he began a teaching career that would span thirty years—with time out for graduate work—to be followed by two careers outside education.[3]

Powell was born June 11, 1882, near Belmont, in Spotsylvania County, Virginia, the son of Captain James Leavette Powell and Carrie Elizabeth Jones Powell of Stafford County, Virginia. His father, who served as a captain in the Confederate Army, had practiced law in West Virginia and Virginia. Captain Powell was twenty-three years older than Carrie when they married. Later he served as commonwealth attorney for Spotsylvania County and in both the Virginia senate and house.[4]

In 1903, fresh out of college, William Powell signed on as an English teacher at Alderson Academy in West Virginia, where he remained for one academic year, moving in 1904 to Fork Union Military Academy. The

COURTESY UNIVERSITY OF RICHMOND

William P. Powell presided over the Department of English during the James B. Eskridge administration. He tried valiantly to keep the journalism program afloat despite a faculty shortage, even to the point of becoming a reporter on the summer *Orange and Black*.

following year he accepted a position as principal of the Morrisville, Virginia, High School, where he remained until he decided to seek his master's degree at the University of Virginia. He began his studies there in 1907 and soon became involved in campus activities. He was secretary of the Jefferson Literary Society, which he represented in two public debates with the Washington Literary Society, and was a literary society speaker on the program of the university's Poe Centennial Celebration. He was awarded the A.M. degree in 1910. Apparently he intended to make a lifetime career of teaching, for he was involved in additional graduate work at Virginia for the next two years, later studying at the University of Chicago three quarters in 1923 and 1924 and at Virginia once again during the summer sessions from 1927 through 1930.[5]

After finishing his post-master's work at Virginia in 1912, Powell, a lifelong bachelor and a Baptist, left the South for an instructorship at Texas A. and M. College. He taught English—probably lower-level grammar, rhetoric and composition courses—for two years followed by a year at Baylor, a Baptist university. At Baylor, he taught Composition and Rhetoric, Argumentation and Debate, Old English, American Poetry, American Prose, Pre-Shakespearean and Elizabethan Drama, and English Poets of the Nineteenth Century, a wide-ranging menu.

While in Waco, Texas, Powell taught on a faculty team that included two rare talents: Andrew J. Armstrong, chairman of the English department, and E. Dorothy Scarborough, who gained fame as a teacher, lecturer and writer. She was affectionately known as "Miss Dottie." Armstrong, during his thirty-year affiliation with Baylor, brought 150 cultural attractions to Waco. Among the notable personalities were Robert Frost, Carl Sandburg, Amy Lowell, Sinclair Lewis, Sherwood Anderson, and Richard Halliburton. He conducted tours to Europe, South America, and the Orient. A Browning Scholar, Armstrong's travels in Europe enabled him to locate many items relating to the famous poet. In 1918 he gave the Baylor library a collection of Browningiana. This was the beginning of Baylor's famous Armstrong Browning Library, now the world's largest collection of material relating to Robert Browning.[6]

Scarborough earned bachelor's and master's degrees at Baylor University. After six years of public school teaching, she joined the English faculty at her alma mater in 1905, taking a year off in 1910 to study at Oxford University. In 1912, the same year that Harry R. O'Brien taught the first journalism course at Oklahoma A. and M. College, she offered Baylor's first journalism course, said to be the first ever offered in a Texas school, and founded the first journalism department in the southwest at Baylor. In 1916 she joined the faculty at Columbia University, where she received her doctorate in 1917. She wrote for the *New York Sun* for a year, then returned to Columbia as an associate professor of English until her death in 1935. She was a poet, as well as a writer of short stories and five novels with a southwestern setting. She also edited three compilations of ghost stories and folk songs and contributed numerous articles and stories to periodicals.[7]

Interacting with two such powerful colleagues gave Powell an appreciation for the teaching of both literature and journalism. At Oklahoma A. and M. College seven years later he would lean more toward Armstrong's interests than Miss Dottie's, although he would try valiantly to serve the needs of journalism in spite of the loss of both Rockey and Getzloe and the lack of interest among most faculty members.

In 1915-16 he served as head of the Department of English and Modern Language at the newly organized Baptist University of Oklahoma at Shawnee. His salary was $133.33 a month. Next he moved to Southwestern State Normal School in Weatherford as department head for two years before his move to Oklahoma A. and M. College[8]

It is likely that Powell had known James B. Eskridge before joining him at Southwestern two years after Eskridge had left the Oklahoma Women's College at Chickasha for the normal school presidency at Weatherford. They may have met while both were teaching in Texas, or perhaps later at an Oklahoma teachers meeting while Powell was at Oklahoma Baptist and Eskridge was just starting his presidency at Southwestern. At any rate, it seems obvious that Eskridge encouraged Powell to join him at Oklahoma A. and M. College following their work together at Weatherford. The fact that both were southerners added to the quality of their friendship.

Eskridge was elected by the board of agriculture on June 1, 1921, at a salary of $4,500 for twelve months. He wanted his own man to handle college publicity. His selection was Wallace Perry, an OU journalism graduate of solid experience. Perry was approved for twelve months at $3,600. Robert E. Bagby, who had served two years under President Cantwell, was given a vacation with pay to September 1 and ordered to turn over all publicity work to Perry immediately.[9]

The dreams of Rockey and Getzloe for a growing and thriving journalism program were reflected in the program that Powell inherited. The first real journalism curriculum, put in place in the academic year 1914-15, had included four courses totalling eight credit hours. During the year prior to Powell's arrival, journalism courses were reevaluated. Getzloe had Rockey's confidence. He assessed the program, probably looking to future plans for a separate department. The result was eight courses totalling twenty-four quarter-hour credits.[10] The growth in journalism offerings during Getzloe's year on campus, reflected in the 1921-22 catalog, must have seemed overwhelming to Rockey's successor.

While it is generally believed that the first work in home economics journalism was begun during the 1921-22 academic year, it had a longer history. Harry O'Brien's journalism instruction, beginning in 1912, had

Mable Caldwell transferred from an English assignment in the secondary school to a position on the college English faculty. She supervised the production of the *A. and Emmer.*

been required of students in the domestic science and arts curriculum. In 1914, junior women in a journalism class had organized a Home Economics Club. Part of their program was to submit stories to *Progressive Agriculture*, in which a domestic science section was begun in September 1913. In addition, the School of Home Economics in 1921 had added a course, 490 Home Economics Journalism, for two credits, giving seniors a chance to explore the field through research and special projects.

Nor is it certain whether the 1921 addition of English 237, Home Economics Journalism, to the list of journalism courses in the School of Science and Literature was due to the interest of President Eskridge and Powell, both newly arrived, or to the ambitious steps of Rockey and Getzloe, who had begun a tentative approach to a separate journalism department in 1920-21, shortly before they left in the political turmoil that cut into faculty ranks.

Only an incomplete picture of the journalism work under Powell can be given. What is known is that English 203, News Writing, was the only course offered during the first semester of the 1921-22 academic year. The class met Tuesdays and Thursdays in Chemistry 306. The third hour apparently was earned by work on student publications, principally the *Orange and Black*. The second semester class schedule was unavailable as this book went to press. That summer the News Writing course was repeated. Powell probably was the teacher. During the remainder of

Powell's short tenure, the college was on the quarter system. While no class schedules for spring and summer were available in library archives, the fall and winter quarters listed only three courses—News Writing I and II and Editorial Writing, all under new numbers—in what obviously was an abbreviated program made necessary by faculty limitations.

As Powell's first academic year got under way, the *Stillwater Gazette* boasted that the city had forty-six blocks of paved streets. Chester Gould had joined the *Chicago Tribune* after a stint as sports cartoonist for the *Daily Oklahoman* and would study at Northwestern University. The college publicity office had sent out a glowing report prior to registration week predicting increased enrollment and the figures had held up. "It has not always been thus," the *Gazette* writer commented. Mr. and Mrs. Freeman Miller had just returned from their usual summer at the foot of Pike's Peak, and Mr. and Mrs. N. W. Rockey were visiting his sister in Oklahoma City prior to leaving for his new duties at Manhattan, Kansas. Another prominent name locally was in the news. Rockey's old friend, Harry O'Brien, had just married Margaret Kingley of Worthington, Ohio, and had recently had an article, "Farmers at Runneymede," published in the *Saturday Evening Post*. Angelo C. Scott had sent word that he would not be able to attend President Eskridge's inauguration. The Oklahoma A. and M. College faculty and staff had been asked to sign oaths of loyalty to the college administration, cars downtown were legally parking in the middle of Main Street, and the Camera Theater proprietor and projectionist had been arrested for attempting to show a Sunday movie. These and similar news reports gave the southerner a hasty view of life in his new environment, a city of 4,701 residents by the 1920 census count.[11]

What perhaps was an indirect reference to journalism appeared in the catalog. Written either by Rockey or Powell, the statement read: "Some courses are made specially practical through definite correlation with certain professions." Powell had an all-female faculty to help him carry out the work of the Department of English. In addition to Grace Mountcastle, associate professor, and Harriet R. Ensworth and Stella I. Priest, instructors, the board of agriculture had elected a new faculty member, Agnes Berrigan, at its September 8 meeting. She was given the rank of associate professor. Among the thirty-seven courses they would be responsible for were nine in composition and grammar, twenty in literature and eight in journalism. The catalog listed them sequentially by number rather than by categories. The program at this point was virtually at a standstill as Powell sought to cover so many courses with so few faculty members. His staffing problem was further complicated by the unexpected death of Priest on November 13. Her physician listed "acute dilation of the heart" as the cause.[12]

Rockey's tenure as department head had lasted for five consecutive years. These had been nurturing years for journalism, years of relative stability. Without Getzloe as major domo of journalism, Powell's first year in office was a patchwork year. He soon saw that he would have to arrange for Mable Caldwell's transfer from secondary school duties to the college English faculty. By the second semester, he had accomplished this. Caldwell was teaching classes in Book Composition and News Writing and had announced a plan to give her students a magazine outlet. Students whose articles were published, she said, would be excused from the final examination in her courses. One student from each section would be selected by instructors to serve on the magazine's management committee with Caldwell. The magazine was named by John Wallace, a student in one of Powell's News Writing classes, in competition with others submitting proposed names. Similarly, Spurgeon Nelson's design for the cover won in that competition. The *A. and Emmer*, with Powell's support, planned a varied editorial menu: articles of local color, poems, jokes, and limericks from freshman composition and sophomore News Writing classes. The first issue was scheduled for thirty-six pages with no advertising and would sell for twenty-five cents.

Powell, with his background in campus journalism and his experience at Baylor, was a strong believer in the motivation provided by being published. He believed the new publication would encourage students in composition classes. The *A. and Emmer*, edited by James W. Bradley

Oklahoma's turbulent 1922 political year signaled the beginning of the end for James B. Eskridge (left). In the summer of 1923, Governor John C. Walton paid a political debt by replacing him with George Wilson, a political leader thought to have socialistic leanings. Eskridge, despite early opposition by alumni leaders, had presided over two successful years as president and had the support of the student body.

and Ivy Burright, was useful to Powell in another way as well. He was in charge of the annual state interscholastic meet and the *A. and Emmer* would be used to generate interest in the college among the high school participants. The masthead of the 1922 issue stated: "The name A. and Emmer suggests the name by which the College is still most generally known, though the name Oklahoma State College is being widely used. The latter name is thought to be more appropriate, because the institution is for girls as well as boys, and offers advanced courses in all sciences, in literature, in languages, in music, in art, in home economics, in business, and in all the subjects offered by other colleges, as well as those indicated by the words agricultural and mechanical.

"Notwithstanding the movement to change the name of the College, the name A. and Emmer for the magazine will link the past with the present, and be significant of the fact that though changing to meet new conditions and new demands, the institution still clings to and preserves sacredly all that was good in its past." The magazine apparently was short lived. Only the 1922 issue remains in the OSU archives.[13]

On the matter of promoting a new name for the college, the *A. and Emmer* was in step with the *Orange and Black*, which earlier had begun a concerted campaign, following the pattern of Iowa State and Kansas State. Angelo Scott had favored the name change fifteen years earlier. While it could not force such a change upon the administration or the board of agriculture, the *Orange and Black* could—and did—require its writers and editors to follow its own style rules. In the paper at least, Oklahoma State College it would be. The idea was adopted by Jess Hoke at the *Stillwater Advance-Democrat* as well.

President Eskridge favored the quarter system, and it went into effect in the fall of the 1922-23 academic year. Journalism students found little change in course titles and descriptions, but now would be required to earn 208 quarter-hour credits instead of 128 semester hours. The new journalism lineup: 228 News Writing, 229 News Writing, 230 Feature Writing, 236 Agricultural Journalism, 237 Home Economics Journalism, 324 Editorial Writing, 325 Magazine Writing, and 326 Current Periodicals. Technical Writing, for engineering students, continued to be taught, but it seems unlikely that it was considered to be anything more than a service course in English composition. English 228 News Writing was listed in the class schedule for the fall quarter to be taught in Room 316 of the new Engineering Building, today known as Gundersen Hall. English 324 Editorial Writing was scheduled in the same room. The winter quarter schedule continued with the second term of the News Writing course, English 229, in Engineering 316. No spring class schedule was found in the archives of the university library. The available class schedules give no indication of who taught the few journalism courses offered.[14] The best evidence from other sources is that Professor

Powell and Caldwell did. They may have had help from Harriet Ensworth, but it is was Caldwell's journalistic know-how that was crucial.

It was clear that Rockey and Getzloe were hard to replace. They had given journalism students a sense of dedication and competence. Powell, despite the fact that he had been a student editor at Richmond, was primarily concerned with the enrollment demands made upon the non-journalism courses in his program while smoothing out a department that was staffed with newcomers. The journalism program that was in place when Powell arrived in Stillwater limped along for the next two years.

Professor Powell, hard pressed for faculty, tried valiantly to carry his share of the journalism load. On one issue of the summer 1922 *Orange and Black*, only four reporters were listed in the masthead. "Prof. Powell" was one of the four.[15] He also took over English 228, News Writing. The *Orange and Black* reported that approximately 100 students were enrolled. Powell assigned campus beats to give his students practical experience. The story suggested that the most successful reporters would have their articles printed in the *Oklahoman* or other state dailies. "This type of practical work will put A. and M. before the people of the State as well as give the ambitious student the thrill of seeing his article in

The *A. and Emmer* was used to stimulate student interest in writing on a wide range of topics as well as to promote the college at the annual state interscholastic meet.

print," the writer stated.[16]

If faculty minutes are a barometer of a president's style, Eskridge saw less need for frequent and prolonged meetings than had his predecessors. In the twenty-two months he led Oklahoma A. and M. College, he presided at only a half-dozen faculty meetings, and the minutes for these reflected a minimum of serious issues and faculty involvement. Either the minutes were sparse or there was little give and take. In his fourth meeting early in 1922, Eskridge cited the college's precarious financial position and asked the faculty to cut expenditures to the minimum. Apparently no faculty minutes exist for October 1922 through August 1923. Researchers will find little information relating to campus journalism in faculty minutes during Powell's leadership of the program.[17]

It was inevitable that Powell's future at Oklahoma A. and M. College was linked with the future of the man who had chosen him. That future was uncertain, almost from the start. First, there was strong alumni resistance to the Eskridge appointment. President Cantwell had been popular and productive, and many prominent citizens, offended by the "politics as usual" stance of the state's political leaders, fought the appointment.[18] Once that unpleasantness had died down, things settled into a somewhat workable but lackluster routine for seven months. But as 1922, the most uproarish year in a long history of wild state politics, began to heat up, tensions and uncertain ties developed on campus. The increasing power of the radical Farmer-Labor Reconstruction League was a matter of concern, as were the various political coalitions beginning to form. Those who had watched Oklahoma A. and M. buffeted by the ups and downs of state politics braced themselves for the inevitable. A brief but tumultuous period was ready to be ushered in. Oklahoma's high-stakes politics, with higher education as one of the pawns, was on the edge of disaster.

Eskridge, described as pompous by a campus journalist, got through the first year. He was reelected by the board in May 1922. But in November, after what was called the most colorful and spectacular election ever held in Oklahoma, John C. "Jack" Walton, former mayor of Oklahoma City, was inaugurated as governor. He paid his debt to the Farmer-Labor Reconstruction League by appointing three of its members to the board of agriculture. John A. Whitehurst, the elected president of the board, had cooperated with Walton in his campaign and expected some reciprocity. He did not get it. Henry M. Stillwell, Pete Coyne, and J. E. Royce voted as a block against him. Whitehurst lost control of the board and felt he had been double-crossed by the dictatorial governor he had helped.[19]

By the end of the second college term in 1922-23, rumors were widespread that George Wilson, a dynamic radical political organizer, would be rewarded for his success in swinging the League vote to Walton.

He clearly was heir apparent to the Oklahoma A. and M. College presidency and was elected by the Walton-dominated board on June 3, 1923. At a board meeting three days later, President Wilson recommended that the salaries of Eskridge and fifty others be ex post facto terminated as of May 31. However, Walton's power politics boomeranged. Walton and the League had underestimated the extent of the unrest, both in Stillwater and across the state. To protect himself, Walton could see it was fence-mending time. Opposition had become so bitter that he decided to acknowledge his blunder in the Wilson appointment. To accomplish this indirectly, he reorganized the board of agriculture. He named two acceptable, public-spirited citizens—Ferne King of Kingfisher and Harry Blake of Duncan—to the board, replacing Pete Coyne and Henry Stillwell. The anti-Whitehurst block had been broken. Whitehurst immediately called a special meeting of the board for the following Friday with the avowed purpose of removing Wilson, as well as his recent rubber-stamp appointees, from office. Among them was Ernest Chamberlain, who had replaced Wallace Perry as editor-in-chief of college publications. The *Stillwater Gazette* accurately predicted that many former employees of the college, removed by Wilson, would be reinstated.[20]

In the first meeting of the reorganized board, Wilson and a number of his appointees were dismissed and Richard G. Tyler was named acting president. Officially, Eskridge's term would expire July 1, 1923. Nevertheless, he remained on campus only a short time after his dismissal. His

Scenes such as this were typical during the James B. Eskridge administration, a period of solid growth at Oklahoma A. and M. William P. Powell found the increase in journalism's student numbers difficult to handle.

request for a temporary injunction restraining Wilson from assuming control prior to July 1 had been dissolved in district court by Judge William H. Zwick. On the other hand, Powell's term was scheduled to last until September 1, 1923. He stayed on until final examinations were over, meantime seeking a new appointment elsewhere.[21]

Powell, with his genteel southern background, must have thought he was figuratively caught in a buzz saw before his tenure at Oklahoma A. and M. College was over. In the second of his two years on campus, four men—Eskridge, Wilson, Tyler, and Bradford Knapp—held the office of president. When he left following the rowdy political slugfest that culminated in Walton's impeachment, Powell accepted an associate professorship at Drake University where he served for one year before moving to Limestone College as head of English for two years. From 1928 to 1933 he was head of the English department at the University of Tennessee junior college at Martin before leaving higher education for good.[22]

In 1934 he began a highly successful twenty-year insurance career in Virginia, West Virginia and Ohio, then returned to the Old Powell Place and Plantation near Belmont. His great-grandfather, Ptolemy Powell, a soldier of the American Revolution, had owned the 500-acre plantation. He passed it on to his son, the Reverend James L. Powell, a Baptist minister. Reverend Powell's son, William Powell's father, was born and lived out his life there. Back to his roots, William Powell began his third career, this time as a tree farmer. His sound forestry practices won him recognition. His two tree farms were certified in a special program to maintain or increase the value of Virginia's forests.[23]

Madelaine Bradley was the best known campus journalist prior to the ascendancy of C. Walker Stone and Paul Miller. *Orange and Black* editor in 1921, she participated in dramatics, held several important student offices, and was widely acclaimed by both peers and faculty as a campus leader.

Just as he had been active in campus affairs as a student, he was both active and dedicated to the organizations that he affiliated with in adult life. He served as president of the Rotary Club in Martin, Tennessee, and attended the Rotary convention in Vienna, Austria. He was a Mason: Blue Lodge, Scottish Rite, and Shrine. He died February 9, 1966, in a nursing home in Fredericksburg, Virginia, and was buried in the Powell cemetery at the ancestral home in Spotsylvania County.[24]

Powell did little to advance journalism education at Oklahoma A. and M. College, but he did the best he could under the circumstances. He managed to keep a minimal offering of courses in motion and to encourage student publications. Following Powell's departure, Edmund E. Hadley also would find that survival was the primary goal in the face of too few faculty and too many time constraints. But Hadley's charisma, plus the support of Powell's successor, J. Frank Dobie, would overcome some of these obstacles.

Endnotes

1. Record Book Committee, compiler, "Selections From the Record Book of the Oklahoma Agricultural and Mechanical College, 1891-1941. Compiled on the Occasion of the Fiftieth Anniversary of the Founding of the College," vol. 2, pp. 121, 122, Special Collections, Edmon Low Library, Oklahoma State University, Stillwater, Oklahoma; *Annual Catalog, Oklahoma A. and M. College, 1921-1922*, pp. 12, 201.

2. Jane S. Thorpe to Harry E. Heath Jr., 7 October 1988, School of Journalism and Broadcasting Centennial History Collection, Special Collections, Edmon Low Library; Richmond College *1899 Spider*, pp. 30, 31.

3. *Catalogue of Richmond College, Richmond, Virginia, 1897-1898*, p. 19; *Catalogue of Richmond College, Richmond, Virginia, 1899-1900*, p. 18; *Catalogue of Richmond College, Richmond, Virginia, 1900-1901*, p. 18; *Catalogue of Richmond College, Richmond, Virginia, 1901-1902*, pp. 20, 26; *Catalogue of Richmond College, Richmond Virginia, 1902-1903*, pp. 20, 23; Alumni-ae Data Blank, University of Richmond, 16 September 1956, pp. 39, 40, School of Journalism and Broadcasting Centennial History Collection.

4. Alumni-ae Data Blank, University of Richmond, 16 September 1956, pp. 39, 40, Individual Biographical Blank of Alumni of the University of Virginia, 11 May 1950, 20 May 1960, and Questionnaire for Members of the Class of 1910, University of Virginia Alumni Association, November 1959, in School of Journalism and Broadcasting Centennial History Collection.

5. *University of Richmond Alumni Bulletin*, Winter 1959, page number not shown on copy; Alumni-ae Data Blank, University of Richmond, and Questionnaire for Members of the Class of 1920, University of Virginia Alumni Association, November 1959, in School of Journalism and Broadcasting Centennial History Collection. A small discrepancy appears in his years at the University of Chicago.

6. Charles R. Schultz to Harry E. Heath Jr., 5 September 1990, and Michael L. Toon to Harry E. Heath Jr., October 1990, in School of Journalism and Broadcasting Centennial History Collection; *Catalogue, Texas Agricultural and Mechanical College, 1912-1913*, pp. 138, 139; *Catalogue, Texas Agricultural and Mechanical College, 1913-1914*, pp. 157, 158; *Armstrong Browning Library, Baylor University, Waco, Texas*, undated, Baylor University Libraries, Waco, Texas; Kent Keeth, "Looking Back at Baylor," undated leaflet, probably reprinted from Baylor alumni publication; *Baylor Bulletin, The Catalogue, 1914-1915*, pp. 85-89.

7. Dayton Kelley, editor, *The Handbook of Waco and McLennan County, Texas* (Waco, TX: no publisher, no date), pp. 9, 239, 240.

8. John W. Parrish to Harry E. Heath Jr., 28 August 1990, and Eunice Short to Harry E. Heath Jr., 29 August 1990, in School of Journalism and Broadcasting Centennial History Collection. See also documentation in endnote 4.

9. Minutes, Oklahoma State Board of Agriculture, 1 June 1921, Special Collections, Edmon Low Library.

10. *Annual Catalog, Oklahoma A. and M. College, 1914-1915*, pp. 84, 85; *Annual Catalog, Oklahoma A. and M. College, 1921-1922*, pp. 202, 203.

11. *Stillwater Gazette*, 2 September 1921, p. 1, 7 October 1921, p. 8, 28 October 1921, p. 1, 4 November 1921, p. 1, 27 January 1922, p. 1.

12. *Annual Catalog, Oklahoma A. and M. College, 1921-1922*, pp. 177, 201-204; Minutes, Oklahoma State Board of Agriculture, 8 September 1921; *Stillwater Gazette*, 9 September 1921, p. 1, 18 November 1921, p. 1; *Orange and Black*, 17 November 1921, p. 1; Class Schedules, Oklahoma A. and M. College, 1921-22, 1922-23, Special Collections, Edmon Low Library.

13. *Orange and Black*, 23 February 1922, p. 3, 9 March 1922, p. 4, 13 April 1922, p. 3, 20 April 1922, p. 1, 27 April 1922, p. 2, 4 May 1922, p. 4; *Annual Catalog, Oklahoma A. and M. College, 1912-1913*, p. 98; *Annual Catalog, Oklahoma A. and M. College, 1919-1920*, pp. 118, 119; *Annual Catalog, Oklahoma A. and M. College, 1920-1921*, pp. 124, 125; *Annual Catalog, Oklahoma A. and M. College, 1921-1922*, pp. 177, 202, 203; Lorene Keeler-Battles, *A History of the Oklahoma State University College of Home Economics* (Stillwater: Oklahoma State University, 1989), pp. 36, 38, 124. Classes in home economics journalism pre-dated the 1927 date cited by Keeler-Battles.

14. *Orange and Black*, 15 December 1921, p. 1; Oklahoma A. and M. College Schedule of Classes, Fall Quarter 1922, Winter Quarter, 1922-1923, Special Collections, Edmon Low Library.

15. *Orange and Black*, 22 July 1922, p. 2.

16. *Orange and Black*, 10 November 1921, p. 3.

17. Minutes, Oklahoma A. and M. College Faculty, 19 September 1921, 11 October 1921, 14 December 1921, 11 January 1922, 22 March 1922, 20 September 1922, Special Collections, Edmon Low Library.

18. *A. and M. College Boomer*, April 1921, pp. 3-9, 11, 12, 18; *A. and M. College Boomer*, May-June 1921, inside front cover and pp. 3, 5, 6, 8, 10-13, 16, 17; *A. and M. College Boomer*, July-August-September 1921, pp. 5, 7, 10, 11, 15-17; Philip Reed Rulon, *Oklahoma State University—Since 1890* (Stillwater: Oklahoma State University Press, 1975), p. 164; *Stillwater Gazette*, 29 April 1921, p. 1.

19. Minutes, Oklahoma State Board of Agriculture, May 1922; *Stillwater Gazette*, 15 May 1922; Rulon, pp. 172, 173.

20. Minutes, Oklahoma State Board of Agriculture, 3 June 1923, 6 June 1923; *Stillwater Gazette*, 5 June 1923, 27 July 1923, p. 1, 3 August 1923, p. 1; Rulon, pp. 172-180.

21. Oklahoma City *Daily Oklahoman*, 2 August 1923, p. 1; *Stillwater Gazette*, 3 August 1923, p. 1; Minutes, Oklahoma State Board of Agriculture, 27 July 1923; Oklahoma A. and M. College *Daily O'Collegian*, 27 March 1942, p. 1, 28 March 1942, p. 1, 31 March 1942, p. 1, 1 April 1942, p. 2; Rulon, p. 175; *Stillwater Gazette*, 1 June 1923, p. 1, 8 June 1923, p. 5.

22. Alumni Data Blank on William P. Powell, University of Richmond, Richmond, Virginia, 16 September 1956.

23. *Alumni Bulletin*, University of Richmond, Winter 1957, copy unpaged.

24. Mary M. Maxwell to Harry E. Heath Jr., 27 November 1991, School of Journalism and Broadcasting Centennial History Collection.

12 A Major Leap Forward

Baseball had its Kenesaw Mountain Landis following the Black Sox scandal of 1919, and Oklahoma A. and M. had its own version of the stern, no-nonsense judge shortly before the impeachment of Governor John C. "Jack" Walton. Walton had stacked the board of agriculture in repayment of political debts he owed the Farmer-Labor Reconstruction League. The board, in turn, had fired President James B. Eskridge and named George Wilson president and had approved Ernest R. Chamberlain, who held A.B. and LL.B. degrees, as editor of college publications. With the board stacked against him, President John A. Whitehurst was impotent. Finally, with his administration in serious trouble, Governor Walton had appointed two new board members, breaking the Farmer-Labor strangle hold. Thus reconstituted, the board had fired Wilson, replacing him with engineering dean Richard G. Tyler as temporary president, and had dropped Chamberlain for Edmund E. Hadley. Walton's blatantly political appointment of Wilson as Oklahoma A. and M. College president had been a fiasco, despite the fact that Wilson was no stranger to the Oklahoma A. and M. campus. He had served from 1914 through 1918 on the Extension Division staff as professor of agriculture in charge of the various farm-related schools under the college's supervision. Wilson held a diploma from Central State Normal, Edmond, but this was not considered to be a college degree. Despite strong support among the laboring classes, he had been unable to command faculty and student acceptance. A touch of elitism at the people's college was apparent. He lasted in office only fifty-eight days.[1]

The Black Sox scandal had led organized baseball to reclaim its good name through the iron will and authoritarian leadership of Landis, a U.S. District judge who became baseball commissioner in January 1921. For Oklahoma A. and M., the problem was to find its own Kenesaw Mountain Landis. The board found its solution in Bradford Knapp, whose unimpeachable record in the land-grant-college movement made him an ideal selection to set things right in Stillwater. He was nationally known for his leadership in the field of agricultural education. He had served as the first director of the U.S. Cooperative Extension Service and had helped plan and carry out World War I overseas food production for the Department of Agriculture followed by three years as dean of agriculture at the University of Arkansas (1920-23). But despite his high standing in national agricultural circles, Knapp would need the top-flight public relations man the board had selected only a month and a half earlier to begin rebuilding the college's tarnished image.[2]

Chamberlain's simple title as editor had become more elaborate. Hadley was given the title of editor-in-chief. He was twenty-eight years old at the time of his appointment, only seven years out of Grinnell College.

The three years served by "Ed" Hadley as major domo of Oklahoma A. and M. journalism is seen by some as the "Camelot" period, providing an aura not unlike the hero worship surrounding the White House days of John Fitzgerald Kennedy, although obviously on a less effusive scale. Some, such as C. Walker Stone, known to his friends and confidants as "Red," would insist that Hadley was the pioneer who brought journalism education to Aggieland. Such was the legend that sprang forth in full flower thirty-five years after Hadley had submitted his resignation to President Knapp.

As pleasant as the myth was at the time, it was inaccurate history. No one had bothered to search out the genesis of Oklahoma A. and M. journalism. That task awaited the book you are reading now. One can make a case for Hadley's having brought "one brief shining moment" to the campus journalism of his day. He was, after all, an inspiration to both Stone and Paul Miller, the university's two most famous journalists of later years. On that basis alone he can hardly be dismissed lightly.

Nor is it difficult to see how the legend developed. Hadley offered a marked contrast to those who had taught journalism before his arrival. With the possible exception of Angelo C. Scott, Harry R. O'Brien, and Lester C. Getzloe, no one ahead of Hadley had been viewed with such respect by those interested in journalism careers. Certainly none of his predecessors had had his extensive experience in "big time" journalism. In his short tenure, he made major contributions both as a teacher and as the institution's chief publicity and publications executive.[3]

An examination of Hadley's background makes it easy to see why he felt at home with students and why students admired him. He was born

August 12, 1895, on a farm near Gilman, Iowa, while Oklahoma A. and M. was still a fledgling college on the plains. His father and mother, Elam J. Hadley and Minnie Boyd Hadley, later moved to Grinnell, Iowa, where they purchased a tract of land bordering the east side of the Grinnell College campus. Elam developed the land, known as Hadley Addition to the city of Grinnell, and soon became active in civic affairs. He was a leading member of the city council when Grinnell's first pavement was poured and when the first modern fire truck was purchased. Thus, young Ed, the first-born of eight children, grew up on the edge of one of the midwest's most-respected liberal arts colleges, learning the lore of campus life from observation.[4]

He attended preparatory school at the old Grinnell Academy, then joined the freshman class, representing the third generation on both sides of his family to attend Grinnell College. He was not long in becoming one of the college's best known students. He decided to focus his studies upon history and economics. Although he found time to participate in freshman football, he failed to make a name for himself later on the varsity team. As a sophomore, he was one of about twenty students on the staff of the student newspaper, *Scarlet and Black*, as a "reporting editor." Apparently he made good strides in campus journalism, for he was employed by the *Des Moines Register* and *Tribune* as campus correspondent while a student.[5]

But journalism was only one of his interests. Music was a strong competitor for his extra-curricular time. He went through the fall tryouts for the Men's Glee Club and after surviving various trials was given a permanent berth as one of five singing second bass. Under Professor G. L. Pierce, the club became known as "The Best in the West." The Grinnell yearbook boasted that "few are the college musical organizations that can rival it." In addition to one weekday practice, Vesper Choir practice on Sundays was required as well as a weekly Oratorio drill. A two-week tour during spring vacation was one of the year's highlights followed by the "Home Concert," the big event of the year in Grinnell music circles. While singing in the Eisteddfod celebration in Des Moines, the club gave a tryout program at the Orpheum Theater and was signed to a summer tour contract.[6]

In the Grinnell College Orchestra, young Hadley was one of six in the second-violin section. He was membership chairman in the Y.M.C.A. Cabinet, and a member of Chrestomathia, the oldest college literary society west of the Mississippi. An all-male group, Chrestomathia sponsored interscholastic debates that were carried on in the name of the society, rather than in the name of the college.[7]

After receiving his bachelor of arts degree in the spring of 1916, Hadley joined the news staff of the *Des Moines Register* and *Tribune* where he remained until the United States entered World War I. Patriotism ran high, and Hadley was not immune. An ambulance unit was being organized at the University of Chicago. He joined it. The 1918 Grinnell class letter placed him in Allentown, Pennsylvania, in the U.S. Ambulance Corps "awaiting transfer to [the] Intelligence Division of the Army." While marking time in Pennsylvania, he enrolled at Muhlenberg College.[8]

Little is known of his wartime service. Whether he remained in the Ambulance Corps or actually was transferred to intelligence is not clear, although it was not uncommon for those with newspaper experience to be assigned to intelligence duties. It is known, however, that he was stationed in New York City following his brief stay in Allentown. To his bitter disappointment, he saw no combat duty. At the end of the war, he joined the staff of Dr. John Hanson Thomas Main, Grinnell's president, who had been named a member of the Near East Relief Commission. He served with Dr. Main at the south end of the Black Sea. Marguerite Feys, his wife-to-be, worked for the commission at the opposite end as secretary to General Maurice Paul Emmanuel Sarrail of the French Army. Miss Feys, a native of Belgium and fluent in French, had met Hadley in connection with their postwar relief work and the two had fallen in love during a moonlit walk on the seashore. They were married in Tiflis, Russia, on February 10, 1920.[9]

Hadley returned to the United States with his Belgian bride soon after the wedding. He joined the staff of the *New Orleans Times-Picayune*, perhaps to provide his young wife an atmosphere in which French was spoken. It was in New Orleans that their first child, Josef, was born on December 31, 1920. Then the Hadleys moved to Memphis, where he worked for the *Times-Scimitar* before getting closer to his roots by moving to the *Kansas City Star*. It was the Kansas City move that ultimately would bring him to Oklahoma. He joined the Kansas City bureau of the Associated Press at 1716 Grand Avenue on June 26, 1922. On July 24, 1922, he was transferred by the AP to Oklahoma City, where he covered the state capitol. It was his work there that brought him to the attention of the board of agriculture when it needed a trouble-shooting public relations man at Oklahoma A. and M. On August 4, 1923, he resigned as AP state editor to accept the board's assignment as publications editor at Oklahoma A. and M.[10] Forty-nine days later, Knapp would replace Tyler. Two months after Knapp's selection, Walton's impeachment would send Martin E. Trapp to the governor's office. Oklahoma politics had never been more feverish.

Knapp and Hadley were a better combination than might have been expected, considering the fact that Knapp had no say in his appointment. The president wanted favorable publicity for the college. Hadley got it. His background in newspaper and wire service work was ideal for general college publicity, although Knapp may have questioned his skills in handling agricultural news. There was a noticeable increase in news about Oklahoma A. and M. both statewide and locally almost immediately after Hadley's arrival on campus. At the same time, the campus newspaper began to take on a more professional tone. It was evident, journalistically speaking, that a new wind was sweeping the campus.

Soon after Hadley drove his sporty Manson into Stillwater with his wife and young son in the fall of 1923—certainly before he was well settled in his office—he found a small but eager group on campus whose chief interest was journalism. What was more important, these students looked forward to a break from journalism's subordinate role as an appendage to the Department of English. They thought the time was ripe for a separate Department of Journalism, with its own faculty and a full-scale major.[11] This goal was not achieved under Hadley. He did, however, bring greater recognition to the journalism program.

Upon reading the first catalog which he was responsible for editing, Hadley found eight journalism courses carried over from the Edwin R. Barrett and Noble W. Rockey years. This fact may have led him to suggest that in the next catalog the Department of English should be renamed the Department of English and Journalism. He was on good terms with J. Frank Dobie, who had joined Oklahoma A. and M. as head of the department soon after Hadley was appointed. Whether the new name was Hadley's idea or was suggested by Dobie is moot. However it came

Edmund E. Hadley, shown here as a Grinnell College student, was still young and energetic when he arrived in Stillwater. His colorful career impressed students, giving him credibility in his teaching, whether in the classroom or in the publicity office.

about, the 1923-24 catalog carried a new title: Department of English and Journalism. After being submerged in the Department of English for a decade, journalism finally had received significant visibility for the first time. The new departmental title would last for thirteen years. A good deal of on-campus "lobbying" by students on the *Orange and Black* staff preceded the catalog change. They had not yet achieved their goal, but an important step forward toward that goal had been taken. In addition to the journalism offerings in English, an advertising course was taught in the School of Commerce.[12]

Among his various duties, Hadley served as chairman of the standing committee on publications. Other members were the deans of the various schools. As student publications had grown, competition for local advertising had increased, and some of the city's businessmen asked for relief from what they considered to be over-solicitation. Thus developed another standing committee, this one on student solicitation for advertising. It was chaired by Dean Clarence H. McElroy with Hadley and three other faculty as members.[13]

Hadley ran his publicity office like a city room, assigning students in his classes to cover stories, then correcting their copy and showing them how to do rewrites. No one flunked Hadley's courses. Students either developed competence or were told to drop out.[14]

One of Hadley's brightest students was Walker Stone, who later would become editor-in-chief of Scripps-Howard Newspapers from the chain's Washington, D.C. headquarters. He credited Hadley with having the most influence in shaping the course of his life. Another of Hadley's students who became a world figure in journalism was Paul Miller, later head of the far-flung Gannett media empire. When Miller came to Oklahoma A. and M. in 1925 he was given a job in the college publicity office writing stories about students, student activities, and various agricultural programs. Miller saw Hadley as a warm and friendly teacher as well as his boss. It was a rare student who was not favorably disposed toward the young Iowan. In nominating Hadley for an alumni award at Grinnell's fiftieth reunion of the class of 1916, Miller wrote: "I have always felt that the coaching and training Ed Hadley gave me in that early period was worth more than I could ever calculate or adequately acknowledge."[15]

Stone and Hadley, though close friends, openly disagreed on at least one occasion. Stone had editorialized against an American Legion endowment drive among students to aid financially depressed war veterans. "Is a group of students of very limited means the place to make up for the government's failure to make those compensations?" he had written. Using the *O'Collegian's* "Firing Line" column, Hadley strongly supported the drive.[16]

The popular Iowan had strong ties with his family. In his second year on campus, Hadley's brother Don spent several weeks in Stillwater, followed later by his father, two sisters, and a brother-in-law. They made the trip from Grinnell by automobile, a considerable journey considering the roads of that period. Don Hadley returned to Iowa with them. Part of the family solidarity was related to their sharing of common experiences. It is noteworthy that two of Hadley's grandparents, his mother, three younger sisters, his younger brother, and a niece all had attended Grinnell College.

Hadley's stay at Oklahoma A. and M. was brief. But for the handful of journalistically inclined students, he was the right man at the right time. He was young, enthusiastic, and aggressive, and he had a special knack for person-to-person communication. There were no faculty-student barriers when he visited or worked with students. His faculty and staff colleagues also were impressed with his style. He was imaginative, and obviously was a self-starter.[17]

To some, Hadley seemed flamboyant. In the vernacular of that day, some saw him as a "dandy." To others, there was nothing particularly noteworthy about him. He was slender, about a size 36, of medium height, with pleasant features and a friendly face. He weighed about 145 pounds. He dressed well and was outgoing in his contacts. One of his contemporaries recalled him as a hale-fellow-well-met type, a good conversationalist, buoyant and well liked. Despite this, he chose those in his social circle carefully. When he was not at his typewriter in the southwest corner of Old Central, he stayed close to home. He had few social contacts with the exception of students in his classes or those handling publicity assignments for him. Hadley's assistant in the College Publications Office, Randle Perdue, recalled that Hadley was "something of a loner." He apparently did not mix much with those in town-and-gown circles, but occasionally he entertained students in his home at 508 Jefferson Street.[18]

Irvin Hurst, who embarked upon a long and successful career in insurance after having earned a solid reputation as a political reporter for the *Oklahoman* and *Times* of Oklahoma City, remembers being invited to dinner by the Hadleys. All of the conversation among Mr. and Mrs. Hadley and their young son was carried on in French. The conversation directed to Hurst was in English.[19]

Among the reasons that Hadley was both liked and respected by students was his World War I background, which to many young people was at once glamorous, mysterious, and exciting. In addition to his impressive personality, he had a consistently enthusiastic, optimistic approach to daily living.[20]

Hadley regularly appeared on campus in tie and jacket, as all faculty were expected to do, but when he worked he was much less formal. Whether sitting at his typewriter turning out publicity for the Knapp administration, supervising student employees writing "home towners," or teaching a copyediting class, he would first remove his jacket, loosen his tie, and roll up his sleeves. Then he would get down to business.[21]

The more comprehensive journalism program which had evolved under Barrett and Rockey, while still shown in the catalog, was considerably reduced during Hadley's years. Faculty changes had left the journalism program short-handed, and only a limited number of basic courses were offered.[22]

He apparently had no academic title. His name did not appear in the catalog as a member of the English faculty. But his involvement with students learning journalistic skills is supported by first-hand reports from those who were associated with him and from various college documents as well, including class rolls bearing his signature.[23]

The late Raymond Fields, one of Oklahoma's best-known publishers and later a business associate of Hadley's, recalled the young college publications head as one who associated freely with students, teaching them journalism on an individual basis. He would sit down with young reporters, criticizing them constructively, praising when possible, and helping them to develop their stories by judicious editing. His advice about how to handle a particular writing problem was welcomed. Not only did he assist those on the weekly campus newspaper, the *Orange and Black*, a fact which was reflected in the paper's improvement, but his careful selection and supervision of student help in the publications office also had a positive effect upon campus journalism.[24]

Only fragmentary evidence exists to support the extent of Hadley's teaching. Certainly it was somewhat limited by his duties as college editor and publicity agent. His first year he taught at least two courses, News Writing and Editorial Writing, both in the fall quarter. No other class schedules for the year were found in the archives. The next available class schedule, for spring quarter 1925, suggests that he had taught part of a new lineup of journalism courses activated in 1924-25. This program, no doubt Hadley's own creation, included three quarters of News-Gathering and Reporting, two of News Editing and one of Special Writing. The latter encompassed editorial, political, and feature writing. In addition there was a course in Agricultural Journalism and one in Home Economics Journalism. Agricultural Journalism was taught by Lacy Wilborn Littlejohn, a member of the agricultural education faculty who held a B.S. in agriculture from Texas A. and M. College. Mable Caldwell, daughter of the legendary Professor James H. Caldwell and an Oklahoma A. and M. graduate, was responsible for Home Economics Journalism. She had recently returned from a journalistic position at Kansas State Agricultural College. Hadley had chosen to handle the general journalism courses. Journalists would note that he had emphasized the importance of *news gathering* rather than simply writing, and that newspaper editing had been stressed for the first time. Most of the courses during the Hadley era were taught in Engineering 316, Morrill 212, Library 203 and 204, and Home Economics 301. Hadley preferred engineering and the new library building for his classes, for they were only a few steps from his office in Old Central.

Some of the journalism courses were extremely small by today's standards. For example, on one occasion when Hadley taught editing his class consisted of only four or five students. He would sit at the desk with them, pass out copy—sometimes a story someone in the class had written—and with a brief introduction to the assignment set the class to editing. Hadley then would lead a critique on the editing of each story. The course, one student recalled, emphasized basics such as sentence structure, paragraphing, headline writing, news judgment "and things of that nature." His reporting class was larger, but of the twenty-one enrolled, seven dropped.[25]

The loyalty of students in chapel attendance had slipped in the postwar period and was a matter of concern to Knapp. Whether he hoped to rebuild positive attitudes toward attendance or was concerned about a possible church-state challenge is not clear. Whatever the reason, on March 12, 1925, Knapp used the chapel period to announce: "I want to impress upon you that we are holding convocation—not chapel." He deplored the conspicuously vacant seats he faced, the *O'Collegian* reported.[26] Later in the term there apparently had been little improvement. Attorney General George Short was scheduled for an Armistice Day convocation in the College Auditorium, but when only seventy-one students had gathered at 1:30 P.M., Knapp cancelled the program. He said

C. Walker Stone (*left*), a powerful student political leader, helped lift student journalism from essays, poetry, and highly subjective news stories to a more professional plane. Paul Miller (*center*) and Irvin Hurst (*right*) were among the outstanding members of the *O'Collegian* staff during the Edmund E. Hadley years. Miller was sports editor and later managing editor, while Hurst served as editor. Later, as a senior, Hurst taught a journalism class to assist the hard-pressed faculty following Hadley's resignation.

Short would not be asked to speak to such a small audience.[27]

While there was less support for convocations during the Flapper Era, there were occasional efforts to show support for Knapp in other ways. The American Association of University Women had taken the lead in establishing Knapp Night, which had some of the characteristics of fall's Harvest Carnival and spring's May Festival. Campus social groups presented skits in competition for $15 in gold, a prize likely to bring a chuckle to students today.[28]

The *Orange and Black* was located in Old Central, as was Hadley's office, a fact which gave him an advantage in scouting talent for part-time help in his publicity duties. An example will bear this out. At a weekly convocation that had attracted "a few conscientious upper classmen and most of the freshmen who had not yet learned to cut," Irvin Hurst perked up with President Knapp's announcement that Madelaine Bradley would welcome reporters for the *Orange and Black*. A senior from Oklahoma City, Bradley had been a leader in dramatics, journalism, and numerous other campus activities. She would qualify for her baccalaureate degree at the end of the winter quarter after four quarters as editor. To the student body, her looming departure was viewed as the end of an era.[29] As will be seen later, the start of the spring quarter proved to be just that for the student newspaper.

Hurst would recall his first encounter with Hadley in these words: "As soon as assembly was over, I dashed over to Old Central. . . . Unable to find Miss Bradley, I literally bumped into Ed Hadley. When I told him I had a year's experience on the *Okmulgee Daily Times*, he invited me back in the afternoon for a tryout in writing home town stories for students rating news mention. Fortunately, I made the grade, and thus for four hours a day through the autumn months I was grinding out local stories—an experience which soon enabled me to identify hundreds of students by home town and local newspaper." Hurst not only developed wide campus contacts, but improved his skills under Hadley's guidance while at the same time gaining statewide publicity for Oklahoma A. and M.[30] Such student help enabled the new editor-in-chief to carry on a general public information program for Oklahoma A. and M. in addition to his responsibility for the production of the college catalog, experiment station bulletins, and other official publications. Such multiple duties also were to be the lot of Clement E. Trout, his successor, for many years.

Two additional examples point up the closeness of the remarkable Ed Hadley to his students. One is the fact that he was embraced as a member of Theta Nu Epsilon (TNE), a secret society made up of leaders from various campus fraternities with the notable exception of Beta Theta Pi members, bitter enemies of TNE. TNE's principal objective was to control campus politics by infiltrating such power centers as the Student Senate, Men's Panhellenic Council, and the boards controlling student publications. It came into being, in all likelihood, to counteract the power of the Betas in campus affairs, and a bitter enmity ensued as TNE began to exert its influence on campus elections, including that of the student newspaper editor. On at least two occasions the sub rosa organization was banned by the Oklahoma A. and M. administration, only to resurface (assuming it had actually disbanded) with its power largely intact.[31]

During Hadley's short time on campus, several of the college's leading student journalists were members, and his closeness to them led to his being invited to join. He was especially close to "Red" Stone, perhaps the most powerful student leader of his day and a TNE member. An anti-TNE handbill which influenced the outcome of the 1926 campus elections, leading to the defeat of Hurst in his bid for reelection as editor, listed Hadley as a TNE member. The handbill named Stone as one of a half dozen TNE senate members, then alleged that "the following members of the publications department. . .were placed there by their TNE brothers. . . ." Listed were Charlie Weathers, business manager, and Ray

The *1927 Redskin* used a visual summary of the previous year's dramatic events in campus journalism. It was a year in which the sub rosa society Theta Nu Epsilon was exposed, leading to an upset in the election of an *O'Collegian* editor, followed by the resignation of an editor who clashed with President Bradford Knapp.

"Gabe" Gierhart, editor, of the *Redskin*, and Hurst, editor of the *O'Collegian*. "And to these," the handbill reported, "is added the name of a faculty member, chairman of the board of publications, Ed Hadley." The handbill continued: "This is just a brief sketch of a society which has stolen and bought its way into control of campus politics and student activities. An organization which stole the presidency of the student senate from [Raymond] Bivert and gave it to [George] Connor; which placed Red Stone in the secretary-treasurership of the student senate. . . ."[32]

While some of the charges in the handbill were excessive and would be difficult if not impossible to substantiate, there is little doubt that TNE had assumed considerable power in campus affairs, and that some of the brightest, most promising student journalists were members. Nor did these students, following graduation, show any reluctance to admit that they had been members. For example, when the college's most famous journalism graduate, Paul Miller, well on his way to national prominence, was asked to send his vita to his alma mater, he readily listed Theta Nu Epsilon membership as part of his campus record, despite the fact that this affiliation may have cost him the editorship in the 1927 all-college elections. Miller had lost to Otis Wile by a narrow margin.[33]

Hadley's membership, too, was a matter of record, as was that of Stone and Hurst.[34] The merits or demerits of their participation and that of others is difficult to assess decades later. Was Oklahoma A. and M. better served by the dominance of a single social fraternity or by the intervention of a sub-rosa political society which itself became dominant? Or was the battle between TNE and anti-TNE forces which erupted in 1926, and which surfaced and resurfaced in a less virulent form for several decades, part of a stimulating give and take that helped prepare students for the much-discussed "real world" that stretched into their future? John Oliver, who resigned his Theta Nu Epsilon membership shortly after being named editor of the *Daily O'Collegian*, summed up his feelings forty years later: "While student politics obviously played a hand in the selection of editors, I have the impression that in general the selections were good ones. Certainly the men who preceded me and followed me were most deserving of the post."[35]

One scholar has written that many were inclined to agree with Oliver's evaluation. "Regardless of the TNE influence, or maybe even because of it," wrote Vera Kathryn Stevens Anderson, "the *O'Collegian* was served by editors who were bright, capable, hardworking young men with gifted talents."[36]

The second example providing evidence that Hadley was held in high esteem by leading student journalists and that his counsel was sought by them is to be found in the story of how the *O'Collegian* got its name. It was, in fact, Hadley, in a huddle with a handful of student journalists, who named the paper on a wintry day in what originally was the president's office in Old Central. The christening took place in December 1923 or January 1924.[37]

The *Orange and Black* had been a six-column weekly printed on slick paper in the college print shop. The shop was reluctant to handle a semi-weekly publication schedule, which the staff was contemplating, so it was decided to change the format to five columns and to contract for printing downtown at the *Advance-Democrat*, a weekly newspaper in which Hadley had invested. (During the next eleven months the paper alternated five- and six-column formats on several occasions, suggesting that its arrangements for printing had shifted as conditions warranted.)[38]

Irvin Hurst, who was present, later described Hadley's role in naming the paper. Others present, Hurst recalled, were Randle Perdue, who worked mornings for the *Daily Press* and afternoons for the Oklahoma A. and M. publications department as Hadley's assistant; Walker Stone, Okemah, a sophomore; and possibly Glen Simmons, Muskogee. Simmons was in line to be editor of the *Redskin* the following year. Hadley insisted that the paper needed a more distinctive name.

"Each of us tried our hand with a name. Some of us tried to work 'Aggie' in. . .but finally Hadley came up with 'The Oklahoma Collegian.' The name was too long for [the nameplate of] a five-column paper. Either the type would be small, or the name had to be shortened.

"How about 'The Okla Collegian?' someone suggested. The name had possibilities, but finally Hadley announced:

"I've got it! Let's call it 'The O'Collegian.' "Thus it was that the *O'Collegian* made its first appearance Sunday, March 16, 1924."[39]

As the weekly *Orange and Black* metamorphosed into the semi-weekly *O'Collegian*, it was led by an exceptional talent, Harold "Ben" Matkin, a Stillwater student whose father was a well-known city official. Matkin was supported by a strong team of student journalists. Stone was his news editor and among his eleven staff members were Houston Overby, Walter Biscup, and Edward Burris, later to become vice dean of the College of Business, where his service lasted for forty-five years. A popular feature on the editorial page was "Ben's Kolem," sub-titled "Just Jabs o' Joy." The paper was blessed with talent, and this was reflected in the quality of its content. It was delivered to subscribers on Thursdays and Sundays. Within a short time, if plans materialized, it would be sent to every high school senior in the state as an indirect recruitment technique.[40]

As Hadley and his students gave birth to the *O'Collegian*, there were 18 major buildings on the Oklahoma A. and M. campus, and about 2,000 resident students, a faculty of approximately 250, and a library of 50,000 books and 125,000 pamphlets. The *O'Collegian's* circulation was more than ten times the total number of Aggie students enrolled in 1895 when the first issue of the *Mirror* appeared.[41]

In the spring elections, Stone won the editorship over Carl Schedler and Simmons was elected to edit the *Redskin*. Stone chose Hurst as managing editor, and they continued the *O'Collegian* on a semi-weekly basis through the fall term of 1924.

Hurst was a young man with initiative. When the Aggies defeated the University of Oklahoma Sooners, 6-0, on Lewis Field, Hurst decided to publish an extra. The papers sold like hot cakes. It was only the second time the Aggies had won in the series. The winning touchdown was scored by Guy Lookabaugh, a returning World War I veteran who had played in the first winning game against OU in 1917.[42]

The *O'Collegian* newsroom was located on the top floor of Old Central in what had been the auditorium. Communication from Hadley to *O'Collegian* editors was simple and direct. Harmony prevailed. Because of Hadley's closeness to such student leaders as Walker Stone, it is not surprising that modern student government at OSU owes a debt to him. The first student constitution, which had created the Student Association in 1915, gave the Senate power to legislate on matters of student interest. An earlier journalism leader, Professor Noble W. Rockey, had played a major role in shaping that constitution, which had served campus needs until 1924. Then the association, with Hadley's assistance, began a revision. Stone, perhaps the most influential student senator of his day, no doubt had a part in Hadley's selection as the faculty

A victory over the University of Oklahoma Sooners was enough to cause Irvin Hurst to get out an extra edition of the student newspaper. It was sold as the crowd was leaving the stadium and had wide distribution in off-campus Stillwater.

member to work on the revision. Their friendship was deep and life-long. The new constitution was the first to give the Senate power to grant and revoke charters of campus organizations. It was also the first to require publication of monthly financial reports by the Student Association. The revised constitution stood up for eight years before being once more revised under President Henry G. Bennett's direction.[43]

The Hadley era was one in which the journalistic ferment on campus was high. This was due in part to Hadley's encouragement and in part to the increasing sophistication of the student body, a far cry from the rustic character of the college's first prep class. It would have been unthinkable for the Aggies of the 1890s to have produced an irreverent, nose-tweeking publication with humor typical of the 1920s. But in its third issue, the new semi-weekly *O'Collegian* reported plans for just such a publication. A decade earlier, Harry O'Brien's students had introduced the campus to the *Earthquake*, a newspaper filled with phoney stories with professors often the butt of the humor. But that publication was issued only for the fall and spring campus carnivals. Now the Oklahoma A. and M. Press Club was proposing a humor magazine published on a regular schedule typical of those at "all of the larger institutions in the country." It would be called the *Aggievator* and would make its first appearance during the annual Interscholastic Meet in May. "Its pages will contain the latest wit of the campus, and the regular student comedy which is alone peculiar to colleges and universities," the *O'Collegian* reported. The Press Club had elected Elmo Flynt to edit and manage the magazine. For the first issue, the club's members would be the staff along with "others who have shown marked talent in former humor papers. . . ." Beginning in the fall, the club planned to relinquish control but would act as an advisory board.[44]

More information on the *Aggievator* was forthcoming in late April. The Press Club announced that all profits from the magazine would go to the stadium campaign. *O'Collegian* readers were told that the first issue would contain "humorous articles, poems, jokes, limericks and the general run of literary output that characterizes a college humor maga- zine," and would sell for 25 cents. In an editorial, the *O'Collegian* praised the Press Club for its "exhibition of sportsmanship and loyalty," the members foregoing private gain "in order that they might aid the worthy cause."[45] The *Aggievator* sales force at the Interscholastic was expected to be the "Peppers," with the probable assistance of the "Wampus Kittens," Press Club President Ben Matkin reported.[46]

The *Aggievator* was the most notable new publication during the Hadley years. It was the brainchild of Houston Overby, a brilliant student who preferred sleeping to going to class. Hadley may have had something to do with the birth of the magazine, but the idea was Overby's. President Knapp, of course, expected his publications chief to look over the collective shoulders of the *Aggievator* staff. Hadley was rather lenient in reviewing *Aggievator* jokes, a fact which was unsettling to Knapp. One joke, about a newly married student couple, was particularly damaging. All appropriations were made individually at that time, and legislators loyal to the Oklahoma A. and M. College or the University of Oklahoma often worked hard to gain an edge in the budget process, which more often than not favored the university. One legislator, standing on the floor waving a copy of the *Aggievator*, insisted on reading the offensive joke to the entire chamber. A well-informed alumnus of the time estimated that it probably cost Oklahoma A. and M. $50,000 in appropriations for that biennium.[47]

There were other journalistic stirrings as well. The *Oklahoma Home* was scheduled to appear for the first time in May. The thirty-six-page magazine would rely upon the talents of the students in Home Economics Journalism under Mable Caldwell. A staff had been organized with Margaret Darlow as editor and Frances Kahle as managing editor. Advertising would be sold by the class and the magazine would contain articles written only during regular laboratory periods. It was patterned after the *Iowa Homemaker*, a monthly published by home economics journalism students at Iowa State College. The May 1925 issue, Volume 2, Number 1, carried a brief editorial by assistant editor Cherry Palmer on the magazine's goals. It would, she wrote, give practice in the field of journalism to juniors and seniors in home economics and make them aware of career possibilities in publications work. Other purposes stated by Palmer were to bring the work done in the classroom and laboratory to the attention of Oklahomans and to interest prospective students through a portrayal of campus life. This 1925 issue included jokes and poetry as well as serious articles. Professor Whittier Burnett contributed four of the poems.[48]

Stone was a builder. He would not be satisfied until he had given the student body a *daily* newspaper. Hadley obviously gave the idea strong support. He may even have planted the notion in Stone's mind.

When President Knapp was approached with the idea, conditions were favorable. Knapp liked Stone's initiative, and he had confidence in Hurst, who was dating his daughter, Marion. He authorized publication of the *O'Collegian* as a daily and gave Stone a good deal of freedom, admonishing him only to tell the truth, to uphold moral standards, and not to print stories which ridiculed or hurt others unless a principle was at stake. Student journalists had, in general, practiced such tenets for years at Oklahoma A. and M.[49]

In a special Saturday meeting April 12, 1924, the *O'Collegian* board approved a new salary scale for the paper's executives. Beginning April 15, the editor-in-chief would receive $45 a month and the business manager $30. The news editor, sports editor, and assistant business

Two new publications emerged during the Ed Hadley years. The *Oklahoma Home* was a serious attempt to develop professionalism among home economics journalism classes. The *Aggievator* had a longer and more colorful life. It was typical of campus humor magazines of that era.

manager were to receive $15. As board secretary, Matkin was directed to prepare filing blanks to be used in the May 6 election by candidates for editor-in-chief, business manager, and junior and senior student board members. The blanks were to be filed with Dean McElroy, Hadley, or Matkin. The board also authorized the weekly summer edition of the *O'Collegian* with Matkin in the dual role of editor and business manager. Then, in what seemed an unusual action, a resolution was passed to be directed to President Knapp. In the resolution, the board called attention to inaction by the *Redskin* board, pointing out that its sister board needed to pass on the qualifications of candidates for elective staff positions "as provided in the student senate constitution."[50]

As a semi-weekly, the *O'Collegian* had increased its coverage of student activities as well as the college's substantial progress under Knapp, but only a third of the student body had subscribed for the fall quarter. In spite of this, Stone and Hadley were determined to pursue their bold plan for a daily campus newspaper. They knew the semi-weekly's voluntary seventy-five cent subscription fee would not be enough. The solution? A *required* student fee. Stone's power in student politics was unquestioned, and he had the ear of Ed Morrison, president of the Student Senate. Hadley also had the solid support of the *O'Collegian* board. Using the publicity office's typewriter with a small-cap "E" instead of the customary lower-case "e"—the same typewriter Clement

Trout would later use for years—Hadley outlined a plan for a daily newspaper. He signed the plan of approximately 865 words with his identifying titles: "Chairman O'Collegian Board, Instructor in Journalism, Editor-in-Chief of College Publications." The document was titled "Report by the O'Collegian Board" and was addressed "To the Student Senate of Oklahoma A. and M. College." In it, Hadley, no doubt reflecting suggestions from students on the board, appealed to student loyalty.

"Its newspaper is a real indication of the loyalty and spirit of the student body. A poor, struggling paper is no credit to our student body. Failure to support it is as bad, exactly, as if we had refused to pay our football team's expenses to Lawrence for the game with Kansas university last Saturday, after it won the game.

"With united support, the staff of the *O'Collegian* is in a position to give this student body a real paper, published daily—a paper which will reflect credit upon the college and which will be more than twice as interesting and valuable to readers as the present paper. . . .

"There is only one apparent way this can be effected. It is by legislation by the student body, guaranteeing to the *O'Collegian* the general support of the men and women on this campus.

"Therefore, the O'Collegian Board recommends that a bill providing for a general subscription to the *O'Collegian* by members of the student body, amounting to one dollar for each student each quarter of the school year except the summer term, be approved by the student senate and submitted to the student body at a special election to be called as soon as possible. . . ."

The board's proposal went on to report Knapp's support of the idea, "providing the students themselves adopt the plan." The proposal ventured the prediction that a daily paper would "knit together our student body as no other instrument could." As an addendum, the proposal included a bill to be submitted at a special senate meeting October 13, 1924. The bill was endorsed by the senate and submitted to a vote of the student body ten days later. It passed handily and was reported in detail by the *O'Collegian*. The student body had made the paper's financial success virtually a certainty.

Moving from semi-weekly to daily was an ambitious undertaking. While today's *O'Collegian* is published five times a week with no home delivery, the late 1924 conversion from two to six editions a week included home delivery. Stone had begun to lay the groundwork for the paper's Associated Press membership in June 1924. Hadley transmitted the application for AP membership with a covering letter in which he said: "Beginning December 1 the *O'Collegian* will be a daily morning publication with a Sunday edition, but not published on Monday of each week.

"Aside from the fact that, with Associated Press membership, we will step to the front among college publications, we believe it may be of interest to you to know that the students of the college, numbering 2,300, have voted upon themselves a general tax of $1.00 each quarter, to be paid at the time of registration, as subscription to the *O'Collegian*. We do not know of another college paper so supported. Our circulation will cover every student in the college. Besides this, twice each week, on Thursdays and Sundays, the college is purchasing 1,000 copies to distribute to high schools of the state on the basis of one paper to each ten students."[51] Oklahoma A. and M. College was probably the only college in the United States to have a daily newspaper without a strong journalism school behind it.

Now Stone and his jubilant staff members settled down to the business of putting out a daily. It was an exciting challenge to all of them—one which required a concerted effort to meet the daily deadlines. The AP membership was put to use immediately. The *O'Collegian* had subscribed to the AP's "pony" service, which provided 2,000 words nightly dictated by telephone from the AP state bureau in Oklahoma City. Mildred Maroney, secretary to President Knapp, was among those who transcribed the brief news reports at the *Advance-Democrat* office.[52]

It seems clear that the combined efforts of Stone and Hadley led to daily status for the *O'Collegian*. The paper's circulation of 2,983 had passed its old rival at OU, the *Oklahoma Daily*, which had a circulation of 1,700. Not only that, but Oklahoma A. and M. entered a select circle with Associated Press membership. Only four other college papers in the United States were affiliated with AP: those at the University of Illinois, Indiana University, the University of Iowa, and Dartmouth College.[53]

The *O'Collegian* was delivered to Hadley's home six days a week. One of his teaching methods was to mark with a soft editing pencil the paper's errors or its misapplication of accepted journalistic practices. The marked copies would go to the staff in Old Central. He had followed the same practice with the *Orange and Black*.[54]

While some faculty were active in the Chamber of Commerce and various civic clubs, Hadley preferred to use his limited free time in other ways. He joined Victor F. Barnett of the *Tulsa Tribune*, chairman, and W. D. Little of the *Ada News* on a committee appointed in November 1925 to prepare a style sheet "for Oklahoma members of the Associated Press and Oklahoma A. and M. College journalism classes." The committee's work was successful. The style sheet was printed by the college and widely distributed. It was a boon to staff members of the *O'Collegian* as well as other publications.[55]

As his professional contacts expanded, Hadley helped form the Payne County Press Association. W. C. Bridwell, publisher of the *Glencoe Mirror*, was chosen temporary head. In addition to Hadley, who represented the *Stillwater Democrat*, those who attended the first meeting were Otis Wile of the *O'Collegian*; Edwin Brown, *Stillwater Gazette*; and Randle Perdue, Hadley's publicity assistant, who also edited the *Stillwater Daily Press*.[56]

Aided by increasing farm prosperity and the college's expanding academic programs, Hadley's dedication to his publicity efforts had begun to show results. By 1925, Oklahoma A. and M. had increased its enrollment by 37 percent, "more than any other institution of its nature and rank in the entire United States."[57] A greatly expanded publicity program, including more frequent contacts with newspapers and radio stations and the use of display advertising, had paid off, just as Knapp's administrative policies and his close cooperation with the board of agriculture had. Not to be overlooked were Knapp's contacts with opinion leaders and key politicians and Hadley's heavy emphasis upon hometown stories detailing the activities of student leaders. On at least one occasion, full-page ads were purchased in the *Daily Oklahoman*, *Oklahoma City Times*, *Farmer-Stockman*, *Oklahoma News*, *Tulsa World*, *Tulsa Tribune*, and the Oklahoma City Chamber of Commerce magazine *Oklahoma*. Smaller ads had appeared in numerous community newspapers and specialized magazines. Riding the tide of these and an increasing number of Hadley-generated news stories and pictures appearing in state papers, Knapp was predicting an enrollment of 3,000 students.[58]

The *O'Collegian* could be expected to lend strong support to any project enhancing the college's growth and reputation. When President Knapp announced plans to raze the wooden grandstand and replace it with a steel-supported unit seating 5,000, the paper gave the story major front-page display and followed the campaign with continuing publicity. The project's goal was construction, on a unit-by-unit basis, of a major stadium. The drive was tied to the college's expectation that it would soon leave the Southwestern Conference to become a member of the Missouri Valley Conference. Knapp said: "We must be able to hold up our heads, knowing we have not only as good a group of teams, but also as good an athletic plant as have the member schools." One of the first AP stories carried by the *Daily O'Collegian* informed Aggies of their election—after years of rejection—to the Valley.

Student publications cooperated with the administration in other ways as well. Not only did the *Redskin* office serve as a clearinghouse for cap-and-gown orders, but the *O'Collegian* was headquarters for lost-and-found articles.[59]

Journalistic surroundings in Old Central were not always tranquil. On the evening of June 30, 1925, a severe windstorm accompanied by rain caught a group in Old Central near Hadley's office. The building creaked and trembled, and a giant strip of plaster fell from the ceiling to the hallway floor. No injuries were reported. Approximately twenty months later, more plaster fell. This time some of it struck Raymond Bivert, general manager of student publications. A bump and a brief headache resulted and caused administrative concern about the building's condition. This concern led later to a new home for student publications.[60]

One reason for Hadley's effectiveness in bolstering the journalism program was the help he received from J. Frank Dobie. Knapp had lured Dobie away from the University of Texas to head the Department of English. His reputation as an expert on Southwestern folklore was gaining public attention and both he and Hadley realized its potential. Both were popular writers and both had shared similar experiences in the Great War. They became close friends. Dobie, who had served in the field artillery for about two years, once said that if he ever wrote an autobiography, one chapter would feature Ed Hadley as the main character.[61]

The warm feelings between Hadley and Dobie can be illustrated by the vignette which follows. It involved a book and two bottles of tequila. Dobie had been saving the tequila from his ranching days near the Rio Grande and had brought them to Stillwater. A student had financed a private printing of Mark Twain's *Conversations in 1601* and had given Dobie a copy. A Hadley colleague from newspaper days—E. H. Taylor of the *Country Gentleman*—was visiting Stillwater and wanted to see Twain's *1601*. Hadley, meeting Dobie by chance as he walked across campus, told him of Taylor's interest.

Dobie later recalled the story of what happened next: "I told Hadley to bring [Taylor] around to our house on Duck Street, which always seemed to me a very appropriate name for a street in Stillwater, about 5 o'clock and we'd have *1601* and tequila together. They came on time. I

J. Frank Dobie, a well-known writer of Southwestern folklore, was head of the Department of English during the Ed Hadley Years. He was a strong supporter of journalism and with Hadley introduced a new unit title: Department of English and Journalism. In his teaching, he marked papers carefully throughout, then added a pithy note on the outside.

had the tequila mixed with lemon juice and sugar and ice and water. Neither Hadley nor Taylor seemed averse to it. Before long, Taylor was inviting me to write a piece for the *Country Gentleman* on cowboy songs. . . . I wrote the piece with care and must say that I thought it sang like a fiddle. . . . I received a telegram saying in effect, 'Your piece on cowboy songs received with enthusiasm. Go to San Antonio and write two articles on trail drivers.'"

Dobie got leave from President Knapp and later said he had had "one of the bully times" of his life with the trail drivers. His contact with the magazine through Hadley led to other lucrative writing assignments. Dobie commented: "Well, the *Country Gentleman* just about paid for the house in Austin that [Bertha and I] have been living in for 34 years. . . . If it hadn't been for Ed Hadley I never would have met E. H. Taylor and if it hadn't been for E. H. Taylor I might still be writing my Ph.D. thesis on 'The Influence of Agricultural and Mechanical Colleges on American Literature.'"

Dobie and Hadley, in the colloquial speech of later years, would have been classed as free spirits. They were somewhat unconventional in the attitudes and pedagogical styles they brought to Oklahoma A. and M., and they probably brought Knapp an occasional sense of discomfort. There is a hint of this in Dobie's description of his resignation around commencement time in 1925.

"I told [Knapp] that I was resigning from Oklahoma A. and M. College to return to Texas. Manifestly he was not interested in where I was going, but if there had been a haystack anywhere near us, the glow and the glee on Bradford Knapp's countenance would have set it afire."[62] Newspaper reports later pointed out that Dobie had left because library resources for his research at Oklahoma A. and M. were less adequate than those at the University of Texas.[63]

In the college's organizational scheme, Dobie and Hadley were equals in one sense, but not in another. In administrative matters, Dobie, as head of the Department of English and Journalism, did not outrank Hadley in the latter's position as head of college publications. But in the classroom, Hadley was under Dobie, for journalism was a sub-section in English. It seems likely, however, that their relationship was one in which neither sought to "pull rank." In a letter years later, Dobie recalled: "I had liked him from the minute I laid eyes on him and, moreover, respected him, which is a lot more than I can say for a lot of men in college journalism that I've met since."[64]

Hadley's mystique, already a popular topic among those students close to him, gained wider campus attention when it was learned that he had befriended the grandson of Count Leo Tolstoy during his postwar duty on the Baltic. The *O'Collegian* reported that five years earlier in war-torn, revolution-swept Red Russia, Hadley had met Ilia Tolstoy, then

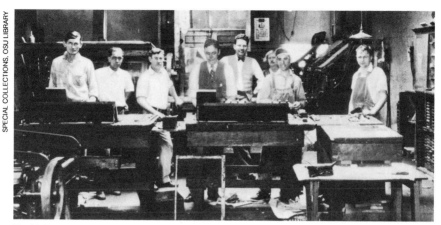

Paul Miller (in bow tie) lost his bid for the *O'Collegian* editorship, then dropped out of school to become editor of the *Okemah Daily Leader*. He is shown with his backshop crew in Okemah. He later returned to campus as assistant to Randle Perdue in the Bureau of Information and Service, taking his degree in 1933. Then Miller began his rapid rise through the Associated Press to international fame.

a youth of seventeen. The meeting was on an American Relief Expedition train for which Hadley had responsibility. For three months, the two worked together. Then they were sent into different areas. Hadley had given Tolstoy his Iowa address. The young Russian had immigrated to Iowa. He was attending Penn College and working three hours a day on Hadley's uncle's farm on the edge of the campus.[65] The conclusion was, of course, that Hadley was a man of wide and unusual experiences. This was true, but the aura that surrounded Hadley because of the stories about his career added a "larger than life" dimension to his reputation.

Hadley's presence as the ranking journalistic model for students on campus had brought an air of hope and optimism reflected especially in the recruiting efforts of Stone. It was Stone, probably more than any other single individual, who encouraged Paul Miller to enroll at Oklahoma A. and M. They continued a warm personal friendship long after both had gained international journalistic acclaim. This lasted until Stone's death in 1973.[66]

Two carbon copies of letters from Stone to Miller are still to be found in School of Journalism and Broadcasting files. In one, Stone encouraged Miller to become part of what the future editor-in-chief of Scripps-Howard Newspapers saw as a great academic adventure: having a part in the growth of the journalism program on the Aggie campus.[67] It is interesting to note that Miller would later become chief executive officer of the largest newspaper group in the United States, Gannett, as well as chairman of the board of directors of the Associated Press. Both men were strongly influenced by Hadley, as were Hurst and others among the outstanding men and women who would launch their journalism careers from the Stillwater campus.

Stone's optimism that a full-fledged journalism program at Oklahoma A. and M. would soon be established is reflected in the first letter to young Miller, then editor of *Wa-Sha-She* at Pawhuska High School. Eight days later Stone temporarily doffed his semi-official Oklahoma A. and M. journalism hat and put on his rushing hat for Kappa Sigma fraternity in a personal, unofficial letter. He obviously was persuasive. Miller came to Oklahoma A. and M., became active in campus journalism, and was initiated by Kappa Sigma on May 18, 1926. He lived in the fraternity house, then located at 240 North Hester, only about 225 Miller-style strides from his publicity work in Old Central. It seems safe to assume that the journalism recruitment program was strongly encouraged, if not actually set in motion, by Hadley, but it was skillfully carried out by Stone, who contacted numerous high school editors in his campaign to bring promising editorial talent to Stillwater.[68]

These efforts had brought about an upturn from inconsistent, often amateurish writing to a more professional approach on the student newspaper. The unusual talent that had come his way, plus Hadley's coaching and setting of standards, made the difference. In addition to Stone, Miller, and Hurst, he had been blessed with such talent as J. Nelson Taylor, Walter Biscup, Harold "Ben" Matkin, Madelaine Bradley, George Milburn, Gus Fields, Otis Wile, Gladys Milne, Robert E. Cunningham, Cecil Williams, Ray "Gabe" Gierhart, Clarence Paden, and Ewing Jones.[69] Rarely does campus journalism find such a constellation in three brief years. Their skillful use of the language as *O'Collegian* staff members would make some current student journalists seem inept.

Hadley's intense loyalty to his cadre of journalism students was apparent in his behavior following the 1926 battle between TNE and its opposition. After the charge presented in the widely-circulated pre-election handbill, Hadley acknowledged his TNE membership, adding: "I could not have been classed with a cleaner, more outstanding group of students on this campus than the men who are victims with me."[70] His choice of the term "victims" suggests that he believed he had become *persona non grata* with President Knapp, who was a conservative in his feelings about academic roles.

Knapp was becoming sensitive to problems related to student publications. Even Stone, who generally was on good terms with President Knapp, found himself in the doghouse. Stone was serving as general manager of student publications at the time. As the 1925-26 academic year drew to a close, Stone had asked the Student Publications Board to attend a meeting May 15 at which the *1927 Redskin* contract for printing and engraving were scheduled to be let by the editor and business manager-elect. Stone had asked Chairman Hadley and the four other board members to attend, for their approval would be required.[71] Knapp got wind of the meeting. He lost little time in putting his feelings in writing to Stone and the board. In a letter that apparently was hastily dictated, he stated:

"The next year's *Redskin* is in the hands of a different Board and you have no right to tie the hands of the next Board. . . . I am insisting that next year's Board let the contracts.

"In order to show you that I mean business I will say that there will be no contracts let on this matter without the approval of myself. I am going to say further that I am disgusted with this year's *Redskin* and I am going to see that it is handled in an entirely different manner next year, or I am going to withdraw the college's support. In fact, I do not see how I can get through approval of it this year when it contains an open and gratuitous insult to the State Board of Agriculture. The thing is going to be handled on a different basis next year or I am going to know the reason why." The basis for Knapp's ire probably was the "Redskin Chaff"

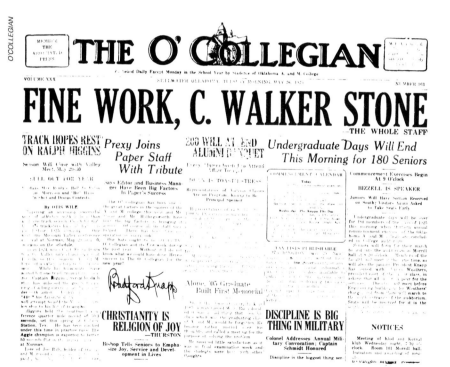

When at the end of the spring term President Bradford Knapp complimented Walker Stone and his staff for having succeeded in giving the campus a lively daily newspaper, Stone unabashedly bannered the kudo.

section, more specifically, "The KA Endeavor" and "An Aggie's Soliloquy."[72]

Knapp's rebuke rankled Stone, who felt he had performed in a responsible way. The *1926 Redskin* had created problems for him as well as Knapp. As fall classes were under way, Stone had written Raymond Bivert a sharply worded letter because obligations to the printers and engravers had not been paid. The most telling paragraph read:

"For the first time in the history of the institution the *Redskin* not only broke even, but laid in a surplus of better than $800. Before leaving, [Charles] Weathers and I checked all the accounts of the *1926 Redskin* completely, turned over the records and financial statement to you, and made out requisitions covering the remainder of our printing and engraving bills except $600 to each. Attached to these requisitions were written authority to the chief clerk to pay $600 each to the engraver and the printers with the $1200 due from the administration. The said $1200 should have been in the chief clerk's office by June 15th, or at latest, by the middle of July; and now—three months later—I receive a hot letter from Hugh Stephens saying that we still owe them $600."

Stone closed by saying he did not wish to interfere with Oklahoma A. and M. affairs, but that he wanted the records "straightened out so as to give a clean record to those who did attend to their affairs in the correct manner." Carbon copies of the letter went to President Knapp and H. A. Andrews, chief clerk.[73]

As his tenure wore on, Hadley looked for new involvements. One of these was a hankering for a newspaper of his own. While serving as editor-in-chief of college publications, he had bought an interest in the Advance-Democrat Publishing Company. Arthur S. McEwen and Hadley formed a partnership, with McEwen as manager and Hadley as editor of the *Stillwater Democrat*. This arrangement offered some advantages, for the *O'Collegian* was printed at this time in the *Democrat's* plant on Eighth Street, but it also made Hadley vulnerable to those who saw in the arrangement a conflict of interest.[74]

Hadley was growing restless and was close to a major decision. The performance of his college duties had been generally acceptable, and in some areas outstanding. But now, after a few days of reflection, Hadley decided he had had enough of higher education. There is no solid evidence that the decision was forced, although President Knapp had expressed concern about faculty participation in TNE, suggesting publicly that faculty members give up TNE membership or submit their resignations. Some faculty and students no doubt felt that the *Aggievator's* occasional indiscretions and Hadley's ties with Theta Nu Epsilon had hastened his departure. It was more likely that other reasons tilted the scales. He was a newspaperman and was itching to return to his first love. His eighteen-month partnership in the *Stillwater Democrat* had been useful in his work at Oklahoma A. and M. and had kept him close to the smell of printer's ink, but Oklahoma City beckoned. He sold his interest in the *Democrat* to McEwen and W. E. Carlson and submitted his resignation as head of the Department of Publications effective August 1 in order to buy the *Capitol Hill Beacon.*[75]

In April 1926, Knapp became edgy over an editorial that appeared in the *Oklahoma City Times* which implied that the administration had censored the *O'Collegian*. Knapp hastily wrote the board of agriculture, denying any attempt to censor the student publication. While there may have been little basis for the specifics on that occasion, students sometimes believed Knapp was too involved in student publications. He did not hesitate to write Stone when he thought an event had not been adequately covered. In addition, he was known to have called *O'Collegian* staff members to his office on more than one occasion to lecture them on journalistic matters.

Some students were slow to forgive Knapp for *O'Collegian* editor Clarence Paden's dismissal for an editorial on sex and for Hadley's departure. But as it became time for his presidential appointment to be renewed, the *O'Collegian* called for a fourth term. The paper reported that "Knapp and his administrative aides have accomplished more during his three years here than any head of the college heretofore." Knapp was reelected on April 6 at the same salary as before, $10,000.[76]

When he left in the summer of 1926, Hadley had served Oklahoma A. and M. for some thirty-two months, had shown considerable skill in carrying out his duties, and had inspired those interested in journalism careers to forge ahead. Whatever his reasons for leaving, he joined Raymond Fields in establishing the *Capitol Hill Beacon*. Ed and Marguerite Hadley had little trouble adjusting to their return to Oklahoma City and his new management duties with the *Beacon*. He would have preferred to have purchased the *Beacon* outright, but did not have enough money. He enlisted the aid of Fields and Ed McIntyre, publishers of the *Guthrie Leader*, who had ties with oil millionaire and philanthropist Lew Wentz. They put up the money and Hadley provided the management, adding sparkle to the paper with his writing and editing skills. He was said to be "a showman type of newspaperman."[77]

Hadley saw a bright future in an encircling ring of papers around the perimeter of Oklahoma City, and set up editions for Moore, Wheatland, Choctaw, Spencer and Britton. D. S. Woodson, who sold to Hadley, agreed to be listed as "associate editor."

Five years passed and the market had not yielded the returns Hadley had hoped for. In March of 1931, he sold his interest in the paper to Fields and McIntyre and left for Washington, D.C. Hadley served first as Washington correspondent for the *Daily Oklahoman* and *London Chronicle* and later for the *Montreal Daily Star*. He represented the *Star* from 1943 until his retirement in 1962, with time out for Navy duty that gave him the combat experience he reluctantly had missed in World War I. There is ample evidence that Hadley, whose office was in the National Press Club Building, was highly regarded by the *Star*. He was featured in house ads praising his abilities, and his stories datelined Washington frequently were given major page-one display with his by-line and identification as "The Star's Resident Correspondent" or "Of the Star's Washington Bureau." Among these stories were President Harry Truman's historic speech to Congress enunciating the Truman Doctrine, Truman's surprising victory over Thomas E. Dewey in the 1948 presidential race, Washington reaction to the U. S. "police action" in Korea, the opening of the McCarthy hearings, and Nikita Khrushchev's visit to New York City for a speech to the U.N. and a Washington conference with President Dwight Eisenhower. His stories carried an overtone of British English, and many were excellent examples of interpretative reporting.[78]

There is an epilogue to the Hadley story. Walker Stone was not one to forget a friend. He had been one of Hadley's closest confidants during their days together on the campus. They had remained close friends in the years that followed. With an assist from his long-time friend, Paul Miller, Stone arranged with Charles L. Allen, then director of the School of Journalism and Communications, for an "Ed Hadley Day" in Stillwater.[79] It was characteristic of Stone and Miller that their friendships ran deep, and their return to red-dirt country to add their prestige to that of other distinguished old grads in honoring Hadley was typical of them. Newspaper executives on the top rung have to have a streak of toughness, but in addition Miller and Stone had a deep reservoir of sentiment in their makeup. They knew they were paying tribute to an aging mentor whom they loved and admired; they knew, too, that they were giving visibility to their alma mater and its growing prominence in journalism education.

Now, on May 24, 1961, as a feature of OSU's annual Journalism Day, Stone had arranged for Hadley to be the honored guest. To most, the day was "Ed Hadley Day." While approximately seventy-five ex-students and ex-colleagues looked on approvingly, Hadley was given a silver tray with an inscription from friends expressing appreciation for his years of service to them and his profession. Stone, representing the Scripps-Howard Foundation, gave $2,500 to be used for scholarships in memory of famed war correspondent Ernie Pyle. Allen said the scholarships would be awarded to students on the basis of need. Randle Perdue, who had served as Hadley's assistant in the college publicity office, paid tribute to Hadley as "a perfectionist in his profession."[80]

Among those taking part in the program were Miller, at that time president and general manager of Gannett Newspapers; Charles Bennett, managing editor of the *Daily Oklahoman* and *Oklahoma City Times*; Sid

Steen, *Tulsa World* executive editor, and Bruce Palmer, KWTV- Oklahoma City news director. In addition, Canada's highly respected *Montreal Daily Star* carried an editorial praising Hadley, who was nearing the end of his career as the paper's Washington Bureau chief.[81]

In his coverage of the event, John Taylor of the *Daily O'Collegian* reported that "the old-timers took the spotlight while the younger set listened with awe."[82] Twenty years later, Harold Hubbard of the Kingfisher *Free Press and Times* recalled that "Charles Allen made a big event of the occasion and a good time was had by all."[83]

Ed Hadley Day was divided into three parts. The morning included panel discussions on "The Challenge to Journalism in the 1960s." During the afternoon, sessions on daily and weekly newspaper problems were featured. The highlight of the day was the banquet honoring Hadley, with Miller as master of ceremonies. Speakers were Miller, Stone, and Allen. President Oliver S. Willham was flanked on his right by Hadley and on his left by Miller.[84]

At the banquet, grey-haired alumni took the floor one by one and reminisced about college experiences in the Roaring Twenties. They relived the days when a student with a car was unheard of and a semester's fees totalled $18.50.[85]

It was, as Taylor had written, a "glorious day." But it had its dark side, too. A senior from Oklahoma City plunged 65 feet to his death on the concrete below the south stands at Lewis Field, eighteen students were arrested in panty raids on Stout and Murray halls, with peace finally settling on the campus at 5 A.M. A fire on the Theta Pond bridge had to be dealt with by campus authorities amidst all the other excitement.[86] Reading their papers over coffee the next morning, Miller, Stone, and Hadley must have confirmed with their comments that Bob Dylan was right when he wrote "The Times They Are a Changing." The belated celebration of Hadley's contributions to journalism education and public information had come thirty-five years after his departure from Oklahoma A. and M. Stone was the prime mover in contacting many of the old grads. He knew that Hadley was close to retirement, and he wanted to give his good friend and mentor one last hurrah.

Despite Hadley's rich background, it is unlikely that he would have been Knapp's choice as editor-in-chief of campus publications. Knapp would have preferred someone with a background in agricultural journalism. But he had no choice. In the turmoil of a controversial new administration at the capitol, Governor Walton's political albatross, George Wilson, had chosen Ernest R. Chamberlain for the job. When Wilson became a political liability, Walton had broken the paralyzing grip of the Farmer-Labor Reconstruction League on the board of agriculture and the revamped board, with a nudge from John Whitehurst, had selected Hadley to replace Chamberlain. It would not have been prudent

As an epilogue to the Hadley story, "Ed Hadley Day" was celebrated at OSU in 1961. Responsible for much of the planning were Walker Stone (*left*) and Paul Miller (*right*), shown here with their early mentor. Both credited Hadley with giving them a good start in professional journalism.

for Knapp, as he replaced Richard G. Tyler after Tyler's interim presidency of two months, to have gone against Whitehurst's choice. Despite Knapp's wait-and-see attitude, Hadley had proved to be successful in carrying out his duties, and in many ways the Knapp-Hadley combination was a good one. Hadley achieved many of the college's publicity goals as it sought to rebuild and expand its public image. But Knapp had highly specific ideas concerning the primary focus of the job. Much of this perception evolved from his illustrious father, Seaman A. Knapp, the early sculptor of the widespread extension program in land-grant institutions. Added to this heritage was Knapp's own USDA leadership in farmers' cooperative demonstration work and later as chief of extension work in the south during a ten-year period ending in December of 1919.[87]

While there may have been a tinge of regret upon Knapp's part when Hadley decided to return to newspapering, there also was the realization that now he could fill the position with an agricultural journalist whose education and professional experience better suited him. Clement E. Trout would be that man.

Hadley died on October 6, 1973, in Winston-Salem, North Carolina, where he and Marguerite had bought a home at 341 Springdale Avenue to be near relatives.[88]

Endnotes

1. *Annual Catalog, Oklahoma A. and M. College, 1914-1915*, p. vi; *Annual Catalog, Oklahoma A. and M. College, 1915-1916*, p. xv; *Annual Catalog, Oklahoma A. and M. College, 1916-1917*, p. xvi; *Annual Catalog, Oklahoma A. and M. College, 1917-1918*, p. v; Author interview with Irvin Hurst, 5 July 1984; *Stillwater Gazette*, 27 July 1923, p. 1, 3 August 1923, p. 1; Walker Stone to Grinnell College Alumni Association, 17 November 1965, and Irvin Hurst to Harry E. Heath Jr., 12 December 1989, in School of Journalism and Broadcasting Centennial History Collection, Special Collections, Edmon Low Library, Oklahoma State University, Stillwater, Oklahoma; L. Edward Carter, *The Story of Oklahoma Newspapers—1846-1984* (Muskogee, OK: Western Heritage Books, Incorporated), p. 202. Carter erred on at least two counts: Knapp did not select Hadley and Hadley was not the founder of journalism education at Oklahoma A. and M.

2. *Stillwater Gazette*, 27 July 1923, p. 1, 10 August 1923, p. 5; Angie Debo, *Prairie City* (New York, NY: Alfred A. Knopf, 1944), p. 166; Philip Reed Rulon, *Oklahoma State University—Since 1890* (Stillwater: Oklahoma State University Press, 1975), p. 184; Floy Farrar Wilbanks, "The Life and Work of Dr. Bradford Knapp" (Master of Arts thesis, Texas Technological College, 1940), introduction; *Stillwater Gazette*, 10 August 1923, p. 5.

3. Oklahoma State University *Daily O'Collegian*, 23 May 1961, p. 1, 25 May 1961, p. 16; Carter, p. 202; Walker Stone to Grinnell College Alumni Association, 17 November 1965, Donald Hadley to Ivyl W. Welton, 3 November 1965, Ivyl Welton to Mary G. Jones, 7 November 1965, Paul Miller to Murray D. Welch, 29 December 1965, Ivyl D. Welton to Journalism Department, Oklahoma State University, 9 October 1965, and Janet W. German to Harry E. Heath Jr., 12 January 1981, in Files of the School of Journalism and Broadcasting, Oklahoma State University.

4. Dorothy Hadley Zeh to Harry E. Heath Jr., 7 February 1992, and Biography of Edmund E. Hadley, 3 November 1965, prepared by his brother Donald Hadley, p. 1, in School of Journalism and Broadcasting Centennial History Collection.

5. Biography of Edmund E. Hadley, 3 November 1965, prepared by his brother Donald Hadley, p. 1, and Anne Kintner to Harry E. Heath Jr., 3 July 1987, in School of Journalism and Broadcasting Centennial History Collection; *1915 Cyclone*, p. 60, Grinnell College Yearbook; *1916 Cyclone*, p. 218.

6. *1915 Cyclone*, p. 60; *1916 Cyclone*, pp. 158, 159; Anne Kintner to Harry E. Heath Jr., 3 July 1987, School of Journalism and Broadcasting Centennial History Collection.

7. *1915 Cyclone*, p. 138; *1916 Cyclone*, pp. 170, 178; Anne Kintner to Harry E. Heath Jr., 3 July 1987, School of Journalism and Broadcasting Centennial History Collection.

8. Dorothy Hadley Zeh to Harry E. Heath Jr., 12 February 1991, School of Journalism and Broadcasting Centennial History Collection.

9. Keelan H. Noble to Harry E. Heath Jr., 17 January 1991, School of Journalism and Broadcasting Centennial History Collection.

10. *Newport [Rhode Island] Daily News*, 18 July 1980, p. 10; William S. Busik to Harry E. Heath Jr., 12 May 1987, Irvin Hurst to Harry E. Heath Jr., 2 October 1969, Joe Somma to Harry E. Heath Jr., 28 March 1988, and Fred L. Lee to Harry E. Heath Jr., 14 July 1989, including p. 741 from 1923 City Directory for Kansas City, and Biography of Edmund E. Hadley, 3 November 1965, prepared by his brother Donald Hadley, p. 2, in School of Journalism and Broadcasting Centennial History Collection; Rulon, p. 184; Hurst interview.

11. Author interview with E. E. Johnson, 15 June 1980; Author interview with Walker Stone, 13 May 1972; Author interview with Randle Perdue, 6 June 1984; Author interview with Irvin Hurst, 5 July 1984; R. A. Young to Harry E. Heath Jr., 4 April 1988, School of Journalism and Broadcasting Centennial History Collection; Walker Stone to Paul Miller, 22 April 1925 and 30 April 1925, Files of the School of Journalism and Broadcasting; *Stillwater Gazette*, 10 August 1923, p. 5, 14 October 1923, p. 5.

12. *Annual Catalog, Oklahoma A. and M. College, 1937-1938*, p. 102; *Annual Catalog, Oklahoma A. and M. College, 1923-1924*, pp. 191, 269; Walker Stone to Paul Miller, 30 April 1925, Files of the School of Journalism and Broadcasting.

13. *Annual Catalog, Oklahoma A. and M. College, 1923-24*, p. 13; *Annual Catalog, Oklahoma A. and M. College, 1924-25*, p. xiii.

14. Walker Stone to Awards Committee, Grinnell College, Alumni Association, 17 November 1965; Carter, p. 203.

15. Paul Miller to Murray D. Welch, 29 December 1965, and Walker Stone to Grinnell College Alumni Association, 17 November 1965, in Files of the School of Journalism and Broadcasting; Carter, p. 203.

16. *Daily O'Collegian*, 15 May 1925, p. 4. Walker Stone's close friendship with E. E. Hadley is underscored by a lengthy account of their one-month fishing trip to the Chama and Bronzo River valleys of New Mexico published on page one of the *O'Collegian* for 9 July 1925.

17. *Stillwater Gazette*, 12 September 1924; Author interview with Walker Stone, 13 May 1972; Paul Miller to Harry E. Heath Jr., 29 June 1984, and Mildred Maroney to Harry E. Heath Jr., 28 December 1989, in School of Journalism and Broadcasting Centennial History Collection.

18. Wandalee Basore interview with Bernadine Brock, 6 July 1984, School of Journalism and Broadcasting Centennial History Collection; Author interview with Sid Steen, 24 March 1981; Hurst interview; Author interview with Randle Perdue, 6 June 1984; Johnson interview.

19. Hurst interview.

20. Stone interview; Hurst interview.

21. Hurst interview.

22. Oklahoma A. and M. College Class Schedules, 1923-24, 1924-25, 1925-26, Special Collections, Edmon Low Library.

23. Walker Stone to Grinnell College Alumni Association, 17 November 1965, Files of the School of Journalism and Broadcasting.

24. Author interview with Raymond Fields, Summer 1975.

25. Schedule of classes, 1923-24, 1924-25, 1925-26; Hurst interview; Class Roll, vol. 1, Winter 1923-24, stored in the basement of the Student Health Center, Oklahoma State University.

26. *Daily O'Collegian*, 13 March 1925, p. 1.

27. *Daily O'Collegian*, 12 November 1925, p. 1.

28. *Daily O'Collegian*, 29 April 1925, p. 5, 1 October 1925, p. 4.

29. Irvin Hurst to Harry E. Heath Jr., 28 June 1980, Files of the School of Journalism and Broadcasting.

30. Irvin Hurst to Harry E. Heath Jr., 12 September 1969, 2 October 1969, and 28 June 1980, Files of the School of Journalism and Broadcasting.

31. Hurst interview; Vera Kathryn Stevens Anderson, "A History of the *Daily O'Collegian*, Student Newspaper of Oklahoma A. and M. College: 1924-1934" (Master of Science thesis, Oklahoma State University, 1975), pp. 153-155.

32. Anderson, pp. 153-155; Hurst interview; Bonnie E. Emerson, "Democracy in Action on Campus," *Oklahoma A. and M. College Magazine*, vol. 16, no. 9 (April 1944), pp. 3, 8, 15; Irvin Hurst to Harry E. Heath Jr., 11 July 1988, School of Journalism and Broadcasting Centennial History Collection.

33. John Oliver to Kathryn Anderson, 11 January 1974, and Biographical sketch of Paul Miller, 29 September 1942, in Files of the School of Journalism and Broadcasting.

34. Donald Hadley to Ivyl W. Welton, 3 November 1965, Files of the School of Journalism and Broadcasting; Anderson, pp. 153-155.

35. John Oliver to Harry E. Heath Jr., 16 September 1987, School of Journalism and Broadcasting Centennial History Collection; Andersen, p. 166.

36. Anderson, pp. 151-169; Emerson, p. 8.

37. Irvin Hurst to Harry E. Heath Jr., 28 June 1980, School of Journalism and Broadcasting Centennial History Collection.

38. Carter, p. 57; *Orange and Black*, 10 January 1924; *O'Collegian*, 16 May 1924, 30 October 1924, 6 November 1924.

39. Irvin Hurst to Harry E. Heath Jr., 28 June 1980, School of Journalism and Broadcasting Centennial History Collection.

40. *O'Collegian*, 16 March 1924, p. 2; *1924 Redskin*, p. 266.

41. Carter, p. 203; *O'Collegian*, 23 March 1924, pp. 1, 4.

42. *O'Collegian*, 4 September 1924, p. 4.

43. Emerson, p. 3.

44. *O'Collegian*, 20 March 1924, p. 1, 23 March 1924, p. 1.

45. *Orange and Black*, 24 February 1924, p. 2; *O'Collegian*, 24 April 1924, pp. 1, 2.

46. *O'Collegian*, 1 May 1924, p. 1.

47. Johnson interview.

48. *Oklahoma Home*, May 1925.

49. *O'Collegian*, 1 November 1924, p. 1, 19 December 1924, p. 1.

50. *O'Collegian*, 13 April 1924, p. 1.

51. Report by the O'Collegian Board, 1924, E. E. Hadley to the Student Senate of Oklahoma A. and M. College, Milton Garges to C. Walker Stone, 1 July 1924, and other pertinent documents, in Files of the School of Journalism and Broadcasting; *O'Collegian*, 4 September 1924, p. 3, 16 October 1924, p. 1, 26 October 1924, pp. 1, 2; Anderson, pp. 19, 20.

52. Mildred Moroney to Harry E. Heath Jr., 28 December 1989, School of Journalism and Broadcasting Centennial History Collection; *O'Collegian*, 2 December 1924, pp. 1, 2.

53. *O'Collegian*, 2 December 1924, p. 4, 28 January 1925, p. 1; Rulon, pp. 207, 208.

54. Based upon author's personal inspection of papers in Special Collections, Edmon Low Library.

55. *Associated Press Style Sheet* [1925], Files of the School of Journalism and Broadcasting.

56. *Stillwater Gazette*, 23 July 1926, p. 1.

57. Rulon, p. 190; *Stillwater Gazette*, 26 September 1924, 10 October 1924.

58. *Stillwater Gazette*, 20 August 1926, p. 5.

59. *O'Collegian*, 17 April 1924, p. 1.

60. *O'Collegian*, 17 April 1924, p. 1, 4 February 1925, p. 2; *Stillwater Gazette*, 3 July 1925, p. 1; LeRoy H. Fischer, *Oklahoma State University Historic Old Central* (Stillwater: Oklahoma State University, 1988), pp. 169-171.

61. J. Frank Dobie to Walker Stone, 17 May 1961, School of Journalism and Broadcasting Centennial History Collection.

62. J. Frank Dobie to Walker Stone, 17 May 1961, Virginia Knapp to Harry E. Heath Jr., 19 November 1989, and Mildred Maroney to Harry E. Heath Jr., 28 December 1989, in School of Journalism and Broadcasting Centennial History Collection.

63. *O'Collegian*, 18 March 1925, pp. 1, 4.

64. *Stillwater NewsPress*, 25 May 1961, p. 16; J. Frank Dobie to Walker Stone, 17 May 1961, School of Journalism and Broadcasting Centennial History Collection.

65. *O'Collegian*, 30 March 1924, p. 4.

66. Walker Stone Collection, University of Wisconsin, Madison, Wisconsin. See also the Paul Miller Collection, Special Collections, Edmon Low Library.

67. Walker Stone to Paul Miller, 22 April 1925, 30 April 1925, Files of the School of Journalism and Broadcasting.

68. Walker Stone to Paul Miller, 22 April 1925 and 30 April 1925, J. H. Ball to Paul Miller, 20 August 1978, Files of the School of Journalism and Broadcasting; Hurst interview. Don Hadley, later a longtime member of the *Washington Star* staff, spent part of his college time at Oklahoma A. and M. in 1924. See *O'Collegian*, 19 June 1964, p. 3.

69. Irvin Hurst to Harry E. Heath Jr., 5 November 1975, School of Journalism and Broadcasting Centennial History Collection; Author's selective compilation from *O'Collegian* mastheads listing staff members, 1924-1925; "Keeping Pace With the Aggies, *Oklahoma A. and M. College Magazine*, vol. 1, no. 3 (November 1929), p. 20; "Keeping Pace With the Aggies," *Oklahoma A. and M. College Magazine*, vol. 1, no. 6 (February 1930), p. 20; "Keeping Pace With the Aggies," *Oklahoma A. and M. College Magazine*, vol. 1, no. 8 (April 1930), p. 19; "Keeping Pace With the Aggies," *Oklahoma A. and M. College Magazine*, vol. 2, no. 9 (May 1931), p. 275.

70. *Daily O'Collegian*, 14 April 1926, p. 1.

71. Walker Stone to Edmund E. Hadley et. al., 4 May 1926, Files of the School of Journalism and Broadcasting.

72. Bradford Knapp to Walker Stone and Board, 7 May 1926, President's Papers, Special Collections, Edmon Low Library; *Redskin*, pp. 342, 366.

73. Walker Stone to Raymond Bivert, 18 September 1926, President's Papers.

74. Tom R. Hoke to Harry E. Heath Jr., 23 June 1983, Files of School of Journalism and Broadcasting; *Stillwater Gazette*, 10 September 1926, p. 4.

75. *Daily O'Collegian*, 22 April 1926, p. 1; *Stillwater Gazette*, 10 September 1926, p. 4.

76. Rulon, pp. 194, 195; *Stillwater Gazette*, 9 April 1926; Bradford Knapp to Board of Agriculture, 6 April 1926, President's Papers.

77. *Capitol Hill Beacon: Sixty Years of Community Service*, Special 60th Anniversary Edition, pp. 23, 24, 86, 87. Capitol Hill is located in Oklahoma City, Oklahoma.

78. Dorothy Hadley Zeh to Harry E. Heath Jr., 7 February 1992, David Sellers to Harry E. Heath Jr., 17 February 1992, Charles L. Allen to Harry E. Heath Jr., 5 April 1981, and Service des loisirs et du developpement communautaire, Division des bibliotheques, Bibliotheque centrale, 1210, rue Sherbrook Est, Montreal H2L 1L9 to Harry E. Heath Jr., 21 July 1987, in School of Journalism and Broadcasting Centennial History Collection; *Early History of Capitol Hill* (Oklahoma City, OK: Suburban Newspapers, 1965); *Montreal Daily Star*, 13 March 1947, p. 1, 3 November 1948, p. 1, 28 July 1950, p. 1, 11 April 1951, p. 1, 22 April 1951, p. 1, 17 September 1959, p. 1.

79. *Capitol Hill Beacon*, 60th Anniversary Edition, p. 24; *Daily O'Collegian*, 23 May 1961, p. 1; *Tulsa World*, 19 May 1961, p. 19; *Stillwater NewsPress*, 21 May 1961, p. 11; 24 May, p. 1; *Montreal Daily Star*, 26 May 1961, editorial page; Irvin Hurst to Harry E. Heath Jr., 8 January 1981, and Sid Steen to Harry E. Heath Jr., 24 March 1981, in School of Journalism and Broadcasting Centennial History Collection.

80. *Stillwater NewsPress*, 25 May 1961, p. 16; Journalism staff telephone interview with George Hill, 21 May 1981.

81. *Stillwater NewsPress*, 25 May 1961, p. 16; *Montreal Daily Star*, 26 May 1961, editorial page.

82. *Daily O'Collegian*, 25 May 1961, p. 1.

83. Harold Hubbard to Harry E. Heath Jr., 25 March 1981, School of Journalism and Broadcasting Centennial History Collection.

84. "Tentative Program, Oklahoma State University Journalism Day Honoring Ed Hadley," 24 May 1961, School of Journalism and Broadcasting Centennial History Collection; *Stillwater NewsPress*, 25 May 1961, p. 16.

85. *Daily O'Collegian*, 25 May 1961, p. 1; Randle Perdue to Harry E. Heath Jr., 25 March 1981, School of Journalism and Broadcasting Centennial History Collection.

86. *Stillwater NewsPress*, 25 May 1961, p. 16; *Daily O'Collegian*, 26 May 1961, p. 1.

87. *Daily O'Collegian*, 21 March 1925, p. 3, 15 April 1925, p. 3, 21 October 1925, p. 3, 13 November 1925, p. 1; Rulon, pp. 181, 182; *Stillwater Gazette*, 3 August 1923, p. 1; Wilbanks, pp. 14, 15, 18, 19, 30, 31, 34.

88. *Winston-Salem Journal*, 9 October 1973, p. 2; Dorothy Hadley Zeh to Harry E. Heath Jr., 7 February 1992 and 30 March 1992, Virginia E. Hauswald to Harry E. Heath Jr., 23 March 1992, and Irvin Hurst to Harry E. Heath Jr., 26 March 1991, in School of Journalism and Broadcasting Centennial History Collection.

13 The Trout Years Begin

Edmund E. Hadley's departure left a brief gap in the continuity of campus journalism. The 1925-26 catalog, with announcements for 1926-27, had gone to press before his replacement had been named. Randle Perdue, Hadley's assistant, had stayed on, so the publications and publicity activities—though somewhat curtailed—continued without interruption. The academic program in journalism also would limp along on a make-do basis. Despite this, the collaboration of J. Frank Dobie and Hadley had moved the program forward, and Hadley's successor, once selected, would find the gains they had made favorable for further progress.[1]

The move toward a major in journalism had faltered with Noble W. Rockey's dismissal and Lester C. Getzloe's departure during the summer of 1921. Rockey had taken the first step in 1920 by recommending Getzloe as an assistant professor assigned exclusively to the journalism segment of the Department of English. No teacher prior to Getzloe could focus solely upon journalism. Not until Hadley's arrival had a similar arrangement occurred. Hadley's teaching was in journalism alone, but it had been worked into his already busy schedule as publicity agent and editor-in-chief of college publications.[2]

During the brief Dobie-Hadley years, another step leading to greater recognition for journalism had been taken. As Hadley and Dobie's friendship developed, they had decided on two important changes that would be reflected in the catalog. For the first time, with the approval of acting dean Clarence H. McElroy, the 1923-24 catalog carried the title Department of English and Journalism. Rather than being intermixed with the various English and literature courses, journalism was listed under its own subhead as one of the department's three sub-sections: rhetoric and English composition, English literature and language, and courses in journalism. Eight courses awaited the man who would replace Hadley. Who would teach these courses remained a mystery, for a major turnover in the department had followed Dobie's departure for the University of Texas and none of the four newly appointed faculty members were journalism trained.[3]

As the fall semester got under way, only Perdue, who had not been called upon to teach before, and Mable Caldwell, who had recently returned to her alma mater, could be considered to have had any real experience in journalism. From the top down, there had been a major refurbishing of departmental personnel. William F. DeMoss, a gangling Shakespeare scholar considered by students to be a perfect prototype of Ichabod Crane, had succeeded the popular writer-scholar Dobie as professor and head. He had earned the Ph.D. as well as bachelor's and master's degrees at the University of Chicago. Benjamin F. Williams, who had taken the A.B. degree at Harvard and the A.M. at Valparaiso University, signed on as professor and assistant head. Before Williams's years at Oklahoma A. and M. had ended, the first library building, by then converted to other uses, would bear his name. Other newcomers were Grace M. DeMotte and Anna R. Todd, both assistant professors. DeMotte had done graduate work at the University of Oklahoma and Todd had come from Colorado State Normal at Gunnison. Newly appointed as an instructor was Mahala P. Larason, who had earned the A.B. degree at the University of Oklahoma. Holdovers were M. Agnes Berrigan, Mary N. Baucom, Whittier Burnett, Edward S. McCabe, Victor Solberg, Alice Bralley Traver, and John M. Wallace. Of these, Burnett and Berrigan had a strong interest in writing, but that interest was primarily in *creative* writing courses rather than journalistic writing. Nevertheless, it was a relatively strong lineup and students interested in journalism could profit from the rigorous demands some of these faculty placed upon them in English composition.[4]

It was obvious that the English and literature courses were well covered, but journalism was a different matter. For four years—since the Rockey-Getzloe days—there had been too many courses and too few teachers in the journalism area. DeMoss was desperate. His first move was to ask Perdue to add teaching to his other duties. His experience in Muskogee and Stillwater journalism plus Oklahoma A. and M. publicity work made him a logical choice to take up some of the slack. Perdue would handle two courses. But more help would be needed. DeMoss turned to the student ranks. Irvin Hurst, past editor of the *Daily O'Collegian* and now a senior working in the college publicity office, was another logical choice. Hurst related the story this way: "I was surprised one afternoon to have a visit from DeMoss. 'Mr. Hurst,' he tells me, 'we have a class enrolled in journalism and nobody to teach it. Would you teach the class?' I accepted, subject to approval of [President Bradford Knapp]. There were 20 or 25 enrolled in the class, including Virgil D. Curry of Oilton, who later spent years on the *Tulsa Tribune* staff. I used Bleyer's *Newspaper Writing and Editing*. In the spring of 1927, short of required hours, I petitioned for permission to take an examination for credit in the course I had taught and—surprise!—I passed. I told the college council that probably I had learned more than any of my students."[5]

When Knapp went into the market for Hadley's successor, he was sure he had found the right man in Clement E. Trout. Trout was less colorful than such men as Freeman E. Miller, Angelo C. Scott, Harry R. O'Brien, and Hadley, but he had special skills as an organizer. He could pull together campus resources to make programs work in a productive and economical way. It was a special gift that was to produce outstanding results for more than thirty years while Trout himself, self-effacing, remained a low-key administrator who consistently was underestimated until well into his academic career.

The first news of Trout's appointment came in the *Daily O'Collegian* on October 8, 1926. It was a major story in column one at the top of the front page. President Knapp had announced the day before that Trout would be the new head of the publications department. He was due to report on or before November 1. Since August 1, when Hadley's resignation became effective, Perdue had been acting head of the department, dividing his time between the college and the *Stillwater Daily Press.* Now he had elected to accept full-time employment at the newspaper. He would continue to assist from his office at the *Press*, but until Trout's arrival much of the work would be done by Hurst, generally recognized as one of the most talented student journalists on campus.

Knapp told the *O'Collegian* that Trout's broad experience both in general newspaper work and in agricultural journalism made him an especially good choice for the position. Knapp pointed out that Trout, while connected with the United States Department of Agriculture (USDA), had worked in Texas, Louisiana, Mississippi, and other southern states. One week later, a similar story appeared in the *Stillwater Gazette*. Knapp told the *Gazette*: "[Trout] has had experience as a teacher, as an agricultural editor, as a correspondent for metropolitan newspapers, and in the preparation of timely articles and publicity material. . . . He comes to us highly recommended." What Knapp did not say was that Trout had had his choice of three positions at Oklahoma A. and M. He could have chosen to head either the Department of Agronomy or the Department of Horticulture. Instead, he chose the publicity and publications position with its additional responsibility for journalism courses plus the chairmanship of the publications and solicitation for student advertising committees.[6]

As Knapp had indicated, Trout had had a varied and interesting career before accepting his appointment. He was born August 11, 1891, the son of Colmeda James and Velmah Eddy Trout. In his biographical sketches, he sometimes listed Lakewood, sometimes Shelbyville, Illinois, as his birthplace. Lakewood apparently was a Shelby County farming community near Shelbyville. At any rate, it seems clear that he was a farm boy with the usual responsibilities for work on the family farm. This fact would prove to be an advantage in his later professional life. He attended grade school in Lakewood from 1897 to 1906, then advanced to Shelbyville High School, where he was graduated in June 1909. Fresh out of school, he taught in a rural Shelbyville school for a year, then two years as a seventh-grade teacher in the Shelbyville public schools.[7]

Following his experience as a public school teacher, there is a year in which his next move is less well documented. It may have been during this time that he dabbled in early silent movies. He spent one three-month hitch in what was called a roughneck squad in the production of *Sheridan's Ride*, reportedly the first two-reel motion picture ever made. As one of the "extras," he played both a Confederate and a Union soldier. The film's director was Francis Ford, father of the famous modern-day director, John Ford. But fun and games can carry a man only so far, and Trout knew he must continue his education.[8]

In the fall of 1913, he enrolled at the University of Illinois, majoring in agronomy and specializing in soils and crops. Lacking other evidence, it seems likely he spent his summers in farm work. He received his degree in 1917, although his last classes may have been completed in 1916. *Who's Who in America* lists the date as 1916, but an Oklahoma A. and M. "Biographical Record" in Trout's own handwriting reads: "University of Illinois 1913-1916, B.S. in Agriculture, agronomy major, 1917."[9]

Following his studies at the state university, he taught vocational agriculture and manual training at Centralia Township High School for a year, then took a position as science assistant in the USDA Office of Corn Investigations, Bureau of Plant Industry, in Washington, D.C. After a year in Washington, he returned to his home state to accept a position as vocational agriculture teacher at Jerseyville Township High School. One year later, he was off to a new adventure. He had decided to become a farmer and had moved to the Jacksonville, Florida, area to put his soils and crops training to work.

Whatever the reason for his decision, he was never to return to active farming after that year. Instead, he turned to government service, where he remained for the next four years. During this time he served the first few months as a training assistant. He was responsible for a five-state area under the Federal Board for Vocational Education. Then he was classed

Oklahoma A. and M. College made a strong showing among members of the American Association of Agricultural College Editors (AAACE) early in Clement Trout's career. As head of the Department of Publications and college editor, he exhibited the publicity output of his department at the annual AAACE meeting.

as an agricultural training specialist for the U.S. Veterans Bureau. In 1922, the bureau appointed him training coordinator for World War I veterans needing rehabilitation. After two years assisting veterans, he had decided to return to school.[10]

His next move would lead him into his life's work: disseminating technical information through newspapers, magazines, agricultural bulletins, and other media and teaching others how to do the same. The beginning of this new phase in his professional development came in 1924 when he was awarded a graduate assistantship by the University of Wisconsin. While taking graduate courses in the Department of Agricultural Journalism he studied under Andrew W. Hopkins, one of the nation's best-known men in the field, and worked part-time in the College of Agriculture's editorial office. This led to assignments in the farm department of the *Wisconsin State Journal*. In addition, he edited a page of farm news for *Publishers' Auxiliary*, a widely circulated publication of the Western Newspaper Union. Again the record is unclear. Some documents show that Trout was awarded the M.S. in agricultural journalism in 1924. Others, including *Who's Who*, list the date as 1925. This discrepancy notwithstanding, he returned to the USDA in 1924, serving in the Bureau of Agricultural Economics. He was assigned to the bureau's Office of Information, handling news and house organs for marketing officials. Here he pioneered in the use of radio for farm-market reports, thought to be the first such organized effort in the nation. He was promoted to associate economic analyst and information specialist in 1925, holding that title for a year before his move to Stillwater.[11]

To examine the early part of the Trout era at Oklahoma A. and M., it is helpful to know more of the background of the man who hired him and those who worked over him and with him. Trout wore several hats, so he was answerable not only to Knapp for general college publicity and publications but also to Walter D. Bentley for his extension information activities, to Carr T. Dowell for experiment station publications, and to DeMoss for the academic program which he had inherited and would first stabilize and then strengthen.[12]

Bradford Knapp, like Trout, had lived an eventful life in his youth. An unexpected opportunity for his father changed the course of young Knapp's life. Seaman Knapp was president of Iowa State College when the North American Land and Timber Company, a British firm, asked him to take charge of 1,500,000 acres in Southwest Louisiana. Included were about 25,000 head of wild range cattle and a company operating steamboats, dredge boats and sawmills. He resigned his presidency at Ames in 1885 and moved the family to Lake Charles, Louisiana. For the next three years, young Bradford reveled in this unusual learning experience.[13]

There were no public schools in the area, so the future Oklahoma A. and M. president attended a private school from December 1885 to February 1888. It was in session for about five or six months out of the year and was taught by his sister Minnie. Perhaps more important than the private schooling was the practical experience he gained after hours and during the off months. He learned about the cultivation of rice, sugar cane, and cotton, as well as cattle breeding, logging, and lumbering. During this time, he became an expert horseman and an excellent shot with rifle and revolver. He soon adopted the southland as his own.

It would have been unthinkable that Bradford Knapp should not pursue a college education. There was, after all, the family tradition to uphold. In February 1888, he departed for Iowa State College, where he would live with his brother Herman, who held a responsible position in the college's business and financial office. Eight months later he contracted a severe case of pneumonia. Upon recovery, his doctors advised him to return to the less severe winters of the South. At mid-term of that academic year he transferred to Vanderbilt University in Nashville, Tennessee.

At Vanderbilt, he decided to specialize in science. He felt he had learned the practical side of agriculture and now resolved to learn the scientific side as well. He intended to be a chemist in a sugar refinery after graduation, but he was determined to be more than a bookworm until that time. His broad-scale activities as a student offer some insight into his attitudes as president at Oklahoma A. and M. Vanderbilt's first football team was organized in 1890, and he earned one of the guard positions. The next year he shifted to tackle. As for student publications, he served on both the *Hustler* and the *Observer*. He managed the track team for one year and was a member of the Glee Club. In the social swirl, he was a prominent member of Kappa Alpha fraternity. Such a diversity of activities suggests an outgoing if not exuberant personality. Instead, he was considered a quiet, modest person, mature in his habits.

During the summer months, he returned to his father's vast Lake Charles project and assumed many of the duties connected with the farming operations on the plantation. He also spent considerable vacation time punching cattle, a fact which may have contributed to his robust and well-developed physique.

Bradford Knapp was graduated from Vanderbilt in 1892 with a B.S. degree in chemistry. He returned to Louisiana to take charge of a sugar cane and cotton plantation of 1,700 acres, including a sugar refinery, in St. Martin Parish. His responsibilities were heavy, but they gave him valuable training in executive and administrative affairs. He spent several hours in the saddle each day riding over the Huron Plantation on Bayou Teche, where he supervised the large number of Negro employees. The job suited him. It was a pleasant mixture of office routine and work in the open air. But disappointment was just ahead. The Panic of 1893 led to foreclosure of the mortgages on the various North American projects. Seaman Knapp would forge a new career in the United States Department of Agriculture, but this change in his family's fortunes was hard for Bradford to accept. He felt that if he had known more about legal matters, he and his father might have survived the Panic. He was convinced they had lost control of the property through unfair and illegal means. He told his father, "I'll just study law and see how the trick was done."

In 1894, he enrolled in Georgetown University, Washington, D.C., then in February of 1895 entered the University of Michigan law school, where he financed his way by teaching gymnastics. In 1896 he was awarded the bachelor of laws degree. He was broke, and decided to gain some financial stability before starting his law career. Again his brother Herman, now treasurer of Iowa State College, was helpful. He offered Knapp a job as his assistant, a position he accepted and held for about five years.

Finally, in 1899, he had achieved financial stability and decided to "hang out his shingle." He chose Belmond, in Wright County, Iowa, a town of about 2,000, to launch his new career. He quickly established a reputation for fighting crime. Violators rich and poor, high and low, were prosecuted. Soon he had cleaned up rotten politics and graft, giving the county a reputation for law and order.

Belmond was a turning point in Knapp's life for another reason. A young widow, Stella White Davis, was impressed by his singing in the Methodist Church choir, although she did not meet him for several months. She was a milliner, and soon opened her own shop in Clarion, Iowa. Knapp, when in court in Clarion, always made it a point to call on her. Soon the romance blossomed and they were married in Clear Lake, Iowa, at the home of her sister on July 20, 1904. She was to be a capable partner and teammate for the rest of his life.

After the marriage, the couple lived in Belmond for a year, then moved to Clarion, where Knapp entered a law partnership with State Senator Charles F. Peterson. The partnership lasted four years, including two as county attorney. Life in Clarion was good.

From 1909 to 1919, Knapp worked for the federal government. His duties with the USDA included wide travel, with lectures in Europe and throughout the United States. During this period, dozens of his articles and two books on agriculture were published, and the University of Maryland conferred the honorary doctor of agriculture degree upon him. He was in demand for leadership roles in various organizations, and volunteered his time on the National Council of Boy Scouts in America, the Royal Economic Society of England, and the American Economic Association, among others. He was active in the Masonic Lodge, the Rotary Club, and numerous college honor associations. His admiration for William Jennings Bryan led him to switch his allegiance to the Democratic Party.

In 1920, Knapp left the USDA to become dean of agriculture at the University of Arkansas, where he served for three happy and productive years. On a family trip to Enid, where they would visit Mrs. Knapp's relatives, John A. Whitehurst, the president of the Oklahoma State Board of Agriculture, had arranged to meet with Knapp about the upcoming presidential vacancy at Oklahoma A. and M. The meeting took place in Oklahoma City on September 7, 1923. Knapp's reputation was well known in Oklahoma. He had been a guest speaker in Stillwater on several occasions while at the USDA and had helped Walter Bentley during the development of the college's extension programs. The board was pressed for time. Richard G. Tyler, who had been serving as acting president, would be leaving soon to take up his work at the Massachusetts Institute of Technology. The board offered Knapp the Oklahoma A. and M. presidency at $8,000 a year.

Knapp was reluctant to give an immediate answer to Whitehurst. There had been three different presidents within four months. For years the college had been nothing more than a political football, kicked first one way and then another to suit the whims and fancies of each governor. Every change of administration seemed to bring a turn-over in the presidency and faculty. Knapp was secure in his job as dean of agriculture at the University of Arkansas. He would need assurances before moving his wife and five children to Stillwater. The first encouragement came from Henry J. Waters, who himself had once rejected the Oklahoma A. and M. presidency. Waters, who had been president of the Kansas Agricultural College and was now editor of the *Kansas City Star*, had called Knapp long-distance and urged him to accept. The clincher, apparently, was a three-year contract in which the board agreed not to employ, promote, or discharge a faculty member without his approval. Among other crucial considerations was the assurance of a Stillwater delegation that there would be a change to a board of regents similar to that of the University of Oklahoma. (Before this would come to pass, Knapp would complete four years and eight months at Oklahoma A. and M. followed by presidencies at Auburn and Texas Technological College.) Things looked promising. His family and friends were sure he could replace turbulence and demoralization with stability and progress. Knapp liked challenges, and on September 23, 1923, he began the biggest academic challenge of his career.[14]

By the time Trout had replaced Hadley, Knapp had been in office slightly more than three years. It was obvious that he had met the board's expectations. He was firmly in control on the campus and was well known and accepted throughout the state through his many public appearances and radio talks. To smooth the transition, Knapp had called the various student editors and their key staff members to his new Whitehurst office for a get-acquainted session with Trout. Existing policies were discussed and no changes were advocated. The president used the occasion to outline his plans for a proposed student union building which he said would house publication offices.[15]

Trout soon felt comfortable on the Knapp team. He talked Knapp's language. Both had had farm-management experience, though on a vastly different scale. Both had given effective service to the USDA. Trout's knowledge of the USDA's information services was a big plus in his dealings with the Oklahoma A. and M. president. While both were from the North, they had worked in the South and had developed an appreciation for its culture. In fact the thirty-five-year-old Trout had met his future wife, a Georgia miss with a decidedly Southern cultural and social outlook on life, during his USDA service in the South. He married Ruth Lee Brown of Hartwell, Georgia, soon after coming to Oklahoma A. and M. Their two daughters, Ruth Ann and Juanita Jane, would be born and reared in Stillwater's college atmosphere. Professor and Mrs. Trout quickly became active in local church and civic affairs.[16]

A rural setting always appealed to Trout. He could not farm and keep up with the multitude of duties assigned him at Oklahoma A. and M. College, but he could live outside the usual residential setting. It was eight years before his finances and the country home of his choice coincided. The Trouts moved from 1107 West Fourth to a colonial-style home on an acreage overlooking Boomer Lake. It was a rustic setting north of the campus, well beyond the outskirts of Stillwater. He indicated his address on personnel forms with the simple statement: "North of City." Today the city has reached far beyond his rustic setting.[17]

Trout—low-key, serious and goal-directed—had long since confirmed Knapp's judgment. He had brought to the job credentials that Knapp respected. He had had the practical farm experience, had studied in two outstanding land-grant schools, had learned of the multitudinous functions of the USDA at first-hand, and could see a promising future for Oklahoma A. and M. in its three-part mission of teaching, research and extension. He may have been slightly awed by what was expected of him, but he also was challenged by the opportunities the job presented. He was ready to accept the challenge.

President Knapp brought Trout to Stillwater as the only full-time employee in journalism. His official duties were three-fold: teaching journalism, being the college editor for the experiment station, and serving as head of the Department of Publications. This heavy load was carried until the 1954-55 academic year, when publishing and public information duties were split off from his academic responsibilities. His primary title was editor of college publications, but he held academic rank as a full professor in the Department of English, a status Hadley had never achieved. Agriculture professors often had complained about their news coverage during the Hadley era. Trout and his staff got along well with them and the complaints diminished.[18]

One confusing element in Trout's wide range of responsibilities was that of extension information. While he would assist the Extension Division in its publicity function when called upon, this area of the college's concern would remain in Walter Bentley's hands until May 2, 1927, then would shift to Dover P. Trent, Bentley's replacement as director. By contrast, the editorial function of the experiment station was immediately placed in Trout's domain. Apparently Knapp did not want to rock Bentley's boat. The aging extension specialist had returned temporarily to his old directorship following W. A. Conner's resignation in 1926. Bentley had been an associate of Knapp's father, founder of the federal extension program, and Knapp had been Bentley's supervisor and friend during his own years as a U.S. Department of Agriculture extension administrator. Bentley, with Seaman Knapp's support, had become the father of the extension system in Oklahoma, and it was an honor he cherished.

The implementation of the Smith-Lever Act of 1914 had given Bentley a roster of county agents who formed a potent information network. Bentley had assumed a proprietary interest in extension and had ruled it with a strong hand during his years as director. Bradford Knapp may have been reluctant to have Trout take over publicity responsibilities from a close family friend who was in the twilight of his career. Be that as it may, the arrangement was confusing to outsiders and often a matter of concern to Trout as he attempted to coordinate the responsibilities of the publications department. Cooperation improved under Trent.[19] Later, the confusion would be reduced somewhat by a written agreement on information responsibilities.

While Trout knew his immediate success depended upon his work as publications editor, he was convinced that his long-range success was tied to strong academic programs in agricultural and home economics journalism. He was analytical in his approach to any new situation, careful in choosing a plan of action and meticulous in implementing it. Hasty decisions were not part of his administrative style. It seems likely, then, that he reviewed what had been done in the years prior to his arrival. He knew what was expected of him as editor-in-chief of college publications, but he also carried the title "professor of journalism." Wearing that hat would require a careful study of old catalogs. If he went through them carefully, as he almost surely did, he would have noted John A. Craig's pioneering effort in Agricultural Journalism from 1908 until his controversial dismissal in 1910. No journalism would be offered again until 1912, when Edwin R. Barrett, the new head of the Department of English and Public Speaking, would bring it back. This time it had appeared as an English course rather than under the auspices of the School of Agriculture.

President Bradford Knapp conferred the baccalaureate degree upon his daughter Marion in 1927. Another graduate that year was Irvin Hurst, a prominent student journalist, who married Marion the following year. Knapp sought to guide student publications with a stronger hand than any other Oklahoma A. and M. or OSU president.

The new journalism course carried the title English 8a-b-c Advanced Composition and covered three terms. While it was broader in scope than Craig's course, it gave considerable emphasis to agriculture and domestic science because many of Harry O'Brien's students were majoring in those fields. Upon further perusal of the Oklahoma A. and M. catalogs, Trout would discover that the first curriculum in journalism—five courses— had appeared in the 1914-15 academic year, replacing English 8a-b-c. He would note, too, that the titles and course descriptions were closer to those of non-technical schools than those of most land-grant institutions.[20]

Finally, he would notice the changes that had taken place as the college shifted from quarters to semesters and back to quarters again, as well as the influence of Getzloe, first, and then Hadley, both journalists with a liberal rather than a technical orientation. He would be gratified for the return of Agricultural Journalism and the addition of Home Economics Journalism in 1921-22, but he observed that these were service courses and that there was no degree offered in journalism. Getzloe had emphasized news writing and Hadley had emphasized reporting as well as news writing and editing. It was plain to see that the visibility journalism had lost from 1921 to 1923 had been regained under Dobie. Except for Hadley's addition of a second editing course, there were no curriculum changes from 1923 until Trout's arrival near the end of the first semester in 1926. Trout would ride out the year with the program Dobie and Hadley had left him, but by the time the next catalog copy was prepared he would shape the program to his own design.[21]

The 1925-26 catalog had listed eight journalism courses in the School of Science and Literature and one advertising course in the School of Commerce. The journalism courses were largely a legacy from Edwin R. Barrett. These had been telescoped from eight to five courses as the college moved from the quarter to the semester plan just before Trout's arrival. Courses had to be restructured and credit hours reconsidered. A typical entry in the 1926-27 catalog: "213 (228 and 1/2 of 229) News Writing and Reporting." Trout was pleased that DeMoss was agreeable to listing journalism courses under a separate heading in the schedule of classes. As the new man responsible for journalism, he was seeking higher visibility for the program he hoped to build.[22]

When Trout arrived in Stillwater, Oklahoma was only twenty years old and not a single hard-surfaced road spanned the state. There was no such thing as a cold drink of water on a hot summer day in campus buildings. The college's first six graduates were successful businessmen in their prime, Knapp was stressing diversified farming, and oil was coming into its own on a wave of excessive production. Oklahoma A. and M. had conferred 1,789 degrees since its first graduation ceremonies. The college had broken the 100 mark with the class of 1915, and by 1925 the number had grown to 218. Knapp had just moved the administrative offices from Morrill Hall to Whitehurst. As the prairie college in Stillwater was growing, journalism education had shown solid growth nationally. From 1910, when only four schools had four-year programs, the number had increased to twenty-eight by 1920. Within a year after Trout's arrival, the number had jumped to fifty-four.[23] Prospects looked good. The hard work of Rockey and Hadley was about to pay dividends.

C. Walker Stone, Hadley's strong right arm in promoting journalism's growth, had left and was launching what would become a highly successful newspaper career. Raymond E. Bivert had replaced him as general manager of student publications during the transitional period before Trout's arrival. Already Bivert was taking steps to strengthen his domain, which would complement the various programs that Trout soon would restructure and lead. Printing off campus had been too costly for the *O'Collegian*. Bivert knew the paper could not be handled by E. J. Westbrook's busy college printshop, as it had been in the Northup and Gelder days. His solution was a $15,000 printing plant for student publications. It would be controlled by a new state-chartered O'Collegian Publishing Company, which would have both faculty and student representation. Details were worked out with President Knapp and Dean McElroy.

In August 1926, the new printing equipment was installed in the basement of the old library, which had been renamed the Biology Building. A detailed liquidation plan was worked out. Bivert could tell Knapp that the last payment was scheduled on November 10, 1929.[24]

By the fall of 1927, even an outsider reading the catalog would be aware of the direction Trout had mapped for journalism. From the early courses of Craig and O'Brien emphasizing agricultural journalism, the program had evolved with a less specialized emphasis under Rockey, Getzloe, and Hadley. In his first year, Trout had not had the opportunity to change the focus of course titles and descriptions. They continued to be general in tone, not unlike those of such schools as the University of Kansas and the University of Texas. But Trout's studies as well as his professional career had convinced him that Oklahoma A. and M. as a land-grant institution should follow a different path. The 1927-28 catalog reflected this view. Trout had expanded the program to eleven courses. Five of these courses in addition to Agricultural Journalism and Home Economics Journalism were given a *technical* emphasis instead of the more generalized approach Trout had found upon his arrival. He quickly established the idea that a journalism classroom would not be the place to doze off. He would expect competence. In one of his first classes, he assigned four A grades, five Bs, five Cs, two Ds, two Fs, and three incompletes.[25]

Trout was unprepared for the disruption that would come three months after he had settled into his routine in Old Central. Bivert had been slightly injured by falling plaster as he sat at his desk on February 8, 1927. Knapp and college engineers inspected the building within hours. Knapp ordered all activities to be removed from the building. Trout's office was moved to Room 111, Whitehurst, while the *O'Collegian* took up temporary space in the College Cafeteria waiting room and the *Redskin* and *Aggievator* shared the floor above with the Student Senate. Mable Caldwell, editor of the *Boomer*, moved to the Old Engineering Building. While there is no doubt that Old Central needed repairs—it had been declared unsafe for classes as early as 1921—its temporary closing may have been hastened by a ruse. Student journalists had gone to the floor above and pounded heavily enough to precipitate the "accident." Early in his administration, Henry G. Bennett placed Old Central in proper repair and full-time use was resumed.[26]

Trout's concept of building bridges between academic specialties and journalism led to intra-departmental arrangements that were to last for more than three decades. First, inspired by Andrew Hopkins, he carried the University of Wisconsin idea to Dean Carr T. Dowell. The result was a major in agricultural journalism, first listed in the Oklahoma A. and M. catalog for 1927-28. Then he took the idea to Dean Nora A. Talbot and a home economics journalism major was the result. It, too, was formalized in the 1927-28 catalog. Advertising instruction had been offered by the School of Commerce since 1914, but there was not a major program. It took Trout a little longer here because commerce was between deans, but by the academic year 1929-30 his ability to sell an idea was successful once again. He gained the confidence of the new commerce dean, Raymond D. Thomas, and the result was a new major program in Commerce Journalism. While Wisconsin and Iowa State had applied the concept in agriculture and home economics and Kansas State had developed a Department of Industrial Journalism and Printing, the fact that Trout had formed a partnership with the School of Commerce was new among land-grant institutions in mid-America. At the core of the structure was still the course work in the School of Science and Literature, but journalism's presence on the campus was greatly enhanced by the cooperative intra-departmental agreements forged by Trout. In addition to degrees offered in the three colleges, Trout and his faculty set up minor programs across jurisdictional lines leading to a certificate in journalism.[27]

All of this was to lead to confusion in later years when journalism accreditation became important. Most accrediting officials and visiting inspectors were unfamiliar with arrangements which were so atypical of the usual school of journalism. It took considerable work by letter and telephone to clarify the concept for those who found it unusual.[28]

Within a short time, all of the new majors were carefully spelled out, with catalog listings of the required courses. The explicit nature of the programs gave enrollment a boost. Years later, when Oklahoma A. and M. College had reached university status and enrollment had quadrupled, catalogs no longer had the space to spell out each program and students and prospective students had to work harder on their own to discover the requirements in various journalism programs. This may have slowed the growth of journalism enrollment for several years.

Meanwhile, the buffeting about that student publications had faced almost semi-annually was soon to end. In December 1927, the editorial offices and printing plant moved into the recently vacated Creamery Building. It was the first time all student publications and their own printing plant had been housed under the same roof. Bivert called it "the first breath of permanency."

The new *O'Collegian* printing plant was proving to be more than a convenience for student publications. It was an important source of income for financially pressed students. The *Daily O'Collegian* alone carried a student payroll exceeding $12,000 per year. During the year of 1928-29, eighty-two students were regularly employed throughout student publications, receiving an aggregate salary of $14,250, making Bivert's program the largest student employment organization on campus.[29]

Raymond Bivert (*left*), an outstanding Aggie student who later became business manager of student publications, worked closely with the journalism program from 1926 until he entered military service during World War II. Welden Barnes (*right*), a promising student journalist in the 1930s, later became director of the Public Information Division under President Oliver S. Willham.

While taking up his information and publications duties, Trout began to search for teaching talent. He knew he could count upon Mable Caldwell, an assistant professor who had taught both English and journalism off and on for five years and had become active in civic affairs through the Stillwater Woman's Club. But he wanted to provide a broader menu of courses, and he would need more help. Trout found the answer in a former newspaperman who had been working for the Associated Press.[30]

Robert V. Peterson came from a background similar to his own. He had taken his B.S. degree at Iowa State College, where he had studied agricultural journalism. His duties, in addition to teaching, would involve writing and editing for both the experiment station and Extension Service. A native of Ocheyedan, Iowa, Peterson had spent most of his youth in Faribault, Minnesota, where his first newspaper job was writing a high school column for the *Daily News*. After his Iowa State days he had joined the Associated Press in Wichita, Kansas, later working for the AP in Des Moines and Kansas City.

He came to Oklahoma A. and M. in time for the changeover from quarter to semester terms in 1927. Trout assigned him to teach News Writing and Reporting. Agricultural Journalism was taught by Trout, while Caldwell taught two sections of Home Economics Journalism that semester as well as Special Articles. Peterson, later to be known affectionately as "Mr. Pete" during a twenty-two-year tenure in the OU journalism school, entered the graduate program at Oklahoma A. and M. as a part-time student, earning the M.S. degree in 1929 while continuing with his teaching and publications work. His research on the reading habits of Oklahoma farmers was useful to Trout for in-house planning while also providing weekly newspapers positive reinforcement for their use of agricultural news from the college. Trout recommended Peterson's promotion based upon his "good work" for two years.[31]

No sooner had Peterson settled in than Trout was asked to chart the future of journalism at Oklahoma A. and M. In the mid-1920s, students—particularly Walker Stone—had expressed hopes for a journalism department. The subject never was given serious consideration by the higher administration, although Rockey had seen its merits as early as 1920. But by 1928, the talk of a separate department had become official. Trout was restrained in his response to such a possibility. He stated his position in an undated and untitled document. No letter of transmittal was found in the archives. Whether the report went to Knapp or to Bennett is not clear. If it was prepared at Knapp's initiative, it may have been passed on to Bennett, for Knapp soon would submit his resignation. It seems more likely that is was prepared for Bennett—probably one of several similar status reports from other administrators—to help familiarize the new president with the college. Trout's annual reports always carried a title and emphasized the work of the Department of Publications first, with secondary emphasis given to the academic work in journalism. On this occasion, however, journalism education was primary.

"As to the possibilities," he wrote, "there are several ways of looking at it. A common view is that we should give a degree in general journalism. I do not agree with this view for several reasons." Among them Trout cited OU's journalism school of twenty years standing with a strong statewide following and the support of the state press association. He felt it would be better to compete with OU indirectly. Trout cited programs in "Technical" and "Industrial" journalism at Iowa State and Kansas State as examples of indirect competition with state universities. "I believe these courses are very effective, if not more effective than the regular journalism courses. . .," he noted.

"The idea of the Technical Journalism course is that the student takes enough work in some particular line, such as agriculture, to be a specialist in that field, and then takes journalism courses to train him to use his special knowledge on the printed page. That is the idea back of the Agricultural and Home Economics degree courses now offered here."

Students from schools other than agriculture and home economics could take the basic journalism work as electives, but Dean McElroy believed that a student should be allowed to take enough journalism for a major, though he would be registered in English.

With possibly one new course, "Editorial Writing," Trout conceded that "we are offering enough work to justify either a major or a certificate." Whether general journalism should be a separate major was a question to be decided, Trout wrote, adding that the catalog could be changed to show journalism as a major.

In one year, Trout pointed out, the advanced work in journalism would increase the teaching load by nine hours and Professor Caldwell would be needed full-time. Trout felt the experience of his staff would give the work standing with state editors "who insist on practical experience for journalism instructors."

If the administration determined that a major in general journalism should be offered, either in a separate teaching department or school, Trout expressed the opinion that "we have the basis for starting that work." He said it would involve an increase both in the number of courses and in the teaching staff. Additional equipment would be needed as well.[32]

There is nothing in the archives to indicate how Trout's position paper had been received, and by whom, but it had given him a chance to air his views. He clearly had shown a preference for the way Iowa State and Kansas State had developed their curricula. Should departmental status be granted in the future—as it was about nine years later—it seemed clear the direction Trout would go. Meantime, he was flexible enough to leave the door open for a new approach, should the administration and the board of agriculture favor it. The document brought no change in academic alignments and Trout shifted his thoughts from "what might be" to the problems at hand, foremost of which was faculty staffing.

Knapp had been, in terms of the expectations of his time, an effective leader. He had presided over changing student attitudes set off by the broadened horizons of veterans returning from overseas; he had tried to hold the line with the *in loco parentis* concept he had grown up with as the Roaring Twenties with their "flaming youth" began to push social interaction in new directions and to greater lengths. In general, his relationships with the board of agriculture had been good. He was respected as an efficient administrator. But board members at times still exercised powers Knapp did not believe should be in their hands.

During his presidency, Knapp had become a popular spokesman for the kind of education that would contribute directly to earning power, human comfort and personal well-being. His travels throughout the state had made him a favorite with farmers, and his radio broadcasts had gained him a wide following. Then, unexpectedly, old-style Oklahoma politics had surfaced again. First he met resistance from the board of agriculture in his move to reorganize extension work despite earlier assurances that there would be no interference with his personnel decisions. Next his resistance to construction contracts awarded on the basis of board friendships had antagonized some. He also opposed a board effort to gain a preferential appointment for a person he considered to be unqualified. He gained board support for a revamped business office, but when he dismissed Dean Edward P. Boyd of the School of Engineering, Boyd's supporters started a counterattack. Anonymous letters assailing Knapp's character, honesty, and ability were sent to every office-holding politician in Oklahoma. Finally, Knapp felt his only recourse was to submit his resignation.[33]

As his tenure at Oklahoma A. and M. neared its end, Knapp wrote the board of agriculture on two matters concerning journalism. The first was a request for approval of "certain courses in Industrial Journalism." He said the new courses, with a technical emphasis, were "splendid courses and should be authorized." The second matter, relative to the college sharing in the salary of a student publications manager, Knapp chose to leave to his successor.[34] Although he continued officially as president until July 1, 1928, he left on May 1, 1928, to assume the presidency of Auburn Polytechnic Institute. The board of agriculture asked Clarence McElroy to serve until Henry Bennett arrived late in June.[35]

Board members had promised Bennett a free hand in guiding the college's affairs, but with the presidency in limbo, they had decided some heads should roll. Two deans and five faculty members, among them

Trout, found themselves suddenly unemployed. Trout's dismissal, it was said, was linked to *O'Collegian* criticism of board president Harry Cordell. The board apparently felt Trout should have muzzled the campus newspaper. Following the faculty firings, Cordell told the *O'Collegian* that no further interference would take place. Within days, however, the board voted to dismiss forty non-faculty employees. Bennett did not protest the firing of staff, but he did protest the firing of faculty. He saw that several of the "fired" appeared on the payroll again. Apparently there was no board protest of Bennett's action in reinstating them. Trout had continued his work without interruption, although he must have had qualms about his future during the brief period before Bennett quietly reversed the board's action. Heretofore, board members had had a rural boss system some believed to be every bit as tough and encompassing as the machines of such urban bosses as Tweed, Pentergast, Cox, and Curley.[36]

Now Bennett's own political clout began to emerge. In addition to resisting the faculty firings, he drew up a tenure policy based upon the 1915 statement of the American Association of University Professors. The unanimous adoption of the statement brought an end to the annual election of faculty by the board, a pernicious practice that had greatly weakened Oklahoma A. and M. through the years.[37]

Trout soon was considered a notable campus character. Not only had his "doodling" attracted attention, but his office as well. Newcomers were surprised to find him at work behind mounds of papers, tangible evidence of insufficient clerical help. Yet, he seemed to know where everything was. Though overworked and understaffed, Trout still would take time to help students and faculty who came to him for advice. Historian Berlin B. Chapman, who was to become a prolific writer of Oklahoma history, remembered how Trout helped him develop a popular writing style for newspaper articles and how he advised him on typography and design for his first book.[38]

From June through September of 1929 Trout had been in touch with Ralph Lashbrook, a Kansas State journalism graduate working on the *Kansas City Star*. Peterson was on leave until September 1, 1930, and Trout recommended Lashbrook as his temporary replacement. If Robert Peterson did not return, Lashbrook would be his permanent replacement. He would handle sports publicity, editing, and "certain parts of the general news work" at $2,000 per year. DeMoss and McElroy approved the recommendation. Bennett did not. He was considering an overhaul of the public information program and apparently wanted to wait to assess Trout's needs later.[39]

Staffing problems were piling up. Mable Caldwell also had taken leave. On September 2, 1929, she left for Scotland to pursue graduate studies at Edinburgh University. Agnes Berrigan, then attending London

The *Daily O'Collegian* acquired its own printing press when Raymond Bivert convinced President Bradford Knapp and Dean Clarence H. McElroy that it would be cost effective and would stabilize student publications. It began operating in January 1930 and was used for more than thirty years.

University, met her the morning of September 12 as her steamship docked at Plymouth, England. This, too, would require a shift in teaching assignments.[40]

Trout had other concerns as well. It seemed that he had to prove himself over and over again in the new president's office. While Knapp had seen him as the right man in the right place, Bennett seemed to see only the quiet, seemingly timid "doodler" who kept his pencil moving in a small black notebook as he listened—whether in a personal conference or a major meeting surrounded by a large crowd. Bennett himself was outgoing and energetic, with a strong personality. Trout, though his accomplishments brought all of those traits quietly into play, projected a far different image.[41] Trout continued to have problems coordinating his work with extension. He had found it difficult to advance the college's publicity efforts and yet have the Extension Service zealously guard its own public information program. Now, adding to Trout's confusion, President Bennett had announced a new Bureau of Information and Service. He had decided to make the name of Oklahoma A. and M. "a household word." He was quoted as having said it was self-evident that the college's story had not been thoroughly told. Randle Perdue, editor of the *Stillwater Daily Press* and earlier assistant editor of college publications under Hadley, would be in charge effective February 1, 1930. It is not clear, based upon existing documents, whether Trout was consulted before the announcement was made. However, a carefully prepared typewritten proposal preceded Bennett's announcement. At the top of page one was written, in pencil, Perdue's name. No other name appeared. An impressive article by Perdue, "That Man Bennett," extolling the new president's accomplishments, had not missed the presidential eye. Perdue's skills had impressed Bennett.

As a student, Perdue had been an outfielder on the Tiger baseball team, a student manager for the football team, sports editor and editor of the *Orange and Black,* and a correspondent for Tulsa, Oklahoma City and other newspapers, and for the Associated Press. After joining the *Muskogee Phoenix* in 1914, he had served a year as secretary to acting President L. L. Lewis and six years as President James W. Cantwell's personal secretary. He had next applied his energies as editor of the first alumni publication, the *Boomer,* in 1921, and as secretary of the Stillwater Chamber of Commerce. Beginning in 1922 he divided his time between work on the *Stillwater Advance-Democrat* and Oklahoma A. and M. publicity followed by editorships at the *Stillwater Gazette* and the *Press.*

The most extensive public description of the new bureau was carried in the *A. and M. College Magazine.* Perdue's work would supplement Trout's. There was no direct connection between the bureau and the Department of Publications, the magazine article emphasized, but the work of the two offices would be "correlated." For the immediate future, Perdue would concentrate on the $500,000 memorial stadium and fieldhouse campaign. He also would serve as executive secretary of the statewide organization sponsoring the drive. Paul Miller returned to the campus to handle other aspects of the bureau's work with the title of assistant director. By 1932 he had replaced Perdue as director. This was a time in which big dreams ranged far beyond fiscal realities and Perdue was only one of many caught in the retrenchment that was at hand. The bureau soon faltered. Within a matter of months, Governor William H. Murray had insisted that the college's payroll be reduced. He left it up to Bennett to decide where the cuts would come. The bureau was scrapped and responsibility for its services reverted to Trout. That responsibility, taking into account the agreement with extension, would remain in his hands until 1954. Perdue, whose off and on connections with the college had spanned twenty-one years, launched an insurance career and never again held a campus appointment.[42]

On the academic side, Peterson had decided not to return for the 1929-30 school year. He had resumed newspaper work as managing editor and part owner of the *Wewoka Daily Times-Democrat* and as co-owner of the *Sulphur Times-Democrat* and the *Capitol Hill Beacon* in south Oklahoma City. Years later, in 1957, he and his two sons would purchase the *Durant Daily News*, the *Durant Weekly News* and radio station KSEO. Today these properties are part of the Donrey Media Group. In 1945, two years after he had served as president of the Oklahoma Press Association, Peterson joined the OU faculty. During his years in Norman, he began an association with the *Norman Transcript* as associate publisher under Fred Tarman that lasted until 1955. He retired at OU in 1974. Among several honors received in retirement, Peterson was elected to the Oklahoma Journalism Hall of Fame in 1981.[43]

The Trout-Caldwell team soon would be strengthened by Peterson's replacement. In the meantime, another faculty member was borrowed from the English faculty. He was Blaine DeLancey, an assistant professor who had come to Oklahoma A. and M. shortly after Trout. When Trout was finding it difficult to cover the expanded program he had put into motion he called upon DeLancey, who held the A.B. degree from Marietta College, Marietta, Ohio, and the master of arts from Ohio State University. DeLancey taught the Special Articles course.[44]

In his annual report to President Bennett on October 31, 1929, Trout listed both accomplishments and shortcomings in the Department of Publications, which served as an umbrella for teaching personnel in journalism in addition to their affiliation with the Department of English and Journalism. He pointed out that the workload in recent years had permitted only the elective courses in news and feature writing and the required courses in agricultural and home economics journalism to be offered. But now that degree programs in the latter had been approved, more teaching help would be needed to cover the eleven courses. His entire staff at the time consisted of himself, one other faculty member, two half-time student assistants and several students on an hourly basis "equivalent to about one-fourth time for one student." Bivert's time was fully occupied in supervising the finances of student publications, a semi-autonomous position.

Trout stated that the demand by students for more recognition of journalism had led to a certificate in technical journalism awarded for twenty-four hours in the subject. The program was open to students in any school of the college. In the School of Science and Literature, it would take the place of the requirement that two minors be completed. During the first semester of the 1928-29 academic year, Trout and Peterson had done all of the teaching. In the second semester, Caldwell had provided a big lift by teaching nine credits. One additional full-time staff member would be required by September 1930, and more equipment—including tables and typewriters for students—would be needed as well as a reading room and laboratory. Other needs included a budget for supplies and newspaper and periodical subscriptions and a larger press room for student publications. Trout asked that the college help finance the press-room expansion.

Trout made fifteen recommendations for the 1929-30 fiscal year. Most of these related to non-academic matters. The most important recommendation called for the addition of an extension editor to be paid from the Extension Service budget but assigned to Trout's publications staff. Other personnel needed, Trout said, were a full-time copy editor-proofreader to be shared by the experiment station and extension,

A newspaperman who had served the campus in many capacities, including editing the first alumni publication and serving as assistant editor for college publications, Randle Perdue became director of a new Bureau of Information and Service in 1930. While his work was to supplement that of Clement Trout's, the venture only added to Trout's confusion as to his role in the Henry G. Bennett administration.

a college photographer (to be supported by the various departments using the service), and full-time stenographic help in his office to reduce but not eliminate the student employees. Trout also recommended that he be given "standing" in both the experiment station and the Extension Service. Other recommendations were that information services in a number of categories be increased and that additional space and office equipment be made available. "At some time in the future," Trout wrote, "it may be desirable to consolidate the mail rooms of the College, Experiment Station and Extension Service under the Publications Department. The same is true of mimeographing, now scattered." They were slow in coming, but many of Trout's suggestions and recommendations eventually became reality.[45]

As the 1930-31 academic year began, journalism was once more in Old Central. The historic building had stood empty for two years and had been restored and redecorated at a cost of about $40,000. Hundreds of students brought their laughter and banter back to its halls daily. Geology was on the first floor. The second floor housed journalism in two offices and a classroom, plus classrooms for the English and agricultural education departments. The new Bureau of Information and Service adjoined the journalism offices. The third floor was occupied by the Former Students Association, agricultural education, and the Graduate School.[46]

Peterson's replacement was one of the most talented of Trout's staff as the 1920s were ending. Carl A. Rott brought to Oklahoma A. and M. a solid background in both agriculture and journalism. It is likely he was recommended to Trout by Professor Hopkins. Rott was born November 15, 1902, in Sauk County, Wisconsin, and was graduated by the University of Wisconsin in a non-degree program in agriculture in 1924. He earned the B.S. degree in agricultural journalism in 1926, and added the M.S. in 1928, majoring in journalism and economics. Following graduation he had worked as a reporter for the *Milwaukee Journal* and the *Milwaukee Times*. He was editor of the *Shawano County (Wisconsin) Advocate* for three years and was an assistant editor on the *Wisconsin Agriculture and Farmer* staff.[47]

As was true of most of the earlier journalism teachers who had come and gone during the development of the curriculum, Rott had been a student leader. He was on the editorial staff of *Country Magazine*, served on a publicity committee for the 1926 prom, was general chairman of the Little International Livestock Show during his senior year, and was on important committees planning the show in his sophomore and junior years. He was a member of Delta Theta Sigma and FarmHouse fraternities, was secretary-treasurer of the Saddle and Sirloin Club, and was elected to Alpha Zeta, national honorary agricultural fraternity. Rott's agricultural journalism professor, the same Hopkins who had taught Trout and was greatly admired by him, was a faculty member of all of these organizations.[48]

Rott was in his late twenties when he came to Stillwater in his dazzling big sports car. That car led to difficulties on one occasion. He was stopped by officers who thought he was Pretty Boy Floyd, a notorious Oklahoma criminal of the 1930s.[49]

The Depression had a decided effect upon Rott's future. It cut his teaching career at Oklahoma A. and M. short. He had joined the faculty in 1929 and had taught most of the news-editorial courses for four semesters. In June of 1931 there was a 37 percent cut in teachers' pay at Oklahoma A. and M., and twenty-eight faculty members, including Rott, were released. He was not only professionally competent but personable as well and would have been a valuable asset to the journalism program on a long-term basis had conditions been different.[50]

After losing out at Oklahoma A. and M., Rott moved to Enid, where he had a brief tenure in radio at KCRC. He had assisted in radio work at Oklahoma A. and M. and the growing importance of broadcasting fascinated him. His experience in the new medium would be a plus in his later political career, assessed in these words: "Probably no other young Republican who was not a native Kansan ever exerted as much influence in Kansas politics as did Carl Rott. . . . "

Arriving in Topeka from Enid in January 1932, Rott soon became acquainted with Alf M. Landon, then serving his first term as governor. His experience in journalism, radio, and economics soon made him

Key faculty members in Clement E. Trout's first decade were (*left to right*) Robert V. Peterson, Carl A. Rott, and George F. Church. All were seasoned journalists with strong credentials.

invaluable to the man who was later to be the Republican nominee for president. He became an important member of Landon's campaign team. After Landon's landslide loss to Franklin D. Roosevelt despite his strong showing in the *Literary Digest* poll, Rott continued with Landon as his private secretary. Later, when Senator Payne Ratner announced his candidacy for governor, Rott was among the first chosen for his headquarters staff. Rott's growing influence in Kansas politics resulted in his appointment as secretary of the State Highway Commission following the election. Governor Ratner held him in high regard throughout his service to the state.[51]

Upon leaving Kansas politics in August 1940, Rott moved to Nebraska as managing editor of the *Hastings Tribune*. After three years there, he returned to Kansas as editor and general manager of the *Winfield Courier*. At the time of his death on January 6, 1969, he was editor and publisher of the *Sheridan (Wyoming) Press*, where he had gone in 1946 after three years on the *Courier*. He was president of the Wyoming Press Association in 1952 and had served on the Wyoming Highway Commission.

In his twenty-three years on the *Press*, he set high reportorial standards with an emphasis upon local news. He wanted to be first with the news, but not at the expense of accuracy. He was courageous as well. Shortly after his term on the highway commission had expired, he vigorously fought the Wyoming Highway Department's plan for the location of Interstate 90. I-90 went where the highway department wanted it to go, but Sheridan County's votes defeated Governor Milward Simpson in his bid for reelection. Rott lost the highway battle but "made a lot of friends in the county" in the process. Wyoming was a fitting place for Rott to close out his career. He was an outdoorsman, loved fishing, and knew where to catch them.[52]

Rott's departure in 1931 was bad news for Trout, but there was good news to balance it. Trout could see the first fruits of his initiative in curricular affairs. The first journalism degrees in Oklahoma A. and M. history were awarded that spring to Ben O. Osborn in agricultural journalism and to Bess Allen and Ellen E. Ryan in home economics journalism. A year later he had the satisfaction of watching as the first commerce journalism degree was conferred upon Freman O. Pickle. No official lists of other journalism graduates in these early years were published. The School of Science and Literature and its successors chose not to list graduates by majors until 1964. Despite this, it seems clear from unofficial records in the School of Journalism and Broadcasting that the majority of journalism graduates through the years came from what today is the College of Arts and Sciences. One indicator was the fact that during Trout's first decade, the official lists ran about two to one in favor of commerce journalism degrees over the specialized programs in agricultural and home economics journalism combined.[53]

In a four-page annual report dated October 31, 1931, Trout had submitted to President Bennett a summary of progress both in publications and in journalism. The assumption from the Hadley days forward had been that journalism classes would be taught by publications staff members under the academic aegis of the Department of English and Journalism, and Trout's reports combined the two activities. At this point, his department had added the editing of Engineering Experiment Station publications to its list of responsibilities. In the report's academic section, Trout reported that during the previous year 1,973 students had been enrolled in the degree and certificate courses. Sixty-five of these were in agricultural journalism and six in home economics journalism. During the year, five students received M.S. degrees with minors in journalism. (Major work at the graduate level would not be available for fifteen years.) As noted, one B.S. degree was awarded in agricultural journalism and two in home economics journalism. Two certificates in technical journalism were awarded. It was the first year the senior-level degree and certificate courses in journalism had been offered. Trout noted the increased teaching load Rott's departure had placed upon him and George F. Church. He recommended that Rott's position be filled as soon as possible. Additional recommendations echoed those of the previous year—more space, more equipment, more staff (including a full-time stenographer), more upgrading for both the teaching and publications programs. It must have seemed to Trout that his reports were filed without serious consideration. Such was the nature of the Depression years.[54]

With the losses of Peterson and Rott, Trout went into the market for a man—women on journalism faculties were a rarity—with comparable experience and similar personal characteristics. Each replacement Trout made was made with great care. He patiently reviewed the record of a potential faculty member, usually on the basis of careful discussions with his Oklahoma A. and M. faculty colleagues, but the decision was his. The idea that faculty personnel committees would have a major voice in such matters was totally foreign to the administrative concepts of the day. More than one departmental administrator during the centennial decade wished for the days when such simple administrative procedures prevailed. Trout's search was a resounding success. He found his answer in George Church, a competent writer who would prove to be an excellent teacher.

Church's background was not exceptional, but it was substantial enough to assure Trout that he could adequately fill the current vacancy. He had started his higher education at the Wisconsin State Normal School in Oshkosh, transferring in September 1923 to the University of Kansas to study journalism. He entered with advanced standing as a junior and on his application listed only his mother, Jane N. Church, Rio, Wisconsin, on the blank for parent or guardian. He was quiet, unassuming, friendly, and easy to know. That he met his responsibilities promptly and efficiently soon became apparent. During his second semester at the University of Kansas, he was listed on the *Sunday Kansan* staff. The next semester, he was alumni editor on the *University Daily Kansan*. In his

Members of the 1931 board of publications were (*left to right*) E. E. Johnson, Frank Crews, Earl McCafferty, Ewel Stone, Raymond Bivert, Clement Trout (chairman), James H. Arrington, Joe Griffin, Elmer Woodson, and Leroy McGuirk. Bivert, Trout, and Woodson had long tenures in Oklahoma A. and M. journalism.

final undergraduate semester, 1924-25, he had moved up to editor-in-chief of the daily paper.[55]

Following his undergraduate studies, he had decided upon graduate work. He was awarded the master's degree and had completed all of the class work for a doctor of philosophy degree. He was not only a scholar but a skilled writer as well, so it is difficult to understand why the dissertation was never written. As a graduate student, Church was listed on the Kansas teaching staff for the academic years 1926-27 and 1927-28. He apparently stayed on with faculty duties for a year following the M.A., received in 1928. The second semester of that year the class schedule listed him as teacher of a required two-hour course, History of American Journalism. In addition, it appears likely that during that year, and probably during his graduate studies as well, he was *Daily Kansan* lab supervisor and advisor, riding herd on *Kansan* staff members and cub reporters.

The *1925 Jayhawker*, the University of Kansas yearbook, reveals Church to have been highly focused. He did not scatter his energies. In the senior section he was listed as a journalism major who had been active in Sigma Delta Chi, the sixteen-year-old national journalism fraternity for men, and one of thirty-three members of the *Daily Kansan* board. The yearbook stated: "Members of the Kansan Board, with the assistance of students enrolled in the department of journalism and faculty counsel, conduct this news enterprise. Students are elected upon the merits of their journalistic work and professional spirit. An editorial staff is elected monthly by the board." The *Kansan* of that day was a seven-column newspaper with five daily issues and a Sunday edition. It leased "regular United Press Service."[56]

Church's senior portrait pictures a ruggedly handsome young man with a full head of wavy hair parted on the right side, slightly protruding ears, a mouth fixed in a slight smile, expressive eyes, and a Cary Grant chin. In the vernacular of the day, he was well groomed. While he was developing his journalistic skills on Mount Oread, Church had met an energetic journalism student who was to become his wife. She was Alice Van Meesel, a member of the campus newspaper staff. They were married in September 1929. Her father, in charge of caring for campus laboratory animals, was widely and affectionately known as "Van the Animal Man." One day, trudging across campus, probably with a sack of feed across his shoulder, he came face-to-face with Chancellor Lindley. In response to Lindley's "How are you, Van?" Van Messel had replied: "I'm fine, but I had never expected to see the day when the head and tail of the university would meet!" His daughter had the same frank openness in her day-to-day contacts.[57]

Trout had good reports on George Church. He had gained reporting and editing experience on the *Reporter* at Fon du Lac, Wisconsin, and was completing a year as city editor of the *Winfield Courier*. Trout invited him to Stillwater to look the campus over. He took him to visit with Professor DeMoss, then to President Bennett's office. The meeting with Bennett went well. They discovered they had mutual friends. The upshot of this was that he was offered more money than had earlier been suggested by Trout. Shortly after, he accepted the offer and the Churches prepared for the ninety-two-mile move south from Winfield.[58]

In September 1930, Church moved into Old Central, where Trout also was officed. Almost from his first day on the campus, Church's duties were split into at least three segments. During his early years, he divided his time among sports publicity, teaching, and experiment station bulletin editing. For a man who most wanted to teach—and preferred to concentrate on a single goal—this may have been disquieting. Like Trout, Church was a workaholic. After a full day on the campus he would work evening hours at home on unfinished college tasks. This was a year-around pattern, and included more than paper grading.[59]

As a teacher, the energetic Church had "spark." One alumnus recalled him as "a small, thin, pleasant person" who had a proclivity for puffing on a pipe. He had an identifying chuckle along with his soft-toned but snappy conversation. Church was respected as a professional, practical newspaperman by those who knew him.[60] Among the courses he taught were History of Journalism, Ethics of Journalism, Advanced Special Articles, Technical News Writing, Editing and Copyreading, Agricultural Journalism, and Methods and Problems. Church prepared thoroughly for his classes, most of which were taught on the second floor of Whitehurst Hall. Faculty and students both rated him as an excellent teacher. He was a careful reader of student output. John Oliver, editor of the *Daily O'Collegian* in 1933-34, told this story: "I remember sitting in the back row of [a class in History and Ethics of Journalism] with Scoop Thompson and Harry Long. On one examination, I remember we gave each other a bit of help. My paper came back from Church with cross references to identical errors which had appeared in Thompson's and Long's papers. . . . I'm not sure how much of the ethics he taught sunk in."[61] Enrollments often were small, running from ten to thirty in the pre-World War II years. In one of the last courses Church taught following the war, he looked into the faces of 181 students in one section of Agricultural Journalism.[62]

During the Depression years especially, Trout relied upon student help to keep the work of the publications department moving. A good example was Dorothy McCue, a part-time secretary whose record probably was unsurpassed for a combination of student activities, scholarship, and work. She worked for Trout four years, held two major presidencies, was a member of the Manuscript Club and Chi Delta Phi, another writers' group, and on two important student boards. She completed her work with a minor in journalism in 1932.[63]

Trout and Church were expanding their influence. They participated in Oklahoma Press Association meetings, and their desire to help high school teachers and to attract students led them to active participation in the journalism section of the Oklahoma Education Association. Church delivered a lecture—"Visualizing News for the School Paper"—at the 1933 Oklahoma Education Association meeting in Tulsa. As was consistently true of Church, he had prepared well and his talk was both stimulating and perceptive. The following year, in Oklahoma City, Trout spoke on "Desirable School Publicity." Another speaker was H. H. Herbert of the University of Oklahoma School of Journalism. Herbert discussed the proper limits of journalism courses in high schools and small colleges.[64]

After years of confusion over the division of responsibilities for extension information, a working agreement between Trout's department and the Extension Service was developed. It outlined the responsibilities each would have as well as those areas in which responsibility would be shared. No doubt the first extension editor, Duncan Wall, had a major role in preparing the document. It was titled "Memorandum of Agreement on Handling Publicity Between the Publications Department and the Extension Editor" and probably was worked out after a series of discussions between Trout and Wall. Trout's department would be responsible for the clip sheet, the mimeographed service to daily newspapers, the sports service, "special services" and other services as requested by college officials and the experiment station. Extension, using the federal franking privilege for its mailings, would provide a regular service to weekly newspapers, a news service to county agents, stories for daily newspapers concerning extension activities, and radio programs.

As to subject matter, Trout's staff would cover all college and experiment station material, while Wall would be responsible for all extension activities and "such experiment station subject matter as may be necessary to supplement the Extension Division subject matter material." All experiment station material, was to be "cross-checked with the Publications Department." When desirable, by agreement, duties on particular projects could be transferred from one department to the other.

Radio was largely the responsibility of the Extension Service, although subject matter talks by faculty and experiment station personnel which were used as the basis of news stories were to be divided between Trout's and Wall's departments on the basis of the agreement, which left ample opportunity for disputes and rumpled feelings. Wall's department would have the responsibility for deciding when faculty and experiment station personnel were needed for a broadcast.

In all cases, print or broadcast, the two departments were to cooperate "to the best advantage of the College and the Extension Division." This suggests that the agreement may have been written by Wall. Whether it ever was ratified by both parties is unknown, although it must have been of some value in reducing ambiguity if not territorial rights. There is no evidence as to Bennett's views on the matter. The document was somewhat vague, even inconsistent in some places, but it may have helped reduce friction and the embarrassment caused earlier by duplication of services to state news media.[65]

In 1936, President Bennett and Dean Schiller Scroggs had suggested that Oklahoma A. and M. student publications should have someone to "advise and supervise" their editorial work. Trout delayed his response to the suggestion for at least two reasons: the administration had suggested that student publications should finance the plan, which would be impossible under current conditions, and Trout was uneasy about the possibility that student journalists would see such a move as infringing upon their editorial prerogatives. The original idea called for the person hired to be responsible solely to the Board of Publications. As the months passed, Trout knew he must submit a more realistic plan to the administration. The editorial freedom of the *O'Collegian* was his primary concern. He reevaluated the proposition in a letter addressed jointly to Bennett and Scroggs, offering suggestions as to funding for the position and indicating his willingness to search for a qualified person to fill the slot.[66]

The man who was to become the first professional advisor to the *O'Collegian* was Leon H. Durst. A Texas newspaperman, Durst had spent sixteen years with the Associated Press with assignments from Oklahoma City to Sioux Falls, South Dakota, and then to Kansas City. He left on friendly terms after one year, but a precedent that would be followed in later years had been established.[67]

As the first decade of Trout's unprecedented administrative tenure in Oklahoma A. and M. journalism neared its end, he and Dean Scroggs had had several conversations about "the work of the Publications Department, including Journalism teaching." In a letter of approximately 1,290 words, Trout had pointed out that he and Church were able to spend less than half of their time on teaching. This was too little, he said, because of the number of students enrolled and the "large number of papers to be graded regularly." Both publications and academic duties suffered because of inadequate help. He told Scroggs of the success of "our plan for specialized journalism," citing demands for graduates that could not be filled "for lack of trained men and women."

Whether Scroggs or Trout had initiated the latest idea for an independent Department of Journalism can not be determined from available evidence. Certainly the conversations Trout had had with Scroggs must have encouraged the possibility. Trout, always conservative in his

One of the *O'Collegian's* strongest staffs was available during the 1930-31 school year. At the copy desk are Clara Neal, Aubrey McAlister, and Lyle Dunigan. Others are (*from left*) Leroy McGuirk, Elmer Woodson, Chrystal Seitz, Harry Long, Ralph Runnels, George Crain, Sam Hoover, Roberta Whitworth, Virginia Doniphin, Paul Williams, Manly Humphrey, Lawrence Thompson, and E. E. Johnson.

approach, had written: "While I do not think we will develop a large department, if we can graduate each year 10 to 15 superior students divided between the various specialties, we can fill a definite need in the Southwest." He estimated that only one new course—in newspaper business management—would need to be added in the School of Arts and Sciences. More advertising also would be needed, he pointed out, and this work "should be strengthened in cooperation with the School of Commerce, which at present teaches the advertising." Trout felt that only one additional faculty member would be needed. During most of the decade he had been working under the burden of the Great Depression, the worst of budget times, and he had learned to cut corners in every possible way. This included using the clean side of once-used paper that in normal times would have been considered trash and, when possible, sending news releases on penny post cards. Conservation had become a way of life, reflected through the years even in monetary rewards for Trout and his staff.

A matter that would become crucial later was alluded to as well. It was a need for closer contact with house organ editors in Oklahoma. Already Trout was thinking about an annual conference for this group of "highly intelligent and educated workers." Trout's view was that Oklahoma A. and M. could develop an exclusive contact with prospective employers having "highly important influences." This, eventually, would lead to a new curriculum in industrial editing.

In a postscript, he cited the need to meet a recent state requirement that those planning to teach English must have a course in journalism.

Such students were taking the beginning news writing course, which Trout felt had weakened it. He proposed that a three-hour course in general newspaper study be added for these and other students who might be interested. "It should be taught by the entire staff," he said, "each member taking his particular field." Such a team-teaching approach was relatively new at that time. In view of the range of topics covered in the letter, Trout's estimate that only one new faculty member would be needed seemed far short of realistic.[68]

After Mable Caldwell's return from Edinburgh and her commitment to full-time English teaching, Trout had employed women primarily for non-teaching duties. Ruth E. Dunham, for example, had been an editorial assistant writing for the news and information services in Trout's domain. When Dunham had decided to move on, Trout almost immediately thought of Helen Freudenberger. She had been a star reporter and campus editor for the *Daily O'Collegian* in 1935 and 1936, and had spent four months editing the *Maud Daily Enterprise*. Trout had phoned her on September 17, 1936, to discuss the Dunham position and had followed up that day by sending an information blank, which served as a job application document. She returned it the following day with a covering letter expressing concern about leaving Fred T. Smith, her publisher, after such a short time.[69] In a telegram September 21, Trout offered her the job at $80 a month through June 30. In a follow-up letter that day he pointed out that he expected the job to continue beyond the end of the fiscal year, "but the College does not make contracts beyond July 1." He added: "Arrange things to make them agreeable there."[70]

Freudenberger had arranged to break in her replacement, and Smith had agreed that her last day at the *Enterprise* would be October 5. Trout responded that he had not expected her to come in less than two weeks. He urged her to "do whatever is necessary to treat Mr. Smith right." As was consistently true of his behavior in such a situation, he wrote Freudenberger: "If it would be advisable to stay there a little longer, do so. However, let me know if you change your plans. Otherwise we will look for you the fifth. . . ." Things worked out. Freudenberger joined the staff as an editorial assistant or, as she stated, a publicist.[71]

Freudenberger was only one of many students who had had a part in the journalism of Trout's first decade. Among the others were Bess Allen, Ellen E. Ryan, Ben O. Osborn, Louis Blackburn, Orlando Blackburn, Robert E. Cunningham, Lyle C. Dungan, Hazel Watkins, Dorothy Callahan-Patterson, Freman O. Pickle, Dean B. Yount, Welden Barnes, Paul Miller, Sylvester F. Hughes, Max E. Stansbury, James C. Rumfelt, Elmer Woodson, Fred Barlow, Ray B. Baggett, Billie Mary Behrendt, Foreman Carlile, Velma B. Clark, N. S. DeMotte, Curtis Ellis, Samuel C. VanCuron, F. E. "Wally" Wallis, David O. Crist, Ina Bell Ryserson, Chad C. Durham, William H. Feather, Ivy Milton Howard, Virginia Pope,

Margaret E. Heiser, Earl Richert, David P. Johnson, Willis A. Lansden, Henry J. Osborn, Phil G. Perdue, Richard Venator, and Milo R. Klopfenstein.

Trout's greatest strength during his early years at Oklahoma A. and M. was his organizational ability. He had intense concentration and, while his demeanor could be described as lackluster when compared with his predecessor, he was an original and creative thinker. He began to develop close contacts with the deans of the various schools on campus, knowing that his philosophy of journalism education called for an appropriate combination of courses in other fields, mostly technical, to which he would add the basic journalism concepts. His students would bridge the gap between these technical fields and the public. Many of these "bridge builders" with words on paper would cast long shadows in the journals of their day—some locally, some regionally, a few nationally, and at least one internationally. Trout and his teaching staff could look upon the results of their early efforts with satisfaction.

Endnotes

1. *Annual Catalog, Oklahoma A. and M. College, 1925-1926*, pp. xiii, xiv, xv, 182, 183.

2. Noble Warren Rockey, undated and untitled handwritten historical review, 1911-1921, family papers of Esther Rockey Jones, School of Journalism and Broadcasting Centennial History Collection, Special Collections, Edmon Low Library, Oklahoma State University, Stillwater, Oklahoma; *Annual Catalog, Oklahoma A. and M. College, 1920-1921*, pp. 124, 125.

3. *Annual Catalog, Oklahoma A. and M. College, 1923-1924*, pp. 191, 194, 195.

4. *Annual Catalog, Oklahoma A. and M. College, 1924-1925*, pp. v, vi, viii, ix, x; Miscellaneous letters to the Harry E. Heath Jr. from alumni who had studied under the professors listed, School of Journalism and Broadcasting Centennial History Collection.

5. Irvin Hurst to Harry E. Heath Jr., 26 March 1991, School of Journalism and Broadcasting Centennial History Collection.

6. Oklahoma A. and M. College *Daily O'Collegian*, 8 October 1926, p. 1; *Stillwater Gazette*, 15 October 1926, p. 9; Irvin Hurst to Harry E. Heath Jr., 26 March 1991, and John W. Hamilton to Harry E. Heath Jr., 29 May 1981, in School of Journalism and Broadcasting Centennial History Collection; *Annual Catalog, Oklahoma A. and M. College, 1926-1927*, pp. v, xvi, 191, 192; Author interview with John Hamilton, 8 June 1984, Stillwater, Oklahoma.

7. Biographical data sheets of Clement E. Trout, Files of the School of Journalism and Broadcasting, Oklahoma State University.

8. David W. Bakker, "Clement E. Trout: Portrait of Pioneer," term paper completed for Journalism 311: History of Journalism at the University of Oklahoma in May 1969, Library of the School of Journalism, University of Oklahoma, Norman, Oklahoma; Author interview with Ann Trout Blinks, 21 and 22 May 1984, Stillwater, Oklahoma; *Stillwater NewsPress*, 23 March 1971, p. 3; *Daily O'Collegian*, 27 June 1958.

9. Clement E. Trout, "Biographical Record" (12 February 1937), John W. Hamilton, "Biographical Statement on Clement E. Trout (29 May 1981), and Biographical data sheets of Clement E. Trout, in Files of the School of Journalism and Broadcasting; *Who's Who in America, 1956-1957* (Chicago, IL: Marquis Who's Who, Incorporated, 1956), vol. 29, p. 2605; *Who's Who in America, 1958-1959* (Chicago, IL: Marquis Who's Who, Incorporated, 1958), vol. 30, p. 2799.

10. Biographical data sheets of Clement E. Trout, Files of the School of Journalism and Broadcasting.

11. Biographical data sheets of Clement E. Trout, Files of the School of Journalism and Broadcasting.

12. *Annual Catalog, Oklahoma A. and M. College, 1926-1927*, pp. v, vi, xvii, xviii; Floy Farrar Wilbanks, "The Life and Work of Dr. Bradford Knapp" (Master of Arts thesis, Texas Technological College, 1940).

13. Wilbanks, p. 7.

14. Wilbanks, pp. 7-15, 18, 19, 28, 30, 31, 34, 35, 47; Philip Reed Rulon, *Oklahoma State University—Since 1890* (Stillwater: Oklahoma State University Press, 1975), p. 184.

15. *Daily O'Collegian*, 2 November 1926, p. 1.

16. Biographical data sheets of Clement E. Trout, Files of the School of Journalism and Broadcasting; Blinks interview; Author interview with Muriel Groom, 22 June 1984, Stillwater, Oklahoma. The information in this citation has been verified with numerous other sources.

17. *Oklahoma A. and M. College Directory of Students and Faculty, 1933-34*, p. 5; *Oklahoma A. and M. College Directory of Students and Faculty, 1934-35*, p. 1.

18. Irvin Hurst to Harry Heath, 26 March 1991, School of Journalism and Broadcasting Centennial History Collection.

19. Author interview with John W. Hamilton, 21 January 1988, Stillwater, Oklahoma; Dover P. Trent to Clement Trout, 14 November 1927, Clement E. Trout Collection, Special Collections, Edmon Low Library.

20. *Annual Catalog, Oklahoma A. and M. College, 1908-1909*, pp. 71, 72; *Annual Catalog, Oklahoma A. and M. College, 1909-1910*, pp. 38, 39; *Annual Catalog, Oklahoma A. and M. College, 1912-1913*, p. 98; *Annual Catalog, Oklahoma A. and M. College, 1913-1914*, p. 103; *Annual Catalog, Oklahoma A. and M. College, 1914-1915*, pp. 84, 85; *Annual Catalog, Oklahoma A. and M. College, 1915-1916*, pp. 96, 97.

21. *Annual Catalog, Oklahoma A. and M. College, 1921-1922*, pp. 177, 202, 203; *Annual Catalog, Oklahoma A. and M. College, 1923-1924*, pp. 191, 194, 195.

22. *Annual Catalog, Oklahoma A. and M. College, 1925-1926*, pp. 182, 183; *Annual Catalog, Oklahoma A. and M. College, 1926-1927*, pp. 191, 192.

23. *Stillwater NewsPress NewsPlus*, 6 March 1985, p. 1B; *Oklahoma A. and M. College Boomer* (April-May 1926), p. 3; Minutes, Oklahoma A. and M. College Faculty, 7 September 1926, Special Collections, Edmon Low Library; William R. Lindley, *Journalism and Higher Education: The Search for Academic Purpose* (Stillwater, OK: Journalistic Services, 1975), pp. 3, 4.

24. Raymond E. Bivert, "Another Enterprise Goes Over," *Oklahoma A. and M. College Magazine*, vol. 1, no. 2 (October 1929), p. 20.

25. Class Roll, Journalism 213, First Semester 1927-28. Early class rolls are stored in the basement of the OSU Student Health Center.

26. *Daily O'Collegian*, 9 February 1927, p. 1; Rulon, p. 193; Oklahoma City *Daily Oklahoman*, 20 February 1927; 1941 Oklahoma A. and M. College news release in connection with the 50th anniversary of Old Central, School of Journalism and Broadcasting Centennial History Collection.

27. *Annual Catalog, Oklahoma A. and M. College, 1927-1928*, pp. 59, 60, 76, 162, 163, 204, 209-211, 295; *Annual Catalog, Oklahoma A. and M. College, 1929-1930*, pp. 292-294.

28. Clement E. Trout to Walter Wilcox, 14 September 1956, Files of the School of Journalism and Broadcasting; Author interview with Marlan D. Nelson, 10 December 1991, Stillwater, Oklahoma.

29. Bivert, p. 20.

30. Mable Caldwell, editor, *Stillwater Woman's Club Cook Book* (September 1926), Sheerar Center, Stillwater, Oklahoma. Mable Caldwell also helped organize the Stillwater Writers' Club and participated actively in campus organizations.

31. *JB News* (1983-86), p. 19; "1929-30 Annual Report, Department of Publications," p. 10, School of Journalism and Broadcasting Centennial History Collection.

32. Clement Trout, undated report [1929], Clement E. Trout Collection.

33. Wilbanks, pp. 61, 62; Rulon, pp. 196-198.

34. Bradford Knapp to Oklahoma State Board of Agriculture, 4 April 1928 and 28 May 1928, President's Papers, Special Collections, Edmon Low Library.

35. Wilbanks, p. 62; Rulon p. 197 and eighth page in photo section inserted between pp. 140 and 141.

36. Rulon, pp. 197, 224; Hamilton interview, 8 June 1984; Blinks interview; Philip Reed Rulon to Harry E. Heath Jr., 21 August 1984, School of Journalism and Broadcasting Centennial History Collection.

37. Rulon, p. 224.

38. Berlin B. Chapman to Harry E. Heath Jr., 11 April 1987, School of Journalism and Broadcasting Centennial History Collection. Descriptive material in this citation is based upon numerous conversations with individuals who worked for Trout, among them Dorothy Rickstrew Nixon, Sam Whitlow, John W. Hamilton, and James C. Stratton.

39. Ralph Lashbrook to Clement E. Trout, 4 May 1929, C. E. Rogers to Clement E. Trout, 5 May 1929, Clement E. Trout to Ralph Lashbrook, 5 May 1929, Clement E. Trout to Ralph Lashbrook, 4 November 1929, Clement E. Trout to Henry G. Bennett, 7 December 1929, Clement E. Trout to Ralph Lashbrook, 10 December 1929; Clement E. Trout to Ralph Lashbrook, 21 December 1929, and Clement E. Trout to Ralph Lashbrook, 8 January 1930, in Files of the School of Journalism and Broadcasting.

40. "On the Campus," *Oklahoma A. and M. College Magazine*, vol. 1, no. 2 (October 1929), p. 16.

41. Hamilton interview, 8 June 1984.

42. Undated and unsigned plan for expanded information service, Clement E. Trout Collection; Randle Perdue, "That Man Bennett," *Oklahoma A. and M. College Magazine*, vol. 1, no. 1 (September 1929), pp. 8, 29; Hamilton interview, 21 January 1988; Author interview with Welden Barnes, 19 April 1992, Stillwater, Oklahoma.

43. *JB News* (1983-86), p. 19.

44. *Annual Catalog, Oklahoma A. and M. College, 1929-1930*, p. xii; Schedule of Classes, Oklahoma A. and M. College, 1929-30, p. 8, Special Collections, Edmon Low Library.

45. Clement E. Trout, "Annual Report, Department of Publications" (31 October 1929), pp. 6-14, Clement E. Trout Collection.

46. Helen E. Johnson, "Old Central Has New Lease on Life," *Oklahoma A. and M. College Magazine*, vol. 1, no. 1 (September 1929), p. 9; Genevieve Braley, "Classes Resume in Old Central," *Oklahoma A. and M. College Magazine*, vol. 1, no. 8 (April 1930), p. 5; "On the Campus," *Oklahoma A. and M. College Magazine*, vol. 2, no. 2 (October 1930), p. 46.

47. *Tulsa Tribune*, 7 January 1969; *Stillwater NewsPress*, 7 January 1969, p. 1; Personnel data on Carl Rott, Files of the School of Journalism and Broadcasting.

48. *1927 Wolverine*, pp. 147, 462, 497, 559, University of Wisconsin Yearbook; *1928 Wolverine*, p. 415; *1929 Wolverine*, pp. 393, 503; Bernard Schermetzler to Harry E. Heath Jr., 22 February 1988, School of Journalism and Broadcasting Centennial History Collection.

49. Author interview with Alice Church, 21 October 1987, Stillwater, Oklahoma.

50. *Stillwater Daily Press*, 12 June 1931; Church interview.

51. *Highway Highlights*, Kansas Department of Transportation, Topeka, August 1940, p. 1; Connie Hafenstine to Harry E. Heath Jr., 11 February 1988, and Lew Ferguson to Harry E. Heath Jr., 4 November 1987, in School of Journalism and Broadcasting Centennial History Collection.

52. Author interview with David Seaton, 5 October 1988; Dick Redburn to Harry E. Heath Jr., 8 April 1988, and Nancy R. Shelton to Harry E. Heath Jr., 10 February 1988, in School of Journalism and Broadcasting Centennial History Collection; Laramie *Wyoming Press*, January 1952, p. 2, March 1952, p. 1, January 1953, p. 1, February 1953, p. 1.

53. *Annual Catalog, Oklahoma A. and M. College, 1930-1931*, pp. 338, 339; *Annual Catalog, Oklahoma A. and M. College 1931-1932*, p. 292. The number of graduates was based upon author's careful inspection of graduation lists for 1927-1937.

54. Clement E. Trout, "Annual Report, Department of Publications" (31 October 1931), Clement E. Trout Collection.

55. Mrs. "BJ" Pattee to Harry E. Heath Jr., 11 March 1988, School of Journalism and Broadcasting Centennial History Collection; *1925 Jayhawker*, pp. 42, 238, 288, University of Kansas Yearbook.

56. *1925 Jayhawker*, p. 42; Thomas C. Ryther to Harry E. Heath Jr., 14 June 1988, School of Journalism and Broadcasting Centennial History Collection; Personnel data on George Church, Files of the School of Journalism and Broadcasting; University of Kansas *Alumni Magazine* (January 1952), p. 22.

57. Church interview; *1925 Jayhawker*, p. 42; Thomas C. Ryther to Harry E. Heath Jr., 14 June 1988, School of Journalism and Broadcasting Centennial History Collection.

58. Church interview.

59. Church interview; Personnel data on George Church, Files of the School of Journalism and Broadcasting.

60. Author interview with Earl Richert, 10 November 1984, Stillwater, Oklahoma; Hamilton interview, 21 January 1988; Gladys Toler Burris to Harry E. Heath Jr., 21 March 1989, Aubrey McAlister to Harry E. Heath Jr., 23 March 1989, and Dave Johnson to Harry E. Heath Jr., 9 July 1987, in School of Journalism and Broadcasting Centennial History Collection.

61. John Oliver to Harry E. Heath Jr., 16 September 1987, School of Journalism and Broadcasting Centennial History Collection.

62. Class Rolls, 1938-39 through 1948-49, in author's files. These may be verified in bound volumes stored in the basement of the Student Health Services.

63. "Who's Who and Aggie Boosters," *Oklahoma A. and M. College Magazine*, vol. 3, no. 4 (January 1932), p. 7.

64. Dated manuscripts for these talks are in the Clement E. Trout Collection.

65. "Memorandum of Agreement on Handling Publicity Between the Publications Department and the Extension Editor" [1934], probably worked out in conferences between Duncan Wall and Clement E. Trout. A copy of this agreement may be found in the Clement E. Trout Collection.

66. Clement E. Trout to Henry G. Bennett and Schiller Scroggs, 21 April 1937, Files of the School of Journalism and Broadcasting.

67. Personnel data on Leon Durst, Files of the School of Journalism and Broadcasting.

68. Clement E. Trout to Schiller Scroggs, 11 May 1936, Files of the School of Journalism and Broadcasting.

69. Clement E. Trout to Helen Freudenberger, 17 September 1936, and Biographical notes on Helen Freudenberger, in Files of the School of Journalism and Broadcasting.

70. Helen Freudenberger to Clement E. Trout, 18 September 1936, Clement E. Trout to Helen Freudenberger, 21 September 1936, and Clement E. Trout to Helen Freudenberger, 21 September 1936 (two letters in one day), in Files of the School of Journalism and Broadcasting.

71. Helen Freudenberger to Clement E. Trout, 22 September 1936, Clement E. Trout to Helen Freudenberger, 23 September 1936, and Helen Freudenberger Holmes to Marlan Nelson, 5 March 1987, in Files of the School of Journalism and Broadcasting.

14 Journalism Gains Its Spurs

Noble W. Rockey had faced the staffing problems that came with World War I. Now, as the Great Depression began to wane, Clement E. Trout would face the World War II years with their vastly different student mix and the problem of keeping a competent faculty together. He managed well, all things considered.

During his first decade on campus, Trout had built strong programs in three schools—agriculture, home economics and commerce—although most of the courses in the various journalism majors were taught in his home administrative unit, the School of Science and Literature. Later, in 1940, he would be instrumental in shaping a course known as engineering journalism. It would last for fifteen years and would be taught by Ruth Howard, some of that time co-jointly with the Department of English.[1] The visibility Trout had given journalism through his cooperative arrangements plus his creative use of the journalism certificate program had produced more students than his hard-pressed teaching team could comfortably handle. The various programs now in place also called for greater recognition of the technical emphasis he was giving journalism. The 1937-38 catalog had listed Trout's new unit as the Department of Journalism. As the decade ended, however, he amended copy for the 1939-40 catalog to read Department of *Technical* Journalism.[2] In this he was in step with Iowa State and Kansas State, two of the leading land-grant journalism programs in the plains states. He was not simply following the lead of those schools, although it may have appeared so to the casual observer. He truly believed that success in journalism at Oklahoma A. and M. depended upon the approach he had taken almost from his first day in Stillwater, that of linking technical subject-matter areas with journalism. Certainly this would give the program an identity of its own. There was little chance that one could argue duplication of curricula in Stillwater and Norman. But Trout knew, too, that he could not overlook the state's newspaper industry. He chose to concentrate upon community newspapers—weeklies and small dailies—and leave the metropolitan press to the university. The fact that some Oklahoma A. and M. graduates became highly successful in the major leagues of newspaper journalism was not the point. He was proud of their success, but he wanted it clearly understood that the Aggie focus was upon small newspapers.[3]

Departmental files give a hint of the many tasks that faced Trout as his first year of expanded responsibilities began. He was chairman of the High School Vocational Guidance Conference Committee, a position that required him to coordinate program details for the estimated 1,300-plus high school seniors who would attend the annual meeting. He continued as chairman of the standing committees on publications and advertising solicitation. Off campus he was on the board of directors of the Wesley Foundation. All of this in addition to his teaching duties, his administrative responsibility for the publications department, general publicity, experiment station editing—and, now, as head of a new academic department. He was making plans to attend the national meeting of Sigma Delta Chi in Topeka, hopeful that he could pave the way for an Oklahoma A. and M. chapter, a long-sought goal. While in Topeka, he would talk with other journalism administrators about transfer credits. The reason: the University of Missouri had disallowed journalism credits from Oklahoma A. and M. when N. S. DeMotte, who took the B.S. degree in 1935, had enrolled in the bachelor of journalism program at Missouri.[4]

As the 1937-38 academic year opened, Trout reported directly to Dean Schiller Scroggs on academic matters while continuing to wear his other administrative hats. The big challenge now, however, was to make a success of an academic program that had too long hidden its light under a bushel. It had taken ten and a half years, but Trout finally had achieved Rockey's goal.[5]

Although the departmental name did not yet reflect the fact, Trout was determined to increase the emphasis upon technical journalism. This had become evident as early as 1928, when he began to use the term in copy he prepared for the college catalog. He refined the concept in subsequent years and strengthened it in the first catalog issued following the department's independence from the old Department of English and Journalism.[6] Non-majors who wanted to prepare for a career in technical journalism could now earn a "certificate of proficiency" in addition to a degree in history, English, political science, or any other major. The certificate in the School of Arts and Sciences—formerly the School of

Part of the journalism education of students during the 1930s came from their close cooperation with the backshop crew of the O'Collegian Publishing Company. Having their own press in the Student Publications Building was crucial as students developed skills in production techniques.

Science and Literature—required the regular lower division program for the first two years. In the upper division, students selected a major but, instead of selecting a minor, elected twenty-four hours of journalism. The degree was conferred in the major selected, with the certificate awarded in technical journalism. Journalism majors in the School of Arts and Sciences were not eligible for the certificate. Instead, they selected a minor approved by the journalism staff.

Students from other schools on campus could earn the certificate by completing twenty-four hours of journalism in addition to the regularly required work. However, majors in agricultural or home economics journalism were denied the certificate just as were journalism majors in the School of Arts and Sciences. Majors in commerce journalism combined the general business course under the School of Commerce with twenty-four hours of journalism.[7]

In its last year as a sub-section of English, journalism had listed fourteen courses. In its first year as a separate academic unit, a fifteenth course, Newspaper Management, was added. The course lineup would remain unchanged for the next three years.[8]

Trout entered the new era with a small but strong faculty. George F. Church and Sam E. Whitlow, both well-tested and talented teachers, shared the load with him. Church, promoted to associate professor in

1936, had been with Trout since 1930, usually handling three courses a semester plus some supervision of special problems work. In addition, he continued to add strength to the publications department, for he was a competent editor of technical writing. Whitlow, on the other hand, was new. He had joined Oklahoma A. and M. after seven years on the State College of Washington journalism faculty. He held the A.B. degree from Baylor University, where he had served a year as editor of the *Baylor Lariat*. He had earned the master's degree at the University of Missouri School of Journalism, studying under Roscoe B. Ellard, one of the best-known journalism teachers of that time. His early professional work had been in sports for the *Temple Daily Telegram*, *Houston Post*, and *Port Arthur News*. During his years in Pullman, Washington, he was a special correspondent for several papers while teaching and handling public information duties. In 1931, he spent four months on the advertising research staff of the *Spokane Spokesman Review and Chronicle*. Three years later he represented United Press for a year at Washington State in addition to his college duties. In all he had had five years of newspaper experience. One year of work on his Ph.D. was another plus.[9]

Whitlow's career at Oklahoma A. and M. covered a wide range of duties. As a teacher, he was exceptionally successful, inspiring his students and giving them a solid professional background, whether in advertising, management, or news. He was able to get results. In addition, Whitlow started the department's first student advisement program, not only counseling students on curricular and vocational matters but on their personal and social problems relating to college life as well. His success in establishing the advisement system was praised by Trout.[10]

After two years, Whitlow left teaching to become a principal state field assistant in the USDA's Agricultural Adjustment Administration. Meanwhile, journalism staffing problems had developed. Church was planning to take a one-year leave of absence for further study and Leslie W. McClure had accepted an appointment and then had resigned before it had become effective. The 1940 fall term was fast approaching when Whitlow agreed to return to the faculty. Trout was on summer leave at the time, studying at the University of Minnesota. Church, as acting head, handled the appointment details.[11]

Upon his return, Whitlow had publicity duties as well as his teaching. Trout had assigned him responsibility for "college promotion." In this work Trout rated him superior, both original in planning and effective in execution. A year later Whitlow was promoted to associate professor after turning down a promising opportunity with the USDA. In all, he spent seven years in Stillwater, four in teaching, two as associate editor of agricultural extension and one with the USDA.[12]

Trout's second decade might well be described as the Whitehurst Hall years. The publications department had returned to Whitehurst

Two key members of the journalism faculty during this period were Donald D. Burchard (*left*) and Sam E. Whitlow (*right*). They had excellent professional credentials in both news and journalistic management. Students rated them highly in their teaching skills.

from Old Central in 1932 and this meant that the academic program in journalism moved its headquarters to Whitehurst, too. Available class schedules for nine of the ten years show 120 classes in journalism offered, with 101 or 84 percent of those taught in Whitehurst Hall. Room 205 was most frequently used, followed by 232C, 230, and 232B. In addition, seven other Whitehurst rooms resounded with journalism lectures from time to time, as did classrooms in Morrill Hall, the Dairy Building, Williams, Old Central, Home Economics, Engineering, Life Sciences, and the Student Publications Building, once known as the Creamery.[13]

Trout and Whitlow carried the load during the year Church was away. His sabbatical concluded, Church returned the following year to become part of journalism's best-rounded teaching team in the years of limited faculty resources. The variety offered through Trout's connection with four schools was rewarded with increasing enrollments. Growth called for additional faculty. Church was less available, for in 1940 he had been given additional duties as associate experiment station editor. As the 1940-41 academic year opened—a year in which Oklahoma A. and M. would celebrate its fiftieth anniversary a week after the bombs had fallen at Pearl Harbor—two new names joined those of Trout, Church, and Whitlow in the catalog. Helen Freudenberger and Virginia Pope had been appointed as instructors. Both had proven to be talented members of the publications department staff, although they lacked the professional experience that Church and Whitlow had brought to journalism.[14]

The English faculty had depended heavily upon male teachers until World War I, when it began to take on a more balanced look. When William P. Powell signed on as head in 1921, the board of agriculture had hired an all-female English faculty. But only rarely had journalism classes seen a woman's face at the lectern since Mary Mustain's short tenure from December 1918 to April 1919 and Mable Caldwell's work during the Edmund E. Hadley era and the early Trout years. When Trout decided to add women to his staff, he did it without any urging from the administration or a need to comply with federal equal opportunity standards, for none existed. His principal concerns appeared to be immediate need plus the qualifications of the candidate, although he also may have anticipated the manpower crunch that loomed ahead.[15]

The 1940-41 catalog listed three new courses: Journalism and Society, Typography, and Engineering Journalism. Typography did not replace Printing, but concentrated upon elements of design for advertising as well as news and information media, including bulletins and other publications. Two course names were changed that year. Survey of Journalism became Journalism for High School Teachers and Writing and Editing Bulletins became Editing Publications. Only minor changes in course descriptions accompanied the new names. As the academic year began, only Trout and Pope were listed in the class schedule. No faculty member was shown for three of the most vital courses: Technical News Writing and Reporting; Special Articles, Technical and General; and Editing and Copyreading. Whitlow returned in time to fill those gaps. Whitlow taught a particularly heavy schedule during the second semester. He was responsible for reporting, editing, ethics, history, and management classes, while Pope taught Printing and Freudenberger Advanced Special Articles. Trout took charge of Home Economics Journalism, Editing Publications, and Agricultural Journalism. Whitlow shared the Methods and Problems work with other staff members.

All journalism courses had been taught in the upper division for nine years. In 1941-42 an important change in policy took place. Whether it was dictated from above or simply was a way for journalism to compete on even terms with other academic units is not clear. Whatever the reason, there now were two courses listed at the freshman level, four at the sophomore, eight at the junior and eight at the senior level. None of the freshman and sophomore courses counted in the professional program, but were prerequisite to all upper division journalism courses. Printing and Typography, formerly two courses with one credit each, were now combined into one two-credit course. That year, in contrast with his earlier teaching assignments, Whitlow taught only three courses. In his final semester on the faculty, he was responsible for only Typography and Newspaper Management.[16]

Both Freudenberger and Pope, though continuing to work in publications, had contributed substantially to the academic program in journalism. They were Oklahoma A. and M. graduates, but both had added to their expertise on other campuses. In 1939, Freudenberger had taken a leave of absence to work toward the master's degree in agricultural journalism at the University of Wisconsin. It was awarded in the spring of 1940. Teaching would not be her only responsibility. For example, on October 14, 1941, Trout wrote A. M. Patterson, manager of the American Livestock Show in Kansas City, that Oklahoma A. and M. College would be represented by Freudenberger "to assist with publicity concerning Oklahoma."[17]

Trout was pleased with Freudenberger's versatility. He had good reports on her classroom work and he could call upon her for public relations duties as well. But she was below the standard salary scale for her tenure and rank. On April 9, 1942, Trout recommended that she be increased from $1,400 for twelve months to the $1,592 standard effective July 1. "Miss Freudenberger," he informed Dean Scroggs, "handles a large volume of work, devotes long hours to her work, and does an excellent quality of work. She carries heavy responsibilities."[18]

Her reward for excellence did not last long. On July 14, 1942, she applied for a leave of absence without pay from July 20, 1942, "for the

1943 REDSKIN

Under its longtime chairman, Clement E. Trout, the 1942-43 board of directors of student publications was made up of eight voting members—four students and four faculty. From the left (seated) are Bob Odom, Virginia Mershon, Clement E. Trout, Adeline Fox, and Joe Kennedy; (standing) William C. Stone, Clarence H. McElroy, Carl P. Thompson, George White, and Aubrey McAlister. Stone, editorial advisor to the O'Collegian, and McAlister, general manager of student publications, were non-voting members.

duration of the war, plus 6 months, for the purpose of becoming [an] Officer Candidate in the Women's Army Auxiliary Corps." The following day Trout recommended that the leave be approved. She became the first WAAC member selected in July 1942. She was commissioned a second lieutenant in August 1942 and remained in the service until 1949, achieving the rank of major. She was retired for disability that year.[19]

During her teaching career at Oklahoma A. and M., she assisted Trout in the Publicity Methods and Agricultural Journalism courses. She also taught a class in Magazine Article Writing. In this class she required the sale of a freelance article for a passing grade. "I am proud to say all of my students passed," she recalled years later. She also was a founding sponsor of Fourth Estate, a club for women journalism students. The club, founded in 1937, successfully petitioned for a chapter of Theta Sigma Phi in 1942.[20]

As for the second female faculty member at this time, Pope had worked for the *Fairfax Chief* for three years and held B.S. and M.A. degrees from Oklahoma A. and M. She had studied two summers at the Medill School of Journalism, Northwestern University, and had been a correspondent for the *Oklahoma News* and, it appears likely, for the *Daily Oklahoman.* She had joined the Oklahoma A. and M. staff in 1935 as an assistant in the publications department. On May 29, 1940, when she was earning $1,500 for twelve months, Trout had added her to the teaching staff to meet the demands of increasing enrollments. She would hold a dual appointment in journalism and publications while teaching Printing and Typography—later combined as one course—and Journalism for High School Teachers. In both jobs she was considered to be hard working and highly satisfactory. Meanwhile, she had married Elmer L. Hartman. On September 21, 1942, she submitted her resignation effective October 10 to join her husband, who was on active military duty. The Hartmans later operated a horticulture business in Enid and would send a daughter, Carol, to OSU, where she became an outstanding student journalist, taking the B.A. degree in 1964. Like her mother, Carol was outgoing and popular with her peers.[21]

The help Freudenberger and Pope had brought to the short-handed teaching staff was brief but important. Wartime staffing at best was unpredictable, at worst virtually impossible. To make matters worse, Whitlow had submitted his resignation only a short time earlier. It would be effective June 30, 1942, when he would join radio station WKY in Oklahoma City. The farm program he was to start was deferred because of the war and he was given a job in the Oklahoma Publishing Company (OPUBCO) promotion department. When an opening occurred on the *Farmer-Stockman*, editor Ferdie J. Deering chose Whitlow as his associate. After several years in Oklahoma City with Deering, Whitlow was transferred to Dallas when the Oklahoma Publishing Company opened a

Farmer-Stockman office there. He served as editor of the Texas edition until his retirement in 1971.[22]

Soon after the surprise Japanese attack on Pearl Harbor, many journalism faculties across the country were largely decimated. The Oklahoma A. and M. losses were less cataclysmic because they did not come in one fell swoop. In spite of the war emergency, Trout was, fortunately, holding the faculty together fairly well. The Trout-Church nucleus was still in place, and the new faces had been phased in with a minimum of disruption.

Whitlow's replacement was C. Edward Bounds, a native of Hannibal, Missouri, who stood six feet two and one-half inches barefoot and at 162 pounds could have been classed as more than slender. He was to become closer to Trout than any other faculty member of that period. Bounds had earned the bachelor's degree in journalism from the University of Missouri in 1939 and had followed it with the M.A. there in 1941. He had worked for twelve years on various newspapers and publications before seeking a degree. His biographical data revealed that he had served as a reporter and feature writer on the *Philadelphia Bulletin*, as wire editor and later city editor of the *Wilmington [Delaware] Morning News*, and as editor and publisher of five weekly newspapers in Delaware and Maryland. After a short period in government work, he returned to journalism as advertising and promotion manager of the Manchester Paint Corporation and as editor of a trade journal. During this period he free-lanced articles for the North American Newspaper Alliance and the Public Ledger Syndicate. At Missouri he was responsible for special editions of the *Columbia Missourian*.[23]

Bounds came to Oklahoma A. and M. from an instructorship at the Texas College of Mines, El Paso. His appointment was as an assistant professor with a salary of $2,500 for twelve months, typical for the times. Three months after his arrival in Stillwater, the United States was at war and faculty duties underwent unexpected changes as the campus became a center for Army and Navy training programs. Bounds taught his regular classes, assisted the School of Arts and Sciences with advisement, instructed in the Army Specialized Training Program, and directed the War Emergency Training Course in Printing and Publishing.[24]

After two years at Oklahoma A. and M., he was granted a leave of absence for the 1944-45 academic year to serve with the Office of War Information (OWI) in New York City. Returning to the campus in the fall of 1945, he served one year as World War II wound down and the impact of demobilization began to be felt.[25]

Bounds was an inspirational teacher and friendly advisor. He was responsible for turning Mary Goddard from a dietetics career to a long and highly respected career in Oklahoma journalism at the *Lawton Constitution* and the *Daily Oklahoman*. Bounds helped other students as well to move from doubt to certainty about devoting their lives to journalism. Drawing heavily upon his solid professional background, he lectured from limited notes. Students appreciated him for his relaxed classroom style. Those who participated remembered him especially for a two-day publishing trip in March of 1946 when he supervised their work on a special edition of the *Drumright Journal*, one of the features of news-editorial training in that era. Based upon course assignments listed in three catalogs, Bounds had assumed Whitlow's mantle as the journalism faculty's work horse. For two years he taught eight different courses—ten counting special war-time vocational sections—with all the preparation and paper grading such diversity suggests. Half of the courses were at the lower division level, half upper division. All but Journalism for High School Teachers were considered basic news-editorial courses. His load was somewhat lighter after his return from OWI duty.[26]

While on the Oklahoma A. and M. faculty, Bounds wrote for the *Oklahoma Publisher, Publishers' Auxiliary, Editor & Publisher,* and occasionally for the United Press, later known as United Press International. He took some graduate courses as well. He was on the editorial advisement committee of the Southwestern Association of Industrial Editors, on two arts and sciences committees, and was active in the American Association of Teachers of Journalism. He often represented Oklahoma A. and M. at professional meetings, including those of the Oklahoma Press Association, the American Advertising Federation, and the Oklahoma Circulation Managers Association.[27]

Bounds, exuding enthusiasm, "fired the kids up and sent them out full charge." He was breezy and casual, not a conventional teacher. Furthermore, he was able to relate to Trout as no one else on the faculty could. Those who worked with Trout knew him as a no-nonsense boss who abhorred the idea that anyone might be wasting time. But with Bounds things were different. Bounds was able to get his boss to take a coffee break with him. Suddenly, for the first time, Professor Trout was one of the boys, more relaxed, more outgoing. Bounds had loosened him up. As time went on, this made Trout even more efficient in his work. But Bounds observed Trout's office etiquette, as did everyone else. No smoking was allowed in the office, so Bounds would step outside the building to have a cigarette now and then.[28]

To Bounds, Trout was always "The Boss." (Journalism and publications staffers often referred to Trout that way. Elsewhere on campus he sometimes was called "The Big Fish," an appellation with no well-documented history. He certainly was not large in physical stature.) Bounds' considerable correspondence with Trout while on OWI duty always carried the salutation "Dear Boss." For his part, Trout always opened his responses with "Dear Bounds," a habit he usually followed even in personal conversations. He rarely referred to any male by his given name.[29]

Trout had been fortunate in hiring Bounds at a time when war mobilization was peaking. At about the same time, he began to search for an advertising teacher who would hold a split appointment in journalism and the School of Commerce.

He was successful despite the wartime emergency. Resourceful and unerring when he had an opening, Trout was an effective recruiter. Those he hired proved consistently to be both hard-working and competent. This was due in part to the patient, methodical way he went about filling each full-time faculty position. The case of Donald Burchard offers a good example. Trout had learned that Burchard might be interested in Oklahoma A. and M. and invited him to apply. It had been six-and-a-half months since Pearl Harbor, and with the widespread drafting of able-bodied men, qualified teachers were hard to find.

Burchard, born in Chicago, November 22, 1900, had attended New

C. Edward Bounds brought a breezy style and unbridled enthusiasm to his teaching. Students respected his professional competence and tried hard to live up to the standards he set in his news laboratories. He was an excellent advisor as well and led many undecided students into journalism careers.

Trier High School at Kenilworth, Illinois, a school with a reputation for innovative and progressive curricula, then had spent a year at Northwestern University. In 1921 he switched to Beloit College, where he took the A.B. degree in 1925. Following graduation he had worked for the *Evanston [Illinois] News-Index* for five years, *Radio Digest Magazine* in Chicago for two years, and the *Chicago Herald and Examiner* for four years. Finally, he had been owner-publisher of the *Oak Grove [Missouri] Banner* from 1934 to 1937. With thirteen years of newspaper experience behind him, he had decided to teach, and had signed on as an assistant professor with Butler University, where the Department of Journalism was under C. V. Kinter. He had taught "nearly every journalism subject in the catalogue." He also had freelanced some articles for the *Indiana Publisher* and the *American Press.*[30]

To further his educational goals, he had studied at the University of Missouri during the summers of 1938, 1939, and 1940 and had been awarded the A.M. degree. His master's thesis was titled "Reader Interest Problems in Business Papers." His undergraduate work had been in journalism, history, and political science and his graduate work in journalism and history. He was a member of Kappa Tau Alpha, Sigma Delta Chi, the American Association of Teachers of Journalism, and the American College Publicity Association.[31]

Burchard had studied "very little advertising," but had had considerable practical experience planning, writing, and selling it while operating his own newspaper. At Butler he had studied and taught advertising and had worked closely with the Indianapolis Advertising Club. During the academic year 1941-42 at Butler, he had been acting publicity director, and in that position had handled the university's advertising program as well as much of the radio work.[32]

Trout immediately got off letters to Burchard's references, then wrote him with details about the job. He always was careful to proceed step by step with a series of letters that would elicit information he needed in order to form a judgment while at the same time filling the candidate in on information about the college, job requirements and the community. In his first such letter to Burchard he had explained that the person hired would teach "all the advertising for our School of Commerce." This would involve three courses: basic principles, copy writing, and a new problems course on advertising for weekly and small daily papers. "All Journalism students go thru the marketing and advertising courses in Commerce," Trout pointed out. "In addition we have a course in business management for small dailies and weeklies which we would want you to teach. Depending on the enrollment, these courses would not make a full load as they are not all taught each semester. For your additional work, we would have to work it out between your desires and the Departmental needs."[33]

With a growing program in a developing institution, Trout was not afraid to experiment. He had decided to offer journalism in the freshman year for the first time that fall and give only advanced "application" courses in the upper division. He had started newspaper management and advertising work the previous year at the request of the Oklahoma Press Association, and plans had been worked out with association leaders. The goal was a practical course of training for the business side of small newspapers. "Our department is growing in enrollment but of course we are not sure what the war will do," he had written.[34]

After studying Burchard's letters and transcripts, Professor Trout had decided that his background was right for the goals he had in mind. He had discussed Burchard's background with the two deans involved—Raymond D. Thomas of the School of Commerce and Schiller Scroggs of the School of Arts and Sciences—along with Professor F. E. Jewett, head of the business administration department, in which the advertising courses were offered. Trout had been given the go-ahead in negotiations by all three. He told Burchard the position would pay $3,000 for twelve months, that the appointment as assistant professor would be for three years (with the first year a trial period), and that promotion opportunities were "better than in many of the longer established institutions where the rankings are pretty well set. Producing on the job is the important consideration." Whether Burchard would teach full time or have publications work "as necessary" to fill out his program was not settled at this point.

Then Trout turned to another subject. He was, as usual, giving the prospective faculty member, letter by letter, a stream of insights into the Oklahoma A. and M. journalism philosophy. He wanted Burchard to know what he considered to be crucial. About professional contacts, he wrote: "We have always considered that off the campus contacts were very important for all of our journalism work. Under the present restrictions on tires and travel, we will probably not be able to make as many contacts as we have in the past, but we will have provision for off campus contacts with newspapermen and advertising people." Apparently Burchard had raised a question about taking students to community newspapers on publishing trips. Trout responded that this had never been done at Oklahoma A. and M. before, but that "we are certainly open-minded in developing plans along that line if they are favorable to the war conditions ahead."[35]

On July 16, 1942, Burchard wrote that he was glad to accept the assistant professorship with teaching duties in advertising and newspaper management courses plus "whatever [other] teaching and publicity work [is] necessary."[36] Trout recommended Burchard's appointment effective September 1. President Henry G. Bennett had told Trout that he would recommend Burchard to the board of agriculture at its meeting in early August. The appointment was, as expected, approved by the board. Burchard would replace the popular Sam Whitlow. During the summer, Burchard had worked on the *Indianapolis Star* while supervising Butler University's publicity efforts on a part-time basis. Meanwhile, Professor Bounds was trying to find housing for the Burchards.[37]

Burchard soon proved himself to be the able faculty member Trout had expected him to be. In his first year's Faculty Record report he listed eleven published articles, three in the Oklahoma A. and M. State News Service, and the others in trade and farm journals with wide circulation. Most of the articles dealt with problems in newspaper advertising and circulation, although some were more general. He was studying the relationship between advertising and trade-area circulation and its effect on Oklahoma weekly newspapers, was serving on the Constitution Committee of the American College Publicity Association, and had delivered a talk on "New Trends in Advertising" at a meeting of the Tulsa Advertising Federation. In addition, he had attended four statewide meetings of the Oklahoma Press Association plus one regional meeting. He had bypassed a summer vacation and "taught on campus straight through." He had had numerous contacts with newspaper publishers, advertising clubs, and OPA officials; had been a counselor to Cub Scouts; and had maintained active contacts with Kappa Tau Alpha, Alpha Delta Sigma, and Sigma Delta Chi, all journalistic societies.[38]

To meet the emergency needs of community newspapers, the Department of Technical Journalism added a two-year vocational diploma curriculum which would last throughout the war years. It was intended to prepare individuals for practical newspaper work but, as the catalog indicated, was not intended to take the place of the more extensive training required for technical or professional journalism. The emergency diploma added two weekly four-credit courses with six hours of laboratory work plus theory in each. In addition to basic courses in reporting and editing, diploma students took "enough English, history, and other generally needed courses [to give them] a reasonable and logical appreciation of, and ability to interpret, current news." The streamlined program included all phases of newspaper work except mechanical production and plant operation.[39]

While the catalog descriptions of degree work in Agricultural Journalism, Home Economics Journalism, and Business Journalism, formerly known as Commerce Journalism, were straight-forward and easy to understand, requirements of the general journalism program in the School of Arts and Sciences were complicated and confusing. This was due in part to the fact that journalism was headquartered in one college but provided course work for degrees in three others. Despite the confusion, a growing number of students wanted a traditional journalism curriculum.[40]

The 1942 Press Club, later to become a chapter of Sigma Delta Chi, the national professional journalism society, was decimated by the Selective Service soon after this *Redskin* picture was made. From the left (*seated*) are Charles King, Weldon Kerri, Bob McIlwain, Tom Morford, Norman Bridwell, and Lloyd Zacharaie; (*standing*) are Samuel L. Botkin, Warren Cooke, Aubrey McAlister, Leon Vanselous, Don Looper, Eugene Henderson, Joe Hodges, and Douglas Benbrook. Several became successful journalists following World War II.

By 1943, World War II had dug deep into male civilian enrollment at Oklahoma A. and M. College. The changing male-female ratio is clearly evident in this photo of the *1944 Redskin* staff, typical of the ratio on the *Daily O'Collegian* staff and in journalism classes as well. Seated (*from left*) are Peggy Howard, Bonnie Emerson, Gordon Casad, and Dorothy Drew; standing, Betty Sue White, Ruth Seamands, Helen Kilgore, Mary Willbanks, Norman Bridwell, Claire Cox, Alice Holton, Betty Bruce, and Anita Cummings.

As the 1942-43 academic year got under way, the impact of World War II was evident in many ways. Male students who had not volunteered or been drafted were waiting for their notices from Selective Service; a diminishing number of men and an increasing ratio of women populated classes; Oklahoma A. and M. had geared up to serve the war effort through various training programs that turned the campus into a large military base in a civilian setting. The mixture of regular students in their traditionally informal campus garb—men with letter jackets and pleated trousers, women with pleated skirts and bobby sox—seemed increasingly incongruous as Army and Navy uniforms grew in number and cadence counts rang out across campus while training units marched from class to class. A student in one of these classes was a future Oklahoma State University president: Robert B. Kamm. The war had brought with it a similar upheaval in student publications. Women dominated the staffs and held top editorships in larger numbers than ever before. While two other wars—in Korea and Vietnam—were yet ahead, they would bring no comparable change in the male-female ratio.[41]

For civilian students, the year also brought class schedules for three semesters of work rather than the usual two. The nation's hurry-up tempo was reflected in the classroom as well as in war production. Church returned to the lectern to teach a course in Journalism and Society, but Trout and Bounds carried the bulk of the work. Virginia Pope, now Virginia Hartman, taught History of Journalism, and Ruth Howard continued her course in Engineering Journalism. Bounds, taking over the heavy load formerly carried by Whitlow, was joined in the second semester by Donald Burchard. The third semester lineup of six courses was handled largely by Bounds, with Burchard picking up the History of Journalism course. Burchard also taught advertising in the School of Commerce.[42]

The Department of Technical Journalism had stabilized. Few changes appeared in the catalog from 1942-43 until the end of the war, the most notable being the addition of the word *advertising* to the Business Journalism major, which in 1943 became known as Advertising and Business Journalism.[43]

Without the heavy loads carried by Bounds and Burchard in 1943-44, journalism would have been severely handicapped. Except for Trout's classes in Publicity Methods and Home Economics Journalism, the work was almost totally in the hands of the Bounds-Burchard team. The following year would be more difficult. Bounds had left for duty in the Office of War Information. Burchard and Trout were the only regulars left. The word "staff" appeared following three courses in the fall and two in the spring schedule. If Trout had expected to fill these "staff" assignments, help never came, for all courses that year were taught by Trout and Burchard alone.[44]

By January of 1944, Burchard had succeeded in launching the student publishing trips he had asked about before coming to Stillwater. The first was from January 17 to January 19 at Pawnee, where his students took charge of an issue of the *Pawnee Courier-Dispatch*. While on the trip, he consulted with publishers at Pawnee, Cleveland, and Fairfax on course content and publicity problems. Later he would take publishing

Bill Stone (*left*) came to Oklahoma A. and M. College as editorial advisor to the *O'Collegian* during World War II. He was relaxed and friendly and a favorite among campus reporters. John W. Hamilton (*right*) worked primarily in publicity but assisted in teaching. Demanding but fair, he led several students to professional success. Later, he became head of the Department of Publishing and Printing.

teams to Drumright and Chandler where students under his supervision would write news and sell advertising for the *Drumright Journal, Drumright Derrick,* and *Chandler News-Publicist.*[45]

Trout was hard pressed for teachers. As World War II increasingly made staffing uncertain, he drew upon the talents of two men close at hand to augment the faculty. The first was John W. Hamilton, who had joined the publications department in the summer of 1942. Hamilton once described his background by saying he had gone directly from Broken Bow High School into a managing editor's job on the *Idabel Gazette,* had attended Southeastern and Northeastern Teachers Colleges later, then had taught in a mountain, one-room school where "might made right," followed by a job as principal of a Drumright elementary school. He first served as an editorial assistant handling institutional publicity at Oklahoma A. and M. before adding teaching duties in September 1944.

Hamilton taught Interpreting the News as the war continued. Later he would add other courses, including Agricultural Journalism. He was promoted to assistant professor during the summer of 1946. Students considered him to be demanding but fair and praised his ability to challenge them through his constructive criticism. Two students who received individual attention while assisting Hamilton with publicity assignments later became outstanding journalists, praising him for teaching them how to seek out and develop stories. One was Holmes B. "Brad" Carlisle, who became a legendary city editor on the *Nashville Banner.* The other, Chester Frazier, became president of the Agricultural Division of one of the nation's best-known advertising agencies, Bozell, Jacob, Kenyon, and Eckhardt.

Hamilton was a utility man on Trout's team. He wrote news releases, contributed to the clip sheet, assisted the alumni magazine staff, later becoming editor, and helped plan and carry out Trout's well-known workshops for industrial editors. In addition to all this, he was an unofficial liaison worker between the journalism department and its graduates. For a time he edited the low-budget but effective *Journalism Bulletin*, and throughout the years, even after leaving Trout's staff, kept in touch with alumni, helping build loyalty and pride in journalism.[46]

The second man recruited from other campus duties was Richard M. Caldwell, who had established a solid record in newspaper work before coming to Oklahoma A. and M. in 1944. He had earned a journalism degree from the University of Oklahoma in 1926, then had joined the Texas Cotton Cooperative Association in Dallas. After a year in co-op public relations, he moved to the *Sapulpa Herald*, where he served as news editor and managing editor for sixteen years. In 1942, he became assistant city editor of the *Tulsa Tribune*. President Bennett could see that the postwar period would require extra help in his office. He tapped Caldwell as his in-house public relations advisor. In that capacity, he wrote personality profiles and other feature stories for President Bennett and acted as a "trouble shooter" as well. His assignment carried an assistant professorship in journalism, and Trout assigned him to teach Writing and Editing the News.[47]

Meanwhile, Burchard had established himself as a teacher with a notable reputation in the plains states and the University of Kansas was interested in exploring his availability. Trout dreaded the possibility of losing Burchard, but indicated he wanted to see his staff members advance. In his letter of recommendation, he went on to praise Burchard's teaching ability, his professional experience, and his ability to work with people.[48] Soon after this, A. A. Applegate of Michigan State College asked about Burchard. Again, Trout praised Burchard and wrote that "we would hate very much to lose him." Trout predicted that only a real promotion would cause his valued faculty member to move. "Our salary situation has not been too satisfactory," he wrote, "but we expect it to get much better this year."[49]

As other schools contacted Burchard, Trout hoped to hold him with an associate professorship in journalism and business administration. He had recommended the promotion, subject to approval of the School

In 1938, Clement E. Trout founded the Southwestern Association of Industrial Editors, which under a new name became the largest such group in the nation. He traveled widely to provide leadership in the field, as in this planning session at the University of Texas. Far left is Dewitt Reddick, who later became director of the University of Texas School of Journalism and supported Trout in raising professional standards in industrial editing.

of Commerce. He was not successful. Burchard resigned effective September 1, 1945, to head the Department of Printing and Rural Journalism at South Dakota State College.[50]

Meanwhile, World War II had reached a decisive stage. General Anthony McAuliffe's brave troops at Bastogne had held firm in the face of a last-ditch German offensive in the deadly December cold of 1945. Victory in Europe was near at hand. On May 8, 1945, Nazi Germany surrendered and redeployment to the Pacific Theater had begun. With the new school year only three months away, Trout told Scroggs what he already knew: that Burchard's loss "[had created] a problem of meeting the teaching load and other work of the Journalism and Publications Departments." Trout's temporary solution was to continue Evelyn Drimmer on the payroll beyond her scheduled cutoff September 1. Trout explained, "This will relieve Miss [Lois] Elliott and Mr. Hamilton of some work so they can assist in teaching." He also suggested arranging for Elmer Woodson, director of student publications, to teach an advertising course. The arrangement would be on a month-to-month basis until Burchard's loss could be dealt with in a more permanent way.[51] In retrospect, it is difficult to place importance upon such seemingly crucial academic concerns while reflecting upon the fact that only sixteen days before Trout's letter the atomic bomb had been used as a weapon of war for the first time and that eleven days later, on September 2, 1945, Japan had surrendered, ending the costliest and most terrible war in history. The routine of academic life continued, though surrounded by the euphoria of a long-awaited victory.

Despite the loss of Burchard and the mounting difficulties in staffing his programs, Trout launched a new academic venture. He announced a degree program in industrial editing—the first university to do so—in 1945. It had been thirteen years since Trout had taken the lead in organizing the Southwestern Association of Industrial Editors. Now he was recognized nationally as the leading academician in the corporate journalism field. It would have seemed illogical, he reasoned, not to establish both undergraduate and graduate work in this rapidly growing segment of professional journalism. Time and again he had heard editors call for better-trained industrial editors. Oklahoma A. and M. was the logical place to launch the work. Trout had long advocated combining specialization in a subject-matter area with journalism training to give the writer a thorough background in the field he would write about. This philosophy led him to think in terms of students who could be given business, management, and personnel training along with journalism to prepare for careers in industrial editing. The new program was quickly endorsed by professionals and drew national attention and support.[52]

The man who eventually was to be Burchard's replacement was on active military duty in Europe, and Trout continued with a temporary solution to his staffing problem for nine and a half months. Finally, almost by happenstance, he found his man. It was late in World War II, following V-E Day. The faculty member he added would serve Oklahoma A. and M. and OSU for thirty-two years, matching Trout's own long years of dedication. His name was Lemuel D. Groom, and he had the credentials that Trout wanted. First, he had worked on at least five community newspapers, a high priority in Trout's scheme of things. Second, Groom had had solid experience in newspaper advertising and management as well as news-side exposure. The newspaper advertising experience appealed to Trout. Finally, he was married and anxious to settle down following more than two years in the European Theater of Operations. An added plus was two years at the University of Oklahoma as an advertising manager for the *Oklahoma Daily*.[53]

Groom was born to Oscar Downing and Margaret Callaway Groom on November 4, 1911, in Davenport, Oklahoma, a town of about 200. When he was nine the family moved to Tulsa, where his father was associated with the Producer's National Bank. Nine months later, they moved to Bristow. His father had purchased an interest in the First National Bank there. Groom completed his public school work and was graduated from Bristow High School in 1929.

He spent the first semester of his collegiate career at the University of Tulsa, where he chose a major in petroleum engineering. The next semester he returned home to attend Bristow Junior College, then dropped out for a year. The Great Depression had set in, and he worked at odd jobs, hoping to earn enough to return to college. The jobs ranged from delivering groceries to part-time work clerking in a hardware store.

Next Groom enrolled at the University of Arkansas, where he had decided to try civil engineering. When he returned to Bristow in June 1932, he began looking for a job. The state highway department was the most likely place to look, but it was laying off even seasoned engineers.

Meanwhile, his father had acquired the *Davenport Dispatch*, a hand-set weekly with a paid circulation of 217—paid in money, groceries, or farm produce. While looking for a job, Groom helped his father on the *Dispatch*. He learned enough from the tramp printers who handled the paper's mechanical needs that he could work in other print shops in Lincoln and surrounding counties. He had learned the California job case by being given a five gallon bucket of pied type to sort and distribute.

In September 1934, he entered the University of Oklahoma. He had been promised a part-time janitorial job in Albert Pike Hall, the Masonic dormitory, in exchange for his room, as well as a job in the journalism library clipping items about state newspapermen for the *Sooner State Press*.

Groom had wanted to "build high bridges and broad highways in faraway lands and help in the onward march of civilization." But working his way through college, he was diverted from his original goal. He worked in the job shop of the *Norman Transcript*, and in the photo-engraving plant of the University of Oklahoma's student newspaper, the *Oklahoma Daily*. He also had the not-so-glamourous job of sweeping out a pool hall after it closed at midnight. He got through the first semester on $105 and the second on $108.75, the difference being a fifth of Rittenhouse Square rye bought to celebrate final exams.

His jobs with the journalism school library and the *Oklahoma Daily* had led him to journalism. In order to get those jobs, he had to be a journalism student, so he enrolled in some journalism courses, but he still wanted to go into engineering—until he met Professor John Casey and something clicked. In September 1936, he became an advertising-manager on the *Daily*. In his new job, he handled some accounts and supervised the work of three assistants on others. He also worked for Casey, a popular member of the journalism faculty. For $19.20 per month, supposedly paid by the National Youth Administration, Groom graded papers. Several years later he realized that Casey probably was paying him out of his own pocket to keep him in school. Casey would help him again—under unusual circumstances—as World War II was nearing its end.

In spite of Professor Casey's aid and his income from the *Oklahoma Daily*, Groom found in 1936 that he would not be able to stay in school.

He and his wife, Muriel, were expecting a baby and he had to earn more money. He lacked five hours of completing his journalism degree.

O. H. Lochenmeyer, publisher of the *Cushing Daily Citizen*, owned half interest in the *Texas City Sun*. He and his partner, John Gordon, the *Sun's* ad man, had bought the *Houma [Louisiana] Courier* and Gordon had moved to Louisiana to manage the paper.

Lochenmeyer, visiting Casey, had asked him to recommend a qualified person for Gordon's old job in Texas City. Groom was working in a corner of the office grading papers with his back to the two men. Casey pointed to Groom as the man Lochenmeyer was looking for. In February 1936, Lochenmeyer sent Groom to Texas City to replace Gordon. Groom went to work for $25 a week.

Two years later Groom had picked up an additional advertising salesman to help him with a special edition of the paper. The work of this "helper" so impressed Lockenmeyer and Gordon that they offered him Groom's job. Groom went to work for the Lowe Finance Company, the *Sun's* next door neighbor. Then came news that the twin weeklies in Hominy would need a replacement if their managing editor, Roy Harding, could find a chamber of commerce position. Groom's father heard of an opening in the Okmulgee Chamber of Commerce and arranged an interview for Harding. He got the job. The Hominy newspapers, the Tuesday *Journal* and Thursday *News*, hired Groom in June 1938.

The Grooms stayed in Hominy until early December 1938. Business was slow. "It was one of those years when people ate Thanksgiving dinner on the porch, dressed in their shirt sleeves," Groom would recall years later. Advertising business was bad because the merchants were out of summer clothes and the people were not buying winter clothes. The publisher, Vera Moreland, kept him for as long as possible but finally had to let him go.

After being out of work one week, Groom got a job as ad man on the *Bristow Citizen*, published by I. L. Cook. He began work for $18.50 a week plus his Rotary Club dues. He started on December 5, 1938, and stayed until December 21, 1939, when Cook himself began to handle the advertising for the next six weeks—a slack period. It was not a happy Christmas for the Groom family.

Next he worked briefly at a Wilcox Refinery, then took a job in Arkansas on the *Springdale News*, a family-owned enterprise. Edward R. Stafford, the publisher, was ill and unable to manage the newspaper. Groom was advertising manager, managing editor, circulation manager, "everything but society editor and business manager." His news policy was to print all the news he could gather, told as accurately as possible. His advertising policy was governed by Professor Casey's admonition to "sell advertising, not just inches." The purpose of advertising, Casey had taught Groom, was to make informed buyers as well as to play a silver symphony on the cash register.

The future Oklahoma A. and M. professor held this job from February 1940 until April 17, 1944, when he entered military service. While in Springdale he had served as the newspaper's representative at meetings of such groups as the Library Board, Jaycees, Rotary Club, and Chamber of Commerce. Circulation had gone from 1,700 to 2,900, despite a subscription price increase.

Then came the break that would determine his future in journalism education. Late in his overseas duty in the field artillery, Groom was given military leave in Edinburgh, Scotland. He was taking a shower at the YMCA when someone in an adjoining shower started humming "Boomer Sooner." Groom picked up the tune and hummed along. He finished his shower and emerged to find Professor John Casey toweling down. At dinner, after reminiscing about their days at the University of Oklahoma, they began talking about their prospects after the war. Casey told Groom about a possible job. Oklahoma A. and M. College was looking for an instructor with the kind of community newspaper background Groom had.

After returning to Arkansas, Groom wrote to Trout and was invited to Stillwater for an interview, still wearing his GI suntans. On May 15, 1946, he moved his family to Stillwater, where he would spend the rest of his life.

Ten years before, Groom had left the University of Oklahoma short of money and five hours short of graduation. He needed two courses— Editorial Writing and Editorial Interpretation—to get his bachelor's degree, and he needed his bachelor's degree to become a full-time instructor at Oklahoma A. and M. He enrolled in the two courses he lacked, both of which were being taught by H. H. Herbert. Herbert and Groom made a deal. Groom would do the work in Stillwater and mail in his assignments. With Herbert's help he completed his degree requirements and in June 1947 attended graduation exercises at the University of Oklahoma. It had been sixteen years since he had started as an engineering student at Tulsa. He was to become one of those upon whom Trout would build during the final decade of his remarkable era.[54]

Meanwhile, as the 1945-46 academic year neared its end, Trout reflected a sense of desperation in pleading with Dean Scroggs for quick action on the appointment of Don Looper, an Oklahoma A. and M. journalism graduate who was reared in Stillwater. He could see that the influx of veterans—already under way—would bring dramatic changes to the campus, perhaps more so to journalism than to many other departments. The second semester enrollment in the beginning journalism course had grown from 40 to 105 in one year, while the sophomore course had shown a similar gain. As laboratory courses, this lower division work would require "many sections of small groups" in the coming year. Bounds was teaching seven lecture hours, directing the advertising laboratory and advising 130 students. Thirty advisees was considered a quarter-time load. Hamilton was handling the daily news service, the clip sheet, special news—with some student help—and was teaching five hours of class and laboratory in addition to fourteen students working on individual projects in the Methods and Problems course. "I am trying to handle the duties as head," Trout told Scroggs, "and also a two-credit course and sixteen hours per week of laboratory." While work in the publications department was expanding, Evelyn Drimmer had resigned to join her husband, who had returned from military service. A large backlog of work on catalogs and brochures remained to be done. No one was available to drop other assignments to meet these demands. To make matters worse, in September Trout would lose another publications worker, Lois Elliott.[55] Similar letters in which Trout had virtually begged for personnel, equipment and supplies had been written repeatedly through the years. Too often the outcome was too little too late.

Under Bennett, Oklahoma A. and M. had placed growing emphasis upon the need for a stronger faculty college-wide. This meant that fewer faculty could survive with only a baccalaureate or master's degree plus teaching skills. Bennett knew that national recognition for the college could not be achieved without greater emphasis upon research, and that meant more faculty members with doctorates. In more than thirty years of Oklahoma A. and M. journalism instruction there had been no Ph.D. teaching the subject. Trout had been on the trail of his first Ph.D. prospect since 1944. He was Richard B. Eide, who was awarded the M.A. degree by the State University of Iowa in 1930. His thesis was titled "History of Minnesota Newspapers, 1848-1865." He had added the doctorate at the University of Missouri in 1942, with research on the growth of the *St. Paul Pioneer Press* from 1849 to 1909. Eide had written Trout saying he wanted to relocate. He probably had heard about the Oklahoma A. and M. situation from Bounds or Burchard, both of whom were his friends from the Missouri days. At the time, Eide was working on the copy desk of the *Tucson Daily Citizen*. He had taught at state colleges in Minnesota and Wisconsin and later, while working on his doctorate, at the University of Kansas. For the past two years he had been on the University of Texas faculty, but things there had "faded out" with the war. He informed Trout that he was working on a book for high school journalists.[56]

In his response, Trout said he was looking for someone to develop contacts with high school journalism teachers and their publications. He enclosed an application form. Eide followed up by expressing an interest in Oklahoma A. and M. and said he would visit Stillwater on his way north "in a couple of weeks." Apparently nothing definite developed during that visit.[57]

Trout's prolonged postal contacts with Eide underscore both his persistence and the difficulties of planning during the war years, for teachers as well as journalism administrators. Eide, too, had found it desirable to make adjustments as the war progressed.

When Trout next heard from Eide, who had served in the Navy from 1917 to 1919 as a musician first class, it was early 1946. He had been at Shrivenham University in England, where Dean Kenneth E. Olson of the Medill School of Journalism was in charge of a special Army educational program. Eide now had moved to Biarritz American University, APO 268, where he was teaching in another of the Army's special schools established as the tempo of the war in Europe was stepping up. Postwar planning called for such constructive educational opportunities for servicemen during the redeployment period. Before Dr. Eide had gone to Europe to teach servicemen he had served as head of the Department of Journalism at the University of North Dakota and as a professor of journalism at the University of Iowa, where he had resigned to take the overseas assignment. He was highly praised by his European colleagues. During 1945-46 he had served as an Army civilian in England, France, and Germany, both teaching and advising editors of Army newspapers in the American Zone. He earlier had confided to Trout that "Iowa got peeved at my leaving so I do not hope to hear anything more from them." Eide's continuing interest encouraged Trout, for already servicemen in increasing numbers were returning to the campus.[58]

Eide had been reassigned once more, this time to the Unit Publications Branch of the Information and Education Division of USFET, APO 757, Postmaster, New York, N.Y. He expected to be back in the states about June 1. The correspondence continued in May. Trout was looking for an advertising teacher (Groom would end that search) and "four new staff for editorial work." He had an associate professorship in mind for Eide and reported that "our salary situation has improved here over what it was when I talked to you a couple of years ago." Trout was building his staff on a projection of 250 to 300 journalism majors by 1948. Meanwhile, Eide had been delayed in sailing and would not arrive until mid-June. Finally Eide had written on June 22, 1946, to inform Trout that he was back. Trout promptly offered an associate professorship at $3,600 for ten months including one month's vacation, or $4,320 if Eide chose to teach during the summer session. Dean Scroggs, he pointed out, was reluctant to approve a full professorship, which meant a lifetime appointment. The lesser appointment was for five years, but promotion to full professor would not have to be delayed the full five years.[59]

Trout's letters as he sought to build his postwar faculty tell the story of a college in transition. Journalism enrollment at Oklahoma A. and M. had virtually doubled during the war years. For four years, Trout's department had been one of the two or three largest in the School of Arts

Students often gained experience covering agricultural field days, short courses, and other events on campus. J. Edwin Harvey (*left*) takes notes from the scene by walkie-talkie in order to meet a deadline during a major farm event. Across the desk, an unidentified editor polishes a story.

and Sciences. In addition, journalism students majoring in the Schools of Commerce, Agriculture, and Home Economics added to the teaching load, as did a substantial enrollment in courses for non-majors. Trout wrote Eide: "We are estimating some 300 students, at least, in journalism this fall with nearly 200 of them far enough along to be definitely committed to journalism as a major. The load will increase, materially, the following year. We are adding three new instructoral positions. Yours is the top. I have been planning for you to handle advanced courses and start building up a journalism major for the master's degree. We have a demand for it and I believe we will be in a position to start it. We feel that we have increased our standing in the state and nation and the job ahead is one of building into something bigger and better than we have had."[60]

Dean Scroggs was strongly behind journalism. In addition, the Veterans Administration was pushing the new course in industrial editing, which Trout was planning to add to the graduate program. He predicted this would give Oklahoma A. and M. national leadership in that field. He felt the ground work had been laid to give the college one of the strongest journalism units in the country. He was ready to capitalize on the opportunity. The support of both the college and state newspapers would be crucial, and Trout believed he had such support. Enrollment in the fall would be limited only by housing facilities, and housing was short. However, the college was building a block of apart-ments reserved for faculty. They would not be elaborate, but would be comfortable and the rent reasonable.[61]

Trout asked Eide to phone him collect at the Hotel Statler, St. Louis, where he would be attending a meeting of the American Society of Journalism School Administrators on June 27 and 28, or in Stillwater June 30 or July 1.[62] He enclosed a 750-word statement of his department's aims and objectives. The principal theme was technical journalism, that is, preparation for some *specialty* within the field of journalism. To achieve this goal, Trout believed that a good specialist would need "some general newspaper experience." Trout knew that some candidates for faculty positions might not be familiar with the technical journalism approach. He was careful to spell out the characteristics of the program:

"As I see it, we are trying to emphasize the two extremes in the journalistic field. To meet the needs of our state, we are trying to give training for editorial work, management, and advertising for weeklies and small town dailies. We have not more than four or five newspapers in Oklahoma which do not fall in that class.

"At the other extreme is our industrial editing [curriculum]. . . . We work with the School of Commerce to give training in general business and journalism which we believe would fit students for such positions as financial writers on newspapers, and particularly for the trade press, and for administrative positions in business firms which involve a knowledge of press relations, news promotion, and so on. We also work with the Schools of Agriculture and Home Economics to give training in those special fields which would prepare the students for work with experiment stations, extension service, as farm editors on newspapers and so on. Our idea is that all of these fields involve, [among other things], the basic knowledge of news [and] the techniques of editing. The basic difference is that [these individuals have] enough knowledge in their field to exercise. . .initiative in the development and selection of material for publication and in its presentation. Also, they have developed an appreciation of the place of this information and specialized material in the news stream of the nation and in the lives and activities of special groups of people."

Trout could see that the expansion in Oklahoma A. and M. journalism might threaten the closeness of students and faculty. He wanted that cooperation to continue as the faculty and student body continued to grow. Newcomers would need to adjust to the program as it developed. "In other words," he wrote,"they should be ready to do whatever is needed." This would be a daunting prospect for some applicants, as suggested by the next part of Trout's statement:

"This department handles the college news and promotion and editing as well as the teaching; and on occasion, a staff member, whose primary responsibility is teaching, may be asked to help on some of these other activities. It would be difficult or impossible to definitely allocate certain courses to an instructor in advance. . . . Our plan is to do all we can to enable the staff member to do what he is best fitted to do and what he is interested in doing and in return to expect him to be ready to fit into the needs of the work as they come along. We want our staff members to assist in making contacts with state editors and in giving them services when possible. We want a staff member to study the problems involved in our field, including southwestern newspapers, and make conscious adjustments of his attitude, presentation, and background to the situation here."[63]

Apparently Eide had not been put off by Trout's frank presentation of the Oklahoma A. and M. situation. On July 1, 1946, Trout recommended that Eide be appointed an associate professor in the Department of Technical Journalism, effective September 1. The two had worked out details by telephone. Eide would replace Bounds, who had resigned effective September 1 to become head of the Department of Journalism at the University of Alabama. On July 2, Trout confirmed Eide's terms of employment. He asked Eide for a new application (he had submitted one in 1944) and new letters of reference to "give us a corrected record for your file." Six days later Trout informed Eide that his appointment had been approved. The college was rebuilding some military barracks for apartments at $40 a month and Trout had put in an application for Eide, who said he had no objection to barracks living. Eide had, however, expressed a preference with reference to his teaching duties. He asked to be assigned to advanced courses such as history, law, and editorial writing.[64]

Trout was in agreement with Eide's desire to teach seniors and graduate students, but that might not be possible for at least a year. Trout explained: "I am trying to work out the class assignments for this year. As you know, our student load runs about 8 or 10 seniors, about 20 juniors, probably 100 to 125 sophomores and no one knows how many freshmen but we are guessing a minimum of 150. This gives small classes and limited offerings of senior work, complete offerings for the medium size classes in junior work, and the heavy load in freshman and sophomore classes. To balance this, at present, everyone is going to have to handle some of the lower division work. As our classes move up, the demand for the advanced work will increase so that I expect next year, all of your work will be with the advanced students. We need to offer two or three new advanced courses to supplement what we already have. For this fall, I am tentatively scheduling you to handle a new one credit course which we are calling a seminar. We want it as a method of rounding out advanced students before graduation. I also want you to handle the course in History and Principles, which includes ethics. As we are shifting some of our work we are going to have to get together and plan content of each course so that we will cover the field without overlapping.

"I think I would like to have you handle our course in Interpreting the News. This is an open elective for the entire college and is really a study of current events. I will try and write you in more detail concerning these courses in about a week."[65]

Eide reported for duty on September 1, 1946, just four days after James C. Stratton and ten days before Vera Wood Gillespie. Along with Groom, who had joined the faculty three and a half months earlier, they were the last major teaching additions made during the build-up in anticipation of swelling enrollments.[66]

Gillespie would serve for only one year and Eide for three. Groom and Stratton would become long-time faculty members, contributing much to both campus and community. Both would play significant roles in the final twelve years of the Trout administration and in the administrations of C. Ellsworth Chunn, Charles L. Allen, and Harry E. Heath Jr.

With the war's end, the influx of veterans returning to the campus or enrolling for the first time posed a challenge for all journalism faculties. The GI Bill of Rights had made a college education available to millions who otherwise might not have been able to seek a college degree.

COURTESY JOHN HAMILTON

Shortly after joining the faculty in 1946, James C. Stratton, with a national reputation in scholastic journalism, began a highly successful annual workshop for high school students and advisors. The work covered writing, editing, and, as shown here, intensive work in typography and design.

Journalism was a popular subject among returning veterans as well as high school students who had lived in a news-hungry homefront throughout the war. Tooling up to meet the pressing enrollment demands had begun as World War II neared its end. Trout continued to build his faculty as he moved into the exhilarating postwar period.

Trout's middle years in his long tenure saw several new courses added to the curriculum. However, the guts of the program during these years—reporting and editing—remained virtually unchanged. These courses were given slightly different refinements depending upon the background and interests of those who taught them, but the basic principles were well taught even as the faces at the lectern changed. If proof of this fact is needed, the success of Oklahoma A. and M. graduates of this period should be sufficient. Many of them became outstanding in a variety of jobs on newspapers and magazines, in radio, public relations, advertising, and promotion, in both the commercial and government sectors of mass communication.

An undated Press Club and journalism student check list, perhaps prepared in connection with the club's interest in gaining a Sigma Delta Chi chapter, included 187 names, many of them well known for their

1943 REDSKIN

Three of journalism's outstanding students in early 1943 were (*left to right*) Sam L. Botkin, Holmes B. "Brad" Carlisle, and Patsy Horner. Carlisle later became an outstanding city editor on the *Nashville Banner* in Tennessee.

achievements in journalism. Among those listed were Beverly Bennett, Walter Biscup, Orlando Blackburn, Robert Bridges, George Casey, Eldon Cates, Kay Cowan, Robert E. Cunningham, Virgil Curry, Loa Le Davis, N. S. DeMotte, Curtis Ellis, George Ewing, William H. Feather, Philip Fordice, Ray "Gabe" Gierhart, Joe Griffin, D. L. Harbour, J. Edwin Harvey, Leonard Herron, Russell Hester, Irvin Hurst, Emery Jacobs, Carl Jenkins, David Johnson, E. E. Johnson, Wallace Kidd, David Knox, Theodore Lorenz, Veeda Massey, Clifton Mayfield Jr., Aubrey McAlister, Paul Miller, Clara Neal, Earl Richert, Richard Smith, William Tharp, Lawrence Thompson, Samuel C. VanCuron, Richard Venator, and Otis Wile. In addition to those named—some in public relations but most in newspaper work—there were numerous high school and college journalism teachers and others with public relations duties in colleges and universities. Among these were Welden Barnes, R. A. Brigham, John Hamilton, Harold Matkin, Helen Freudenberger, Sylvester Hughes, Orval C. Husted, Cora Belle Knearl, Marjorie Moore, Phil Perdue, Virginia Pope, Wayne Puckett, Eugene Shepherd, Joe Synar, Sue Van Noy, and Raymond Swartz. The list was, of course, incomplete and included some who had not majored in journalism but had been included for their work on student publications. A notable absentee was Thomas Heggen, whose brief year on campus in 1937-38 marked him as a writer with a distinctive style but inconsistent in carrying out *O'Collegian* assignments. Following World War II, his book *Mr. Roberts* became a best seller. It was followed by the Broadway and motion picture hits of the same name, with Heggen and Joshua Logan collaborating.[67]

With the end of the spring semester, Trout closed the second decade of his three-part story. As he did, he watched with pride as fifteen journalism graduates received their degrees, adding to the growing evidence of the department's success. The pace would slacken but there would be little time for Trout to relax during the summer months. He would attend the annual American Society of Journalism School Administrators meeting, plan the program for the faculty Social Sciences Club, of which he was chairman, welcome the High School Journalism Short Course, begin laying preliminary plans for accreditation, and continue with his busy public information and publications schedule. He had reached the two-thirds mark in his remarkable, multivaried career. He still was looking for new and better ways to advance the fortunes of the college in general, and technical journalism in particular.[68]

Endnotes

1. *Annual Catalog, Oklahoma A. and M. College, 1940-1941*, p. 363. Engineering journalism finally was dropped from the 1955-1956 catalog when Professor Cecil Williams introduced a junior-level course in report writing for engineering students. For two years, 1945 through 1947, a junior-level journalism course in engineering publications also was offered.

2. *Annual Catalog, Oklahoma A. and M. College, 1937-1938*, p. 102; *Annual Catalog, Oklahoma A. and M. College, 1939-1940*, p. 115.

3. L. Edward Carter, *The Story of Oklahoma Newspapers—1846-1984* (Muskogee, OK: Western Heritage Books, Incorporated, 1984), p. 203.

4. Clement E. Trout to Schiller Scroggs, 12 October 1937, and Clement E. Trout to Schiller Scroggs, 25 October 1937, in Files of the School of Journalism and Broadcasting, Oklahoma State University, Stillwater, Oklahoma.

5. *Annual Catalog, Oklahoma A. and M. College, 1937-1938*, pp. xiii, 102, 289, 290.

6. *Annual Catalog, Oklahoma A. and M. College, 1927-1928*, pp. 209-211; *Annual Catalog, Oklahoma A. and M. College, 1937-1938*, p. 102.

7. *Annual Catalog, Oklahoma A. and M. College, 1937-1938*, p. 102.

8. *Annual Catalog, Oklahoma A. and M. College, 1937-1938*, p. 290.

9. *Annual Catalog, Oklahoma A. and M. College, 1937-1938*, pp. xiv, xix, 102; Sam Whitlow to Harry E. Heath Jr., 7 May 1988, and Sam Whitlow to Harry E. Heath Jr., April 1988, School of Journalism and Broadcasting Centennial History Collection, Edmon Low Library, Oklahoma State University; Undated, informal vita prepared by Sam Whitlow, Clement E. Trout to Schiller Scroggs, 11 May 1937, Sam Whitlow to Clement E. Trout, 12 May 1937, and Sam Whitlow to Clement E. Trout, 9 August 1937, in Files of the School of Journalism and Broadcasting.

10. Clement E. Trout, "To Whom It May Concern," 8 May 1944, and Personnel data on Sam Whitlow, in Files of the School of Journalism and Broadcasting.

11. Undated, informal vita prepared by Sam Whitlow, and Oklahoma A. and M. College Recommendation for Change in Staff for Sam Whitlow, 27 July 1940, in Files of the School of Journalism and Broadcasting.

12. Oklahoma A. and M. College Recommendation for Change in Staff for Sam Whitlow, 26 July 1941, and Clement E. Trout, "To Whom It May Concern," 8 May 1944, in Files of the School of Journalism and Broadcasting; Sam Whitlow to Harry E. Heath Jr., April 1988, School of Journalism and Broadcasting Centennial History Collection.

13. Author's tabulation based upon course schedules in Special Collections, Edmon Low Library.

14. *Annual Catalog, Oklahoma A. and M. College, 1940-1941*, p. 116; Personnel data on Helen Freudenberger and Virginia Pope, Files of the School of Journalism and Broadcasting.

15. *Annual Catalog, Oklahoma A. and M. College, 1921-1922*, pp. 8, 9, 12, 201.

16. *Annual Catalog, Oklahoma A. and M. College, 1940-1941*, pp. 362-364; *Annual Catalog, Oklahoma A. and M. College, 1941-1942*, pp. 120, 121, 366-368; Oklahoma A. and M. College Departmental Schedule of Courses, First Semester 1940-41, p. 21; Oklahoma A. and M. College Departmental Schedule of Courses, Second Semester, 1940-41, p. 24; Oklahoma A. and M. College Departmental Schedule of Courses, First Semester, 1941-42, p. 20; Oklahoma A. and M. College Departmental Schedule of Courses, Second Semester, 1941-42, p. 20.

17. Helen Freudenberger Holmes to Harry E. Heath Jr., 5 March 1987, School of Journalism and Broadcasting Centennial History Collection; Clement E. Trout to A. M. Patterson, 14 October 1941, Files of the School of Journalism and Broadcasting.

18. Clement E. Trout to Schiller Scroggs, 9 April 1942, and Oklahoma A. and M. College Recommendation for Change in Staff for Helen Freudenberger, 25 April 1942, in Files of the School of Journalism and Broadcasting.

19. Oklahoma A. and M. College Request for Leave of Absence for Helen Freudenberger, 14 July 1942, Clement E. Trout to Schiller Scroggs, 15 July 1942, Edwin M. Martin to Clement E. Trout, 9 August 1944, Clement E. Trout to Edwin M. Martin, 19 August 1944, and Oklahoma A. and M. College Resignation or Discontinuance Form, 3 July 1948 for Helen Freudenberger, in Files of the School of Journalism and Broadcasting; Helen Freudenberger Holmes to Harry E. Heath Jr., 5 March 1987, School of Journalism and Broadcasting Centennial History Collection.

20. Helen Freudenberger Holmes to Harry E. Heath Jr., 5 March 1987, School of Journalism and Broadcasting Centennial History Collection; Oklahoma A. and M. College *Daily O'Collegian*, 18 April 1942, p. 1; Record Book Committee, compiler, "Selections from the Record Book of the Oklahoma Agricultural and Mechanical College, 1891-1941. Compiled on the Occasion of the Fiftieth Anniversary of the Founding of the College," vol. 3, p. 397, Special Collections, Edmon Low Library.

21. Personnel data on Virginia Pope, Oklahoma A. and M. College Recommendation for Change in Staff for Virginia Pope, 29 May 1940, and Oklahoma A. and M. College Resignation or Discontinuance Form for Virginia Pope, 21 September 1942, in Files of the School of Journalism and Broadcasting; Sam Whitlow to Harry E. Heath Jr., 7 May 1988, School of Journalism and Broadcasting Centennial History Collection; Author interview with Alice Church, 21 October 1987, Stillwater, Oklahoma.

22. Clement E. Trout to Paul E. Thomson, 16 June 1948, Files of the School of Journalism and Broadcasting; Ferdie J. Deering to Harry E. Heath Jr., 27 June 1988, School of Journalism and Broadcasting Centennial History Collection.

23. *JB News* (1983-86), p. 19; Oklahoma A. and M. College Request for Information Concerning Training and Professional Experience of C. E. Bounds, 5 May 1941, and C. E. Bounds to Sam Whitlow, 5 August 1941, in Files of the School of Journalism and Broadcasting.

24. Oklahoma A. and M. College Recommendation for Change in Staff for C. E. Bounds, 13 June 1941, C. E. Bounds to Clement E. Trout, 7 June 1941, C. E. Bounds to Clement E. Trout, 17 June 1941, and Clement E. Trout to Local Board No. 8, Selective Service, Kansas City, Missouri, 17 January 1944, in Files of the School of Journalism and Broadcasting.

25. Clement E. Trout to "President's Office," 4 August 1944, Files of the School of Journalism and Broadcasting; *JB News* (1983-86), p. 19.

26. Mary Goddard to Harry E. Heath Jr., 3 November 1987, Mary Goddard to Harry E. Heath Jr., 13 November 1987, in School of Journalism and Broadcasting Centennial History Collection; *Annual Catalog, Oklahoma A. and M. College, 1941-1942*, pp. 366-368; *Annual Catalog, Oklahoma A. and M. College, 1942-1943*, pp. 357-359; *Annual Catalog, Oklahoma A. and M. College, 1943-1944*, pp. 352-354; Oklahoma A. and M. College Request for Permission to be Absent from Duty and/or for Travel, C. E. Bounds, 4 March 1946, Files of the School of Journalism and Broadcasting.

27. Faculty Record of C. E. Bounds, 1 October 1942 to 1 October 1943, Files of the School of Journalism and Broadcasting.

28. Author interview with John W. Hamilton, 5 January 1987, Stillwater, Oklahoma; *JB News* (1983-86), p. 19.

29. Berlin B. Chapman to Harry E. Heath Jr., 11 April 1987, School of Journalism and Broadcasting Centennial History Collection; *JB News* (1983-86), p. 19; Based upon thirteen letters exchanged by the principals in 1945, regarding C. E. Bounds, Files of the School of Journalism and Broadcasting.

30. Oklahoma A. and M. College Request for Information Concerning Training and Professional Experience of Donald D. Burchard, 25 June 1942, Clement E. Trout to Donald D. Burchard, 3 July 1942, Clement E. Trout to Donald D. Burchard, 10 July 1942, and Clement E. Trout to Donald D. Burchard, 20 July 1942, in Files of the School of Journalism and Broadcasting.

31. Oklahoma A. and M. College Request for Information Concerning Training and Professional Experience of Donald D. Burchard, Files of the School of Journalism and Broadcasting.

32. Donald D. Burchard to Clement E. Trout, 1 July 1942, Files of the School of Journalism and Broadcasting.

33. Clement E. Trout to James A. Stuart, 2 July 1942, Clement E. Trout to Wray Fleming, 2 July 1942, and Clement E. Trout to Donald D. Burchard, 3 July 1942, in Files of the School of Journalism and Broadcasting.

34. Clement E. Trout to Donald D. Burchard, 3 July 1942, Files of the School of Journalism and Broadcasting.

35. Clement E. Trout to Donald D. Burchard, 10 July, and Clement E. Trout to Donald D. Burchard, 11 July 1942, in Files of the School of Journalism and Broadcasting.

36. Donald D. Burchard to Clement E. Trout, 16 July 1942, Files of the School of Journalism and Broadcasting.

37. Clement E. Trout to Donald D. Burchard, 8 August 1942, Recommendation for Change in Staff for Donald D. Burchard, 21 July 1942, and Donald D. Burchard to Clement E. Trout, 23 July 1942, in Files of the School of Journalism and Broadcasting.

38. Faculty Record, Donald D. Burchard, October 1943, Files of the School of Journalism and Broadcasting.

39. *Annual Catalog, Oklahoma A. and M. College, 1941-1942*, p. 121.

40. *Annual Catalog, Oklahoma A. and M. College, 1941-1942*, pp. 86, 87, 120, 121, 151, 152, 250.

41. Philip Reed Rulon, *Oklahoma State University—Since 1890* (Stillwater: Oklahoma State University Press, 1975), pp. 261-265.

42. Oklahoma A. and M. College Schedule of Classes, First Semester 1942-43, p. 19; Oklahoma A. and M. College Schedule of Classes, Second Semester, 1942-43, p. 19; Oklahoma A. and M. College Schedule of Classes, Third Semester, 1942-43, p. 11.

43. *Annual Catalog, Oklahoma A. and M. College, 1943-1944*, pp. 148, 149.

44. *Annual Catalog, Oklahoma A. and M. College, 1944-1945*, p. 121; Class Rolls, 1944-45, stored in the basement of the OSU Student Health Center.

45. Travel requests of Donald D. Burchard, 15 January 1944, 7 April 1945, 26 April 1945, Files of the School of Journalism and Broadcasting.

46. *Oklahoma State Engineer*, vol. 11, no. 3 (March 1946), pp. 8, 24; Departmental Schedule of Courses, Second Semester, 1945-46, p. 24, and Personnel data for John W. Hamilton, Files of the School of Journalism and Broadcasting. See also various Hamilton documents in the School of Journalism and Broadcasting Centennial History Collection.

47. *Stillwater NewsPress*, 31 May 1992, p. 2; Departmental Schedule of Courses, Second Semester, 1945-46, p. 24, Files of the School of Journalism and Broadcasting.

48. Clement E. Trout to Elmer Beth, 15 May 1945, Files of the School of Journalism and Broadcasting.

49. Clement E. Trout to A. A. Applegate, 18 June 1945, Files of the School of Journalism and Broadcasting.

50. Oklahoma A. and M. College Recommendation for Change of Staff for Donald D. Burchard, 19 June 1945, and Donald D. Burchard to Henry G. Bennett, 27 August 1945, in Files of the School of Journalism and Broadcasting.

51. Clement E. Trout to Schiller Scroggs, 22 August 1945; Carolyn Gonzales, "OSU's Sixth Decade: A World War Brings Sudden Maturity," *Oklahoma State University Outreach*, vol. 57, no. 2 (Winter 1985), pp. 2-11.

52. *Annual Catalog, Oklahoma A. and M. College, 1944-1945*, p. 152; *Annual Catalog, Oklahoma A. and M. College, 1950-1951, Commerce*, pp. 28, 29. In the 1944-1945 catalog, industrial editing was an option allowed under business journalism. Five years later it was listed independently as one of three distinct majors: advertising, business journalism, and industrial editing. All were under business administration in a cooperative program with the Department of Technical Journalism.

53. Liz McCarty, Untitled biography of Lemuel D. Groom (27 February 1970), Library of the School of Journalism, University of Oklahoma, Norman, Oklahoma.

54. McCarty, Untitled biography of Lemuel D. Groom.

55. Clement E. Trout to Schiller Scroggs, 10 April 1946, Files of the School of Journalism and Broadcasting.

56. Richard B. Eide to Clement E. Trout, 8 May 1944, Files of the School of Journalism and Broadcasting; Toni Kaiser to Harry E. Heath Jr., 19 June 1992, School of Journalism and Broadcasting Centennial History Collection; *Journalism Quarterly*, vol. 13, no. 3 (September 1936), p. 342; *Journalism Quarterly*, vol. 22, no. 3 (September 1945), p. 243. The University of Missouri lists Eide's doctorate as 1940. The citation in the September 1945 *Journalism Quarterly* lists 1942.

57. Clement E. Trout to Richard B. Eide, 13 May 1944, and Richard B. Eide to Clement E. Trout, 13 May 1944, in Files of the School of Journalism and Broadcasting.

58. Clement E. Trout to Richard B. Eide, 12 February 1946, Richard B. Eide to Clement E. Trout, 25 February 1946, Military Service Record of Richard B. Eide, 6 December 1948, and Clement E. Trout to Schiller Scroggs, 1 July 1946, in Files of the School of Journalism and Broadcasting.

59. Richard B. Eide to Clement E. Trout, 22 April 1946, Clement E. Trout to Richard B. Eide, 3 May 1946, Clement E. Trout to Richard B. Eide, 21 May 1946, Margaret Eide to Clement E. Trout, 10 June 1946, Clement E. Trout to Margaret Eide, 13 June 1946, Richard B. Eide to Clement E. Trout, 22 June 1946, and Clement E. Trout to Richard B. Eide, 25 June 1946, in Files of the School of Journalism and Broadcasting.

60. Clement E. Trout to Richard B. Eide, 25 June 1946, Files of the School of Journalism and Broadcasting.

61. Clement E. Trout to Richard B. Eide, 8 July 1946, Files of the School of Journalism and Broadcasting.

62. Clement E. Trout to Richard B. Eide, 25 June 1946, Files of the School of Journalism and Broadcasting.

63. Clement E. Trout to Richard B. Eide, "Statement of Departmental Aims and Objectives," 25 June 1946, Files of the School of Journalism and Broadcasting.

64. Clement E. Trout to Richard B. Eide, 2 July 1946, Clement E. Trout to Richard B. Eide, 8 July 1946, and Richard B. Eide to Clement E. Trout, 12 July 1946, in Files of the School of Journalism and Broadcasting.

65. Clement E. Trout to Richard B. Eide, 26 July 1946, Files of the School of Journalism and Broadcasting.

66. Clement E. Trout to Schiller Scroggs, 7 September 1946, Files of the School of Journalism and Broadcasting.

67. Undated Press Club and journalism student check list, [1946], Clement E. Trout Collection, Special Collections, Edmon Low Library; Thomas O. Heggen, *Mr. Roberts* (Boston, MA: Houghton-Mifflin, 1946), throughout.

68. Clement E. Trout to Schiller Scroggs, 30 April 1947, Clement E. Trout to Schiller Scroggs, 26 May 1947, and Clement E. Trout to Faculty, 24 May 1947, in Files of the School of Journalism and Broadcasting.

15 Postwar Growth and Development

After twenty years and one month, Clement E. Trout was entering his final chapter of service to Oklahoma A. and M. College. The first had been one of establishing goals, reorganizing programs, and working out relationships in several interfacing academic and service units. The second was a period of maturation, highlighted by the formation of an independent academic department, national impact in the field of industrial editing, and a rapidly increasing number of students dedicated to professional careers in the various facets of journalism, whether print or electronic. He was at the high tide of his career during a time many believed to be the most crucial years of the century.

Trout's third period, following World War II, was an exciting time on American campuses. Men and women came out of the military services ready to learn. Eager to make up for lost time in reaching their career goals, they set high standards for themselves and challenged the younger non-veterans. The nation's classrooms crackled with electricity, a kind of intellectual excitement not often apparent in college and universities today.

As Oklahoma A. and M. College entered the postwar years, Trout could look with satisfaction at what had been accomplished. Athletic titles alone were not the college's sole claim to fame. It had gained national attention for its back-to-back NCAA basketball championships, adding to the luster of its perennial No. 1 position in wrestling. But these were less important to Trout than the college's recognition as the undisputed leader in industrial editing and the successful petition of the Press Club for a chapter of Sigma Delta Chi, the national professional journalism society, a long-sought goal of male journalism students.

During the 1946-47 academic year, Trout had received favorable reports on all of his new faculty members. Lemuel D. Groom had taken hold in the advertising and management courses and was gearing up for typography. He was winning student support with his tall tales from the Ozarks, as well as his wide-ranging journalistic experience. Richard B. Eide had spurred interest in graduate work while winning praise for his undergraduate teaching as well. James C. Stratton had quickly established himself as the new leader in the news-editorial program and as the faculty specialist in scholastic journalism, a field in which he already had earned national stature.

Stratton, son of a druggist father and a mother steeped in the fine arts, had left Pueblo for studies at the University of Colorado, where he was awarded the B.A. in journalism cum laude. He had followed this with the M.S.J. degree from the Medill School of Journalism, Northwestern University, in 1940. Between degrees he had taught English and journalism for eight years at Pueblo Central High School, where he had been a student from 1921 to 1925. Following the master's from Northwestern, he had directed journalism studies at the University of Wyoming and had written two manuals that were popular in high school journalism instruction.

For three years during the war he had been given permission to serve as editor of the *Laramie Bulletin* while continuing his teaching duties at the university. Among his personal friends and references were Ralph Crossman, journalism head at Colorado, and James L. Morrill, president of the University of Minnesota, whom he had served under at the University of Wyoming.[1]

Another 1946 arrival, Vera Wood Gillespie, had just completed her master's at the University of Minnesota School of Journalism following fourteen months as editor of the *Richmond Daily Register* in Kentucky. A Phi Beta Kappa from the University of Kentucky, she came with high recommendations from Minnesota, where she had compiled an outstanding record while serving as a teaching assistant as she completed her M.A. degree. When she elected to join the journalism faculty at the University of Texas she was replaced by Elsie Shoemaker, who would become a key member of Trout's staff.[2]

Shoemaker had taught at Southwestern State College in Weatherford, Oklahoma, for twenty years, followed by a headship in journalism at Winthrop College, Rock Hill, South Carolina. She returned to Oklahoma A. and M. as a graduate assistant in order to teach journalism and study home economics. She would become Trout's specialist in home economics journalism, but she also assisted in the news-editorial program. By 1950, she was an assistant professor. In all, she served eleven years before "retiring" to her next job as a feature writer for the *Stillwater NewsPress*

Three new faculty members helped meet the demands of increasing enrollments following World War II. Vera Wood Gillespie (*left*) was an energetic and enthusiastic personality in reporting and editing classes, but her tenure was short. Lemuel D. Groom (*center*), a dependable and versatile teacher for thirty-two years, served under four journalism administrators. Elsie Shoemaker (*right*), whose specialties were home economics journalism and feature writing, helped bring stability to the department during the 1950s.

for more than a decade.[3]

The postwar period brought not only a flood of students to the campus but demands for more administrative space in Whitehurst Hall as well. The Department of Technical Journalism and the closely aligned Department of Publications would have to move to new space. Trout and his staff would no longer be at the seat of power, directly above the president's office. Rather, they would be in a surplus military barracks, one of many President Henry G. Bennett had acquired to handle the influx of veterans. The building, known as TF-8, would be home for eleven years, despite the fact that the letters TF stood for "Temporary Frame."

Planning for the move into TF-8, nestled between Whitehurst and Life Sciences, was disruptive, coming as it did as Trout was preparing for something new in journalism education: accreditation. While the building itself was far less impressive than Whitehurst Hall, the space and arrangement of work areas would be an improvement, and the pending move would be to the department's advantage in the soon-to-come accreditation inspection.[4]

Trout was glad that the new and somewhat threatening matter of journalism accreditation was one of the principal topics at the first meeting of the Southwestern Journalism Congress after its World War II hiatus. All 13 member schools were represented by approximately 170 students and faculty members, including Trout, Eide, and Marquetta Griswold, a graduate assistant. In a special session for faculty members, Trout believed he had received some help on his plans for accreditation. The congress passed a resolution to be forwarded to the accrediting council "outlining a plan for inspection which we think would be fair and equitable."[5]

For Trout, the summer months—leading to one of the most important years of his career—had been full. One major event was behind him. The first annual Industrial Editors Short Course had been held May 17-22 at the college's Okmulgee branch. The meeting had been successful and would grow in size and influence in the years to come.[6]

Also during the summer, at James Stratton's initiative, a six-day short course for high school journalism students was held. It, too, would become an annual event. In addition, discussions with Dean Daniel C. McIntosh of the Graduate School had gone forward. Trout had informed McIntosh that the M.S. degree would fit the needs of the Department of Technical Journalism better than the M.A.[7]

Trout saw the meeting of the American Society of Journalism School Administrators (ASJSA) as crucial because it focused upon accreditation. Earl English, executive secretary of the American Council on Education for Journalism (ACEJ), clarified the new accreditation program's procedures. Trout discussed the college's petition for accreditation with him. ASJSA members were concerned about the possibility that accreditation would "regiment" journalism teaching. English and other council representatives assured the society that there was no such intention. The meeting was widely covered by trade publications, airing for the first time several accreditation concerns. Trout believed that ASJSA had been responsible for many of the "liberating attitudes of the council."

He also used the Chicago trip to look for faculty. Dean Kenneth Olson and Professor Albert Sutton of Northwestern University's Medill School of Journalism suggested two possible staff members. Trout interviewed one of the men that evening without success, and had followed up by letter with the second. He also had used the trip to discuss the future of the Southwestern Association of Industrial Editors (SAIE) with the president of the International Council of Industrial Editors. The SAIE, born on the Oklahoma A. and M. campus in 1938, was the most powerful single industrial editing group in the country and eventual merger was being considered.[8]

While Stratton and Groom would contribute more to the success of journalism studies over the long pull, Eide's was a crucial appointment at the time, for Trout's hopes for a successful graduate program depended upon him. His doctorate carried weight with Dean McIntosh.

Eide's first year had been a busy one. In the fall semester, he represented the college at numerous meetings, including those of the Oklahoma Agricultural Writers Association, the Junior-Senior College Press Association, the reorganization meeting of the Northeastern Oklahoma Professional Chapter of Sigma Delta Chi, the Southwestern Association of Industrial Editors, and the annual meeting of the American

Society of Teachers of Journalism. His teaching load consisted of three junior level and two senior level courses. Enrollment ranged from six to twenty-six. Among his students who would later make successful journalism careers were Wandalee Hinkle, Byron Lehmbeck, James H. Scott, Richard Snider, Hall Duncan, Holmes B. "Brad" Carlisle, Mac Hefton, Bruce Heydenburk, Bill Byrd, Marquetta Griswold, Don Looper, and Bobbie Shoemaker. Groom and Elmer Woodson, director of student publications, were among his seminar enrollees.[9]

The fast pace continued during the second semester. Eide's case, in microcosm, simply reflected the coming to maturity of journalism education at Oklahoma A. and M. It had been a slow but steady building process for the first twelve years, culminating in departmental status. The next decade, despite the war, had brought increased enrollment plus a revamping of programs, with a growing emphasis upon industrial editing. This new emphasis did not replace, but was added to, the other specialized journalism curricula and the community journalism program. Trout obviously wanted to introduce Eide to the department's important publics, and so his attendance at various meetings continued. He represented Oklahoma A. and M. at the annual meeting of the Journalism Section of the Oklahoma Education Association, a meeting of the Oklahoma Chapter of SAIE, a planning session in Guthrie for the

COURTESY JOHN HAMILTON

James C. Stratton (*left, at front of room*) and lab assistant D. Earl Newsom (*with student at lectern*) conduct a newswriting class in TF-8 shortly after World War II. The aging manual typewriters continued in use well into the 1970s. Stratton served journalism for more than thirty years and later as music director for KOSU. Newsom became a longtime faculty member at the University of Maryland.

Industrial Editors Short Course, and the Southwestern Journalism Congress in Ft. Worth. He conducted the annual Junior-Senior College Press Association meeting (this time at the college's Okmulgee branch, because of crowded conditions on the main campus), attended the district Oklahoma Press Association (OPA) meeting in Perry, and went to the state Associated Press (AP) meeting in Norman, where he extended an invitation to the AP editors to meet in Stillwater in 1948.[10]

Eide had returned to Wisconsin for the summer to be with his wife, who was recovering from surgery. Trout wrote him with the good news that the College Council had officially approved graduate work in journalism. It was scheduled to start in the fall. He also reported that he had talked with K. Starr Chester, director of research for the college's Research Foundation, about a project Eide was pursuing on the Norwegian and French underground press movements. Said Trout: "I am suggesting that it might be published as a book or a Research Foundation bulletin."[11]

Eide had been a full professor earlier, but had accepted the Oklahoma A. and M. offer at a lesser rank. Now, with a year's performance behind him, he was ready to press for a full professorship. He had, he thought, good reasons: his wife would have to give up her mathematics headship at a state college to come to Stillwater, and with the graduate program approved and his projected leadership in it, the rank was justified. Trout had not opened the subject. His most recent letter had mentioned possible housing for the Eides. Virginia Pope Hartman was leaving to accompany her husband to Ohio State, where he would work toward a doctorate. Their home would be available for $75 to $80 a month. Eide's response was to the point. He was reluctant to ask his wife to give up her position until he had been promoted to full professor. "I might add, too," he wrote, "that such a rank would enhance the standing of the new graduate work. . . ." Mrs. Eide was being pressed for a decision at River Falls within two weeks. "Could you wire us?" he asked.[12]

Trout lost no time in acting. On June 30 he wired that the recommendation had gone forward and no doubt would be approved. Eight days later, President Bennett confirmed Trout's prediction. Trout wrote Eide about his promotion and added that Elsie Shoemaker was looking for an apartment for him. The promotion was effective September 1 at no change in pay. Eide was the first person advanced to full professor in journalism in twenty-one years.[13]

As the 1947-48 academic year opened, Trout needed at least three additional faculty members, but was not likely to find them. If he moved John Hamilton to full-time teaching he would have to replace him in publications. Whether Richard M. Caldwell would be available full-time was doubtful. Graduate fellowships would have to supply part of the answer. He would count primarily upon Eide, Stratton, and Shoemaker, with part-time assistance from George F. Church, Hamilton, and Caldwell. Trout, as usual, would carry part of the teaching load. In other departments, supporting courses would be taught by Stuart B. Seaton in advertising; Haskell Pruett in photography; and John Woodworth, radio.[14]

The first degree programs had been outside the School of Arts and Sciences, but once a major program with a community journalism emphasis was established it was in greatest demand. In one way, the program had had less visibility than the others. Each year the School of Science and Literature and its successor, the School of Arts and Sciences, had listed graduates without designating majors. It was not until 1964 that journalism majors in the liberal arts were identified in commencement programs. In a lengthy national trade paper article, Hamilton underscored the growth in community journalism. He wrote: "With more than 300 weekly newspapers and 50 dailies to serve, the Technical Journalism Department at A. and M. is fully dedicated to training workers for the community journalism field. This is the main sequence offered. . . . It combines courses in writing, editing, advertising and business management tied in with [the social sciences]." Then Hamilton mentioned agricultural journalism, home economics journalism, advertising, business writing, and industrial magazine editing as other sequences, pointing out that Oklahoma A. and M. was the first college or university to offer a four-year program in industrial editing.

"For the regular community journalism students," Hamilton wrote, "courses in history, economics, government, political science, sociology and psychology are 'musts.' For the specialized fields, students take a major in journalism and another in their field of specialization. . . ."[15]

That fall, 182 students had declared themselves majors in journalism. Although Trout had encouraged the programs in agricultural and home economics journalism, these programs had lagged. The number of liberal arts students in journalism, 116, far exceeded those in other programs, followed by commerce journalism majors, 54. The atypical war-years ratio of women to men had reverted to a more normal distribution. Of those enrolled in one or more journalism classes, 166 were men and 103 women. Six had declared majors in the new industrial editing curriculum, including two graduate students. The flexibility of the journalism program was illustrated by the fact that students from fourteen different majors ranging from music to political science were taking twin majors.

During the fall semester, 382 students were instructed in journalism plus 27 in advertising and 146 in non-professional service courses for a grand total of 555 in all courses combined. The first postwar graduates, twenty-one in all, had included only three with the B.S. degree. All others had taken the B.A. Shortly after graduation, fifteen were gainfully employed in journalism, some on newspapers and magazines, others in public relations and radio.

During the year, Stratton had been responsible for 148 advisees, 74 men and 74 women. This was a clue to the growth of the community journalism program. Although he had some help with advisement the following year, he still personally supervised the scheduling of 77 men and 61 women.[16]

With the 1947-48 academic year only a little more than a month away, Trout was perplexed. Vera Gillespie had resigned to go the University of Texas at a substantial increase in salary. Hamilton was being tempted by a job at the University of Tennessee, and Don Looper was shifting to the radio services department under H. H. Leake. But Trout was assured by Eide's plans to be on deck the first week in September following a summer studying Norway's press in Minneapolis, New York City, and Washington, D.C.[17]

True to Trout's prediction, enrollment in upper division courses was increasing. In Journalism 352, Interpreting the News, Eide had thirty-five students. He taught three junior-level courses that fall, but he also continued with the work Trout considered his long suit: his seminar and his supervision of master's theses. In the spring he had forty students in Journalism 342, Interpreting the News, plus less spectacular but solid increases in Journalism 343, Community Reporting; 383, Community Editorial Problems; and 462, Law of the Press. He also was supervising three master's candidates. His service report showed 104 students taught and he had averaged 44 hours a week in college-related duties. He had the assistance of one of his best students, Wesley Leatherock, grading papers. In addition the students referred to earlier, those who would later make successful journalism careers included Charles C. Anderson, David Ryker, Donal Walters, Carl Meyerdirk, and James Reid.[18]

With classes under way, Trout and his faculty turned their attention once more to accreditation. The American Council on Education for Journalism, a new organization with a starter grant from the Rockefeller Foundation, was made up of recognized leaders in journalism education in cooperation with five professional organizations: the American Newspaper Publishers Association, American Society of Newspaper Editors, Inland Daily Press Association, National Editorial Association, and Southern Newspaper Publishers Association. Trout had applied for accreditation in community journalism, agricultural journalism, home economics journalism, and business journalism. On October 17, 1947, a five-man team arrived for two days of classroom observations, interviews, scrutiny of physical facilities, library holdings, and a myriad of other concerns. The visitors were O. C. Brown, advertising director of the *Oklahoma City Times*; Bruce Palmer, a respected former newspaper man who had become an Oklahoma City leader in radio journalism; Aaron G.

Benesch, city editor of the *St. Louis Star-Times*; Ralph Lashbrook, head of the Department of Industrial Journalism and Printing at Kansas State College; and Earl English, ACEJ executive secretary.

The accreditation team had made a favorable report on Oklahoma A. and M. journalism, but no public announcement would be forthcoming for nearly eight months. Of twenty-four categories in which specific ratings were given, the department rated high in eight, median high in nine, median in six, and median low in one. Among the high ratings were the special objectives, regional validity, student morale, faculty teamwork, and credit requirements. The visitors noted, seemingly with surprise, that the involvement of four deans did not seem to be a serious handicap. The lowest rating came in the news-editorial category, community journalism, where the program was graded down as to "suitability." In addition to sitting in on several classes, the visitors had had conferences with President Bennett and his assistant, Earle Albright, as well as Dean Schiller Scroggs and Trout, before writing their report.[19]

In February, at the opening of the second semester, Oklahoma A. and M. added its first course in public relations, a fact that received widespread publicity. It would be for advanced seniors and graduate students and was planned to strengthen the industrial editing program. Trout felt that no existing textbook was right for the course. He intended to experiment with his approach in the beginning. He wrote that such studies would be valuable only if the ideal of public relations in its highest sense could be made basic. "I hope to point out many of the skills, techniques, devices and psychological principles which will be used in sound public relations."[20]

Oklahoma A. and M. had sponsored the Southwestern Association of Industrial Editors from its founding, and Trout felt a sense of urgency about the upcoming meeting of the International Council of Industrial Editors (ICIE) in Milwaukee May 3-8. Talk of a merger was in the air, and Trout had official duties in both organizations. In addition, he intended to use the meeting to promote the new undergraduate and graduate programs in industrial editing as well as the national short course he had launched in 1947.[21]

Soon after came Trout's involvement in a Washington conference brought about through his position on the executive committee of ICIE. Invitations were issued by the White House and committee members met with President Truman's executive staff, Secretary of Defense Forrestal, Speaker of the House Martin, and top officials of the FBI. ICIE had maintained liaison with the government throughout World War II. Trout reported in detail upon the conference. He was one of "about eighteen" who had come from all parts of the country to help reactivate information channels between the government and industrial editors. Oklahoma A. and M. was the only college represented, giving Trout an opportunity for contacts "not easily secured in other ways." The most productive meeting of the two days had been with Paul Hoffman, head of the Economic Cooperation Administration, where the groundwork was laid for a constructive exchange of information.[22]

In his annual fiscal year report to President Bennett, Trout reviewed the accomplishments of both the publications department and the Department of Technical Journalism, including a supplement covering the work of Richard M. Caldwell, "working primarily with the Office of the President." It provided impressive statistics in all areas of public information and public relations. One paragraph in the report gave an overview of Trout's academic perspective: "In general, the work of the department has continued along the lines developed over many years. Probably the major changes during this year were the establishment of graduate work, moving into a new building, and the accreditation by the National [sic] Council on Education for Journalism. . . .in four sequences. This accreditation was based on the work of the department over a period of years and the ability and training of the staff now handling the work."[23]

The fact that Trout had not slowed his pace was reflected in his Faculty Record report for the past year. Among his honors, he had been listed in *Who's Who in America* and *Who Knows and What.* He had served on six committees and as chairman of the student publications board, had attended numerous professional meetings, and had been active in eleven professional societies. In addition, he continued as a director of the International Council of Industrial Editors, served as secretary of the Southwestern Association of Industrial Editors, as president of the Oklahoma Agricultural Writers Association, and was responsible for planning the Industrial Editors Short Course and the annual meeting of the Junior-Senior College Press Association, known in later years as the Oklahoma Collegiate Press Association.[24]

The most important news, however, came soon after the close of the spring semester. Earl English, carrying out ACEJ instructions, notified Trout that "your sequences in Business-Advertising, Home Economics Journalism, Agricultural Journalism, and Community Journalism have been accredited." Public release of the information was scheduled for June 10. English included a visitors' report of twenty-one pages and pointed out that accreditation information used in college catalogs, brochures, and other publications should specify the sequence or sequences accredited. He indicated that he would call for another list of June graduates about December 1, 1948, and that accredited programs would be required to submit to re-examination within five years.[25]

In all, thirty-five colleges and universities had been accredited in one or more academic programs. Although English's letter to Trout had mentioned business-advertising as an accredited sequence, the news release English provided used the term advertising-management, listing

Home for the Department of Technical Journalism during the final stage of the Clement E. Trout era was TF-8, one of many surplus military barracks moved to the campus in 1947 to meet the postwar enrollment boom. Though "temporary," it was home for journalism students and faculty for eleven years.

Oklahoma A. and M. as one of seven institutions accredited in this specialty. Eight schools were accredited in community journalism, six in agricultural journalism, and four in home economics journalism. Trout sought to clarify terminology in the advertising area. "We make no claims for having an adequate sequence in management," he wrote English. "We do teach a semester's work in that field, but we do want the emphasis on our business journalism."

On December 17, Trout submitted his follow-up report on 1948 graduates to English. It included thirty-eight names, seventeen of them female, including summer graduates. In the covering letter, he indicated an interest in applying for accreditation in industrial editing.[26]

Following the accreditation visit, Trout had written English to express his satisfaction over the visitors' report. Since the visit, he said, "we have moved into our new building (TF-8) and many of the points raised by the Committee have been improved. We are, of course, expecting to continue to improve our program and facilities." He also wrote members of the accreditation team in a similar vein. He gave special thanks to Ralph Lashbrook, whose thorough understanding of technical journalism had been valuable to other ACEJ visitors.[27]

As journalism was moving into the graduate area, the Oklahoma State Regents for Higher Education had submitted some data that had piqued Dean Scroggs's interest. It showed eight students doing graduate work in journalism at the University of Oklahoma and four at Oklahoma A. and M. In contrast, the University of Oklahoma had only four-and-a-half graduate credits cataloged compared to twenty-five at Oklahoma A. and

M. "Why should we have so many more hours offered than OU?" Scroggs asked. He wondered if "an unwarranted expansion of graduate work" was occurring, and asked Trout for comments on the data, adding: "Unless there is an acceptable reason to the contrary, it is requested that graduate offerings in Journalism be sharply reduced in the forthcoming catalog." Copies of Scroggs's letter went to President Bennett and Dean McIntosh, among other interested officials.

Trout's response stressed the difference between Oklahoma A. and M. and the University of Oklahoma in terms of specialized journalism versus general journalism. In a modern context, his rationale seemed to fall short of a satisfactory explanation. Graduate work in journalism and mass communication today is more restrictive. The Oklahoma A. and M. approach, in which several courses could be taken for either graduate or undergraduate credit, was followed by a number of colleges and universities at that time. Neither the journalism files nor the university archives, carefully examined, revealed any administrative action as a result of the questions raised.[28]

One of Trout's concerns in 1951 was his role as chairman of an ethics committee representing industrial magazine editors. The committee met in Chicago the day before the annual ICIE convention, and Trout would report upon the committee's progress in developing a code of ethics. He also was serving as chairman of the education committee and would be called upon for that report. Trout considered the work of the latter committee to be especially important because of Oklahoma A. and M. leadership in education for industrial editing. He continued as an officer of the Society of Associated Industrial Editors, which had substituted the word *Society* for *Southwestern* as its membership took on a national character. Trout also served on the board of directors and, as usual, planned to attend that group's convention in Biloxi, Mississippi, in October. At the meeting, he was elected secretary-treasurer for the fourteenth consecutive year.[29]

An indication of the widespread acceptance of Trout's leadership in industrial editing may be illustrated by a request he received from an editor in Eindhover, Holland, seeking information on a twenty-point program for promoting industrial magazines. Trout sent the requested material promptly, saying it had been of great value in the United States and expressing the hope that it would be useful in Holland.[30]

For reasons unknown, the publications department was now being referred to as the editorial and publicity department in correspondence and reports. No explanation for this was found in the archives of the university library. The use of the new name was somewhat inconsistent, as the earlier designation frequently was interspersed with use of the new name.

Trout was still interested in accreditation for industrial editing and had written Earl English asking for an application form. With his letter he had included a summary of recent graduates showing twenty-one working in journalism-related jobs in Oklahoma and eleven in other states. Five in the latter category were not employed in journalism, and the employment of two was unknown.[31]

Now that Oklahoma A. and M. was a school with accredited programs, it was invited to become a member of a once-exclusive group, the former American Association of Schools and Departments of Journalism (AASDJ), which had drastically limited recognition of schools seeking membership. The AASDJ now was known as the Accredited Schools and Departments of Journalism. Trout wrote Elmer F. Beth, secretary-treasurer, saying that the school was happy to accept the invitation.[32]

The third annual Industrial Editors Short Course, once again held on the Okmulgee campus, had been a success. Trout reported that thirty-five editors and six Oklahoma A. and M. students had attended and that, though the geographic spread was not as great as in the past, it was "still wide enough to give us a broad contact with editors."[33]

Meanwhile, the Oklahoma A. and M. *Journalist's Bulletin* had reached its fourth volume. Edited by John Hamilton, it had been started four years earlier by Donald D. Burchard "to keep students out in the field in summer jobs informed of what the department was doing and also to let the students know about each other." Hamilton predicted it would be

COURTESY JOHN HAMILTON

In the years 1947-1958, the Industrial Editors Short Course became a national success story. It had its meager beginnings on the Oklahoma A. and M. branch campus at Okmulgee. At the second annual short course, K. C. Pratt, a national leader in industrial editing from New York City, was the lead instructor.

a permanent part of the department's work, but he confessed that it had to be "worked in between other chores" and some alumni had been remiss in keeping in touch. Despite this, the publication was filled with news about Aggies in new jobs, weddings, births—in short, a miscellany that reaffirmed the success of the Department of Technical Journalism in educating students not only for print and broadcast news work, advertising, and public relations, but for life itself. Of particular note was an item about Matrix Table, sponsored by Theta Sigma Phi, which that year had attracted a statewide audience of 300 to hear the famed syndicated columnist Dorothy Thompson.[34]

In the past, Trout had prepared annual reports that covered both the Department of Publications and the Department of Technical Journalism. In 1949, at the request of Dean Schiller Scroggs, a separate annual report on the academic program had been prepared. In it, Trout covered department-sponsored meetings such as those of the Oklahoma Junior and Senior College Press Association, the annual Industrial Editors Short Course, the Oklahoma Agricultural Writers Association, and Professor James Stratton's summer clinic for high school journalism students and sponsors. In addition, he reported on the activities of Theta Sigma Phi and Sigma Delta Chi in bringing speakers to the campus, and departmental sponsorship of a convocation featuring Curtis MacDougall of Northwestern University, a noted author of journalism textbooks.

Trout detailed the offices held by faculty members, their judging activities, speeches given, and his own committee activities in industrial editing, various journalism education associations, and on the board of the newly formed American Public Relations Association. Departmental growth, he reported, had been steady: 1945-46, 140; 1946-47, 196; 1947-48, 187; 1948-49, 235. Fifty students had been graduated in the various journalism programs in 1949. The enrollment in service courses was up, and Trout expected it to continue high. With the large number of graduates and a decreasing enrollment in the freshman and sophomore years, Trout predicted that enrollment would drop unless lower-division totals increased.

As journalism numbers had increased, the old system of using most journalism teachers in publications department activities was fading. Trout wrote: "There are two departments, Technical Journalism and Editorial and Publicity, overlapping. . . . However, most of the staff is definitely assigned to one field or the other. Miss Elsie Shoemaker, James C. Stratton, Lemuel Groom and Dr. R. B. Eide devote practically all of their time to teaching. Occasionally they act as consultants on special problems. Mr. Hamilton usually works with a few students, and Mr. Caldwell does occasionally. The head of the department regularly does some teaching, handles some individual project students, and works on the promotion and editorial phases of the departments." Trout pointed out that, statistically speaking, the teaching load may not have seemed heavy, but that "so much of our work is of a laboratory nature [requiring] individual attention. . . . that our teachers are really handling at least a full load and probably devoting more than full-load time and effort." Trout confessed that his busy faculty was doing "very little research" and that scholarly publications were few and far between.

Concluding his report, he asked for additional office furniture and filing cabinets. "In our teaching, we would like to have some sort of sound recording equipment. . . . We could also use a reflectoscope type of slide machine and screen. We need very much to increase our equipment for printing laboratory work, but along with it must go increased space, and that is a part of the problem. Also, we need staff to offer any additional work. Twelve more typewriters are urgently needed for our laboratories, this is our most urgent equipment needed."[35]

That year, for President Bennett's benefit, Trout also prepared a separate fiscal-year report covering the Department of Editorial and Publicity as well as the academic program. The former covered activities ranging from news services to promotional materials, from the alumni magazine to special events, from the "Weekly Calendar" and "Official Bulletins" to the college catalog. One noteworthy statistic was that 9,116 home town stories about student achievements had gone out, averaging 30 a day for 300 working days and mentioning approximately 20,500 names. In the teaching section of the report, Trout reported that 1,402 students had enrolled in 53 classes, excluding summer school, and that fifty-seven had received degrees, including five graduate students.[36]

During the summer of 1949, innovation was in the air. Trout was adding special equipment to permit students to hear amplified telephone conversations in connection with reporting and news writing laboratories. This arrangement in Room 102, TF-8, opened the door for creative laboratory exercises stressing telephone interviewing techniques. At the same time, the department was planning for a series of professional convocations with attendance required of all journalism majors. The meetings would feature "outside speakers in the various communications media [discussing] vocational problems in their fields." The meetings were scheduled monthly except for January and would be held in Old Central.[37]

During the war years, the Oklahoma Junior and Senior College Press Association had met on the Okmulgee campus, but as the 1949-50 academic year opened, Trout had decided that expanded Oklahoma A. and M. facilities would permit its return to Stillwater. The delegates were housed and the meetings held in the short course center on West Sixth Street on October 14 and 15, and Trout judged the program to be successful, though attendance was down because of conflicting events at some of the member schools.[38]

After a summer as visiting professor at the University of Oklahoma, Eide opened his last year on the Oklahoma A. and M. faculty with a $500 salary boost. That fall he taught three junior-level classes and one senior-level class plus two 500-level graduate courses. He had a total of 113 students and estimated his Oklahoma A. and M. duties required 50 work hours weekly. He had completed two books, *Norway's Press 1940-1945* and *Formulas For Publishing*, both published privately. His professional obligations were increasing. He was secretary of the curriculum committee and its sub-committees, editor of the *Pi Gamma Mu News*, district governor of Toastmasters Club, had taken on committee work for the American Legion, and had agreed to serve as advisor to Alpha Tau Omega fraternity. He obviously had became well entrenched in both campus and community affairs.[39]

Postwar interest in journalism was growing. Upper-division enrollment continued to be up. In the spring, Eide had 33 enrolled in Journalism 342, Interpreting the News; 25 in 383, Community Editorial Problems; 47 in 462, Law of the Press; and 5 in a senior special problems course, 430. He was supervising the work of two graduate students as well. He had 119 students and was spending 45 hours a week—22 of them in paper grading and class participation—on his official duties. He also

Delegates to the 1950 Sigma Delta Chi convention in Miami, Florida, were (*left to right*) Charles Stiver, Gerald Eby, and Bill Baker. This photo was taken by Professor Claron Burnett around midnight in Tallahassee. "We drove straight through in a car provided by Gerald Eby's grandad," Burnett recalled. "We jumped around the capitol grounds to get the blood circulating before continuing to Miami Beach."

had added to his list of promising future professionals such names as Max Batchelder, Jack Lynch, Forrest Boaz, Bill Boykin, William Harmon, Robert McCulloh, James Reynolds, Steve Washenko, Peter DeFelice, William O'Donnell, Warren Shull, William Ward, and Joe Woolard.[40]

Once again, he traveled. In November he supervised journalism students at the national Sigma Delta Chi Convention in Milwaukee, conducted the annual conference of the Junior-Senior College Press Association at the branch campus in Okmulgee, and attended an OPA district meeting in Fairview. In May, he sought jobs for upcoming graduates at an OPA Advertising Clinic in Oklahoma City.[41]

Soon new opportunities beckoned. Eide resigned effective June 30, 1949, to organize a journalism major at Florida State University, the former state women's college in Tallahassee.[42]

Reviewing an earlier discussion about regular contacts with state newspapers, Trout wrote President Bennett suggesting that Oklahoma A. and M. take the lead in providing a series of training programs for rural correspondents. Tom Rucker, secretary of the state press association, was urging newspapers to hold such schools, and Trout and several faculty members had assisted the *Perry Journal* in one of the first. It had included, in addition to rural newspaper correspondents, reporters for the various extension clubs and 4-H and women's clubs. Trout called this "a part of the regular activity which the college and extension service should carry on."

In proposing that Oklahoma A. and M. College take the lead in assisting the Oklahoma Press Association, Trout told Bennett that he would need at least one additional staff member. Trout wrote that even if Eide's replacement could be found "our regular work will be too heavy to send someone out on these trips and visits regularly. . . . It seems to me our general promotion program has expanded smoothly and we are in better position to furnish more services than we have been. The question is how far to go and when."[43] Bennett may have expected Trout to answer such questions himself, but he rarely attempted to provide specific solutions.

Meanwhile, Trout had limped along with temporary graduate and undergraduate instructors while he looked for Eide's replacement. In March he hired Claron Burnett. Burnett had taken his degree in agricultural journalism at Oklahoma A. and M. College in 1942, then had gone into the Army with the Corps of Engineers. At war's end he had enrolled at the University of Wisconsin in the Department of Agricultural Journalism, earning his M.S. degree in 1947. For the next three years he had worked as an associate editor for the Olsen Publishing Company, specializing in trade papers for the dairy industry, before joining Trout's faculty in March of 1950. He was a valuable asset as a teacher and advisor, giving Trout the help he needed both in agricultural journalism and publications. He was well remembered at Wisconsin, and after four years in Stillwater was offered an associate professorship there. He resigned effective January 31, 1955. Meanwhile, the graduate courses had been rearranged to cover Eide's loss. Most of this responsibility had fallen upon Stratton and Trout.[44]

In his report to Dean Scroggs covering the 1949-50 academic year, Trout reported that the monthly convocations had been successful, as had the journalism-sponsored short courses. Enrollment of majors was down, but was growing in such service courses as Agricultural Journalism, Advanced Engineering Journalism, and Interpreting the News. Arts and sciences led in majors, with seventy, followed by commerce, agriculture, and home economics. Trout reported heavy committee and public service work by faculty, but no research. "This is the weakest spot in our entire set-up," Trout commented. The only research was being done by graduate students.

Once again Trout asked for more typewriters, more space, and additional equipment for the typography laboratory. He reiterated the need for recording and playback equipment for reporting laboratories and added his hope that an opaque projector might be provided. Such simple requests, reflected upon by students and faculty members during the Centennial Decade, would seem mundane in an age of computers, camcorders, electronic videotape editing stations, up-links and down-links, and a myriad of other devices for which words did not exist in 1950. In his fiscal-year report covering editorial and publicity work as well as the Department of Technical Journalism, Trout had summarized the teaching area with these figures: number of students in journalism classes, 1,242; number of bachelor's degrees, 59; number of master's degrees, 4.[45]

Another publishing trip, this one to the *Perry Journal*, had given journalism students a chance to produce a community daily. Publisher Milo Watson had written to commend Max Batchelder, Dorothy Harvey, Calvin Chick, Ann Trout, and Virginia McConnell, who had "unusually impressed" Watson and his staff. Graduate assistant Mark A. Clutter, who had been assigned to teach two junior-level courses—Community Reporting and Community Editorial Public Relations—supervised the students.[46]

In mid-summer, a police action in Korea soon became a deadly serious war. While it would mean that some students and faculty would be called to active duty, leaving others to speculate upon their own personal involvement in the months ahead, things on campus remained essentially unchanged. The impact of World War I and World War II had been tremendous. The Korean War, though costly in men and materiel, made hardly a ripple upon the campus. Things went on as usual. Whatever the crisis, whether local or national, Trout would not be deterred from his interest in professional development. At about this time, he took the initiative in getting a group of Tulsa-area public relations people together for lunch. That session later would lead to a Tulsa chapter of the Public Relations Society of America. In a campus-wide memorandum, Trout reported that during the past year more than 1,104 stories of college events and more than 14,200 hometown stories about Oklahoma A. and M. students had been sent to newspapers, magazines, and radio stations. Chester J. Frazier, who had earned B.S. and M.S. degrees in agricultural journalism at Oklahoma A. and M., was doing much of the news services work under John Hamilton, as were others in the publicity department.[47]

With the fall semester under way, Hamilton, editor of the *Journalist's Bulletin*, was beating the drums for journalism graduates to return for the big homecoming game with Missouri October 28. Everyone on campus was anxious to show off the college's magnificent new Student Union, and journalism had planned to set up a registration desk on the first floor. The nine-page *Bulletin*, as usual, was full of news about the busy lives of Aggie journalism graduates.[48]

By 1951, Trout had so firmly established himself as the leading authority on industrial journalism that his correspondence load was heavy. He received letters frequently from throughout the United States and some from Canada. These were full of questions about books that would help editors, ideas for meeting topics, use of symbols and slogans, and numerous other concerns. In each case, Trout would answer with suggestions, sometimes sending examples he had collected, at other times a bibliography or a personal experience that might fit the situation.[49]

By 1952, as Trout adjusted to Henry Bennett's tragic death in Iran and Oliver S. Willham's new presidency, his devotion to greater professionalism in industrial editing had begun to reap personal rewards. As the climax of the Industrial Editors Short Course that year, the Society of Associated Industrial Editors recognized its founder for his fifteen years as secretary. At a Clement E. Trout Appreciation Dinner, President Luther Williams, editor of *Sunray News*, praised him for his vision and foresight. SAIE president Charles Inglis gave Trout an impressive plaque. Engraved upon it was this message: "In Appreciation of Inspirational Service, Leadership and Vision Dedicated to Industrial Journalism and Industrial Communications The World Over." Governor Johnston Murray, through a member of his staff, certified him as a "Commodore in the Oklahoma Navy," and personal tribute was paid through hundreds of letters and telegrams mounted in a scrapbook and presented to Trout. One national trade magazine referred to him as the "grand old man of company publications."[50]

The surprise recognition by SAIE was followed by a fellowship at the

At a 1952 testimonial dinner, Donalene Young, an Oklahoma City editor, presented a scrapbook containing about 100 letters of appreciation from industrial editors throughout the United States to Clement E. Trout. The letters attested to Trout's role in the Society of Associated Industrial Editors (SAIE) in bringing greater professionalism to the field. Such honors and awards mounted in the next eight years.

Foundation for Economic Education, Irvington on Hudson, New York. In twenty-five years, Trout had rarely taken a vacation. The only extended period away from campus was for eight weeks of study at the University of Minnesota during the summer of 1941. The fellowship would be for six weeks at the United States Steel Corporation in Pittsburgh, where Trout would work in public relations and industrial communications. During his absence, John Hamilton, assistant college editor, was in charge of the editorial and publicity department and Professor Claron Burnett handled academic matters.[51]

Trout wrote to Dean Scroggs from Pittsburgh describing his fellowship duties and the beauties of the Blue Ridge Parkway he and Mrs. Trout had enjoyed en route to Pittsburgh. It was a challenging time for corporate communications. The mills were closed because of a national railway strike, necessitating changes in scheduling and a heavier work load, but he remarked, "It is a wonderful experience. We ask what we wish and usually get an answer that is satisfactory."[52]

Trout submitted an extensive report of his experiences at U.S. Steel to Scroggs, who said he intended to pass it on to President Willham. In the report, Trout commented upon communication channels and their effectiveness, showing a keen understanding of the communications process. It seemed obvious that the experience would be translated into more effective teaching.[53]

As Trout's academic duties demanded more and more of his time while his work in the industrial editing field continued to expand, he was wondering about a solution to his problem. Briefly put, he had never been able to get enough staff and budgetary support to keep pace with the growing responsibilities in his two departments. There are gaps in existing documents that would help to clarify what was happening, but a hint came in a letter to Vice President Randall T. Klemme. After discussing summer work plans, Trout said that "some permanent policy" concerning publicity and editing should be established. "Everyone is looking for a move and the problems of the present situation become greater. A clear allocation of responsibility with corresponding authority is necessary for any plan to be successful. . . . I have suggested a small committee to study plans and make recommendations. I am ready to help and cooperate in any action taken."[54] While it is difficult to be certain, based upon available documentation, this may have been one of the first steps leading to a major reorganization in 1954 that would free Trout to concentrate upon academic responsibilities while giving up his publicity and publications duties.

A summer action that may have seemed routine was the appointment of Dorothy Rickstrew to assist with secretarial duties during June, July, and August. As OSU celebrated its 100th anniversary in 1990, Dorothy Rickstrew Nixon was still at work, having served during five administrations in the School of Journalism and Broadcasting. Few individuals have given the institution such longevity and loyalty.[55]

In August, another honor came Trout's way. He was named "Communications Man of the Month" by *Industrial Marketing* magazine, and in October he was re-elected secretary of the SAIE at its national meeting in Carlsbad, New Mexico. The famous typographer, Otto Forkert, was on the program, and Trout's friendship with him led to important acquisitions by the Edmon Low Library later, including a skillfully reproduced copy of the Gutenberg Bible and books and manuscripts on typography.[56]

As the first semester of the 1952-53 academic year neared its end, Trout found himself in a minor skirmish over territorial rights. The Oklahoma Institute of Technology had prepared a certificate for students who had worked on the *Oklahoma Engineer* magazine. It was to be signed by the president, dean of engineering, and faculty advisor to the *Engineer*, certifying that the recipient had attained "Highest Proficiency in the Field of Journalism." Presumably the student had studied and mastered story content, magazine layout, business organization, photography and art. Trout protested to Dean Scroggs that "in most, if not all cases," the students had had no more than a two-credit course devoted to work on the magazine and that the instructor and magazine supervisor had not been trained in the fields mentioned. He feared the certificate would be confused in job contacts with the comprehensive training offered in the Department of Technical Journalism. Trout requested that the certificate be modified to eliminate the possibility that it might be mistaken for certification or training in the field of journalism.[57]

A more pleasant matter helped to balance his concern over the engineering transgression. Trout no doubt chuckled at a letter from William A. Sumner, one of his favorite professors during his student days at Wisconsin. "Seems like I can hardly pick up a magazine in the industrial and printing trades this year without finding your face smiling out at me. . . . Business publications. . . . are certainly recognizing the good work you have done with them."[58]

With the meeting more than a year away, Oklahoma A. and M. was looking forward to the 1954 Southwestern Journalism Congress. The journalism faculty and students would be hosts to the thirteen-member organization which had played an important role in its four-state area since the middle twenties. Trout figured $500 above the budget for non-hosting years would be needed, mainly for outside speakers. Before attending the 1953 Congress, he wanted definite assurance of the administration's support.[59]

The next big event on the agenda was the seventh annual Industrial Editors Short Course, combined with the second Alumni Editors Short Course, March 23-28, 1953. The four-and-a-half-million-dollar Student Union Hotel was to be used, with single rooms at $4.25 up. Fifty-seven editors registered plus four guests, the short-course staff of seven, nine members of the Oklahoma A. and M. staff, and twelve journalism students. Sixteen firms were represented for the second time or more, strong evidence of the value of the program. The short course had wide coverage in the trade press. It had paid out, not only in income but in the recognition it brought to Oklahoma A. and M. as the leader in this field.[60]

As the spring semester moved along, Trout was involved in his usual round of meetings, speeches, articles. A source of good news was money contributed for four industrial editing scholarships. Donors were the McCormick-Armstrong Company, Wichita; R. C. Walker of Southwestern Engraving Company, Tulsa; Semco Color Press, Oklahoma City; and Harry Turner and Associates, Topeka. Two of the scholarships were for four years, two for one year. Plans were going forward on the summer high school short course, the 1954 short course for industrial editors and a clinic "on agriculture and its place" in the news stream. Stratton would handle the high school clinic, Burnett the agricultural meeting and, as usual, Trout the annual industrial editing course.[61]

Trout returned from the ICIE and SAIE conventions with news that overshadowed his continuation on both boards, his committee involvements, and other duties. In a report that went to Dean Scroggs and, probably, to President Willham as well, he stated: "Through Mr. Low and the Library, we offered. . .the facilities of the library as a depository for [ICIE] records, ICIE to furnish storage equipment and pay for maintaining the files and catalog listing. This was accepted, so we are the historical center for ICIE. They also set up some money to pay for a trial of a loan reference library. Material which they possess and other which we have, will be cataloged and made available on loan to editors. . . . This will make us an international center of information on industrial editing with practically no cost to us. It will also enable us to catalog our material. This committee was also authorized to use some funds to underwrite expenses of graduate theses in. . .industrial editing. . . ."[62]

During the summer, Trout was asked by the U. S. Steel Corporation to prepare some brochures. He requested a leave of absence to accept the assignment, with Burnett to "act as head of the Departments of Technical Journalism and Publications while I am gone."

This news, plus Trout's report on the industrial editing conventions, had brought a glowing response from Dean Scroggs congratulating him on the "substantial achievements which you have accomplished both for the College and for the field of journalism. . .It is good to know that we have on our staff one who so ably and consistently establishes himself as a leader in his field."[63]

All of the above suggests an academic department serving needs at home and reaching out to be of service both in its primary area and nationally. Such events were building a name for Oklahoma A. and M. journalism, but the biggest news of the year came shortly after the end of

COURTESY JOHN HAMILTON

An important feature of journalism instruction in the 1940s was the emphasis upon practical, hands-on experience. Publishing trips were taken to various towns, where Oklahoma A. and M. students would spend several days writing the news and selling the advertising for community newspapers. Student staff members on this trip listen to a critique by Gordon Rockett, editor of the *Drumright Derrick*. Faculty members in the background are James C. Stratton and John Hamilton.

the second semester. It was the tip of the iceberg, but a portent of a major reorganization in the public information area that would come a few months later. Trout's letter to Edward L. Morrison in the president's office revealed the first part of the plan, a plan which Trout called the "most logical," noting that he had helped work it out and had recommended it. For a year there had been no money allocated to arts and sciences for editorial work. Trout's department had handled publications on a time sheet maintained in the president's pffice. Now the publications work would be part of the printing department under John Hamilton, who had worked closely with Trout for ten years.[64]

A little over a month later, while Trout was on leave at U.S. Steel, Scroggs wrote a seemingly routine letter with a big final paragraph. He told of "quite a flood here—five and a half inches of rain in about an afternoon." It had flooded the sub-basement of the library. He spoke of summer pay details for Burnett, Stratton, and Robert McCulloh, and that he hoped Trout was enjoying his work in Pittsburgh. Then: "By the way, the President has indicated that he eventually contemplates complete separation between the editorial and publicity and the journalism work. The editorial and publicity budget has been withdrawn completely from the Arts and Sciences budget and is being handled somewhere else."[65]

For nearly three decades Trout had been the pivotal figure in Oklahoma A. and M. public relations work. Now the college's expanding enrollment and the more complex administrative structure that had evolved called for a new look at Trout's duties, not the least of which was his responsibility for the growing academic programs in journalism.

A committee was formed to study the consolidation of all information agencies on campus. After several meetings, Randall Klemme, vice president for agricultural and industrial development, prepared a statement based upon the discussions. It would be the basis for a proposal to be presented to President Willham. Welden Barnes, secretary to the president, circulated the statement to all committee members with a request for revisions. Another meeting was called for June 23 in the Student Union. Members would consider proposed revisions, which Barnes had circulated with a memorandum calling the meeting. After the revised proposal had been studied by an ad hoc committee, President Willham announced a plan to consolidate the six separate college information offices into one division under the directorship of Barnes, a well-qualified journalist with experience in both print and broadcast media as well as public relations. The new plan called for Edd Lemons, who had directed extension information, to head agricultural public information activities, with George F. Church, experiment station editor, as editor of agricultural sciences. McCulloh would continue his responsibility for general college news. The Oklahoma A. and M. regents had approved the reorganization, which would become effective January 1,

1954. Willham wrote that the purpose was "to coordinate and improve. . .existing public information services." He said all public information employees would be retained. Barnes continued in the president's office until his replacement was named, then opened his new office in the basement of the Classroom Building in April 1954. In the reorganization, Barnes's consolidated administrative unit became one of several non-academic divisions of the university.

The work of the division consisted of the duties and responsibilities carried on previously by several separate offices at the university, including the General University News Bureau, the Office of the Agricultural Experiment Station Editor, the Office of the Agricultural Extension Editor, the Office of the Agricultural Radio and Television Specialist, the General University Radio and Television Services, the Office of Extension Visual Aids, the Office of Alumni Publications, and the Office of Athletic Publicity.[66]

Trout probably was ambivalent about the reorganization. He had been "the Big Fish" while heading his multifaceted activities as college editor, head of the Department of Publications (later Editorial and Publicity), and head of the Department of Technical Journalism. He was overworked, but a central figure on campus. His workload had become more realistic with the recent changes, but his ego may have been bruised. He had been proud of his titles. Now he raised a question with President Willham: "Would it be in line with administrative procedure and policy to designate the 'emeritus' status for these titles which no longer represent my responsibilities. I would like to have some recognition of my service in these positions on the continuing record. . . . The titles Professor of Journalism and Head of the Department of Technical Journalism would continue as the active designations."[67] The emeritus titles apparently were not approved, for they were not used.

The reorganization of public information at Oklahoma A. and M. was not without problems. Dean Scroggs related one of these to President Willham: "The separation of the joint department into Publicity under Mr. Barnes and Technical Journalism under Professor Trout leaves our relations with SAIE stranded. They are not of any immediate concern to Publicity in its new orientation, neither are they directly related to classroom instruction." Scroggs reasoned, however, that Trout's ties with major industries through his industrial editing short courses were of "large value" to the college. The solution was a small direct addition to the maintenance budget of the School of Arts and Sciences.[68]

Now Trout was free to concentrate upon the academic program and his continuing love affair with industrial editing. In building the graduate program, he had requested funds from the Graduate School for the fiscal year 1954-55. Dean Robert W. MacVicar had responded that funds were limited, and that Trout should consult with Dean Scroggs in seeking to add graduate teaching assistants from the Arts and Sciences budget. MacVicar urged Trout to reapply for support the following year, presumably after a stronger commitment to graduate work had been shown by journalism.[69]

It was a year of meetings. The Department of Technical Journalism and the School of Commerce, along with Associated Industries of Oklahoma and the National Association of Manufacturers (NAM), co-sponsored a conference on industrial communication. Among the twenty-six participants was C. Ellsworth Chunn, education director for the NAM, who four years later would replace Trout as the guiding hand in journalism at what by then would be Oklahoma State University. Soon after, another major meeting was held. Oklahoma A. and M. had played host in 1938 to the Southwestern Journalism Congress. Now it was time once more, on a rotation plan, for the congress to meet in Stillwater. Trout received approval from Dean Scroggs for all journalism students to be excused March 19 and 20 to participate in the meetings.[70]

Space on the second floor of TF-8 had become available and journalism was able to take over Rooms 210 and 211, providing more suitable space for previously cramped news writing and editing laboratories. In addition, with the college news service moving, Trout was able to assign two additional rooms on the first floor to academic use. He also recommended that Room 212 be continued as the *Agriculturist* office. These changes would be favorable for the re-accreditation visit that would be scheduled in coming months.[71]

Soon after he had appeared on an SAIE program in Kansas City, Trout wrote President Willham about a problem that had persisted too long: unrealistic catalog listings. He asked Willham for "a clarification of policy and instructions for guidance." The instructional staff at that time actually consisted of Trout, Stratton, Lemuel D. Groom, and Elsie Shoemaker. Yet the catalog under instructional staff in journalism had included Richard Caldwell, Hamilton, and Church.

"None of these men," Trout pointed out, "have done any teaching for some time. Mr. Church was a major instructor at one time, but has handled no course work for more than ten years. Mr. Hamilton did some teaching and was related to Journalism until his transfer to his present position a year ago. Mr. Caldwell taught one course for one or two semesters some ten years ago." Trout believed that these false listings had given the impression that journalism was adequately staffed, when the contrary was true. In addition, "these non-teachers have increased the number of higher ranking staff members, [inhibiting promotions]." Complicating matters further, Elmer Woodson, director of student publications, felt that he deserved faculty rank in journalism. If he were given academic rank, he would add to the apparent staff. Asking for a policy clarification, Trout stated: "If it is the policy to give academic rank to individuals in administrative work related to instruction, [Woodson] would deserve consideration. However, adding him to the ranks would increase the problem of building and promoting the actual instructional staff. . .I will appreciate your. . .instructions as to policy for the Department of Technical Journalism as we strengthen the instructional work."

Why the first problem, that of misleading catalog listings, was not handled by Trout directly is not clear. As college editor, he had been responsible for the catalog. As to the second problem, no response by President Willham was found in School of Journalism and Broadcasting files. That fact notwithstanding, Woodson was not given an academic title, but subsequent catalogs resolved Trout's other concern.[72]

Toward the end of Trout's academic career, Oklahoma A. and M. was scheduled to be reexamined for accreditation by the American Council on Education for Journalism. He had visited with Walter Wilcox, the council's executive secretary, in Chicago, and Wilcox had asked that Trout send him "a more definite purpose" for the college's journalism work. Wilcox's background in journalism education had been general rather than specialized. It was not uncommon for those unfamiliar with land-grant institutions to be mystified by such terms as "agricultural journalism" and "industrial editing." Responding to Wilcox's request, Trout wrote a three-page, single-spaced letter presenting the rationale for the Oklahoma A. and M. programs. He indicated he would ask for accreditation in four sequences: agricultural, home economics, and community journalism, and industrial editing. The degree program in industrial editing had been created after the council's 1947 visit.[73]

As the accreditation picture came into focus once more, Trout was dealing with Ira W. "Bill" Cole, who had replaced Wilcox as the ACEJ contact. Cole had suggested a re-accreditation visit for the fall of 1954. Trout responded that Oklahoma A. and M. was working on plans to strengthen the advertising curriculum and to set up some work in radio and television. "There will probably be some reorganization of the department," he wrote, suggesting that the ACEJ visit be postponed for a year. By then, he believed, "we will know for sure about the strength of these courses and any changes."[74]

In preparation for re-accreditation, Trout had asked for one additional staff member "to bring our offerings into balance." He said work needed to be offered in photography, advanced typography, and radio and television. "We have practically nothing in these fields," he wrote. In addition, he requested $1,000 to equip a type laboratory. Oklahoma A. and M. had been criticized in the original accreditation visit for inadequate typography facilities and these had not been upgraded in the past seven years. The request certainly was modest. Trout predicted it would provide minimum equipment "for the most elementary work" often or twelve laboratory students.[75]

Wandalee Hinkle and Jim Reynolds "ham it up" in front of a prop used for an event sponsored by journalism students. Both were among the most talented *O'Collegian* staff members following World War II.

When he submitted his yearly Faculty Record report in November, Trout once more appeared to be one of the college's busiest administrators. He was on four campus and seven off-campus committees, had spoken on programs in Albuquerque and Kansas City, had attended six major off-campus meetings or conventions, sponsored three major meetings on campus, served on two church boards, continued as secretary of SAIE, and was an active member of ten professional organizations.

Trout had been among the college's senior department heads for years but had gone largely unrewarded. His salary had lagged to "a bottom position for that group." Dean Scroggs sought corrective action. Trout's pay was raised to $5,900 for ten months plus $1,180 for the summer months.[76]

As the second semester was getting under way, Trout once more was making adjustments in personnel. Donald Burchard had resigned, but it was too late to replace him with a permanent faculty member. Trout would make do with graduate assistants. Meanwhile, he was in touch with a man he was considering as Burchard's replacement in the fall. "I have been considering a man who is interested in industrial editing," he wrote Jess Covington at Louisiana Tech State College. "I will be coming up for retirement some of these days. . . . When I leave, there will be a question of how to keep our specialized programs going." Trout was looking for someone who could gradually take over his leadership in the national industrial editing organizations. Covington had the potential, Trout believed. Covington never came to Oklahoma A. and M. As it turned out, however, Trout continued his work on the national scene until his death. No one ever truly assumed his leadership in education for industrial editing.[77]

In March, shortly before the ninth annual short course for industrial editors, Trout had written Ira Cole once more. He intended, he said, to ask for re-accreditation in the same sequences as before. "From the developments in view, we would prefer a visit in 1956-57. However, we might consider a visit next year."[78]

Trout had been widely recognized in trade and industrial publications for fifteen years. In April 1955 he gained a national mainstream journalism audience for his missionary work in industrial editing with a major article in *Quill* magazine. *Quill*, in identifying him, cited him for pioneering "classroom training in journalistic specialties."[79]

Now that he was giving more attention to the academic program and was less distracted by his earlier duties, Trout began to recognize that the many activities of his department were cutting into the teaching time of the faculty. One by one Trout recited the faculty's involvements that "take a considerable amount of time. . .and increase the problem of adequate handling of [teaching] responsibilities." It was not easy to pull away from some of these involvements. For example, the state professional chapter of Sigma Delta Chi in Oklahoma City had been organized "at the instigation of our College chapter and our staff members," Trout wrote Dean Scroggs, "and we feel we should carry responsibility." Claron Burnett had been secretary of the state professional chapter, and with his departure that role had been filled by George Church, who would not want to carry the responsibility permanently. Item by item—from supervision of the *Agriculturist* to sponsorship of the campus chapters of Sigma Delta Chi and Theta Sigma Phi, from the short courses to sponsorship of the Oklahoma Collegiate Press Association, which had been continuous for twenty-eight years—Trout recited the pressures upon his faculty. He recited the campus involvements in Varsity Revue and Matrix Table and the off-campus participation in the Oklahoma Press Association and the time he was giving to the two national industrial editing groups. Then, as was his custom, he raised a question for those above him which called for a more definite recommendation of his own. Referring to his work with ICIE and SAIE, he wrote: "We have built a world wide reputation through these activities but in setting up a staff and a budget for the Department, they need to be taken in consideration. Should we continue to put in the time, the effort and finances that are necessary to keep up this work?" During Trout's time, none of these activities diminished. It is doubtful that any major budgetary adjustments were made as a result of his having raised such issues without recommending a course of action. The journalism and broadcasting faculty years later seemed similarly committed to such ancillary activities. Reduced teaching loads rarely were made to accommodate the extra time spent keeping the various service activities vibrant and alive in the eyes of interested groups on campus and off.[80]

It is unclear how much thinking Trout had given the future of journalism at Oklahoma A. and M. once he was ready to retire. Apparently he had been increasingly concerned as he saw television developing rapidly both in academic programs and campus facilities at schools such as Michigan State University, the University of Illinois, the University of Florida and Stanford University. He had called upon one of the academic visionaries in television, William K. Cumming, for advice. Cumming was television producer-coordinator at WKAR-TV, Michigan State, with faculty duties in the Department of Journalism. He had looked at Oklahoma A. and M.'s possibilities and had given Trout rough cost estimates on equipment and facilities, excluding renovations, air conditioning, and office equipment. He also provided an elaborate plan for campus-wide interfacing in communications activities and a schematic diagram for the organization of a proposed School of Journalism and Communications at Oklahoma A. and M. Whether Cumming's five-page letter to Trout was shared with the administration and played a role three years later in the formation of the School of Communications under Ellsworth Chunn is not known. Apparently Trout had been primarily interested in bringing Cumming in for a television workshop that would complement the Industrial Editors Short Course. There is a hint, however, that Trout may have hoped to add Cumming to his faculty. Cumming was considering a move to Stephens College. "Before I make a final decision," he wrote, "I shall phone you long distance."[81] Cumming later accepted the Stephens offer.

As Oklahoma A. and M. increased its international involvements, Trout saw an opportunity for journalism to have a small part in such outreach. He suggested that the college offer a number of guest scholarships, perhaps one to a nation, "to assist and encourage international attendance at our short course." Dean Scroggs liked the idea, and suggested to President Willham that, should he approve the project, the invitations be written over Willham's signature. If the idea was implemented, there is no evidence that it was reflected in later short course registrations.[82]

As the 1955-56 academic year opened, Trout still had not found a permanent replacement for Claron Burnett, who had joined the Department of Agricultural Journalism at the University of Wisconsin. He had written the USDA for suggestions. Louis Hawkins, experiment station director, wanted Trout to develop a research program in agricultural communications. Now Trout was looking for Burnett's replacement in agricultural journalism at the undergraduate level plus another person to teach at the graduate level and direct a research program for Hawkins.[83]

The move by Hawkins suggested a growing recognition of graduate work in journalism, a feeling also reflected by the department in gradually adding graduate courses to its work. The latest addition was a course in General Semantics taught by Professor Stratton. In its first semester it was listed as Journalism 493, but Trout quickly recognized that it appealed most to graduate students and a few advanced seniors. His petition to renumber the course 593 was approved. Stratton was well read in the field and had developed a strong interest in it. A few of the class projects in General Semantics still exist. They reflect a well-taught course with rigorous standards.[84]

In early 1956, Trout spoke to a clinic of trade association magazine editors in Chicago and used the trip to confer with Dean Kenneth E. Olson of the Medill School of Journalism at Northwestern University. He was serving as chairman of special sequences for the Association for Education in Journalism and would appear on that group's convention program during the summer. At Northwestern he also observed the use of closed circuit television in Professor Baskett Mosse's laboratory. On his way home he stopped at Ames, Iowa, to study both the operation of the Iowa State University Press and the work of Ben King in the use of television to teach chemistry. Trout began to see possibilities for science instruction at Oklahoma A. and M. with the equipment used for television news instruction as well.[85] This was typical of early thinking about the multi-purpose use of television equipment on campus, but later would be found to be unrealistic.

At about that time, Associated Business Publications invited Oklahoma A. and M. to associate membership, largely on the basis of its work in industrial editing. Other early associate members were the University of Minnesota, University of Missouri, Montana State University, Northwestern University, Syracuse University, and the University of Wisconsin.[86]

Trout was still looking for someone to teach agricultural journalism and to work on experiment station research. Instead of two positions, he had scaled down his search to one faculty member who would handle both undergraduate and graduate courses as well as research. He made an offer to Eldon M. Drake at Utah State, but Drake declined. Following this attempt, Trout turned to a puckish, balding forty-six-year-old bachelor who had had the kind of experience that would meet both technical journalism's needs and Hawkins's research requirements. Maurice R. Haag was a 1938 agricultural journalism graduate of the University of

Loftin Mann, co-director of the 1948 Varsity Revue, takes a break from rehearsals in front of a mock-up of a newspaper page used to promote the show, co-sponsored by the two professional journalism societies, Sigma Delta Chi and Theta Sigma Phi. Mann was active on the *Aggievator*, the campus humor magazine.

Wisconsin. After twenty-two months as assistant extension editor at Wisconsin, he had served forty-one months in the Army—including two and a half years in French Morocco and Algeria—rising from private to staff sergeant. Following the war he became experiment station editor at the University of Wyoming. After two years he moved on to the American Society of Agronomy, where he served for twelve years as editor of technical publications before moving to OSU in January 1957 as an associate professor.

For Trout, this was a triumph of patience. He had followed Haag's career for years and had sought to hire him on several occasions. Haag would become a popular leader of the agricultural journalism program and a friend and advisor of students. His office was in the Communications Building, where he was a fully accepted colleague, but he was well known and appreciated in both the College of Agriculture and the experiment station. From 1957 to 1962 he was faculty advisor to Sigma Delta Chi and, in that role, supervised Varsity Revue. He was founder of, and advisor to, the Agricultural Journalism Club. Despite these involvements, he gave Hawkins the research he wanted.[87]

The tenth annual short course for industrial editors had been successful. Forty-six editors registered to hear the views of seven instructors, including three of national stature. Promotion pieces went to 8,000 editors and about twelve trade journals carried articles announcing it.

The result was the widest geographic distribution of participants in the course's history.[88]

For months Trout had appealed to Earle C. Albright, assistant to President Willham, for fresh paint, inside and out, at TF-8. He knew the building would be used for at least two more years and wanted it spruced up before the next accreditation visit. He tried once more shortly before he would attend a Los Angeles meeting of the ICIE and then go to Honolulu to speak to an employee communications conference sponsored by the Hawaii Employers Council. Trout told Albright that students resented the surroundings and faculty members felt the department was losing students because of the building's run-down condition.[89] There may have been legitimate reasons for the delays, but they were not discovered in existing files.

Trout's honors continued to mount. The most recent—an award for twenty-five years of service to the American Association of Agricultural College Editors—brought a letter of praise from President Willham. Trout's recognition would continue to add up as he neared retirement.[90]

With the fall semester under way, he was off to Chicago to work on a constitutional amendment for the ICIE that would lead to the dissolution of his beloved SAIE. Shortly after, he reported to President Willham that the organization he had nurtured since 1938—now with approximately 700 members scattered over twenty-four states—had voted at its convention in Dallas to dissolve. It had been a major influence in the development of the International Council of Industrial Editors. The SAIE directors expressed their appreciation to Oklahoma A. and M. for its sponsorship and then voted to present the college an emblem as permanent recognition of its service. Trout's eighteen years as secretary had ended. No other person had filled the office.[91]

Once more, as 1956 neared its end, Trout was asking Albright for fresh paint for the war surplus barracks journalism had occupied since 1947. "We feel we are not asking too much," he wrote, reminding Albright that an accreditation visit was upcoming.[92]

Trout was due to retire under college policy on July 1, 1957, but Dean Scroggs had asked that he stay on for an additional year. After discussing the matter with various faculty members, Willham approved Scroggs's request. Trout would be at the helm as journalism faced an accreditation inspection once more. The months leading up to accreditation were busy ones. Trout continued his committee work with ICIE and appeared on various programs, frequently receiving formal recognition for his leadership. The Oklahoma Collegiate Press Association cited him for thirty years of devoted and constructive sponsorship. Next came new accolades to Trout from the recently dissolved SAIE, with that group's last president presenting a plaque to President Willham before an audience of about 2,000 at the 1957 Varsity Revue. The plaque read: "In appreciation to the Oklahoma A. and M. College for excellent service to Industrial Editing and its professional organization. SAIE 1938-1956." In addition, the Industrial Editors Short Course had been a resounding success with fifty-nine on its roster and outstanding instruction from such national figures as Otto M. Forkert, the famous Chicago typographer, and H. B. Bachrach, General Electric Company public relations leader from New York.[93]

All of this was well and good, but the big news of 1957 was the re-accreditation of Oklahoma A. and M. College journalism. Its sequences in agricultural, home economics, and community journalism had been accredited for a second time, while the industrial editing program had been newly accredited. John E. Stempel, ACEJ secretary-treasurer, requested that no local publicity be released prior to the general release of the accredited list. The visiting team had included Burton Marvin, University of Kansas, chairman; Lewis H. Rohrbaugh, provost, University of Arkansas, generalist; Lester G. Benz, State University of Iowa; Donald D. Burchard, Texas A. and M. College; Raymond H. Gilkeson, editor, Capper Publications, Inc., Topeka; Robert S. Gillespie, supervisor of employee publications, Sandia Corporation, Albuquerque; and Helen Hostetter, Kansas State College. They had visited Oklahoma A. and M. on January 7 and 8; Stempel's covering letter for the visitation report was dated May 21, 1957.

The program was rated median high in agricultural journalism, community journalism, industrial editing, and service to the profession. Home economics journalism received a median rating, as did administration. The faculty rating was divided, with three median ratings and three median low, the latter based upon insufficient professional experience. Research, housing, and facilities were rated low. The visitors described administration within the department as "loose and passive." Student, alumni, and placement records were incomplete, the visitors believed, calling for more careful and continuous record keeping. Also criticized was the lack of a central file of course outlines. In some cases, no course outlines existed at all. Students noted that faculty members were involved in other jobs and service activities "to the point where office hours were few." The visitors observed that teaching loads were heavy and "topped off by a rather large service load for a faculty as small as this one." They suggested a "tightening up" of administrative policies and procedures.

The committee also cautioned against the overload of outside activities by some faculty members. It recommended that an additional full-time faculty member replace some of the part-time help being used.[94]

Shortly after the accreditation challenge had been met, the Oklahoma Legislature passed a bill authorizing the Board of Regents for A. and M. Colleges to give Oklahoma A. and M. a new name: Oklahoma State

University of Agriculture and Applied Science. The goal of a new name in the early 1920s—Oklahoma State College—was never achieved. Now, a shortened version of the official new name, Oklahoma State University, was in common use almost overnight.[95]

Meanwhile, the honors continued to pile up for Trout, despite the fact that the accreditation team had faulted him, albeit indirectly, for diverting too much administrative time to his widespread participation in industrial editing matters. At Toots Shor's famous New York restaurant, the House Magazine Institute Award was given to Trout—a plain, unsophisticated man from small-town Oklahoma—as 350 New York City and area editors applauded. Two recent winners had been *Fortune* magazine and Standard Oil of New Jersey. Trout was the second individual honoree in the award's history. Mrs. Ludel B. Sauvageot had written President Willham praising Trout's service on the President's Advisory Committee and congratulating the university on having the nation's first accredited industrial editing sequence.[96]

On May 17, Gerald T. Curtin, an Aggie alumnus, had written Dean Schiller Scroggs, enclosing a copy of OPA President George Hill's letter setting up a committee under Curtin to offer assistance to Oklahoma A. and M. journalism. Curtin requested a luncheon meeting on campus for May 25. Scroggs thanked Curtin by letter and said he would attend. Curtin, editor of the *Watonga Republican*, chaired the meeting. Committee members attending were Gareth Muchmore, *Ponca City News*; Jim Pate, *Madill Record*; and Marsden Bellatti, *Stillwater NewsPress*. Absent were Bob Breeden, *Cleveland American*, and Wheeler Mayo, *Sequoyah County Times*. Dean Scroggs represented the college, and Trout, Lemuel Groom, Maurice Haag, Elsie Shoemaker, James Stratton, and Elmer Woodson represented OSU journalism. The meeting was exploratory in nature. Curtin expressed concern over the increasing shortage of trained journalists because of decreasing journalism enrollment at Oklahoma A. and M. and other schools. Various reasons for the drop were discussed. Early in the discussion, organizational structure was mentioned. Should Oklahoma A. and M. have a department or a school of journalism? Scroggs said this question would require "a long look" by the administration. He did not close the door on a change in name. Trout explained the department's structure and budgeting, and various faculty members described their responsibilities. Before the meeting ended, a preliminary two-part resolution had been adopted.[97]

Trout sent a copy of the minutes to Curtin and promised to send other materials he had requested. He told Curtin he had reported to President Willham on the meeting and that Willham had asked for a statement on space needs, both minimum and desirable, and had wanted an appraisal of employment opportunities in newspaper work. Could Trout and others go to work wholeheartedly on that aspect of the problem? Trout told the president, "We can."[98]

Five weeks later, Trout prepared a space report. He said the minimum space requirement, without expansion of the journalism program, would be 1,100 square feet for radio and photography laboratories, plus space for typography, news and editing laboratories, and a reading room. Space needed in the near future, he said, would include nine offices, two typography and two news laboratories, and one editing and one layout laboratory. A 500 square foot work room, a reading room of 1,000 square feet, two or three classrooms, an auditorium seating 100, a photography laboratory of 3,000 square feet, and radio and TV labs and offices totalling 5,000 square feet were on his "desirable" space list. "This does not provide for student publications offices with an editing room and production space," he wrote. Scroggs forwarded Trout's space report to Vice President MacVicar, calling it a fair estimate of space needs. He suggested "more adequate attention to the requirements of the department in all ways, but better housing is becoming a major consideration."[99]

Trout attended the ICIE convention in Boston, then stopped overnight in Tulsa before going to Sequoyah State Park for the mid-summer OPA meeting. At that meeting, Curtin reported on the earlier luncheon meeting in Stillwater. Trout gave Scroggs details on the OPA meeting, saying a strong resolution had been presented by Curtin's committee urging the boards of regents involved to "strengthen both the physical situation and the prestige of the department." The resolution was adopted unanimously "with many expressions of approval," including that of Fayette Copeland, director of the School of Journalism at the University of Oklahoma. Trout called the action "a significant step forward for our work."[100]

The OPA's five-part prescription for building interest in OSU journalism included backing for the summer high school short course offered by Stratton, encouragement of high school journalism instruction throughout the state, a speakers program stressing the satisfactions of the profession, creation of a summer program of internships on state newspapers, and a general effort to increase participation in journalistic studies. The earlier resolution had been reworded: "Be it resolved that, the Oklahoma Press Association hereby goes on record requesting the Oklahoma State Regents for Higher Education to assist in this program by providing for better housing and status for Journalism at Oklahoma State University and that the Oklahoma Press Association hereby approves and endorses the recommendations set out in the Committee Report." The document was signed by Curtin.[101]

Three days later, a major front page story in the *O'Collegian* reported on the OPA action. Another page one story reported that seventeen high school students and their journalism sponsors would meet for a week of instruction in the Classroom Building. One day would be devoted to yearbooks and six to newspapers. The *O'Collegian* went all out. In a strongly worded editorial of approximately 420 words, the editorial staff criticized the administration for laxity in its support of journalism, pointing out that $460,000 in state funds plus $100,000 in savings accumulated over twenty-seven years by student publications and $41,000 contributed by editors was making a modern journalism building possible at the University of Oklahoma. TF-8 and the ancient dairy building occupied by student publications should have been condemned years ago, the editorial stated, describing them as a disgrace to both journalism and the university.[102]

Trout's report on his trip to Boston for the ICIE's annual convention gave the first indication of the success of the group's Resource and Reference Library housed at OSU. "This library brings 700 to 800 personal requests for help and information on industrial editing each year," Trout wrote. "It also provides us with copies of all [industrial editing materials] ICIE can accumulate." Trout pointed out that OSU classes had access to the library and that requests had come from Europe and Australia as well as Canada and the United States.[103]

With the fall semester of his last academic year under way, Trout was still depending upon part-time faculty. But one part-timer was participating in an innovative venture with Trout. Kenneth Weaver, a *NewsPress* editor, was lecturing one hour a week and working with a group of OSU

Even in retirement, Clement E. Trout continued advancing the professionalism of industrial editing. To do this, he founded and published the monthly *Trout's Communication Research Reports*. The publication, off to a promising start in 1959, ended with his death in 1960.

journalism students on the downtown paper. Weaver and Trout had tried the idea out with a small group the previous year. The idea was popular and more students were participating. Trout told Scroggs that Weaver was "doing a full two credits and more."[104]

Trout's Faculty Report for September 1, 1956 to September 1, 1957, showed the usual crowding of events into his schedule. It included his most recent honors, of course, including his appointment as an editorial adviser to *Industrial Editor* magazine.[105]

Dean Scroggs no doubt had visited with Trout on more than one occasion about Trout's upcoming retirement, probably asking if he had anyone in mind as a possible successor. On September 23, 1957, the farm-bred Illinois journalist put his suggestions in writing. Without seeming to strongly favor one over another, he suggested three men "who might be considered for the headship of the Department of Technical Journalism." Two of them—Albert A. Sutton and Baskett Mosse—were on the faculty of the highly rated Medill School of Journalism at Northwestern University. Both had Oklahoma ties. Sutton, well known for his work in photography, typography, and newspaper design, had been on the OU journalism faculty from 1937 to 1940. Mosse, a University of Tulsa graduate, had worked four years under B. A. Bridgewater on the *Tulsa World* sports desk before earning the M.S.J. degree at Northwestern. From 1941 to 1945 he had been a writer-editor in the NBC Newsroom in Chicago. Medill Dean Kenneth E. Olson had asked Mosse to teach a radio news course, which soon developed into a full-scale sequence in radio and television news. Among such programs, it was generally considered to be one of the best, if not the best, in the country. Trout saw Mosse's broadcasting expertise atop a newspaper career as a solid plus.

The third name suggested was that of Robert S. Gillespie, employee publications supervisor for the Sandia Corporation, Albuquerque, New Mexico. Gillespie had taken the B.S. in journalism at Illinois and the M.S. at the State University of Iowa after about fourteen years' experience on an Iowa weekly, the *La Mars Sentinel*. After teaching four semesters at the University of New Mexico he had logged six years with Sandia. He was active in the International Council of Industrial Editors, a fact which had brought Trout into close and favorable contact with him.

The administration received suggestions from other sources as well. For example, Paul Miller, OSU's rising star in the national journalism firmament, had written favoring Elmer Woodson, director of student publications, as Trout's successor. In addition, a number of individuals had written expressing interest even before a formal call for applications had gone out. Trout's successor would not be among the three men he had suggested.[106]

On September 1, 1958, Trout became professor and head emeritus. He continued on half pay while assisting with the Industrial Editors

Short Course and a variety of campus duties. Trout also continued to serve journalists on a national scale. He founded *Trout's Communication Research Reports*, a newsletter summarizing the latest communications research of interest to writers, editors, and public relations executives. His reputation as a pioneer in corporate communications had given the publication a receptive audience and a promising start-up circulation. In addition, honors continued to come his way. On January 30, 1959, a certificate of appreciation "in grateful recognition of service and friendship to the weekly and daily newspapers of Oklahoma" was presented to him. It was signed by Lou S. Allard, president of the OPA, who had been an Oklahoma A. and M. student, and Ben Blackstock secretary-manager. The next month the Industrial Press Association of Greater St. Louis ordained him a member of the Royal Order of the Scribes of Saint Louie for "bestowing benefits over and above the moral obligations of his calling." Trout's last honor during his lifetime came only five months before his death. At the arts and sciences banquet on February 15, 1960, Dean Robert B. Kamm presented him with a "certificate of appreciation for thirty-two years of service to the faculty of the College."

Perhaps Trout's most meaningful honor was one he did not live to see. The Clement E. Trout Communicator of the Year Award was established by industrial editors in 1961, to be made each year to "any prominent executive who symbolizes through development, promotion or inspiration a current, outstanding program of effective communications."[107]

For months Trout had taken medication for a heart ailment. At the time of his death on July 16, 1960, he was making $330 a month—$121.50 from account number 2223, communications; $108.50 from Social Security; and $100 from the teachers' retirement fund. His pay was not impressive, but his service to journalism was.[108]

The final decade of Trout's unequaled thirty-two-year career in campus journalism had been momentous. It had brought a postwar boom in enrollment, national accreditation, personal triumph and long-delayed recognition for Trout, a major change in his responsibilities, freeing him to focus his attention upon curricular matters—and it brought, too, changing attitudes and relationships, retirement, and university status for the college. It had brought, as well, an underfinanced effort to elevate "communications" into the major leagues of American journalism education.

Endnotes

1. Oklahoma A. and M. College Request for Information Concerning Training and Professional Experience for James C. Stratton, 13 April 1946, and Clement E. Trout to Schiller Scroggs, 25 November 1946, in Files of the School of Journalism and Broadcasting, Oklahoma State University, Stillwater, Oklahoma.

2. Oklahoma A. and M. College Request for Information Concerning Training and Professional Experience of Vera W. Gillespie, 15 May 1946, Files of the School of Journalism and Broadcasting.

3. *National Publisher*, 8 June 1968, p. 1; Oklahoma State University *Daily O'Collegian*, 30 July 1976, p. 7.

4. Clement E. Trout to Richard B. Eide, 9 July 1947, and Dorothy Rickstrew Nixon to Harry E. Heath Jr., 22 June 1984, Files of the School of Journalism and Broadcasting.

5. Clement E. Trout to Henry G. Bennett and Schiller Scroggs, Report on the Southwestern Journalism Congress [25 April 1947], and Schiller Scroggs to Clement E. Trout, 28 April 1947, in Files of the School of Journalism and Broadcasting.

6. Clement E. Trout to L. K. Covelle, 28 May 1947, Files of the School of Journalism and Broadcasting.

7. Clement E. Trout to D. C. McIntosh, 24 April 1947, Files of the School of Journalism and Broadcasting.

8. Clement E. Trout to Schiller Scroggs, 26 May 1947, and Clement E. Trout to Schiller Scroggs, 31 July 1947, in Files of the School of Journalism and Broadcasting.

9. Travel requests for 25 September 1946, 27 September 1946, 24 October 1946, 4 November 1946, and 12 November 1946 for Richard B. Eide, in Files of the School of Journalism and Broadcasting; 1946 Class Rolls for Journalism 343, 352, 373, 401, 442, Basement of the OSU Student Health Center.

10. Travel requests for 22 February 1947, 27 February 1947, 28 February 1947, 15 April 1947, 5 November 1947, 15 November 1947, and 26 November 1947 for Richard B. Eide, Files of the School of Journalism and Broadcasting.

11. *Annual Catalog, Oklahoma A. and M. College, 1945-1946*, p. xii; Clement E. Trout to Richard B. Eide, 6 June 1947, Files of the School of Journalism and Broadcasting.

12. Clement E. Trout to Richard B. Eide, 15 July 1947, and Richard B. Eide to Clement E. Trout, 26 July 1947, in Files of the School of Journalism and Broadcasting.

13. Clement E. Trout to Richard B. Eide, 30 June 1947, Henry G. Bennett to Clement E. Trout, 8 July 1947, Clement E. Trout to Richard B. Eide, 8 August 1947, and Oklahoma A. and M. College Recommendation for Change in Staff for Richard B. Eide, 30 July 1947, in Files of the School of Journalism and Broadcasting.

14. Clement E. Trout to Schiller Scroggs, undated memorandum, Clement E. Trout to Schiller Scroggs, 26 May 1947, Clement E. Trout to Schiller Scroggs, 31 July 1947, Clement E. Trout to Charles C. Anderson, 3 July 1947, Clement E. Trout to Charles C. Anderson, 31 July 1947, and Clement E. Trout to Margie Lausten, 8 August 1947, in Files of the School of Journalism and Broadcasting; *Annual Catalog, Oklahoma A. and M. College, 1947-1948*, pp. 140, 280, 281, 365, 411, 412.

15. *Publishers' Auxiliary*, 6 September 1947, p. 8.

16. Department of Technical Journalism Summary of Enrollment, Fall Semester, 1947, Files of the School of Journalism and Broadcasting.

17. Clement E. Trout to Richard B. Eide, 1 August 1947, Richard B. Eide to Clement E. Trout, 15 August 1947, Clement E. Trout to Richard B. Eide, 12 August 1947, and Faculty Record, 1 October 1946 to 1 October 1947, in Files of the School of Journalism and Broadcasting.

18. *Annual Catalog, Oklahoma A. and M. College, 1946-1947*, pp. 358-359, Undated service report, Richard B. Eide, second semester, 1947-1948, and Official class rolls and final grades for Richard B. Eide, 30 January 1948, in Files of the School of Journalism and Broadcasting.

19. Visitors report to the Accrediting Committee, American Council on Education for Journalism, 18 October 1947, Files of the School of Journalism and Broadcasting.

20. Clement E. Trout to William H. Taft, 22 December 1947, Files of the School of Journalism and Broadcasting.

21. Clement E. Trout to Henry G. Bennett, 16 April 1948, Files of the School of Journalism and Broadcasting.

22. Alfred E. Greco to Clement E. Trout, 15 May 1948, and Clement E. Trout to Schiller Scroggs and Henry G. Bennett, 15 July 1948, in Files of the School of Journalism and Broadcasting.

23. Annual Fiscal Year Report, Department of Publications and Department of Technical Journalism, July 1948, Files of the School of Journalism and Broadcasting.

24. Oklahoma A. and M. College Faculty Record, Clement E. Trout, 1 October 1948, Files of the School of Journalism and Broadcasting.

25. "Journalism Department Nationally Recognized," *Oklahoma A. and M. College Magazine*, vol. 20, no. 1 (October 1948), p. 19; *Reports on Schools of Journalism, Special Bulletin*, Southern Newspaper Publishers Association, November 8-10, 1948, and Earl English to Clement E. Trout, 1 June 1948, in Files of the School of Journalism and Broadcasting.

26. Confidential news release for afternoon newspapers, 19 June 1948, Clement E. Trout to Earl English, 6 October 1948, and Clement E. Trout to Earl English, 17 December 1948, in Files of the School of Journalism and Broadcasting.

27. Clement E. Trout to Earl English, 22 June 1948, Clement E. Trout to Ralph Lashbrook, 26 June 1948, and Clement E. Trout to Aaron G. Benesch, 28 June 1948, in Files of the School of Journalism and Broadcasting.

28. Clement E. Trout to Schiller Scroggs, 27 November 1948, Clement E. Trout to Schiller Scroggs, 16 December 1948, in Files of the School of Journalism and Broadcasting.

29. Clement E. Trout to Schiller Scroggs, 17 April 1951, Clement E. Trout to Schiller Scroggs, 16 October 1951, in Files of the School of Journalism and Broadcasting; *Daily O'Collegian*, 16 October 1951.

30. Clement E. Trout to Anthony J. D. Sips, 20 September 1921, Files of the School of Journalism and Broadcasting.

31. Clement E. Trout to Earl English, 14 January 1949, and Schiller Scroggs to President's Office, 3 March 1949, in Files of the School of Journalism and Broadcasting.

32. Clement E. Trout to Elmer Beth, 28 February 1949, Files of the School of Journalism and Broadcasting.

33. Clement E. Trout to Schiller Scroggs, 30 March 1949, Schiller Scroggs to Clement E. Trout, 13 April 1949, in Files of the School of Journalism and Broadcasting.

34. Oklahoma A. and M. College, *Journalist's Bulletin*, (May 1949), pp. 1, 8.

35. "Report of the Department of Technical Journalism, 1948-49," Files of the School of Journalism and Broadcasting.

36. "Report of the Departments of Editorial and Publicity and Technical Journalism, Fiscal Year 1 July 1948 to 30 June 1949," Files of the School of Journalism and Broadcasting.

37. Clement E. Trout to E. E. Brewer, 18 July 1949, and Clement E. Trout to A. A. Arnold, 21 July 1949, in Files of the School of Journalism and Broadcasting.

38. Clement E. Trout to Schiller Scroggs, 17 October 1949, Files of the School of Journalism and Broadcasting.

39. Undated Service Report, Richard B. Eide, first semester 1948, and Faculty Record, 6 December 1948, in Files of the School of Journalism and Broadcasting.

40. Undated class rolls and final grades of Richard B. Eide, Spring 1949, and Undated Oklahoma A. and M. College Service Report of Richard B. Eide, Spring 1949, in Files of the School of Journalism and Broadcasting; *Annual Catalog, Oklahoma A. and M. College, 1946-1947*, pp. 358-359.

41. Oklahoma A. and M. College Request for permission to be absent from duty and/or for travel for Richard B. Eide, 30 October 1948, 3 November 1948, 22 November 1948, 22 May 1949, Files of the School of Journalism and Broadcasting.

42. Author interview with James C. Stratton, 25 November 1987, Stillwater, Oklahoma; Oklahoma A. and M. College Resignation or Discontinuance Form for Richard B. Eide, 19 July 1949, Files of the School of Journalism and Broadcasting.

43. Clement E. Trout to Henry G. Bennett, 2 January 1950, Files of the School of Journalism and Broadcasting.

44. Request for information, 22 January 1950, and Oklahoma A. and M. College Personnel Action Form for Richard B. Eide, 16 December 1954, in Files of the School of Journalism and Broadcasting.

45. "Report of the Department of Technical Journalism, 1949-50" (June 1950), and "Summarized Report of Departments of Editorial and Publicity and Technical Journalism, 1 July 1949 to 30 June 1950," Files of the School of Journalism and Broadcasting.

46. Milo Watson to Mark Clutter, 13 May 1950, Undated Oklahoma A. and M. College Official Class Roll and Final Grades of Mark Clutter, Second Semester, 1949-50, Files of the School of Journalism and Broadcasting.

47. *PRSA Tulsa 1990 Membership Directory*, p. 24; Undated memorandum to Oklahoma A. and M. College Faculty, Summer 1950, Files of the School of Journalism and Broadcasting.

48. *Journalist's Bulletin*, October 1950, p. 1.

49. Eugene L. Price to Clement E. Trout, 2 February 1951, Eugene L. Price to Clement E. Trout, 25 April 1951, Clement E. Trout to Eugene L. Price, 4 May 1951, Eugene L. Price to Clement E. Trout, 9 May 1951, Clement E. Trout to Eugene L. Price, 13 June 1951; A. D. Tomlinson to Clement E. Trout, 17 May 1951, and Clement E. Trout to A. D. Tomlinson, 20 May 1951, in Files of the School of Journalism and Broadcasting. This small sampling of letters from industrial editors is typical of hundreds received by Trout from 1938 until his death.

50. Society of Associated Industrial Editors, *Sounding Board* (May 1952), pp. 1, 3; *Greater Oklahoma News*, 7 March 1952; *Daily O'Collegian*, 29 March 1952, p. 1; International Council of Industrial Editors, *Reporting* (July 1952), pp. 28, 30; *Industrial Marketing*, August 1952, p. 64. By actual count in the Clement E. Trout Collection, Special Collections and Archives, Edmon Low Library, Oklahoma State University, there were seventy-nine letters and seven telegrams.

51. Clement E. Trout to Schiller Scroggs, 24 April 1952, Oklahoma A. and M. College Application for Leave of Absence for Study or Travel, 24 April 1952, Clement E. Trout to Oliver S. Willham, 20 July 1952, and Clement E. Trout to Randall Klemme, 21 July 1952, in Files of the School of Journalism and Broadcasting.

52. Clement E. Trout to Schiller Scroggs, 23 July 1952, Files of the School of Journalism and Broadcasting.

53. Clement E. Trout to Schiller Scroggs, 2 September 1952, and Schiller Scroggs to Clement E. Trout, 23 September 1952, in Files of the School of Journalism and Broadcasting.

54. Clement E. Trout to Randall Klemme, 21 July 1952, Files of the School of Journalism and Broadcasting.

55. Clement E. Trout to E. C. Albright, 28 May 1952, Files of the School of Journalism and Broadcasting.

56. *Industrial Marketing*, August 1952, p. 64.

57. Clement E. Trout to Schiller Scroggs, 18 November 1952, and Schiller Scroggs to Oliver S. Willham, 25 November 1952, in Files of the School of Journalism and Broadcasting.

58. William A. Sumner to Clement E. Trout, 16 September 1952, Files of the School of Journalism and Broadcasting.

59. Clement E. Trout to Schiller Scroggs, 6 January 1953, and Schiller Scroggs to Oliver S. Willham, 30 January 1953, Files of the School of Journalism and Broadcasting.

60. Undated registration list, seventh annual Industrial Editors Short Course, and Clement E. Trout, "Report to the Higher Administration" (7 April 1953), in Files of the School of Journalism and Broadcasting.

61. Clement E. Trout to Schiller Scroggs, 7 April 1953, Clement E. Trout to Schiller Scroggs, 11 April 1953, Clement E. Trout to Schiller Scroggs, 13 April 1953, Clement E. Trout to Schiller Scroggs, 20 April 1953, and Clement E. Trout, general announcement, 13 April 1953, in Files of the School of Journalism and Broadcasting.

62. Clement E. Trout to Schiller Scroggs, "Report on ICIE and SAIE Conventions, Houston, Texas, May 19-23, 1953," Files of the School of Journalism and Broadcasting.

63. Clement E. Trout to Schiller Scroggs, 8 June 1953, and Schiller Scroggs to Clement E. Trout, 22 June 1953, in Files of the School of Journalism and Broadcasting.

64. Clement E. Trout to Edward L. Morrison, 18 June 1953, Files of the School of Journalism and Broadcasting.

65. Clement E. Trout to Schiller Scroggs, 14 July 1953, and Schiller Scroggs to Clement E. Trout, 24 July 1953, in Files of the School of Journalism and Broadcasting.

66. Oliver S. Willham to Deans, Directors and Department Heads, 12 December 1953, Files of the School of Journalism and Broadcasting.

67. Clement E. Trout to Oliver S. Willham, 21 June 1954, Files of the School of Journalism and Broadcasting.

68. Schiller Scroggs to Oliver S. Willham, 14 June 1954, and Clement E. Trout to Welden Barnes, 27 October 1954, in Files of the School of Journalism and Broadcasting.

69. Robert MacVicar to Clement E. Trout, 21 January 1954, Files of the School of Journalism and Broadcasting.

70. Clement E. Trout to All Deans, Department and School Heads, Program, Industrial Communication and Education-Industry Conference, 9 March 1954, Clement E. Trout to Schiller Scroggs, 10 March 1954, and Schiller Scroggs to Clement E. Trout, 12 March 1954, in Files of the School of Journalism and Broadcasting.

71. Clement E. Trout to Rooms Committee, 5 May 1954, Files of the School of Journalism and Broadcasting.

72. Clement E. Trout to Oliver S. Willham, 12 June 1954, Files of the School of Journalism and Broadcasting.

73. Clement E. Trout to Walter Wilcox, 14 September 1956, Files of the School of Journalism and Broadcasting.

74. Clement E. Trout to I. W. Cole, 28 June 1954, Files of the School of Journalism and Broadcasting.

75. Clement E. Trout to Schiller Scroggs, 13 November 1954, Files of the School of Journalism and Broadcasting.

76. Faculty Record, Clement E. Trout, 1 October 1953 to 1 October 1954, Schiller Scroggs to Oliver S. Willham, 31 November 1954, and Oklahoma A. and M. College Recommendation for Change in Staff for Clement E. Trout, 13 November 1954, in Files of the School of Journalism and Broadcasting.

77. Clement E. Trout to Jess Covington, 21 January 1955, and Clement E. Trout to Jess Covington, 14 February 1955, in Files of the School of Journalism and Broadcasting.

78. Clement E. Trout to I. W. Cole, 8 March 1955, Files of the School of Journalism and Broadcasting.

79. Clement E. Trout, "An Understanding of Business Aids Command of Communication Skills," *Quill Magazine*, vol. 43, no. 4 (April 1955), pp. 12-14.

80. Clement E. Trout to Schiller Scroggs, 12 May 1955, Files of the School of Journalism and Broadcasting.

81. William K. Cumming to Clement E. Trout, 24 July 1955, Files of the School of Journalism and Broadcasting.

82. Clement E. Trout to Schiller Scroggs, 2 August 1955, and Schiller Scroggs to Oliver S. Willham, 2 August 1955, in Files of the School of Journalism and Broadcasting.

83. Clement E. Trout to Lester Schlup, 23 September 1955, Files of the School of Journalism and Broadcasting.

84. Clement E. Trout to Robert W. MacVicar, 13 December 1955, Files of the School of Journalism and Broadcasting; Class projects in General Semantics, School of Journalism and Broadcasting Centennial History Collection, Special Collections, Edmon Low Library.

85. Clement E. Trout to Schiller Scroggs, 19 March 1956, Files of the School of Journalism and Broadcasting.

86. *Daily O'Collegian*, 21 March 1956.

87. Clement E. Trout to Eldon M. Drake, 21 March 1956, Clement E. Trout to Schiller Scroggs, 10 January 1957, and Files of the School of Journalism and Broadcasting; *Daily O'Collegian*, 15 October 1963, pp. 1, 6.

88. Clement E. Trout to Schiller Scroggs, 16 April 1956, Undated promotional brochure, tenth annual Industrial Editors Short Course, and Clement E. Trout to Schiller Scroggs, 19 April 1956, in Files of the School of Journalism and Broadcasting.

89. Undated story by Oklahoman and Times Bureau, June 1956, and Clement E. Trout to Earle C. Albright, 11 June 1956, in Files of the School of Journalism and Broadcasting.

90. Oliver S. Willham to Clement E. Trout, 13 July 1956, Files of the School of Journalism and Broadcasting.

91. Clement E. Trout to Oliver S. Willham, 31 October 1956, Files of the School of Journalism and Broadcasting.

92. Clement E. Trout to Earle C. Albright, 27 November 1956, Files of the School of Journalism and Broadcasting.

93. Schiller Scroggs to Oliver S. Willham, 11 March 1957, Oliver S. Willham to Schiller Scroggs, 15 April 1957, Clement E. Trout to Schiller Scroggs, 25 February 1957, Clement E. Trout to Schiller Scroggs, 27 May 1957, and Undated program and roster, Industrial Editors Short Course, in Files of the School of Journalism and Broadcasting; *Stillwater NewsPress*, 25 April 1957, 1 May 1957; Alva *Northwestern News*, 26 April 1957; *Daily O'Collegian*, 8 May 1957.

94. Visitors report to the Accrediting Committee, American Council on Education for Journalism, 7-8 January 1957, and John E. Stempel to Clement E. Trout, 21 May 1957, in Files of the School of Journalism and Broadcasting; *Stillwater NewsPress*, 26 May 1957, p. 2; *Greater Oklahoma News*, 13 June 1957.

95. "Name of Oklahoma A. and M. Changed to Oklahoma State University," *Oklahoma A. and M. College Magazine*, vol. 28, no. 10 (June 1957), p. 5.

96. Ludel B. Sauvageot to Oliver S. Willham, 21 June 1957, Robert W. MacVicar to Ludel B. Sauvageot, 26 June 1957, Oliver S. Willham to Trout, 24 June 1957, Schiller Scroggs to Clement E. Trout, 3 June 1957, Clement E. Trout to Mae D. Aucello, 5 June 1957, and Undated report from Clement E. Trout to Schiller Scroggs, June 1957, p. 1, in Files of the School of Journalism and Broadcasting; *Stillwater NewsPress*, 21 June 1957; *Tulsa World*, 21 June 1957; *Greater Oklahoma News*, 13 June 1957.

97. Gerald T. Curtin to Schiller Scroggs, 17 May 1957, Schiller Scroggs to Gerald T. Curtin, May 1957, and Minutes of OPA-Oklahoma A. and M. journalism meeting, 25 May 1957, in Files of the School of Journalism and Broadcasting.

98. Clement E. Trout to Gerald T. Curtin, 30 May 1957, Files of the School of Journalism and Broadcasting.

99. Two reports from Clement E. Trout to Schiller Scroggs, estimating journalism space needs, July 1957, and Schiller Scroggs to Robert MacVicar, 8 July 1957, Files of the School of Journalism and Broadcasting.

100. Clement E. Trout to Schiller Scroggs, 15 June 1957, with copy of Oklahoma Press Association resolutions, Files of the School of Journalism and Broadcasting. The resolutions also were sent to Vice President Robert MacVicar at his request.

101. Gerald T. Curtin, "Resolutions Unanimously Adopted at the Annual Meeting of the Oklahoma Press Association, Sequoyah State Park, June 15, 1957," Files of the School of Journalism and Broadcasting.

102. *Daily O'Collegian*, 18 June 1957, p. 1, 28 June 1957, p. 2.

103. Clement E. Trout, "Report of Trip to Boston to Attend the Annual Convention of the International Council of Industrial Editors, July 11-15, 1957," forwarded to Schiller Scroggs, July 1957, Files of the School of Journalism and Broadcasting

104. Clement E. Trout to Schiller Scroggs, 22 November 1957, Files of the School of Journalism and Broadcasting.

105. Service Report, 1 October 1956 to 1 October 1957, submitted 25 November 1957, and Oklahoma State University news release, 3 October 1957, in Files of the School of Journalism and Broadcasting.

106. Clement E. Trout to Schiller Scroggs, 23 September 1957, and Paul Miller to Clement E. Trout, 7 April 1958, in Files of the School of Journalism and Broadcasting.

107. Oklahoma State University Request for Personnel Action for Clement E. Trout, 29 July 1958, Oklahoma Press Association Certificate of Appreciation, 30 January 1959, Industrial Press Association of Greater St. Louis, "Royal Order of the Scribes of Saint Louie," 24 February 1959, Oklahoma State University news release, 27 April 1959, Certificate of Appreciation, College of Arts and Sciences, Oklahoma State University, 15 February 1960, and Mrs. Clement E. Trout to subscribers of *Trout's Communication Research Reports*, 13 August 1960, in Files of the School of Journalism and Broadcasting.

108. Oklahoma State University Request for Personnel Action, 29 July 1958, and Separation Notice (Death) for Clement E. Trout, 20 July 1960, in Files of the School of Journalism and Broadcasting.

16 A School Is Formed

The Clement E. Trout era was coming to an end. It had brought stability to the journalism program, and with that stability a measure of security. The threat that the state's two major journalism programs might be merged had lessened. Trout's emphasis upon *technical* journalism was not likely to cause major concern to the University of Oklahoma with its more generalized approach. Earlier talk of combining the programs was almost nonexistent, now rarely heard above a whisper.

Oklahoma's land-grant institution and its journalism program had reached a promising crest. Both were firmly established. There was no question now that the once struggling agricultural college was indeed the university's sister institution, in fact as well as name. But the approaching retirement of Trout posed new problems. What direction would—or should—the nationally accredited program in journalism take? This was a question inseparable from the future of Oklahoma State University itself.

The university long since had shed its image as a technical institution only. It was a full-service university with growing prestige in a wide array of programs and in the breadth and depth of its research efforts. Who would be the ideal replacement for Trout, and what emphasis should the program have? If the institution was to nurture its new role as a comprehensive university, might it not wish to reflect the growing importance of the nation's mass media system by a more comprehensive program in mass communication. Or should it stick to its last; should it continue to stress the specialized journalism that had led to accreditation and to a place of high standing in technical journalism along with such schools as Iowa State University, Kansas State University and the University of Wisconsin, with its much respected Department of Agricultural Journalism?

It takes time to hire a new department head, especially at a turning point such as Oklahoma State University now faced. It seemed wise to be deliberate in thinking the matter through. The vice president in charge of academic affairs, Robert W. MacVicar, a talented biochemist, was aware that the consolidation of communication programs had certain advantages. It would be economical, for example, to merge administrative duties and budgets which currently were spread among several related units.[1]

Why not a new configuration for the journalism program? Why not a School of Communications, with a broader combination of disciplines under one umbrella? Other schools—notably Boston University and Michigan State University—had moved to the broader approach. Under the school structure, it would be possible to join the collegiate trendsetters as well as to keep in step with the converging of mass media industries.

With these and perhaps other considerations in mind, MacVicar urged consolidation upon Schiller Scroggs, dean of arts and sciences. In MacVicar's own words, the idea was to create an inter-disciplinary unit that would bring together relatively small but closely related elements in the broad field of communications.[2] While the concept simmered, the

SPECIAL COLLECTIONS, OSU LIBRARY

Vice President Robert W. MacVicar took the lead in creating the School of Communications. He saw it as a way to combine related academic units and reduce costs while improving efficiency.

Department of Technical Journalism went into a holding pattern.

Trout's plans to retire June 30, 1958, had been no secret. He had been scheduled to retire a year earlier, but Dean Scroggs had asked that he continue for a year. Scroggs explained that his own retirement was only one year away, and he believed the new dean should be involved in the selection of Trout's successor. President Oliver S. Willham had concurred in the recommendation.[3] As 1958 wore on with no official announcement as to the department's future, a number of Oklahoma newspaper executives, especially those who were Oklahoma A. and M. graduates, became restive. One of these, Gerald T. Curtin, publisher of the *Watonga Republican* and active in the Oklahoma Press Association, showed his concern for the future of journalism at OSU in a letter to Dean Scroggs dated February 26, 1958. "Cowboy" Curtin had been a football hero and student leader at Oklahoma A. and M. from 1928 to 1931. He had led a small group of Aggies on a foray to recover the clapper from Old Central's Victory Bell after a group of Sooner fraternity men had stolen it following the Oklahoma A. and M. gridiron triumph over OU on November 22, 1930. Later, he was to send a son and daughter to the journalism school.

In the letter, he told Scroggs that he had heard several unofficial reports of improvements planned for the journalism program, and that one report was alarming. Pending the appointment of a new administrator, Curtin wrote, he had been told by recent graduates that plans for improvement were being held at status quo, if not drifting. One may assume Curtin was speaking not just for himself but for numerous editors and publishers—OU graduates as well as those from Oklahoma A. and M.

He pointed out that Trout, on the verge of retirement, must judiciously avoid aggressive new policies and plans that might go counter to the wishes of his successor. If such "drifting" were true, Curtin wanted Scroggs to be aware of it and to press the search for a competent person to head the department.

Curtin, again no doubt representing the views of other state journalistic leaders as well as his own, indicated that the person selected might already be in the department, but that it could be necessary to import administrative talent. His one caveat: the new leader should be a good organizer with practical experience in newspaper journalism. Curtin believed newspaper journalism to be the foundation in any communication field, including "radio, television and industrial communications as well." Not only did Curtin believe journalism would provide such a foundation, but he stressed that with 60 daily and 230 weekly newspapers in Oklahoma, newspapers were "the basic employment field for state-trained journalists." Nor was course work alone sufficient. Curtin wanted Scroggs to understand that training on a campus newspaper should be a laboratory requirement. Students with such experience, he asserted, were better qualified than those with theory alone.

Curtin's letter held special significance, for he was chairman of the Oklahoma Press Association committee assigned to assist the OSU journalism program, and he intended to call a meeting of his committee as soon as he returned from a two-week vacation trip.[4]

Dean Scroggs responded immediately in a two-page letter of approximately 750 words. He sought to assure Curtin that things were not drifting. Already three highly qualified men had been brought to the campus for interviews. These candidates were "accorded full opportunity" to discuss projected plans with President Willham and Vice President MacVicar as well as with other administrative officers who would be involved in the expanded program. Members of the journalism faculty, Scroggs emphasized, had visited with each of the candidates. Other faculties which were expected to become part of the new and broader structure were not mentioned in connection with the interviews.

Of the three possible successors to Trout, one failed to impress university officials, another priced his services beyond reach, and the third candidate, who had visited on February 20, was offered the position. The university could not expect an answer for another week or possibly longer. Two additional possibilities—"one of these an almost sure candidate"—would be invited for interviews should the university's choice, an advertising man with first-hand experience in "most of the [communication] fields," fail to accept its offer.

Scroggs's forthright letter to Curtin made it clear that Vice President MacVicar's plan for consolidation was well under way. The plan obviously had figured prominently in the selection process. It was clear, too, that the evolving academic unit would encompass more than journalism. First, the selection of an advertising man suggested that advertising courses would likely be moved from the College of Business to the new unit, located in the College of Arts and Sciences. In addition, Scroggs had specifically mentioned the integration of photography, broadcasting and speech with the journalism program. At no point did he name the unit, which within a short time would be known as the School of Communications.

Scroggs wrote Curtin: "It has been my position that the specific planning of the new school should be left in detail to the new man. Effectuating the general policy will call for considerable liaison work and even transfer of some functions. Long-term effectiveness can best be gained by having the new administrator responsible both for detail planning and execution. He will need your help, and it is my judgment that your committee has been formed just in time to assist us a lot. My only regret is that we cannot possibly have our new man available to meet with you and your committee when you return from Mexico."

How rapidly and successfully the new approach to communication studies at Oklahoma State University would move ahead was dependent upon the economic recession and more especially the cut in the oil allowables for Oklahoma. But recession or no, the university had decided to move ahead. "You may be sure," the dean wrote, "that we have in mind as one of our first moves the strengthening of the newspaper wing of the school." Elaborating, Scroggs stated that he considered newspaper training to be fundamental. "We have felt our newspaper sequence planned primarily for the smaller town dailies and weeklies is on a sound basis. It needs to be strengthened in some areas and probably expanded." He suggested that Curtin's committee could be especially helpful in this area, and in the decision as to the place of advertising in the program.[5]

These were crucial days for Scroggs. He was now only five months away from retirement and was hurrying to develop a unified and functional College of Arts and Sciences out of Oklahoma A. and M.'s old School of Science and Literature, which had been largely a service unit.[6] Time was running out for him, and he wanted to refine the college's structure before turning it over to his successor. Unification of the communications disciplines was one of the keys to a more streamlined organizational structure college-wide.

Scroggs knew that the entire matter was being rushed. Ideally, there should have been much more time for discussion among all concerned. But events were closing in on him and there was not enough time for mutual give and take. This lack was to contribute to serious conflicts later. The favored candidate, despite the strong support of Vice President

Schiller Scroggs had been a strong supporter of Clement E. Trout since 1938. Shortly before retirement, Scroggs had carried on negotiations for Trout's successor, C. Ellsworth Chunn.

Albert E. Darlow and Professors Trout and Maurice R. Haag, declined the appointment after he had given considerable thought to the pros and cons of accepting. It was necessary to reopen the search, time to turn to the "almost sure candidate."

On April 7, 1958, C. Ellsworth Chunn and his wife, Florence, were invited to visit the campus.[7] Files maintained by Dean Scroggs suggest that Chunn had indicated an interest earlier, for his vita was circulated to Vice President MacVicar and Professor Trout along with a copy of the letter of invitation. Chunn probably was the fourth man to be considered, and it is likely that there had been consensus among at least a dozen administrators that he was a viable candidate.

In his letter inviting the Chunns to visit Stillwater, Dean Scroggs for the first time referred to the new unit by name. "The imminent retirement of Professor Clement E. Trout," he wrote, "makes this a strategic time to reorganize certain functions, such as journalism, public relations, photography, radio and television writing and technique, into a School of Communications." Considerable thought had been given to the proposal, although "details of the reorganization" had not been fixed. Scroggs said that what remained was for a competent leader to come in as soon as practicable "to plan and effectuate the organization." Scroggs saw the job as one requiring cooperative relations with every division on campus as well as with the state's newspapers. It would pay in the range of $9,000 to $10,000 for twelve months with two weeks paid vacation. "The key fact is that this is a strategic time for the constructive and rewarding exercise of leadership in a promising academic situation," Scroggs concluded.

Eight days after Scroggs had written him, Chunn was on the OSU campus. The Union Club was full and Scroggs had made reservations at the Circle D Motel on North Main Street. At 2 o'clock in the afternoon of April 15, Chunn began two days of thirty-minute visits with the various deans, other high-ranking university officials, plus representatives of the speech faculty, including those with an interest in broadcasting. At a 12:15 luncheon on April 16 in the Student Union's Gnu Room, he met with thirteen university officials, including three he had talked with earlier in the day. Attending the luncheon were Trout; MacVicar; Randall Jones, of the College of Agriculture; Evelyn Rebecca Pate, vice dean of the College of Home Economics; Haag, James C. Stratton, and Lemuel D. Groom, all journalism faculty; Welden Barnes, director of public information; Hans Andersen, head of the Department of English, Foreign Languages and Speech; Harry Anderson, chairman of the speech faculty; Scroggs; Chunn; Walter W. Hansen, vice dean of arts and sciences; and George F. Church, Agricultural Experiment Station editor and a former member of the journalism faculty.[8]

Following the luncheon, Chunn went to MacVicar's office for his final scheduled one-on-one meeting. MacVicar was not sure that Chunn was right for the job, but he knew that this candidate had the strong support of Scroggs and chose not to stand in his way.[9]

Ellsworth and Florence Chunn returned to their home at 931 Peachtree Battle Circle, N.W., in Atlanta with assurances from Dean Scroggs that the job was Chunn's if he wanted it. Two days after the last of the campus meetings, Dean Scroggs had written Chunn that he was awaiting his final word "with keenest anticipation, hoping that it will be that you both will speedily join forces with us." The letter also contained this significant paragraph: "You will be interested to know that the Speech people have agreed to cast their lot in the School of Communications. I just ended my conference with Professor Harry Anderson a few minutes ago."[10] Scroggs's soon-to-be named successor as dean of the College of Arts and Sciences would not select Trout's replacement after all. Circumstances had ruled this out.

Scroggs's replacement, Robert B. Kamm, dean of students at Texas A. and M. University, arrived at OSU two months after Chunn had taken up his duties with the School of Communications. Chunn was clearly Scroggs's man. The timing had been slightly off.

The man Scroggs had invited to become the first director of the School of Communications was no newcomer to higher education. Born in Jonesboro, Arkansas, on April 8, 1915, he had taken a B.A. degree at the University of Arkansas with a major in journalism and a minor in geology in 1937. Then he moved on to Northwestern University's Medill School of Journalism where he earned the master's one year later with a journalism major and a political science minor. With an M.S.J. degree in hand, he accepted an instructorship in journalism and English at the University of Tulsa. He taught for a year and a half, acutely aware of the war raging in Europe. He was a reserve officer, having been commissioned a second lieutenant after completing the ROTC program at Arkansas. As the U.S. strengthened its military posture, he knew he was likely to be called. When ordered to active duty, he was immediately assigned to the Philippine Scouts and soon was en route to Manila. His duty permitted him to study part-time at the University of Manila. In a letter to friends in Tulsa, Chunn pictured the life army men were leading in the Philippines. He had been called into service shortly before Christmas and was stationed at Fort McKinley on Luzon. Chunn wrote:

"We sit on a powder keg here. When or if it will blow no one knows. We are always ready. For instance this week we expect a practice alert. An emergency signal will sound and we [will] quickly go to our assigned battle stations. A couple of weeks ago our regiment had a reconnaissance in. . .a defense jungle in the mountains. Often we cut our way with bolo knives and walked circumspectly lest a python drop on us. As we crept through the bamboo, acacias, and vines all of us mused, 'I never thought this would happen to me.'

"I thought these scenes were only for the movies, which make it so romantic. If fighting bramble, or marching in 100 degree temperature, or taking 10 grains of quinine daily is romantic, Hollywood's tropic atmosphere was gained from a trip to Catalina. We did find much of interest, however, to-wit: The most picturesque spot I have ever encountered at Subig [sic] bay on the China Sea." Then came Pearl Harbor followed close on by the overwhelming Japanese invasion of the Philippines. He was a prisoner of war from the fall of Corregidor to the Japanese surrender, ending World War II.

On April 21, 1958, Dean Scroggs wrote to President Willham with carbon copies to Vice President MacVicar, Dean J. Andrew Holley, Dean Eugene Swearingen, and Professor Hans Andersen stating that at noon that day Chunn had phoned from Atlanta to accept appointment as director of the new School of Communications. He expected to arrive in Stillwater to take up his duties on May 15, he said, but preferred that no announcement be made prior to that date.[11] The dean immediately prepared and forwarded under separate cover the necessary appointment papers.

The letter to President Willham expanded upon earlier statements about the new unit, bringing them into clearer focus. It was time to put recent understandings into writing. Dean Scroggs recommended to Willham that a School of Communications be established "as soon as practicable," but not later than May 15, 1958, the day of Chunn's projected arrival. Chunn's title, also part of the recommendation, would be "Director of the School of Communications and Professor of Journalism."

The scope of the plan virtually doomed the new director to personnel problems. He would have to be a genius in interpersonal relationships to succeed without full, tough-minded support from the upper echelons of the university hierarchy. There obviously were built-in ego problems, for some units with departmental status must shed that status for the larger good. The personnel, equipment, facilities, and fund balances of the various units would be transferred to the umbrella agency under Chunn. The University of Oklahoma's H. H. Herbert School of Journalism would find at the sister institution an academic unit of broader scope than its own. The competition now would be school vs. school, rather than department vs. school. In the process, OSU programs in journalism, public relations, speech, photography, and radio-television would constitute the new school. With the president's approval, these were to be transferred "not as organized departments but as constituent units (as, for example, Meteorology is a constituent unit of the Department in [sic] Physics)."

The dean felt he had touched the necessary bases. He had conferred with Dean Holley about the photography unit, with Vice Dean Edward

C. Ellsworth Chunn was not a stranger to Oklahoma when he was named director of the new School of Communications in 1958. An Arkansas native, he had taught at the University of Tulsa and the University of Oklahoma.

Burris (in the absence of Dean Swearingen) about the "advertising and public relations aspects," with Professor Hans Andersen and representatives of the speech staff relative to their concerns, and with Vice President MacVicar about the radio and television units on Sixth Street as well as the "entire plan of organization." The status of advertising courses, located in the College of Business, seemed ambiguous, for Scroggs had not mentioned advertising as a "constituent unit" of the school.[12]

Not only was a new and exciting concept being worked out. The new school's units, scattered both on and off campus, would be brought together in a new home. The old Science Hall, dedicated in 1920 and for years occupied by the Department of Chemistry, would now be the seat of the School of Communications. Chemistry was moving across campus to new quarters in the recently completed Chemistry-Physics Building.

The selection of Chunn to head the communications program seemed, in some ways, to present shortcuts in administrative protocol. For example, his application for the position was dated April 21, 1958, the same day he phoned his acceptance. His transcripts had not arrived when the request for personnel action naming him director was signed by Scroggs on April 21 and by President Willham two days later.[13] Perhaps Scroggs was rushing to complete as much important business as possible before yielding responsibility to his replacement. Looming in the background was the fact that the selection committee already had gone through at least four interviews, including Chunn's, trying to gear up for the advent of a new academic organization by fall semester. Time was short. A building must be refurbished, curricula agreed upon, promotional materials prepared and circulated, a new organizational structure set into motion. Little wonder that Scroggs felt a sense of urgency, even if it meant the use of some unorthodox procedures. Quick action seemed necessary while understandings were fresh in the minds of the various faculty and staff members involved in the bold new direction their programs would take.

Now that a director had been selected, OSU officials could move ahead with details. Vice President MacVicar mailed Chunn floor plans for the old Science Hall, then known as the Chemistry Building and "soon to be designated as the Journalism Building." Chunn began work on the floor plans, juggling to accommodate administrative space, faculty offices, classrooms, and laboratories in a forty-year-old structure that would be badly over-crowded from the start. On April 30, President Willham huddled with MacVicar, Holley, Barnes, and Scroggs "to discuss the Communications set-up." It was agreed that photography, speech, radio, and television would be moved to the School of Communications, but that the radio taping service, largely funded by the Extension Service, would remain under Barnes. MacVicar felt the taping service should fall under Chunn, but did not press the point. All other radio and television programming was to become a function of the School of Communications.[14]

Dean Scroggs had mailed the summer and fall class schedules to Chunn and was on the alert to locate adequate housing. Meanwhile, a copy of the new director's approved appointment was in the mail to him, with regents' approval a formality. Scroggs received Chunn's application and transcripts on May 2, the same day he had mailed documentation of the appointment to Chunn.[15]

Ten days after the April 30 meeting, President Willham reported to the board of regents on plans for the new school. The regents approved the proposal subject to the availability of funds. Willham then called upon MacVicar for a clearer picture of the school's organizational structure.[16] On May 12, MacVicar drafted a comprehensive memorandum to be sent later to Willham. Its subject was "Organization of the School of Communications," and it was marked in underscored capital letters with the words "Draft for Comment." Copies were sent to ten of OSU's top administrators, including all deans. They were asked to respond with comments "as promptly as possible" because of Chunn's expected early arrival.[17] Scroggs wrote MacVicar that the document had his full approval, then forwarded his copy to Chunn "to be sure I have made no oversight."[18]

1959 REDSKIN

"Backshop" personnel worked closely with journalism majors, often serving as unofficial teachers of the techniques of publishing. In this typical scene, Noel Corser, production superintendent, took time to discuss the *O'Collegian's* press with Frances Mayfield.

The draft stood up well. When the final document was issued to all deans, directors and heads of academic departments on June 25, few changes had been made. The opening paragraph had been reshaped by Willham's office because the memorandum was now issued in the name of the president. In the organization section, there was one addition: the non-academic Division of Radio and Television Services had been assigned to the school. Under function, "the preparation of school administrators in the broad area of public relations" had been added to other responsibilities interfacing with the College of Education.

The school was to be an integral part of the College of Arts and Sciences, and the dean was to have responsibility for its administration and control. It was to begin operations with three academic segments "as a unified group for administrative purposes": the Department of Technical Journalism; the speech section of the Department of English, Foreign Languages and Speech; and the Department of Photography.

The school's academic administrator was to have the title "Professor and Director," and—at least for the present—no formal departmentalization would be effected. Chunn, as the first director, would oversee both undergraduate and graduate courses in journalism, speech and drama, radio and television, photography, advertising copy (including design and layout), and public relations. But there was more. He also would bear responsibility for the supervision of the University Auditorium and the Prairie Playhouse, intercollegiate forensics, and the student-operated radio station. He was charged with development and production of radio and television programs for off-campus use by the Division of Public Information, and the development and coordination of closed-circuit television programs by other instructional departments using "any all-university facilities." An appropriate extension program would be carried out under the direction of Arts and Sciences Extension, and communications research would be conducted as well.

This was more than a big order. Considering the limitations of faculty, staff, space, and equipment, the document might well have carried the title of a later popular television program, "Mission Impossible." In short, without vastly larger resources than the university was prepared to commit to the school, it could not possibly carry out all of the activities assigned to it.

But there were yet other responsibilities. The new director must coordinate his various programs with five colleges as well as with other administrative units. With the College of Business, he was to coordinate industrial journalism, and advertising as an aspect of merchandising; with the College of Engineering, industrial journalism and the technical aspects of radio and television; with the College of Home Economics, industrial journalism and the training of demonstration specialists; with the Division of Agriculture, agricultural journalism and communication research sponsored by the Agricultural Experiment Station; with the College of Education, the training of speech, journalism and communication arts teachers as well as the preparation of school administrators in the broad area of public relations.[19]

In addition to the colleges, Chunn would be expected to work with

C. Ellsworth Chunn checks over remodeling plans for the Communications Building as work is rushed for fall classes.

Centennial Histories Series

the Board of Publications "in relation to the student newspaper, the yearbook and other student publications." Traditionally, Chunn's predecessors had served as chairman of the board, and he would inherit that mantle. With the publishing and printing department of the Division of Auxiliary Enterprises, he would coordinate "the use of this university facility for instructional purposes whenever practicable." But the greatest demands came in connection with the Division of Public Information. The school was to assist in preparation of material for release to the press "where appropriate use can be made of the material in the instructional program." It also was to prepare and produce radio and television programs for release through public information, except in agriculture, "which responsibility [would] remain in the Agricultural Information Section of the Division of Public Information." Finally, the school would prepare and/or produce "such other radio and television programs as may be arranged for the Division of Public Information in connection with the public relations program of the University."

The effective date for "implementation of the reorganization" would be June 1, 1958, for functional purposes and July 1 for budget purposes. Appropriate funds would be transferred by the comptroller from existing accounts to the School of Communications, and administrators involved would initiate the necessary personnel action documents through the dean of arts and sciences to transfer personnel to the school from their home departments. Responsibility for the student radio station and all auxiliary equipment was to be transferred from public information to the School of Communications "at the earliest possible date," and physically moved to what the administration had earlier referred to as the Journalism Building but now was calling the Communications Building.

Because other academic units still occupied some areas in the building, assignment of available space would be the responsibility of MacVicar. The school was to be moved "with minimum delay" from its temporary frame building, TF-8, located immediately north of Whitehurst Hall. TF-8, a surplus World War II Navy barracks, had been journalism's home since 1947, when it was brought to the campus as one of the many "temporary" emergency buildings in Henry G. Bennett's program to accommodate the flood of World War II veterans.[20]

The plan for a School of Communications was enough to frighten away anyone but a gutsy workaholic, and its scope, though not then in writing, may have been a factor in the rejection the university received from its earlier favored candidate. In late May, Chunn left his position as education director of the National Association of Manufacturers' Southern Region, a twelve-state area, and started the journey to Stillwater. An exciting adventure was about to begin.

Endnotes

1. Schiller Scroggs to Harry E. Heath Jr., 1 September 1970, and Robert W. MacVicar to Harry E. Heath Jr., 10 August 1987, in School of Journalism and Broadcasting Centennial History Collection, Edmon Low Library, Oklahoma State University, Stillwater, Oklahoma.
2. Robert W. MacVicar to Harry E. Heath Jr., 10 August 1987, School of Journalism and Broadcasting Centennial History Collection.
3. Schiller Scroggs to Oliver S. Willham, 11 March 1957, Files of the School of Journalism and Broadcasting, Oklahoma State Univeristy.
4. Gerald T. Curtin to Schiller Scroggs, 26 February 1958, Files of the School of Journalism and Broadcasting; Oklahoma City *Daily Oklahoman*, 25 December 1930, p. 15; *Stillwater Gazette*, 19 December 1930, p. 1; Doris Dellinger, *A History of the Oklahoma State University Intercollegiate Athletics* (Stillwater: Oklahoma State University, 1987), p. 91.
5. Schiller Scroggs to Gerald T. Curtin, 28 February 1958, Files of the School of Journalism and Broadcasting.
6. Schiller Scroggs to Harry E. Heath Jr., 1 September 1970, Files of the School of Journalism and Broadcasting.
7. Schiller Scroggs to Gerald T. Curtin, 28 February 1958, and Schiller Scroggs to C. Ellsworth Chunn, 7 April 1958, in Files of the School of Journalism and Broadcasting.
8. Schiller Scroggs to C. Ellsworth Chunn, 7 April 1958, undated and unsigned handwritten copy of telegram to C. Ellsworth Chunn, and undated and unsigned roster of those to attend luncheon for C. Ellsworth Chunn in the Gnu Room, Student Union, 16 April 1958, in Files of the School of Journalism and Broadcasting.
9. Robert W. MacVicar to Harry E. Heath Jr., 10 August 1987, School of Journalism and Broadcasting Centennial History Collection.
10. Schiller Scroggs to C. Ellsworth Chunn, 18 April 1958, School of Journalism and Broadcasting Centennial History Collection.
11. "A New Dean for Arts and Sciences," *Oklahoma State University Magazine*, vol. 2, no. 3 (September 1958), p. 7; *Tulsa Collegian*, 9 May 1941, p. 1; Undated biography of C. Ellsworth Chunn, Oklahoma A. and M. College Request for Information Concerning Training and Professional Experience, 21 April 1958, and Schiller Scroggs to Oliver S. Willham, 21 April 1958, in Files of the School of Journalism and Broadcasting.
12. Schiller Scroggs to Oliver S. Willham, 21 April 1958, Files of the School of Journalism and Broadcasting.
13. Oklahoma State University Request for Personnel Action for C. Ellsworth Chunn, 21 April 1958, Files of the School of Journalism and Broadcasting.
14. Schiller Scroggs to C. Ellsworth Chunn, 25 April 1958, C. Ellsworth Chunn to Schiller Scroggs, 29 April 1958, and Schiller Scroggs to C. Ellsworth Chunn, 30 April 1958, in Files of the School of Journalism and Broadcasting.
15. Schiller Scroggs to C. Ellsworth Chunn, 2 May 1958, and Schiller Scroggs to C. Ellsworth Chunn, 2 May 1958, in Files of the School of Journalism and Broadcasting (two letters of same date).
16. Summary statement, "School of Communications, College of Arts and Sciences," 10 May 1958, and Conference in which President Willham asked Vice President MacVicar to draft a detailed statement on the organization of the School of Communications, Files of the School of Journalism and Broadcasting. It is probable that this was the conference of 30 April 1958 referred to in the text (p. 386). Minutes, Board of Regents for Oklahoma A. and M. Colleges, 10 May 1958, Special Collections, Edmon Low Library, Oklahoma State University.
17. Robert W. MacVicar to Oliver S. Willham, President, Subject: Organization of the School of Communications, with cover memorandum dated 12 May 1958, Files of the School of Journalism and Broadcasting.
18. Schiller Scroggs to Robert W. MacVicar, 13 May 1958, with carbon copy to C. Ellsworth Chunn, Files of the School of Journalism and Broadcasting.
19. Oliver S. Willham to Deans, Directors, and Heads of Academic Departments, Subject: Organization of the School of Communications, 25 June 1958, Files of the School of Journalism and Broadcasting.
20. Oliver S. Willham to Deans, Directors, and Heads of Academic Departments, Subject: Organization of the School of Communications, 25 June 1958; Pictures and captions, *Oklahoma State University Magazine*, vol. 2, no. 11 (May 1959), p. 29; Gene Allen to Harry E. Heath Jr., 29 June 1989, School of Journalism and Broadcasting Centennial History Collection.

17 Tensions and Breakup

C. Ellsworth Chunn was exhilarated by the prospect of a new educational challenge. It had taken a little longer than he had expected to wind things up in Atlanta. Among other professional matters, he had to look after National Association of Manufactures (NAM) conferences at the University of Georgia and the University of South Carolina.

As he traveled westward, he thought of his scheduled appearance June 13 at the annual summer outing of the Oklahoma Press Association (OPA). Ben Blackstock, the OPA executive secretary, had phoned on May 19 to invite him. Blackstock suggested he speak on "plans for the School of Communications, especially, the Division of Journalism." Thanks to information from both Schiller Scroggs and Blackstock, Chunn had written to Gerald T. Curtin the following day asking for suggestions on the scope of his remarks. Curtin, publisher of the *Watonga Republican*, was chairman of the OPA-OSU Advisory Committee.[1]

No doubt Chunn also turned over in his mind the sketches of the Communications Building floor plans he had drawn for Vice President Robert W. MacVicar. These would help the architects in preliminary planning before his arrival, but he knew there would be wrinkles to be ironed out with Clement E. Trout, who also had been asked by MacVicar to suggest changes in the structure. Chunn had planned for a minimum of carpentry on the first floor, but the need for more than routine privacy in the office of the speech therapist on the second floor would call for important renovations. The third floor would require a larger women's room. He thought, too, of how to adjust space for radio and television production and how he would need to arrange space for the "student radio station."[2]

How to use the first floor was a puzzle. He would have some space, but just how much was uncertain, for chemistry and psychology still held claims on parts of it. Throughout the building, lighting needed to be blue-white fluorescent, flooring must be repaired, walls painted, window air conditioners installed in his office and in the office of Dorothy Rickstrew, his secretary. Would the administration allow air conditioners in dark-rooms and radio control rooms? At least one classroom should be equipped with blackout blinds and projection screen for audio-visual aids. Bannisters needed to be tightened for safety and venetian blinds added on the third floor's south and southwest rooms. So many details.[3]

Between brief conversations with his wife as the drive to Stillwater continued, Chunn's mind drifted—as it would for the rest of his life—to the good and bad days in the Philippines. The bad days especially. The retreat to Bataan, the Japanese assault on Corregidor, his combat wounds, the Death March, the seemingly endless days at Cabanatuan, the mercilessly packed and stinking holds in the Japanese prison ships, the days in a Japanese prison camp in Korea, the liberation by American troops, the thin veneer between civilization and savagery.[4]

It was June 1, 1958, and the Chunns were nearing the end of their journey. The move was, in fact, a homecoming. Florence, a Tulsan, had met Ellsworth in his first teaching assignment at the University of Tulsa, where she was a hometown student living with her parents. Ellsworth was from Jonesboro, a Northeastern Arkansas trade center 215 miles east of the Oklahoma border as the crow flies. A reserve officer, Chunn cut a

SPECIAL COLLECTIONS, OSU LIBRARY

The old Science Hall with its stately Georgian columns became the home of the new School of Communications in the fall of 1958. After eleven years in TF-8, a "temporary" wooden structure, this was viewed by students and faculty as a major improvement.

dashing figure in his Army uniform at the 1940 Christmas season Pan-Hellenic Ball, Florence Jenkins on his arm, "making the girls breathless and the boys jealous."[5] He was awaiting orders that would take him to the Pacific months before Pearl Harbor and the Japanese invasion of the Philippines. She would wait throughout the uncertain days of his long years as a prisoner of war. Then VJ Day, his return, and the wedding.

Chunn, the young Tulsa journalism professor of twenty years before, was well equipped for his newest challenge when he reported to Dean Scroggs on June 2.[6] He had a rich background in educational pursuits, and journalistic experience as well. His interests were catholic. He was a competent violinist, a poet, an author, a leader.

While Chunn had not been the first choice of OSU officials, he was well qualified to succeed Trout. Among others, he had the high regard of John E. Drewry, dean of the University of Georgia's Henry W. Grady School of Journalism, with whom he had cooperated for four years in two yearly education-industry conferences co-sponsored by the journalism school and the NAM. Copies of Scroggs's letter to Dr. and Mrs. Chunn inviting them to visit Stillwater had been sent to MacVicar and Trout along with a biographical sketch of the prospective director.[7] That sketch showed a relatively good balance of professional and academic experience.

Despite his seemingly oriental name, Chunn was of Irish descent. Among his forebears, Sylvester Chunn of the 10th Virginia Continental Line, one of twenty-one Revolutionary War ancestors in the family, had served with General Washington at Valley Forge. Chunn had spent the first twenty-two years of his life in Arkansas, and had earned the B.A. degree from the University of Arkansas in 1937 with a major in journalism and minors in geology and German. In 1938, he was awarded the master of science degree in journalism by the Medill School of Journalism, Northwestern University, where he had won a full graduate scholarship. His minor had been in political science and his thesis was titled "A Digest of Illinois Laws Affecting Newspapers."[8]

Then came two years as chairman of journalism courses at the University of Tulsa, followed by his call to active duty as an infantry officer. Before the Japanese invasion and the fall of the Philippines, he had studied at the University of Santo Tomas in Manila during his off-duty time, developing a speaking knowledge of Spanish.[9]

After five years as a prisoner of war, he had returned as a major to the United States wearing the Silver Star, Bronze Star with oak leaf cluster and Purple Heart with two oak leaf clusters, among other military decorations. He had married Florence Jenkins and had begun his adjustment to civilian life. He accepted a National Association of Broadcasters internship at KPRC, Houston, then picked up where he had left off as head of the newly created Department of Journalism at Tulsa with the

Journalism faculty and staff assisted physical plant employees in the move from TF-8 to the old Science Hall. Dorothy Rickstrew and Maurice Haag share a moment of conversation as they pack office belongings.

rank of assistant professor. His promotion to associate professor came quickly. Two years later, he joined the journalism faculty at the University of Oklahoma, then accepted an assistant professorship the following year at the University of Missouri, where he began work on the doctorate and soon was promoted to associate professor. After earning the Ph.D. degree in history with a minor in journalism (his dissertation was titled "History of News Magazines"), Chunn accepted a position as director of public relations and professor of journalism and marketing at Texas Christian University. He remained there until joining the NAM in 1953.[10]

For five years, Chunn handled educational matters for the NAM in the Southern states, including Oklahoma, contacting industrialists and educators, making speeches, arranging institutes, writing booklets, and counseling industry. Although he had been away from campus life, he had not been away from education.[11]

As for media experience, Chunn had dabbled in food-product sales and advertising and had worked part-time for the *Jonesboro Daily Tribune* throughout his high school and college days. He had been a stringer for the Associated Press from 1935 to 1937 and for International News Service in 1937. While at Northwestern, he had done some reporting for the *Chicago Herald-Examiner* and had assisted the staff of Northwestern's public relations department.[12]

He was a Democrat, a Methodist, a Mason, a Kappa Sigma, and a member of the Military Order of the World Wars. Along the way, he had been selected for membership by ten honorary and/or professional societies, and had received a 1951 research grant from the Carnegie Foundation for the Advancement of Teaching. He had conducted Austrian newspaper editors on a tour of the United States for the University of Missouri and the U.S. State Department, and had written two books, a pamphlet on news style, and several magazine articles and short stories. Alpha Kappa Psi fraternity had selected him as the Georgia honorary initiate of 1955. His biography had appeared in *Who's Who in America* and *Who's Who in the South and Southwest*, and his list of references was solid but not ostentatious.

Despite the debilitation of life in prisoner of war camps, he now considered his health to be excellent and at six feet tall he carried 180 pounds, a gain of some fifty pounds since POW days. In considering Scroggs's offer, Florence's desire to see her parents more often no doubt influenced Chunn. Her parents still lived in Tulsa, only a brief drive away.[13]

Chunn no sooner had found his way to his TF-8 office than he faced a myriad of routine details: a June 17-20 meeting of the International Council of Industrial Editors in Washington, D.C., at which Professor Trout would be honored; the need to revise floor plans for the Communications Building to provide three additional faculty offices ("even with these we will be doubling up two or three professors to an office"), finding a replacement for Professor Elsie Shoemaker to teach home economics journalism; getting air conditioners approved for Rooms 201 and 203; evacuating TF-8 without needless delay; and checking on a temporary change in plans as to transfer of the Arts and Sciences Multilith Service to the School of Communications.[14]

Then Chunn began the other duties the time demanded. He worked on fall teaching assignments, applied for admission to the graduate faculty, prepared promotional materials, held his first faculty meeting, wrote a pamphlet to help county agents with their media contacts and expanded his correspondence to smooth the transition from the Trout administration to his own.

Lou S. Allard, publisher of the *Drumright Derrick* and a former Aggie, was president of the state press association as Chunn warmed to the tasks ahead. Allard may have inquired as to Chunn's plans for community-newspaper service, for the new director wrote Allard on July 21 reiterating the school's desire to conduct research that would benefit the state press. He called upon Allard to make suggestions for research "that you would want to see done in Oklahoma." The journalism director envisioned research being carried out by both graduate students and advanced undergraduates on projects "that would be of direct benefit to you and other papers." Originals of the same letter went to each of the seven members of Curtin's OPA committee, with carbon copies to Scroggs and MacVicar.[15] There is little evidence that suggestions poured into the office.

When Chunn queried Scroggs as to funds for radio-television maintenance, the dean suggested he wait and "talk this out with Dean [Robert

B.] Kamm after next Friday."[16] Scroggs was now deeply involved in his move to Florida and was ready for Kamm to handle such problems.

There was only one major staffing decision to be made as the 1958-59 academic year approached. Except for graduate assistants, the teaching staff was largely in place. But Chunn must find Shoemaker's replacement in the home economics journalism area, a difficult task at such a late date. The most likely prospect on short notice was twenty-four-year-old Doreen Cronkite Clair, a Kansas State home economics journalism graduate with four years of newspaper and publicity experience in Kansas and Texas. She was a five-time winner of the K-Key Award for her work in campus journalism and had won the Journalism Memorial Award as well.[17]

Mrs. Clair, a widow with an infant son, had completed her degree in home economics journalism in January of 1956. She was a member of Phi Kappa Phi, Mortar Board, Theta Sigma Phi, and Omicron Nu and had graduated with honors. Before enrolling at K-State she had spent a year as society editor of the *Abilene [Kansas] Reflector-Chronicle* and while in school had worked as a copy writer in the college news bureau. Following graduation she served for several months as a secretary in Eighth Air Force Headquarters and had returned to the college as assistant editor of the *Kansas 4-H Journal.* She had enrolled in the Kansas State graduate school just before being contacted by Chunn.[18]

On July 22, Mrs. Clair drove alone to Stillwater to be interviewed for the position. She visited with Vice President MacVicar for half an hour, then met with Pauline Cunningham, assistant to the dean of home economics, and Dean Scroggs. At 4:00 P.M. she sat down with the journalism faculty to exchange views on the position, her apprehensions relieved by the friendliness of the group. She saw possibilities for expanding the curriculum. At 1:45 P.M. on July 29, Chunn phoned Mrs. Clair, offering her a ten-month appointment at the rank of instructor. Two hours and fifteen minutes later she phoned her acceptance. Two days later her appointment papers had been signed. Chunn announced on July 30 that Mrs. Clair would join the faculty on September 1 as an instructor.[19]

She was both conscientious and productive in her work at OSU. In addition to Home Economics Journalism, she taught four other courses: Introduction to Journalism Fields, Publicity Methods, Interpreting the News, and Agricultural and Home Economics Promotion. She contributed to school efforts in other ways, such as advising students, speaking on the program of the Oklahoma Collegiate Press Association, and assisting in various promotional efforts.[20]

That problem solved, Chunn turned his attention to the recruitment of students. One of his first efforts was an attractive but brief brochure in which this statement appeared: "OSU's School of Communications offers training for a wide variety of interesting careers. The Oklahoma

Doreen Clair joined the faculty as a specialist in home economics journalism. She was effective but had a short tenure.

State student may choose specializations in community journalism, industrial editing, advertising, photography, speech, radio-TV, drama, public relations, agricultural journalism or home economics journalism." The four sequences—journalism, speech, photography, and radio-TV—were emphasized on the cover along with inter-disciplinary programs in advertising, public relations and industrial editing. Dean Eugene Swearingen of the College of Business took exception to the mention of advertising and industrial editing, noting that the brochure "may be slightly misleading." These two programs were still a part of his domain. Neither had been reassigned in the formation of the school, although they would be relinquished by business after the arrival of Chunn's successor a few months later.[21]

The pending move from TF-8 to the new Communications Building posed other problems of a quite different nature for the new school. For one thing, badly needed space in the basement was being held by chemistry for laboratory work and storage. But worse still was the stench from psychology's "hundreds of rats." Haskell Pruett, recalling this transition period, said the odor was "terrible—worse than going to the hog pens."[22]

Despite these frustrations, or perhaps because of them, the new director took to the road to make media contacts. He wanted to cover as much ground as possible before fall classes began. In Tulsa, he visited seven top media executives, four on the metropolitan dailies, two in television and one in radio. He also visited the publishers of the *Sapulpa*

Daily Herald and the *Sapulpa Democrat* and the publisher of the *Drumright Journal.*

Reporting to Scroggs on the trip, with carbons to Oliver S. Willham, MacVicar, and Trout, Chunn told of establishing a summer internship on the *Tulsa Tribune* and eliciting a promise from editor Jenkin Lloyd Jones to "speak to our students this fall." As to the internship, he commented: "This is significant in as much as *The Tribune*, like the *Daily Oklahoman*, has limited its internships in the past to students of the University of Oklahoma." He also spoke of the interest of Bill Henthorne and Sid Steen of the *World* "in talking with any of our qualified graduates." At KOTV and KVOO-TV he gathered technical advice on OSU's proposed television facilities, while his visit with Frank L. Lane, manager of KRMG radio, revealed that Lane's "greatest needs from us will be time salesmen, writers and announcers."

The visit with publisher R. P. Matthews in Sapulpa was especially pleasing to Chunn. Matthews was jubilant over having successfully defended himself in a $100,000 libel suit the day before. "Mr. Matthews showed me how he did it," Chunn wrote. "He read passages from my book on Oklahoma newspaper law to the court." Editor Matthews told him OSU was doing the best job of training newspaper personnel of any school in the state. Publisher Gordon R. Rockett of the *Drumright Journal*, who also was part owner of radio station KUSH in Cushing, expressed an interest "in both our journalism and radio sequences." Rockett also said he would like to use some OSU tape programs on KUSH. Summing up, Chunn reported: "Reaction to the visits was so good that I believe we can capitalize on similar trips to other stations and newspapers in the state."[23] Responding to his letter, Dean Scroggs praised Chunn for taking hold of his duties "with so much imagination and energy."[24]

About two weeks later, Chunn was on the road again, this time to visit newspapers and radio stations in Ponca City, Newkirk, Blackwell, Tonkawa, and Perry. His purpose, he wrote his new dean, Robert Kamm, was to build rapport with the state's newspaper and radio leaders. His report to Dean Kamm and Vice President MacVicar carried the same enthusiastic tone as his first tour report. It also had produced some positive results. Editor Gareth Muchmore of the *Ponca City News* told Chunn he would deliver some type fonts and a job press to the school soon, but declined an offer to teach a journalism class for fall "because of [the pressure of his] many other professional activities." At Blackwell, Chunn proposed that senior journalism students edit the *Journal-Tribune* one day during spring semester. Publisher Milo Watson of the *Perry Journal* offered to allow Fred G. Beers, his managing editor, to have an afternoon off each week to act as a laboratory instructor in newswriting courses.[25] Chunn accepted the offer.

On July 29, in what probably was his first faculty meeting, Trout's successor covered thirteen items of business. The only record of that meeting is labeled "Agenda," but its style and content suggest it was the minutes of the meeting. Curricular matters were given the greatest attention, but the faculty may have found plans for the move into new quarters of more personal interest. An air of anticipation filled the room.

Now that the new school was a reality, Chunn wanted to study all course offerings for overlapping and duplication. A second reason may have been to assure himself that teaching outlines had been prepared for all courses. The outlines were to be arranged topically, "so that—if you had to be away because of illness or a professional trip—someone could step in your place and teach the course without too much confusion to the students." He called for the outlines by October 1.

Chunn then announced the appointment of curriculum committees in the various areas to go over the outlines, "not to tell you how to teach, but to arrange the course content in the most efficient manner." In the speech area, Harry Anderson, Leslie R. Kreps, and Glenna Wilson were appointed; in radio-television, John Woodworth, Darrel Woodyard, and Frederick Kolch; in journalism, James C. Stratton, Haag, and Lemuel D. Groom; in photography, Pruett, Harry Hix, and Haag.

After outlines had been submitted, Chunn indicated he would call upon the faculty to consider possible curriculum revisions. "Are there courses we need and do not have?" he asked. "Do we have courses that we should eliminate?" Reflecting upon the last accreditation report, he wondered about adding the requirement of press photography to the print sequences and the advisability of "some sort of photography" for television students. He informed the faculty, too, that the accrediting team had suggested that "some of our courses that list two credit hours need actually three hours credit."

Then Chunn, the first person to carry the title *director* in the communication area, noted the need for stronger efforts to attract qualified majors in all of the school's specialties. To accomplish this, he urged faculty members to "travel about, talk with guidance counselors...", speak before civic clubs, present programs in high schools, etc." He told the faculty that he wanted them to have comfortable, adequate, dignified quarters, but expressed his regret that it would be necessary to share office space. On the brighter side, each office was to have a telephone, good lighting and clean surroundings. Chunn said his policy would be to have regular faculty meetings, but that they would be brief. He would limit debate, he said, if it went on too long. He promised that he would work for the faculty, saying he wanted them "to have the best." For a proposed newsletter, he called for faculty members to submit items about alumni as well as about their own successes such as authorship of books and articles, speeches delivered, or progress in graduate work.[26]

For some there was a wait and see attitude following the meeting, but

Haskell Pruett, a bouncy, energetic sixty-three-year-old known campuswide as "Doc," was jubilant over his escape from the College of Education to the School of Communications. He had chafed for years under the lip service he felt photography had received. His dean, J. Andrew Holley, although a personal friend, had told Pruett on one occasion, "I don't want a course in tennis and I don't want a course in photography." As a result, photography had been given meager budgetary support, with Pruett often buying equipment and supplies from his own pocket. "Andy Holley was delighted to tell me in no uncertain terms that he was finally getting the photography department out of education," Pruett said. The move was good news for Pruett as well as his dean. He immediately received a $25 a month raise, and on the faculty ratings kept by Chunn, his score was among the highest. Pruett liked the open communication he had with Chunn. He felt he could talk with him about anything. Harry Hix, Pruett's laboratory instructor, made the move with him, but until all of the basement space could be transferred to the school, photography labs would continue to be located in Morrill Hall.[27]

For the speech faculty, the shift in academic fortunes was one to be assessed slowly. Speech studies had started in 1898 with the arrival of Angelo C. Scott, who had a strong interest in oratory. Scott, even as president, continued to teach public speaking until his informal work was formalized in 1906 with the appointment of Howard G. Seldomridge, who set up a speech program in the Department of English. One year later, the Department of Public Speaking was established with Seldomridge as head. But in 1910, the new department returned to English in a joint program now called the Department of English and Public Speaking. "Seldy," as he was affectionately called by students, continued to teach speech until 1912 when he left Oklahoma A. and M. for a teaching position at James Millikin University, Decatur, Illinois. His replacement, Isadore Samuels, after two years on campus was named to head a resurrected Department of Public Speaking.[28]

In 1917, John R. Pelsma replaced Samuels, directing the work in Public Speaking until 1920 when D. Terry Martin started a thirty-three-year tenure. One year after taking over the program, Martin changed the unit's name. It now was the Department of Speech. Martin was a strong personality with dogmatic ways, but he had developed and nurtured the department to a position of prominence on campus. With his retirement in 1953, the speech faculty once again lost its autonomy. It was absorbed into what then became a tri-partite unit, the Department of English, Foreign Languages and Speech. That arrangement had worked fairly well. Hans Andersen had named Martin's long-time sidekick, Harry Anderson, chairman of the speech faculty and a relaxed relationship existed among Andersen as head and his faculty chairmen.[29]

Now speech once again was called upon to adjust to a new home department in which it did not have departmental status. There was some uneasiness as the shift of authority took place. Some speech faculty felt that, despite the agreements forged by Dean Scroggs, Hans Andersen, and Harry Anderson, they had had too little to say about the transfer. In addition, there was some question of whether moving from old and picturesque Williams Hall, home of the Prairie Playhouse, would best serve the interests of the faculty, which included drama as well as speech and radio-television professors. Whether Chunn would continue with Anderson as speech chairman was another uncertainty.

The answer to the latter question was not long in coming. Chunn set up a conference with Anderson and Professor Frederick Kolch, a competent and effective speech generalist. Among their colleagues, they appeared to be the most likely possibilities for the appointment. Chunn informed the two that he was about to name a speech chairman, and that it would be neither of them. On September 18, Chunn appointed four faculty chairmen, announcing the appointments to the communications faculty by inter-office memo four days later. Leslie Kreps, who had come to OSU only a year before, was to replace Anderson as chairman of the speech faculty. Other chairmen named were Haskell Pruett, photogra-

The speech faculty in the School of Communications included (*from the left*) Lee Gilstrap, Frederick Kolch, Glenna Wilson, Martha Sharp, Vivia Locke, Harry Anderson, and Leslie Kreps. The merger was not popular with speech faculty, who pressed Dean Robert B. Kamm for recognition as a separate department.

phy; Professor Robert Johnson, radio-television, and Chunn himself, technical journalism. In this arrangement, radio-television had been given coequal status with speech, but drama had not. It remained in the speech area.[30]

There may have been other reasons the speech faculty was restive. For one thing, the student credit hours generated by the speech faculty were far larger than those of the other constituent units. For another, its faculty of ten outnumbered the faculties of the other *sequences*. Journalism had four, including Chunn, and photography and radio-television two each. The term "sequence" was in common use at Northwestern University, where Chunn had earned his master's, and in journalism accreditation circles as well. Because Chunn's instructions from the administration had not allowed departmental status for the various units, he had decided to use the term in his organizational structure.[31] Less important, perhaps, was the fact that speech had moved somewhat piecemeal into the Communications Building because much of the top floor had been gutted to make room for radio and television studios formerly located on Sixth Street. It was not immediately available for occupancy.

By early fall, speech faculty luncheons in the Prairie Playhouse had become rump sessions. Most outspoken was Vivia Locke, a talented dramatics professor. As the year progressed, she increased the intensity of her demands that speech and drama attempt to get out from under the communications umbrella. She and others felt that Dr. Chunn's desire to review scripts to be staged was a form of censorship that high school drama teachers might accept, but that such behavior was untenable at the university level. There appeared to be a clash, too, between Chunn and Martha Sharp, whose breezy style and high visibility somehow rubbed him the wrong way.[32]

Added to all of this was the fact that several members of the speech faculty believed they had been coerced into another amalgamation. They thought that their productivity and teaching effectiveness deserved greater recognition. While their earlier merger into Hans Andersen's department had been a comedown of sorts, the relaxed atmosphere between Hans Andersen and Harry Anderson had produced only minimal problems for speech and drama personnel. Yet there was smoldering resentment that on that occasion they had simply been told by Dean Scroggs that they would no longer be a separate department. There had been more faculty involvement this time, but too little to suit some faculty and staff.[33]

Chunn's frustrations mounted. Mrs. Clair resigned effective January 31, 1959, to return to Manhattan, where she was to be married on February 5. He would have to make do with a patchwork solution to cover her courses while seeking to resolve the growing dissent in the speech wing of the school.[34]

Faculty members in speech had been dissatisfied even before they had been moved to the School of Communications. Ten months earlier Harry Anderson had put into writing "the needs and wishes which we have had for the past several years." Top priority was to break free of the Department of English, Foreign Languages and Speech and to reestablish a free-standing Department of Speech. Next was their desire to step up course offerings in speech correction, including clinical facilities, and to introduce a lineup of courses in radio and television. Thirdly, the speech faculty called for more adequate space, including private offices, a clinical area, a combination laboratory and reading room equipped with sound recording equipment, and a room for debate squad meetings, study and practice. The statement of needs included a suggestion that KVRO be returned to the campus and used as a laboratory for the application of classroom theory. If the journalism program was to be moved to the Chemistry Building, Anderson wrote, "we suggest that Speech be moved there also in order to facilitate greater cooperative efforts."

The dissatisfaction of the speech faculty can best be understood in the context of the times. Faculty involvement in decision making was on the upswing nationally. At OSU, a Faculty Council had been established in 1953 following years of authoritarian administration from the top down. Faculty members generally, not simply speech faculty, wanted more involvement in the decisions that would affect them in a significant way.

Chunn's military background and his fondness for using frequent memoranda to announce decisions or to set policy—a procedure not foreign to the National Association of Manufacturers—may have played a part in the growing gap within the school. But one must remember that Chunn had inherited an organizational structure that neither his new dean, Robert Kamm, nor Chunn himself had a part in forming. Some of the units involved were open and receptive, but that attitude was not true of most of the speech faculty.[35]

It was clear that Chunn had sought to respond to various dissatisfactions in the speech and broadcasting areas. Several letters and memoranda had reflected this, as had two reports that otherwise were largely critical. In an undated report, "The Administration of the Speech Area," received by Dean Kamm shortly before the end of the spring semester, Kreps had predicted that "speech will not receive proper administration under the present arrangements." The seven-page report summarized the speech faculty's frustrations in their relationships with Chunn, his dismissal of Sharp, faculty recruitment, budget, censorship of theatre productions, and favoritism for journalism over speech in brochures and public pronouncements.[36]

In a seven-page "Report from Radio-Television, School of Communi-

In addition to Robert M. Johnson, who headed radio-television, the heads of the other areas of the new School of Communications were Leslie R. Kreps in speech (*left*) and Haskell Pruett in photography (*right*).

cations," dated April 6, 1959, Robert M. Johnson, faculty chairman, referred to "stifling conditions [the report would detail] as an honest attempt not to destroy but to correct." These included too few faculty meetings, lack of needed consultation on budgetary and technical matters, misquoting of OSU officials to prevent action that Chunn did not wish to see carried through, and Johnson's own dismissal. "I was fired," he wrote, "for doing the job for which I was hired." He said he had written the report "for what value it may have in restoring the accepted quality and reputation of academic standards and basic integrity in human relations which have come to be disregarded."[37]

One or both of the reports apparently had been called to Chunn's attention. Four days after Johnson's report had gone to Dean Kamm, Chunn wrote a memorandum to President Willham, with carbon copies to Vice President MacVicar and Dean Kamm. He charged that unimportant differences of opinion had been magnified, and that more time was needed to make the school concept work. He told Willham that disagreements had been enhanced "by difficulties of combining speech with journalism, or anything else. Speech does not want to fit in, it wants to stand alone." Chunn gave his reasons for having dismissed Sharp and Johnson, both of whom later would be retained, then outlined six alternatives for Willham to consider, one of which was to abolish the School of Communications. His first choice was to remain as director of the school, with each of the four specialty areas given departmental status.

From Chunn's point of view, the problems of the first year were related to organizational structure rather than to human relations. He asked President Willham for an opportunity to confer about any anticipated change "in order to protect my professional reputation."[38]

The speech faculty's search for a separate identity such as it had enjoyed for so many years under D. Terry Martin was not new. More than two months before Chunn had been hired, Harry Anderson had informed MacVicar that "Our first desire is the reestablishment of the Department of Speech."[39]

Dean Kamm, a strong believer in faculty participation in academic matters, was aware of the difficulties Chunn faced. He had listened to speech and radio-television faculty air their grievances individually and collectively. He had met several times with Chunn, seeking to find a way to promote collegiality in the school. But as the months passed, Chunn sensed that he was presiding over an unworkable combination of talents. Kamm was certain that he was. Finally, over coffee in the Student Union on May 26, 1959, Dean Kamm told Chunn that the school must be dismantled. The frustrations Chunn had faced in what he felt had been an even-handed approach to the various faculties had not been kind to his ego. He had signed on to direct a school. To stay on in a lesser capacity did not appeal to him. He told Kamm he would submit his resignation. The journalism faculty tried unsuccessfully to get him to stay, but he had had enough. A complete break with the university was, he felt, the proper response. In a terse, one-sentence letter June 8, he confirmed his verbal resignation, effective July 1, 1959. His separation notice was signed by Vice Dean Walter A. Hansen the next day and on June 17 by President Willham. His period of service was recorded as "5-15-58 to 6-30-59."[40] What had started as an exciting challenge for the sensitive Arkansan had ended in frustration and disillusionment.

It did not take Chunn long to relocate. His credentials were sound and his public relations experience solid. On July 20, 1959, little more than a year after his move to Stillwater, he was writing his former OSU colleagues on the letterhead of the American Academy of Pediatrics in Evanston, Illinois, where he now was director of the Department of Health Education and Information.

The typewritten letter was addressed "Dear Friends," but in pencil he had noted that it was for journalism and photography faculty members only. His new office overlooked the Northwestern University campus. "Across the hall from me," he wrote, "I can see the blue-green waters of Lake Michigan." The Stillwater home had been sold and he was awaiting the arrival August 1 of his wife and two children. He was living temporarily in the Library Plaza Hotel, but had purchased a four-bedroom house at 724 Jonquil Terrace, in nearby Deerfield.

Chunn directed parts of the letter individually to Dorothy Rickstrew,

C. Ellsworth Chunn addresses high school journalists at the second annual J-Day program. On the panel (*left to right*) are Bruce Palmer, Betty Brenz, Bob Allen, and Roland Sodowsky. The panel represented television, public relations, and newspapers.

"Lem" Groom, "Maury" Haag and "Jim" Stratton, commenting on the things they would like about his new location and facilities. Then he turned to a new theme. He said he had reliable information that "all the communications schools are having difficulties and wish they had never been set up. Speech is the trouble. Even some of the big J schools are having problems with budgets and strife." A brief, offhand remark indicated that, as he perceived things, there had been coolness toward him by Dean Kamm. But there was a lighter note, too. "It's not true what they say about Yankees. These are all very friendly. They talk funny but you know they mean well even if they can't speak right."[41]

Endnotes

1. John E. Drewry to S. M. Berry, 28 May 1958, and C. Ellsworth Chunn to Gerald T. Curtin, 20 May 1958, in Files of the School of Journalism and Broadcasting, Oklahoma State University, Stillwater, Oklahoma.
2. Schiller Scroggs to Gerald T. Curtin, 28 February 1958, and C. Ellsworth Chunn to Robert W. MacVicar, 13 May 1958, in Files of the School of Journalism and Broadcasting. Chunn's letter had referred to the basement, first, and second floors. In this book, those references were changed to first, second, and third floors in keeping with Physical Plant designations.
3. C. Ellsworth Chunn to Robert W. MacVicar, 13 May 1958, Files of the School of Journalism and Broadcasting.
4. *Tulsa Tribune*, 24 July 1945, copy unpaged.
5. *1941 Kendallabrum*, p. 1, Administration Section University of Tulsa Yearbook; Florence Chunn to Harry E. Heath Jr., 29 July 1989, School of Journalism and Broadcasting Centennial History Collection, Special Collections, Edmon Low Library, Oklahoma State University.

6. Schiller Scroggs to Oliver S. Willham, 2 June 1958, Files of the School of Journalism and Broadcasting; Oklahoma State University *Daily O'Collegian*, 14 May 1958, pp. 1, 6.

7. John E. Drewry to S. M. Berry, 28 May 1958, and Schiller Scroggs to C. Ellsworth Chunn, 7 April 1958, in Files of the School of Journalism and Broadcasting; *Daily O'Collegian*, 2 December 1958, pp. 1, 3.

8. *JB News* (1983-86), p. 24; C. Ellsworth Chunn, *Not By Bread Alone* (Society of the Descendants of Washington's Army at Valley Forge, 1981), inside back cover; Response to "Oklahoma A. and M. College Request for Information Concerning Training and Professional Experience" (Application for Position) by C. Ellsworth Chunn, 21 April 1958, and Undated biographical sketch [1958] of C. Ellsworth Chunn, transmitted by carbon copy to Vice President Robert W. MacVicar and Clement E. Trout by Schiller Scroggs, Files of the School of Journalism and Broadcasting.

9. *JB News* (1983-86), p. 24; Application for Position as Director, School of Communications of C. Ellsworth Chunn, 21 April 1958, Files of the School of Journalism and Broadcasting.

10. Undated biographical sketch of C. Ellsworth Chunn [1958], and Biography of C. Ellsworth Chunn, typewritten manuscript, 4 October 1981, Files of the School of Journalism and Broadcasting; Lieutenant General S. E. Smith, editor, *The United States Marine Corps in World War II* (New York, NY: Random House, 1969), p. 105; *Who's Who in America 1980-1981* (Chicago, IL: Marquis Who's Who, Incorporated), vol. 1, p. 620.

11. John E. Drewry to S. M. Berry, 28 May 1958, and Undated biographical sketch [1958] of C. Ellsworth Chunn, Files of the School of Journalism and Broadcasting.

12. Undated biographical sketch [1958] of C. Ellsworth Chunn, Files of the School of Journalism and Broadcasting; *Who's Who in America 1980-1981*, vol. 1, p. 620.

13. Application for Position, 21 April 1958, Undated biographical sketch [1958] of C. Ellsworth Chunn, and Florence Chunn to Harry E. Heath Jr., 29 July 1989, in Files of the School of Journalism and Broadcasting.

14. C. Ellsworth Chunn to John W. Heusel, 2 June 1958, C. Ellsworth Chunn to Oliver S. Willham, 6 June 1958, C. Ellsworth Chunn to Robert W. MacVicar, 9 June 1958, Oliver S. Willham to C. Ellsworth Chunn, 17 June 1958, and Schiller Scroggs to Robert W. MacVicar, 7 July 1958, in Files of the School of Journalism and Broadcasting.

15. C. Ellsworth Chunn to Oliver S. Willham, 6 June 1958, C. Ellsworth Chunn to Robert W. MacVicar, 9 June 1958, Oliver S. Willham to C. Ellsworth Chunn, 17 June 1958, C. Ellsworth Chunn to Mr. Bullen, 27 June 1958, Schiller Scroggs to Robert W. MacVicar, 7 July 1958, and C. Ellsworth Chunn to Lou S. Allard, 21 July 1958, in Files of the School of Journalism and Broadcasting.

16. Undated handwritten note from Schiller Scroggs at the bottom of a memorandum from C. Ellsworth Chunn dated 25 July 1958, Files of the School of Journalism and Broadcasting.

17. Oliver S. Willham to C. Ellsworth Chunn, 17 June 1958, C. Ellsworth Chunn to John Stevens, 30 July 1958, Doreen Clair Burbank to Harry E. Heath Jr., 10 October 1990, and Oklahoma State University Request for Information Concerning Training and Professional Experience (job application form) of Doreen C. Clair, 3 August 1958, in Files of the School of Journalism and Broadcasting.

18. Oklahoma State University Request for Information Concerning Training and Professional Experience (job application form) dated 3 August 1958, and Transcript, Kansas State College, 7 August 1958, in Files of the School of Journalism and Broadcasting.

19. Interview schedule, Doreen C. Clair, 22 July 1958, Doreen C. Clair to C. Ellsworth Chunn, 23 July 1958, Handwritten notes by C. Ellsworth Chunn at bottom of Doreen C. Clair letter dated 29 July 1958, Request for Personnel. Action, New Appointment of Doreen C. Clair, 31 July 1958, C. Ellsworth Chunn to Communications faculty, 30 July 1958, C. Ellsworth Chunn to Julia Stephens, 30 July 1958, C. Ellsworth Chunn to John Stevens, 30 July 1958, and C. Ellsworth Chunn to Doreen C. Clair, 1 August 1958, in Files of the School of Journalism and Broadcasting.

20. Based upon letters from Doreen C. Clair to four book publishers, 8 August 1958, and Schedule of Classes, First Semester, 1958-59, in Files of the School of Journalism and Broadcasting.

21. *The School of Communications at Oklahoma State University*, undated brochure,

probably published between July and September 1958, Files of the School of Journalism and Broadcasting. A file copy of this brochure includes a handwritten note on the cover from Dean Swearingen to Dean Kamm raising a question as to the locus of advertising and industrial editing courses.

22. Author interview with Haskell Pruett, 21 October 1987, Stillwater, Oklahoma.

23. C. Ellsworth Chunn to Schiller Scroggs, 18 July 1958, Files of the School of Journalism and Broadcasting.

24. Schiller Scroggs to C. Ellsworth Chunn, 29 July 1958, Files of the School of Journalism and Broadcasting.

25. C. Ellsworth Chunn to Robert B. Kamm, 5 August 1958.

26. Harry H. Anderson to Robert W. MacVicar, 3 March 1958, and Agenda [Minutes], Faculty and Staff Meeting, School of Communications, 29 July 1958, in Files of the School of Journalism and Broadcasting.

27. Pruett interview.

28. *Annual Catalog, Oklahoma A. and M. College, 1906-1907*, pp. 69, 70; *Annual Catalog, Oklahoma A. and M. College, 1907-1908*, pp. 7, 49, 88, 89; *Annual Catalog, Oklahoma A. and M. College, 1910-1911*, pp. vii, 105, 107, 108; *Annual Catalog, Oklahoma A. and M. College, 1914-1915*, pp. ix, xiv, 83-85; *Annual Catalog, Oklahoma A. and M. College, 1915-1916*, pp. viii, 109, 110; *Annual Catalog, Oklahoma A. and M. College, 1916-1917*, pp. vii, xxi, 118, 119.

29. *Annual Catalog, Oklahoma A. and M. College, 1917-1918*, pp. vi, xviii, 117, 118; *Annual Catalog, Oklahoma A. and M. College, 1920-1921*, pp. vi, xvi, 135, 136; *Annual Catalog, Oklahoma A. and M. College, 1921-1922*, pp. 8, 215, 216; *Oklahoma A. and M. College Bulletin, Catalog Issue for Arts and Sciences, 1952-1953*, pp. 14, 64, 72-74; *Oklahoma A. and M. College Bulletin, Catalog Issue for Arts and Sciences, 1953-1954*, pp. 14, 64, 72, 73.

30. Author interview with Leslie Kreps, 19 July 1989, Stillwater, Oklahoma; C. Ellsworth Chunn to Communications Faculty, 22 September 1958, Files of the School of Journalism and Broadcasting.

31. C. Ellsworth Chunn to Faculty of School of Communications, 20 October 1958, and Typewritten roster of School of Communications compiled in late summer or early fall of 1958 with marginal notes by C. Ellsworth Chunn, in Files of the School of Journalism and Broadcasting.

32. Based upon author interviews with two members of the 1958 speech faculty. These interviews were supported by a seven page report, "The administration of the Speech Area," submitted to Dean Robert B. Kamm by Leslie R. Kreps. It was stamped "Received April 6, 1959," Files of the School of Journalism and Broadcasting.

33. Harry H. Anderson to Robert W. MacVicar, 3 March 1958, Files of the School of Journalism and Broadcasting.

34. Doreen C. Clair to Oliver S. Willham, 14 January 1959, Oklahoma State University Separation Notice of Doreen C. Clair, 15 January 1959, and Doreen Clair Simpson to "Dr. Chunn, Stratton, Haag, Johnson, Rickstrew, et al," 6 March 1959, in Files of the School of Journalism and Broadcasting.

35. Based upon the author's confidential interviews with faculty members in both speech and journalism over a four-year period.

36. Leslie R. Kreps to Robert B. Kamm, 6 April 1958, Files of the School of Journalism and Broadcasting.

37. Robert M. Johnson to Robert B. Kamm, 6 April 1958, Files of the School of Journalism and Broadcasting.

38. C. Ellsworth Chunn to Oliver S. Willham, 10 April 1959, Files of the School of Journalism and Broadcasting.

39. Harry H. Anderson to Robert W. MacVicar, 3 March 1958, Files of the School of Journalism and Broadcasting.

40. Author interview with Robert B. Kamm, 30 June 1989, Stillwater, Oklahoma; C. Ellsworth Chunn to Robert B. Kamm, 8 June 1959, and Oklahoma State University Separation Notice, Resignation of C. Ellsworth Chunn, 9 June 1959, in Files of the School of Journalism and Broadcasting..

41. C. Ellsworth Chunn to "Dear Friends," 20 July 1959, Files of the School of Journalism and Broadcasting.

18 A Major in Radio and Television

While hobbyists were building crystal sets from coast to coast and radio was in its infancy, colleges and universities had begun to see its educational promise. Experimentation with "wireless" had captured the attention of faculty members at several colleges and universities. Soon radio components were being sold by the Radio Corporation of America, and the U.S. Department of Commerce was struggling with the uncontrolled proliferation of broadcasting stations with overlapping signals. "Fishing" for long-distance programs and logging them had become a national fad. Certainly there was potential for educational goals in what some announcers called "the great unseen radio audience."[1]

Telephony had been a basic engineering course complemented by studies in physics for nine years before the magic word *radio* appeared in the 1923-24 Oklahoma A. and M. catalog. The turning point came with the arrival of James C. Kositzky, an assistant professor who had taken an electrical engineering degree at the University of Nebraska. Since 1916, Nebraska had used a spark transmitter to send out weather and market reports, and the year before Kositzky's move to Stillwater it had been awarded a broadcasting license by the U.S. Department of Commerce. He probably had taken Nebraska's first radio course under J. O. Ferguson in 1919-1920. Kositzky's interest in radio was high. That fact may have been responsible for his election to the faculty. It was more than coincidence that with his arrival a new course, Electrical Communication and Radio, entered the catalog. Later, as the radio mania spread across campus, he added Elementary Radio, a non-technical engineering course open to all students. Another professor interested in the technical aspects of broadcasting was Edwin Kurtz. In 1923, Kurtz succeeded Robert B. George as head of the Department of Electrical Engineering. George, who held an M.S. in electrical engineering from the Massachusetts Institute of Technology, had left Oklahoma A. and M. after only one year. Kurtz had earned a B.S. degree at the University of Wisconsin, an M.S. at Union College, and an electrical engineering degree at Iowa State College. He gave Kositzky strong support as he developed radio work in the department. (Kurtz was destined later to be one of the nation's pioneers in experimental television broadcasting from his University of Iowa laboratory.)

One year after Kositzky's first course was offered, the Department of Physics joined in with Physics 332, Radio. Both departments continued their courses as the radio industry developed, capturing the imagination of students and general public alike with the same sense of excitement television would bring to the nation twenty-five years later.[2]

On August 22, 1923, Richard G. Tyler recommended to the board of agriculture "the installation of a radio broadcasting station." Nothing came of the acting president's recommendation. The board's lack of interest was unfortunate, for at that time Oklahoma A. and M. could have become a leader in the use of radio to relay extension information on a

SPECIAL COLLECTIONS, OSU LIBRARY

HEAR

Dr. Bradford Knapp

by

RADIO

MONDAY, FEBRUARY 23
BETWEEN 7 AND 8 O'CLOCK P. M. AT BRISTOW
396 Meters

We still have time to install three Atwater Kent receiving sets complete. Get this program and future programs for you.

HOKE ELECTRIC CO.

Oklahoma A. and M. College's pioneer in radio was James C. Kositzky, shown here with the first transmitter. Kositzky was an electrical engineering professor and taught the first course in radio. President Bradford Knapp, a radio enthusiast, appointed Kositzky as the technical director of Oklahoma A. and M.'s outreach by radio. Knapp tried hard for a licensed station but failed. He instead turned to remote broadcasts by telephone lines.

broad scale. The college's interest peaked during the presidency of Bradford Knapp, who saw radio both as an extension and a public relations tool. By then, it was too late for Oklahoma A. and M. to receive a license. Knapp relied upon other stations, principally KVOO, with a hook-up by telephone lines. The college's limited radio efforts featured student musical and dramatic talent plus faculty expertise in various academic specialties, with agriculture and home economics given top priority. Kositzky supervised technical matters, and D. Terry Martin, head of the Department of Speech, was program director without portfolio. Kositzky left Oklahoma A. and M. in 1928 and was replaced by Benjamin A. Fisher, who had joined the faculty in 1927 as an assistant professor of electrical engineering. He held the B.S. from the University of Missouri and the M.S. from Iowa State College.

Six years after Kositzky had developed the first engineering course in radio, the Department of Speech offered a non-technical course covering radio performance. Whether the course was Martin's brainchild or was urged upon him by the School of Commerce remains a mystery. It was first listed in the 1929-30 catalog and was labeled Speech 401, Effective Business Expression. It was specifically for commerce juniors and seniors. The course covered a wide range of topics, including a unit on "radio and telephone speeches."

In other words, Martin, who held an A.B. degree from Emery and Henry College and an M.A. degree from Cornell University, had used Angelo C. Scott's approach. Scott had introduced newspaper writing as a unit in rhetoric, and Martin had chosen to introduce a radio unit into a wide-ranging service course for commerce students. He had the assistance of Dorothy DeWitt, a recently hired instructor with her A.B. degree from Grinnell College and an M.A. from the University of Michigan. Martin was in his eighth year on the campus and had become the dominant figure in speech since its 1915 break from the Department of English.[3]

The following year, the course was solely in Martin's hands where it remained for the next sixteen years. Only two changes took place in those years. In the 1932-33 academic year it became Speech 402; three years later the restriction limiting enrollment to commerce majors was lifted, and the course was opened to all students.[4]

The breakout from this meager bill of fare was slow in coming, especially so when one considers the widespread popularity of radio as a news and entertainment medium during the Great Depression. It was not until shortly before the Japanese attack upon Pearl Harbor that broadcasting courses at Oklahoma A. and M. began to reflect the changing character of radio. The day was long past when radio speeches filled the airwaves. Music, drama, variety shows, comedy, documentaries, commentaries, news—a wide-ranging menu—had developed with the rapid growth of national and regional radio networks. Finally, recognition of this had come in the 1941-42 academic year.

Martin's course had devoted only a relatively small amount of time to broadcasting techniques. Now a full-scale radio course, Speech 283, Radio Production, was being offered. The course description read: "An introductory course in the theory and practice of speaking, acting, directing, announcing, and writing for radio communication." It was taught by Joseph W. Wetherby. Wetherby held a bachelor of arts and a master of arts degree from Wayne University. He had been on the faculty since 1936 and had recently been promoted to assistant professor. The following year, as the course's popularity grew, Wetherby was joined by James G. Barton. Barton, a newcomer to the speech faculty, had taken a bachelor of fine arts degree from Nebraska State Teachers College and a master of arts degree from the University of Michigan.[5]

Facilities for the course were all but non-existent. James H. "Jimmie" Baker, later to gain national prominence as an award-winning producer for ABC Television in Hollywood, remembered the crude beginnings in the Prairie Playhouse, an appendage to turret-clad Williams Hall with its old world charm. A hole was drilled through the stage floor. With microphones and an amplifier below, students would broadcast to members of the class above, followed by suggestions on writing, delivery, and production techniques by students and teacher. It was not much, but a number of the students from those lackluster beginnings went on to success in commercial broadcasting.[6]

World War II was keenly felt on college campuses, and Oklahoma A. and M. was no exception. The regular academic program continued, though somewhat curtailed, while the college became a training center for the various military services with special courses underwritten by the federal government. The war cut deeply into non-military male student enrollment and into the younger faculty ranks as well. Both Wetherby and Barton now were on military leave. Martin continued to teach his course in Effective Business Expression, but Radio Production, now considered a basic course by the School of Arts and Sciences, was not scheduled for the 1945-46 academic year. Radio was a subject for discussion in various journalism courses, as it had been for years, but only in Survey of Journalism, and later in Journalism for High School Teachers, was a study unit assigned to it.[7]

With the end of the war, a new era in radio began. Martin gave up his course to Harry H. Anderson. Barton returned and was promoted to assistant professor, but he no longer taught radio. Wetherby went on to fields of endeavor elsewhere. Three credits in Radio Production had evolved into Radio Speech and would fill two semesters for a total of six credits, taught by one of the new faces on campus, John Woodworth, a man with a strong personality and with a range of professional radio experience earlier teachers had lacked.[8]

Woodworth joined the faculty in 1946, coming from Baylor University. He had taken a year off from his Oklahoma City radio job to paint and write. The year off stretched into three. Meanwhile, he had caught the attention of Harold H. Leake, a short man with a big voice, a classical piano player with friends on the literary scene. Leake had come to Oklahoma A. and M. in 1943 as a civilian instructor in the U.S. Naval Training School. When that program was phased out, he remained on the faculty. He held a fine arts degree from the University of Oklahoma and had been chosen to lead the new radio services department established at President Henry G. Bennett's initiative on July 1, 1945. Once again, a perceptive outsider might have wondered about the logic of the college structure. Leake, best known on campus as "H. H.," was pushing radio as an extension vehicle while the catalog listed H. A. Graham as extension editor and radio director. Leake had Bennett's support in bringing Woodworth to the campus. They no doubt had known one another on the Norman campus, where Leake had been program director at the University of Oklahoma station, WNAD. He had had less professional experience than Woodworth and his methods did not mesh with Woodworth's. Woodworth chomped at the bit. The lines of authority were, he thought, not sufficiently defined. The situation eventually improved as Leake gave Woodworth some of the creative freedom he felt he needed.[9]

Soon after his arrival, Leake wrote an article for the *Oklahoma A. and M. College Magazine* in which he foresaw a 10,000-watt college station to be known as KOAG. A transmitter, amplifiers, tubes, and various other parts already were on hand. As his department got under way, his staff included Woodworth as program manager; Kenneth Rupe, chief engineer; Robert P. Ledbetter, assistant chief engineer; Don Looper, radio farm director; and Martha Ingram, secretary. The professional staff was supported by five students who had shown talent, some in radio engineering and some in writing and announcing.

Leake had a well organized morning schedule of five programs over various Oklahoma stations. An hour and a half of broadcasting—from 5:15 to 6:45—was completed each day before the campus would come to life. In two-and-a-half years the amount of regular broadcasting from the college had increased from fifteen minutes per week to eight and three quarters hours per week; from one program over one station to thirty-five over fifteen stations. Before Woodworth's departure, radio services was turning out 250 programs a month for 32 Oklahoma stations. This achievement was made possible by Ledbetter and his colleagues, who built a double-speed copier that simultaneously duplicated three tapes from a master copy. Approximately seventeen miles of tape a week was processed for shipment to various radio stations in Oklahoma and border states. Among the programs were those featuring campus news reported by Oklahoma A. and M. student reporters from the areas of the stations airing the tapes.

Woodworth was always trying to get things done in a hurry. By contrast, Leake's slow pace—an alumnus of that period said he was "slipping in molasses a lot of the time"—frustrated Woodworth and Ledbetter. They wanted to get a full-blown station on the air. A ten-watt General Electric transmitter was available but had never been uncrated. It remained in storage for at least five years. Finally, about five years after he had resigned, Ledbetter rejoiced when he learned that KAMC was on the air. The unit held together extremely well during Leake's years on campus, but he had decided upon a career change. As the 1951-52 academic year began, Woodworth was acting director of the Department of Radio Services, then later director.

Woodworth was interested in—and made an effort to learn—about almost everything. For example, he drew up plans and blueprints for a house that he and a carpenter built for his wife and three children at 2116 College Avenue. He was an avid gardener. As a decorator and builder he "re-did" some of the fine homes the family lived in at various times through the years. He was an accomplished artist with a preference for oil painting. He and his wife, Becky, were active in scouting and church work and found time to teach various skills to their children and other youngsters who gathered at their Stillwater home. They participated in parent-teacher meetings. In short, they were energetic and committed parents.

Like Edmund E. Hadley, Woodworth had a special aura, a mystique that fascinated the students around him. He was a John Barrymore-type without the bottle. He had had a multi-varied career ranging from bookkeeper to Broadway actor. Following graduation from the University of Oklahoma with an English major he had spent a year at Princeton, followed by a year in Florida as a surveyor. Then he returned to Oklahoma City as a bookkeeper. Next came a job as proofreader for the Haldeman-Julius publishing house in Gerard, Kansas.

Returning to the University of Oklahoma, he wrote a prize-winning play in state competition, the only play ever published by the University of Oklahoma Press, *A Certain Young Widow*. His course work led to a teaching certificate.

He lived for a while in the colorful "French Quarter" of New Orleans as jazz was gaining a following, and although he did not realize it at the time, he heard some of the "jazz masters." One of his acquaintances while he was there was William Faulkner.

He became a school teacher in Shawnee, with classes in French, English, and mathematics, and started a little theater. Portraying more than sixteen different voices, he also created a serial, "Jones's Millions," over an NBC outlet. It was considered for purchase by a national network but lost out to "One Man's Family."

As the Depression deepened, Woodworth was program director for KOMA, and from there went to Arkansas where he raised chickens and wrote a play called "The Private Life of Tunis Jones." Returning to Oklahoma City, he took a job as a speech teacher and wrote plays for a federal theater project. His "Cheat and Swing," a story about Belle Starr, played New York, Atlanta, and San Antonio, as did his play "Man in the Tree."

In addition to the University of Oklahoma, Princeton, and Baylor, Woodworth had studied at the University of Iowa, the University of Michigan, Iowa State College, and Northwestern University. He received his master's degree at Michigan State where he was awarded the Avery and Julie award for writing a three-act play titled "Madame LaFarge."

Somewhere in this chain of events, he found time to give speech training to some of the actors and actresses he was appearing with in "Missouri Legend," a story about the notorious James boys. Among those he instructed in the art of talking with a western accent were Jose Ferrer, Mildred Natwick, Dean Jagger, Dan Duryea, Karl Malden, and Dorothy Gish. Woodworth had a part in the production for a year and a half.

Before his arrival in Stillwater, he had taught speech, drama and radio at both the University of Oklahoma and Baylor University. While at Baylor, he had completed a novel. His New York agent was unable to sell the manuscript because it was too sexually explicit for the times.[10]

COURTESY JOHN HAMILTON

An Aggie journalist who later had a large and loyal following as a farm broadcaster was Sam Schneider (*left*), shown here interviewing Ephraim Hixson of the entomology faculty. As farm editor for KVOO, Tulsa, he became a leader in the National Association of Radio Farm Directors.

The first impression some students had of Woodworth was that he was disorganized, "a blithering idiot." But once they had worked with him a while they could see that any long-term thing he planned was carefully conceived. He was, it turned out, a good organizer, and was responsible for much of the student interest in radio from 1946 to 1958. He would button-hole anyone he could—people like John H. Green and Norman DeMarco of the speech faculty—to get things done.

Woodworth got along well with his students if they were making a real effort to improve. But he could be cranky, though even-handed, otherwise. He played no favorites. He believed strongly in theory with practice and soon saw a void in his academic duties. Journalism students had the *O'Collegian* as a training facility that could give them the authentic flavor of newspaper work, but speech students had nothing comparable on which to try their broadcasting talents. Woodworth was determined to change that. He wanted a practical, hands-on outlet for the talent in his classes. His long-range goal was an FCC-licensed station on campus, but for the immediate future he could settle for a *wired-wireless* facility. Engineering students had been involved in short-wave radio activity for years, but Woodworth's plan for a student broadcasting facility was both new and exciting. To expedite matters, he organized a Radio Club, later known as the Kampus Varsity Radio Organization (KVRO became the call letters of the station-to-be).[11]

The fact that Woodworth had a dual appointment in the radio services department, a unit within the Cooperative Extension Service, and the Department of Speech, part of the School of Arts and Sciences, was an advantage. As one of the key figures in the development of the wired-wireless station recalled, "If combining two things would work, Woodworth melded them together." In this case, the melding involved a group of enthusiastic students on one hand, and on the other, the technical know-how and cooperation of Paul McCollum and Robert Ledbetter, recent electrical engineering graduates who now were on the Oklahoma A. and M. staff. McCollum would supervise electronics and engineering students handling the radio frequency responsibilities, and Ledbetter those working the audio side. They were good friends and worked well together. Over the entire operation was the enthusiastic and hard-driving Woodworth, who would provide the student talent to develop a variety of programs and support services. Chief source of this talent would come from the Radio Club. Among the eager club members was Vernon Trexler, a natural leader whose vocabulary did not include the word "impossible." Woodworth was both teacher and club sponsor, and most of the club members took the two courses he taught. As one student said with no sense of criticism, "We couldn't do anything without his OK." He thought all broadcasts should be tied in with the radio courses.[12]

The first year of the club was summed up in the *1949 Redskin*. The yearbook listed seventy-eight members and reported that the club was started during the summer of 1948 and chartered during the fall semester. Then the *Redskin* reported: "The object of the club is to give students who expect to go into the radio field practical experience in the operation of a radio station, in the writing and production of plays and in building and maintaining a wired-wireless radio station to cover the campus. The station. . .is known as KVRO, and began its operation during the spring semester. KVRO is self-supporting through advertising. . .and is on the air at peak listening hours, bringing a balanced program of drama, music, elections, campus news, [student] senate reports, sports events and addresses by guest speakers." Thirty-nine men and fifteen women were pictured, with Woodworth in the center on the front row flanked by Ledbetter and Trexler. Officers listed were Trexler, president; Jack Lynch, vice president; Marilyn Harper, secretary; Ruth Ann Schneekloth, corresponding secretary; and Ted Ferguson, treasurer.[13]

Behind the *Redskin* narrative, which made the entire project seem disarmingly simple, was a more complicated story. A lot of wire had to be strung. McCollum supervised this phase of the operation. Clovis Bolay was one of the students who contributed his time to the grimy job, using surplus 110-B Army field wire unreeled in the steamy tunnels under campus sidewalks. He would lift a manhole cover and climb down into the heat below. It was a risky job, with 2300 volts in some of the power distribution lines that looped the campus. He would stay underground as long as he could and then come out through another manhole to cool off. When Bolay and his sweating helpers came to a dormitory, they would lead the wire up through a rain spout and put a couple of loops on top of the building and then go on to another reception site. The wire was strung in the winter, and Bolay sometimes waded through water up to his waist. At intervals, he hurried past spouting steam, protecting himself with a quilt or a shield of asbestos board to avoid being scalded. On one occasion, when he emerged near the Armory to cool off, the cold air shattered his hot eyeglasses. This incident typifies the dedication of many who worked to make KVRO operational by spring.

Lines were stretched from the auditorium to the stadium and field house, for KVRO planned to do remote broadcasts covering events at all of those sites. There were fraternity and sorority houses still to be reached, and the Army surplus wire was plentiful. At the corner of College and Monroe, wire was strung from the campus to the top of the Sigma Chi house, and from there rooftop to rooftop until all Greek houses were covered. Then the Woodworth-McCullum-Ledbetter team turned its attention to the sprawling Veterans Village. McCollum and Ledbetter decided to use capacitors to tie the signal into Village power lines. KVRO fed the Village through its electrical system rather than by running wire from building to building.

The low-power 6L6 transmitter, with an output of about five watts, was designed by McCollum and located in a small chassis in the Industrial Arts Building, from which the wires through the tunnels were fed. For a brief time a small studio near the transmitter was used, then Woodworth was able to get more commodious space in the attic of Williams Hall. The place was a mess. Pigeons had entered through the broken windows and had roosted there for uncounted months. Woodworth believed in learning by doing, whether it involved writing a script or wielding a hammer. There was plenty of hammering to do. Radio Club members were undaunted. They went to work with lumber and fiberboard to create a studio. They completed the unfinished floor, put in glass panels and hung curtains. Club dues did not pay for everything needed. The college administration helped some, but was dubious about having a stream of students running up and down the stairs to the attic tower. The students accepted as a minor irritation the fact that they were unable to make the studio totally soundproof. Ledbetter designed the console and Trexler built it. High-quality UTC linear standard transformers were used, and the signal had first-class fidelity. The board had four input

COURTESY ABC-TV, HOLLYWOOD

Although radio facilities on campus were primitive in the early 1940s, classes in the Prairie Playhouse simulated broadcasts for experience. Several students of that period, including Jimmie Baker (*center*), went on to outstanding careers in broadcasting. One of Baker's prize-winning shows, "The University in America," featured Jack Lemmon (*left*) and Paul Newman (*right*). In more than four decades with ABC-Television in Hollywood, Baker has won five "Emmys," among numerous other awards.

channels of broadcast quality, two turntables with pre-amplifiers and Clarkston pickup heads.[14]

Woodworth finally had achieved his goal. He had given Oklahoma A. and M. its first radio station, limited in reach to comply with FCC regulations for unlicensed stations. Now he could give his radio classes hands-on experience while at the same time expanding access to news of interest to students. To further this goal, the station added the Associated Press radio wire and the Capital transcription service. KVRO complemented the work of the radio services department. The wired-wireless station served the campus community while agricultural and home economics extension efforts across the state were handled by Leake's radio services unit. Woodworth and Ledbetter were on Leake's staff, so there was close cooperation. Equipment was shared when necessary.[15]

Woodworth would let students try anything he thought they could do. The result, in addition to student-written drama, was coverage of special events to augment the regular broadcast schedule. All sports events on campus were covered play-by-play. Basketball games away from home were carried remote by special arrangement with KOCY. The Oklahoma City station allowed these live pickups so long as KVRO agreed to carry the commercials. KVRO was glad to comply in order to provide the service to Oklahoma A. and M. students. When talent such as the Oklahoma City Symphony Orchestra performed on campus, KVRO was there with live coverage.[16]

Early in his twelve years at Oklahoma A. and M., Woodworth took a group of students to the National Intercollegiate Radio Conference at Baylor. They could not believe the amount and quality of the equipment students from other schools told of working with. Muriel Groom recalled: "Our engineers had *made* our equipment and had gotten permission to get on the roofs to string wires. And these students from other schools had money for their stations. We couldn't believe it. We had one girl, Patricia Spellman, who had a 'ticket.' Because of that we could stay on the air at night and let the engineer go home. We would sign the station off. We had a lot of fun. In programming we seemed to be far ahead of the people we met at this conference."[17]

There was no shortage of electrical engineering students willing to help in the wired wireless operation. Some, such as Ledbetter, had their "tickets" by the time they were sophomores. These students found other opportunities to gain experience. Ledbetter handled the engineering on KVOO remotes and served as chief engineer for KSPI during Paul McCollum's year-long sabbatical. Seven Oklahoma A. and M. students handled KSPI engineering under Ledbetter. The FCC inspector would shake his head in dismay. No other station of that size had so many engineers. Obviously KVRO had not problem in that department. In a sense, Ledbetter was "quarterback" for the student-engineers team.

Equipment was shifted back and forth freely to meet the needs of radio services, KVRO, remote broadcasts for Tulsa and Oklahoma City stations, and KSPI.[18]

Most of the work outside classes was done by the Radio Club. Paul Price and Muriel Groom wrote a program call "Strictly Weird." A catch-phrase "Never fear, Paul Price is here" had wide circulation on campus. Together the two programmed music for listening during study hours. Mrs. Groom loved writing commercials, timing them, and finding the right people to read them. The commercials were saleable, because the wired-wireless station was popular. Calls requesting numbers were frequent from the dormitories, fraternity houses, and sororities. Because the station was popular on campus, it was an excellent advertising vehicle for dry-cleaning establishments, florists, theaters, and other businesses appealing to the college market.[19]

Occasionally, Woodworth's students would go to KSPI and air a program they had produced. He encouraged such opportunities and had a hand in setting them up. He not only believed in hands-on experience but in the value of field trips as a way to enhance classroom instruction. On one of these trips Woodworth's students visited Oklahoma City's first television station, WKY-TV, at the Civic Center.[20]

In the community, Woodworth was well known and had many close friends, among them Helen Sittle, Idress Cash, and Rena Penn Brittan. He was one of the founders of Town and Gown, a community

During radio's golden days of the late 1940s and early 1950s, two of the key figures in the academic program were Darrel Woodyard (*left*) and John Woodworth, shown with a group of his radio speech students in the radio services studio in Life Sciences East. Woodworth believed in learning by doing and developed a large and devoted cadre of future professionals. Woodyard was his assistant.

theater-in-the-round that has established itself through the years as one of Stillwater's principal cultural assets. His home atmosphere reflected his taste in decor. He loved textures and colors. As an artist, he knew how to use both. His wife developed her artistic skills in pottery. Their three children grew up listening to the world's great symphonies.[21]

When he came to Oklahoma A. and M., it did not take long for him to become involved in campus affairs. This led to dissonance. He was somewhat dissatisfied that he did not have the clear-cut responsibility for the college's radio policy. He understood the potential of FM better than anyone on campus, but this fact seemed to matter little. He had an "in" politically with friends who trusted him with certain inside information. Either through these contacts, or intuitively, he know that Oklahoma A. and M. would someday be Oklahoma State University. He immediately urged that an application be sent to the FCC asking for the call letters KOSU. He wanted to make sure that the college had a chance for a full-fledged station. Meantime, it was his goal to maintain what was possible until the college could have something better.[22]

As radio expanded, Woodworth was to have a co-worker. He was Darrel Woodyard, a product of the live-broadcasting era—an era of studio orchestras, choral groups, and solo singers on network staffs, an era when recordings were taboo on the major networks. He had been a singer for NBC for six years in Radio City followed by eleven years as a singer for CBS at 485 Madison Avenue. A native Oklahoman who had tired of the big city, Woodyard was ready to return to his roots. He was born in Pond Creek and was a product of Guthrie, Oklahoma City, Enid, and Pawnee public schools. He signed on in 1949 as a radio program consultant in the Department of Radio Services. The next year, following Leake's resignation to enter church work, Woodworth was advanced to director and Woodyard became Woodworth's program manager. He served in that capacity until, at the age of fifty-four, he was appointed as an instructor in the Department of Speech on July 1, 1957. It was said that President Bennett had personally engineered Woodyard's job in radio services, as he had the appointment of Richard Caldwell as a special writer when Caldwell had become disenchanted at the *Tulsa Tribune*.[23]

There is no record of how effectively the Woodworth-Woodyard team functioned. Apparently, they worked in harmony, for the relationship lasted eight years. Woodyard's concept of programming probably worked fairly well in his early years at Oklahoma A. and M. But as the college was prepping for university status, broadcasting was undergoing vast changes of its own. The rise of television had changed the face of radio programming. It was time for personal as well as personnel changes. As the administration contemplated the structure of the new School of Communications and its role in broadcasting, Woodworth had decided to seek new challenges.[24]

Robert M. Johnson succeeded the dynamic John Woodworth as the driving force in radio studies when the School of Communications was formed in 1958. He lost no time in getting KAMC-FM back on the air after many months of inactivity and gave direction to KVRO, the wired-wireless AM station, as well. His main interest was drama, and he left to return to theater work in Dallas after a short tenure.

When the Woodworths left Stillwater, they settled in Boise, Idaho, where he was named head of the speech and drama department at Boise Junior College, later to become Boise State University. Boise was a repeat performance of the Stillwater years. He built armor and appeared on stage in the Shakespeare Festival in Ashland, Oregon, and was active in Boise Little Theater and Boise Music Week, both as actor and director. He revived his interest in painting, and built from "scratch" a beautiful cabin on Payette Lake, fifty miles north of Boise. He was named "Distinguished Citizen" and unanimously voted "Teacher of the Year" in 1972, one year before he retired to emeritus status at seventy-one. Three years later, the college asked the Woodworths to serve at its "Campus in Spain." Just before their scheduled return from Spain, Woodworth died suddenly on April 13, 1975.[25]

Among the many students who made careers in broadcasting following their experience under Woodworth were Leon Matthews, Gene Allen, Jake Lockwood, Susan DeMarco, Bob Nance, Bill Platt, and Ed Slater. Matthews, as was true of so many others, had his promising start interrupted by military service. He was tagged by his peers for national prominence in radio, but chose to spend his professional life with KSPI in Stillwater following the war.[26]

Woodworth's move came before all of the plans for the new School of Communications had been worked out. On July 24, C. Ellsworth Chunn began seeking his replacement. He had phoned a friend, M. Blair Hart, chairman of speech and dramatic arts at the University of Arkansas, for leads. Hart mentioned Robert M. Johnson, who had just completed a one-year appointment filling in for Norman DeMarco. Working both on the faculty and in the Department of Radio-TV Production, Division of General Extension, Johnson had been exceptionally effective. Hart had recruited Johnson a year earlier; he sent Chunn three letters of recommendation from Johnson's file. All were exceptionally laudatory. Johnson was praised not only for his creative abilities in radio and television but for his pleasing personality, high personal standards, and his ability to work with others.

Chunn was impressed by Hart's appraisal. He phoned Johnson and encouraged him to apply. For his part, Johnson was equally prompt. He no sooner had completed his telephone conversation with Chunn than he posted a letter briefly reviewing his year at Arkansas. "As you will notice," he wrote, "I have seven years in commercial broadcasting as announcer and director. This past year, I was head of the Radio-Television Department and directed experimental educational TV projects. . . ." He had taught courses in broadcast production, announcing, and acting, the latter in the Department of Drama, in addition to his extension duties. A penciled note in Chunn's handwriting at the top of the letter indicated that an offer had been approved by Robert W. MacVicar.

In the meantime, Chunn had received the various items Hart had sent as well as Johnson's letter of interest. He had written Johnson: "Dr. Hart sent me your papers and we are very much interested in you."[27]

Johnson had attended Austin College from 1948 to 1952, taking part in a wide variety of activities. He had served as president of three groups, two of which he had organized, was on the yearbook staff, judiciary committee and community council. In addition, he had played in the band and orchestra. But his first love seemed to be dramatics. He had played the lead in five major college productions and supporting roles in three others. He had written for two Sherman, Texas, radio stations and had worked actively in the Sherman Community Players. This interest had drawn him to Baylor University in 1954 for work in the Baylor Theater under Paul Baker, where he learned lighting, set design, and other production basics.

After completing his B.A. at Baylor in 1956 he spent four months with WRGF-TV in Chattanooga. The job included weather and news reporting and duties as commercial announcer and master of ceremonies on an hour-long variety show. As a television personality there were personal appearances as well. Despite the fast pace and excitement of a promising television future, he decided to return to Baylor for graduate work under Baker.

He had been active in broadcasting throughout his college years. While at Austin College he had been staff announcer for KRRV-AM in Sherman. In addition, he wrote and announced a weekly variety program originating on the Austin College campus. Then he took a year off for work at KTBC radio and television in Austin before enrolling at Baylor.

While finishing his bachelor's degree at Baylor, he had worked at KCEN-TV in Temple as chief announcer. In addition to daily news and weather reporting, he was master of ceremonies for an interview and variety program, did extensive commercial work, sometimes manned the studio cameras, and sometimes directed the action. He seemed to be a junior version of Orson Welles, writing, directing, acting, having a hand in every conceivable creative effort of the station's work day.

By August 12, Chunn was trying to set an interview date with Johnson. Classes would begin September 10, and he wanted to replace Woodworth as soon as possible. His plans were for Johnson to teach only two courses the first semester. He would need to move equipment into the Communications Building and put KAMC-FM and KVRO back into operation. Chunn made it clear to Johnson that his full-time duties would be in broadcasting. "I am seeking a radio-television person for this opening, not a drama teacher," he had written.[28] Johnson visited with Chunn and other Oklahoma A. and M. faculty members on August 19. The appointment came quickly. Johnson formally applied two days later and accepted an instructorship on August 23. He had completed all course work for the M.A. at Baylor, but had yet to complete his thesis requirement with an original drama, a full-length stage play. He was active in the Masonic Lodge, Presbyterian Church, the Naval reserve, and Junior Chamber of Commerce. His professional affiliations were with the Speech Association of America, Southern Speech Association, and the Associated Television Artists and Crafts Guild.[29]

The college's venture into frequency modulation broadcasting had begun in 1955 when the FCC licensed KAMC-FM. Only two FM stations were broadcasting in Oklahoma when KAMC went on the air with test programming on December 29, 1955. The original concept had been for a powerful transmitter near the campus with call letters KOAG and satellite transmitters throughout the state relaying the programs. It would have given Oklahoma A. and M. College a statewide voice twenty-four hours a day, a visionary concept for the time. But the estimated cost was $70,000 and the money was not immediately available. President Bennett died before the plan could be approved. KAMC had been off the air for two years when Johnson arrived. It resumed daily broadcasting at 91.7

As KOSU gained stature as an affiliate of National Public Radio—Oklahoma's first NPR station—it was led by two skilled broadcasting professionals: Philip E. "Ed" Paulin (*left*) and Larry Miller (*right*). Paulin later became chairman of the radio-television-film faculty.

megacycles on February 8, 1959, when Chunn threw the switch dedicating the station to "fine music, the faithful monitoring of the progress of Oklahoma State University, and to factual messages of foremost meaning to all of you." Shortly after its return to the air, the FCC approved KOSU-FM as the station's call letters. The 250-watt station had a reach of only 30 miles, but it gave students a wider audience than wired-wireless could offer. Its primary aim was to provide training for students interested in radio. Tom Blair, a student, was station manager and Johnson served as faculty coordinator.[30]

At first, things had gone well for Johnson. He had worked with his usual enthusiasm and vigor to pick up where Woodworth had left off. The radio stations were back on the air and student interest was building. It was clear, however, that Johnson felt more at home with speech and drama than with the journalism wing of the new School of Communications. As dissent among the speech faculty was building, Johnson, too, was critical of the school's administration. As matters came to a head, Chunn dismissed Johnson and Martha Sharp. Upon his own resignation soon after, they were given an opportunity to remain in their jobs. Sharp stayed on, but Johnson took a position at the Dallas Theater Center under his Baylor mentor, Baker. At that point Leslie Kreps, head of the newly independent Department of Speech, assumed a caretaker role for the academic program in radio and television. It limped along for a year with the help of Darrel Woodyard before Kreps found the man who would lead the program in what soon would be an independent department.[31]

His choice was Robert P. Lacy, a man with a strong speech orientation and good credentials in broadcasting as well. He had been manager of WOSU, Ohio State University, while enrolled in graduate work. Earlier, as a student at Indiana State University, he had produced and directed "Midwest Jamboree," a high-spirited program with a Nashville flavor. At thirty-six, he had logged twelve years in radio, mostly as program director on various stations, and held an ownership interest in WVTS, Terre Haute. He planned to pattern the Oklahoma State curriculum after that of Ohio State, stressing audience psychology, programs and audiences, program building, broadcast law, and a new course in research. During the summer, Kreps had prepared the way for Lacy's arrival in the fall by moving KVRO and KOSU from Sixth and Walnut into remodeled studios on the third floor of what was now the Communications Building. An estimated $60,000 had gone into the improved radio facilities, plus about $8,000 for equipment. Now theory and practice would be available in one location. Kreps expected the fifteen new majors in radio and television to be followed by another hike in enrollment with Lacy's arrival. He was correct. From Lacy's appointment on May 6, 1960, broadcasting began a strong recovery.[32]

He would be assisted by Woodyard, who had decided three years earlier to leave the broadcasting services department for teaching. Woodyard's change of duties might not have been possible had he not enrolled as a student while working in radio services. In 1957, the year of his academic appointment, he received his B.S. degree. Three years later, largely by summer work, he was awarded the M.S. degree by Kansas State University.[33]

When Lacy replaced Johnson in the fall of 1960, he was excited about the prospects for the radio and television program he would head. Not only did he have a licensed FM radio station for his students to operate, but the popular wired-wireless station, KVRO, had been in place for a dozen years and had a loyal following in the campus dormitories as well as in fraternity and sorority houses. He was inheriting a new department with an opportunity to expand and refine its curriculum. His work and contacts at Ohio State University would help, but more important was the cooperation extended by Kreps. Kreps had considered the speech department's radio-television role as temporary.[34]

As soon as the Department of Radio and Television had been approved by the OSU regents, Lacy began searching for a new man. Woodyard had felt uncomfortable in his radio-television role. Students knew that he was well steeped in the techniques and lore of earlier broadcasting, but both teacher and students knew that he had had no experience in the newer, fast-paced, disc jockey-dominated radio that

Once the Department of Radio and Television became an independent academic unit, it flourished under the leadership of Robert P. Lacy (*left*) and Malachi C. Topping (*right*). Student spirit ran high as broadcasting majors filled all major positions on KOSU and KVRO. The department had become the main source of entry-level employees on Oklahoma radio stations.

had evolved in answer to television's now dominant position. Woodyard was glad to shift gradually to a full teaching load in speech, clearing the way for Lacy to seek his replacement.[35]

Lacy chose Malachi C. Topping, a man with both print and broadcasting experience, a wry sense of humor, and two academic degrees including strong supporting course work in sociology and psychology. He had taken the A.B. in journalism from Washington University, St. Louis, in 1947 and fourteen years later had added the M.S. in speech at Ohio State University. When he came to Stillwater, he had completed all of his course work for the Ph.D. in speech, with a radio-television emphasis, at Ohio State. Lacy, too, was working on the Ph.D. at Ohio State and the two had become friends. Topping's appointment began on August 1, 1961, and Lacy announced that he would teach courses in television as well as Programs and Audiences and a new course, largely for non-majors, Broadcasting in Daily Life.

Topping had solid professional credentials. He had worked following his journalism studies as a desk editor on the *St. Louis Star-Times* and as a managing editor of the *Southern Illinoisan*. From 1954 to 1959, a period of rapid growth for television, he had been program director and manager of WKYB-TV in Paducah, Kentucky. From 1959 to 1961, Topping had been a teaching assistant at Ohio State and the year before coming to Oklahoma State had been a research assistant on an Air Force communications project. Lacy said Topping would provide most of his own teaching materials because in the rapidly changing broadcasting field most textbooks were quickly outdated.[36]

Both KOSU and KVRO had studios on the third floor of the Communications Building. KOSU had the studio next to the stairs, and KVRO one to the north. An announcer's booth diagonally between them was wired for both sides, but used primarily by KVRO for news. The large studio commonly faced by the two studio consoles was used for production occasionally, but mostly for KOSU news announcers. The record library was between the studios, behind the announcer's booth. Almost all radio-television classes were held in one large classroom in the northeast corner of the building off the KVRO studio.

The radio studios were as well equipped as those in medium-sized markets. Large full-track tape decks had been acquired the spring of 1961 from KVOO. There were no cartridge decks, but KVRO had a machine with a wide belt of audio tape and a movable head that allowed the selection of about 100 spots, up to 90 seconds in length.

In the fall of 1962, KOSU acquired a state-of-the-art stereo console and multiplex transmitter. This gave the station the distinction of being one of the first FM stereo stations in the state. The newsroom, located across the hall behind the KVRO studio and overlooking the Student Union, had a leased UPI teletype printer and two typewriters. Also in the fall of 1962, radio-television purchased some police radios, which gave students a new outlook on news. Some students became ambulance chasers, with portable tape recorders that today would be considered bulky. Cassette recorders had not yet been developed. Some broadcasting students even bought 16mm Bolex and Bell and Howell movie cameras to pick up a few dollars as stringers for Tulsa and Oklahoma City television stations.

Laboratory facilities were fairly well equipped for radio, but non-existent for television until the fall of 1962. To describe that first year of television as primitive would be giving it the benefit of the doubt. There was no equipment to speak of except for a start on the lighting grid. There were two small Dage videcon cameras and a video switcher. A portable audio console also had been moved in. To capture some flavor of a booth, students erected wood frames, covered them with burlap as walls, then installed a glass window frame for a view of the floor. Rather than calling it a director's booth, students referred to this simulated structure—with a touch of affection—as "Spanky and Our Gang's Club House." In case the intercom between director and cameraman failed, it was no trouble to hear the director's voice through the burlap.

The programming, of course, was not seen anywhere except on the video monitors in the control booth. There was no way to preserve these efforts for posterity, as kinescopes would have been expensive and impractical and video tape recorders had not been invented.[37]

The next major step in the department's development came in 1966. Complaints of interference with other radio signals caused Lacy to convert KVRO to licensed FM status. He got the FCC to move an unused channel from Shawnee to Stillwater, only to realize that commission rules made it impossible for the university to own two stations in the same town. To solve that problem he worked out a plan whereby a group of former broadcasting students, all of whom had been KVRO student managers, formed a non-profit corporation to own the station. The university provided space and utilities, while the station continued to be operated entirely by students and programmed for students. The board submitted a document to stress this point. It was dated June 10, 1966, and entitled "The Understandings By Which the University Furnishes Facilities for KVRO, Inc." In its statement, the board emphasized that the Varsity Radio Organization had owned and operated the wired-wireless station in an atmosphere of complete freedom. The university's only requirement was that the station operate within legal limits. It was conceded that the university administration had been critical on one occasion, after the fact, when KVRO had broadcast an exuberant appeal for a Monday walk-out following victory in an "extremely important" football game. On this occasion the administration simply had informed the station that the bounds of propriety had been exceeded. The station management was asked never again to encourage a student walk-out. Had an off-campus station been guilty of the same conduct, the university no doubt would have filed a similar protest, the board pointed out.

In its request to the FCC, the KVRO board of directors stated: "Demonstrative of the 'station's' freedom to program as it has seen fit is the fact that it has for many years programmed rock and roll music on a top forty program. Stated in the very mildest terms, the administration and faculty of the University do not agree that this is the most desirable music. The students who operate the 'station,' however, have gone right along in the programming. . .as determined by their own knowledge of the desires of the audience they serve. They have, in fact, utilized the results of the research on music preferences done by the University's academic departments to help guide their programming. The board of directors of KVRO, Inc. will continue to set the programming policies and control the station's facilities and all rights or interests in the license, and the University will merely continue to furnish operating space and some equipment. . . . Upon permission to construct the. . .proposed facility, KVRO, Inc. will purchase its own transmitter and its own antenna without any aid whatsoever from university funds. There are no documents, instruments or contracts between the university and KVRO, Inc. and the only verbal understanding is as stated above."[38]

On June 20, 1966, Lacy had written the KVRO board of directors that he was pleased to know of their application for an FM license, which he said would benefit both students and the Stillwater community. He assured the board that the university would continue to furnish at no charge all the services and facilities it had for nearly two decades. Lacy wrote: "As has always been the policy, you will be free to operate your own station as you see fit and without interference. We ask only that. . .you operate within legal limits and in accordance with the laws of the United States. . .and the state of Oklahoma."

Lacy expressed pride in the accomplishments of the old wired-wireless station. He predicted the new setup would change nothing except the method used to transmit the signal.[39]

The success of the early academic program in radio and television was evident in Lacy's Christmas newsletters to alumni. These clearly showed that both the Oklahoma City and Tulsa markets were infused with OSU graduates, and that no other Oklahoma college or university was called upon so regularly for new talent. The expanding military establishment, stimulated by the Cuban missile crisis and the U.S. involvement in Vietnam, required more junior-grade officers, and many broadcasting graduates were advancing in the military ranks both at home and abroad. Several already held the rank of captain, and in many cases they were involved in supervising radio and film work.[40]

The Department of Radio and Television had shown impressive growth under Lacy and Topping. By 1967, more than 300 students had passed through the department, but never before had 100 majors been enrolled at the same time. The magic number was reached that year when Nik Jones declared a radio-television major. His father, Jay Jones, was program director for KVOO radio in Tulsa. The curriculum had had only

SCHOOL OF JOURNALISM AND BROADCASTING

Michael Flanagan, a student in the early 1970s, operates the controls from the KOSU announcer's booth on the third floor of the Communications Building. At that time, KOSU was a unit within the School of Journalism and Broadcasting and was an important training adjunct for many students each semester.

five majors the year before Lacy's arrival. Lacy had taken over a curriculum with ten courses, two of a journalistic nature. Soon it had grown to twelve, but the two dealing with broadcast news had been transferred to the journalism curriculum. The first degree in radio and television had been awarded to Theron Dixon just before Lacy's arrival. By 1963, the number had grown to thirteen and by 1968 to nineteen. The names of broadcasting graduates soon were sprinkled throughout state and regional radio and television stations, advertising agencies, and film production houses. Among the frequently heard names were Ed Dobson, Karen Cowell, Bob Callaway, Ed Turner, Ed Brocksmith, Louis Vanlandingham, John Elsner, Richard Chegwin, Bill Engler, Karen Mullendore, Ted Leitner, and Jim Back.[41]

To serve the growing number of broadcasting majors, Lacy added a new faculty member, Jack W. Deskin, a 1964 OSU graduate who had majored in radio and television with a speech minor. He had served as general manager of KNFB in Nowata for two years and before returning to OSU for graduate work had briefly been a sales consultant for KVIN in Vinita. While working toward the M.A. degree in speech, Deskin had helped with television laboratory duties and had been assistant supervisor of KVRO and KOSU. He also had taught Radio and Television Speech, Broadcast Sales, Radio Production, and Station Participation. Upon completion of his master's in 1968 (his qualifying paper was "A Curriculum for Radio and Television"), he was appointed with the rank of instructor in what was now the Department of Radio, Television and Film. During the next two years he added Introduction to Broadcasting, Television Production and Directing, and Problems in Radio and Television to his earlier courses. He also taught two seminars, one dealing with current problems in broadcasting and the other covering cable television.

From 1968 to 1970, in addition to his teaching duties, the energetic young teacher was academic advisor to radio-television students, advisor to KVRO, and advisor to the OSU chapter of Iota Beta Sigma, an honorary broadcasting fraternity in which he served as a member of the national council's governing board. He also was publisher and executive editor of the *Journal of College Radio* and a board member and vice president of the Intercollegiate Broadcasting System. He held memberships in the National Association of Broadcasters and the Association for Professional Broadcasting Education and was active in the Oklahoma City Advertising Club, the Oklahoma City Press Club, and the Oklahoma Broadcasters Association.[42]

The department continued to gain industry approval as well as recognition on campus. Then, in September 1969, the unexpected happened. Lacy's close friend and business associate at WVTS in Terre Haute, Indiana, had died in an Indianapolis plane crash. Lacy was torn between two loyalties. Should he abandon his ownership interest in

WVTS? Should he stay at OSU? Could he manage both responsibilities, commuting by air? Out of a sense of loyalty to his dead partner, Jerry Kulinski, he resigned to go to Terre Haute, where he was desperately needed. At a departmental farewell party in cooperation with KOSU and KVRO, students and faculty presented Lacy a plaque citing his years of "devotion, leadership and friendship."[43] With strong help from Deskin, Topping served out the remainder of the academic year as acting head, then resigned to accept a position at Bowling Green State University.

Deskin had worked well with both Lacy and Topping and was popular with students. He had been an important asset to the department. As he looked to his future, he had decided to pursue the Ph.D. at the University of Oklahoma. It would be, he wrote, "advantageous to both our new program and my future."

After a year at the University of Oklahoma, Deskin moved to the University of Southern Mississippi, where he taught part-time while continuing work on his doctorate, awarded six years later. In the meantime, he had shifted his base to Central State in Edmond, Oklahoma, where he has been a valuable faculty member since 1973.[44]

The changing situation following Lacy's resignation called for prompt action. President Robert B. Kamm consulted with Dean George Gries, then decided to move the program Lacy and Topping had built into a new academic alignment with the School of Journalism and Communications. Both programs were housed in the Communications Building. Both had cooperated on various projects since the 1967-68 academic year. Gries was streamlining the administrative structure in the College of Arts and Sciences and the move would fit into that objective. The change would bring new leadership, but it would not stop the work started by Kositzky and Martin, energized by Woodworth and developed by Lacy. Their successors had been given a strong foundation for future development.

Endnotes

1. *ACE*, American Association of Agricultural College Editors (October-November 1959), pp. 1-3; Robert C. Fite, *A History of Oklahoma State University Extension and Outreach* (Stillwater: Oklahoma State University, 1988), p. 22; Gene Allen, "Voices in the Wind: Early Radio in Oklahoma," manuscript submitted to Oklahoma Heritage Association for publication, pp. 40-42, 47, 48.

2. Oklahoma A. and M. College *Orange and Black*, 14 December 1922, p. 3; *Annual Catalog, Oklahoma A. and M. College, 1914-1915*, pp. 53, 96; *Annual Catalog, Oklahoma A. and M. College, 1923-1924*, pp. 10, 134, 135, 144; *Annual Catalog, Oklahoma A. and M. College, 1924-1925*, pp. vi, 128, 129, 214; *Annual Catalog, Oklahoma A. and M. College, 1925-1926*, pp. 128, 129, 222; *Annual Catalog, Oklahoma A. and M. College, 1926-1927*, pp. 141, 232; *Annual Catalog, Oklahoma A. and M. College, 1927-1928*, pp. 137, 252; *Annual Catalog, Oklahoma A. and M. College, 1928-1929*, pp. 136, 139, 247. Before the Telephony course was introduced, work in Wireless Telegraphy was listed for the first time in the 1909-1910 catalog. Knowledge of Kurtz's work was based, in part, upon the author's visit with Kurtz in Iowa City during his doctoral research.

3. *Annual Catalog, Oklahoma A. and M. College, 1929-1930*, pp. vii, xiv, 252, 253.

4. *Annual Catalog, Oklahoma A. and M. College, 1932-1933*, pp. 215, 216; *Annual Catalog, Oklahoma A. and M. College, 1935-1936*, pp. 230, 231.

5. *Annual Catalog, Oklahoma A. and M. College, 1941-1942*, pp. xxvii, 137, 408; *Annual Catalog, Oklahoma A. and M. College, 1942-1943*, pp. xv, xxviii, 142, 397, 398.

6. Author interview with James H. "Jimmie" Baker, 21 October 1988, Stillwater, Oklahoma.

7. *Annual Catalog, Oklahoma A. and M. College, 1936-1937*, p. 265; *Annual Catalog, Oklahoma A. and M. College, 1944-1945*, pp. 139, 432.

8. *Annual Catalog, Oklahoma A. and M. College, 1946-1947*, pp. 118, 401-403.

9. *Annual Catalog, Oklahoma A. and M. College, 1943-1944*, p. xxviii; *Annual Catalog, Oklahoma A. and M. College, 1945-1946*, pp. xx, xxxii; *Annual Catalog, Oklahoma A. and M. College, 1946-1947*, p. xix; *Stillwater NewsPress*, 23 March 1952, p. 18; John Hamilton, "Aggie Views and News," *Oklahoma A. and M. College Magazine*, vol. 18, no. 1 (October 1945), p. 9; Author interview with Muriel Groom, 22 June 1984, Stillwater, Oklahoma; Rebecca Woodworth to Harry E. Heath Jr., 10 February 1991, and Don Looper to Harry E. Heath Jr., 27 December 1991, in School of Journalism and Broadcasting Centennial History Collection, Special Collections, Edmon Low Library, Oklahoma State University, Stillwater, Oklahoma.

10. *Stillwater NewsPress*, 9 December 1955, p. 12; *Idaho Statesman*, 22 July 1972, p. 5A; *Boise Round-Up*, 9 December 1958; Rebecca Woodworth to Harry E. Heath Jr., 12 January 1991, and Don Looper to Harry E. Heath Jr., 27 December 1991, in School of Journalism and Broadcasting Centennial History Collection; Groom interview; Author interview with Robert P. Ledbetter, 28 August 1991, Oklahoma City, Oklahoma.

11. Ledbetter interview, 28 August 1991; Groom interview.

12. Author interview with Robert P. Ledbetter, Clovis Bolay, and Gene Allen, 28 August 1991, Oklahoma City, Oklahoma.

13. *1949 Redskin*, p. 479, Oklahoma A. and M. College Yearbook.

14. Ledbetter, Bolay, and Allen interview.

15. *Oklahoma A. and M. College Student Directory, 1947-48*, p. vii; Oklahoma A. and M. College *Daily O'Collegian*, 13 December 1949, p. 1.

16. Ledbetter, Bolay, and Allen interview.

17. Groom interview.

18. Ledbetter interview, 28 August 1991.

19. Groom interview.

20. Ledbetter interview.

21. Rebecca Wordworth to Harry E. Heath Jr., 12 January 1991, School of Journalism and Broadcasting Centennial History Collection; Groom interview.

22. Ledbetter interview, 28 August 1991.

23. Biographical sketch of Darrel Woodyard, Files of the School of Journalism and Broadcasting, Oklahoma State University; Author interview with Malvina Stephenson, 31 May 1991, Tulsa, Oklahoma; *Oklahoma A. and M. College Student Directory, 1951-52*, pp. A-12, A-46; *Oklahoma A. and M. College Student Directory, 1952-53*, pp. 16, 59.

24. *Oklahoma State University Catalog, 1959-1961*, p. 73.

25. Rebecca Woodworth to Harry E. Heath Jr., 12 January 1991, and Alan Virta to Harry E. Heath Jr., 15 February 1991, in School of Journalism and Broadcasting Centennial History Collection; *Idaho Statesman*, 22 July 1952, p. 5A.

26. Author interview with Leon Matthews, 3 July 1992, Stillwater, Oklahoma; Author interview with Robert P. Ledbetter, 3 July 1992, Oklahoma City, Oklahoma; Author interview with James R. Bellatti, 3 July 1992, Stillwater, Oklahoma.

27. M. Blair Hart to C. Ellsworth Chunn, 24 July 1958, Robert Johnson to C. Ellsworth Chunn, 24 July 1958, and C. Ellsworth Chunn to Robert Johnson, 31 July 1958, in Files of the School of Journalism and Broadcasting.

28. Biographical sketch of Robert M. Johnson from M. Blair Hart to C. Ellsworth Chunn, C. Ellsworth Chunn to Robert Johnson, 12 August 1958, and Robert M. Johnson to C. Ellsworth Chunn, 16 August 1958, in Files of the School of Journalism and Broadcasting.

29. Oklahoma State University Request for Information Concerning Training and Professional Experience of Robert M. Johnson, 21 August 1958, Robert M. Johnson to C. Ellsworth Chunn, 23 August 1958, Oklahoma State University Request for Personnel Action of Robert M. Johnson, 2 September 1958, and Laurlee Thorn to C. Ellsworth Chunn, 18 November 1958, in Files of the School of Journalism and Broadcasting.

30. "A Venture into Radio's Educational Broadcasting," *Oklahoma State University Magazine*, vol. 2, no. 11 (May 1959), pp. 16, 17; Allen, pp. 199, 200.

31. Oklahoma State University Separation Notice of Robert M. Johnson, 21 August 1959, Files of the School of Journalism and Broadcasting; Author interview with Leslie Kreps, 19 July 1989, Stillwater, Oklahoma.

32. *Stillwater NewsPress*, 8 May 1960; *Daily O'Collegian*, 10 May 1960, p. 3, 24 May 1960, p. 8, 26 May 1960, p. 1, 13 September 1960, p. 1.

33. Information request of Darrel Woodyard, Oklahoma State University Division of Public Information, 18 September 1962, Files of the School of Journalism and Broadcasting; *Daily O'Collegian*, 5 August 1960, p. 3.

34. *Daily O'Collegian*, 24 May 1960, p. 8, 26 May 1960, p. 1.

35. Richard Risk to Harry E. Heath Jr., 12 December 1987, and Mal Topping to Harry E. Heath Jr., 13 February 1991, in School of Journalism and Broadcasting Centennial History Collection; Ledbetter, Bolay, and Allen interview; *Daily O'Collegian,* 26 May 1960, p. 1.

36. *Oklahoma State University Catalog, 1963-1965*, p. 78; Biographical sketch of Malachi C. Topping, Files, Office of Public Information, Oklahoma State University; Malachi C. Topping to Harry E. Heath Jr., 13 February 1991, and Richard B. Risk Jr. to Harry E. Heath Jr., 12 December 1987, in School of Journalism and Broadcasting Centennial History Collection.

37. Richard B. Risk Jr. to Harry E. Heath Jr., 12 December 1987, School of Journalism and Broadcasting Centennial History Collection.

38. Board of Directors, KVRO, to the Federal Communications Commission, 10 June 1966, School of Journalism and Broadcasting Centennial History Collection; Allen, p. 200.

39. Robert P. Lacy to Board of Directors, KVRO, 20 June 1966, Files of the School of Journalism and Broadcasting.

40. Annual newsletters, Department of Radio and Television, 1965-1969, in School of Journalism and Broadcasting Centennial History Collection.

41. *Oklahoma State University Catalog, 1959-1961*, pp. 73, 239; *Oklahoma State University Catalog, 1963-1965*, pp. 78, 281; Annual newsletters, Department of Radio and Television Centennial History Collection; *Stillwater NewsPress*, 19 November 1967, p. 7.

42. Vita of Jack W. Deskin, 20 January 1970, Files of the School of Journalism and Broadcasting.

43. Annual newsletter, Department of Radio and Television, December 1969, School of Journalism and Broadcasting Centennial History Collection.

44. Jack W. Deskin to Harry E. Heath Jr., 28 April 1970, Harry E. Heath Jr. to Jack W. Deskin, 20 May 1970, Vita of Jack W. Deskin, 20 January 1970, Oklahoma State University Request for Personnel Action of Jack W. Deskin, 11 May 1970, Oklahoma State University Separation Notice of Malachi Topping, 17 July 1970, Jack W. Deskin to Harry E. Heath Jr., 1 August 1972, and Jack W. Deskin to Harry E. Heath Jr., 9 January 1991, in Files of the School of Journalism and Broadcasting.

19 A Time to Regroup

Following the departure of C. Ellsworth Chunn in the summer of 1959, the journalism program was administered by a triumvirate: Lemuel D. Groom, James C. Stratton, and Maurice R. Haag. Nominal leader of the group was Haag, an agricultural journalist who had divided his time between the classroom and experiment station research involving the agricultural information program. Haag handled administrative contacts with Dean Robert B. Kamm.[1]

Kamm was not ready to fill the directorship of the School of Communications and chose to assume those duties—without the title—in addition to his deanship. This may be seen as a holding action. He had not given up on the school concept and perhaps hoped later to find the right person to assume the title and its attendant duties. Meanwhile, the School of Communications lived on in the college catalog. While it was established in time for the 1958-59 academic year, it was created too late to permit its name and other basic information to be used in that year's catalog. But in the next two two-year catalogs, 1959-61 and 1961-63, the name did appear, despite the breakup that followed Chunn's resignation. The first had gone to press before the breakup had come, and Chunn's name appeared as director. In the second, the school's name was retained but no director was listed. There was only a loose relationship of separate departments. During this period, Dean Kamm continued to serve informally as coordinator. This may have been Kamm's way of establishing academic equilibrium during a period when emotions were decompressing. In addition, there were other adjustments yet to be made.[2]

While the name lived on for four years, Kamm had made it clear to all concerned that the various units formerly serving under Chunn's leadership were to continue a close and cooperative relationship, but that each would function as a separate academic unit with unit administrators reporting directly to him.[3]

The impasse between Chunn and the speech faculty had been a disappointment to Kamm. He had had high hopes for the School of Communications but he knew the rift that had developed, leading to Chunn's departure, would need some time to heal. His options were limited. It would be neither practical nor desirable to select another school director from the constituent units. Nor would it be wise to ask the speech faculty to return to its former status as part of the old Department of English, Speech and Foreign Languages. In addition, it would be risky to name a new department head for journalism in the short time that remained before the 1959-1960 academic year began. And so the temporary arrangement with Haag as spokesman for the journalism faculty would have to do until a national search could be carried out.

The chain of events that eventually brought Chunn's successor to Stillwater began in 1957, some seventeen months before the School of Communications was formed. Charles L. Allen, an advertising and journalistic management specialist who had served as assistant dean and director of research at Northwestern University's highly regarded Medill School of Journalism, had failed to win the prize he had expected—and felt he deserved. Upon the retirement of Dean Kenneth E. Olson at Medill, Allen had been passed over for an outsider, Ira W. "Bill" Cole. Cole chose his own administrative team, and Allen was no longer a member of the inner circle. A proud man with a distinguished career, Allen chafed but continued his teaching, writing, and research. His books and research brought him into contact with media leaders and he often was invited to speak at their meetings. One such speaking engagement brought him to Oklahoma City, where he addressed members of the Oklahoma Press Association (OPA) on January 24, 1957. He was impressive. Not only was Allen well informed, Oklahoma editors learned, but he had a skillful command of the language plus the ability to inject low-key, George Gobel-style humor into a serious professional presentation.[4]

In the meantime, Clement E. Trout had retired, and Chunn had served a year and had resigned. Five months passed while the search for a new department head continued.

On June 30, 1959, the secretary-manager of the Oklahoma Press Association wrote Kamm suggesting Allen as a person deserving consideration as the new leader of OSU journalism. "If Oklahoma State University can get a man with the stature of Dr. Allen," Ben Blackstock wrote, "I feel certain it would soon be known throughout the country for the excellence of its work. Dr. Allen has a rare combination of education, large practical experience and the dynamic leadership and ability of self-expression desirable for a person charged with directing a journalism school." Blackstock suggested that Allen had the ability to inspire both students and faculty and that graduates under him would be "exceptionally qualified." With his letter he enclosed a copy of the March 1958 *Oklahoma Publisher* in which appeared in full Allen's 1957 OPA speech. In the speech, Allen took a close look at the economic climate, using statistics and logic, then offered fifteen predictions for newspaper advertising revenues in 1958. Summing up, he said: "1958 will be a year in which courageous, able newspaper publishers do very well, and those who are prophets of doom will be victims of their own prophecies."[5]

The same issue of the *Publisher* related the progress of the OPA in its drive to equip the University of Oklahoma journalism school. Ned Shepler, fund chairman, had told a joint meeting of the University of Oklahoma regents and OPA officials that $38,672.39 had been raised toward the drive's $40,000 goal. "We expect the rest of the press association's contributions to put us over the goal within the next few days," Shepler reported. OPA members had brought in pledges earlier totaling less than half of a $100,000 goal. Despite an agreement that contributions would be refunded if the building did not materialize, donors left $31,000 in the fund. Between 1953 and 1956, interest increased this amount to $42,000. In 1956, principally through the efforts of University of Oklahoma regent and publisher Joe McBride, the board of regents appropriated $475,000 for the new building. Other donations were added. The largest contributor was the *Oklahoma Daily*, which put in $77,000 of its reserve fund. This support by the OU regents reflected a kind of assistance from the top unknown in OSU journalism education.[6]

Apparently Blackstock and Kamm had talked about the opening earlier. One day before the OPA manager had written, Kamm had dispatched a letter to Allen's Northwestern University address. He told Allen that he had been recommended "as one to whom we should give consideration." Among other things, Kamm stressed that the candidate should have both sound formal training and practical experience. He underscored the importance of collegiality in the educational setting and the ability to work well with the state's newspapermen.

"We have a good small department," Kamm wrote, "but believe that much more can and should be done. We believe the opportunity is an unusually good one." He asked Allen to indicate whether he might be interested in a twelve-month appointment for a salary in the $8,500 to $10,000 range.[7]

It took two weeks for the letter to catch up with Allen at his home address, 1935 Greenwood Street, in Wilmette, Illinois. Allen, in responding, wrote of a Monday evening dinner he had had with Blackstock, Lawrence Bellatti, and Charley Rhodes in Chicago. Interestingly, as the four men were engrossed in their discussion, a motorcade for Queen

Elizabeth drove by the restaurant. Because the conversation was so intense, they did not go outside and join in the excitement.[8]

At that dinner, Allen noted that he had learned for the first time of Kamm's plans. "As I told those gentlemen, I am honestly interested. . .[but] I am well situated at Northwestern. . . . I could not feel justified in coming to Oklahoma State for $10,000, but let me hasten to assure you that salary would not be a major consideration. . . . I want above all a chance to develop a fine, creditable journalism program, geared to the practicalities of good weekly and small daily publishing, and based upon the bed rock of an excellent education in the liberal arts, and both the social and physical sciences."

Allen praised the dedication of OPA members, told of his years as a specialist in the weekly and small daily newspaper field, and of his books and articles. "I know quite well the journalism of states like Oklahoma," he wrote. He indicated a willingness to "discuss these matters with you at your convenience."[9]

On July 17, Dean Kamm wrote thanking Allen for his continuing interest but pointed out that, because of the lateness of the season, it would not be wise to make an appointment before mid-year. Allen's next letter, undated, indicated that a mid-year appointment would not be out of the question, but that the university might benefit from finding the "best man" for the position by the opening of the school year. He kept the door open by saying he would be pleased to hear further from Kamm.[10]

As the dialogue continued, interest was growing. On August 28,

SCHOOL OF JOURNALISM AND BROADCASTING

The Student Union Commons was a popular meeting place for gab session among journalism students in the 1960s. Sharing fun are (*left to right*) Ann Worley, Marsha Eddins, Ann Larason, J. P. Smith, and Jerry Williams.

1959, Blackstock wrote Milo Watson, publisher of the *Perry Daily Journal*. He said he would like to review his request that Allen be considered for the directorship. He enclosed a note he had received from Allen and urged that the Medill professor and any other candidates be interviewed as early as possible. Blackstock did not want efforts to slacken. He felt it would be a mistake to wait until mid-year "and then [go] into the matter again."[11]

Blackstock's letter to Watson was more than routine, for Watson was chairman of the OPA's OSU Journalism School Committee. He had sent a copy of the letter to Dean Kamm "so that he may know my feeling." Blackstock and other interested parties had attended a luncheon on the campus and it had left him with a sense of frustration. He wrote: "Personally, it seems to me that my nomination of Dr. Allen to Dean Kamm was not handled in the manner in which it courteously should have been. I was serious in nominating him and I am still serious in recommending him. It was my understanding we were asked for suggestions and nominations and that is why I made this one. If the school really was not interested in the feelings of those invited to the luncheon, then they should not have asked us to make suggestions."

Blackstock went on to point out that "the newspaper industry needs the services of an alive, alert and realistic journalism school, not just to train casual students going through the courses, but to keep in touch with the actual needs of the industry these students are supposed to eventually serve." This limited view, though understandable, was at odds with the wider career opportunities journalism graduates across the nation were beginning to seek.[12]

It had been two months since Kamm had first called the opening to Allen's attention. While the OPA was speaking of a journalism *school*, Kamm consistently used the term *department*. He wrote Allen that the selection of Chunn's successor had been slow because key personnel had been away for the summer and he was depending upon the journalism faculty to assist in the selection. "At any rate," he wrote, "we are at the point of going to work seriously in making the appointment."

Kamm commented upon Allen's "wealth of background and experience," but listed three concerns. He wondered if Allen would be satisfied to work with a small program after "doing things in a much bigger way"; be willing to confine most of his activities to "the local program and to service to our Oklahoma newspapers"; and accept the fact that OSU could not match his salary (the lower cost of living in Stillwater would, Kamm believed, offset the salary differential).

Having raised these questions, Kamm sought to reassure Allen that "ours is a genuinely fine opportunity." He noted that he wanted to see the program improve both in size and quality. "We believe there is tremendous potential for service in the Oklahoma newspaper field, and especially to the publishers of the small town dailies and the weeklies. The Oklahoma Press Association recognizes the need for us to move ahead rather aggressively and to give badly needed leadership throughout the State."[13]

In a response of approximately 930 words six days later, Allen reassured Kamm of his continued interest. He answered Kamm's three concerns by citing past experiences at Rutgers and Northwestern where small programs had experienced rapid growth during his tenure. "I do not tremble at a small start unless there exists at OSU a philosophy which glorifies smallness and obstruct growth," he wrote. As for his off-campus research and consulting, he cited the recognition these would bring to OSU and his policy of scheduling such activities during recess and vacation periods. He pledged that he would visit all state newspapers as fast as possible. Finally, he indicated that "we are not too far apart on salary, and perhaps a study of the cost of living in Stillwater may convince me that I would not lose by the move." Allen closed by expressing interest in a visit to Stillwater, "if invited," and satisfaction at Blackstock's confidence in him, stressing the importance of OPA support for the program.[14]

Allen was invited and received unanimous support during a three-day visit. This was followed by a telephone conversation during which an offer was made. It was confirmed in writing by Kamm on September 18, 1959. The appointment would be effective January 1, 1960, "at a twelve months salary of $11,100.00."

Kamm's letter adds credence to the fact that the School of Communications was not yet dead. He stated: "You inquire with regard to the annual budget for the Department of Journalism. This is a little hard to "pull out"' in that there are some items which (as a result of discussion of the various Heads in Communications) we are keeping in the central office, which provides services for each area. This includes budget for clerical staff and certain operations funds. I think it is fair to say, however, that a figure of $40,000.00 is about right. Most of this, of course, is for salaries of Journalism personnel."

There must have been one more telephone conversation. At the bottom of the file copy of the letter was a handwritten notation by Kamm: "Accepted 9-18-59."[15] Allen confirmed his acceptance in a letter dated September 20. In addition to the $40,000 Kamm had mentioned, Allen asked for an additional $10,000 "in the immediate future" for equipment. He included his plans for upcoming meetings, including a speech to the American Marketing Association on December 29. His topic: "Documentary Film Records of the Television Audience." Prior to that and other speaking engagements in New York and Washington, the Allens planned to attend the OPA advertising round tables in Oklahoma City on November 21, followed by a visit to Stillwater and the Kamms for "two or three days." They planned to look for suitable housing, and to store in his journalism office "a lot of books, etc. which we shall bring with us."

To assist in publicity on the appointment, Allen enclosed a comprehensive biographical sketch of five pages and a photograph. On this point he wrote: "I will announce nothing here until I get a copy of your University release, which I hope will go out very widely, to all papers and on the wire. Please send a release to the *Evanston Review*, *Wilmette Life*, and *Chicago Daily News and Sun-Times*.[16]

What were the hopes and aspirations, the successes and disappointments, the central events in the development of the style and character of this man who would change the direction of OSU's journalism curricula? In a minor way, his was the typical Horatio Alger story: from modest means to professional success and acclaim. In the jargon of the 1990s his persona radiated material success and a sense of confidence. He drove a Caddy, wore well-tailored suits, and headed an orderly household in a large home that was tastefully decorated and exuded warmth and charm. He liked having the best, and his beautiful wife could have been a strong contender for the Mrs. America title. His children, now in young adulthood, were handsome.

Charles Allen's teaching experience was solid. He had served from 1925 to 1937 on the journalism faculty at the University of Illinois, and as director of the School of Journalism at Rutgers University from 1937 until the move to Northwestern in 1940. A Phi Beta Kappa and a one-time high school principal, he was a talented professional with a strong ego, one that had been bruised when he was passed over in his bid to succeed Olson. For twenty years he had been a key member of the Medill faculty, during many of those years as assistant dean. But the search committee had settled on Cole, whose relatively modest background in journalism education was overshadowed by his reputation as a man who could get things done. He had proved this in military public relations at Fifth Army Headquarters in nearby Chicago. The Allen children were well established and on their own, and Allen decided to save face and heal his bruised ego by taking on a new challenge. He was well fixed financially and could afford to take the cut in income that the move to Oklahoma State entailed. He promised his lovely and gracious wife, Lida, that he would build her a new home in Stillwater to replace the commodious home they had enjoyed so much in Wilmette. As a couple, they liked to entertain, and a new home planned with that in mind was essential to the move.[17]

As a youth in Towner, North Dakota, Allen lived a vigorous outdoor life. In a letter to the Reverend Herbert Ananestad, his teacher, he recalled borrowing Ananestad's canoe, and tents, stoves and "miscellaneous gear from other people," so he could live on the banks of the Mouse River as soon as the ice went out each spring. He continued to enjoy outdoor life until his declining years. In those carefree days, the future teacher was nicknamed "Prof" by two of his boyhood buddies because he was tall and gangling and resembled Ananestad.[18]

In high school, Allen had aspirations to become a physician. He enrolled in a pre-medical course at Jamestown College, but lack of funds caused him to change his career goals. Falling back on his interest in printing and publishing, he enrolled in journalism at his home-state University of North Dakota, taking the B.A. there in 1924. Allen never ceased being a student, even after he had earned his terminal degree. While a full-time faculty member at the University of Illinois in 1933, he took a second B.A., this one in English, after two years as a part-time student. While at Rutgers, he commuted to Columbia University, where he studied English and political science for three years on a part-time basis. Five years later, he resumed his studies while a faculty member at Northwestern, earning the Ph.D. in psychology and school administration in 1947.[19]

The new OSU journalism leader knew his field from the ground up. He had been a printer's devil at thirteen, and he never outgrew his love for the magic of ink on paper. He became a recognized authority on printing and was the author of *The Journalist's Manual of Printing*, a book used during the 1930s and 1940s in many universities and in the trade as well. Allen began "sticking" type on the *Towner News* in 1912. Six years later he became foreman of the *Mouse River Farmers Press* and worked for a short time on the *Granville Herald* and *Maxbass Monitor*. He also tried his hand at ownership briefly, buying the *Upham Star*.[20]

SCHOOL OF JOURNALISM AND BROADCASTING

Field trips were an important part of journalism in the 1960s. This group is studying letterpress production methods at the Oklahoma Publishing Company in Oklahoma City. An employee explains stereotype casting and shaving in preparing plates for the press. Students were expected to be well informed about all printing processes.

While attending Jamestown College, he was a printer and makeup editor on the *Jamestown Daily Alert*. After transferring to the University of North Dakota, he worked nights on the telegraph desk of the *Grand Forks Herald*. He also was assistant manager of the university radio station, which played an important role in agricultural extension. In the summer of 1924, Allen became a general assignment reporter for the *Minneapolis Tribune*, but soon decided to continue his education as a part-time student at the University of Minnesota while teaching in a junior high school there. In 1925, he joined the journalism faculty at Illinois.[21]

While at the University of Illinois, he purchased and operated three weekly newspapers in Champaign County. It was this type of practical experience combined with his academic background that prepared him to write one of his most successful books, *Country Journalism*, published by Thomas Nelson & Son, a prominent New York publishing house, in 1928.

During World War II, while on a leave of absence from Northwestern, Allen accepted appointment as head of the Office of War Information's news bureau under the leadership of the internationally known Elmer Davis. The bureau was set up like a newspaper city room, with 196 newswriters and other employees. Approximately 800 pieces of domestic and war news moved across his desk each week. Among the items he handled was a monthly communique via trans-Atlantic cable or short-wave radio from Winston Churchill. The messages were in cablese and required some deciphering and fleshing out. "Once in a while Mr. Churchill would put in an expletive, with which he was expert," Allen recalled later.[22]

The longtime journalism educator was a leader in his field, serving in several offices and on numerous committees. Fourteen years into his academic career, he was elected to two consecutive terms as president of the American Association of Teachers of Journalism, forerunner of today's Association for Education in Journalism and Mass Communication. Twenty-three years later, in 1963-64, he held the presidency of the American Society of Journalism School Administrators and for three years was dean of the Southwest District of the American Academy of Advertising. In the latter capacity he visited seventeen universities and delivered speeches at thirty-four meetings.[23]

As one of the nation's most widely known journalism educators, he was a featured speaker at conventions and workshops in major cities throughout the United States and Canada. On one occasion, he addressed a joint session of the North Dakota Senate and House of Representatives. His remarks on some occasions gained wide circulation through various professional and trade publications. In addition, he frequently reported his research in scholarly articles. Typical of these was "Measuring

Advertising Effectiveness by DynaScope Methodology" in the *Journal of Advertising Research*. Whether speaking extemporaneously before an audience or writing a personal letter, Allen had an exceptional command of the language. He was a model for any person who really cared about effective expression.[24]

To keep in touch with trends in journalism, he regularly attended meetings of the American Newspaper Publishers Association, the Advertising Research Foundation, the Association of National Advertisers, the Magazine Advertising Bureau, the Newspaper Advertising Executives' Association, state and regional press associations, and other media-related groups.[25]

One of his interests was readership, and he directed more than ninety such studies on newspapers of all sizes, ranging from small weeklies to metropolitan dailies, such as the *St. Louis Post-Dispatch* and the *Kansas City Star*. The surveys dealt with both news-editorial and advertising content. In addition to his early experience as a newspaper executive, he once served as editor of the *National Publisher* and the *Alpha Tau Omega Palm*, and as associate editor of *Journalism Quarterly*. The National Editorial Association gave Allen its highest honor, the Amos Award, in 1941. He was first listed in *Who's Who in America* in 1946, and later was included in *Who's Who in the Southwest* and *Who's Who in American Education*.[26]

Allen was an excellent teacher. He also was a gifted leader—intelligent, poised, articulate, and well informed in his fields of expertise. To top off these advantages, he brought to the classroom a sense of humor that was clever and often subtle but very much in touch with student attitudes. His excellent command of the English language was impressive to students. He was demanding, making assignments that stretched the minds and energies of those enrolled in his classes. Term papers and research reports were commonplace. He taught no "pud" courses. As a result, his students were in demand, and some made uncommonly fast progress into challenging professional positions.[27]

In bringing to OSU this wide variety of journalistic and educational experiences, Allen had the advantage of strong support from the small faculty he was to lead. Haag wrote Allen on September 23 saying that "Jim, Lem and I are delighted to know you have accepted." Haag promised to keep Allen informed on departmental affairs and volunteered the journalism faculty's help "in [your] getting established here."[28]

Now that the selection had been made, it did not take long for the news to get out. OSU leaders knew they could trade upon Allen's reputation, and they obviously were enthusiastic about the prospects ahead. Both the journalism faculty and the administration were proud that they had landed a national figure to head the program. Allen's prominence appealed to news editors, too, and they were willing to play

The Agricultural Journalism Club in 1963 included several men who would establish successful journalism careers. Standing is the club's popular advisor, Maurice R. "Maury" Haag. Seated (*from left*) are James K. Steward, James O. Williams, Ovonual Johnston, Robert C. Steinberg Jr., Rex Wilmore, Don L. Wooley, Anthony J. Solow, and LeRoy Wilkerson.

the story with more than the usual space for such an appointment. As soon as the news broke, Kamm received congratulatory messages from several OPA members and educators, among them Leslie Moeller, director of the State University of Iowa School of Journalism, and Fayette Copeland, director of the University of Oklahoma School of Journalism. They praised Allen as a vigorous leader who not only "would get things done" but would bring OSU "considerable prestige." John Hamilton, director of OSU's publishing and printing department, expressed his views in a letter to Dean Kamm: "As an alumnus of the technical journalism department here and as a former journalism faculty member, I am keenly aware of the importance of the work of the Department of Journalism to our state and to my work. I appreciate the consideration you exercised in choosing a man of Dr. Allen's caliber for the position. I feel that he will continue the progress made under Professor Trout and will bring new distinction to the institution nationally. Also, new emphasis upon layout and typography will indirectly assist us in this department as [some of our journalism] graduates take positions with the Division of Public Information and in turn use that training [in publications we produce]."[29]

On September 28, 1959, Dean Kamm wrote to Allen, enclosing the official request for his appointment as professor and head of the Department of Journalism plus clippings from the *Daily Oklahoman* and *Stillwater NewsPress* announcing his selection. Kamm also projected confidence in prospects for additional equipment funds. One day later, Haag had written Allen with reference to the spring semester.[30] Allen, in reply, agreed to teach the Methods and Problems courses at both the senior and graduate levels and to direct the theses of those in Journalism

500. As for the other courses, Allen wrote that he would be agreeable to "whatever selection of courses you men make for the next semester."

Heavy rains had brought flooding to Stillwater, so Allen closed his letter with typical banter: "And if it's all the same to you fellows, combine your prayers and your physical strength and your political powers in a last ditch effort to keep Oklahoma State University out of Boomer Creek. You have no idea what a ribbing I have taken recently about 'living in a houseboat,' 'building a Noah's ark,' 'joining the river people,' etc., etc."[31]

Kamm was able to get some additional money. On October 12, he wrote assuring Allen that he had just added $5,000 for instructional equipment to the maintenance budget, and that he hoped for additional monies "after you arrive." He added: "The waters have receded and all goes well here."[32]

Allen's potential value to OSU was reaffirmed even before his arrival. On October 8, he was appointed to the education committee of the Advertising Federation of America, and the Advertising Education Foundation had agreed to a $500 grant for Allen's nationwide study of advertising courses. "It will bring us fine publicity and many contacts with teachers and schools of journalism," Allen told Kamm.[33]

Following his appointment, the flow of letters from Stillwater and

A summer advertising class hears Charles L. Allen, director of the School of Journalism, explain the DynaScope, Allen's patented device to study television audiences as well as to determine traffic patterns in newspapers and magazines. Allen's research brought national attention to OSU.

Evanston continued unabated. Haag wrote suggesting improvements in physical facilities and equipment that "should be purchased." Allen responded sending a carbon copy of his response along with a letter to Dean Kamm. In both letters he asked that expenditures for instructional equipment be deferred until he could discuss the matter thoroughly after his arrival. He also covered his travel plans for the November trip to Stillwater and Oklahoma City. He thanked Haag for storing forty-one boxes of books he had sent, and said at last fifteen more boxes would be coming. He had, "with great reluctance," given away more than 200 volumes. He also described personal equipment he would put to use in the journalism program, for example, a Benday machine, a mimeograph machine and "a great deal of old, but serviceable photographic gear" for both still and motion pictures. He asked Haag to make arrangements for space to park his house trailer.[34]

Haag wrote Allen on October 27, enclosing descriptions of forty journalism courses. Linwood S. Pye, a graduate student, was assisting Groom, Haag, and Stratton. The letter discussed various proposed expenditures for minor items, but suggested that the major expenditures for equipment would await his arrival. Haag explained OSU policy on book purchases and the prohibition of departmental libraries, reported that Clement Trout or Leslie Kreps could provide space for his trailer, and that he would be invited to speak to the Oklahoma Collegiate Press Association during his November visit. Haag closed by suggesting funding of more field trips to Oklahoma City and Tulsa. "[We] have needed closer contact between our students and the working newsmen," he wrote.[35]

The language of these letters reflected male dominance in the media of the day as well as in journalism education. This sexual bias would be drastically altered as females escaped from the women's pages and sexually determined roles in other media to wide-ranging assignments in print and broadcasting a few years later.

In an undated "Dear Bob" letter in mid-November, Allen sent the $500 check from the Advertising Educational Foundation, Incorporated, made out to OSU, along with a letter from the foundation president, William Mapel. It was one of the first two grants made by the foundation and, Mapel wrote, was based upon Allen's professional reputation.[36] The grant was well publicized. Welden Barnes, director of the Division of Public Information, sent Allen copies of five news releases, four of them tailored to the needs of specific newspapers and the other for general release. Barnes's staff had photographed Allen during his visit a few days earlier and the photo would accompany some of the releases. In his letter, Barnes invited Allen to make changes in the stories as he saw fit.

Barnes wrote: "Our Division is making local releases of the picture and story the week of December 1-6, and will follow up with copies to professional and technical publications later."[37] A new flurry of publicity would begin when Allen arrived to assume his duties as department head.

On December 10, based upon measurements supplied by Haag, Allen sent Dean Kamm sketches of his tentative plans for use of the north and south sections of the Communications Building's ground floor. He urged that the entire area be devoted to journalism.[38] On the south side he planned a typography and graphics art production laboratory, seminar room and a library and periodical room. On the north he proposed four rooms for photography—developing, drying, printing and studio—and creative advertising design and copy writing laboratories. Less than half of the plan would be carried out as space demands were adjusted upon his arrival.

The journalism program had been without a permanent leader for a year and a half. The small staff had managed to keep things moving, but Haag and his colleagues were anticipating the Allen era with enthusiasm. A new chapter in journalism education at OSU was beginning.

Endnotes

1. Author interview with Lemuel D. Groom, 2 June 1989, Stillwater, Oklahoma.

2. *Annual Catalog, Oklahoma State University, 1958-1959*, pp. 26, 27, 69, 70, 77, 78, 91, 92, 127, 128, 197, 198, 199, 200, 201, 213; *Annual Catalog, Oklahoma State University, 1959-1961*, pp. 27, 28, 72, 73, 74, 79, 80, 137, 138, 216, 217, 219, 231, 232; *Annual Catalog, Oklahoma State University, 1961-1963*, pp. 31, 32, 61, 69, 70, 74, 77, 78, 93, 94, 143, 144, 153, 240, 241, 242, 257, 265. In the 1963-65 catalog, the name School of Communications no longer appears. The School of Journalism now included options in news-editorial, advertising-journalistic management, agricultural journalism, broadcast journalism, community journalism, home economics journalism, industrial editing, photo-journalism, teaching high school journalism, and graduate work in journalism

3. Robert B. Kamm to Charles L. Allen and Leslie Kreps, 7 April 1961, Files of the School of Journalism and Broadcasting, Oklahoma State University, Stillwater, Oklahoma.

4. Author interview with Baskett P. Mosse [1957], Files of the School of Journalism and Broadcasting; *Oklahoma Publisher*, March 1958, pp. 4, 10, 19. Evaluation based upon personal experience of the author in professional association with Charles L. Allen.

5. Ben Blackstock to Robert B. Kamm, 30 June 1959, Files of the School of Journalism and Broadcasting; *Oklahoma Publisher*, March 1958, pp. 4, 10, 19.

6. *Oklahoma Publisher*, March 1958, pp. 4, 10, 19; L. Edward Carter, *The Story of Oklahoma Newspapers—1846-1984* (Muskogee, OK: Western Heritage Books, Incorporated, 1984), p. 198.

7. Robert B. Kamm to Charles L. Allen, 29 June 1959, Files of the School of Journalism and Broadcasting.

8. Charles L. Allen to Robert B. Kamm, 11 July 1959, Files of the School of Journalism and Broadcasting; Ben Blackstock to Harry Heath, 20 May 1991, School of Journalism and Broadcasting Centennial History Collection, Special Collections, Edmon Low Library, Oklahoma State University.

9. Charles L. Allen to Robert B. Kamm, 11 July 1959, Files of the School of Journalism and Broadcasting.

10. Robert B. Kamm to Charles L. Allen, 17 July 1959, and Charles L. Allen to Robert B. Kamm [20 July 1959],in Files of the School of Journalism and Broadcasting.

11. Ben Blackstock to Milo Watson, 28 August 1959, Files of the School of Journalism and Broadcasting.

12. Ben Blackstock to Milo Watson, 28 August 1959, Files of the School of Journalism and Broadcasting.

13. Robert B. Kamm to Charles L. Allen, 31 August 1959, Files of the School of Journalism and Broadcasting.

14. Charles L. Allen to Robert B. Kamm, 6 September 1959, Files of the School of Journalism and Broadcasting.

15. Robert B. Kamm to Charles L. Allen, 18 September 1959, Files of the School of Journalism and Broadcasting.

16. Charles L. Allen to Robert B. Kamm, 20 September 1959, accompanied by an undated biographical sketch of Charles Laurel Allen, Files of the School of Journalism and Broadcasting. Dr. Allen also called attention to his inclusion in *Who's Who in America*, *Who's Who in Education*, and *Who's Who in Chicago and Illinois*.

17. Undated biographical sketch, Charles L. Allen, September 1959, Files of the School of Journalism and Broadcasting. Author's personal communication with Charles L. Allen. Author's personal experience as chief of Special Events, Department of the Army, the Pentagon, Washington, DC. In this capacity he frequently coordinated programs with Cole, an officer in public information at Fifth Army Headquarters, Chicago.

18. *JB News* (1983-86), pp. 21, 26.

19. Undated biographical sketch of Charles L. Allen, September 1959, Files of the School of Journalism and Broadcasting.

20. *JB News* (1983-86), pp. 21, 26; Undated biographical sketch of Charles L. Allen, September 1959, Files of the School of Journalism and Broadcasting.

21. *JB News* (1983-86), pp. 21, 26; Undated biographical sketch of Charles L. Allen, September 1959, Files of the School of Journalism and Broadcasting.

22. *JB News* (1983-86), pp. 21, 26.

23. *JB News* (1983-86), pp. 21, 26; Edwin Emery and Joseph P. McKerns, *AEJMC: 75 Years in the Making* (Columbia, SC: Accrediting Council for Education in Journalism and Mass Communication, 1987), pp. 29, 47, 82, 83.

24. *Jamestown [North Dakota] Sun*, 26 January 1963, p. 6; *JB News* (1983-86), pp. 21, 26; Author's personal knowledge through professional association from 1946-1985.

25. *JB News* (1983-86), pp. 21, 26.

26. Undated biographical sketch of Charles L. Allen, September 1959, Files of the School of Journalism and Broadcasting; *JB News* (1983-86), pp. 21, 26.

27. *JB News* (1983-86), pp. 21, 26.

28. Maurice R. Haag to Charles L. Allen, 23 September 1959, Files of the School of Journalism and Broadcasting.

29. Leslie Moeller to Robert B. Kamm, 24 September 1959, Fayette Copeland to Robert B. Kamm, 25 September 1959, and John W. Hamilton to Robert B. Kamm, 28 September 1959, in Files of the School of Journalism and Broadcasting.

30. Robert B. Kamm to Charles L. Allen, 28 September 1959, and Maurice R. Haag to Charles L. Allen, 29 September 1959, in Files of the School of Journalism and Broadcasting.

31. Charles L. Allen to Maurice R. Haag, 6 October 1959, Files of the School of Journalism and Broadcasting.

32. Robert B. Kamm to Charles L. Allen, 12 October 1959, Files of the School of Journalism and Broadcasting.

33. Charles L. Allen to Robert B. Kamm, 16 October 1959, Robert B. Kamm to William Mapel, 21 October 1959, Robert B. Kamm to William Mapel, 2 December 1959, and Welden Barnes to Charles L. Allen, 30 November 1959, in Files of the School of Journalism and Broadcasting.

34. Charles L. Allen to Maurice R. Haag, 23 October 1959, and Charles L. Allen to Robert B. Kamm, 23 October 1959, in Files of the School of Journalism and Broadcasting.

35. Maurice R. Haag to Charles L. Allen, 29 September 1959, Charles L. Allen to Maurice R. Haag, 6 October 1959, Maurice R. Haag to Robert B. Kamm, 8 October 1959, and Maurice R. Haag to Charles L. Allen, 27 October 1959, in Files of the School of Journalism and Broadcasting.

36. William Mapel to Charles L. Allen, 16 November 1959, and Charles L. Allen to Robert B. Kamm [13 November 1959], Files of the School of Journalism and Broadcasting.

37. Welden Barnes to Charles L. Allen, 30 November 1959, Files of the School of Journalism and Broadcasting.

38. Charles L. Allen to Robert B. Kamm, 10 December 1959, Files of the School of Journalism and Broadcasting.

20 Reaching for Broader Horizons

Finally, after eighteen months in which Maurice R. Haag, Lemuel D. Groom, and James C. Stratton had presided over a difficult period in the institution's journalism history, a new department head was on the scene. Expectations were high both on campus and off. Charles L. Allen was confident he could bring both prominence and growth to the program.

With his arrival, Allen began urging Dean Robert B. Kamm to find new storage space for chemistry and to remove psychology's experimental rats from the ground floor of the Communications Building. A year and a half would pass before all of this space belonged to journalism. As the transition evolved, only parts of Allen's proposed plans were carried out. Allocation of space in succeeding months involved speech, broadcasting, the *Daily O'Collegian,* and educational television, as well as journalism. Allen made space adjustments a step at a time, based upon already overcrowded conditions.[1]

Dean Kamm had not closed the door on the possibility of eventually turning the leadership of the School of Communications over to a new administrator. It is unlikely he wanted to wear this second hat indefinitely. But he had not considered Allen for this role at the time he was hired, and events over the year and a half since had convinced him that his early assessment had been correct. He held the veteran journalism educator in the highest regard—in fact acknowledged that he was one of the nation's top leaders in journalism education—but he knew it would take a different type of personality to bring smooth and effective interaction to the constituent faculties of such an organization.[2]

Meanwhile, Allen's efforts to consolidate all campus journalism, broadly defined, under his own wing, had alienated at least five colleagues across campus with what Kamm looked upon as "bull-dozing" tactics. Allen's outspoken resistance to the speech program as a part of the School of Communications was 180 degrees away from the dean's viewpoint, nor was Kamm ready to accept the idea that both broadcasting and student publications should become part of the Allen domain. He was agreeable to earlier concessions made in the advertising, industrial editing, public relations and photography areas, but further consolidation seemed undesirable for the present.[3]

The matter was brought to a head by a bellicose letter of approximately fourteen hundred words that Allen had written and had asked his faculty members to sign stating agreement. It was written twenty years to the day after Pearl Harbor, and in it Allen had dropped a few bombs of his own. The strident and intemperate tone of the letter had offended Kamm, who found parts of it unreasonable and degrading of others. He saw it as an attempt to apply unnecessary pressure through both demands and threats. In addition, he was disturbed because Allen had had a conference with Vice President Robert W. MacVicar—one in which Allen stated that MacVicar had supported his curricular views and his plan for space allocations in the Communications Building. Kamm was understandably chagrined that Allen had skipped channels to discuss substantive issues with MacVicar without his dean's presence.[4]

Lemuel D. Groom had been a country printer and editor and felt at home in the journalism school's typography laboratory. With him at the proof press are Janet Reams and an unidentified student.

Allen, at fifty-eight, was in a hurry. He wanted to accomplish the impossible tomorrow. He sought opportunities comparable with these of the University of Oklahoma journalism program, offering the opinion that he was asking "nothing which the majority of accredited schools have not had for 15 to 30 years."[5] He was neither totally right nor totally wrong. Journalism under Clement E. Trout had been under-budgeted for years, but it was a successful program and the administration had grown accustomed to its hard-work-and-low-pay formula.

Kamm had grown increasingly concerned over the past several months as Allen's administrative style had evolved. It seemed to Kamm that each concession to Allen brought forth a request for additional concessions. Allen's direct contacts with President Oliver S. Willham on matters which sometimes went beyond Allen's role as chairman of the student publications board plus his recent conference with MacVicar had convinced Kamm that he must act. The catalyst was Allen's long letter laced with over-strong assertions, for example, "We, the journalism faculty, find the present situation unsatisfactory, unfair, and intolerable. We cannot live with it." Most of this invective apparently referred to recent changes in the speech and broadcasting curricula that Allen viewed as encroachment upon sequences under his jurisdiction. Not only did he feel that it had been a mistake to establish a separate radio-television department, but he accused speech of crashing into "fields where we have been established for 35 years." He stated: "We think that no *course* impinging on anything now taught in the School of Journalism and Communications should be added to any curriculum at OSU without giving our faculty an outline, a syllabus, etc., and adequate time to study these materials."[6]

Kamm's immediate response was a five-and-a-half page single spaced memorandum to Willham and MacVicar. In it, Kamm showed restraint in outlining problems in the communications area. He wrote that he would like the memorandum to serve as background for a needed meeting which he hoped the three could have in the immediate future. Kamm said he was writing in a spirit of good will and friendship toward all concerned. Then he got to the point: "The fact is, however, we do have problems, some of which stem from Charley and his ways of operating. Because we are at a point of making some decisions relating to Charley's future responsibilities, we three need to consider his activities to date. The present memorandum is for the purpose of presenting such as fairly and as accurately as I am able.

"The major issue which we must consider, I believe, is that of *how far* we wish Dr. Allen to go. We have a very able, ambitious, persuasive and powerful man in Charley Allen. He has definite goals in mind, and 'goes all out' in attempting to achieve them. There is no doubt but what we have a great asset in Charley, both professionally and personally—if we can agree on the limits of his role, and if he is willing to observe those limits."

Dean Kamm believed that Allen had resorted to pressure tactics in seeking concessions, using the Oklahoma Press Association; the threat of non-accreditation unless certain debatable goals were reached; and resignations, his own among others. In reviewing recent developments, Kamm alluded to the Department of Journalism having been renamed the "School of Journalism and Communications." Prior to formally recommending the change, Allen, Leslie R. Kreps, Robert P. Lacy, and Kamm conferred. Kamm wrote that there had been a great deal of "give and take." A considerable concession was made by Lacy and Kreps when it was agreed that the established name of "School of Communications" would be used as the vehicle by which the Department of Journalism would become a school. At the same time it was expressly stated and understood that *communications*, in its fullest sense, would continue to be shared in, and be a continuing concern of all three parties—and not solely within the jurisdiction of the new School of Journalism and Communications. "Admittedly, such was more than we probably should have hoped for, but it was agreed upon in good faith, I felt, and I assumed, the understanding would be honored. Such has not been the case, however, and Charley now takes the position that anything of a communications nature is his concern, in view of the fact that he heads the School of Journalism and *Communications*. . .I suggest that to resolve this problem, we ask Charley to confine his activities to only the 'School of Journalism' aspect of the title. If possible, I'd like to go so far as to drop the two words 'and Communications' from the title. I would hope this might be done locally, as a means of clarifying responsibilities, without having to submit a name change."

Kamm also recommended continuing cooperative efforts "in the broad area of communications" and making clear to all concerned "that Radio-TV will continue as a separate department, serving both Journalism and Speech, as well as its own majors and others at the University." Kamm concluded with his opinion that the time had come to "draw the line," so that Allen would understand that journalism alone was his responsibility.[7]

A written record of the meeting which followed Kamm's memorandum to Willham and MacVicar was unavailable, but the dean followed it up with a memorandum to Allen in which he put down in writing "several understandings which will serve to guide our future activities." These understandings, he wrote, "are fully concurred in by both President Willham and Dr. MacVicar." Dean Kamm used the memorandum to praise the progress of the journalism program and to inform Allen that on January 1, 1962, he would have a salary increase and a new title. He would, on that date, be *director* rather than *head* of his school.

Kamm noted that he had said "School of Journalism." The words "and Communications" were dropped from the title. Allen was to be the director of the School of Journalism within the larger framework of journalism and communications. Coordination and leadership relating to certain shared, interdisciplinary communications activities would continue to come from Kamm's office. No unit administrator under the *communications umbrella* would be assigned such responsibility.

"Along with the School of Journalism," Kamm stated, "we will continue to operate a separate Department of Speech and a separate Department of Radio-TV." The three unit leaders would each report administratively to Dean Kamm.[8]

One of the concessions the administration had made in Allen's move to Stillwater was to end the split appointment in advertising with the College of Business. Advertising was placed under the journalism umbrella. Allen moved quickly to give advertising more support than it had had before, and added courses in journalistic management, which he considered to be one of his fortes. Under his direction an advertising-management sequence evolved and was accredited by the American Council on Education for Journalism (ACEJ).[9]

Before leaving Northwestern, Allen had studied the OSU catalog. He found five courses at the lower division level, twenty-two upper division courses, and ten graduate courses. Of the undergraduate courses, eleven were news-editorial, three advertising, two public relations, and others less focused. The graduate courses included Thesis, two courses in Specialized Reporting, Principles of Modern Editing, Public Relations, Extension Information, Current Typographical Problems and Trends, House Magazine Editing, and General Semantics in Journalism. When the 1963-1965 catalog was issued, it reflected the direction he would take

SCHOOL OF JOURNALISM AND BROADCASTING

At the 1965 journalism banquet, Charles L. Allen announced outstanding students in three curricula. From the left, David Lyon was recognized in advertising, William Harmon in graduate studies, and Anthony J. Solow in the news-editorial program.

the program. Technical journalism had been given less visibility in C. Ellsworth Chunn's year as director of the School of Communications, and under Allen it was de-emphasized more.[10]

Courses in agricultural and home economics journalism still were taught, but they were downplayed in promotional materials. The programs the new administrator knew best, those at Illinois, Rutgers, and Northwestern, were broad-gauged in approach rather than with the highly specialized focus that Trout had emphasized. Allen was careful to continue community journalism as part of the program, for he had a sentimental feeling for weeklies and small dailies although his professional career had veered in the direction of advertising, management, and readership research. He was aware, too, of the large number of weekly papers that held membership in the Oklahoma Press Association, and what they expected, often unrealistically, of the state's journalism schools. Many of the state's weeklies were published by Oklahoma A. and M. graduates, and some upcoming OSU graduates would find it necessary to start their careers on small newspapers.[11]

To give him a feel for journalism opportunities in the southwest, the first research under Allen at OSU focused upon the job market for journalism graduates in the various media fields. Among these studies were those of James A. Butts and Gregg S. Bond, graduate students in journalism. Allen wrote a series of five articles based upon Butts's data covering the years 1924-60. The stories were distributed by the Division of Public Information with a covering memorandum to editors signed by Robert L. McCulloh, editor and head of the OSU News Bureau. The research results formed the basis for news releases that often found their way into the state's leading newspapers. These stories sometime bypassed the Division of Public Information, a fact which caused consternation in that office.[12]

The small faculty Allen had inherited could not keep up with the increasing enrollment and curricular expansion that followed the widespread publicity and promotional activities Allen had set in motion. Now he could begin to add new faculty. His first move was to find a versatile teacher whose background he knew. He turned to a forty-two-year-old Iowa State University associate professor, Harry E. Heath Jr. Heath had written his master's thesis at Northwestern under Allen's supervision and had gained a reputation for his work in broadcast journalism during twelve years at Iowa State less a year-and-a-half out for a return to active duty during the Korean conflict.[13]

Allen wanted Heath to bring more realism to the work in broadcast journalism, a difficult task with only one Vidicon film camera and an industrial type television camera, both of which were in demand in two non-news courses. Heath borrowed an antiquated 16 mm motion picture camera, an editing viewer and splicer from Guy M. Pritchard, director of audio visual services, to give his small class experience shooting and editing news film. Later, when he became director, Heath added a Bolex and three Bell and Howell cameras and set up an editing laboratory with four editing stations. With careful scheduling, these proved adequate for TV news and cinematography classes.[14]

Allen wanted to add Heath for several other reasons as well. He had been educated from the fourth grade through his undergraduate university studies in Tulsa and had newspaper contacts in both Tulsa and Oklahoma City. Although he was the principal teacher of broadcasting and film courses at Iowa State, he had taught, among other courses, reporting, editing, and typography and had served as major professor on several master's theses. In addition, he had been adviser to all agricultural journalism majors, a fact that would appeal to the OSU administration. Such a teacher would be valuable as Allen launched a broadcast journalism curriculum. But, in a program such as was now under way, Allen would need someone with skills in both print and broadcasting. Heath had the versatility he sought.[15]

From Heath's point of view, the change would be a good one. He had been stretched too far, he thought, at Iowa State. Allen's description of the job seemed to offer a chance for Heath to improve his effectiveness because he would not be teaching the wide range of courses he had taught

In addition to his classroom teaching, Glenn A. Butler worked as editorial advisor to the *O'Collegian*. Discussing a story with him are (*left to right*) Alan Krug, Linda Ray, and Linda Maule. Butler later became a faculty leader at the University of Florida.

at Iowa State. Then, too, there was the fact that the move would bring him and his wife closer to home. His parents still lived in Tulsa and were well into retirement. His wife's mother lived in Houston. It would mean a considerable loss in salary, but it offered offsetting advantages that appealed to both. Mrs. Heath would be a graduate assistant and later an instructor in the Department of Family Relations and Child Development. The Heath family visited Stillwater in July and agreed to accept the appointment. Heath would be a full professor at a salary of $8,000.[16]

Another new faculty member was Glenn A. Butler, who had served Oklahoma A. and M. as a graduate assistant under Clement Trout and was returning to continue work toward his doctorate. Butler was a graduate of Okmulgee High School and had followed with an associate arts degree from Northern Oklahoma College. Then he had enrolled at the University of Oklahoma, where in 1950 he was awarded the bachelor's degree in journalism and three years later, following military service, a master's degree in education. He had served in Japan and Korea as a medic with the 45th Division and before returning home after twenty-two months overseas had been a battalion sergeant major. When he returned to Norman from the Far East to begin work on his master's, he served part-time as a journalism librarian, and following graduate studies accepted a position as director of publications and instructor in journalism at Central State College in Edmond.

In 1956, he took a year's leave of absence to start work on his doctorate in higher education with a minor in journalism at Oklahoma A. and M., then returned to his work at Central State. His appointment became effective on September 1, 1956, as a part-time temporary instructor; on May 8, 1957, Trout filled out Butler's discontinuance notice.[17]

Butler continued at Central State until 1961, when he resumed resident study on his doctorate at Oklahoma State University. On July 27, 1961, Allen appointed him as a graduate assistant for one year. He was terminated on May 31, 1962. His next academic year was spent at Findlay College, Findlay, Ohio, as director of public relations, where his work was praised by the administration.[18]

Meanwhile, a faculty need had developed in photography. Wesley Calvert, thirty-five years old, stocky, energetic, and personable, had earned a reputation for designing and running one of the finest photojournalism laboratories in the country at Texas A. and M., where he had worked under Donald D. Burchard. He had learned that Allen was seeking a replacement for Haskell "Doc" Pruett, who was retiring. The popular Pruett had brought photography from the College of Education to the School of Communications in 1958, and it had remained in the Department of Journalism following the 1959 reorganization. Through the years, Pruett had become a campus legend and his courses attracted enough students to keep him and Harry L. Hix, his assistant, well occupied. Following military service, including eighteen months in the Philippines, Calvert had earned the bachelor of journalism degree from the University of Missouri in 1951 and had completed the course work for his M.A. there in 1953. He had had both reportorial and production experience in his native California and a wide range of duties on the *Columbia Missourian*, including news, advertising, circulation, and promotion. In addition, he had been on the business staff of the *Columbian* magazine and had been a graduate assistant and laboratory instructor in typography.

In the 1953-54 academic year, he was given a one-year appointment as instructor at Iowa State College. His principal responsibility was typography, but he had taught news and advertising courses as well. The following year he joined the Texas A. and M. journalism faculty. Although he taught a wide range of courses, he had succeeded in building the highly regarded photojournalism program praised by ACEJ officials.

Calvert had written Allen on December 3, 1961, expressing interest in the Pruett position. Heath had worked with him at Iowa State and urged Allen to give him serious consideration. Calvert came to Stillwater for an interview on April 6, 1962. Soon after he had lectured in one of Allen's classes on a "trial run," Allen offered him an assistant professorship at $6,800 for nine months. The appointment papers were sent forward on June 6, 1962.

The new photography teacher added strength to OSU's offerings. Hix, as had been true of Pruett, was an excellent generalist in photography, but was not news oriented. Calvert knew photojournalism and brought greater realism to photo assignments. Calvert and Hix, both well schooled in their separate brands of the art, complemented one another.

Calvert, a member of the National Press Photographers Association as well as six other professional journalistic societies, took an active part in departmental affairs. He was well liked by students, although some thought him to be too demanding in his photo assignments. Unfortunately, Pruett's loss was reflected in sagging enrollments in photography courses. Allen felt he could no longer justify a second professor in that specialty. Calvert resigned effective June 30, 1964, to become general manager of student publications at Washington State University, where in succeeding years he was recognized as a national leader in the field.[19]

Calvert's resignation cleared the way for Allen to add one of his most outstanding faculty members, William J. Roepke. He had been on the faculty at Arizona State College, Flagstaff, since 1960, and was concerned about the reorganization in mass communication there. The placement bureau of the Association for Education in Journalism had tipped him off about the opening created at Oklahoma State University by Haag's death. After an exchange of letters and a personal interview, Allen offered Roepke an assistant professorship at $7,000 for the regular school year

Two popular photography teachers during Charles L. Allen's administration were Wesley D. Calvert (*left*) and Harry L. Hix. Calvert replaced the legendary Haskell "Doc" Pruett, but he had a short tenure. Hix stayed on until retirement. During his years as principal photography teacher, he had the second largest enrollment in the nation in the 1970s.

effective September 1.[20]

Roepke had had excellent experience with McCann-Erickson, Incorporated, one of the nation's leading advertising agencies, as well as in private industry. He had earned both the B.S. and M.S. degrees at the Medill School of Journalism, Northwestern University, majoring in advertising and business management. Though not an agricultural specialist, Roepke did creditable work in the service courses in agricultural journalism. However, his greatest contribution was in advertising, a field in which he excelled. Allen considered him to be the best teacher on his staff, youthful, personable, and "a splendid lecturer in the classroom." Unfortunately, he was contemplating a move west, based upon climate, geography, and his wife's health. He resigned, effective at the end of May 1967.[21]

President Willham had authorized a new budget position with half of the salary coming from the student publications account. Allen apparently had been in contact with Butler, for in early March Butler had written expressing an interest in returning to OSU. In his letter he referred to "the position [Allen had] mentioned." Allen must have felt sure he would have the new budget position, for he and Butler had agreed upon terms before President Willham had officially authorized it. The salary would be $8,000 for twelve months. Butler would work in the mornings teaching and completing work on his Ed.D., and in the afternoons as editorial advisor to the *O'Collegian*. Allen, Elmer Woodson, and Butler would work out the details.[22]

Butler returned as an assistant professor, teaching two freshman courses, Introduction to Journalism Fields and Journalistic Style and Structure, and a sophomore-level course, Agricultural Journalism. In addition, he assisted Allen with the Oklahoma Collegiate Press Association and various administrative duties.[23]

By 1965, other schools were interested in Butler. In response to an inquiry from the University of Houston, Allen wrote: "He is the most promising member of my faculty. I think he is going to be at the top of our profession." Meantime, Butler had not only received an attractive offer from Houston, but "several others as well." He told Allen he hoped for at least $9,600, but said he would stay for $8,800.[24]

Heath, too, had other offers. In the summer of 1965 he visited the University of Florida, where Rae Weimer was building one of the nation's top-ranked journalism schools. Allen had painted a less than optimistic picture about the future of journalism at OSU, and had encouraged Heath to consider the move. When Heath decided to accept Weimer's offer, Allen scrambled to cover the bases for fall. He reduced Butler's load on the *O'Collegian* and gave him additional teaching time, then added John L. Griffith as a part-time graduate teaching assistant.[25]

Butler stayed on for another year, then asked for a leave of absence without pay to serve as executive director of the Foundation for Senior Citizens in Oklahoma City. He returned briefly to Oklahoma State University, then accepted a position in the School of Journalism and

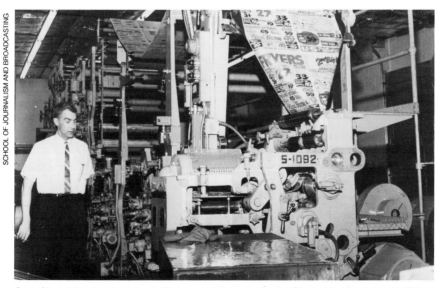

One of journalism's most talented faculty members during the Charles L. Allen era was William J. Roepke, who took an interest in all phases of journalism, both print and electronic. His specialty was advertising, but he studied and valued the presswork that enhanced it.

Communication at the University of Florida, where he had a long tenure, including a position as chairman of the public relations faculty.[26]

Griffith had decided to work toward the doctorate, and the Oklahoma State University opening created by Heath's departure appealed to him. The Chicago native was thirty-four years of age when he decided to apply. He carried 155 pounds on a five foot, ten inch frame and was in good health. He had attended the University of Louisville for a year, then served in the Air Force for three years before taking up his studies at Southeastern Oklahoma State College, where he earned his B.A. degree in 1956. A year later, in Trout's last year as department head, he had earned the M.S. with a thesis titled "A Critical Content Analysis of Selected Oklahoma High School Newspapers." James C. Stratton had supervised his work. He had been an outstanding undergraduate, making Blue Key and *Who's Who in American Colleges and Universities* at Southeastern. Following his master's at Oklahoma State University, he had taught at Northeastern Oklahoma A. and M. College for a year, joined the *Ardmore Daily Ardmoreite* as a reporter for four years, then had returned to teaching at Northern Oklahoma College for three years.[27]

With Heath's departure for Florida, Griffith was a timely replacement. He took over some of the work that had been Heath's, and some that Elsie Shoemaker had handled, including home economics journalism. Among the courses were Agricultural News Writing and Agricultural Communications. By April 1966, Allen valued his work so much that he recommended a title change from graduate teaching assistant to temporary assistant professor. Later he removed the word "temporary." The same month, Griffith began working on the Ed.D. degree in higher education with a journalism concentration. Shortly before Heath returned from Florida as Allen's successor, Griffith resigned. He had signaled his intention to Allen in February, saying he would resign "at the end of this school term." His resignation was effective May 31, 1967. From Oklahoma State University he went to the University of Florida, where he later became chairman of the Department of Journalism in the College of Journalism and Communications.[28]

Allen was a man who evoked strong reactions. He was liked or disliked. There were few who fell midway in the attitude continuum. As a handsome young professor at the University of Illinois, Allen was aware that many a coed had cast a romantic eye in his direction. Even into his sixties, his style and bearing were attractive to women. Men appreciated Allen for his leadership skills and his informality in dealing with students as well as with faculty colleagues. At Northwestern he was well known for his outings with small groups of students to nearby water spots where boating and a good supply of beer would make a long, mellow day. Another side of Allen was not so well known. His charity was not a matter of common knowledge, but numerous Northwestern students who were about to drop out of school were given personal loans to see them through. This charity would later be extended to OSU journalism students. Other students, especially at Medill, where his pantry surveys were an important marketing tool for Chicago advertising agencies, earned much-needed financial aid and learned at the same time as field workers in the surveys. OSU students received similar financial help in readership surveys during the 1960s.[29]

The graduate program prior to Allen's arrival had depended primarily upon funding to give the journalism faculty relief from excessive paper grading and increasing laboratory duties or to assist in the department's experiment station research. It rarely numbered more than three students. Under Allen, the graduate program began to grow. His reputation helped attract students, but his recruitment efforts played a part, too, as did the increasing interest in graduate work nationally. If there were weaknesses, and these were not fatal, they were related to the limited number of courses with graduate-level rigor and to the limited faculty available to handle existing courses. To some, an additional shortcoming was Allen's consistent use of his chronophotographic invention, the DynaScope, for both print-media and television-viewing

The School of Journalism and Communications had replaced its old Duplex letter press with a modern Goss Suburban offset press in the early 1960s. Three of the most talented students of that period were (*left to right*) Jean Kygar, Rex Wilmore, and Pat Musick. They learned newspaper production in the *O'Collegian* press room.

behavior. Numerous graduate students during Allen's tenure carried out their studies by using the DynaScope as their basic research tool. Some students thought that a wider range of research topics and methodology would have been a better approach.[30]

Allen's television research, which documented the fact that television sets often were turned on when no one was in the room, rubbed broadcasting trade publications the wrong way, for it suggested that commonly accepted viewership data might well be overestimated. Robert Lacy, head of the new Department of Radio and Television, which had spun off from the Department of Speech one year after the breakup of the School of Communications, joined the debate by publicly attacking the validity of Allen's data.[31]

Lacy appealed to Dean Kamm to put the damper on Allen's television research. Kamm diplomatically suggested that more attention might be given to print research and less to broadcasting. Allen's rejoinder was that Lacy was welcome to do newspaper research. He saw communications research as an open field with no boundaries, a field in which such scholars as sociologists, psychologists, anthropologists, political scientists, and semanticists had played a role, and he saw no reason to place limits upon communications research at OSU. This was an argument that was difficult to refute.[32]

In the wake of this disagreement over research, some of the conflict that had existed in the School of Communications began to surface again. Speech was no longer in the Communications Building, but conditions still were crowded. Journalism was using the sub-surface first floor as well as the second floor while radio-television controlled most of the third floor, although some journalism classes were held in the large classroom in the southwest corner. Broadcast news courses were under Allen, but Lacy was bootlegging news instruction in his program without such a course having been approved for listing in the radio-television section of the catalog. Perhaps the final straw for Lacy was Allen's use of a single-system Vidicon sound camera to give students experience in producing television commercials in his advertising classes. Because of the inter-departmental rivalry plus limited enrollment in the course, broadcasting majors were missing this opportunity to expand their television advertising know-how. In addition, broadcasting students interested in news were not getting the advantage of instruction from a professional broadcast journalist. Conversely, journalism students interested in broadcasting felt unwelcome in the KOSU and KVRO newsroom and studios on the third floor.[33]

The Lacy-Allen hostility had spread among some of the students. Apparently acerbic comments were injected into some lectures or conferences, for soon students from the third floor were defacing journalism announcements and promotional materials posted on the second floor bulletin boards. The atmosphere was not good. It was not until Allen's retirement that relationships within the building took an upturn.

The thaw began in late summer 1967, when Harry Heath returned from his professorship at the University of Florida to replace Allen, who would retire on August 31. Heath had been the unanimous choice of the journalism faculty.[34]

Allen's interests were broad, and sometimes far-reaching. He was widely known for his research, and during the Oklahoma State University years his DynaScope had attracted national attention. He was founder and first president of Pi Alpha Mu, a national professional fraternity for students in advertising and management. He established a chapter at OSU soon after his arrival. Several prominent Oklahoma journalists as well as students were initiated, building a bond with state media leaders. One of his favorite philanthropies was an annual gift to the Charles Allen Journalism Scholarship at his alma mater, and for a few years he provided an annual accuracy award in Oklahoma Collegiate Press Association competition, which he served as executive director from 1960 through early 1967.

For Allen, still energetic and highly motivated, there was work yet to do. After leaving OSU in 1967, he directed Texas Tech's graduate

Charles L. Allen (*left*) sought ways to bring his students into contact with well-known figures in journalism. Chet Huntley (*right*) of the famous NBC Huntley-Brinkley team was one of them. After students had visited with Huntley, Allen stepped forward to exchange views at a reception at the Student Union.

program in journalism for two years. Then he accepted an assignment as visiting professor of journalism and director of the Mass Communications Centre at the Chinese University of Hong Kong. During that year, he wrote his ninth book, *Communication Patterns in Hong Kong*.[35]

Upon leaving Hong Kong, the Allens retired to Santa Barbara, California, where he continued with a limited schedule of consulting. His time now permitted him to return to one of his favorite hobbies, music. He sang in both the Santa Barbara Chorus and the Bible Presbyterian choir. In addition, he played the baritone horn in the community band once a week, and operated his own job press on which he did printing "for charity and for a bunch of relatives."[36]

Then his health began to break. He underwent surgery in 1978, but made a good recovery. The diabetes that had been under control worsened. In 1984, a foot was amputated, but he adjusted and was able to care for himself. His wife, incapacitated by a brain tumor, was in a nursing home. After his adjustment to his second surgery, he suffered two small strokes and then deteriorated rapidly. He died on February 7, 1985, at the age of eighty-two.[37]

Allen's principal contributions to OSU journalism had been his emphasis upon graduate work and his strengthening of the courses in advertising and journalistic management. In addition, he had given the curriculum a broader reach and had strengthened the school's contacts with major media organizations. It was a time of regrouping following the tensions and hostilities that had developed during Chunn's year as director of the ill-fated School of Communications. In a sense, the Allen years—though not without tensions of their own—had represented a transition from technical journalism to a more general approach. The idea had originated in the mind of Vice President MacVicar, had germinated under Chunn and finally began to mature under Allen.[38] Whether it had been the right road to follow would not be known for years to come.

Endnotes

1. Charles L. Allen to Robert B. Kamm, 10 December 1959, and Charles L. Allen to Robert B. Kamm, 15 December 1959, in Files of the School of Journalism and Broadcasting, Oklahoma State University, Stillwater, Oklahoma.

2. Robert B. Kamm to Charles L. Allen and Leslie Kreps, 7 April 1961, Files of the School of Journalism and Broadcasting.

3. Robert B. Kamm to Oliver S. Willham and Robert W. MacVicar, 11 December 1961, Files of the School of Journalism and Broadcasting.

4. Charles L. Allen to Robert B. Kamm, 7 December 1961, with endorsement of agreement signed by James C. Stratton, Maurice R. Haag, Lemuel D. Groom, and Harry E. Heath Jr., and marginal notes by Kamm, Files of the School of Journalism and Broadcasting.

5. Charles L. Allen to Robert B. Kamm, 8 December 1961 (cover letter to letter of 12 July 1961), Files of the School of Journalism and Broadcasting.

6. Charles L. Allen to Robert B. Kamm, 7 December 1961, Files of the School of Journalism and Broadcasting.

7. Robert B. Kamm to Oliver S. Willham and Robert W. MacVicar, 11 December 1961, Files of the School of Journalism and Broadcasting.

8. Robert B. Kamm to Charles L. Allen, 13 December 1961, and Request for Personnel Action, 12 December 1961, in Files of the School of Journalism and Broadcasting.

9. Oliver S. Willham to Baskett Mosse, 21 December 1961, Baskett Mosse to Oliver S. Willham, 30 December 1961, and ACEJ Accreditation Report, in Files of the School of Journalism and Broadcasting.

10. *Oklahoma State University Catalog, 1963-1965*, pp. 69-71.

11. Ben Blackstock to Milo Watson, 28 August 1959, and Robert B. Kamm to Charles L. Allen, 31 August 1959, in Files of the School of Journalism and Broadcasting; *Annual Catalog, Oklahoma State University, 1960-1961*, pp. 216, 217.

12. Gregg S. Bond, "1961-1962, Job Census of Men and Women on Daily and Weekly Newspapers in Oklahoma" (Master of Science thesis, Oklahoma State University, 1962); James A. Butts, "A Job Census of Oklahoma State University Journalism Graduates" (Master of Science thesis, Oklahoma State University, 1962).

13. Biographical data on Harry E. Heath Jr., Files of the School of Journalism and Broadcasting.

14. Narrative of events in which the author participated.

15. Biographical data on Harry E. Heath Jr., Files of the School of Journalism and Broadcasting.

16. Oklahoma State University Request for Change in Staff, appointment, Harry E. Heath Jr., 1961, Files of the School of Journalism and Broadcasting.

17. Oklahoma State University Request for Change in Staff, leave of absence of Glenn A. Butler, 1 September 1956, and Discontinuance, 8 May 1957, in Files of the School of Journalism and Broadcasting.

18. Oklahoma State University Request for Change in Staff, appointment of Glenn A. Butler, 27 July 1961, Terminated, 31 May 1962, and Arthur Eakin to Charles L. Allen, 19 April 1963, Files of the School of Journalism and Broadcasting.

19. Author interview with Baskett Mosse, 1961, seven letters exchanged by Charles L. Allen and Wesley D. Calvert from 31 January 1962 to 9 April 1962, Request for Personnel Action, appointment of Wesley D. Calvert, 6 June 1962, and Separation Notice of Wesley D. Calvert, 25 May 1964, in Files of the School of Journalism and Broadcasting; Washington State University *Daily Evergreen*, undated 1981, p. 1; *JB News* (1983), p. 2.

20. William J. Roepke to Charles L. Allen, 10 February 1964, Charles L. Allen to William J. Roepke, 14 February 1964, Charles L. Allen to Robert B. Kamm, 2 February 1964, William J. Roepke to Charles L. Allen, 25 February 1964, William J. Roepke to Charles L. Allen, 26 February 1964, Charles L. Allen to William J. Roepke, 6 March 1964, William J. Roepke to Charles L. Allen, 17 March 1964, Charles L. Allen to William J. Roepke, 6 April 1964, William J. Roepke to Charles L. Allen, 8 April 1964, Western Union Roepke to Charles L. Allen, 8 April 1964, and Oklahoma State University Request for Personnel Action, appointment of William J. Roepke, 26 May 1964, in Files of the School of Journalism and Broadcasting.

21. Resume of William J. Roepke, Charles L. Allen to Theodore E. Conover, 10 January 1967, William J. Roepke to Robert B. Kamm, 30 March 1967, William J. Roepke to James Scales, 30 March 1967, William J. Roepke to Charles L. Allen, 30 March 1967, William J. Roepke to Harry E. Heath Jr., 30 March 1967, James R. Scales to William J. Roepke, 3 April 1967, and Oklahoma State University Separation Notice of William J. Roepke signed by V. B. Monnett, 11 May 1967, in Files of the School of Journalism and Broadcasting.

22. Glenn A. Butler to Charles L. Allen, 5 March 1963, Glenn A. Butler to Charles L. Allen, 12 April 1963, Oliver S. Willham to Charles L. Allen, 12 April 1963, Charles L. Allen to Glenn A. Butler, 19 April 1963, Arthur Eakin to Charles L. Allen, 19 April 1963, Charles L. Allen to Glenn A. Butler, 1 May 1963, Glenn A. Butler to Charles L. Allen, 7 May 1963, and Recommendation for Change of Status of Glenn A. Butler, 14 May 1963, in Files of the School of Journalism and Broadcasting.

23. Class rolls of Glenn A. Butler, Files of the School of Journalism and Broadcasting.

24. Patrick Welch to Charles L. Allen, 1 April 1965, Charles L. Allen to Patrick Welch, 8 April 1965, Glenn A. Butler to Charles L. Allen, 31 May 1965, and Charles L. Allen to Robert B. Kamm, 1 June 1965, in Files of the School of Journalism and Broadcasting.

25. Author interview with Charles L. Allen, Summer 1965, Charles L. Allen to Robert B. Kamm, 8 July 1965, and Request for Information Concerning Training and Professional Experience of John Griffith, 9 July 1965, in Files of the School of Journalism and Broadcasting.

26. Request for Leave of Glenn A. Butler, 25 July 1966, and Charles L. Allen to James Scales, 21 July 1966, in Files of the School of Journalism and Broadcasting.

27. Request for Information Concerning Training and Professional Experience of John Griffith, 9 July 1945, Files of the School of Journalism and Broadcasting.

28. Salary Adjustment for John Griffith, 13 December 1965, Request for Change in Title, 20 April 1966, Charles L. Allen to James R. Scales, 20 April 1966, Change of Status, 16 May 1966, 27 November 1966 of John Griffith, John Griffith to Charles L. Allen, 21 February 1967, and Notice of Resignation of John Griffith effective 31 May 1967, in Files of the School of Journalism and Broadcasting.

29. Author interview with Mrs. Leonard Feinberg, once a student of Charles L. Allen at the University of Illinois, summer 1963; Author's numerous conversations with Northwestern University faculty colleagues of Allen; JB News (1983-86), p. 21; Author's observations during six years as student and faculty colleague of Allen.

30. Based upon comments of Charles L. Allen's graduate students and titles of 1960-1967 theses on file in the OSU Library and in the School of Journalism and Broadcasting.

31. Broadcasting Magazine, 23 July 1962, p. 57.

32. Charles L. Allen to Robert P. Lacy, 7 November 1962, and Charles L. Allen to Robert B. Kamm, 24 July 1962, in Files of the School of Journalism and Broadcasting.

33. Based upon class exercises left in journalism laboratories and personal observations of the author.

34. Frequent results of defacement observed by author and other faculty and students; James R. Scales to Charles L. Allen, 10 April 1967, Files of the School of Journalism and Broadcasting.

35. JB News (1983-86), pp. 21, 26.

36. Charles L. Allen to Harry E. Heath Jr. [1971], Files of the School of Journalism and Broadcasting.

37. Madge Allen Bridgeman to Harry E. Heath Jr. 2 June 1984, and Harry E. Heath Jr. to Madge Allen Bridgeman, 6 June 1984, in School of Journalism and Broadcasting Centennial History Collection, Special Collections, Edmon Low Library, Oklahoma State University.

38. Schiller Scroggs to Harry E. Heath Jr., 1 September 1970, and Robert W. MacVicar to Harry E. Heath Jr., 10 August 1987, in School of Journalism and Broadcasting Centennial History Collection.

21 Rapid Growth and Diversity

Through the years, Charles L. Allen's successor as director of the School of Journalism had become so identified with Oklahoma State University that most people assumed he had been an undergraduate there. He had long since stood and sung the OSU alma mater with obvious warmth, and even a touch of emotion. The truth was, however, that he had set foot on the Stillwater campus only once—to cover a football game for the *Tulsa Tribune*—before he was interviewed late in the summer of 1961 for a faculty vacancy.

Harry E. Heath Jr., the new director, was graduated in 1937 from Tulsa Central High School, where he won national honors as sports editor of *Tulsa School Life*. He was offered a scholarship by Drake University, but elected to enroll at the University of Tulsa, where as a freshman he served as sports editor of the *Tulsa Collegian* and continued his work as Tulsa correspondent for *The Sporting News*, a national baseball weekly. While at the University of Tulsa, he worked in the publicity department and as campus correspondent for the *Tulsa Tribune* to help pay for his tuition. In his senior year he was *Collegian* co-editor with Baskett Mosse, who was later to become a leader in journalism education. He also created and edited two sports publications. These papers—*Softball News* and *Tulsa Sports News*—gave him valuable experience but were only break-even enterprises. He took the few journalism courses available and earned his bachelor of arts degree in English and psychology in 1941.[1]

While Adolf Hitler strutted over his conquest of Europe and the Battle of Britain raged on, he enrolled at Northwestern University to work toward a master's degree in the Medill School of Journalism. He was widening his appreciation of scholarly effort under Curtis D. MacDougall, Kenneth E. Olson, Floyd Arpan, and Albert A. Sutton. His living expenses were greater than he had anticipated and he had taken a job in the Central Division of the National Broadcasting Company, located on the fourteenth floor of Chicago's Merchandise Mart, to help pay for the master's. He wrote and edited network news broadcasts for Dave Garraway, Durward Kirby, Jim Campbell, Cleve Conway, Lynn Brandt, and other staff announcers, and on one occasion assisted the internationally famous H. V. Kaltenborn, passing through Chicago and using NBC's WMAQ facilities for his highly rated nightly commentary. Then the Japanese attack on Pearl Harbor plunged the United States into World War II. Within weeks Heath was on his way to Fort Sill, Oklahoma, for induction into the Army.[2]

Four-plus years later he was a civilian once more and faced a choice. Bill Ray, director of news and special events at NBC-Chicago, wanted him to return to the news staff there. The University of Tulsa wanted him to head its News Bureau, including responsibility for sports publicity. In Chicago before the war he was single. Now he was married and had a young son. He passed up the chance to grow with NBC and the promising new television industry, opting for an environment he thought would be better for family living. He took the Tulsa job, returning to Northwestern for two summers to complete his course work for the master's. His thesis—a survey of college public relations programs and procedures—was written in absentia.

At Tulsa, where C. Ellsworth Chunn had returned after surviving the Bataan Death March and nearly five years as a Japanese prisoner of war, Heath was asked to teach journalism part-time. He enjoyed teaching. After he had spent a year and a half at Tulsa, Dean George Turnbull at the University of Oregon School of Journalism, one of the west coast's most respected programs, offered him a full-time teaching job. He accepted. His replacement at Tulsa was Jack Murphy, a talented young sports writer who had been best man at Heath's wartime wedding. Murphy later was to gain national fame as sports editor of the Copley newspapers in San Diego, where today Jack Murphy Stadium attests to his veneration. At Oregon, Heath taught both in the print and broadcast news curricula, but was chiefly responsible for the latter. During his year there, his program in broadcast journalism was accredited by the American Council on Education for Journalism (ACEJ). It was one of only five in the nation so recognized.[3]

Next came an offer from Iowa State College, later to be renamed the Iowa State University of Science and Technology. Once more, he was hired to teach in both the print and broadcasting areas, with major responsibility for broadcast journalism. Less than two years after he had settled into his new routine at Iowa State, a "police action" in Korea became the Korean War. He was recalled to active duty. Returning to Iowa State a year and a half later, he had decided that his future in education demanded further study. He immediately began work toward his doctorate on a part-time basis.

For most of the next four years, he taught three-quarters time and took graduate courses in a program that permitted a blending of mass communication with behavioral sciences. Finally, as he reached the dissertation stage, he gave up his teaching duties and spent one term as a full-time graduate student. His dissertation research validated the effectiveness of television as a medium for off-campus teaching.[4]

In 1956, with Secretary of State John Foster Dulles as the commencement speaker, President James Hilton conferred the doctor of philosophy degree upon Heath. Although an average student academically as an undergraduate, his doctoral studies in vocational education, sociology, psychology and mass communication had earned him membership in Phi Kappa Phi, the most prestigious scholastic honorary society on campus. Part of his doctoral program had included work at the University of Iowa on a grant from the Iowa State University Research Foundation. He took courses in cinematography and communications research methods and participated in a seminar on media ethics and responsibility. The grant carried with it an agreement that he would teach a minimum of two years at Iowa State following completion of his graduate work. Heath had no other intention. He returned to the classroom full-time, teaching the university's first courses in basic motion picture techniques and televi-

The faculty team early in Harry E. Heath Jr.'s administration included (*in the back, left to right*) James L. Highland, L. Edward Carter, Lemuel D. Groom, Ronald Dyke, Heath, James C. Stratton, and Walter J. Ward. In front are C. Dennis Schick (*left*) and Harry L. Hix. Groom, Stratton, Ward, and Hix would serve throughout the Heath years. This faculty team brought the first of two successful accreditations in journalism to OSU during the Heath era.

sion news and supervising radio news broadcasts by journalism students over a local commercial station, KASI, from remote facilities in the Press Building on campus.[5]

By now, Heath was one of the nation's best known teachers of broadcast journalism. His two terms as president of the national Council on Radio and Television Journalism led to his participation in a UNESCO seminar at the University of Strasbourg, where he was one of the featured speakers. His remarks were translated simultaneously in four languages so that members of the multi-national audience could select which translation they would hear on their headphones. The dean of journalism at the University of Moscow brought his own interpreter, but the English translation of his remarks was not transmitted by headphones.[6]

Heath continued to carry a heavy load on the print side as well, teaching required courses in reporting, editing, and typography in various journalism curricula and a service course in publicity methods for agriculture students. In addition, he served as advisor to all agricultural journalism majors, taught an occasional graduate course and supervised the research of several master's candidates. He had been offered a department headship in a reputable liberal arts college, but Director Ralph Casey of the University of Minnesota School of Journalism had advised him to wait for better opportunities, and he had taken Casey's advice. When he later was passed over upon the retirement of Kenneth R. Marvin, head of the Iowa State Department of Technical Journalism, he was ready to consider a move.[7]

In the summer of 1961, the man who had been his thesis advisor at Northwestern, Charles Allen, wrote to ask if he would be interested in making a change. Allen had completed a year and a half as OSU journalism head and wanted to strengthen broadcast journalism. He had turned to Heath as a likely candidate to develop that specialty. After visiting the campus with his wife and daughter, Heath accepted Allen's offer of a full professorship and arrived in time for the opening of the fall semester. Again he taught courses in both print and broadcast journalism and assisted with the graduate workload. He also continued his interest in the behavioral sciences, taking post-doctoral courses in psychological interviewing, marriage counseling, and family crises.[8]

By 1965, Allen had become disillusioned. He felt hemmed in by the higher administration and saw little hope for developing a School of Journalism of the magnitude he had earlier thought possible. When an offer came to Heath from Rae O. Weimer, director of the School of Journalism and Communications at the University of Florida, Allen encouraged Heath to accept it.[9]

Heath spent two academic years at Florida. Again he taught both print and broadcasting courses, but the scales tipped to print. His reporting, public relations, and company publications courses were popular. He taught a graduate course and was major professor for several master's candidates. But the work that attracted the most attention was his public opinion course. That course required two major term papers, and those who finished it with a grade higher than average looked upon their success as a badge of honor. It was one of the two or three "Purple Heart" courses in the school.

During his two years at Florida, Heath had introduced a new teaching technique in reporting. He tape recorded a critique for each news story written in his laboratories and students would listen to the critiques on headphones in the journalism library. Students told him they learned more that way than by relying solely upon comments written upon their papers in red ink.[10]

The Florida experience was valuable in an unexpected way. As a member of several journalism school committees, Heath had an opportunity to study Weimer's administrative style. His leadership skills were remarkably effective. He was dynamic and could get to the heart of an issue without wasted motion. He was widely recognized for having built one of the nation's outstanding journalism schools. Weimer respected Heath as well. By the time Oklahoma State had contacted Heath as a possible replacement for Allen, who soon would retire, Weimer himself was nearing retirement. Robert M. Mautz, vice president for academic affairs, met with Heath over lunch at the Gainesville Country Club to talk about his future at Florida. Clearly he was one of the leading candidates to succeed Weimer. Plans called for a College of Journalism and Communications presided over by a dean. Heath was flattered, but the chance to return to his Oklahoma roots won out.[11]

Prior to becoming a journalism administrator, Heath had had a respectable record in the fight to publish or perish. He had co-authored *How to Cover, Write, and Edit Sports; A Guide to Radio-TV Writing;* and *Modern Sportswriting.* He also had headed the Audio-Visual Committee of the Association for Education in Journalism, and in that capacity had served as editor of *Directory of Journalism Films,* an extensive annotated bibliography. His articles had appeared in *Journalism Quarterly, Journal of Broadcasting, College Public Relations Quarterly, Quill, Adult Leadership, School Press Review, Scholastic Editor, Modern Medicine, Science of Mind,* and other professional and popular publications. Among booklets and pamphlets he had written or edited were *A Guide to Newspaper Page Makeup, Typography Specimen Sheets, Directory of Journalism Tapes, Broadcast Journalism Handbook, Five Talks on Broadcasting Journalism,* and *Careers in Public Relations.* Later, which came as a surprise to many, he wrote and designed three small books of poetry, some of it with a metaphysical flavor, while serving as director.

Administrative experience was not entirely new to Heath. He had been a company commander and later a staff officer during World War II.

He had learned to organize training programs and delegate responsibilities. At the University of Tulsa he had been responsible for the News Bureau and, as a part-time journalism teacher, had written the course descriptions for that school's first Department of Journalism. During the Korean War he had been assigned administrative duties, first in the Office of the Chief Chemical Officer at Gravely Point in the nation's capital, and later in the Pentagon as chief of the Army's Special Events Branch, part of the Public Information Division. In this assignment Heath wore the insignia of the Army's General Staff. But, he was to find, experiences such as these had taught him little about managing a tight budget and, with too little money, hiring competent teachers.[12]

Nevertheless, Heath hired his first faculty member before leaving Florida for Oklahoma. Walter J. Ward had just completed his first year of teaching on the Florida faculty following completion of his Ph.D. at the University of Iowa. He had solid professional credentials including four years in daily newspaper work and four years in corporate public relations.

Heath and Ward had discussed journalism education over lunch on numerous occasions and their views were compatible. One of Heath's first goals at Oklahoma State was to increase the size and quality of the

Graduate student Robert Dimery (*left, left photo*) and other members of a graduate seminar listen to an amplified telephone hookup with Brigadier General S. L. A. Marshall, a famous military analyst for the Washington Post-Los Angeles Times Syndicate, on Vietnam War coverage. Harry E. Heath Jr. relayed student questions to Marshall. Such hookups brought famous journalists into the classroom at a low cost. In the right photo, Walter J. Ward, coordinator of graduate studies in journalism and broadcasting, explains a problem in computer data analysis to a group of graduate students. Left to right are Morris Ruddick, Ward, Roger Klock, and Lee Gray.

graduate program. Ward seemed ideal for the job. He had just been offered a position on Notre Dame's marketing faculty. It would pay more than Heath could offer. But Heath had told Ward he would put him in charge of the graduate program and that he would have a free hand to shape it. Ward was excited by the challenge and accepted.[13]

Heath's first troublesome staffing problem was to replace William J. Roepke, an outstanding advertising teacher. After Heath's selection as director but while he was still at the University of Florida, Roepke had written that he had accepted a position at the University of Wyoming. Health problems had contributed to the decision. Heath was fulfilling his contract at Florida and would not make the move to Stillwater until late June. He could not wait that long to begin negotiations for Roepke's replacement. Neither was he likely to have time to carry out a search, line up interviews at OSU, and hire a permanent faculty member once he reached Stillwater. His solution was to locate an experienced person who would consider a one-year appointment as a visiting professor. Heath found that the position was budgeted at about $4,000 less than the going rate in other accredited journalism schools. After several unsuccessful contacts and one on-sight interview, he found a temporary solution. Someone on the Florida faculty, probably Weimer, had suggested Manning D. Seil as a possibility. Although he would be sixty-five in July, Seil was not ready to retire. His background was impressive. He had completed twenty years of full-time professional experience plus twenty-three years of full-time college teaching. He had been an Army Air Corps pilot and later public relations officer for the Central Flight Training Command at Randolph Field, Texas. He had retired as a colonel in the United States Air Force. Seil was not pressed financially for he was drawing retirement pay from both Florida and the U.S. Air Force plus a pension from the International Typographical Union.

Seil's academic credentials were sound. He had taken his B.S. in journalism with strong supporting work in business administration at the University of Illinois in 1928. When Charles Allen left Illinois in 1937 to become director of the School of Journalism at Rutgers, Seil had replaced him and by 1940 had earned an M.S. in economics as a part-time student while teaching a full load in journalism. He had been on active military duty from 1941 to 1946, when he returned to the Illinois faculty. In 1952 he had moved to the University of Florida, where he was head of the advertising curriculum until retirement in 1963. He had studied law for two years and then had moved to Spring City, Tennessee, in 1965 upon becoming a visiting professor of economics and business administration at the University of Chattanooga. Among his references was the widely respected Dean Fred Siebert of Michigan State University, who had been a faculty colleague at Illinois.

Seil's newspaper experience was extensive. He had worked on eight newspapers, including the *Houston Press* and *Atlanta Journal*, and his experience had covered editorial, advertising, and mechanical positions. He had worked for the Ludlow Typograph Company and the Mergenthaler Linotype Company and still carried his card in the International Typographical Union.

His writing at Illinois included two publications: *Advertising Copy and Layout* and *Exercises in Proofreading*. He also had written *Guide for Air Force Writing* and while serving in Ecuador for the U.S. State Department had authored *Publicidad y Relacionas Publicas*, a book on public relations. That year, 1961, he also had lectured on advertising and public relations in Jamaica. He held memberships in Alpha Delta Sigma, Sigma Delta Chi, Alpha Epsilon Rho, the Association for Education in Journalism, the American Academy of Advertising, and the Advertising Federation of America.[14]

Heath's contact with Seil by telephone April 11, 1967, was right for both parties. Heath had determined to place high emphasis upon professional experience, and Seil met that criterion. Seil wanted to be closer to his wife's relatives in Paris, Texas. The move would help on that score. The timing was right. On July 13 he would complete his two-year stint at the University of Chattanooga as a visiting professor and would be available. On May 4, 1967, Heath had wired his offer of a twelve-month appointment as a visiting associate professor. Seil had accepted by letter on May 5. The appointment would start on July 1, 1967, and continue through June 30, 1968. Heath had bought a year's time to continue the search for Roepke's replacement.[15]

Seil's year at Oklahoma State was productive. He spoke on "Newspaper Advertising Headlines" at an Oklahoma Press Association (OPA) short course, participated in OSU's annual High School Journalism Day and the widely acclaimed Industrial Editors Short Course, and had accompanied students from his advertising classes on two trips. The first, Advertising Career Day, was sponsored by the Oklahoma City Advertising Club, and the second, Red Carpet Day, was a project of Tulsa Industrial Advertisers. Although sometimes taciturn in student conferences, Seil was a good team player and carried his share of the load in the school's service programs.[16]

One of the first things Heath tried to accomplish, once immediate staffing problems had been settled, was to rebuild bridges that had been in disrepair since Clement E. Trout's retirement. He arranged a conference with Wayne Meinhart, head of the Department of Marketing. He knew that advertising majors should have at least six hours—preferable nine—in marketing, and that marketing majors were shortchanged if they did not include advertising in their program. The close cooperation between journalism and the College of Business, (formerly the School of Commerce), had weakened under Chunn and had all but disappeared under Allen. Meinhart was receptive to Heath's overture and both marketing and advertising students profited by the new collegiality.

Next, Heath sought to ease the tensions between the Department of Radio and Television and journalism. Similar tensions, though less severe, existed between journalism and the fledgling educational television unit located on the third floor. First Leslie R. Kreps, then Robert P. Lacy, had inherited broadcasting in the realignment of the School of Communications following Chunn's departure. Heath's first move was to volunteer the services of a talented graduate student, David Houser, to help with editorial duties on *College Broadcasting* magazine, a national organ with headquarters in radio-television. This helped to thaw the cold war that had existed between Charles Allen and Lacy. A few months later, educational television had been moved from radio-television to a separate budgetary unit under Marshall Allen, fresh from his educational television experience at Southern Illinois University. Educational television was fighting for space and budget and needed equipment. To newcomers during the Centennial Decade at OSU it would seem inconceivable that the well equipped and beautifully housed Educational Television Services (ETS) of today could have once been so hard up. The fact is, however, that Heath's willingness to lend journalism's single-system Vidicon motion picture equipment to ETS was a much-appreciated gesture that improved relationships on that front. Later, Allen and Vice President James H. Boggs conferred with Heath on space problems. Heath sacrificed some of his own badly needed space to give ETS relief, minimal though it must have seemed to Allen. Conditions in the Communications Building were far from ideal, but Heath's fence-minding had improved the working environment. The fences that had been built to keep others out now had gates that opened to permit others in. President Robert B. Kamm's hopes for closer cooperation among communications programs was far from being realized, but there had been progress.[17]

The big plus from all this was that Heath's creative energies could now be directed toward building a stronger School of Journalism. Lacy, too, must have felt greater freedom to get on with the work of his growing department, including both KVRO and KOSU, which were integrated into his academic program more closely than the *Daily O'Collegian* had been incorporated into campus journalism education under Allen.

Heath had been named publisher of the *Daily O'Collegian* by President Kamm, who wanted to minimize the influence of student politics on the paper. The new journalism school director did not take the added responsibility lightly. He wanted the paper to become an important teaching laboratory in addition to its responsibility to provide news and information to the campus. Trout had sought a similar goal in 1937 with Leon Durst as newsroom supervisor, and later when Warren Shull, James Stratton and others had integrated their reporting and editing laboratories with the *O'Collegian*. The Student Senate had asked for a study of *O'Collegian* operations. In response, Edward C. Burris, chairman of the Oklahoma State University Board of Student Publications, had organized a committee with Norman N. Durham, dean of the Graduate College, as chairman. The O'Collegian Study Committee included Ralph Sewell, assistant managing editor of the *Daily Oklahoman* and *Oklahoma City Times;* L. Edward Carter, city editor of the *Lawton Constitution*; Heath; and students Robert L. Cox and George O'Reilly.

The committee had worked through the fall of 1968 and spring of 1969, and its recommendations were submitted to the board of publications in May. The board asked the directors of the O'Collegian Publishing Company to consider the sections of the report dealing with personnel and equipment.

Concerning personnel, the directors reaffirmed the committee's recommendations that Heath, as director of the School of Journalism, be designated publisher of the *Daily O'Collegian* and that he be made a member of the board of directors of the O'Collegian Publishing Company. The directors also favored the creation of three new positions: associate publishers for news and business and a retail advertising manager. The associate publisher for news would serve as a faculty advisor to the editor and news staff of the *O'Collegian*. The associate publisher for business would be responsible for practices and policies of the retail advertising manager and would be in charge of the personnel and details of the production department. In addition, this individual would serve as business manager of the *Redskin* and other publications. The retail advertising manager would be responsible for conducting a well organized and planned advertising program to further the training of advertising majors—a much needed improvment—and would be responsible for all local advertising. The positions were to be filled by the beginning of the 1969-70 school year.[18]

The committee had recommended that the paper become an extension of journalism school instruction with a professional journalist empowered to guide the news staff in "real world" publishing procedures. The brief job description on the university's recruitment report read: "Supervision of *Daily O'Collegian* newsroom with specific responsibility for copy desk, plus teaching certain editing and reporting classes, which are to be integrated with the production of the student newspaper." Minimum qualifications were three years of full-time work on a daily newspaper plus a master's degree or its equivalent.

Heath considered seven candidates and, in consultation with faculty members, chose Carter, who shortly before had enrolled for graduate work and had served briefly as advisor. Carter held two baccalaureate degrees from the University of Oklahoma, one in journalism and the other in history. He had earned twelve hours on his master's at the OU graduate center at Fort Sill and wanted to complete the degree while teaching journalism. He presented outstanding transcripts for two years at Cameron State Agricultural College and three years at the University of Oklahoma.[19]

Following his undergraduate work at OU, Carter had served two years in the Army, then joined the *Ardmore Ardmoreite*, where in two years he had advanced from reporter-photographer to city editor. While in Ardmore he had been named outstanding Associated Press correspondent in Oklahoma for 1956. He then spent a year as newswriter and editor with the Associated Press in Oklahoma City, and in 1958 joined the *Constitution* as city editor. One special assignment took him to Europe for six weeks to cover an Air Force troop transfer from Oklahoma with daily interviews and pictures on former area residents living in six European countries. Heath also liked the fact that Carter had been a Linotype operator and printer during his college years and summer vacation periods. He was, at age thirty-eight, well rounded both educationally and professionally and had highly respected references.

Upon Carter's selection as associate publisher for news, Heath informed him that he was being recommended for a part-time instructorship. "Your work would involve running the copy desk on the *O'Collegian* and handling an editing course," Heath wrote. "You can make of the editing course what you wish. This is the first time [in recent] years it has had lectures with it (two a week), and I hope that some of the lecture time each week can be devoted to a discussion of the strengths and weaknesses

Edson Perry (*left*), *O'Collegian* production superintendent, and pressman Mark Perry, an OSU journalism student, check an early run on the paper's new $160,000 Web Leader, a high speed web-perfecting offset press that increased both the page and color capacity of the newspaper.

Oklahoma State University 479

of *O'Collegian* editing. For the lab, we will require each student enrolled to work three hours each week on the *O'Collegian* copy desk, under your supervision."[20] In mid-June the OSU regents approved Carter's appointment. Meanwhile, Heath had named Elmer Woodson, director of student publications since 1944, as associate publisher for business, and a long-time faculty member, Lemuel D. Groom, as retail advertising manager. Groom would divide his time between teaching and his work on the *O'Collegian*.

As for the study committee's recommendations on equipment, the publishing company appointed Heath and Woodson to select a subcommittee to study *O'Collegian* printing equipment and make recommendations for improvements. Members of the board of directors of the O'Collegian Publishing at that time were President Kamm; Heath; Burris; Woodson; Robert G. Schmalfeld, dean of student affairs; Sam Satterfield, OSU budget director; and Philip Sutton, editor of the *Daily O'Collegian*.[21]

Heath's faculty was taking shape. Carter would be a valuable member for four years, returning to his alma mater after completing both his M.S. in journalism and his Ph.D. in history while on his part-time appointment.[22]

C. Dennis Schick, working on his doctorate and teaching half time at Southern Illinois University at Carbondale, had been told by Bryce Rucker of Heath's search for an advertising professor to replace Seil. On December 1, 1967, he wrote expressing interest and sent a personal data file. He would be available in the fall. One week later, Heath wrote asking Schick to come to Stillwater for an interview. He made a favorable impression. The regents approved an assistant professorship effective September 1, 1968.[23]

Fresh out of high school, Schick had served three years in the Army before entering Temple Junior College, where he was an honor graduate. At Temple, he had been business manager, managing editor, reporter, and columnist for the campus newspaper. During the next two years at Texas Christian University, he made the dean's list, was active in student publications, and compiled a long list of honors. He had served as president of Alpha Delta Sigma, the men's professional advertising fraternity, and had received its outstanding service key. He was president of the student section of the Southwestern Journalism Congress, had won a Sigma Delta Chi citation for his column, and had earned the B.A. degree in June 1962.

At the University of Illinois where he had been awarded the M.S. degree during the summer of 1964, he had held a James Webb Young graduate assistantship and had served both as a research assistant and an administrative assistant. He had served in two other campus agencies and had handled the Illini correspondence course in Principles of Advertising. His thesis was titled "Attention Given to Advertising

Education by Trade Journals."

Following his master's work at Illinois, Schick spent two years at Texas Christian University where he taught eight different courses in all, mostly in advertising and public relations. He continued to teach advertising half time at Southern Illinois, where he served as co-sponsor of Alpha Delta Sigma, promotion director for the journalism department, and associate editor of *Linage*, the ADS national quarterly. As part of his job as promotion director, he originated and edited *Hotline*, an internal publication. Throughout his college years, he had worked part-time in advertising sales on newspapers, first at the *Temple Daily Telegram*, then the *Fort Worth Star-Telegram*, and later the *Champaign-Urbana Courier*.

Schick was the kind of creative person Heath needed. They soon became a team in promoting the School of Journalism. More important, Schick was assigned responsibility for advertising studies. Unofficially, he was chairman of the sequence in advertising and public relations.[24]

In December 1968, Heath had begun correspondence with Ronald W. Dyke, a University of Oklahoma graduate who had completed the B.A.

Because the faculty was made up entirely of veteran teachers upon his arrival, Harry E. Heath Jr. emphasized youth in his early faculty appointments. Three of the first new arrivals were (*left to right*) James L. Highland, C. Dennis Schick, and James W. Rhea. All were energetic and competent and soon gave the school a reputation for innovative progress.

degree in 1957 and the M.A. in 1968. He would fill the vacancy created by William Harmon's move to Southern Illinois University. His professional experience was varied. He had been assistant editor of *Metronome Magazine* in New York City, had eight years in advertising at the Lawton Publishing Company, and additional advertising experience on the *Oklahoma Journal*. He served as advertising manager for the *Oklahoma Daily* and handled advertising layout laboratories at the University of Oklahoma while he was a graduate student. He joined the faculty on September 1, 1968, but his tenure was short, ending January 31, 1969. His son had dyslexia, and special education in Stillwater proved to be minimal. The family moved to California.[25]

Dyke's replacement would become one of the strongest members of the Heath faculty for the remainder of his directorship. Heath had known William R. Steng Jr., at the University of Florida, where Steng had been a graduate assistant. He had corresponded with him off and on over several months, and Steng had expressed an interest in coming to OSU. However, there was no opening at the time. Meanwhile, he had accepted an assistant professorship in journalism at Florida Southern College. Now the time was right, and Steng was available. On July 16, 1969, Heath informed Steng that the regents had approved his appointment as an assistant professor effective September 1, 1969.[26]

Steng's background was unusually strong. In high school, he had been president of the Student Council, was named to the National Honor Society, and had held class offices. As an undergraduate at Rutgers University, he made the dean's list six times, was elected to Kappa Tau Alpha, served as sports announcer for four years—two of those years as sports director on the campus radio station—had been a sports writer on the yearbook two years, and had graduated cum laude in 1956 as a Henry Rutgers Scholar with a major in journalism and a minor in economics. His undergraduate thesis covered the history of advertising regulation.

Following graduation, he had joined the *Hackensack Record*, where he served for eight years in various capacities—reporter, rewrite chief, copy editor, editorial writer, editor of the midweek section, and assignment editor. Then he took time out to travel before joining the *Sarasota Florida Herald-Tribune* in April 1965. For eighteen months he was a sports writer and columnist before enrolling as a graduate student in the University of Florida's School of Journalism and Communications, majoring in journalism and minoring in political science. The M.A. degree was awarded in August 1968 following acceptance of his thesis on the free press-fair trial controversy. Then he had begun his teaching career at Florida Southern, where he also served as sports publicity director and advisor to the student newspaper. He taught seven different courses there, including reporting, editing, advertising, public relations, newsroom management, and journalism history.

Steng's versatility and his strong recommendations from employers gave Heath confidence that he was ideal for the program OSU was building. Heath was not disappointed. Steng was a tower of strength, along with Walter Ward and others, giving the school a reputation for high standards in its upper division and graduate work. He soon was recognized as the state's leading teacher of communications law, while gaining recognition in journalistic management, ethics, and media responsibility. His contributions to research and service efforts were among the most productive and his classroom appraisals were among the three highest from the start. He was, students said, tough but fair.[27]

As soon as he had pulled together a faculty team to build the program around, Heath formed an administrative council to contribute to his consideration of major issues. Each member represented a special area or areas within the school: Schick (advertising and public relations), Steng (news-editorial), and Ward (graduate studies). Later, as changes in personnel and structure dictated, the council membership was changed as well as enlarged to include the school's chief academic advisor and the extension coordinator.

One of Heath's early goals in building the School of Journalism was to bring together a variety of talents from different locales. He felt there had been a tendency toward in-breeding on the campus for years. He had appointed a bearded look-alike for Fidel Castro, James Pecora, a former UPI staffer from Indianapolis, to teach both professional and service courses in news. Pecora had quickly decided that teaching was not for him and had resigned to return to wire service work. Meanwhile, Heath had received a tip on a young West Virginia journalist. He wrote James L. Highland to see if he might be interested. He told Highland that OSU had an enrollment of 16,500, with 170 journalism majors. Highland responded that he was "deeply interested." His credentials showed promise for a leadership role in the news-editorial curriculum.[28]

Highland had majored in journalism at the University of West Virginia, one of that region's most successful programs, from 1958 to 1960. The next year he was an English major at Salem College, then he returned to complete both a B.S. and an M.S. in journalism at West Virginia, finishing in 1967. As an undergrad he had taken a minor in political science and in his graduate work a minor in speech with a radio-television production emphasis. His thesis was titled "Survey of Editorial Practices of West Virginia Television Stations." Heath believed firmly in the value of cross-media skills, but there also were other interesting aspects to his vita. From 1960 to 1961 he had covered the courts for the *Clarksburg Exponent* and for the next four years, while a student, had covered the courts and politics for the *Morgantown Post*. He obviously was a workaholic—a characteristic Heath understood—for Highland was a graduate assistant at West Virginia in 1965-66 while working for the *Post*. The need to support a wife and two small children no doubt contributed to his willingness to take on such a heavy schedule.[29]

Here was a young, aggressive applicant who not only had studied journalism and the political system, but had gained experience in both. From 1965 to 1968, when he signed on with the *Charleston Daily Mail*, he had worked for the state director of purchasing, first as press secretary and later as buyer-inspector and coordinator of the department's computer service. On the side he had served on special assignment as aide to James M. Sprouce, state Democratic Executive Committee chairman, and as coordinator for the Morgantown phase of Vice President Hubert Humphrey's visit to West Virginia University in 1967. Heath also noted the miscellaneous information on his application: he was a member of Kappa Tau Alpha, journalism scholarship honorary, and Sigma Delta Chi, professional journalism society; he had been named "Outstanding Collegiate Reporter," and was a member of the Clarksburg Masonic Lodge; his current salary would not be a problem.[30]

From 1963 on, his transcript—earlier inconsistent—showed steady improvement. His graduate record was outstanding. Heath forwarded to V. Brown Monnett, acting dean, the necessary documents with his recommendation that Highland be appointed at the rank of instructor to replace Pecora. The appointment was approved by President Kamm and seventeen days later by the regents, effective September 1, 1968. Heath notified Highland by Western Union, following up with a letter listing the

Trips to news centers, supported in part by a grant from the *Reader's Digest*, became a feature of the Harry E. Heath Jr. administration. This group looks over a simulated moonscape at NASA in Houston, where they interviewed officials and astronauts in the space program. Some wrote special stories to carry out the purpose of the grant.

Centennial Histories Series

four courses he would teach and the textbooks for them.[31]

In seven months, Highland's energetic approach to teaching had made a difference in OSU journalism. Field trips and follow-up seminar discussion sessions enabled students to understand problems of administrative, legislative, and judicial branches of government. Reporting classes were spending several days each semester covering the capitol. On one trip OSU journalists spent approximately an hour with Oklahoma Governor Dewey Bartlett discussing state problems and how the governor thought they could be solved.

The university's student newspaper, the *Daily O'Collegian*, was represented at the launching of Apollo 8 in Houston, Texas, during the Christmas recess. The student reporter, Bob Beck, was afforded complete press credentials and enjoyed the same privileges as representatives of the national wire services and major metropolitan newspapers. Two other students attended the inauguration of Richard M. Nixon in Washington, D.C., and provided state newspapers and the OSU daily with first-hand reports of events there.[32]

Locally, city council meetings, city planning and zoning commission sessions, school board meetings, the police department and county offices, and the various problems facing each were being covered both objectively and interpretatively. The city manager, the mayor, the chief of police, and all county officials had been interviewed by student reporters. These same journalists sat in on criminal and civil court sessions. They covered major murder trials and even traveled with political candidates. It was clear that Highland had added a vigorous tone to the news-editorial program.[33]

Heath was well aware that the students were benefiting from Highland's practical approach. To show his appreciation for the advances made in the eighteen months since Highland's arrival, Heath recommended him for promotion to assistant professor. An earlier recommendation had been held up because the search for a dean to replace James R. Scales was in progress. This time it had cleared all channels following approval on April 15, 1970, of the new arts and sciences dean, George A. Gries. Highland's promotion and the usual three-year appointment had been approved simultaneously. Two months earlier the personnel committee of the School of Journalism and Communications had given Heath a thoroughly documented report recommending the promotion. The committee cited Highland's progress on his Ed.D. program, his heavy teaching load, his chairmanship of the Hearst Awards and internship committees and membership on three other committees, his interest in research, and such off-campus efforts as the OPA Newswriting Short Course, the Southwestern Journalism Congress and various field trips. The committee added a cautionary note on "the number of projects he is willing to undertake."[34]

Under Dean George A. Gries, faculty members were relieved of many of their advisement duties. Linda McDonald became chief advisor for the School of Journalism and Broadcasting, increasing efficiency in academic record keeping as well as student and faculty morale.

With the departure of Harmon, who had held a split appointment in public information and journalism, Highland had become coordinator of the annual six-day OPA Newswriting Short Course in Oklahoma City, one of the school's most important services to state newspapers. The OPA appreciated Highland, assisting him financially with the costs of his graduate work during the summers.[35] He consistently scored high in short course evaluations.

The young professor, whose breezy manner was infectious with both students and professionals, was a willing participant in school affairs. Typically, he represented Heath at the AEJ convention at the University of South Carolina in August 1971 when Heath was unable to attend because of illness. He also was ambitious. He wanted to serve as head of the news-editorial sequence in preparation for a future department headship "at some small college or university." But Heath planned to "continue to wear that extra hat for now."[36]

By the spring of 1972, Highland's alma mater was showing an interest in him. He was forging ahead with his doctoral studies, and by the opening of the fall semester had completed his dissertation proposal. He was working Saturdays at the *Stillwater NewsPress* and getting ready to accompany ten students to the national Sigma Delta Chi meeting in Dallas. Despite his tendency to take on too many responsibilities, Heath recommended him for reappointment because of his teaching skills with news-editorial undergraduates.[37]

Highland was creative in his classroom approach. Perhaps not typical, but certainly suggestive of this, was one surprise final examination he had given. The Associated Press described the exam:

"Highland decided to scrap the usual true-false or multiple choice test. [His version of a more realistic test began] when a student came into the class and started arguing with Highland as the class waited. . .the test. The instructor argued back and finally the student pulled out a gun and fired point-blank.

"Highland slumped to the floor as the class rose in panic. Another teacher, hearing the shots, came running in and he too was shot. The gunman then ran from the classroom and out of the building as the students stared in shock.

"That's when Highland rose from the floor, and with the acrid smell of gunpowder pervading the classroom, told his students. . .their final exam would be [to] write about what they had just seen.

"'Each student's grade depended on how well he wrote the details of what he saw and heard,'" Highland explained. 'After observing their actions and reading their news stories, I could see that the majority of the first semester reporting students had learned their lessons well. . . .'

SCHOOL OF JOURNALISM AND BROADCASTING

A field trip to the nation's capital brought journalism and broadcasting students close to national leaders, historic sites, and media enterprises. Bill Orendorff, June Lester, and Nancy Nunnally (*left to right*) were among the larger group interviewing Speaker of the House Carl Albert.

"The instructor said most students were exceptionally accurate in describing the gunman but there was some disagreement on how many shots were fired. . . .

"'I had warned the class that the final examination would be different. . . . However, I don't think any of the students expected the preliminaries to be so drastic.'"[38]

Sometimes Highland would find himself in controversies that Heath would have to deal with. OPA President D. Jo Ferguson, publisher of the *Pawnee Chief*, complained that Highland in his *NewsPress* moonlighting had violated a release date. Ferguson considered this to be an ethical lapse. It had created a problem for Ferguson with his co-workers on the board of the Indian Meridian Vocational-Technical School, located on the edge of Stillwater. Highland's view was that he had informed a *NewsPress* official of the release date but had been overruled. Heath instructed Highland to phone Ferguson and explain what had happened.[39]

No sooner had this died down than Heath was settling a dispute over Highland's proposal that he teach a graduate-level course through Arts and Sciences Extension at Western Electric Company in Oklahoma City. Highland had neglected to discuss this with Ward. Heath resolved the problem by vetoing the graduate course but approving a junior-level course, Principles of Public Relations.[40] Meanwhile, Highland had completed his third annual short course for OPA and had received high praise from secretary-manager Ben Blackstock: "As usual, Jim did an excellent job and you can well be proud of him. . . . [Our] students fill out a critique sheet on each of the instructors and, as always, Jim scored higher than any of the others—all excellent marks." Heath forwarded Blackstock's letter to Dean Gries who wrote Highland: "Sometimes we feel that these 'above and beyond' activities go unrewarded, but I want to assure you that we do take notice of them. They are most vital to the total program of O.S.U."[41]

Less than two months away from severing his connections with the university, Highland was working full-time for the *NewsPress* during the summer. Corporate attorney Clee Fitzgerald had initiated legal proceedings against the city commission for violation of the state open meetings law. Highland was about to become a complaining witness against the commission, which included two high-ranking OSU administrators. E. Moses Frye, the university's legal counsel, saw "no possible conflict of interest." Highland had the support of the *NewsPress* co-publishers, who had instructed Fitzgerald to act. Highland wrote Heath:

"If, for any reason, the University decides it would not be in its best interests for me to act as a complaining witness, I will withdraw. Otherwise, I will proceed as per the instructions of my summer employ-

Sheila Wisherd (*right*) discusses creative advertising with Linda Eckles. Wisherd later joined the College of Arts and Sciences staff to help develop television outreach. Her work in advertising instruction came during a period of rapid growth.

ers." The conflict was settled out of court. The commission would be more cautious in the future.[42]

By early August, Western Kentucky University had made Highland an attractive offer that would give him approximately $3,600 more than his OSU salary. Although it was late to secure a replacement, Heath did not want to stand in the way of Highland's advancement. He gave Western Kentucky a strong recommendation on Highland, summing up his contributions to the School of Journalism and Broadcasting: "He has taught reporting at various levels, history of journalism, and has conducted seminars with students on our daily newspaper. For two years he ran a project in conjunction with the downtown daily in which his students put out the paper once a week. In addition, he has carried his share of committee work.[43] "He is," Heath wrote, "hard working, available to students, easy to work with and competent." Five days later, Heath wrote a warm personal letter to Highland, thanking him "for the many things you have done to help us build the school." Heath wrote Blackstock pledging continued participation in the annual short course and saying that a tight budget had kept OSU from giving Highland an immediate incentive to stay although a raise was promised in a year.[44]

Meanwhile, a faculty member with exceptional cross-media talents was added in the fall of 1972. Leo J. Turner had had a long and distinguished career in journalism. An outstanding writer, he had served as a foreign correspondent for United Press in Jerusalem, and as bureau chief in Chicago and New York. Later he had worked for *Newsweek*

Members of the advanced reporting project at the *Stillwater NewsPress* look over the results of their weekly Tuesday edition. Lee Bell, an OSU journalism graduate and managing editor, discusses the work with (*left to right*) Nita Bridwell, Randy Sumpter, and Deborah Jackson.

magazine and in public relations and advertising in New York City. He also taught at New York University, where he earned an M.B.A. degree and had completed the course work for a Ph.D. Heath saw Turner as especially valuable, for he could handle reporting, editing, or advertising courses. That type of flexibility was especially helpful during a period when faculty changes on journalism staffs were frequent because of the nation's booming economy. At OSU, Turner taught in both the news-editorial and advertising areas, but he preferred the latter.[45]

Turner had helped fill the Highland gap, but he did not replace him. Highland's replacement was Michael O. Buchholz, a young journalist who was opposite in personality but with matching competence. While Highland was outgoing, exuberant, and aggressive, Buchholz was quiet, relaxed, and introspective. Underneath that exterior, Buchholz had a good sense of humor and a sharp mind, with enough assertiveness to handle in his own quiet way any classroom situation. Buchholz held two degrees from North Texas State University. His B.A. in 1966 was in journalism and mathematics with a minor in English. He was chosen the top male journalism graduate in his class and had graduated with honors. He majored in political science and minored in journalism for the master's degree awarded in 1973. North Texas had a well-respected faculty, and Buchholz was ready and qualified. He had joined the *Fort Worth Star-Telegram* in 1968, then left for two years of Army duty, returning to cover government and politics for nearly four years. He accepted an assistant professorship at OSU, effective September 1, 1974. Buchholz was considered by journalism administrators to be an outstanding member of the faculty. His tenure would last throughout the Heath years. While a member of the faculty, he would earn the Ph.D. in sociology. He left as an associate professor with tenure to join the faculty at Texas A. and M. University in 1984.[46]

Things were running smoothly. The journalism faculty had grown, the program had been refined, cooperation among faculty members was excellent, and strong relationships had been established with the OPA. On the latter point, Heath had recognized a fact that Charles Allen had overlooked. Although the OPA had worked diligently for Allen's appointment, he was reluctant to forge strong bonds with the association. This basic error may be illustrated by his ambitious plan for an annual Journalism Forum series. Such an effort largely duplicated the kind of educational program the OPA had successfully pursued for years. The forum series failed for lack of interest—or sense of need—among newspaper people. By way of contrast, Heath and his faculty, from the beginning, had helped with the OPA's workshops and clinics and Heath had contributed a monthly column to the *Oklahoma Publisher.* In other words, Heath knew that OSU's professional outreach could be effective only in a cooperative effort. His budget was too limited to do otherwise and the OPA's professional programs were too well entrenched and too successful to compete with. Everyone stood to gain by such cooperation. Why Allen could not see this is moot. Perhaps he feared OPA infringement upon his academic prerogatives, which never at any time occurred during the Heath years. Or perhaps his ego stood in the way of such cooperation. As a builder, Allen was reluctant to share credit for the building he did.

Heath was pleased with the way things were going. He had strengthened the faculty, had succeeded in getting modest salary increases for faculty and staff, and was working to convince Dean Gries that more maintenance money was essential to upgrade equipment in journalism laboratories. His optimism on the latter was premature.

As he sought to stabilize the growing advertising sequence, Heath got a lucky break. W. Robert Glafcke, a mainstay on the University of Florida advertising faculty, had decided to return to his home state to seek a Ph.D. in marketing at OSU. Heath gave him a half-time appointment beginning in the fall of 1969.[47]

Glafcke, personable and competent, made an important contribution to the journalism program for twenty-three months before becoming

During this period, the school continued to place a high value upon faculty members with extensive professional experience. Three of the many seasoned professionals were (*left to right*) Charles T. "Tom" Ladwig, Jim Files, and John Thomas. Ladwig taught both advertising and news-editorial classes; Files handled introductory writing and public relations; and Thomas was responsible for the large photography enrollment.

disillusioned with delays in his doctoral program. A few months later he held a responsible position in the *New York Times* organization at a big increase in pay. His loss was offset by Marlan D. Nelson and George Rhoades, who had both returned for graduate work and had accepted teaching assignments part-time.[48]

An early challenge to the post-Allen journalism program was that of reaccreditation. Two sequences—news-editorial and advertising—were critically examined in a two-day inspection by John H. Colburn, editor and publisher of the *Wichita Eagle* and *Beacon*; Neale Copple, director of the University of Nebraska School of Journalism; and Wallace E. Garets, head of the Texas Technological College Department of Journalism. On May 5, 1969, OSU learned that its accreditation had been reaffirmed in both sequences. The same curricula had been approved five years earlier. The visiting team recommended reducing the required journalism courses to twenty-six credits and updating the graphic arts course and equipment. OSU was criticized for low salaries and crowded facilities in journalism. Heath said he would seek to correct these deficiencies. While the journalism faculty was glad to have won reaccreditation by the American Council on Education for Journalism, it took greatest pride in the high marks the school had received for its excellent faculty and student morale.[49]

By now, Heath had come to expect the unexpected in his role as an administrator. But he was not prepared for what would come next. On a pleasant fall evening in 1969 as he drove to his home north of Stillwater he experienced a new sensation. His eyes were playing tricks on him. For a split second a stop sign would suddenly appear as two signs, then in a flash would return to a single image. By the time he had reached home, his vision seemed normal, but he awakened the following morning seeing two lamp shades over his bed where he knew there was only one. Consultations with an ophthalmologist and his family physician offered no explanation. At the University of Oklahoma Medical Center a neurologist searched for the answer with brain scans and other sophisticated medical tests. Finally, he referred his patient to James Wise, a Johns Hopkins medical school graduate from Stillwater who was on the OU medical school staff. Wise used the latest medical journal research to conduct a test that he felt might solve the puzzle. The test left no doubt. Heath had a rare neuromuscular disease known as myasthenia gravis.

Medication was prescribed, but the prognosis became guarded. In addition to double vision, Heath now had difficulty in swallowing solid food and his speech was less distinct. In spite of this, he continued to teach, assist with OPA workshops, and lecture upon his research into the evolving "underground" press. Professional groups in Oklahoma City and Tulsa were surprised by Heath's evidence of the growing strength of the various youth-driven activist movements across the country, some of them highly disruptive, if not destructive, on college campuses. He was

SCHOOL OF JOURNALISM AND BROADCASTING

Paula Hall (left), James L. Highland (standing), and Tony Swinney chat with Robert Jordan, National Geographic writer and editor, during his visit to the School of Journalism and Broadcasting as a participant in the "Editor in Residence" program. Jordan's major article on Oklahoma in the magazine had created a wave of enthusiasm across the state. Students reacted favorably to his friendly style and journalistic know-how.

asked to appear on television by Clayton Vaughn of Tulsa's KTUL-TV, Channel 6, but declined. His facial muscles were slack and his facial expressions unpredictable. His ability to enunciate had been affected, too. He told Vaughn he planned to restrict the narrated slide presentation to professional meetings.[50]

Finally the condition grew so threatening that he was referred to the Mayo Clinic in Rochester, Minnesota. He no longer could form his words clearly enough to teach. In addition, he was having respiratory weakness and his diet was largely liquid. If he attempted a deep-knee bend, he could not return to a standing position. He even lost the use of muscles that had permitted him to whistle, one of his favorite diversions. He went on sick leave and placed Ward in charge of the faculty. The university administration considered the possibility that it might soon have to find a permanent replacement.

Then, following numerous tests and a change in medication during his hospital stay in Minnesota, Heath began to regain his strength. It was a slow, day-by-day process involving a study of metaphysics, daily meditations, and a revised medication program. Within a few months he resumed teaching and could give up his mid-morning and mid-afternoon rest periods. The myasthenia was in remission and once more he was working fifty to sixty hours a week.[51]

Heath tried diligently to add minorities to both the student body and the faculty. He had succeeded in recruiting several black students. Efforts to add black faculty were less successful. Recognition of his efforts came in 1970 when the School of Journalism and Communications was one of twenty-eight accredited academic units in the nation chosen for minority grants from the American Newspaper Publishers Association Foundation. Two black students—Anita Day, a sophomore from Lawton, and Carol Fletcher, a Spencer freshman—received $500 stipends. Only one other grant was received by Oklahoma institutions. On the faculty side, he had tried on at least three occasions to hire Carmen Fields, a *Boston Globe* writer with television experience. Her father, Ernie Fields, was a well-known Tulsa dance band leader and Heath had hoped that her Oklahoma ties would work to OSU's advantage. Her on-campus job interview was impressive but she decided to remain in Boston. Other offers were made to talented black media practitioners, but the OSU salary schedule fell considerably short. While he was unable to hire black faculty, he did succeed in adding other minorities. He believed in equal opportuny legislation and sought to build a cosmopolitan faculty.[52]

The Department of Radio and Television had been highly successful in its first ten years, nine of those years under Robert P. Lacy, an energetic leader with a background in radio station management. He had maintained an ownership interest in WVTS, Terre Haute, Indiana, and was available for consultation in its management. When his owner-partner died in a plane crash, Lacy faced a tough decision. Should he continue at OSU or return to WVTS where he was needed to provide full-time direction for the property? He was torn between his sense of responsibility to both. His sense of loyalty to his close friend won out. He resigned and returned to Terre Haute.

Now President Kamm had to make a decision. He still believed that part of the original School of Communications could be salvaged. Should Dean Gries call for a search for Lacy's replacement or consider another plan. Kamm was aware of the improved relations between radio-television and journalism. He also was aware that Heath had been in charge of broadcast journalism at Iowa State. After a brief period during which Malachi C. Topping served as acting head of the department, Kamm and Gries discussed their options. Gries suggested that now might be a logical time to merge the programs under one administrator. Kamm concurred. Gries expressed the view that "an appreciable degree of integration and consolidation in areas such as news, advertising, and sales should be effected." He said a general upgrading in all programs was essential. The merger was announced on March 3 with Heath as director of the realigned programs. In publicity on the merger, as well as in a letter to the parties concerned, Gries had expressed his confidence in Heath and had pledged his continued support for broadcasting. Heath assured Topping and Jack W. Deskin, a popular assistant professor, that he would like them to stay. Both finished out the academic year and then moved on. Heath would have to find a new faculty for the broadcasting wing of the school, which now had a combined enrollment of 325.[53]

Heath spent the summer months seeking faculty replacements in broadcasting. He succeeded in adding two well qualified men: James W. Rhea and J. David Cranshaw. Rhea, who would serve at the outset as acting chairman and later as chairman, had earned degrees at the University of Nebraska and the University of Kansas. He recently had been awarded the Ph.D. by Ohio University and was a member of the broadcasting faculty at Memphis State University. Cranshaw, a graduate of the University of Georgia journalism school, had just completed his master's in broadcast journalism at Northwestern University. Both had solid professional experience in broadcasting. To round out the faculty, Heath would start with part-time help. He had the advantage of excellent television experience in the availability of Marshall Allen and Ken Lane of Educational Television Services. For additional help he called upon Tom Huddleston, a tall Texan who had enrolled in the Ed.D. program. Later, with a strong recommendation from Rhea, Duane V. Smith was added. Smith had been on the Baker University faculty for five years and had logged fifteen years of commercial radio and television experience. He was working on a doctorate in speech communication at the University of Kansas and had been serving as editorial director of KLWN,

Lawrence, while teaching at Baker.[54]

In September 1971, Philip E. "Ed" Paulin arrived on campus from Kentucky to manage KOSU-FM, and from the start he added strength to the radio-television-film faculty. Eventually he would teach full-time and serve as faculty chairman. After nearly thirty years behind him in broadcasting, he had enrolled as a University of Kentucky freshman at the age of forty-two. He was graduated in 1969, then earned his master's shortly before his move to Stillwater. His wife, Micki, would hold a staff position in the School of Journalism and Broadcasting until retirement. Paulin, a popular sports broadcaster with management experience in sales and programming, found a competent staff of four in place upon his arrival: James C. Stratton, music director; J. David Cranshaw, news director; John Mason, engineer, and Delores Myers, secretary.[55]

With the help of the faculty curriculum committee, Heath developed a broad program with ten options—three in broadcasting—for students to choose from. He knew he must compete in the numbers game to protect the journalism and broadcasting budget, and the diverse options available attracted students. He had mixed feelings about the results. He later

SCHOOL OF JOURNALISM AND BROADCASTING

To raise money for a three-story addition to the Communications Building, the School of Journalism and Broadcasting used various special events. At left is a publicity photo set up and shot by advertising and public relations students to promote a benefit golf tournament, the JB Open. At right, motion picture and television star Dale Robertson mingles with the audience at the Dale Robertson Show, produced by OSU alumnus James H. "Jimmie" Baker of ABC-TV, Hollywood. Robertson and other stars contributed their talents without cost to the school.

feared that through such narrow specialization students might be missing some of the basic skills in reporting and writing that would be essential to their careers. Soon, as the Vietnam War and Watergate led hordes of activist-minded students into media studies, the school was to have approximately 750 majors.

With this rapid growth, the faculty had also increased. Unfortunately, support staff did not keep pace with the growth in enrollment. Heath was handicapped with turnovers in the secretarial staff. Most were wives of students and moved on when their husbands completed their studies. The one staff employee of long standing, Dorothy Richstrew Nixon, now was on a half-time basis. Heath pleaded for more clerical help, but without success. To keep things moving he used Clement Trout's solution, hiring student typists on hourly wages to keep up with the heavy volume of paperwork. Throughout the week he accomplished much of this work from 5 P.M. to 7 P.M. or later. His open-door policy meant that much of his time was devoted to conferences with faculty members, students with academic and other problems, *O'Collegian* editors and KOSU personnel. Some of his critics said he did not delegate enough responsibility to others. Heath's view was that his faculty and staff were already overextended and that he could not delegate more without adversely affecting morale. While most other Big Eight schools could add additional staff members to accommodate increasing enrollments, this was not possible for the journalism and broadcasting program at OSU. Heavy teaching loads were the norm because budget constraints did not allow faculty additions to keep pace with the growth.

As for student performance, it was slipping. Too many incoming students in the 1970s were weak in basic writing and vocabulary skills. Many were not able to convey their ideas clearly, either orally or on paper. Following a beginning writing class one day a discouraged student had told Heath how difficult the writing assignments were. He said he had not been required to write more than two or three paragraphs in twelve years of public schooling. Heath's view was that the public schools had failed to require enough reading and writing. "If students are not taught effective communication skills from elementary school on, how can they be expected to make substantial progress in meeting the standards of a first-class university or the demands of society?" he asked. The weakness was magnified because many students seemed unwilling to work to make up the lost ground.

To combat the problem, Heath required all students in the first week of the freshman media writing course to take the Purdue English Competence Examination. Many failed to make the required 60 percent and were placed in non-credit remedial sessions conducted by Barbara Smith and Mary Louise Turner before being allowed to retake the test. Students who had not met the requirement after one or two attempts usually dropped the course. Others received an "I" grade until they made the required score. To defend his position, Heath insisted that there was a close relationship between the ability to express ideas clearly and concisely and intellectual attainment.[56]

Another of Heath's concerns was a weakening of ties with the College of Agriculture. Following Maurice R. Haag's death in 1963, the agricultural journalism effort had begun to lag. Allen had chosen not to fill the position with an agricultural specialist. Later, under Heath, a talented agricultural journalist and alumnus, Anthony J. Solow, joined the faculty for a year, commuting from Tulsa. Following that year, faculty members untrained in the field had taught the courses. The school's participation in the experiment station research effort had all but disappeared. While the service courses in agricultural journalism continued for a time, these were cut back because the rapid growth in majors was placing heavy demands upon teaching loads. Meanwhile, the College of Agriculture had shown no sign of wanting to continue the close relationship Trout had nurtured. Heath, working through Assistant Dean Randall Jones, had spent hours seeking to gain the college's support in a return to the Trout pattern. Finally, when Charles Voyles became head of the Department of Agricultural Information, things began to change.

Born in Okemah on April 27, 1926, Voyles had learned the rigors of farm and timber work by the time he was graduated in 1946 from Haworth High School, where he was president of the senior class. Shortly after graduation, he had joined the Army Air Force in order to qualify for the GI Bill of Rights. After three years, first in Maine and then the Azores, Sergeant Voyles was mustered out.

In the fall of 1949, he came to Oklahoma A. and M. College, where he enrolled as an agricultural education major. The B.S. degree in 1952 led to graduate work in journalism and a job as editorial assistant to George F. Church in the experiment station. His M.S. program emphasized agricultural information and his thesis focused upon the impact of publicity on FFA programs.

Voyles's work with Church was rewarding personally and professionally. He was promoted to assistant agricultural publications editor in 1954, and editor in 1961. Then he was named associate director of public information, extension editor and experiment station editor in 1967. In a reorganization of the university's public information program in 1975, he became head of agricultural information.[57]

Soon Heath began to make progress in his efforts to rejuvenate the agricultural journalism curriculum. Voyles and Jones were sympathetic to Heath's efforts, which earlier had moved at a snail's pace, apparently having a low priority on Dean Frank Baker's agenda. Finally, with the program's rejuvenation in 1977, it would be far more independent than the agricultural journalism major created and sustained by Trout. Rather than being headquartered in journalism it would be an adjunct of the Department of Agricultural Information. But even this gain was a triumph of sorts. Heath cooperated with Voyles in promoting the revived program, which had been moribund. Agricultural information personnel took over the program's advisement function. Soon there were fifteen majors, and by Voyles's retirement in 1987 the enrollment had doubled. Heath's hopes that the close ties of the Trout days could be reestablished had been dashed, but he accepted "half a loaf" as better than none. At least the program had not died.[58] Similar efforts were made in home economics journalism, but with even less success. The degree program there was dead. Only remnants of the Trout effort remained as "suggested electives." Not a single course titled Home Economics Journalism remained.

It was time to reassess the school's immediate space needs. Heath had checked on OSU's long-range building plans and found that the school was far out of the running. His program simply could not wait thirty or more years for tax-supported construction. He would seek private support. Even at the University of Oklahoma, home of the H. H. Herbert School of Journalism, Copeland Hall had been built with the help of a large number of private gifts in a campaign supported by the OPA. But in that case, Anadarko publisher Joe McBride's influence as a member of the board of regents had led to an appropriation of $475,000 in state funds. Tax money for a journalism and broadcasting building at OSU was not likely to be committed.[59]

By 1973, the rapid growth in advertising, broadcasting, public relations, and news-editorial students had created a space crisis in the old Science Hall, begun in 1918, completed in 1920 and redesignated as the Communications Building in 1958. It had been necessary to move the entire advertising program—faculty offices, classrooms, and laboratories—to the fourth floor of Gardiner Hall, a structure dating back to 1911 when it was designated as the Women's Building. There was no other apparent solution. Heath considered himself fortunate to gain approval of the move from the university's space committee and Dean Gries. The move, while practical, was far from ideal. It was then that plans to gain private support for an addition to the Communications Building began. These called for a three-story addition to existing facilities, a one-story case study room, and improvements within the existing structure. The building was structurally sound and would, in Heath's opinion, be good for another fifty years if needed improvements were made.[60]

C. Walker Stone, recently retired editor-in-chief of Scripps-Howard Newspapers, agreed to serve as national chairman of the building campaign. James R. Bellatti, co-publisher of the *Stillwater NewsPress*, led the state fund-raising efforts. The Oklahoma Press Association's board of directors and executive-secretary Ben Blackstock were highly

One of the brightest days in OSU journalism and broadcasting history came on a windy May day in 1974. It was groundbreaking time and manning the shovels were (*left to right*) Robert B. Kamm, James R. Bellatti, Paul Miller, George A. Gries, and Harry E. Heath Jr. Bellatti served as state chairman in the fund raising campaign for an addition to the Communications Building.

supportive in contacts with publishers and through the columns of the *Oklahoma Publisher*. Former OPA presidents J. L. Jennings and D. Jo Ferguson and the current president, Harold Belknap, had added their influence in various personal contacts. Soon after the national campaign began, Stone died of a heart attack. Earl Richert, his successor at Scripps-Howard, picked up Stone's duties in contacting newspaper executives nationally.[61]

During the summer months, the drive to raise $600,000 began in earnest. The School of Journalism and Broadcasting, with the endorsement of both the Oklahoma Press Association and the Oklahoma Broadcasters Association, was seeking $300,000 in gifts. President Kamm had promised to match the campaign dollars.

Much of the drive depended on the person-to-person approach. Heath and Bellatti, chairman of the OPA's Oklahoma State University Journalism Committee, coordinated visits to newspapers and broadcasters throughout the state. About $162,000 already had been committed by media groups, a cable television company, alumni, professionals, friends, faculty, staff and students. Bellatti and Heath made several flights in the

Stillwater Publishing Company's plane, piloted by Leon Matthews, to the state's far corners, selling the need to prospective donors and asking for their support. Hundreds of letters to journalism alumni were sent to back up campaign appeals in *JB News*, the school's tabloid publication for graduates and former students. Most important of all was a formal proposal to the Gannett Foundation seeking a major grant for the building project. The result was a $300,000 stock-transfer gift. That, with other gifts—including money from the sale of university land needed by the city for its medical-center project—assured an attractive three-story addition to the Communications Building.[62]

The Gannett gift caused a flurry in the office. Sally Maune, Heath's secretary, had become so excited by the telephone call announcing the Foundation's decision that she was not sure whether the caller had said $30,000 or $300,000. A letter of confirmation verified the larger figure. The stock had appreciated by a substantial amount before it was sold in accordance with a schedule designated by the Foundation. A visit by Gannett's Vernon Croup had been a preliminary to the decision. He had liked what he had learned in visits with Heath and his faculty. They obviously were competent as well as enthusiastic about their work. But the visit, including conversations with students, had made him dramatically aware of shortcomings in the school's physical facilities. He had carried the word back to Paul Miller that the school needed and deserved the Foundation's support. The Gannett grant would give the beautiful old Georgian structure a new face in keeping with other modern buildings nearby and would become part of a mall leading to Old Central.

Groundbreaking for the three-story addition took place May 3, 1974. The project, in harmony with the architecture of the Student Union's east portico and the nearby Business Administration Building, would include a one-story case study room seating 120. The groundbreaking was a major milestone in the school's history. Spirits soared at the school's annual honors banquet that followed. District Judge R. L. Hert was given the "Friend of Journalism" award by the student chapter of Sigma Delta Chi. Heath's editing students gave him a plaque of appreciation for creative innovations he had introduced in teaching the course.[63]

On September 13, 1974, the OSU regents formally approved a $739,542 contract with Commander Construction Company of Oklahoma City for the addition. Site work was started in mid-August. Approximately $475,000, more than half of the project's cost, had come from contributions, gifts and pledges. Heath recommended to President Kamm that the building be named the "Paul Miller Journalism and Broadcasting Building." The university's regents voted to accept the recommendation. The building was dedicated on Thursday, March 18, 1976, as the highlight of a five-day Communications Week celebration. On three of those days, state, regional, and national media leaders

Thanks to the Gannett New Technology Van, which spent several days adjacent to the construction site for the addition to the Communications Building, students and faculty were introduced to various computerized typesetting systems. Examining the newest in newspaper technology are (*left to right*) Frank Ragulsky, *Daily O'Collegian* associate publisher for news; Leland Tenney, *Daily O'Collegian* associate publisher for business; and William R. Steng, one of the School of Journalism and Broadcasting's top-rated faculty members. Similar equipment soon would be added to the campus newspaper as well as to the school's news lab.

converged upon Stillwater for lectures and panel discussions in the Student Union Theater. Tuesday focused upon advertising and public relations, Wednesday television, radio and film, and Thursday print media and the dedication ceremonies.[64]

The new construction completed Phase I of the school's program to improve its physical plant. A $100,000 challenge gift by Paul and Louise Miller opened Phase II. Students still sat in old chairs that snagged their clothing and worked in laboratories full of ancient manual typewriters. The challenge gift and matching funds would be used for furnishings and equipment. The primary goal was to update reporting, editing, broadcasting, and advertising laboratories with the latest electronic equipment.[65]

At the midway mark in his years as director, Heath still had too little bargaining power when openings occurred on his faculty. Oklahoma State University ranked sixth in average salaries among Big Eight journalism programs at the professorial level and eighth for both associate and assistant professors. These data, compiled by Neale Copple, director of the University of Nebraska School of Journalism, had been circulated to all conference journalism administrators. Higher education in general was underfunded in Oklahoma, and this contributed to OSU's poor showing.[66]

Between 1975 and 1977, conflict with some faculty members had developed over Heath's desire for a core curriculum for all lower division students. In addition, although he was responsible to the administration for both KVRO and KOSU, he was bypassed on all KVRO financial matters. His requests for financial statements had been consistently disregarded. In addition, some of his commitments to President Kamm with reference to KOSU programming had not been fulfilled. These and other concerns had led the director to plan a reassignment of duties within the school. Protests reached Dean Gries' office, and he had put a "freeze" upon any such action until the school's problems could be studied more carefully. Following review by a three-man faculty committee chaired by V. Brown Monnett, who was the associate dean, Gries lifted the freeze and reaffirmed his confidence in Heath as director. In a memorandum to faculty members in the School of Journalism and Broadcasting, he said the school would continue as a single budgetary unit with no change in name and that Heath's responsibilities included not only the academic area of instruction but relationships with the *Daily O'Collegian*, KOSU-FM, and KVRO-FM. He urged faculty members to work together toward common goals. Heath, after giving emotions time to cool, went ahead with reorganization.[67]

Numerous honors were won by both students and faculty during the Heath years. In 1968, Ralph Marler had won first place for newswriting in the national Sigma Delta Chi competition. The same year, Robert Dimery placed first in news photography and Larry Maloney in feature photography. OSU had garnered the most first place awards of any school in the nation. In 1974, Andrew Tevington placed first in the national Sigma Delta Chi editorial writing competition. Jan Berry, Enoch Needham III, Mike Dougan, and Lauren L. Steele, had placed in the top twenty in the highly competitive national Hearst contests, and in 1968, Steve Logue was the only double winner in Southwestern Journalism Congress competition with first places in both news and feature writing. In 1977, Steve Castleberry won a $1,200 Hearst scholarship for first place in spot news coverage.

On the faculty side, Walter Ward received the prestigious Beachy Musselman Award from the Oklahoma Press Association in 1969. Heath received a certificate of appreciation for his service to OPA and for "the OSU journalism school and its growing prestige." In addition, the Oklahoma professional chapter of Sigma Delta Chi chose Heath for its annual "Friend of Journalism" award.[68]

In 1979, Michael J. Bugeja was hired to replace Jack Harrison as newsroom advisor for the *Daily O'Collegian*. Heath wanted someone who would view the newsroom as a classroom. Bugeja was outstanding in this

In 1979, Robert Mackle (*left photo*), editor of the *Daily O'Collegian*, received the Barney Kilgore Award, the highest student honor bestowed by the Society of Professional Journalists, Sigma Delta Chi. The award, named for the famous editor of the *Wall Street Journal*, recognizes the most outstanding performance of a college or university journalist. Nita Bridwell (*right photo*) is presented her William Randolph Hearst certificate by L. Edward Carter. Bridwell finished among the top twenty in the national Hearst writing competition.

capacity for the last three years of Heath's directorship. Liberally educated and with outstanding writing skills sharpened by his work with United Press International, Bugeja contributed greatly to the education of news-editorial majors. Heath's successor, Marlan D. Nelson, assigned Bugeja a full teaching load. Bugeja later was recognized as one of OSU's outstanding professors.[69]

An award that brought more national attention came in 1980, when King D. White, a part-time faculty member, was named Distinguished Campus Advisor by the Society of Professional Journalists, Sigma Delta Chi. One year earlier, Robert Mackle, campus chapter president, had won the Barney Kilgore Award, the top student honor nationally. Known as "Dad" to the students with whom he had worked during his four years as advisor, White assisted the chapter in its strong stand on open meetings and open records on the campus, in the city, and in the state.

Phil Record, the director of region eight, noted that no student chapter had shown OSU's aggressiveness on freedom of information issues. "I doubt if many professional chapters can match its record," he said. For two years in a row the OSU chapter had been judged best in its region. Heath told a *Quill* reporter that White had been advisor, confidant, and friend to his students, providing guidance through wisdom and example." That year, White also was recognized by the society's Oklahoma professional chapter with its "Friend of Journalism" award.[70]

Heath's administration had its exhilarating highs and its depressing lows. Among the highs were the construction of the Paul Miller Journalism and Broadcasting Building, built without a state tax appropriation, and successful accreditation twice in all programs evaluated. Others were the rapid growth of the school, not only in enrollment but in its recognition regionally and nationally, and the success of many graduates in all aspects of the mass media professions. Also high on the list was the acquisition of Paul Miller's personal papers, one of the most important journalism collections in any of the nation's libraries.

But there had been valleys as well as peaks in his leadership. He had not reappointed William Harmon in 1968 and this had led to an investigation by the American Association of University Professors (AAUP) and censure of Oklahoma State University, a censure that lasted until a settlement reached by President Lawrence L. Boger with Harmon and the AAUP in June 1979. The censure may have played a part in thwarting Dean Gries's long and hard efforts to bring a chapter of Phi Beta Kappa to the campus and indirectly may have colored his attitude toward Heath and his sometimes independent style of leadership. Another crisis had developed over the non-reappointment of Duane V. Smith. This had led to a lengthy and bitter series of hearings under the chairmanship of Gerald H. Brusewitz. The appeals committee had recommended to President Kamm that Heath's decision be given further study, but Kamm had chosen to uphold Heath's position.

There had been other actions by Heath leading to tensions which might have been avoided by a more relaxed administrative style. One of these was Heath's decision to replace James W. Rhea as chairman of the radio-television-film curriculum with Philip E. Paulin, manager of KOSU. Rhea had developed strong friendships among some of the state's most influential radio executives and these men were quick to let Dean Gries know that they considered the action unwise. They exerted pressure upon him for Heath's removal as director or for a broadcasting program outside the school structure. Such pressures played a part in a series of assessments of the school's structure, two by off-campus visitors and one by an on-campus faculty committee. Heath saw little justification for such investigations. It seemed to him that the two successful accreditation inspections by the American Council on Education for Journalism should have been sufficient. These time-consuming and tension-building challenges to his direction of the school gradually diminished during the administration of President Boger.

During his years as director of the School of Journalism and Broadcasting, Heath saw the strengthening of faculty as one of his most significant accomplishments. The addition of faculty specialists with strong professional credentials helped to forge a program highly respected nationally as well as throughout the state and surrounding areas.

Many of these faculty members contributed long years to the benefit of their students. Others turned to opportunities elsewhere after only a

Two journalism students walk toward the new Paul Miller Journalism and Broadcasting Building, pristine in its straight-line beauty. The $745,000 structure was built with a major gift from the Gannett Foundation and strong support from Oklahoma newspapers, other state media, alumni, and friends.

few years. Among those with at least four years of duty were H. Ray Wilson, Rey Barnes, Jim Files, Paul Couey, and Mary Louise Turner. All brought strong professional credentials to the university and added to the faculty balance Heath was seeking.

Although some faculty members served only breifly, in many cases their contributions to the success of the various options in journalism and broadcasting were substantial. Among these were John G. Henry, Frederick J. Kosik, Anthony J. Solow, Thomas McCoy, R. Larry Snipes, Charles T. "Tom" Ladwig, Riley Maynard, Frederick L. Kolch, Stephen Lieb, and Richard A. Bergstrom. Part-time teaching help from KVRO and KOSU personnel such as Robert Yadon, Larry Miller, Pat Stout, Richard Ehmen, Don Hoover, and Carolyn Smith had been valuable. In addition, Heath occasionally had called upon such professionals as Oscar Heuser, Al Fiegle, Bob Flournoy, and Max Rodgers when a course was without an available instructor.

Ward, Schick, Steng, Groom, Nelson, Rhea, and Paulin had served as curricula chairmen during the Heath directorship. During this time, the university's administrative procedures had changed drastically. As five-year plans, more and more faculty involvement in the administrative process, frequent statistical reports documenting accountability, and a vast increase in routine paperwork piled up, creative approaches to curriculum and faculty development had suffered. Heath understood administrative burnout and had come to feel that most administrators should stay in one administrative position for no more than ten years. He had decided that a good exit point had arrived with the appointment of Smith L. Holt as dean.[71]

On February 8, 1982, the OSU regents approved Heath's resignation as director and gave him a new title: regents service professor. In letters to the school's alumni and Oklahoma media leaders, Heath said his years as director had been filled with long hours and difficult times, but that they had offered rich personal rewards. He praised the work of the school's secretarial and clerical employees, the dedication of his faculty and the guidance and support of the university's administration. He cited alumni such as Paul Miller, C. Walker Stone, and Hal Phillips, who had made possible "scholarships and other benefits" and had been worthy models for the student body. "In a sense," he wrote, "this represents the traditional changing of the guard." He predicted continued progress under the new director, Marlan D. Nelson, urging faculty support for him in the years ahead.[72]

The most important need of the new director, he believed, would be full cooperation from the faculty. As he left the directorship, Heath said he would like to see a stronger honors program, more money for grants and scholarships to journalism and broadcasting majors, an improved television laboratory, updated newswriting and editing labs, and space for a student-faculty lounge. His successor would achieve most of these goals.

Endnotes

1. Biographical data on Harry E. Heath Jr., Files of the School of Journalism and Broadcasting, Oklahoma State University, Stillwater, Oklahoma.
2. Based upon author's participation in the events described.
3. George S. Turnbull, *Journalism in the Making* (Eugene, OR: School of Journalism, University of Oregon, 1965), pp. 76, 78, 154, 155.
4. Iowa State College Faculty Personnel Information, 19 February 1955, with revisions, Archives, Iowa State University Library, Iowa State University, Ames, Iowa.
5. *Ames* Iowa *Daily Tribune*, 9 February 1967, p. 7; Author's memorabilia; Iowa State College Faculty Personnel Information, Archives, Iowa State University Library; Ann Keane to Harry E. Heath Jr., 3 March 1992, School of Journalism and Broadcasting Centennial History Collection, Special Collections, Edmon Low Library, Oklahoma State University.
6. *News of Iowa State* (1956); Iowa State College Information Service, 6 December 1956; *Sioux City Journal Tribune*, 28 August 1958; Miscellaneous papers, Archives, Iowa State University Library.
7. Iowa State College Faculty Personnel Information, 19 February, with revisions, Iowa State University Library; based upon author's participation in the events described.

8. Charles L. Allen to Harry E. Heath Jr. [July 1961] and Harry E. Heath Jr., to Charles L. Allen [July 1961], in Files of the School of Journalism and Broadcasting; Official transcript of Harry E. Heath Jr., Office of the Registrar, Oklahoma State University.

9. Author's personal communications with Charles L. Allen; Rae O. Weimer to Harry E. Heath Jr., 5 June 1965, Files of the School of Journalism and Broadcasting.

10. Faculty records of Harry E. Heath Jr., Archives, University of Florida Library, Gainesville, Florida.

11. Based upon author's participation in the events described; Lemuel D. Groom to James R. Scales, 29 November 1966, Harry E. Heath Jr. to V. Brown Monnett, 12 April 1968, Files of School of Journalism and Broadcasting.

12. Biographical data on Harry E. Heath Jr., Files of the School of Journalism and Broadcasting.

13. John J. Kennedy to Harry E. Heath Jr., 28 April 1967, Harry E. Heath Jr. to John J. Kennedy, 1 May 1967, Files of the School of Journalism and Broadcasting; based upon author's participation in the events described; News release, 6 January 1967, Office of Public Information, Oklahoma State University.

14. William J. Roepke to Harry E. Heath Jr.[Winter 1966-67], Harry E. Heath Jr. to William J. Roepke [Winter 1966-67], and biographical data on Manning D. Seil, in Files of the School of Journalism and Broadcasting.

15. Author interview with Manning D. Seil, 11 April 1967, Harry E. Heath Jr. to Manning D. Seil, 4 May 1967, and Harry E. Heath Jr. to Manning D. Seil, 5 May 1967, in Files of the School of Journalism and Broadcasting.

16. *Oklahoma Publisher*, September 1967; *Stillwater NewsPress*, 20 September 1967, p. 4; *Tulsa World*, 28 September 1967, p. 59; OSU Faculty Service Report on Manning D. Seil, 1968, Files of the School of Journalism and Broadcasting.

17. Based on author's participation in the events described; Harry E. Heath Jr. to V. Brown Monnett, 23 October 1968, Files of School of Journalism and Broadcasting.

18. Senate Recommendation 122-B, OSU Student Association, 1 May 1968, School of Journalism and Broadcasting Centennial History Collection; Edward C. Burris to Harry E. Heath Jr., 16 July 1968, Files of the School of Journalism and Broadcasting; *Daily O'Collegian*, 27 June 1969, p. 1

19. Personal Data Sheet, 25 March 1968, Application letter, 16 May 1968, and Recruitment Report, 22 May 1968 of L. Edward Carter, in the Files of the School of Journalism and Broadcasting.

20. L. Edward Carter to Harry E. Heath Jr., 16 May 1968, Harry E. Heath Jr. to L. Edward Carter, 22 May 1968, and Harry E. Heath Jr. to L. Edward Carter, 29 May 1968, in Files of the School of Journalism and Broadcasting.

21. *Daily O'Collegian*, 27 June 1969, p. 1.

22. Request for Personnel Action, 15 June 1968, and Separation Notice, 26 April 1972 of L. Edward Carter, in Files of the School of Journalism and Broadcasting.

23. Request for Personnel Action, 15 March 1968, approved by regents 13 April 1968, of C. Dennis Schick, Files of the School of Journalism and Broadcasting.

24. Personal Data Sheet, 1968, of C. Dennis Schick, Files of the School of Journalism and Broadcasting; *Tulsa World*, 14 April 1968, p. 13.

25. Correspondence exchanged by Harry E. Heath Jr. and Ronald Dyke, 8 December 1967 through 15 March 1968, OSU Application for Position on Instructional, Research, or Administrative Staff of Ronald W. Dyke, 25 March 1968, OSU Request for Personnel Action, 26 March 1968, Harry E. Heath Jr. to George Gries, 10 December 1968, Harry E. Heath Jr. to Robert B. Kamm, 16 December 1968, OSU Separation Notice, 2 January 1969, approved by regents, 8 February 1969, in Files of the School of Journalism and Broadcasting.

26. Harry E. Heath Jr. to William Steng, 16 June 1969, OSU Request for Personnel Action, 1 July 1969, and Harry E. Heath Jr. to William Steng, 16 July 1969, in Files of the School of Journalism and Broadcasting.

27. Data on William R. Steng, Files of the School of Journalism and Broadcasting.

28. Harry E. Heath Jr. to James L. Highland, 27 February 1968, and James L. Highland to Harry E. Heath Jr., 4 March 1968, in Files of the School of Journalism and Broadcasting.

29. Vita for James L. Highland, Files of the School of Journalism and Broadcasting.

30. James L. Highland to Harry E. Heath Jr., 4 March 1968, and Application for Position on Instructional Research or Administrative Staff for James L. Highland, 24 March 1968, in Files of the School of Journalism and Broadcasting.

31. Stanley R. Harris to Harry E. Heath Jr., 10 April 1968, Harry E. Heath Jr. to James L. Highland, 19 April 1968, Request for Personnel Action, 16 April 1968, Harry E. Heath Jr. to James L. Highland, 13 May 1968, and Harry E. Heath Jr. to James L. Highland, 13 May 1968; *Stillwater NewsPress*, 22 August 1968.

32. *Daily O'Collegian*, 7 January 1969, pp. 6, 7; Scrapbooks for 1972, School of Journalism and Broadcasting.

33. James L. Highland, "Field Trips Help J-Students at OSU," *Quill*, March 1969, p. 26.

34. Memorandum, School of Journalism and Broadcasting Personnel Committee, 13 February 1970, and Request for Personnel Action for James L. Highland, 13 February 1970, in Files of the School of Journalism and Broadcasting.

35. News release on James L. Highland, 5 April 1971, Office of Public Information, Oklahoma State University; Ben Blackstock to James L. Highland, 24 May 1971, 8 June 1972, Files of the School of Journalism and Broadcasting.

36. James L. Highland to Harry E. Heath Jr., undated memo, and Harry E. Heath Jr. to James L. Highland, 18 January 1972, in Files of the School of Journalism and Broadcasting.

37. Guy H. Stewart to Harry E. Heath Jr., 3 April 1972, Walter J. Ward to James L. Highland, 24 September 1972, Travel Request, 11 October 1972, Request to Engage in Specified Outside Activities, 9 November 1972, and Harry E. Heath Jr. to George A. Gries, 17 November 1972, in Files of the School of Journalism and Broadcasting.

38. Undated teleprinter transmission by the Associated Press, Files of the School of Journalism and Broadcasting.

39. D. Jo Ferguson to Harry E. Heath Jr., 10 February 1973, in Files of the School of Journalism and Broadcasting.

40. Walter J. Ward to Harry E. Heath Jr., 5 March 1973, and Harry E. Heath Jr. to Jack Moore, 15 March 1973, in Files of the School of Journalism and Broadcasting.

41. Ben Blackstock to Harry E. Heath Jr., 24 April 1973, and George A. Gries to James L. Highland, 26 April 1973, in Files of the School of Journalism and Broadcasting

42. James L. Highland to Harry E. Heath Jr., 29 June 1973, Files of the School of Journalism and Broadcasting.

43. Harry E. Heath Jr. to James Wasolowski, 10 August 1973, Files of the School of Journalism and Broadcasting

44. Harry E. Heath Jr. to James L. Highland, 15 August 1973, and Harry E. Heath Jr. to Ben Blackstock, 16 August 1973, in Files of the School of Journalism and Broadcasting; *Stillwater NewsPress*, 16 December 1969, p. 3; *Oklahoma Publisher*, November 1969.

45. *Stillwater NewsPress*, 31 July 1972.

46. Harry E. Heath Jr. to Michael O. Buchholz, 20 February 1974, and Michael O. Buchholz to Harry E. Heath Jr., 15 February 1974, in Files of the School of Journalism and Broadcasting.

47. Harry E. Heath Jr. to Sigley Seil, 14 August 1969, Files of the School of Journalism and Broadcasting.

48. OSU Request for Personnel Action, 1 July 1969, OSU Separation Notice, 26 May 1971, and data on W. Robert Glafcke in Files of the School of Journalism and Broadcasting; *Communigator*, College of Journalism and Communications, University of Florida, Spring 1987, p. 5; *Oklahoma Publisher*, September 1969.

49. *Oklahoma Publisher*, April 1969; *Stillwater NewsPress*, 7 May 1969, p. 4; "The Goal: Meet the Challenge," *Oklahoma State University Alumnus Magazine*, vol. 10, no. 1 (January 1969), pp. 10-13.

50. Author's personal communication with Clayton Vaughn, KTUL-TV, Tulsa.

51. Author's personal biographical file; Biographical data on Harry E. Heath Jr., Files of the School of Journalism and Broadcasting.

52. *Daily O'Collegian*, 19 May 1970, p. 4; *Stillwater NewsPress*, 20 May 1970, p. 7; *Oklahoma City Times*, 21 May 1970, p. 32. Much of the other information is based upon the author's participation in the events described.

53. George A. Gries to Robert B. Kamm, 23 February 1970, and Harry E. Heath Jr. to George A. Gries, 3 March 1970, in Files of the School of Journalism and Broadcasting; *Daily O'Collegian*, 4 March 1970, p. 1; *Stillwater NewsPress*, 3 March 1970, p. 1; *Oklahoma Publisher*, March 1970; *Oklahoma Journal*, 12 March 1970; "The Changing University Scene," *Oklahoma State University Alumnus Magazine*, vol. 11, no. 5 (May 1970), pp. 4, 5.

54. *Stillwater NewsPress*, 12 August 1970, p. 6; Data on Duane V. Smith, Files of the School of Journalism and Broadcasting.

55. *Stillwater NewsPress*, undated clipping from September 1971; *JB News* (February 1983), p. 2.

56. Based upon author's participation in the events described.

57. Data on Anthony Solow, Files of the School of Journalism and Broadcasting; Data on Charles Voyles, Files of the Office of Public Information and the College of Agriculture, Oklahoma State University.

58. Based upon author's participation in the events described.

59. L. Edward Carter, *The Story of Oklahoma Newspapers—1884-1984* (Muskogee, OK: Western Heritage Books, Incorporated, 1984), pp. 198, 199; Author's personal biographical file.

60. J. Lewie Sanderson, R. Dean McGlamery, David C. Peters, *A History of the Oklahoma State University Campus* (Stillwater: Oklahoma State University, 1990), pp. 73, 109, 110, 426-428.

61. *Scripps-Howard News*, April 1973, p. 2, May 1973, p. 19; C. Walker Stone Papers, 1918-1969, State Historical Society of Wisconsin, Madison, Wisconsin.

62. "Communications Seeks Expansion," *Oklahoma State University Alumnus Magazine*, vol. 13, no. 7 (September-October 1972), p. 11; *JB News* (January 1972), p. 1; *JB News* (June 1972), pp. 1, 4; *JB News* (1972-73), p. 1; *Director's Letter to the Alumni* (January 1974), pp. 1-4, Files of the School of Journalism and Broadcasting.

63. "Breaking Ground for New J-B Building," *Oklahoma State University Outreach*, vol. 15, no. 6 (June-July 1974), p. 31; "$300,000 Creates Addition to J-B Building," *Oklahoma Stater*, vol. 1, no. 1 (1974), p. 1; *Daily O'Collegian*, 3 May 1974, p. 3.

64. *Stillwater NewsPress*, 18 March 1976, p. 1; *JB News* (1974-76, two editions), p. 1; *Communications Week March 15-19, 1976*, brochure, Files of the School of Journalism and Broadcasting.

65. *JB News* (1979-80), p. 1; Phase II, Oklahoma State University School of Journalism and Broadcasting flier, 1976, Files of the School of Journalism and Broadcasting.

66. Neale Copple to Big Eight Journalism Administrators, 18 May 1976, Files of the School of Journalism and Broadcasting.

67. Harry E. Heath Jr. to George A. Gries, 10 June 1975, V. Brown Monnett to George A. Gries, 4 March 1976, George A. Gries to Harry E. Heath Jr., 3 May 1976, Harold Niven to George A. Gries, 29 July 1976, George A. Gries to School of Journalism and Broadcasting Faculty, 9 June 1976, and Neale Copple and Harold Niven to George A. Gries, 3 August 1976, in Files of the School of Journalism and Broadcasting; *Daily O'Collegian*, 11 June 1976, p. 1.

68. Scrapbooks, 1968-1977, School of Journalism and Broadcasting

69. Based upon author's participating in the events described.

70. Data on King D. White, Files of the School of Journalism and Broadcasting; "SPJ, SDX Names the Four Distinguished Campus Advisers for 1980," *Quill*, vol. 68, no. 3 (March 1980), p. 17; *MC 1123 Review* (1979), p. 1, School of Journalism and Broadcasting Centennial History Collection.

71. Based upon author's participation in the events described.

72. *JB News* (1981-82), pp. 1, 3; *Director's Letter to the Media* (September 1982), pp. 1-4, Files of the School of Journalism and Broadcasting; *Oklahoma City Times*, 24 November 1981, p. 4.

22 An Alumnus Leads the School

Dean George A. Gries, hard working and innovative, was succeeded on November 1, 1980, by Smith L. Holt, professor and head of the chemistry department at the University of Georgia. The new dean had Oklahoma ties. He was born in Ponca City on December 8, 1938, and took his bachelor's degree in science engineering at Northwestern University, Evanston, Illinois, in 1961. This was followed by a Ph.D. in inorganic chemistry at Brown University in 1965 after Holt had worked six months as a research chemist at the Continental Oil Company in Ponca City. He had built an outstanding teaching and research record both in the United States and abroad before deciding to return to his home state. A brother, James, still lived in Ponca City and was serving in the state legislature.[1]

Holt's acceptance of the deanship seemed to Harry E. Heath Jr. a good time for new leadership in the School of Journalism and Broadcasting. He had held the post since July 1, 1967, and felt that he had accomplished his major objectives. He wrote Holt at Georgia suggesting that once he was on the scene and settled into his new routine he might wish to give serious thought to finding a new director. The job had lost much of its zest for Heath, who felt the school needed new leadership and fresh ideas.[2]

After the new dean's arrival in Stillwater, Heath continued in office for a time, making fund-raising trips with Holt and arranging speaking engagements in various communities for him through his contacts with publishers. Holt intended to build a stronger statewide awareness of his college's role.

While Heath was in his lame duck status, Holt had called for an assessment of the School of Journalism and Broadcasting. The 1976 accreditation report could have given him a reasonably accurate overview of the school's strengths and weaknesses. In addition, the files in his office must have contained details of both the Monnett and Copple-Niven reports as well. Nevertheless, he wanted a fresh look at things before proceeding. He called upon three consultants: Scott M. Cutlip, dean of the University of Georgia School of Journalism, who was a nationally known public relations expert; Richard Gray, director of the Indiana University School of Journalism, who had a strong background in news-editorial functions and research; and Robert Smith, dean of the Temple University School of Communications and Theater, who had been recommended for his broadcasting expertise. Each issued a separate report, and Heath was given an opportunity to share his reactions with Holt. Gray's report was especially cogent. He showed a thorough understanding of industry trends and their relationship to the validity of the OSU program. Holt believed the consensus favored a single unit and that the concept of a core curriculum should be continued.

On February 8, 1982, Heath's title as professor and director was replaced by a new one—regents service professor. He continued his teaching and added extension work to his duties.[3]

Marlan D. Nelson, who had served as chairman of journalism curricula since 1977, was named interim director by Dean Holt on April 5, 1982. Holt needed time to assess the broad-ranging domain he had assumed responsibility for, and he saw no reason to make a hurried appointment. After eighteen months upon the scene, Holt formed a search committee made up of four School of Journalism and Broadcasting faculty members representing four media specialties plus three professional media leaders, one from broadcasting, one from advertising and one from the community newspaper field. Philip E. "Ed" Paulin, the broadcasting faculty leader, was named committee chairman.[4]

A national search was begun in April 1982 through *Advertising Age, Broadcasting, Quill,* and *Editor & Publisher* magazines and the *Chronicle of Higher Education,* a tabloid widely circulated on college and university campuses. Some possible candidates also were contacted by various faculty members. When the committee held its first meeting on April 21, 1982, it had on hand thirty-six applications from throughout the United States, some from candidates at highly regarded schools of mass communication. Committee members spent considerable time studying and discussing the application papers and supporting documents. Student leaders also were consulted. When committee members convened on June 11, 1982, their decision was to submit the names of five candidates to Holt without recommendation. The committee's consensus was that there were no candidates on the list who should be endorsed for the job. Telephone conversations with one of the five led the committee to drop him from the list forwarded to Holt.

Holt apparently had determined to let the school continue for a time without a permanent director while he evaluated its operation. Soon, however, President Lawrence L. Boger suggested that the search be reopened. Advertising was placed once more and all of the original applicants were asked to indicate whether they wished to receive further consideration. Sixteen of the original thirty-six plus three new candidates now made up the pool of applicants. On June 23, Paulin convened the committee to determine the candidates to be interviewed. Members agreed upon three names and Dean Holt asked that a fourth name, that of a previous applicant, be added. The interviews were carried out during June and July. Following the interviews, one of the four surviving contenders dropped out because he felt that "neither the faculty nor the administration truly understood and, therefore, could not be committed to what it would take to build a school of national promise."[5]

Finally, on July 25, the committee recommended to Dean Holt that the school's interim director be elevated to director. Eight days later, Holt informed the school's faculty that he was recommending Nelson's appointment to President Boger. He stated that Nelson "has the complete support of this office." Holt wrote that the college would work with him "to help provide the continued development of your program." The appointment was approved by the OSU regents at their September

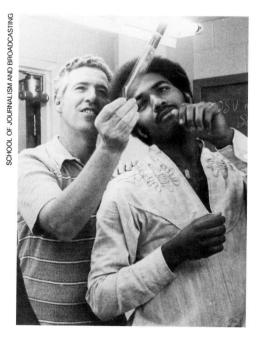

Marlan D. Nelson (*left*) discusses a student's negatives as part of an assignment in the summer Urban Journalism workshop, funded by a grant from Dow-Jones, Inc., publisher of the *Wall Street Journal*. The workshops have been an important part of the School of Journalism and Broadcasting's effort to encourage promising minority students.

meeting, to be effective September 13, 1982. Nelson had become the first OSU alumnus to head the program.[6]

Nelson, ramrod straight at six feet two-and-a-half inches and proud of his Cherokee heritage, already was well-known on campus. He had been in charge of the school's print sequences for five years and had continued those duties after being named interim director. He had logged more than twenty-five years of teaching experience in four states, starting as an instructor at the University of Idaho in 1957. Before he enrolled as a freshman at Oklahoma A. and M. College in 1952, he already had gained two years of experience on his hometown *Haskell News* as a linotype operator and reporter.

Nelson completed his B.A. degree at OSU with a major in journalism in 1956 and returned to Haskell as managing editor. He also worked briefly in production at Tams Bixby's *Muskogee Phoenix* and *Muskogee Times Democrat*. Then he moved west where he was awarded the M.A. degree by Stanford University in 1957. He worked on publications in Colorado and California, then continued his graduate studies at the University of Iowa, and then at Southern Illinois University, while teaching part-time.

From 1963 until 1973, Nelson was chairman of the journalism department at Utah State University, Logan. During most of this period he was assistant and later associate dean in the College of Humanities and Arts as well as journalism chairman. From 1973 to 1977, he was professor and acting head of the Department of Communications, associate dean for instruction, and coordinator of fine arts in the College of Humanities, Arts and Social Sciences at Utah State. He returned to Stillwater in the fall of 1969 for additional graduate work, completing his doctorate in 1972.

His research interests had focused upon the relationship between bar and press. His doctoral study, "Free Press-Fair Trial: An Exploratory Study," had led to a number of publications as well as formal papers delivered to newspaper conferences and at industry and academic meetings. Among his publications was *Free Press-Fair Trial 1950-1969: An Annotated Bibliography*. He and George Rhoades, an OSU graduate teaching at the University of Texas-Arlington, were working on a text-book for use in introductory media writing courses. It was completed in 1984 and has had consistent use since. It is in its second edition.[7]

Nelson's first move was to reorganize the school. He appointed Paulin and William R. Steng as assistant directors. Paulin would be in charge of radio, television and film studies and Steng would replace Nelson as leader of the instructional programs in journalism, advertising, and public relations. They would handle the day-to-day operation of their units, reporting to Nelson. These internal appointments, requiring no action by the OSU regents, would last for nearly four years.

Another veteran professor, Walter J. Ward, was reaffirmed as coordinator of graduate studies and professor in charge of the Bureau of Media Research and Services, which had its embryonic start under Heath and Ward but had increased its outreach when Nelson made it fully operational. Research with outside organizations on a consulting basis would be handled by Ward, while Heath would plan and execute non-research media service programs.[8]

In order to give professors a stronger role in running the school, Nelson set up a new committee system. A student affairs committee was established to handle advising, grade appeals, and scholarships. A graduate affairs committee was charged with admissions and awarding graduate teaching assistantships. A media relations committee was given responsibility for cooperation with regional and state media on projects such as student internships, visiting editors and scholars, and workshops and seminars that would use the talents of media practitioners. The two personnel committees for journalism and broadcasting were combined into one during 1982-83, with equal representation by faculty election. The new committee would recommend faculty appointments, reappointments, promotions and tenure. The reorganization would mean slower action than earlier procedures but, Nelson said, "democracy always is [slower]." The faculty was to participate more actively in the school's programs.[9]

The new director opened the 1982-83 academic year with six new

Charles Fleming (*left*) and Brooks Garner (*right*) are the School of Journalism and Broadcasting's experts in public relations. Fleming is assistant director for graduate studies, while Garner plans such programs as High School Journalism Day and the annual Oklahoma Collegiate Press Association conference. Both have contributed heavily to the school's success in classroom instruction.

faculty members: Charles F. Fleming, Charles W. Overstreet, William J. Rugg, Gregory Stefaniak, Joanne Gula, and Jennifer Rogers. Though popular teachers, Gula and Rogers stayed only one year.[10] Another relative newcomer was Thomas R. Hartley, who had been added by Heath late in his administration.

Hartley, jovial and well groomed, had been a sportswriter, newspaper editor, advertising executive, teacher, co-owner of a radio station, and co-owner of an advertising and public relations agency. Before his most recent advertising agency work in his native Washington state, Hartley had been director of information services and head of the journalism department at Fort Hays State College in Kansas and assistant athletic director at the University of Idaho. He obviously brought a variety of skills to his advanced advertising classes in which, as he said, he drew upon both agency and "street experience." In 1981, he had reintroduced the Addys Awards program honoring the best in student print and broadcast advertising and graphics.[11]

Fleming, a twenty-two-year veteran of the Marine Corps, was chosen to strengthen the school's public relations courses. He had extensive experience in military public relations and had been given a leave during active duty to specialize in that field while earning a master's degree at the University of Wisconsin. His bachelor's degree was from the University of Washington.

Overstreet, who had served as a temporary lecturer, now joined the permanent faculty to complement Hartley's work. Overstreet was responsible for lower division advertising courses. A 1952 graduate of Oklahoma A. and M. College, he had returned to the campus in 1980 to begin work on his master's degree and had completed that work while serving part-time. He had completed four years in the Army followed by experience in both corporate and agency advertising. He came to OSU from the TEAC Corporation of America in Monticello, California.

Rugg, tall and poised, joined the School of Journalism and Broadcasting after work in corporate video and twelve years of teaching experience at Utah State University, Arkansas State University, and the University of Texas-El Paso. He taught courses in cable communication, television directing, production, and advanced television practices, plus seminars on new technologies in the mass media and corporate and industrial video. He held the B.A. in English and theater from Barrington College in Rhode Island, the master's in broadcasting and speech from Utah State, and the Ph.D. in broadcast production and higher education from the University of Mississippi. He had spent the year before coming to OSU as television studio manager for the Raytheon Gulf Systems Company in Kuwait.

Stefaniak, a teacher with a ready sense of humor, had earned the bachelor's degree at Southern Illinois University, the master's at Brooklyn College, and the Ph.D. in journalism at Southern Illinois. He had taught at the University of Evansville, Rutgers University, and Brooklyn College. At OSU, he taught broadcast management, sales and promotion courses, as well as documentary broadcasting and television directing.[12]

The faculty had been strengthened in time to have a part in preparation for the first big challenge of Nelson's administration. The first reaccreditation inspection of OSU journalism was scheduled for February 17, and 18, 1983. The visiting team, headed by Del Brinkman, dean of the University of Kansas School of Journalism, included Paul Janensch, executive editor of the widely respected *Louisville Courier-Journal*, and professors from two other universities with accredited programs. OSU was approved in both news-editorial and advertising sequences, the only programs submitted for consideration. The same programs had been approved in 1976.[13]

In a message to alumni, Nelson expressed satisfaction with early progress under his leadership. Despite a budget shortfall, academic and scholarly accomplishments had been noteworthy. Enrollment had continued high. Nelson applauded the faculty for its recommendation to raise the grade point average required for graduation from 2.5 to 2.75. This would be studied by the faculty and voted upon later. The vote was favorable but the action was vetoed by the central administration based upon Vice President James H. Boggs's interpretation of policies established by the state regents.

Faculty participation in scholarly and professional meetings had also increased. Michael O. Buchholz, Stefaniak, Rugg, Paul Couey, Gula, and Rogers had appeared on the programs of a variety of media-related organizations. In addition to this faculty productivity, Michael J. Bugeja had served as chairman of the 1983 Southwest Cultural Festival, and William Crane had produced a film adaptation of an award-winning short story. Ed Paulin had attended the International Radio-Television Seminar in New York City, columns by Harry Heath and William Steng were appearing regularly in the *Oklahoma Publisher* and Walter Ward had gained his first two research clients for the bureau.

Summing up other progress, Nelson noted that the Paul Miller papers had been received by the OSU library, "primarily through Heath's efforts." Professors Hartley and Overstreet had helped several Stillwater merchants with their advertising and public relations programs, and Hartley had been selected for participation in the AAAA professor-exchange program. He was assigned to Marstellar Advertising in Chicago. Bugeja's article on "Newspaper Policy Concerning Rape Coverage" had been the cover story for the winter issue of *National College Press Review*. Nelson applauded these signs of professional growth by the faculty.

In the extension area, the High School Journalism Day and Oklahoma

Collegiate Press Association (OCPA) conferences were praised by students and advisors. The groundwork for the improved J-Day programs had been laid earlier as Professor Robert Wegener, successor to John Henry, had reshaped the annual event. In addition, the Oklahoma Press Association's newswriting short course chaired by Heath, with help from Steng, Leland Tenney, and Jack Lancaster, was a success. Next up was an Urban Journalism Workshop under a grant from the Newspaper Fund—the sixth such workshop at OSU under Nelson's supervision. To add to this flurry of activity, the faculty had hammered out curricular changes that updated course offerings in journalism and broadcasting. Three new courses were approved for the radio-television-film program and one for journalism.

In the meantime, the expansive spirit of the new Nelson administration had been cooled by the effects of the 1982 oil bust. "Watchdogging" now became a major task in the school, with more conservative planning of programs in undergraduate and graduate teaching, in research, creative work and in extension. Commenting on the debilitating effects of the oil bust, Nelson wrote: "Our resources are limited, and we must view new courses as encroaching on our resources. In a steady-state educational environment, this means that we must view every course in terms of cost—including dollars as well as faculty time. If we have 20 FTE faculty teaching at full load with 60 courses on the books, we cannot add one course without upsetting that workload. The delicate balance can be attained by dropping courses, combining existing courses, offering courses [less often], and by requiring fewer courses for our major sequences. The steady-state economy means we must become better managers. And we will. . . ."[14]

Frederick L. Kolch, a longtime member of the speech faculty, joined the School of Journalism and Broadcasting in 1983 to teach radio and television announcing and performance. He served as coach to student announcers in campus radio activities and cable television, dividing his time with speech and language pathology and audiology. He held the bachelor's and master's degrees from Wayne State University in Detroit and had done doctoral work at the University of Michigan. For several years, he had been a leader of the American Association of University Professors on campus as well as at the state level. Kolch, sophisticated and with perfect diction, was widely known and admired for his skills as a speech critic.[15]

The first change in Nelson's administrative structure came in 1983 when Ed Paulin was put in charge of special projects in broadcasting. Rugg was named acting assistant director with responsibility for the academic programs in radio, television, and film. Later during the academic year, the word "acting" was removed from Rugg's title.[16]

Nelson continued to build his faculty, adding five new members as

The heart of the advertising curriculum during the Marlan D. Nelson administration has been two widely experienced professional practitioners: Thomas R. Hartley (*left*) and Charles "Chuck" Overstreet (*right*). The list of their former students in the advertising field is long and impressive. They have found time, too, to contribute heavily to the school's extension efforts.

the 1984-85 academic year arrived. Brooks Garner, who held B.A. and M.A. degrees in journalism from the University of Oklahoma, had worked for the *Daily Oklahoman* and in corporate public relations with Phillips Petroleum, Southwestern Bell, and Oklahoma Gas and Electric. He taught advanced public relations and the public relations media laboratory and replaced Harry Heath as leader of the school's extension program.

Television news instruction received a boost with the addition of Lisa John, a workaholic who had been a part-time lecturer after starting her doctoral work in higher education with specialization in mass communication. She brought to the campus more than sixteen years experience in radio and television news, newspaper reporting, and public relations. She had been prominent in television news in the Lawton area and later at KWTV and KOCO-TV in Oklahoma City. Her experience included work on the *Daily Oklahoman*. She was well equipped to teach production and advanced news courses in television and contributed much to the internship program in broadcasting. She held a bachelor's degree from the University of Denver and a master's from the University of Oklahoma.

Maureen Nemecek had earned a bachelor's degree in English at the University of Nebraska, followed by a master's degree in broadcasting and a Ph.D. in American studies at the University of Maryland. She was versatile and taught both print and broadcast courses, while adding strength to the graduate program. Her interest in international communication was a plus, for the graduate program was gaining more students from other parts of the world.

Lisa Schillinger was well known to the faculty. She had taken her master's degree in the OSU mass communication program and held a B.A. degree in journalism and Russian area studies from the University of Illinois. She continued working toward an Ed.D. degree on campus, while teaching and serving as *Redskin* advisor. Her strengths were in communication graphics and international communication.

The news-editorial program benefited greatly for the remainder of the Centennial Decade from the addition of a fifth faculty member. Donald U. Reed, a knowledgeable journalist, had long wire service experience which made him "unflappable" in the routine frustrations of the academic world. At the same time, his down-to-earth practicality in class and laboratory gave students a realistic view of the reportorial function and its importance.

Reed had won out over some twenty other applicants, largely on the basis of his professional experience. He taught both lower and upper division courses in the news-editorial curriculum. Most of his professional career following his graduation from Fresno State University was spent with United Press International (UPI), at that time still a strong and vigorous competitor with the Associated Press and other news services around the world. He started as bureau manager and staff writer in Fresno, then was promoted to manager of the San Francisco bureau. In 1969, he moved to Dallas as UPI's Southwest Division news editor. Eight years later, he became the Central Division news manager at the service's key distribution center in Chicago. In 1979, he moved to UPI headquarters in New York, where he served as managing editor, second in command of the worldwide news service. When new owners took over the service in 1983, Reed and his wife began a more leisurely pace in Connecticut, then came to Stillwater. His addition soon was reflected in the increasing number of awards won by student journalists in regional and national competition.[17]

In 1985, Sharon Hartin Iorio was added to teach a course on school publications and assist with the large enrollment in media style and structure. The year before, she had earned her master's in mass communication at OSU. She was a leader in the secondary education section of the Association for Education in Journalism and Mass Communication and had attracted wide attention for her master's research on the status of open meeting laws nationally. A paper based upon her thesis had won the Broadcast Education Association's award for the "top student paper." While teaching part-time, she had begun doctoral work in sociology.[18]

In 1986, for the first time since 1924, the *Daily O'Collegian* was without a press. The O'Collegian Publishing Company, over the protests of the newspaper's staff members and Heath, had decided to sell the press and publish the paper on contract at the *Stillwater NewsPress*. Press room space was converted to an enlarged newsroom, and the old newsroom was taken over by the *O'Collegian*, advertising staff.[19]

That year, two more faculty were added. Terry M. Clark had big shoes to fill. Bugeja, who had departed for Ohio University, had been one of the most popular teachers in the school's history. Nelson had made a good choice. Clark quickly became one of the most effective reporting and editing teachers the school had known. He was friendly and enthusiastic and soon had developed a following among students that rivaled the popularity of Bugeja. A 1966 magna cum laude English graduate of Central State College in Edmond, he had worked on an Iowa weekly, then had earned his master's degree in journalism at the University of Iowa in 1969. He came to OSU from the *Duncan Banner*, where he had served seven months as advertising director after selling his weekly newspaper, the *Waurika News-Democrat*, which he had owned for a dozen years. He remained until the end of the Centennial Decade.

John R. Ellerbach held the master's degree from Drake University and had a background in radio news, freelance writing, and public relations. He had spent three years with the Iowa Hospital Association as public relations director. Ellerbach brought effective cross-media skills to the faculty. He taught classes in broadcast newswriting and assisted in

SCHOOL OF JOURNALISM AND BROADCASTING

The training of hundreds of news-editorial students in recent years has been in the hands of these highly skilled professional journalists (*left to right*): Michael J. Bugeja, Terry M. Clark, and Donald U. Reed. Not only have School of Journalism and Broadcasting students sharpened their writing and editing under their guidance, but working journalists across the state owe much to their workshops, seminars, and on-the-scene consulting.

advertising copy and layout laboratories. He left in May of 1988 for a faculty position at Franklin College in Indiana.[20]

Although other faculty changes would come later, Nelson had built the foundation for the remainder of the Centennial Decade. That foundation included Fleming, Hartley, Overstreet, Garner, John, Nemecek, and Reed.

In 1987, Fleming was named assistant director for graduate studies. Within a year, graduate research became "computerized" with all statistical analysis based upon the OSU standard, "SYSTAT: The System for Statistics." This brought a radical change to graduate research classes.[21]

The school's emphasis upon guest lecturers continued high. The Newspaper Fund, Incorporated, a Dow-Jones creation, was crucial in bringing highly respected journalists to OSU classrooms through its editor-in-residence program. But an even more significant move in enrichment programs was to come later in the Paul Miller Lecture Series, created in 1987 with a gift from Paul and Louise Miller.[22]

It appeared that things were running smoothly under Nelson. For one thing, internal communication had been improved. He was careful to keep both faculty and staff informed on a wide range of subjects: meetings, visiting speakers, committee appointments, upper-echelon administrative decisions, deadlines for faculty and staff participation in various programs, job openings—everything he knew of that others might logically find useful. Faculty meetings were scheduled more frequently, and agenda items were invited. The meetings proceeded in an orderly fashion. In short, the transition from Heath to Nelson had appeared to be more than satisfactory.

Then disaster struck. Within a six-month period, three key faculty members were lost. A vacation stroll in Sarasota, Florida, on the evening of August 3, 1986, ended Steng's career. A drunken motorcyclist speeding in the area jumped the curb and careened into the popular professor, crippling him physically and shattering him emotionally. A dynamic lecturer, he had established a reputation as one of the school's outstanding professors in ethics and responsibility as well as the legal aspects of mass media. His injuries were so severe that he was placed on disability status and never returned to his duties except for a brief, part-time assignment. His loss was a tragedy, not only to himself but also to the hundreds of future students who would miss his stimulating classes.[23]

Ward, the faculty iconoclast who was the keystone of the graduate faculty, was diagnosed with pancreatic cancer. He died on September 17, 1986. William Jackson, the school's film specialist who had taught hundreds of students in the History and Significance of Film and Broadcasting, walked into the office on December 6, 1986, to say he was on his way to the hospital. He drove himself to the Stillwater Medical Center, then died of a heart attack slumped in his car in the emergency area parking lot. Veteran OSU educators could not recall a time when fate had decimated a faculty in such a short time. Nineteen months later, cancer would claim Leland Tenney, who had served the School of Journalism and Broadcasting since August 1, 1974, first as associate publisher and later as general manager of the *O'Collegian* and as lecturer in various courses.[24]

The school's structure changed once more in 1987. Nelson had added Steng's and Ward's duties to his own for a year. Budget cuts, however, required retrenchment. His decision was to eliminate a layer of administration. Assistant directors were dropped at the undergraduate level, eliminating Rugg's administrative duties and giving him a heavier teaching load. Whether he knew it or not, Nelson had created precisely the structure recommended in the 1976 accreditation report. That year, the visiting accreditation committee had written: "The team applauds the new plans to reorganize the administrative structure of the school. Broadcasting and journalism are not separate entities and their direction should be centralized in the hands of the director." Dean Gries had not favored such action then; Dean Holt saw no reason to block it now.[25]

Governor George P. Nigh had been elected for a second term and soon the university was notified of a mandatory five percent cut in all budgets. This fiscal setback was not unexpected, given the state's economic woes.

SCHOOL OF JOURNALISM AND BROADCASTING

The loss of these faculty members was a heavy blow to Director Marlan D. Nelson and their other faculty colleagues. William Jackson (*left photo*) died of a heart attack in 1986. Walter J. Ward (*right in right photo*) died of cancer that year, while William R. Steng was physically disabled when hit by a drunken motorcyclist and was unable to continue teaching. Jackson was the school's motion picture specialist; Ward was coordinator of graduate studies; and Steng, assistant director for journalism, advertising, and public relations, was a valued member of the graduate faculty.

Budget cuts came with regularity for years. The turnaround finally came when the legislature passed House Bill 1017 in a special session called by Governor Henry L. Bellmon in 1990. In the meantime, the College of Arts and Sciences had overbudgeted for several years and was now required to remove the deficit. This meant that faculty who had died, resigned, retired, or had failed to be reappointed could not be replaced except under stringent guidelines that rarely were approved. The budgetary line item for most of these losses went into Dean Holt's "deficit pool." Once the college had established a balanced budget and new monies had become available, Nelson would be able to draw positions out of the pool. He had lost the equivalent of two and a half full-time faculty members during this budget crunch.[26]

Not only had his payroll budget been hit hard, but the same was generally true of his operating budget. It had decreased considerably over a ten-year period. Only one increase came during that time—a distribution of new funds in 1988 to cover the school's part of the costs involved in establishing the new Ericsson telephone system. This system, which eliminated extension phones and gave each employee a specific number as well as computerized records of long-distance use, was projected to cut costs significantly over the long haul. But over the first two years, the School of Journalism and Broadcasting had spent about $150 more monthly on telephone service than in the past. That expense, out of an already reduced operating budget, called for more stringent economy in every aspect of the school's administration.[27]

In the face of the tight budget situation, the major redeeming fact was a decline in the school's enrollment during the first nine years of Nelson's leadership. There were reasons for the decline. For one thing, the activism of the 1960s and 1970s had given way to a growing student conservatism, and the Watergate syndrome that skyrocketed mass media enrollments during Heath's administration had faded into history. In addition, the steady flow of "baby boomers" had begun to slacken early in Nelson's administration. Another factor was a change in the advisement system. No longer did those who intended to major in journalism and broadcasting options enter the school as freshmen. Their advisement was handled in the College of Arts and Sciences. They became journalism and broadcasting majors, statistically speaking, when they reached sophomore standing. With a tight budget and overworked staff, the school itself had, in fact, wanted to see the enrollment decrease. In 1983 it had acted to bring about a more favorable student-faculty ratio. It could do nothing about admission standards. Those were set by the state regents. But retention standards could be changed, and the journalism and broadcasting faculty had voted to upgrade them. All majors in the school would now have to achieve a 2.5 average in their major as well as in all upper-division courses. In addition, transfer students without a 2.0

average would not be accepted unless they had achieved a 3.0 for two semesters in at least twelve credit hours. This action was designed to eliminate those who would reach their scheduled graduation time without the required 2.5 average. It also reduced the flow of transfer students from other business-oriented programs who saw advertising and public relations as a potential major.[28]

From its peak of about 750 during the Heath administration, enrollment had leveled off to about 425. During the Nelson administration it had remained fairly steadily at three percent of the total university enrollment and between nine and ten percent of the total arts and sciences enrollment. It continued as the academic unit with the largest number of majors and the largest number of graduates in the college each year.[29]

As for relationships with other academic units, new cooperative efforts had evolved in some cases, while a live-and-let-live atmosphere had developed in others. The best of the cooperative programs had emerged with the Departments of Art and Theater. Professor Nick Bormann had revitalized art's long defunct commercial art training late in the Heath administration, and Nelson, then chairman of the journalism and advertising options, had worked with Heath to develop cooperation with Bormann and his department head, Richard Bivins. This had matured during the Nelson administration and, in the main, was working well. Art students were taking the school's typography and journalistic design course and performing well. As the course was required of fewer journalism and broadcasting majors, art students made up a significant part of the enrollment. Art students also were enrolling in Advertising Copy and Layout, but in some cases found the prerequisite writing courses to be an obstacle, either real or imagined. Advertising students and some other journalism majors were taking basic design courses in the Department of Art. Both art and journalism and broadcasting were making changes. Art had planned a laboratory for computer graphics, a fast-growing commercial art technique important in advertising and public relations, and journalism was doing the same. Nelson saw the prospect for future cooperation as healthy and growing.

Cooperation with the theater department also had progressed. This was only in the talking stage when Heath had stepped down, but Nelson had carried negotiations forward with Kenneth Cox following the resignation of Jim Woodward. In 1985 Nelson and Cox had worked out a joint venture in which theater students could major in television production and performance in either their home department or the School of Journalism and Broadcasting. It worked both ways. While theater students were taking three broadcasting courses, broadcasting students enrolled in theater courses were learning lighting, staging, and directing, as well as how to evaluate creative theatrical techniques. Nelson consid-

1968 REDSKIN

John Henry (*in apron*) talks printing with a small laboratory group in his graphic arts laboratory. A skilled craftsman, he brought enthusiasm to students with his practical but creative projects. Robert Wegener (*inset*), who was strong in newspaper design, succeeded Henry.

ered this to be an ideal arrangement, and Cox agreed that it was working smoothly and to the advantage of students.

Nor did Nelson feel threatened by the growth of the technical writing and film programs in the Department of English. In his view, technical writing had not replaced the old industrial editing concept nurtured by Clement E. Trout in the Department of Technical Journalism, which had given way to the new School of Communications under C. Ellsworth Chunn. Although the industrial editing program had not survived in its earlier form—highly focused and with degree programs both at the undergraduate and graduate levels—changes in the public relations field since the 1960s had made a broader approach desirable. Many journalism graduates were filling the jobs industrial editing majors had filled earlier. Often, these were entry-level positions on company publications. Technical writing graduates from the Department of English were, in Nelson's view, going largely into publishing houses as assistant editors and into such industries as aircraft production where their skills in preparing instructional manuals and writing and editing technical reports were in demand. While journalism graduates occasionally took the same kinds of positions, most did not. There was a symbiotic relationship rather than an abrasively competitive one. Technical writing students took such courses as Mass Media Style and Structure, Reporting I and Editing I while some journalism majors enrolled in technical writing courses. Some technical writing students used journalism professors as advisors on a major research report required by English.[30]

Tensions had built in the 1970s as English had, in Heath's opinion, encroached upon the claim that journalism had long had upon cinematography instruction. The friction had diminished following a live-and-let-live conference involving Heath, English head Gordon Weaver and faculty members in both units who had film interests. English had expanded upon its original film-as-literature rationale under Peter Rollins after adding another film teacher, Leonard Leff. But as the program evolved, the focus was upon film as popular culture and was a driving force in what now was called film history and criticism. Rollins had produced several documentary films on grants he had received. Some of these were noteworthy and had been well received by critics and audiences as well. Rollins and Leff, however, had not developed production courses for their students. Meanwhile, the death of journalism's motion picture specialist, William Jackson, plus a limited budget, had caused retrenchment. The film history course, earlier know as History and Significance of Film and Broadcasting, had enrolled as many as 300 students in a single mass lecture class under Jackson during film's peak years in the school. It had been dropped from the schedule in 1985. Jackson had not been replaced and no other faculty member was willing to add the course to his teaching load. Soon, the radio-television-film program dropped the word "film" from its title. Any film to be taught would now be included in the television production, documentary, and television news courses. In effect, with the death of Jackson, film instruction would increasingly focus upon news rather than upon its more complex esoteric aspects.[31]

Another factor was the difficulty in contracting for film processing. The school's processing equipment, a secondhand gift, had broken down, and film now was sent to Dallas for processing. This caused delays that hampered work in the course and was costly to students as well. More and more, instruction in pictorial continuity shifted to video tape and away from 16mm film. The last use of film was in an intersession cinematography course taught by William Rugg in the summer of 1990. The demand for a single film production course continued, but there was little vocal support for a major option in film either on the part of students or faculty. Students with a career interest in motion pictures—many of them majors in English or theater pointing toward television drama—were advised to complete their undergraduate work in Stillwater and go elsewhere, usually to California, for graduate or specialized work in film. Nelson viewed his relationships with the technical writing and film programs in English as satisfactory but less structured than those with art and theater.

The long-standing cooperation with the College of Agriculture, started in Trout's first year on campus, had remained strong throughout his thirty-two-year tenure. Even into the Ellsworth Chunn and Charles Allen administrations it had continued, but with the death of Professor Maurice Haag in 1963, it had begun to weaken. Nelson had tried to encourage the agricultural journalism program, now called by what some thought to be a more accurate name: agricultural communications. During Nelson's administration, four different persons had been given responsibility for working with the small program. The administration in agriculture seemed reluctant to give journalism the kind of full cooperation Trout had. Even with such cooperation, the accredited status once held by agricultural journalism would no longer have been possible. Policy changes in the Accrediting Council on Education for Journalism and Mass Communication (ACEJMC), formerly the ACEJ, would require a weakening of the agriculture component in favor of added hours in liberal arts and sciences. Such a problem had not existed when accreditation was gained because of the agricultural journalism program's high professional acceptance under earlier accreditation standards. Now agricultural communications would have to be revised significantly to meet the new ACEJMC criteria. Whether this would be done was unresolved as the centennial year neared its end. Probably there would never be a return to 'the kind of program Trout had nurtured.

There were difficulties in another area that had been strong during the Trout era. The College of Home Economics was under a new dean, Patricia Knaub, and an extensive reorganization had taken place there. Nelson felt that the college's new orientation in the communications area had increased its involvement with the Department of Speech Communication while relations with the School of Journalism and Broadcasting had cooled. The general catalog had not listed a major in home economics journalism since 1968. Elaine Jorgenson, the school's closest contact during the deanship of Beverly Crabtree, was now the college's director of academic affairs. Heath had been unsuccessful in his efforts to reestablish a major program similar to that of the Trout years. Home economics had followed agriculture's lead in dropping the name journalism from the curriculum title. It now was home economics communication and only a minor program. In Dean Knaub's reorganization, a number of departments had been merged and various centers created. The strong ties forged by Charles Allen with the old clothing, textiles and merchandising department had faded away and the new design, housing and merchandising department and its Center of Apparel Marketing and Merchandising, in spite of the obvious use of advertising and public relations in those fields, had shown no interest in cooperative efforts with Nelson's programs. As for the business college's possible participation in programs with a communications thrust—for example, a coopera-

528   Centennial Histories Series

Two productive members of the School of Journalism and Broadcasting during this period were Lisa John and William Rugg. John was the goad and guiding light for many students on the "Cable Magazine" show, while Rugg used his wide experience both in the classroom and as advisor to Alpha Epsilon Rho.

tive program in mass media management or a return to the old business journalism program abandoned after the 1960-61 academic year—no serious discussions had been attempted.

If there was to be interfacing with the Colleges of Agriculture, Business Administration, and Home Economics, Nelson saw the best opportunity for it through the university's new Center for International Trade Development. But such possibilities were not likely to reach fruition without additional faculty and a commitment by the colleges' deans. Within the College of Arts and Sciences, however, Nelson saw more immediate possibilities. He was interested in developing a political science-journalism combination, perhaps awarding the old journalism certificate, as Trout had done. A substantial number of political science majors were taking some journalism and broadcasting courses and he could see a carefully structured intra-departmental program benefiting both disciplines.[32]

Nelson had to learn, as Heath had, to occasionally use patchwork to keep his programs moving. Although he had de-emphasized photojournalism, staffing photography classes continued to be a problem. For years Harry Hix had shepherded hordes of shutterbugs through the cramped semi-basement space where psychology's rats had once scuttled around in their cages. Hix had retired, and for five years John Thomas had been in charge of photography. After Thomas had moved to Memphis

State University, Diane Sears-Bugeja followed by Perla Ward, two emergency part-time teachers, had kept photography afloat. The versatile Terry Clark, a strong member of the news-editorial faculty, had followed Ward with outstanding success. He was succeeded by John Catsis and Gene L. Post. Catsis had been hired to replace Rugg, who had resigned to accept a position at Northern Arizona University. Catsis was a graduate of the Northwestern University Medill School of Journalism and a highly competent broadcast journalist and freelance writer. He was a catalyst in lifting school and faculty morale. Post, who had retired in 1986 after twenty-three years as the College of Education's audio-visual specialist, was ideal both for laboratory supervision and instruction. Photography was no longer a major sequence. It had fallen victim to the budget crunch and tighter accreditation demands. Although now only a service course, public relations and news-editorial majors frequently elected it.[33]

Long-range planning, curricular and faculty adjustments, intensive months of preparing an extensive pre-visit accreditation report, stabilizing the faculty once more, and his work as president of the OSU Credit Union had placed heavy demands upon Nelson. More were to come.

Heath had faced turmoil when a small group of off-campus broadcasters sought either his removal as director or a stand-alone radio-television department with its own budget.

On that occasion, nearly all of the faculty had signed a letter to Dean George Gries supporting Heath. The crisis was resolved and the school's structure preserved. Now Nelson faced a different brand of turmoil. A revolt was brewing within the faculty, encouraged in part by the adversarial mood that had developed campus-wide. An atmosphere of distrust prevailed. The dispute over the showing of the controversial film *The Last Temptation of Christ* had led to the formation of a Committee for the First Amendment and a court challenge. Demonstrations and "teach-ins" were mildly reminiscent of the Vietnam-era turmoil. The regents finally, after a protracted delay, had allowed the film to be shown.

In the spring, the smoldering tensions mounted again, this time over President John R. Campbell's reinstatement of seven football players who had not met the university's academic standards. In the College of Arts and Sciences, the campus unrest had filtered down to various academic units, where the conflict became faculty vs. department head. Factions within various faculties were seeking more power and the administration of at least two departments had been upended. Dean Smith Holt along with other deans had visited their faculties individually to hear grievances. The atmosphere of unrest in some cases increased in spite of the expected catharsis.[34]

With all of this as a backdrop, an outbreak of discontent within a faction of the School of Journalism and Broadcasting can be seen in a broader context. For some, the unrest was related to grievances, often

Radio-TV major Sherry Pankey (*left*) handles the controls in the School of Journalism and Broadcasting's annual cable coverage of the homecoming parade. Professor Lisa John served as producer. Johnny Saied (*right*), an agricultural communications major, does camera work in an Educational Television Services studio. The early morning program is called "Sunup" and is carried on the Oklahoma Educational Television Authority network.

greatly magnified, going all the way back to broadcasting's unsuccessful breakaway efforts during the Heath administration. Others felt that deserved promotions had been thwarted. Still others, without hard facts, felt the school's budget consistently favored print over broadcasting in terms of salaries and equipment. Heath also had faced this complaint, although it was contrary to budget data. There were reservations, too, about the upcoming challenge of re-accreditation. Broadcasting had never been inspected by a visiting accreditation team. Some faculty were lukewarm to the idea, apparently feeling that the accreditation team might be dominated by print interests. But now it was all or nothing. The new *unit rule* required that all academic programs within the communications unit seeking accreditation must submit to the critical eye of the visiting inspection team. To win re-accreditation, OSU would be required to include its curricula in broadcasting and, for the first time, too, its graduate program. Accreditation was, in colloquial terms, a new ball game.

The accreditation issue became the first of several conflicts that would bring months of faculty tension. The unrest became overt when the accreditation team met on Sunday afternoon with a group of the school's students. Apparently word of the special session, to which all students were invited, was given unusual distribution. Not only did current students attend, but a number of former students from Tulsa, Oklahoma City and Wichita were present. What emerged appeared to the accreditation team to be an "orchestrated" attack upon Nelson. A number of graduate students were present. Some said they could not believe what they were hearing.

The accreditation committee had decided the feedback was unrealistic. Too many of the dissatisfied individuals who had spoken out had repeated key words and phrases. The committee concluded the themes had been rehearsed. One member said "[they] sounded like robots." To gain perspective, committee members came to Nelson's office on Monday morning. Would he, they asked, let them take over his 9:30 A.M. Media Style and Structure class and talk with his students? Nelson agreed. The committee spent forty minutes with the class and concluded that much of what they had heard Sunday had, in fact, been orchestrated. The class feedback, in Nelson's absence, was upbeat and laudatory, filled with praise for the school and what the students were looking forward to in the program.

During the committee's remaining days on campus, members were stopped in the hallways by some broadcasting students who repeatedly decried the fact that the cinematography course was not being offered. This was true, although the students did not fully realize why dropping the course had been necessary. But they also persisted in false charges that all of the operating budget was being spent on other curricular options in an effort to "squeeze out the broadcasting major." At times the committee deliberations were briefly interrupted as two or three individuals volunteered to help members with their assessment of the school. David Bartlett, president of the Radio-Television News Directors Association who was a member of the accrediting team, grew weary of being accosted when he would step outside the conference room. He asked students to desist, pointing out that the broadcasting industry was in a state of flux and that OSU was in step with changing times. In effect, he told them they should "get on the bandwagon or ship out."

Even after the accrediting team left Stillwater, the effort to cast doubts on the School of Journalism and Broadcasting's leadership continued. Committee members and even members of the broader Accrediting Council on Education for Journalism and Mass Communication were contacted by long-distance telephone by some faculty members discouraging accreditation, even on a provisional basis. Four months after the January 1990 accreditation visit, the ACEJMC informed Oklahoma State's administration that *provisional* accreditation had been granted. OSU was given one year to upgrade journalism and broadcasting laboratory equipment and to submit a revised report with transcript data covering all graduates of the past two years. It would reveal whether graduates had taken ninety hours outside their major, with sixty-five of these in liberal arts classes.

After the accreditation issue was settled, other concerns emerged. A group of female faculty members scheduled a meeting with Nelson to discuss their salaries. Only hours before the meeting, the group cancelled the appointment. The reason is not clear, even today, but some uninvolved faculty members speculated that the purpose was to broaden the base of their discontent by involving some faculty males and making promotions, salaries and use of maintenance money as well as Nelson's leadership style issues for resolution. One faculty member used a frontal approach, asking Nelson if he thought he had been rewarded adequately for his services at OSU. Nelson's reply was that none of the school's faculty members had been adequately rewarded because of the budget crunch, but that the faculty member in question had been rewarded fairly based upon his performance and available funds. At that point, Nelson believes, the dissident group began to map strategy for a challenge to his directorship.

While an issue with some was the need to adjust salaries, that was a problem Nelson already was aware of. He had consulted with Dean Holt in an effort to make salaries more equitable, and Holt had said he would

1987 REDSKIN

Jack Lancaster, faculty advisor to the *Daily O'Collegian*, OSU's prize-winning newspaper, looks over the shoulders of five of his staff members as they discuss the current issue. Frequent staff critiques are part of the learning process in the news-editorial sequence.

find the money some way. Dissatisfied faculty members may have believed their protests had been responsible, and that the dean had acted to "save Nelson's hide." Such was not the case.[35]

By now the emotions of dissatisfied faculty members had grown, through circular reaction, to encompass other grievances, including what they considered to be manipulation of committee assignments. An informal caucus had formed. This had led to a request that the dean, along with Neil J. Hackett, the associate dean, meet with the faculty. The meeting was arranged for May 7, 1990, shortly before commencement. Now caucus members began to refine their strategy. It was to call for the removal of Nelson as director. Some faculty members outside the caucus had no idea what the meeting was about. They were surprised and shocked at the litany of grievances brought against Nelson, who was not present to defend himself. Some faculty members spoke in his defense, but they obviously were not prepared to match the highly charged emotions of those who spoke for a change in leadership. A motion for Nelson's dismissal got a prompt second. The vote, by secret ballot, included part-time faculty as well as proxies. It favored Nelson's removal as director.

Now Dean Holt faced a tough decision. He had seen a similar pattern evolve in other departments in the wave of unrest on campus. How far was it to go? On May 10, the faculty met with Nelson in the Paul Miller Journalism and Broadcasting Building. Nelson was conciliatory, offering brief comments aimed at peace-making. Emotions had escalated. This time there were volatile remarks with charges and counter charges on the part of both segments of the split faculty. Again, there was a motion for removal. Again, the vote went against Nelson, but this time the gap had narrowed. Faculty members Connie Lawry and Harry Heath were se-lected to report the outcome to Dean Holt. Their reports were made individually.[36]

At first, Dean Holt stated that Nelson would remain as director for the immediate future but that the administration of the school would have regularly scheduled evaluations during the year. He held individual meetings with each faculty member and invited written evaluations on several occasions. After considering the views expressed and allowing time for emotions to cool, Holt, on June 7, 1990, reaffirmed his intention to continue with Nelson as director.[37]

As Nelson reflected upon what had happened he could see many reasons for the stress factors that had played a part in the unrest. The curriculum was changing. The core-courses concept had been approved unanimously, but some faculty apparently harbored resentments about it. A few faculty members had felt thwarted in their desire to advance in the administrative hierarchy. Necessary cutbacks in certain areas were related to the state's economic woes but had added to the discontent.

President Lawrence L. Boger introduces Edwin Newman, the famous NBC newsman and author, to the applause of a crowded room at the dedication of OSU's state-of-the-art Educational Television Services Building in 1983. At left is Marshall Allen, director of ETS since 1967. Newman, calling for better use of the English language, captivated his audience.

With fewer financial problems, faculty salaries could have advanced in a more satisfactory way, but the resources were not there. Added to all of this was the campus-wide uncertainty over the university's new administrative structure.

To make matters worse, Nelson believed there was a "leak" in the dean's office. He had worked out a faculty-promotion schedule, and had discussed it openly with the dean. After he had submitted this confidential information, it had quickly become common knowledge among some journalism and broadcasting faculty. If this had leaked, how was he to know what other confidential information might fuel the fires of discontent?[38]

The year had been an unfortunate one in the history of the School of Journalism and Broadcasting. Nelson had paid heavily in personal stress. The productivity of the faculty as a whole had been adversely affected, too. Although time and effort finally had reduced the polarization of the faculty, it would be a while before the wounds would heal. In the minds of some, they might never heal.

Now it was time for a summing up. Trout and Allen had been careful to use statistical data to keep the higher administration in touch with trends in their programs. Nelson extended this technique through computer technology. Probably no administrator ahead of him had been as adept at supporting the logic of his decisions with data. In meeting with various advisory groups he answered questions with numbers plus his interpretation of what such data meant in terms of his decision-making.

Typical was a report prepared by Nelson for the board of directors of the Oklahoma Association of Broadcasters (OAB) near the close of the centennial year. It might well have served as the manuscript for a "State of the School" message. It was a comprehensive review of the school's development during his administration. A similar report was prepared for the Oklahoma Press Association.

For the year just completed, 419 students had been registered as majors seeking B.A. or B.S. degrees in six options: advertising, broadcast journalism, broadcast production and performance, broadcast sales and management, news-editorial journalism, and public relations. The number of undergraduates receiving baccalaureate degrees in those programs averaged 132 from 1982-83 to 1989-90. Figures for 1989-90 showed a total of 151 graduates with 64 percent in advertising, news-editorial journalism, and public relations, and 36 percent in broadcast journalism, broadcast sales and management, and broadcast production and performance. By options, the figures were fifty-two in advertising (34 percent); twenty-seven in broadcast journalism (18 percent); twenty-four in news-editorial journalism (16 percent); twenty-one in public relations (14 percent); eighteen in broadcast sales and management (12 percent), and nine in broadcast production and performance (6 percent). Twenty-two individuals, including part-time employees, made up the teaching force in 1990. Calculated as the equivalent of full-time teachers, the total was 14.775.

Referring to faculty and student enrichment programs, Nelson reported that students entering the School of Journalism and Broadcasting had garnered their share of scholarship money available in the "honors entrance" category. However, the dollar-value of the scholarships from this source had been limited. He saw a need to expand the scholarship funds available to the school's majors. A limited number of programs for faculty enrichment were in place. Other sources of funding were needed to aid faculty. Through the College of Arts and Sciences Dean's Incentive Grant Program, minimal research proposals for two or three junior faculty members had been funded each year. A number of senior faculty were conducting research or producing either creative or scholarly work as an overload. Because of decreases in state appropriations, faculty workloads had remained heavy in order to serve the large number of majors.

Nelson's report continued on a more optimistic note. During the 1987 fall semester, the school had launched four enrichment campaigns through outside funding.

The first was for a lecture series bringing distinguished journalists to the campus. This developed from a proposal to the Paul Miller family and the Gannett Foundation, creating the Paul and Louise Miller Endowment. The endowment was funded to provide "caretaking" for the OSU library's extensive collection of Miller's papers and memorabilia as well as to enrich various programs offered through the school. As a result, the annual Paul Miller Lecture Series began in 1988.

The second campaign was to increase the Oklahoma Press Association-OSU Print Journalism Endowment Fund to $200,000. The endowment was created in 1984 with a beginning balance of $70,000. During October 1990, the $200,000 goal was reached. Interest from the endowment would be used for scholarships, faculty enrichment programs, and equipment not funded through state appropriations. Five scholarships were set up to honor faculty members who had served the school with distinction during the past fifty years.

The third effort sought an endowed professorship. A proposal presented to the Donald W. Reynolds Foundation was funded in June 1989, creating the Donald W. Reynolds Centennial Professorship in Journalism. Under the grant, the Reynolds Foundation pledged payment of $125,000 over a three-year period. The state pledged $125,000 in matching funds. The centennial professorship will provide funds to bring distinguished reporters and editors to campus for classroom presentations of from two to six weeks as well as for workshops and seminars.

A research and scholarly writing award was the fourth enrichment effort. This award, when fully funded, will be for outstanding work that evaluates the career of Paul Miller, the university's most distinguished journalism alumnus.

Nelson reported that an advisory committee, covering all media specialties had formed. He encouraged the OAB, with the assistance of those on the advisory committee, to establish an endowment fund comparable to that of the press association. The interest earned would be used for broadcasting equipment. Such an endowment would be an investment by the OAB and the school in the future of telecommunications as well as in the career development of promising young broadcasters.

During the centennial year, all of the school's curricula were approved by the Accrediting Council on Education for Journalism and Mass Communication. Suzanne Shaw, executive director, notified OSU that the council in its Chicago meeting May 10 and 11 had unanimously accepted the recommendation of the site team chair and the accrediting committee that the earlier provisional rating be lifted. The school had brought three areas that were "flagged" into full compliance. The accreditation would be effective through 1996. Areas that had been evaluated included curricula, faculty, student records and career counseling, laboratory equipment, operating budget, alumni relations, school governance and faculty input in decision making, affirmative action policies, fiscal resources to attract qualified faculty, quality of instruction, and internships and/or work experience.

The base of the school's academic program still was a core curriculum cutting across print and broadcast lines. Courses required of all students were JB 1393, Mass Media Writing; JB 2393, News Reporting; JB 3163, Law of Mass Communications; JB 3173, History of Mass Communications, and JB 3553, Radio and Television News Writing and Reporting. In addition to the core courses, majors were required to select up to eighteen credit hours in courses in their option area or in areas closely related to the option, for a total of thirty-three hours.

As for liberal arts and sciences requirements, Nelson's report stated that graduates from ACEJMC-accredited programs must complete a minimum of ninety hours in courses outside the School of Journalism and Broadcasting, sixty-five of them in traditional liberal arts and sciences, including general education requirements.

The school's internship program, as Nelson's report to the broadcasters stated, had been cited by numerous organizations as a "model," and most students who complete the work found it easier to obtain their first job and advance more quickly. In its 1990 site visit, the Accrediting Council on Education for Journalism and Mass Communication praised the number, quality, and range of internships available to radio, television, and print students. Approximately 80 percent of the school's graduates had earned internship credits, most within driving distance of the campus. However, in special cases, internships had been filled at network news stations in New York City; at advertising agencies in Dallas and Chicago; at newspapers in Florida, California, Indiana, Missouri, Arkansas, Texas, Nevada, and Washington, D.C.; at consumer magazines in New York City; and at public relations firms and organizations such as the American Heart Association, the International Jaycees, and the U.S. Olympic Committee.

While student internships were widespread geographically, there were in-town opportunities as well. A limited number of students worked at KOSU-FM, housed in the journalism-broadcasting building, as interns and as part-time employees. Educational Television Services, now in a large, modern facility located across campus, was not available for general school instructional purposes, but internships were available for several students each semester, and its staff worked closely with the school in various production programs. KKND, once located on campus as KVRO, accepted students for internships, as did KSPI-AM and KSPI-FM and the *Stillwater NewsPress*.

As the Centennial Decade ended, the school maintained nine laboratory facilities for students. The Macintosh Computer Laboratory was used for news reporting, advertising copy and layout, radio-television advertising, radio-television news reporting, graphics, public relations media writing, and advanced radio and television news. It was equipped with a seventeen-station, networked bank of Apple Macintosh computers with various software. Plans were under way for two more Macintosh laboratories to accommodate all laboratory courses. An older news and editing laboratory included a CompuGraphic One system and was linked with the *Daily O'Collegian* newsroom computer. This gave students in reporting laboratories, as well as *Daily O'Collegian* staff members, an opportunity to see the best of their work in print. Broadcasting laboratories included a television studio for advanced production and broadcasting classes, two radio carrels for radio production classes, and editing consoles for students in television production, television news and related classes. In addition, a newly installed studio was being used in radio news writing and in daily audiocasts over Cable Channel 30, and a photography laboratory with twelve stations was available to students in all curricula. A computer-assisted writing laboratory, established with outside grants, provided computers and software. It was used in all courses within the school for drill and practice on language skills and writing.[39]

It takes many individuals with a diversity of skills to make a professional program work. Important in this sense was Jenkin Lloyd Jones Jr. of the *Tulsa Tribune*, a frequent guest lecturer. Adjunct, part-time, or short-term faculty members from 1982 through 1990 included

Maureen Nemecek, in the People's Republic of China on a 1988 Fulbright-Hays grant, shows her home town newspaper to two young friends. One of her special research interests is international communications.

Larry R. Adkisson, Debra D. Bendler, Jean Devlin, Douglas Drummond, Donald O. Forbes, Stephen M. Neumann, Matt Skinner, Keith M. Swezey, John B. Tiger, Susan E. Tomlinson, Al W. Wiggins, William Willis, Fritz W. Wirt, and L. Douglas White. In addition to his part-time faculty role, Wirt served as general manager of the *Daily O'Collegian*, following the death of Leland Tenney. Also, Forbes directed the student advertising staff. Wirt brought to the campus an outstanding background in executive leadership both in the Harte-Hanks newspaper organization and in the Gannett group. He taught courses in news editing and newspaper management. Forbes, who taught graphic arts and advertising copy and layout, had sharpened his skills in the advertising department of the *Denver Post*. Graduate assistants were used to supervise laboratories as needed and greatly helped to make up for the shortage of faculty.[40]

Since the 1960s, Dorothy Rickstrew Nixon had faithfully maintained scrapbooks covering activities of the school's students, faculty, and staff. As the school grew, these volumes became larger and larger. Not all of this was due to numbers alone. As the school became more widely known, opportunities for leadership increased. Thus, both students and faculty found the doors to leadership and service more open. The scrapbooks spanning the Nelson era present a panorama of success. Throughout the Centennial Decade, many students in the school's various programs had earned prestigious scholarships, national-level awards for their writing and electronic media production, as well as local, regional, and national recognition for their internships.

Faculty honors during the Nelson administration had been frequent and impressive. Paulin had won the Fred Jones Outstanding Teacher Award; Bugeja received the AMOCO Award for outstanding teaching; and Nemecek, winner of a Fulbright-Hays grant to study communications in China, had been named outstanding teacher in the College of Arts and Sciences. In 1987, Lisa John had been named "National Advisor of the Year" by Women in Communications, Incorporated, and had been similarly honored by the Oklahoma City professional chapter for excellence in her field. Earlier she had won the Radio-Television News Directors Association graduate scholarship. In addition, she was the only broadcast journalist to win a national award from the National Federation of Press Women in 1986.

In 1987, Hartley was named "Educator of the Year" in the southwest district of the American Advertising Federation, Rugg was named national "Advisor of the Year" by Alpha Epsilon Rho, repeating the 1978 award won by James Rhea, and Jack Harrison had been given the "Ag Communicator in Education" award by Agricultural College Editors for his work with OSU students. Overstreet's paper on advertising ethics had been judged best in the nation by the International Association of Business Communicators, and Bugeja had continued to add to his honors. In addition to his earlier award as arts and sciences teacher of the year and his successful direction of the Southwestern Cultural Heritage Festival, he had been the grand prize winner in a *Writer's Digest* contest. Before resigning at OSU, he had received a total of twenty teaching and writing awards in five years. In addition, Garner had passed a rigorous examination and was accredited by the Public Relations Society of America. He now had the right to add the letters APR to his signature. Recognition had come to Heath as well. He had won the Beachy Musselman and H. Milt Phillips awards from the Oklahoma Press Association, for distinguished service, and had been named to the Oklahoma Journalism Hall of Fame.

A combination student-adjunct faculty honor had come to Jenifer Reynolds and news director Don Hoover in 1985. Their KOSU-FM program, "Selling the Public Spectrum" won the highly prized duPont-Columbia University broadcast journalism award, the "Pulitzer" of broadcasting.

Among student honors, OSU frequently placed in the Hearst "top twenty" list with outstanding writing by Miles Moffeit, Marla Johnson, Ziva Hobson, Joan Smith, and others. Laura Cupp won the Lowe-Runkle advertising scholarship. Douglas Drummond and Andy Williams captured the E. K. Gaylord Award for in-depth reporting. Amy Hudson was named a D. W. Reynolds Scholar. In regional Alpha Epsilon Rho competition in 1989, OSU won twelve of the twenty-five awards presented. Earlier, a first place award was won for outstanding television production in the southwest regional competition. Typical of the annual honors and awards banquets was the 1983 event in which twenty-seven scholarships and awards were presented. Not typical was the fact that K. C. Moon was recognized four times during the luncheon.

Scholarly output had been meager during the 1980s, as had been true before, but faculty service was at a high level. Hartley was a leader, with frequent workshops and seminars on advertising techniques for small businesses. On a broader scale he reached an international audience through satellite television distribution in the Arts and Sciences Extension advertising-for-business series. Fleming presented a series of public relations workshops for educators, business people, and non-profit groups, then teamed up with Garner for intensive seminars in which Southwestern Bell Telephone community relations managers sharpened their skills. This project was an annual event for four years. The Fleming-Garner team gave additional workshops on planning and managing communication.

Nemecek and Bugeja had presented a six-program television series on "Mass Communication and Social Change" as part of the expanding television outreach of the College of Arts and Sciences. Rugg's "Home Video" workshops were popular, and the summer Urban Journalism

Workshop for minorities, started in 1978, was in its seventh year. The Southwestern Journalism congress had met on the campus under the leadership of Buchholz, and Bugeja, Heath, Reed, and Clark had conducted numerous workshops in cooperation with the Oklahoma Press Association. In addition, Reed, Heath, Overstreet, and Hartley had consulted with state newspapers as "visiting professors."

There were other outreach services by journalism and broadcasting faculty members as well. Overall, it was a commendable showing.

In terms of faculty enrichment, Fleming, John, and Clark attended a Gannett-sponsored teaching workshop in Indiana, and Nemecek, John, and Clark attended seminars at the Poynter Institute, St. Petersburg, Florida. Hartley kept current and sharpened his teaching skills at Marsteller, Incorporated, and at Cunningham and Walsh, both well-known advertising and public relations firms in New York City, during two summers. Schillinger added to her international depth by spending seven weeks in Moscow studying Soviet communications agencies.

In a different way, individual faculty members such as Hartley and Heath enriched their knowledge of journalistic techniques by judging contests involving news and advertising at the request of various groups. Team judging by many faculty members contributed in a positive way to

Gregory Stefaniak *(left)* visits with Kelley and Scott Emigh at the school's golden anniversary celebration in 1987. Journalism became an independent department in 1937. Scott was chapter president of Alpha Epsilon Rho, professional broadcasting society.

relationships nationally with the Donrey Media Group and Scripps-Howard and, on the state scene, with the Oklahoma Collegiate Press Association.

Special events included the annual Addy and Broady awards. The Addy competition recognized creative student work throughout the school, while the Broady awards were limited mainly to broadcasting majors. Journalism and Broadcasting Week often attracted outstanding speakers, as in 1985, when David Lawrence Jr., publisher of the *Detroit Free Press*, and Jenkin Lloyd Jones, publisher of the *Tulsa Tribune*, were among the speakers. Under Rugg's supervision, broadcasting students "took over" Radio Station KSPI one day a year to gain experience in all aspects of local station operation. A unique program brought about by Schillinger's contacts in the Soviet Union led to an exchange of articles by the *Daily O'Collegian* and the Moscow State University *Messenger*.

Perhaps the most important special event of the decade took place in 1987. It was the fiftieth anniversary of the School of Journalism and Broadcasting as an independent academic unit within the College of Arts and Sciences. It was incorporated into homecoming activities.[41]

As the Centennial Decade ended, Marlan D. Nelson could reflect upon eight years filled with promise and disappointment, cooperation and strife, goals fulfilled and goals unreached. He was convinced he had steered the program in a direction that would best meet the needs of students facing vastly different mass media technologies and interrelationships. Certainly it was a period shaped by an electronics revolution far beyond the imaginations of the program's earlier administrators: Edwin R. Barrett, Freeman E. Miller, Noble W. Rockey, William P. Powell, Edmund E. Hadley, Clement E. Trout, C. Ellsworth Chunn, Charles L. Allen, and Harry E. Heath Jr. Nelson would have to rest his case, as had his predecessors, with the often incomplete and sometimes flawed fabrics woven by history.

Endnotes

1. *Stillwater NewsPress*, 29 June 1980, p. 9A.

2. *Oklahoma Observer*, 25 October 1981; Oklahoma State University *Daily O'Collegian*, 24 November 1981, p. 1; *Stillwater NewsPress*, 24 November 1981, p. 1; "Harry E. Heath, Jr., A Profile," *Arts and Sciences Reports*, vol. 1, no. 4 (April 1982), pp. 7, 8; *JB News* (1981-82), pp. 1, 3; *Tulsa Tribune* [February 1982], School of Journalism and Broadcasting Centennial History Collection, Special Collections, Edmon Low Library, Oklahoma State University, Stillwater, Oklahoma; "Harry Heath Steps Down as J/B Director After 15 Years," *Oklahoma State University Outreach*, vol. 53, no. 4 (Summer 1982), p. 25.

3. Oklahoma State University Personnel Action Form of Harry E. Heath Jr., *Director's Letter to the Media* (1982), and Harry E. Heath Jr. to Jone Hawkins, Doris Stokes, Micki Paulin, Dorothy Nixon, and Jennifer Cray, 22 March 1982, in Files of the School of Journalism and Broadcasting, Oklahoma State University; *Stillwater NewsPress*, 12 February 1982, p. 4; Reports of Scott Cutlip, Richard Gray, and Robert Smith to Smith L. Holt (1981), Files of the College of Arts of Sciences, Oklahoma State University.

4. *Stillwater NewsPress*, 29 March 1982, p. 8; Oklahoma State University Personnel Action Form of Marlan D. Nelson, 24 March 1982, approved by regents, 21 April 1982, Files of the School of Journalism and Broadcasting; Author interview with Philip E. Paulin, 28 April 1991, Stillwater, Oklahoma; *JB News* (1981-82), pp. 1, 5.

5. Paulin interview; Edmund B. Lambeth to Philip E. Paulin, 21 July 1982, Files of the School of Journalism and Broadcasting.

6. Oklahoma State University Payroll Action Form of Marlan D. Nelson, 17 August 1982, and Smith L. Holt to Faculty of the School of Journalism and Broadcasting, 2 August 1982, in Files of the School of Journalism and Broadcasting; *Stillwater NewsPress*, 27 June 1982, p. 7B, 12 September 1982, p. 5A; *JB News* (February 1983), pp. 1-3; Paulin interview.

7. Biographical information on Marlan D. Nelson, and Marlan D. Nelson to Charles Fleming, 25 October 1988, in Files of the School of Journalism and Broadcasting. A useful status report covering the School of Journalism and Broadcasting may be found in *Arts and Sciences Reports*, vol. 1, no. 4 (April 1982), pp. 8-11.

8. *Stillwater NewsPress*, 15 December 1982, p. 24; *JB News* (February 1983), p. 1; News Release on Marlan D. Nelson, December 1982, Files of the School of Journalism and Broadcasting; *Oklahoma State News*, 16 December 1985.

9. *JB News* (February 1983), p. 1.

10. *Stillwater NewsPress*, 12 September 1982, p. 16C; *JB News* (February 1983), p. 3; *JB News* (1983-86), p. 27.

11. *JB News* (1981-82), p. 4; *Daily O'Collegian*, 26 September 1981, p. 5.

12. *Stillwater NewsPress*, 12 September 1982, p. 16C; *JB News* (1983-86), p. 27.

13. *Daily O'Collegian*, 17 February 1983, p. 3; Accreditation Report, American Council on Education for Journalism, 16-17 February 1976, and Milton Gross to Robert B. Kamm, 4 May 1976, in Files of the School of Journalism and Broadcasting.

14. *JB News* (February 1983), pp. 1, 2; Author interview with Marlan D. Nelson, 4 June 1991, Stillwater, Oklahoma; *Daily O'Collegian*, 17 June 1983, p. 8; "Paul Miller: His Gift Is a One-of-a-Kind Story of American Journalism," *Oklahoma State University Outreach*, vol. 54, no. 4 (July 1983), p. 20.

15. *JB News* (1983-86), p. 27.

16. Author interview with Marlan D. Nelson, 20 July 1992, Stillwater, Oklahoma; *JB News* (1983-86), p. 17.

17. *Stillwater NewsPress*, 22 July 1984, p. 2; *JB News* (1986), p. 3; *JB News* (1983-86), p. 27.

18. *JB News* (1983-86), p. 27.

19. *Daily O'Collegian*, 26 August 1986, p. 5, 28 August 1986, p. 4; Harry E. Heath Jr. to Board of Directors O'Collegian Publishing Company, 21 August 1986, and Minutes, Board of Directors of O'Collegian Publishing Company, 13 May 1987, in Files of the School of Journalism and Broadcasting; Jana Boler, "The *O'Collegian*. . .Surveying the OSU Community," *Oklahoma State University Outreach*, vol. 58, no. 2 (Winter 1987), p. 21. At this meeting, the board voted to continue the arrangement with the Stillwater Publishing Company to print the paper. An estimated annual saving of $20,273 was projected. Marlan D. Nelson was authorized to represent the company in finding a buyer for the *O'Collegian* press.

20. *Stillwater NewsPress*, 25 September 1991, p. 2, 12 September 1992, p. 2, 22 July 1984, p. 2; *JB News* (1981-82), p. 4; *JB News* (1986), pp. 1, 3, 4, 9, 12; *JB News* (1983-86), p. 27.

21. Charles Fleming to Harry E. Heath Jr., 20 June 1992, School of Journalism and Broadcasting Centennial History Collection.

22. *Stillwater NewsPress*, 2 March 1988, p. 6, 18 March 1988, pp. 1, 3; *Tulsa World*, 6 March 1988, p. 12A; *Daily O'Collegian*, 18 March 1988, pp. 1, 3.

23. *Stillwater NewsPress*, 8 December 1985, p. 2, 12 August 1986, p. 2; *JB News* (1983-86), p. 1; *JB News* (1986), p. 1.

24. *Daily O'Collegian,* 7 December 1985, p. 2, 18 September 1986, p. 2; *Stillwater NewsPress,* 17 September 1986, p. 2, 18 September 1986, p. 2, 26 September 1986, p. 2; *Atchison [Kansas] Daily Globe,* 1 October 1986; *JB News* (1983-86), pp. 22, 25.

25. Thomas Hartley to Harry E. Heath Jr., 22 June 1992, Charles Fleming to Harry E. Heath Jr., 20 June 1992, and Journalism Accreditation Report, American Council on Education for Journalism, 16-17 February 1987, with cover letter from Milton Gross to Robert B. Kamm, 4 May 1976, in Files of the School of Journalism and Broadcasting; Author interview with Marlan D. Nelson, 17 July 1992, Stillwater, Oklahoma.

26. Author interview with Marlan D. Nelson, 4 June 1991, Stillwater, Oklahoma.

27. Author interview with Marlan D. Nelson, 10 June 1991, Stillwater, Oklahoma.

28. *JB News* (February 1983), pp. 1, 2; Nelson interview, 4 June 1991.

29. Marlan D. Nelson, "Report to Oklahoma Association of Broadcasters, 13 May 1991" (covering School of Journalism and Broadcasting data through 1990), Files of the School of Journalism and Broadcasting.

30. Nelson interview, 10 June 1991.

31. Based upon author's participation in the events described.

32. Nelson interview, 10 June 1991.

33. Charles Fleming to Harry E. Heath Jr., 20 June 1992, School of Journalism and Broadcasting Centennial History Collection; *JB News* (1986).

34. *Daily O'Collegian,* 28 September 1989, p. 1, 5 October 1989, p. 1, 17 October 1989, pp. 1, 8, 23 January 1990, p. 1, 24 January 1990, p. 1, 25 January 1990, p. 1, 26-27 January 1990, p. 1, 29 January 1990, p. 1, 15 February 1990, p. 1, 28 February 1990, pp. 1,5; *Stillwater NewsPress,* 13 October 1989, pp. 1, 3.

35. Nelson interview, 10 June 1991.

36. Based upon information supplied by faculty members who attended the two meetings in question. The author also was present at the meetings described.

37. Smith L. Holt to the Faculty of the School of Journalism and Broadcasting, 7 June 1990, Files of the School of Journalism and Broadcasting.

38. Nelson interview, 10 June 1991.

39. Marlan D. Nelson, "Report to Oklahoma Association of Broadcasters, 13 May 1991," Files of the School of Journalism and Broadcasting; *JB News* (1983-86), p. 1; *Daily O'Collegian,* 24 March 1989, p. 10.

40. List of faculty compiled by Joy Stewart from files of the School of Journalism and Broadcasting.

41. Scrapbooks for the years 1982-1990, Files of the School of Journalism and Broadcasting.

Selected Bibliography

COLLECTIONS

Archives, Baylor University, Waco, Texas.

Archives, DePauw University, Greencastle, Indiana.

Archives, Emporia State University. Emporia, Kansas.

Archives, Grinnell College, Grinnell, Iowa.

Archives, Iowa State University, Ames, Iowa.

Archives, Marietta College, Marietta, Ohio.

Archives, Michigan State University, East Lansing, Michigan.

Archives, Ohio State University, Columbus, Ohio.

Archives, Ohio Wesleyan University, Delaware, Ohio.

Archives, Park College, Kansas City, Missouri.

Archives, State Historical Society of Wisconsin, Madison, Wisconsin.

Archives, University of Illinois, Champaign-Urbana, Illinois.

Archives, University of Kansas, Lawrence, Kansas.

Archives, University of Pennsylvania, Philadelphia, Pennsylvania.

Archives, University of Richmond, Richmond, Virginia.

Oklahoma State University Edmon Low Library, Special Collections, Stillwater, Oklahoma:

    Board of Regents for the Oklahoma Agricultural and Mechanical Colleges Minutes.

    Berlin B. Chapman Collection.

Ferdie Deering Collection.

Henry S. Johnston Collection.

Paul Miller Collection

Oklahoma Agricultural and Mechanical College Faculty. "Minutes of the First Faculty, March 17, 1892, to June 2, 1899." Typed manuscript in two volumes.

Oklahoma State Board of Agriculture Minutes.

James Clinton Neal Collection.

President's Papers.

Record Book Committee, compiler. "Selections from the Record Book of the Oklahoma Agricultural and Mechanical College, 1891-1941. Compiled on the Occasion of the Fiftieth Anniversary of the Founding of the College." Vols. 1-2.

School of Journalism and Broadcasting Centennial History Collection.

Angelo C. Scott Collection.

Clement E. Trout Collection.

Oklahoma State University, Public Information Services, Stillwater, Oklahoma:

Files.

Oklahoma State University, School of Journalism and Broadcasting, Stillwater, Oklahoma:

Files.

Sheerar Cultural and Heritage Center, Stillwater, Oklahoma.

Stillwater Public Library, Stillwater, Oklahoma.

NEWSPAPERS

Oklahoma State University Student Newspaper:

Oklahoma A. and M. College Mirror. 1895-1898.

College Paper. 1899-1907.

Brown and Blue. 1908.

Orange and Black. 1908-1924.

O'Collegian. 1924-1927.

Daily O'Collegian. 1927-1992.

Stillwater Daily Press. 1914, 1938-1941.

Stillwater Eagle-Gazette. 1894-1895.

Stillwater Gazette. 1983-1894, 1895-1956.

Stillwater NewsPress. 1941-1992.

Stillwater *Peoples Progress.* 1906-1907.

INTERVIEWS

Author interviews with Marshall Allen, 17 June 1991 and 10 December 1991, Stillwater, OK.

Author interview with James H. "Jimmie" Baker, 21 October 1988, Stillwater OK.

Author interview with Welden Barnes, 19 April 1992, Stillwater OK.

Author interview with Wandalee Basore, 6 July 1984, Stillwater, OK.

Author interview with James R. Bellatti, 3 July 1992, Stillwater, OK.

Author interviews with Raymond Bivert, 8 June 1984 and 25 March 1987, Stillwater, OK.

Author interviews with Ann Trout Blinks, 21 May 1984 and 22 May 1984, Stillwater, OK.

Author interview with Forrest Boaz, July 1989, Stillwater, OK.

Author interview with Alice Church, 21 October 1987, Stillwater, OK.

Author interview with Mrs. Leonard Feinberg [Summer 1963].

Author interview with Glee Miller Garnett, 30 May 1987, Stillwater, OK.

Author interview with Leonard Herron, Jr., 21 October 1987, Stillwater, OK.

Author interview with Raymond Fields, Summer 1975, Wagoner, OK.

Author interview with J. O. Grantham, 25 June 1991, Stillwater, OK.

Author interview with Lemuel D. Groom, 2 June 1989, Stillwater, OK.

Author interview with Muriel Groom, 22 June 1984, Stillwater, OK.

Author interviews with John W. Hamilton, 8 June 1984, 5 January 1987, 20 January 1988,and 21 January 1988, Stillwater, OK.

Author interview with Roy T. Hoke, 15 March 1988, Stillwater, OK.

Author interview with Irvin Hurst, 5 July 1984, Stillwater, OK.

Author interviews with E. E. Johnson, 15 June 1980 and 24 June 1982, Stillwater, OK.

Author interview with Robert B. Kamm, 30 June 1989, Stillwater, OK.

Author interview with Leslie Kreps, 19 July 1989, Stillwater, OK.

Author interviews with Robert P. Ledbetter, 28 August 1991 and 3 July 1992, Oklahoma City, OK.

Author interview with Robert P. Ledbetter, Clovis Bolay, and Gene Allen, 28 August 1991, Oklahoma City, OK.

Author interview with Leon Matthews, 3 July 1992, Stillwater, OK.

Author interview with L. D. Melton, 29 July 1987, Oklahoma City, OK.

Author interview with Sid Miller, 19 October 1988, Stillwater, OK.

Author interview with Baskett P. Mosse [Winter 1957], Deerfield, IL; telephone interview [Fall 1961], Evanston, IL.

Author interview with Pat Musick, 14 July 1991, Stillwater, OK.

Author interviews with Marlan D. Nelson, 4 June 1991, 10 June 1991, 10 December 1991, 17 July 1992 and 20 July 1992, Stillwater, OK.

Author interview with Lorraine Miller Newkirk, 12 May 1987, Stillwater, OK.

Author interview with Dorothy Rickstrew Nixon, 22 June 1984, Stillwater, OK.

Author interview with Philip E. Paulin, 28 April 1991, Stillwater, OK.

Author interview with Randle Perdue, 6 June 1984, Stillwater, OK.

Author interview with Ed Pharr, 9 December 1991, Stillwater, OK.

Author interviews with Haskell Pruett, 26 January 1985, 21 October 1987 and 22 October 1987, Stillwater, OK.

Author interview with Earl Richert, 10 November 1984, Stillwater, OK.

Author interview with David Seaton, October 1988.

Author interview with James M. Springer Jr., 2 August 1984, Stillwater, OK.

Author interview with Sid Steen, 24 March 1981, Stillwater, OK.

Author interview with Malvina Stephenson, 31 May 1991, Tulsa, OK.

Author interview with Walker Stone, 13 May 1972, Stillwater, OK.

Author interview with James C. Stratton, 28 May 1984, Stillwater, OK.

Author interview with Elizabeth Oursler Taylor, 23 October 1987, Stillwater, OK.

Author interview with Elmer Woodson, 11 December 1991, Stillwater, OK.

Author interview with Leon York, 24 July 1984, Stillwater, OK.

Wandalee Basore interview with Bernadine Brock, 6 July 1984, School of Journalism and Broadcasting Centennial History Collection.

THESES AND DISSERTATIONS

Anderson, Vera Kathryn Stevens. "A History of the *Daily O'Collegian*, Student Newspaper of Oklahoma A. and M. College: 1924-1934." Master of Science thesis, Oklahoma State University, 1975.

Bond, Gregg S. "1961-1962, Job Census of Men and Women on Daily and Weekly Newspapers in Oklahoma." Master of Science thesis, Oklahoma State University, 1962.

Butts, James A. "A Job Census of Oklahoma State University Journalism Graduates." Master of Science thesis, Oklahoma State University, 1962.

Flanders, Henry J. "A Newspaper Is Born: The Genesis of the Stillwater News-Press." Master of Science thesis, Oklahoma State University, 1982.

Gilmore, Francis Richard. "A Historical Study of the Oklahoma Agricultural Experiment Station." Doctor of Education dissertation, Oklahoma State University, 1967.

Goodwin, Loretta. "The Origin and Development of Journalism Education at Iowa State University." Master of Science thesis, Iowa State University, 1984.

Lindsay, Leon William. "A Biography of David R. McAnally Jr." Master of Arts thesis, University of Missouri, 1956.

Wagner, Nancy Jane. "A History of the University School of Journalism: The First Fifty Years, 1913-1963." Master of Arts thesis, University of Oklahoma, 1964.

Wilbanks, Floy Farrar. "The Life and Work of Dr. Bradford Knapp." Master of Arts thesis, Texas Technological College, 1940.

BOOKS

Beal, William J. *History of the Michigan Agricultural College*. East Lansing: Michigan Agricultural College, 1915.

Beckman, Frederick W.; O'Brien, Harry R.; and Converse, Blair. *Technical Journalism*. Ames: Iowa State College Press, 1942.

Brill, H. E. *The Story of Oklahoma City University and Its Predecessors*. Oklahoma City: Oklahoma City University Press, 1938.

Carter, L. Edward. *The Story of Oklahoma Newspapers*. Muskogee, OK: Western Heritage Books Incorporated, 1984.

Chapman, Berlin B. *The Founding of Stillwater: A Case Study in Oklahoma History*. Oklahoma City, OK: Times Journal Publishing Company, 1948.

Cunningham, Robert E. *Stillwater Through the Years*. Stillwater, OK: Arts and Humanities Council of Stillwater, Oklahoma, Incorporated, 1974.

Cunningham, Robert E. *Stillwater: Where Oklahoma Began*. Stillwater, OK: Arts and Humanities Council of Stillwater, Oklahoma, Incorporated, 1969.

Dellinger, Doris. *A History of the Oklahoma State University Intercollegiate Athletics*. Stillwater: Oklahoma State University, 1987.

Dusch, Willa Adams. *The Sigma Literary Society, 1893-1897: A Chapter in the History of the Oklahoma A. and M. College*. Edited by Berlin B. Chapman. Stillwater: Oklahoma A. and M. College, 1951.

Emery, Edwin and McKerns, Joseph P. *ACEJMC: 75 Years in the Making*. Columbia, SC: Accrediting Council for Education in Journalism and Mass Communication, 1987.

Emery, Edwin and Smith, Henry Ladd. *The Press and America*. New York, NY: Prentice Hall, incorporated, 1954.

Fischer, LeRoy H. *Oklahoma State University Historic Old Central*. Stillwater: Oklahoma State University, 1988.

Fischer, LeRoy H., editor. *Oklahoma's Governors, 1907- 1929: Turbulent Politics*. Oklahoma City, OK: Oklahoma Historical Society, 1981.

Fite, Robert C. *A History of Oklahoma State University Extension and Outreach*. Stillwater: Oklahoma State University, 1988.

Foreman, Carolyn Thomas. *Oklahoma Imprints*. Norman: University of Oklahoma Press, 1936.

Foreman, Grant. *A History of Oklahoma*. Norman: University of Oklahoma Press, 1942.

Green, Donald E. *A History of the Oklahoma State University Division of Agriculture*. Stillwater: Oklahoma State University, 1990.

Lindley, William R. *Journalism and Higher Education: The Search for Academic Purpose*. Stillwater, OK: Journalistic Services, 1975.

Marable, Mary Hays and Boylan, Elaine. *A Handbook of Oklahoma Writers*. Norman: University of Oklahoma Press, 1939.

Mott, Frank Luther. *American Journalism*, third edition. New York, NY: The Macmillan Company, 1962.

Murphy, Patrick M. *A History of Oklahoma State University Student Life and Services*. Stillwater: Oklahoma State University, 1988.

Newsom, D. Earl. *A Pictorial History of Stillwater, One Hundred Years of Memories*. Norfolk, VA: The Donning Company, 1989.

O'Dell, DeForest. *The History of Journalism Education in the United States*. New York, NY: Teachers College, Columbia University, 1935.

Oklahoma A. and M. College Catalog and Announcements, 1891-1957.

Oklahoma State University Catalogs, 1958-1991.

Redskin. Oklahoma State University Yearbook, 1910-1991.

Rulon, Philip Reed. *Oklahoma State University—Since 1890*. Stillwater: Oklahoma State University, 1975.

Scott, Angelo C. *A Boyhood in Old Carlyle*. Iola, KS: Iola Register Press, 1940.

Scott, Angelo C. *The Story of an Administration of the Oklahoma A. and M. College*. Oklahoma City, OK: no publisher, 1942.

Scott, Charles F. and Duncan, L. Wallace. *History of Allen and Woodson Counties*. Iola, KS: Allen County Historical Society, 1901.

Technical Journalism at Iowa State College 1905-1955. Ames: Department of Technical Journalism, Iowa State College, 1955.

Thoburn, J. B. *A Standard History of Oklahoma*. Chicago and New York: The American Historical Society, 1916.

Thoburn, J. B. and Sharp, John Winthrop. *History of the Oklahoma Press and the Oklahoma Press Association*. Oklahoma City, OK: Industrial Printing Company, 1930.

Turnbull, George S. *Journalists in the Making*. Eugene, OR: The School of Journalism, University of Oregon, 1965.

ARTICLES

Adams, J. Homer. "In Retrospect and Prospect." *Oklahoma A. and M. College Magazine*, vol. 13, no. 4 (January 1942), pp. 8, 15.

Adams, J. Homer. "When the College Was Young." *Oklahoma A. and M. College Magazine*, vol. 1, no. 4 (December 1929), pp. 9, 21.

Bivert, Raymond E. "Another Enterprise Goes Over." *Oklahoma A. and M. College Magazine*, vol. 1, no. 2 (October 1929), p. 20.

Braley, Genevieve. "Classes Resume in Old Central." *Oklahoma A. and M. College Magazine*, vol. 1, no. 8 (April 1930), p. 5.

"Breaking Ground for New J-B Building." *Oklahoma State University Outreach*, vol. 15, no. 6 (June-July 1974), p. 31.

Chapman, Berlin B. "Author Discovered by A. C. Scott." *Oklahoma A. and M. College Magazine*, vol. 17, no. 6 (March 1945), pp. 3, 4, 13, 14.

Chapman, Berlin B. "Literary Records Preserved in Library." *Oklahoma A. and M. College Magazine*, vol. 17, no. 7 (April 1945), pp. 4, 13.

Chapman, Berlin B. "The Neal Family and the Founding of the Oklahoma A. and M. College." *Chronicles of Oklahoma*, vol. 68, no. 4 (Winter 1990-1991), pp. 349-369.

"China: The Door Opens Wider." *Oklahoma State Alumnus Magazine*, vol. 13, no. 9 (December 1972), pp. 3-6.

"Communications Seeks Expansion." *Oklahoma State Alumnus Magazine,* vol. 13, no. 1 (September-October 1972), p. 11.

"E. J. Westbrook Retires." *Oklahoma A. and M. College Magazine*, vol. 17, no. 6 (March 1945), pp. 1, 4.

Emerson, Bonnie E. "Democracy in Action on Campus." *Oklahoma A. and M. College Magazine*, vol. 16, no. 9 (April 1944), pp. 3, 8, 15.

"Harry Heath Steps Down as J/B Director after 15 Years." *Oklahoma State University Outreach*, vol. 53, no. 4 (Summer 1982), p. 25.

Hastings, James K. "Oklahoma A. and M. College and Old Central." *Chronicles of Oklahoma*, vol. 28, no. 1 (Spring 1950), pp. 81-84.

Hazen, W. B. "Some Corrections of 'Life on the Plains.'" *Chronicles of Oklahoma*, vol. 3, no. 4 (December 1925), pp. 295-318.

Highland, James L. "Field Trips Help J-Students at Oklahoma State University." *Quill*, vol. 57, no. 3 (March 1969), p. 26.

Holter, George L. "When the School Was Young." *Oklahoma A. and M. College Magazine*, vol. 1, no. 3 (November 1929), pp. 12, 31.

Johnson, Helen E. "Old Central Has New Lease on Life." *Oklahoma A. and M. College Magazine*, vol. 1, no. 1 (September 1929), p. 9.

"Journalism Department Nationally Recognized." *Oklahoma A. and M. College Magazine*, vol. 20, no. 1 (October 1948), p. 19.

Little, Blanche. "The Oklahoma A. and M. College." *The School Journal*, vol. 74, no. 2 (1907), p. 664.

Miller, Freeman E. "Founding the College Library." *Oklahoma A. and M. College Magazine*, vol. 1, no. 3 (November 1929), pp. 18, 19, 27.

Nettleton, Kay. "Vingie Roe." *Oklahoma State University Outreach*, vol. 52, no. 2 (December 1980), p. 17.

"A New Dean for Arts and Sciences." *Oklahoma State University Magazine*, vol. 2, no. 3 (September 1958), p. 7.

"New Department of Information and Service Formed This Month." *Oklahoma A. and M. College Magazine*, vol. 1, no. 6 (February 1930), p. 21.

Northup, Frank D. "First Consolidated School Law in the United States." *Chronicles of Oklahoma*, vol. 27, no. 2 (Summer 1949), pp. 162-169.

Northup, Frank D. "An Incident in the Early History of Dewey County." *Chronicles of Oklahoma*, vol. 3, no. 4 (December 1925), pp. 289-294.

Perdue, Randle. "That Man Bennett." *Oklahoma A. and M. College Magazine*, vol. 1, no. 1 (September 1929), pp. 8, 29.

Reggio, Michael H. "Troubled Times: Homesteading in Short Grass Country, 1892-1900." *Chronicles of Oklahoma*, vol. 57, no. 2 (Summer 1979), pp. 196-211.

Roe, Vingie E. "Former Aggie Is Famous Writer." *Oklahoma A. and M. College Magazine*, vol. 1, no. 3 (November 1929), pp. 8, 9.

"A Venture into Radio's Educational Broadcasting." *Oklahoma State University Magazine*, vol. 2, no. 11 (May 1959), pp. 16, 17.

Index

Brusewitz, Gerald H.: 505.
Bryan, William Jennings: 266.
Bryant, Ray: 174.
Buchholz, Michael O.: 490, 491, 517, 542.
Bugeja, Michael J.: 503, 504, 517, 521, 540-542.
Bullen, Harry B.: 185.
Burchard, Donald D.: 150, 301, 307-310, 312, 314-316, 345, 360, 366, 458.
Bureau of Information and Service: 247, 281.
Burke, J. J.: 63.
Burks, Garnett: 34.
Burnett, Claron: 348-350, 352, 354-356, 361-363.
Burnett, Whittier: 240, 260.
Burright, Ivy: 218.
Burris, Edward: 237, 385, 478, 480.
Bushnell, C. J.: 107.
Business Journalism: 272, 299, 310, 312.
Butler, Glenn: 457, 458, 460-462.
Butts, James A.: 456.
Byrd, Bill: 337.

C

Caldwell, James H.: 232.
Caldwell, Mable: 126, 211, 214, 217, 219, 232, 240, 260, 272, 274, 275, 277, 280, 291.
Caldwell, Richard M.: 314, 338, 339, 346, 358.
Callahan-Patterson, Dorothy: 291.
Callaway, Bob: 431.
Calvert, Wesley: 458-460.
Campbell, C. B.: 166.
Campbell, Jeff: 173.
Campbell, Jim: 470.
Campbell, John R.: 530.
Campbell, Kellis: 70.
Canfield, Jesse J.: 133.
Cantwell, James W.: 144, 145, 157, 158, 161, 163, 166-169, 172, 180, 181, 185, 200-202, 204, 214, 279.
Cantwell, Mrs. James W.: 144.
Capper, Arthur: 87, 88.
Carlile, Foreman: 291.
Carlisle, Holmes B. "Brad": 314, 326, 337.
Carlson, Avery L.: 147, 148, 151.
Carlson, W. E.: 251.
Carlton, Oscar: 174.
Carlyle, Katherine: 161.
Carter, L. Edward: 471, 478-480, 504.
Casad, Gordon: 311.
Casey, George: 327.
Casey, John: 317-319.
Casey, Ralph: 472.
Cash, Idress: 420.

Castile, Eric L.: 173.
Castleberry, Steve: 503.
Cates, Eldon: 327.
Catsis, John: 530.
Caudell, Andrew: 52.
Chafin, Robert C.: 143.
Chamberlain, Ernest: 221, 225, 226, 253.
Chapman, Berlin B.: 89, 277.
Chase, Ward: 205.
Chegwin, Richard: 431.
Chemistry Building. *See* Communications Building.
Chemistry-Physics Building. *See* Physical Sciences Building.
Chester, K. Starr: 338.
Chick, Calvin: 350.
Chilton, J. S.: 163, 164.
Chunn, C. Ellsworth: 325, 358, 362, 381-406 423-425, 435, 436, 439, 456, 466, 470, 476, 477, 526, 528, 543.
Chunn, Florence Jenkins: 382, 383, 392, 393, 395.
Chunn, Sylvester: 393.
Church, Alice Van Meesel: 286.
Church, George F.: 283-288, 299-302, 305, 339, 356, 358, 361, 382, 498.
Church, Jane N.: 285.
Churchill, Winston: 443.
Clair, Doreen Cronkite: 396, 397, 402.
Clark, Edward F.: 14, 15, 22, 41.
Clark, Frank J.: 72.
Clark, Terry M.: 521, 530, 542.
Clark, Velma B.: 291.
Clay, John: 115.
Cleveland, Grover: 36.
Clutter, Mark A.: 350.
Colburn, John H.: 492.
Cole, Ira W. "Bill": 359, 361, 436.
College Building. *See* Old Central.
College Paper: 64, 65, 71, 73, 83-86, 99, 160.
College Press Bureau: 24, 32, 38, 39, 45, 47, 51, 53, 63, 64, 164.
Commerce Journalism. *See* Business Journalism.
Communications Building: 192, 385, 386, 389, 391, 392, 394, 395, 397, 402, 424, 426, 428, 430, 432, 448, 451, 452, 464, 477, 496, 499, 500-502, 504, 506. *See also* Paul Miller Journalism and Broadcasting Building.
Connell, John H.: 73, 81, 95-99, 101-107, 110, 111, 119, 120, 137, 143, 157.
Conner, W. A.: 268.
Connor, George: 236.
Connors, John P.: 99, 105.
Converse, Blair: 135.
Conway, Cleve: 470.

Cook, I. L.: 318.
Cooke, Warren: 311.
Copeland, Fayette: 368, 445.
Copple, Neale: 492, 502.
Cordell, Harry B.: 277.
Corser, Noel: 387.
Couey, Paul: 506, 517.
Covington, Jess: 360, 361.
Cowan, Kay: 327.
Cowell, Karen: 431.
Cox, Claire: 311.
Cox, Kenneth: 525, 526.
Cox, Robert L.: 478.
Coyne, Pete: 220, 221.
Crabtree, Beverly: 528.
Craig, John A.: 3, 11, 97, 98, 105, 112, 115, 119, 120, 126, 269-271.
Crain, George: 290.
Crane, William: 517.
Cranshaw, J. David: 495, 496.
Crews, Frank: 285.
Crist, David O.: 291.
Crossman, Ralph: 334.
Crout, Vernon: 501.
Cruce, Lee: 89.
Cumming, William K.: 362.
Cummings, Anita: 311.
Cunningham, Pauline: 396.
Cunningham, Robert E.: 248, 291, 327.
Cupp, Laura: 541.
Curry, Virgil D.: 261, 327.
Curtin, Gerald T.: 367, 368, 379-381, 391, 395.
Cutlip, Scott: 512.

D

Daily O'Collegian: 102, 242, 243, 273, 278, 290, 379, 477-480, 503, 521, 539.
Dairy Building: 301.
Darlow, Albert E.: 382.
Darlow, Margaret: 240.
Darnell, Lewis J.: 14.
Davis, Arthur J.: 185.
Davis, Elmer: 443.
Davis, Loa Le: 327.
Davis, P. J.: 103.
Day, Anita: 494.
Dean, John: 129.
Debate and Oratory Club: 26.
Deering, Ferdie J.: 304.
DeFelice, Peter: 349.
DeLancey, Blaine: 280.
DeMarco, Norman: 416, 423.
DeMarco, Susan: 422.
DeMoss, William F.: 260, 261, 264, 270, 277, 287.

DeMotte, Grace Marion: 260.
DeMotte, N. S.: 291, 298, 327.
Department of Printing: established, 83.
Deskin, Jack W.: 431, 432, 495.
Devlin, Jean: 540.
Dewey, Thomas E.: 252.
DeWitt, Dorothy: 411.
"Dick Tracy": 199.
Dimery, Robert: 474, 503.
Dixon, Theron: 431.
Dobie, J. Frank: 223, 229, 245, 246, 259, 260, 270.
Dobie, Bertha: 246.
Dobson, Ed: 431.
Donald W. Reynolds Centennial Professorship in Journalism: 537.
Donald W. Reynolds Foundation: 537.
Donart, Clarence R.: 21, 52.
Doniphin, Virginia: 290.
Dougan, Mike: 503.
Dowell, Carr T.: 264, 272.
Drake, Eldon M.: 363.
Drew, Dorothy: 311.
Drewry, John E.: 393.
Drimmer, Evelyn: 315, 320.
Drummond, Douglas: 540, 541.
Dulles, John Foster: 471.
Duncan, Hall: 337.
Dungan, Lyle C.: 290, 291.
Dunham Ruth E.: 291.
Dunlavy, George Washington: 190.
Dunn, Jesse J.: 157.
Durham, Chad C.: 291.
Durham, Norman N.: 478.
Durst, Leon H.: 289, 477.
Duryea, Dan: 415.
Dyer, Ray J.: 89.
Dyke, Ronald W.: 471, 481, 482.
DynaScope: 446, 463-465.

E

Earthquake: 128, 165, 239.
Eby, Gerald: 348.
"Ed Hadley Day": 252-254.
Eddins, Marsha: 438.
Educational Television Services: 477, 495, 535, 538.
EFC Debating Club: 17.
Ehmen, Richard: 506.
Eide, Richard B.: 320-325, 334-338, 340, 346, 348-350.
Eisenhower, Dwight D.: 252.
Eliot, Charles W.: 8.
Ellard, Roscoe B.: 300.
Ellerbach, John R.: 521, 522.

Elliott, Lois: 315, 320.
Ellis, Arthur: 174.
Ellis, Curtis: 291, 327.
Elsner, John: 431.
Emerson, Bonnie: 311.
Emigh, Kelley: 542.
Emigh, Scott: 542.
Engineering Building (1902): 160, 272.
Engineering Building (1912). *See* Gundersen
  Hall.
Engler, Bill: 431.
English, Earl: 336, 342, 343, 345.
English, W. L.: 97.
Ensworth, Harriet R.: 216, 219.
Eskridge, James B.: 200, 202-204, 207, 212,
  214-218, 220-222, 225.
Ewing, Amos A.: 14.
Ewing, George: 327.

F

Farmer-Labor Reconstruction League: 220,
  225, 253.
Feather, William H.: 291, 327.
Ferguson, D. Jo: 488, 500.
Ferguson, J. O.: 409.
Ferguson, Ted: 417.
Ferrer, Jose: 415.
Fiegle, Al: 506.
Fields, Carmen: 494.
Fields, Carol Emmerson: 86.
Fields, Ernie: 494.
Fields, Gus: 248.
Fields, John: 64, 66, 85-92, 95, 96, 106.
Fields, Raymond: 232, 251.
Files, Jim: 492, 506.
Finnell, H. H.: 174.
Fisher, Benjamin A.: 411.
Fitzgerald, Clee: 488.
Flanagan, Michael: 430.
Fleming, Charles F.: 515, 516, 522, 541, 542.
Fletcher, Carol: 494.
Flournoy, Bob: 506.
Flynt, Elmo: 239.
Forbes, Donald O.: 540.
Ford, Francis: 262.
Ford, John: 262.
Fordice, Philip: 327.
Forkert, Otto: 366.
Fourth Estate: 304.
Fox, Adeline: 303.
Frazier, Chester J.: 314, 351.
Freudenberger, Helen: 291, 301, 303, 304,
  327.
Frost, Robert: 213.
Frye, E. Moses: 488.

G

Gallagher, Edward C.: 129, 160.
Gannett: 230, 247, 252, 502.
Gannett Foundation: 501, 536.
Gannett Newspapers: 542.
Garets, Wallace E.: 492.
Garner, Brooks: 515, 519, 522, 541.
Garraway, Dave: 470.
Gault, Frank M.: 158, 161, 163, 164, 166,
  169, 172, 200.
Gelder, George B.: 86, 87, 92, 99, 165.
George, Robert B.: 410.
Getzloe, Bertha Matthews: 196.
Getzloe, Lester C.: 186, 194-198, 200, 201,
  204-206, 211, 214, 215, 217, 219, 226,
  259, 260, 270, 271.
Getzloe, Margaret Stribling: 197.
Getzloe, W. J.: 196.
Gierhart, Ray "Gabe": 236, 248, 327.
Gilbert, Norris T.: 47.
Gilkeson, Raymond H.: 366.
Gillespie, Robert S.: 366, 370.
Gillespie, Vera Wood: 325, 334, 335, 340.
Gilstrap, Lee: 182.
Gish, Dorothy: 415.
Glafcke, W. Robert: 491, 492.
Glazier, Henry E.: 24, 25, 43, 44.
Gloeckner, Gus: 174.
Goddard, Mary: 305.
Gordon, John: 318.
Gore, Thomas: 185.
Gould, Chester: 199, 216.
Graham, H. A.: 413.
Graves, Lloyd M.: 145, 146, 148.
Gray, J. T.: 156, 170, 173, 176.
Gray, Lee: 474.
Gray, Richard: 512.
Gray, Ruth: 156.
Green, George H. C.: 200.
Green, John H.: 416.
Green, W. J.: 203.
Greer, Frank Hilton: 61, 87.
Gries, George A.: 432, 485, 486, 488, 491,
  495, 499, 500, 503, 504, 511, 523, 530.
Griffin, Joe: 285, 327.
Griffith, John L.: 461, 462.
Griswold, Marquetta: 335, 337.
Groom, Lemuel D.: 150, 316-319, 325, 334-
  337, 346, 358, 367, 382, 399, 406, 435,
  444, 447, 451, 452, 471, 480, 506.
Groom, Margaret Callaway: 316.
Groom, Muriel: 318, 419, 420.
Groom, Oscar Downing: 316.
Gula, Joanne: 516, 517.
Gundersen, Carl: 108.
Gundersen Hall: 116, 117, 127, 159, 160,
  218, 233, 301.

Guthrey, E. Bee: 33.
Guthrey, Patrick H.: 33.

H

Haag, Maurice R.: 363, 364, 367, 382, 394,
    399, 406, 435, 436, 444, 445, 447, 448,
    451, 459, 498, 528.
Hackett, Neil: 534.
Hadley, Don: 231.
Hadley, Edmund E.: 179, 223, 225-254, 259-
    261, 267, 270, 271, 278, 284, 302, 414,
    543.
Hadley, Elam J.: 227.
Hadley, Josef: 228.
Hadley, Marguerite Feys: 228, 251, 254.
Hadley, Minnie Boyd: 227.
Halbrook, James M.: 20.
Hall, Homer G.: 188, 189, 205.
Hall, Paula: 493.
Halliburton, Richard: 213.
Hamilton, Fearn Bernard: 159, 163, 184,
    188, 195, 205.
Hamilton, Hays: 159.
Hamilton, John W.: 313-315, 320, 327, 338,
    339, 345, 346, 351, 352, 355, 356, 358.
Hamilton, Ralph: 136.
Hansen, Walter W.: 382, 405.
Harbour, D. L.: 327.
Harding, Roy: 318.
Harmon, William: 349, 455, 482, 486, 505.
Harnden, M. G.: 167.
Harper, Marilyn: 417.
Harrison, B. F.: 174.
Harrison, Benjamin: 13, 61.
Harrison, Jack: 503, 540.
Hart, M. Blair: 423.
Hartenbower, A. J.: 170, 173.
Hartley, Thomas R.: 516-518, 522, 540-542.
Hartman, Carol: 304.
Hartman, Elmer L.: 304.
Hartman, Thomas J.: 36, 52.
Hartman, Virginia Pope: 291, 301-303, 327,
    338.
Harvest Carnival: 128, 129, 161, 165, 234.
Harvey, Dorothy: 150, 350.
Harvey, J. Edwin: 322, 327.
Haskell, Charles N.: 156.
Hawkins, Louis: 363.
Hayes, Phil: 174.
Heath, Harry E. Jr.: 325, 456-459, 461, 462,
    465, 469-507, 511, 512, 515-519, 522,
    524, 525, 527-531, 534, 541-543.
Hefton, Mac: 337.
Heggen, Thomas: 327.
Heiser, Margaret E.: 292.
Henderson, Eugene: 311.

Henry, John: 506, 518, 526.
Henthorne, A. J.: 86.
Henthorne, Bill: 398.
Herbert, H. H.: 195, 288, 319.
Herron, Leonard: 327.
Hert, R. L.: 501.
Hester, Russell: 327.
Heuser, Oscar: 506.
Heydenburk, Bruce: 150, 337.
Hickham, John P.: 156, 169.
Highland, James L.: 471, 481, 483-490, 493.
Hilgenbert, L. W.: 203.
Hill, George: 367.
Hilton, James: 471.
Hinkel, John P.: 69.
Hinkle, Wandalee: 337, 360.
Hinson, Marcus: 205.
Hix, Harry: 399, 400, 458-460, 471, 529.
Hixson, Ephraim: 415.
Hobson, Ziva: 541.
Hodges, Joe: 311.
Hoffman, Paul: 342.
Hogg, James S.: 32, 33.
Hoggard, Paul: 174.
Hoke, Jess: 203, 218.
Hoke, Roy T.: 169, 173, 174.
Holley, J. Andrew: 384, 386, 400.
Holt, James: 511.
Holt, Smith L.: 507, 511-513, 523, 524, 530,
    533.
Holter, George L.: 16, 18, 19, 24, 25, 37, 46,
    104, 105.
Holton, Alice: 311.
Holtzclaw, Henry F.: 146.
Home Economics East: 233, 301.
Home Economics Journalism: 214, 215, 232,
    240, 270, 271, 274, 275, 299, 302, 310,
    312, 499, 528.
Hoover, Don: 506, 541.
Hoover, Sam: 290.
Hopkins, Andrew W.: 263, 272, 282.
Hopkins, Mark: 204.
Horner, Patsy: 326.
Hostetter, Helen: 366.
House, Ada Belle: 103.
House, H. C.: 53.
Houser, David: 477.
Houston, Temple: 31.
Howard, Ivy Milton: 291.
Howard, Peggy: 311.
Howard, Ruth: 297, 312.
Hubbard, Harold: 253.
Huddleston, Tom: 495.
Hudson, Amy: 541.
Hughes, Sylvester F.: 291, 327.
Humphrey, Hubert: 484.
Humphrey, Manly: 290.
Hunt, DeWitt: 194.

Huntley, Chet: 465.
Hurst, Dick: 205.
Hurst, Irvin: 231, 233-238, 247, 248, 260, 261, 269, 327.
Husted, Orval C.: 327.
Hutto, Frank: 19, 35, 36.
Hutto, Maggie: 18, 37.
Hutto, Myrtle May. *See* Myrtle May Hutto Northup.
Hutto, Willis W.: 15, 16, 19, 20, 36, 37, 38.

I

Iba, Henry: 191.
Industrial Arts Building: 418.
Industrial Editors Short Course: 336, 345, 351, 354, 362, 364, 365, 366, 370, 476.
Inglis, Charles: 351.
Ingram, Martha: 413.
International Council of Industrial Editors: 336, 341, 342, 344, 354, 361, 365, 368, 369, 395.
Iota Beta Sigma: 431.
Iorio, Sharon Hartin: 520.

J

Jackson, William: 522, 523, 527.
Jacobs, Emery: 327.
Jagger, Dean: 415.
Janensch, Paul: 517.
Jardot, Louis J.: 35, 36.
Jenkins, Carl: 327.
Jennings, J. L.: 500.
Jewett, F. E.: 309.
John, Lisa: 519, 522, 529, 531, 540, 542.
Johnson, David P.: 292, 327.
Johnson, E. E.: 285, 290, 327.
Johnson, Harry E.: 173.
Johnson, Joseph F.: 7, 8.
Johnson, Marla: 541.
Johnson, Robert M.: 402, 404, 422-425.
Johnston, Ethelyn Genevieve Thorne: 101, 102, 108-110.
Johnston, Henry S.: 99, 101, 104.
Johnston, Jennie May Lodge: 100.
Johnston, Matthew: 100.
Johnston, Ovonual: 445.
Johnston, William W.: 99-112, 116, 119, 120, 122, 184, 186.
Jones, Esther Rockey: 3, 206.
Jones, Ewing: 248.
Jones, Fred L.: 167.
Jones, Jay: 430.
Jones, Jenkin Lloyd: 398, 543.
Jones, Jenkin Lloyd Jr.: 539
Jones, Nik: 430.

Jones, Randall J.: 382, 498.
Jones, W. R.: 169.
Jordan, Robert: 493.
Jorgenson, Elaine: 528.
Journalism: first classroom instruction, 65, 66; recognized as full-term course, 97; first rudimentary curriculum, 119-121; become part of departmental name, 229, 230; first degrees awarded in journalism, 284; as a separate academic unit, 299; lower division courses first offered, 302, 303; offers first degree in nation in industrial editing, 316; first Ph.D. on faculty, 320, 321; graduate work offered, 336, 342; first accreditation, 340-342; formation of School of Communications, 384; Chunn named first director in communication area, 399.
Journalism Building. *See* Communications Building.
Journalist's Bulletin: 345.
Journalism Club: 165, 167.
Journalism Day: 252, 406, 476, 515, 517, 518.

K

Kahle, Frances: 240.
Kaltenborn, H. V.: 470.
KAMC: 414, 422, 424.
Kamm, Robert B.: 312, 371, 383, 396, 398, 401, 403-406, 432, 435-440, 445-448, 451-455, 464, 477, 480, 484, 495, 500, 501, 503, 505.
Keller, Floyd: 174.
Kelsey, S. H.: 44.
Kennedy, John F.: 226.
Kennedy, Joe: 303.
Kern, Weldon: 311.
Khrushchev, Nikita: 252.
Kidd, Wallace: 327.
Kilgore, Helen: 311.
King, Ben: 363.
King, Charles: 311.
King, Ferne: 221.
Kinter, C. V.: 308.
Kirby, Durward: 470.
KKND: 538.
Klemme, Randall T.: 353, 356.
Klock, Roger: 474.
Klopfenstein, Milo R.: 292.
Knapp, Bradford: 207, 222, 226, 228, 231, 233-235, 239-246, 248-251, 253, 254, 261, 262, 264-272, 274, 276, 278, 410, 411.
Knapp, Herman: 264, 265.
Knapp, Marion: 240, 269.

Knapp, Minnie: 264.
Knapp, Seaman: 264, 265.
Knapp, Stella White Davis: 266.
Knaub, Patricia: 528.
Knearl, Cora Belle: 327.
Knipe, William A.: 43.
Knox, David: 327.
Kolch, Frederick L.: 506, 518.
Kosik, Frederick: 399, 401, 506.
Kositzky, James C.: 409, 410, 432.
KOSU: 425, 427, 428, 430-432, 464, 477, 496, 497, 503, 505, 506, 538, 541.
Kramer, Mary E. *See* Mary E. Mustain.
Kreps, Leslie: 399, 401, 403, 404, 425, 426, 447, 454, 477.
Krisher, Sherman: 174.
Krug, Alan: 457.
KSPI: 419, 420, 423, 538, 543.
Kulinski, Jerry: 432.
Kurtz, Edwin: 410.
KVOO: 411, 415, 419, 430.
KVRO: 416, 417, 419-421, 424, 426-429, 431, 432, 464, 477, 503, 506, 538.
Kygar, Jean: 463.

L

Lacy, Robert P.: 426-432, 454, 464, 477, 494, 495.
Ladwig, Charles T. "Tom": 492, 506.
Lahman, W. L.: 101, 102.
Lancaster, Jack: 518, 533.
Landon, Alf M.: 282, 283.
Lane, Frank L.: 398.
Lane, Ken: 495.
Lansden, Willis A.: 292.
Larason, Ann: 438.
Larason, Mahala P.: 260.
Lashbrook, Ralph: 277, 341, 343.
Lawrence, David Jr.: 543.
Lawrence, James F.: 68.
Lawry, Connie: 534.
Layne, J. P.: 14.
Leahy, W. T.: 110, 111.
Leake, H. H.: 340, 413, 414, 419.
Leatherock, Wesley: 340.
Ledbetter, Robert P.: 413, 414, 416-419.
Lee, Robert E.: 3-5, 77, 92.
Leff, Leonard: 527.
Lehmbeck, Byron: 337.
Leitner, Ted: 431.
Lemmon, Jack: 418.
Lemons, Edd: 356.
Lester, June: 487.
Lewis, E. G.: 47.
Lewis, Lowery L.: 24, 25, 46, 119, 122, 144, 155, 157, 173, 198, 199, 279.

Lewis, Mrs. Lowery L.: 144.
Lewis, Sinclair: 213.
Library Building (1901). *See* Williams Hall.
Lieb, Stephen: 506.
Life Sciences East: 301, 335, 420.
Literary Societies: 17-26, 47, 50, 63, 86, 99, 107, 132.
Litsinger, Joe E.: 80.
Little, W. D.: 169, 243.
Littlejohn, Lacy Wilbourn: 232.
Lochenmeyer, O. H.: 318.
Locke, Vivia: 401, 402.
Lockwood, Jake: 422.
Logan, Joshua: 327.
Logue, Steve: 503.
Long, Harry: 287, 290.
Lookabaugh, Guy: 238.
Looper, Don: 311, 319, 337, 340, 413.
Lorenz, Theodore: 327.
Lowell, Amy: 213.
Lowry, Robert: 43.
Lynch, Jack: 349, 417.
Lyon, David: 455.

M

Mackle, Robert: 504.
MacDougall, Curtis: 346, 470.
MacVicar, Robert W.: 357, 358, 368, 378, 380, 382, 384-386, 389, 391, 393, 395, 396, 398, 404, 405, 423, 452-454, 466.
Magruder, Alexander C.: 14, 16, 19, 20, 40, 43, 44.
Magruder Medal: 16, 19, 20, 36.
Main, John Hanson Thomas: 228.
Makovsky, Boh: 160.
Malden, Karl: 415.
Malone, Paul G.: 206, 503.
Mann, Loftin: 364.
Mapel, William: 447.
Marler, Ralph: 503.
Maroney, Mildred: 243.
Marshall, S. L. A.: 474.
Martin, D. Terry: 400, 405, 411, 412, 432.
Martin, Frank: 205.
Martin, J. E.: 167, 174.
Marvin, Burton: 366.
Marvin, Kenneth R.: 472.
Mason, John: 496.
Massey, Veeda: 327.
Matkin, Harold "Ben": 237, 239, 241, 248, 327.
Matrix Table: 346, 361.
Matthews, Leon: 422, 423, 501.
Matthews, R. P.: 398.
Maule, Linda: 457.
Maune, Sally: 501.

Mautz, Robert M.: 473.
May Day Carnival: 165, 191, 234.
Mayfield, Clifton Jr.: 327.
Mayfield, Frances: 387.
Maynard, Riley: 506.
Mayo, Wheeler: 367.
McAlister, Aubrey: 290, 303, 311, 327.
McAnally, David R. Jr.: 5-8.
McAnally, David Rice: 5.
McAuliffe, Anthony: 315.
McBride, Joe: 437, 499.
McCabe, Edward S.: 260.
McCafferty, Earl: 285.
McClure, Leslie W.: 300.
McCollum, Paul: 416-419.
McConnell, Virginia: 350.
McCoy, Thomas: 506.
McCue, Dorothy: 287.
McCulloh, Robert L.: 349, 356, 456.
McCutchen, J. E.: 103.
McDonald, Linda: 486.
McElroy, Clarence H.: 207, 241, 259, 271, 275-278, 303.
McEwen, Arthur S.: 162, 250, 251.
McGuirk, Leroy: 285, 290.
McIlwain, Bob: 311.
McIntosh, Daniel C.: 336, 344.
McIntyre, Ed: 251.
McKinley, William: 60.
McLish, R. H.: 166, 169.
McNeely, O. D.: 167.
McReynolds, Arthur B.: 21, 115.
Mechanics Building: 83.
Meinhart, Wayne: 476, 477.
Melton, C. A.: 110, 111.
Merrell, Maggie: 148.
Merrell, Oscar J.: 147-151.
Merritt, Fred D.: 146.
Merson, Virginia: 303.
Meyer, O. J.: 174.
Meyerdirk, Carl: 340.
Milburn, George: 248.
Miller, Ada M. Kelly: 157.
Miller, Allee Carey: 32, 33, 156, 173.
Miller, Estelle Shroyer: 31-33, 52.
Miller, Floyd E.: 33, 173, 175.
Miller, Freeman E.: 3, 11, 19, 22, 24, 29-42, 44, 45-49, 51-54, 59, 63-65, 77, 82, 83, 91, 92, 104, 110, 115, 133, 144, 155-159, 161-176, 180, 186, 201, 205, 216, 261, 543.
Miller, H. P.: 105.
Miller, Larry: 425, 506.
Miller, Lewis: 157.
Miller, Louise: 502, 522, 536.
Miller, Paul: 163, 222, 226, 230, 233, 236, 247, 248, 252-254, 279, 291, 327, 370, 500-502, 504, 507, 517, 522, 536, 537.

Miller, Roy F.: 110, 163, 167-169, 175.
Miller, Stella: 156.
Milne, Gladys: 248.
Mittendorf, Oscar: 174.
Mittendorf, T. H.: 174.
Moeller, Leslie: 445.
Moffeit, Miles: 541.
Monnett, V. Brown: 484.
Moon, K. C.: 541.
Moore, Marjorie: 327.
Moorhouse, Harold W.: 141-146, 151, 152.
Moorhouse, L. A.: 105.
Moreland, Vera: 318.
Morford, Tom: 311.
Morgan, Dick Thompson: 89.
Morrill Hall: 71, 117, 127, 149, 159, 191, 233, 271, 301, 400.
Morrill, James L.: 334.
Morrison, Edward L.: 241, 356.
Morrow, George E.: 37, 38, 43, 44, 46, 49-52, 59, 60, 66-68, 82, 83, 85.
Morton, J. S.: 39.
Mosse, Baskett: 363, 370, 469.
Mountcastle, Grace: 193, 194, 206, 216.
Muchmore, Gareth: 367, 398.
Mullendore, Karen: 431.
Murdaugh, Edmund D.: 38, 39, 42, 43, 49, 51, 82, 92.
Murdock, Victor: 69.
Murphy, Daniel W.: 79.
Murray, Johnston: 351. .
Murray, William H.: 96, 175, 279.
Musick, Pat: 463.
Mustain, Mary E.: 183, 190-193, 205, 302.
Myers, Delores: 496.

N

Nance, Bob: 422.
National Public Radio: 425.
Natwick, Mildred: 415.
Neal, Clara: 290, 327.
Neal, James C.: 14, 19, 35, 37, 38, 40, 41.
Neal, Kate: 19, 20, 36.
Needham, Enoch III: 503.
Neerman, C. F.: 80.
Nelson, Albert H.: 108, 130, 131, 158, 159, 163, 183, 184-189, 205.
Nelson, Lillian Bass: 186.
Nelson, Marlan D.: 492, 504, 506, 507, 512-515, 517-519, 521, 522-525, 527-530, 532-536, 538, 540, 543.
Nelson, Spurgeon: 217.
Nemecek, Maureen: 519, 520, 522, 539-542.
Neumann, Stephen M.: 540.
New Education: 107.

Platt, Bill: 422.
Platt, C. C.: 173.
Pope, Virginia. *See* Virginia Pope Hartman.
Post, Gene L.: 530.
Powell, Carrie Elizabeth Jones: 212.
Powell, James L.: 212, 222.
Powell, Ptolemy: 222.
Powell, William P.: 205, 211-223, 302, 543.
Pratt, K. C.: 345.
Press Club: 167, 239, 311, 326, 333.
Price, Paul: 420.
Priest, Stella: 193, 194, 198, 206, 216.
Printing: 47, 67, 68, 77, 81, 99, 100, 162, 271.
Pritchard, Guy M.: 456.
Progressive Agriculturist: 119, 120, 215.
Pruett, Haskell: 339, 397, 399-401, 404, 458-460.
Puckett, Wayne: 327.
Pulitzer, Joseph: 7, 8.
Pye, Linwood S.: 447

Q

Querry, Samuel R.: 47.

R

Radio and Television: 362, 363, 398, 409-432, 453, 454, 464, 477, 494-496.
Radio Club: 416, 417, 418, 420.
Ragulsky, Frank: 502.
Ralls, Joseph Green: 143.
Ranes, G. O.: 174.
Rapp, Workman: 167.
Raque, Henrich Nickel: 182.
Ratner, Payne: 283.
Ray, Bill: 470.
Ray, Linda: 457.
Reams, Janet: 452.
Record, Phil: 504.
Reddick, Dewitt: 315.
Redlich, Frederick W.: 207.
Redskin: 102, 106, 107, 128, 160, 165, 205, 241, 248, 249.
Reed, Donald U.: 520-522, 542.
Regnier, Charles E.: 47.
Reid, James: 340.
Renfrow, William C.: 17, 36.
Reynolds, James: 349, 360.
Reynolds, Jenifer: 541.
Rhea, James W.: 481, 495, 505, 506, 540.
Rhoades, George: 492, 514.
Rhodes, Charley: 437.
Richert, Earl: 292, 327, 500.
Rickstrew, Dorothy. *See* Dorothy Rickstrew Nixon.
Ridpath, John Clark: 29, 30, 31, 49.

Riley, James Whitcomb: 30, 53.
"Riverside Review": 22, 23.
Roberts, Clarence: 119, 202, 203.
Robertson, Dale: 496.
Robinson, Joseph L.: 133, 134.
Rockett, Gordon: 355, 398.
Rockey, Edna: 183.
Rockey, Elizabeth Snyder: 182.
Rockey, Henry S.: 182.
Rockey, John: 182.
Rockey, Julia Maria Patridge: 182.
Rockey, Ned: 201.
Rockey, Nellie: 130, 182.
Rockey, Noble W.: 103, 104, 120, 125-127, 130, 131, 137, 146, 155, 158, 159, 162, 165, 169, 179, 180-186, 188, 191, 193-195, 199-207, 211, 214, 216-217, 219, 229, 232, 238, 259, 260, 271, 274, 297, 543.
Rodgers, Max: 506.
Roe, Vingie: 69.
Roepke, William J.: 459, 460, 475, 476.
Rogers, Bertha: 161.
Rogers, Jennifer: 516, 517.
Rohrbaugh, Lewis H.: 366.
Rollins, Peter: 527.
Roosevelt, Franklin D.: 134, 283.
Rott, Carl A.: 281-284.
Royce, J. E.: 220.
Rucker, Bryce: 480.
Rucker, Tom: 349.
Ruddick, Morris: 474.
Rugg, William J.: 516-518, 523, 527, 529, 530, 540, 541, 543.
Rumfelt, James C.: 291.
Runnels, Ralph: 290.
Rupe, Kenneth: 413.
Ryan, Ellen E.: 284, 291.
Ryker, David: 340.
Ryserson, Ina Bell: 291.

S

Saied, Johnny: 531.
Samuels, Isadore: 130, 137, 158, 159, 163, 181, 203, 400.
Sandburg, Carl: 213.
Sarrail, Maurice Paul Emmanuel: 228.
Sater, J. E.: 79.
Satterfield, Sam: 480.
Sauvageot, Ludel B.: 367.
Savage, J. J.: 166, 169.
Sawyer, Hamlin W.: 62.
Scales, James R.: 485.
Scarborough, E. Dorothy: 213, 214.
Schedler, Carl: 237.
Schick, C. Dennis: 471, 480, 481, 483, 506.

Schillinger, Lisa: 520, 542, 543.
Schmalfeld, Robert G.: 480.
Schneekloth, Ruth Ann: 417.
Schneider, Sam: 415.
School of Communications: 192, 378, 380, 382-389, 391, 396, 399-406, 421-423, 425, 435, 436, 456, 458, 464, 466, 495, 526.
School of Journalism: 455, 469, 477, 478, 483.
School of Journalism and Broadcasting: 496, 500, 503, 505, 511, 512, 514, 515, 518, 524, 535, 536; golden anniversary, 542, 543.
School of Journalism and Communications: 453, 454, 463, 494.
Science Hall. *See* Communications Building.
Scott, Angelo C.: 3, 11, 29, 38, 43, 53, 54, 59-74, 77, 82-85, 92, 95-98, 100, 102-104, 106, 115, 145, 155, 216, 218, 226, 261, 400, 411.
Scott, Charles F.: 60, 61, 66.
Scott, James H.: 337.
Scott, John W.: 60.
Scott, Winfield W.: 62.
Scripps-Howard Foundation: 252.
Scripps-Howard Newspapers: 230, 247, 499, 500, 542.
Scroggs, Schiller: 150, 289, 298, 309, 319-322, 341, 343, 344, 350, 352-358, 360-362, 365, 367, 368, 370, 378-386, 391, 395, 396, 398, 401, 402.
Seamands, Ruth: 311.
Sears-Bugeja, Diane: 530.
Seaton, Stuart B.: 339.
Seay, Abraham J.: 36, 78.
Seil, Manning D.: 475, 476, 480.
Seitz, Chrystal: 290.
Seldomridge, Howard G.: 102, 103, 121, 122, 127, 130, 137, 400.
Self, D. H.: 169.
Sewell, Ralph: 478.
Sharp, Martha: 401-404, 425.
Shaw, Suzanne: 537.
Shepherd, Eugene: 327.
Shepler, Ned: 437.
Shoemaker, Bobbie: 337.
Shoemaker, Elsie: 334, 335, 338, 346, 358, 367, 395, 396.
Short, George: 233, 234.
Shull, Warren: 150, 349, 477.
Siebert, Fred: 475.
Sigma Delta Chi: 30, 135, 165, 167, 298, 311, 326, 333, 346, 348, 361, 364, 484, 486, 501, 503, 504.
Sigma Literary Society: 18-26, 46, 47, 50, 63, 86, 89.

Sigma Literary Society 1893-1897: 23.
Simmons, Glen: 237, 238.
Simpson, Milward: 283.
Sittle, Helen: 420.
Skinner, Matt: 540.
Skinner, Ray: 174.
Slater, Ed: 422.
Smith, A. L.: 174.
Smith, Barbara: 497.
Smith, Carolyn: 506.
Smith, Duane V.: 495, 505.
Smith, Fred T.: 291.
Smith, G. C.: 174.
Smith, J. P.: 438.
Smith, Joan: 541.
Smith, Richard: 327.
Smith, Robert: 512.
Snider, Beulah: 199.
Snider, Richard: 337.
Snipes, R. Larry: 506.
Snow, Frances Huntington: 60.
Society of Associated Industrial Editors: 344, 351, 352, 354, 358, 363, 365. *See also* Southwestern Association of Industrial Editors.
Society of Professional Journalists: 167.
Sodowsky, Roland: 406.
Solberg, Victor: 260.
Solow, Anthony: 445, 455, 498, 506.
Soule, J. S.: 92.
Southwestern Association of Industrial Editors: 315, 316, 336, 337, 341. *See also* Society of Associated Industrial Editors.
Spellman, Patricia: 419.
Springer, James: 175, 176.
Sprouce, James M.: 484.
Stafford, Edward R.: 318.
Stallard, Fred: 35.
Stansbury, Max E.: 150, 291.
Star-Crescent Literary Society: 17.
Steele, George W.: 13, 14.
Steele, Lauren L.: 503.
Steen, Sid: 253, 398.
Stefaniak, Gregory: 516, 517, 542.
Steinberg, Robert C. Jr.: 445.
Stemmons, Walter: 120, 121, 145, 185.
Stempel, John E.: 366.
Steng, William R. Jr: 482, 483, 502, 506, 514, 517, 518, 522, 523.
Stephens, Hugh: 250.
Steward, James K.: 445.
Stewart, L. Frank: 103.
Stillwell, Henry: 220, 221.
Stiver, Charles: 348.
Stone, C. Walker: 222, 226, 230, 233, 235-238, 240-243, 247-254, 271, 274, 499, 500, 507.

Wallace, John M.: 217, 260.
Wallace, Lew: 30.
Wallis, F. E. "Wally": 291.
Walters, Donal: 340.
Walton, John C. "Jack": 220, 221, 225, 253.
Ward, Perla: 530.
Ward, Walter J.: 471, 474, 475, 483, 488, 494, 503, 506, 515, 517, 522, 523.
Ward, William: 349.
Washenko, Steve: 349.
Waters, Henry J.: 267.
Watkins, Hazel: 291.
Watson, James E.: 30.
Watson, Milo: 350, 398, 439.
Waugh, Frank A.: 15, 16, 18, 19, 37, 41, 43, 44, 86, 90-92.
Weathers, Charlie: 235, 250.
Weaver, Gordon: 527.
Weaver, Kenneth: 369, 370.
Weaver, Walter: 199, 200.
Webster Debating Society: 17-26, 50, 63, 91.
Wegener, Robert: 518, 526.
Weimer, Rae: 461, 471, 472, 475.
Wentz, Lew: 251.
Wertz, Leo B.: 205.
West, E. M.: 174.
West, W. E.: 174.
Westbrook, Edward J.: 100, 107, 271.
Wetherby, Joseph W.: 412.
White, Betty Sue: 311.
White, Ewers: 96, 105, 157.
White, George: 303.
White, King D.: 504.
White, L. Douglas: 540.
White, William A.: 118.
Whitehurst Hall: 271, 272, 287, 300, 301, 335, 389.
Whitehurst, John A.: 220, 221, 225, 253, 254, 266.
Whitlow, Sam E.: 299-302, 304-306, 310, 312.
Whitworth, Roberta: 290.
Wiggins, Al W.: 540.
Wikoff, Frank J.: 66.
Wilbourn, Verda V.: 194, 195, 205, 206.
Wilcox, Walter: 359.
Wile, Otis: 236, 244, 248, 327.

Wilkerson, LeRoy: 445.
Willham, Oliver S.: 253, 273, 351, 352, 354, 356-359, 362, 365, 367, 379, 380, 384-386, 398, 404, 405, 453, 454, 460.
Williams, Andy: 541.
Williams, Benjamin F.: 260.
Williams, Carl: 120.
Williams, Cecil: 248.
Williams Hall: 103, 174, 193, 233, 260, 271, 301, 401, 402, 412, 418.
Williams, James O.: 445.
Williams, Jerry: 438.
Williams, Luther: 351.
Williams, Paul: 290.
Williams, Robert L.: 155, 161.
Williams, Walter: 9, 10.
Willis, William: 540.
Wilmore, Rex: 445, 463.
Wilson, George: 217, 220-222, 225, 253.
Wilson, Glenna: 399, 401.
Wilson, H. Ray: 506.
Wilson, Woodrow: 185.
Wimberly, John A.: 14.
Wirt, Fritz W.: 540.
Wise, James: 493.
Wisherd, Sheila: 489.
Women In Communications, Incorporated: 135. *See also* Theta Sigma Phi.
Woodson, D. S.: 251.
Woodson, Elmer: 285, 290, 291, 315, 337, 358, 359, 367, 370, 460, 480.
Woodson, Mortimer: 167.
Woodward, Jim: 525.
Woodworth, Becky: 421.
Woodworth, John: 339, 399, 412-425, 432.
Woodyard, Darrel: 399, 420, 421, 426, 427.
Woolard, Joe: 150, 349.
Wooley, Don L.: 445.
Worley, Ann: 438.

XYZ

Yadon, Robert: 506.
Yost, Casper S.: 7.
Young, Donalene: 352.
Yount, Dean B.: 291.
Zacharaie, Lloyd: 311.
Zwick, William H.: 222.

A History of the
Oklahoma State University
School of Journalism
and Broadcasting

is a specially designed volume of the Centennial Histories Series.

The text was composed on a personal computer, transmitted by telecommunications to the OSU mainframe computer, and typeset by a computerized typesetting system. Three typefaces were used in the composition. The text is composed
in 10 point Melliza with 2 points extra leading added for legibility. Chapter headings
are 24 point Omega. All supplemental information contained in the endnotes,
charts, picture captions, appendices, bibliography, and index are set in either 8 or
9 point Triumvirate Lite.

The book is printed on a high-quality, coated paper to ensure faithful reproduc-
tion of historical photographs and documents. Smyth-sewn and bound with a
durable coated nonwoven cover material, the cover has been screen-printed with
flat black ink.

The Centennial Histories Committee expresses sincere appreciation to the
progressive men and women of the past and present who created and recorded the
dynamic, moving history of Oklahoma State University, the story of a land-grant
university fulfilling its mission to teach, to research, and to extend itself to the
community and the world.